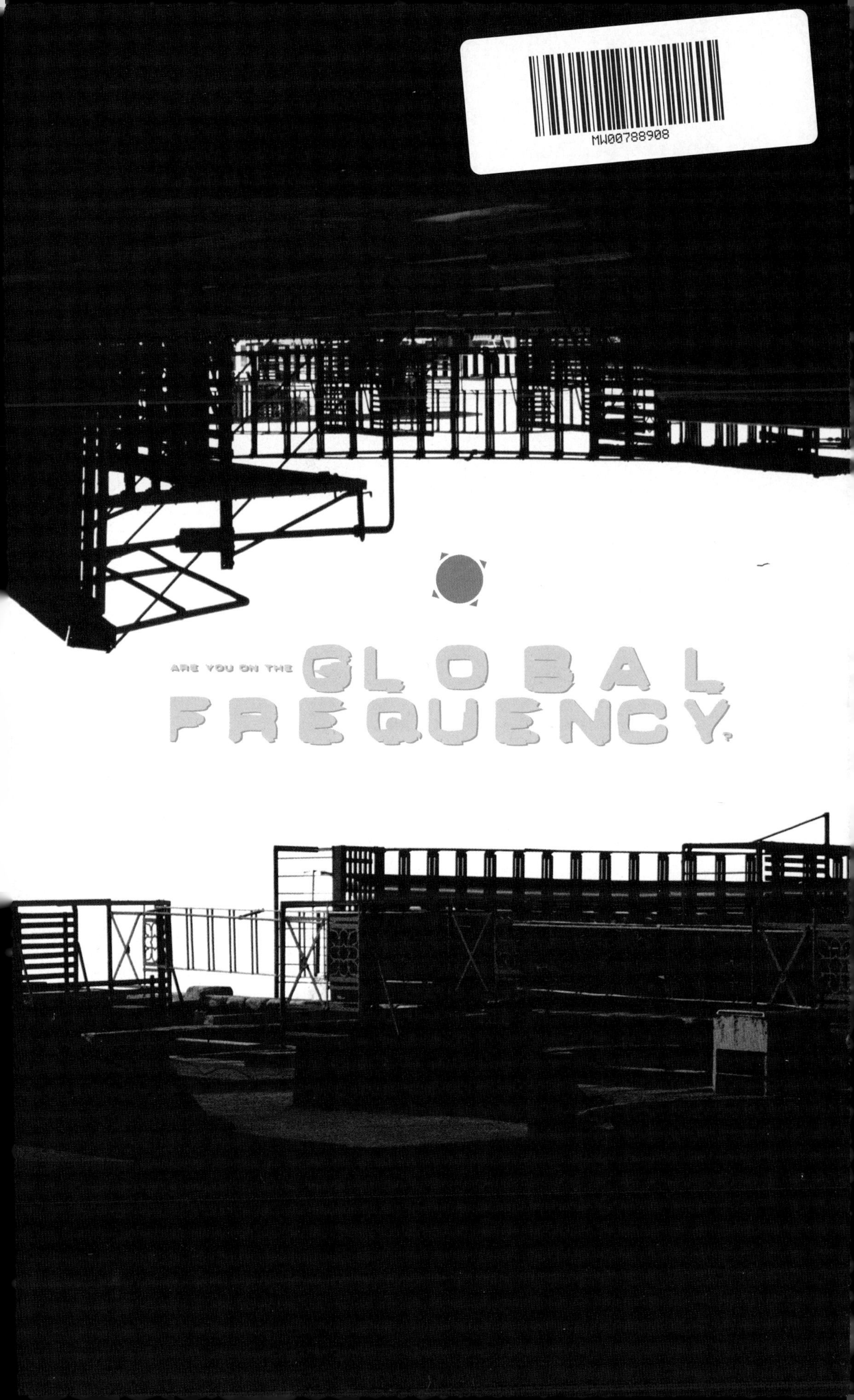
ARE YOU ON THE GLOBAL FREQUENCY?

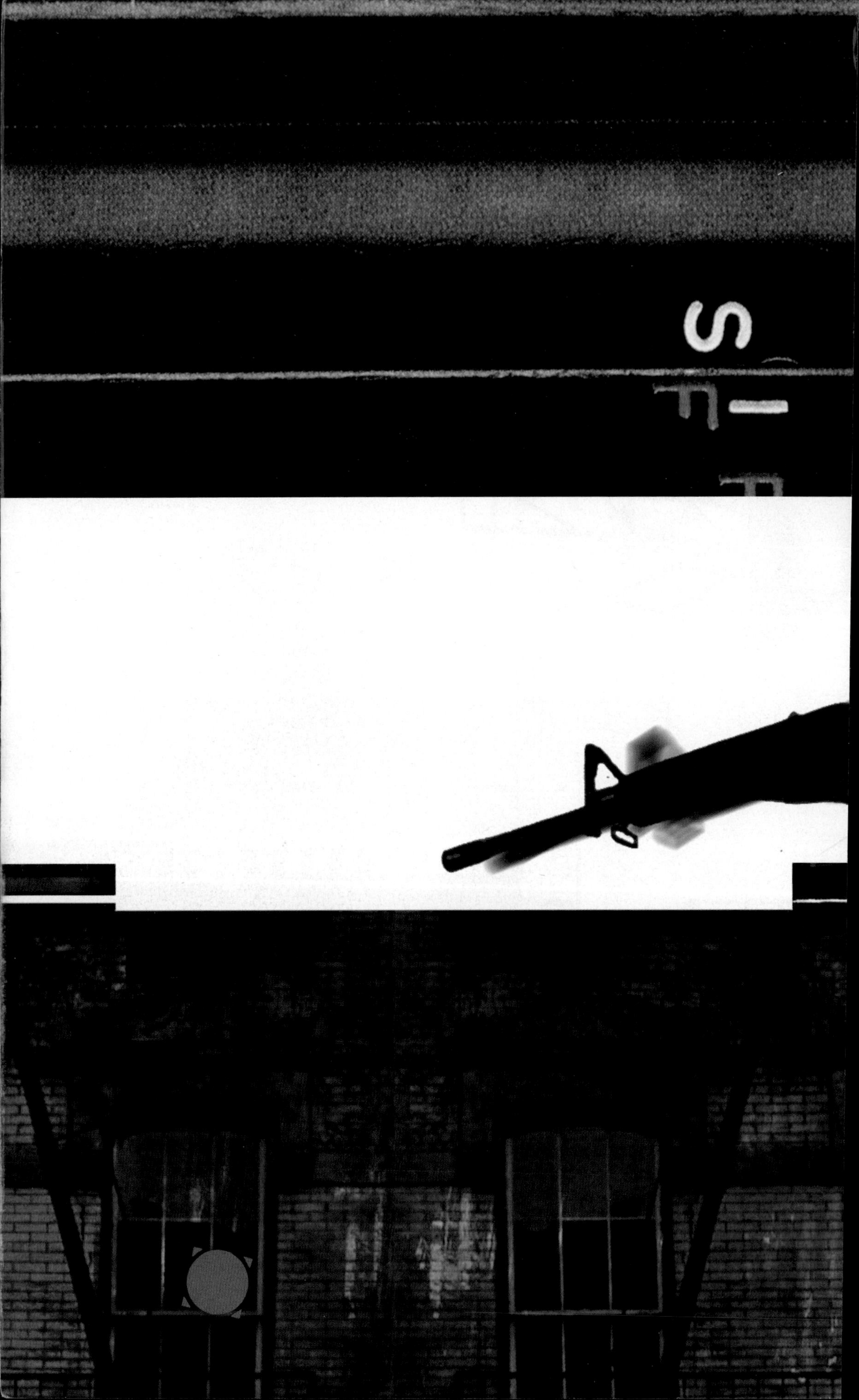

ARE YOU ON THE **GLOBAL FREQUENCY?**

WARREN ELLIS
WRITER

GARRY LEACH	SIMON BISLEY
GLENN FABRY	CHRIS SPROUSE
LIAM SHARP	KARL STORY
ROY ALLAN MARTINEZ	LEE BERMEJO
JON J MUTH	TOMM COKER
DAVID LLOYD	JASON PEARSON

GENE HA
ARTISTS

DAVID BARON   ART LYON
COLORISTS

MICHAEL HEISLER
LETTERER

BRIAN WOOD
ORIGINAL SERIES & COLLECTION COVER ARTIST

GLOBAL FREQUENCY CREATED BY
WARREN ELLIS

SCOTT DUNBIER	EDITOR–ORIGINAL SERIES
KRISTY QUINN	ASSISTANT EDITOR–ORIGINAL SERIES
ROWENA YOW	EDITOR
ROBBIN BROSTERMAN	DESIGN DIRECTOR–BOOKS
CURTIS KING JR.	PUBLICATION DESIGN
KAREN BERGER	SENIOR VP–EXECUTIVE EDITOR, VERTIGO
BOB HARRAS	VP–EDITOR-IN-CHIEF
DIANE NELSON	PRESIDENT
DAN DIDIO AND JIM LEE	CO-PUBLISHERS
GEOFF JOHNS	CHIEF CREATIVE OFFICER
JOHN ROOD	EXECUTIVE VP–SALES, MARKETING AND BUSINESS DEVELOPMENT
AMY GENKINS	SENIOR VP–BUSINESS AND LEGAL AFFAIRS
NAIRI GARDINER	SENIOR VP–FINANCE
JEFF BOISON	VP–PUBLISHING OPERATIONS
MARK CHIARELLO	VP–ART DIRECTION AND DESIGN
JOHN CUNNINGHAM	VP–MARKETING
TERRI CUNNINGHAM	VP–TALENT RELATIONS AND SERVICES
ALISON GILL	SENIOR VP–MANUFACTURING AND OPERATIONS
HANK KANALZ	SENIOR VP–DIGITAL
JAY KOGAN	VP–BUSINESS AND LEGAL AFFAIRS, PUBLISHING
JACK MAHAN	VP–BUSINESS AFFAIRS, TALENT
NICK NAPOLITANO	VP–MANUFACTURING ADMINISTRATION
SUE POHJA	VP–BOOK SALES
COURTNEY SIMMONS	SENIOR VP–PUBLICITY
BOB WAYNE	SENIOR VP–SALES

GLOBAL FREQUENCY

DC Comics, 1700 Broadway, New York, NY 10019
A Warner Bros. Entertainment Company.
Printed by RR Donnelley,
Salem, VA, USA. 12/21/12.
First Printing.
ISBN: 978-1-4012-3797-4

Library of Congress Cataloging-in-Publication Data

Ellis, Warren.
  Global frequency / Warren Ellis.
     p. cm.
  "Originally published in single magazine form in Global Frequency 1-12."
  ISBN 978-1-4012-3797-4
  1. Graphic novels. I. Title.
  PN6728.G55E66 2012
  741.5'973—dc23
                       2012040864

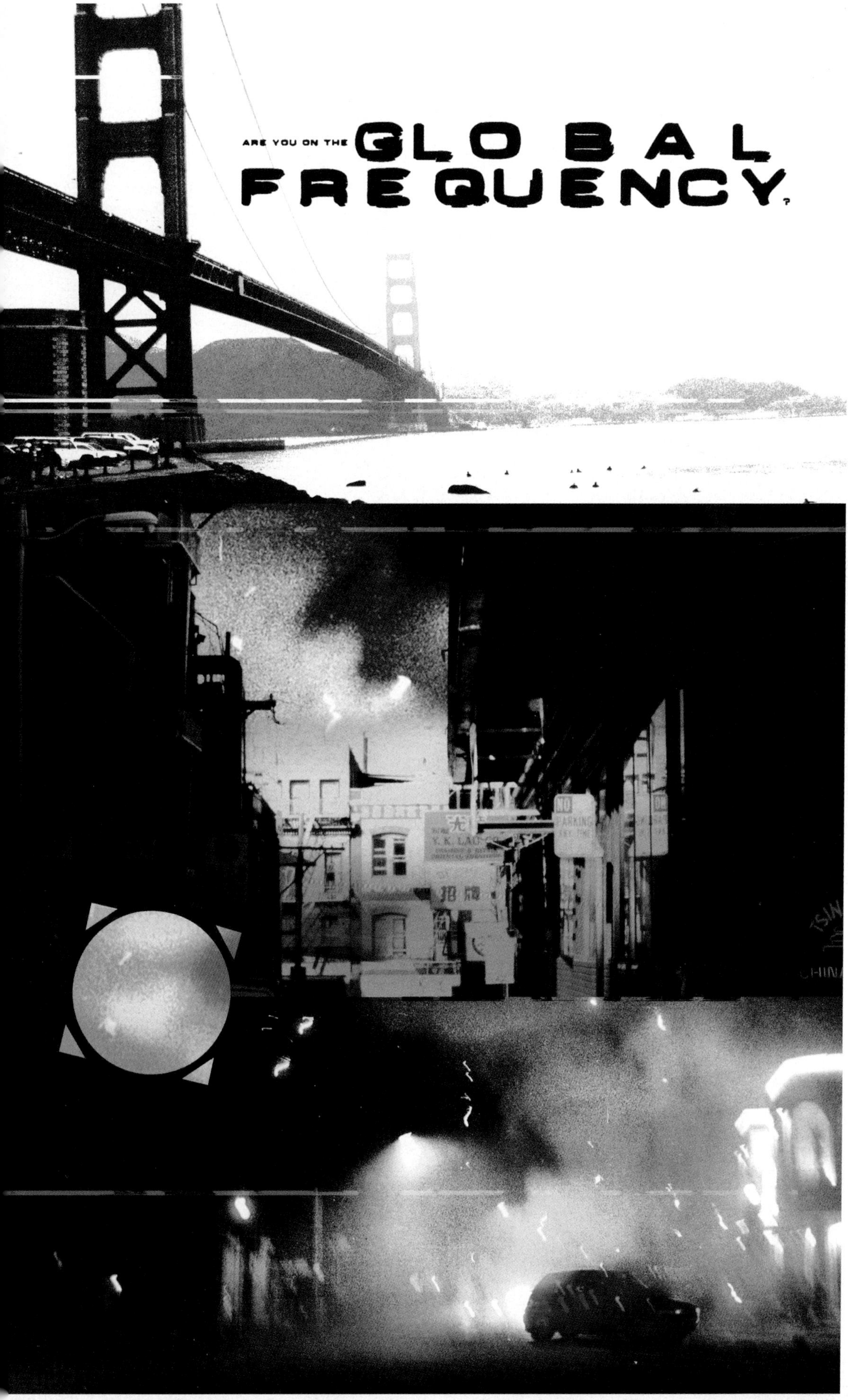
ARE YOU ON THE GLOBAL FREQUENCY?

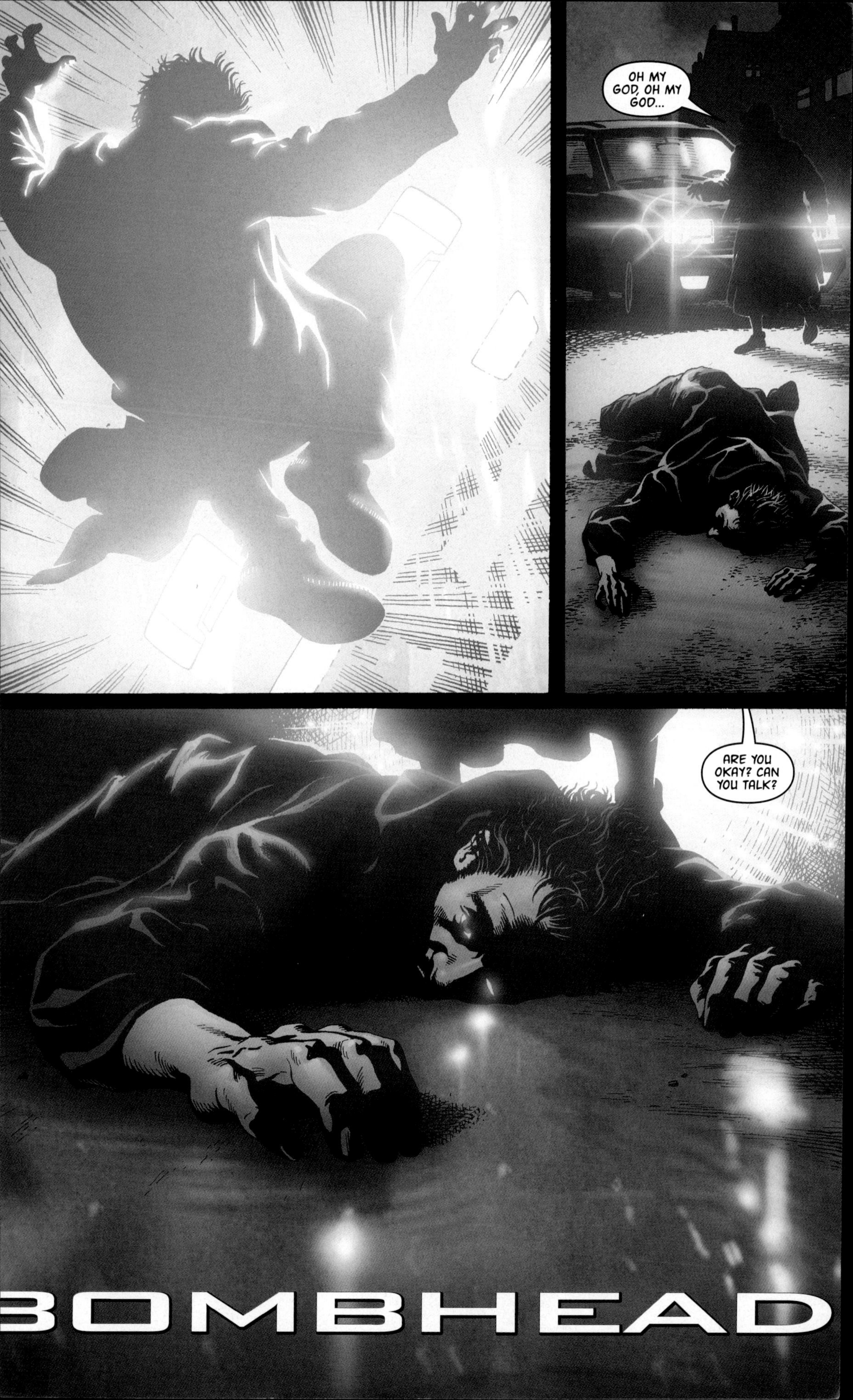
OH MY GOD, OH MY GOD...
ARE YOU OKAY? CAN YOU TALK?
BOMBHEAD

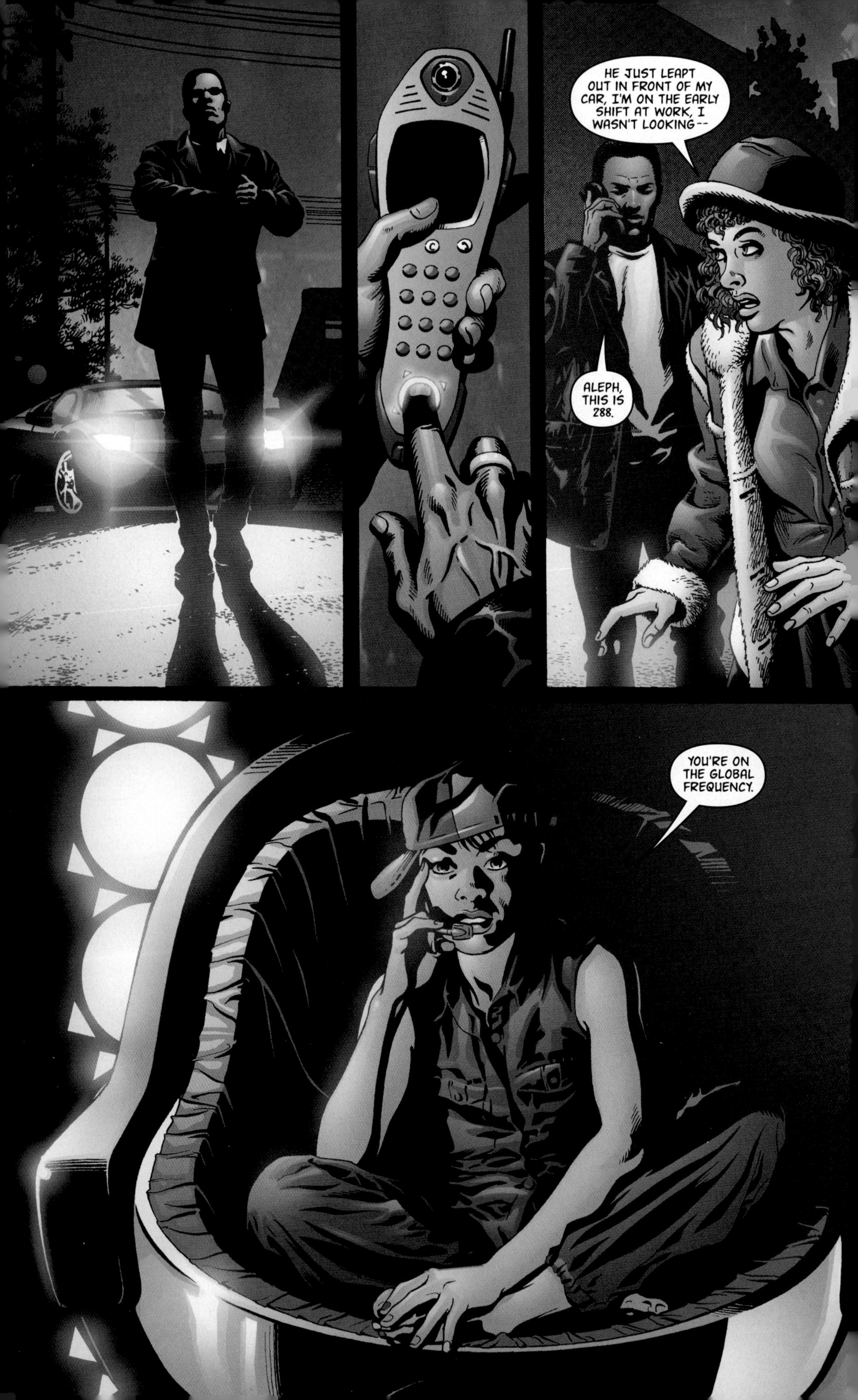
HE JUST LEAPT OUT IN FRONT OF MY CAR, I'M ON THE EARLY SHIFT AT WORK, I WASN'T LOOKING--
ALEPH, THIS IS 288.
YOU'RE ON THE GLOBAL FREQUENCY.

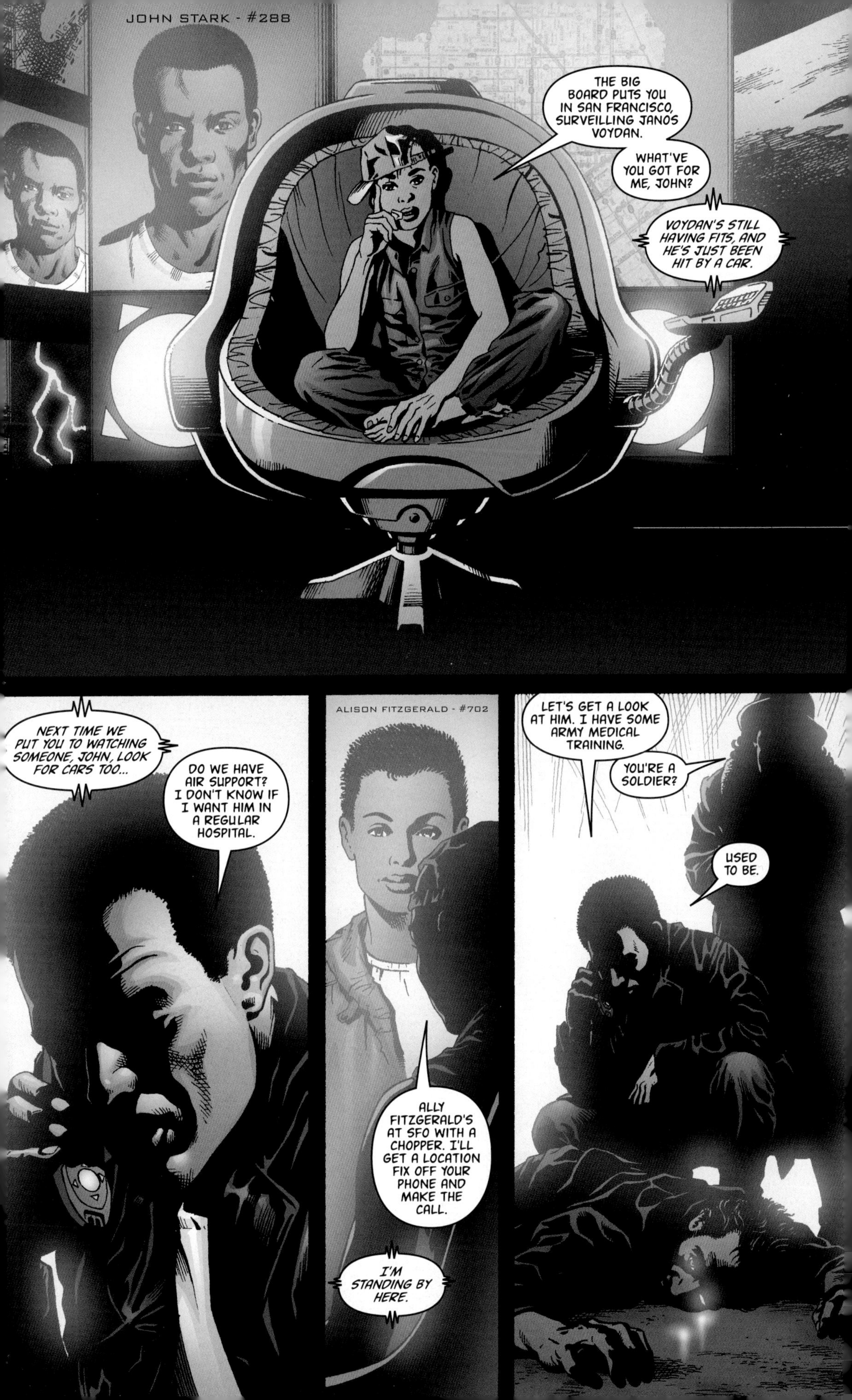
JOHN STARK - #288
THE BIG BOARD PUTS YOU IN SAN FRANCISCO, SURVEILLING JANOS VOYDAN.
WHAT'VE YOU GOT FOR ME, JOHN?
VOYDAN'S STILL HAVING FITS, AND HE'S JUST BEEN HIT BY A CAR.
NEXT TIME WE PUT YOU TO WATCHING SOMEONE, JOHN, LOOK FOR CARS TOO...
DO WE HAVE AIR SUPPORT? I DON'T KNOW IF I WANT HIM IN A REGULAR HOSPITAL.
ALISON FITZGERALD - #702
ALLY FITZGERALD'S AT SFO WITH A CHOPPER. I'LL GET A LOCATION FIX OFF YOUR PHONE AND MAKE THE CALL.
I'M STANDING BY HERE.
LET'S GET A LOOK AT HIM. I HAVE SOME ARMY MEDICAL TRAINING.
YOU'RE A SOLDIER?
USED TO BE.

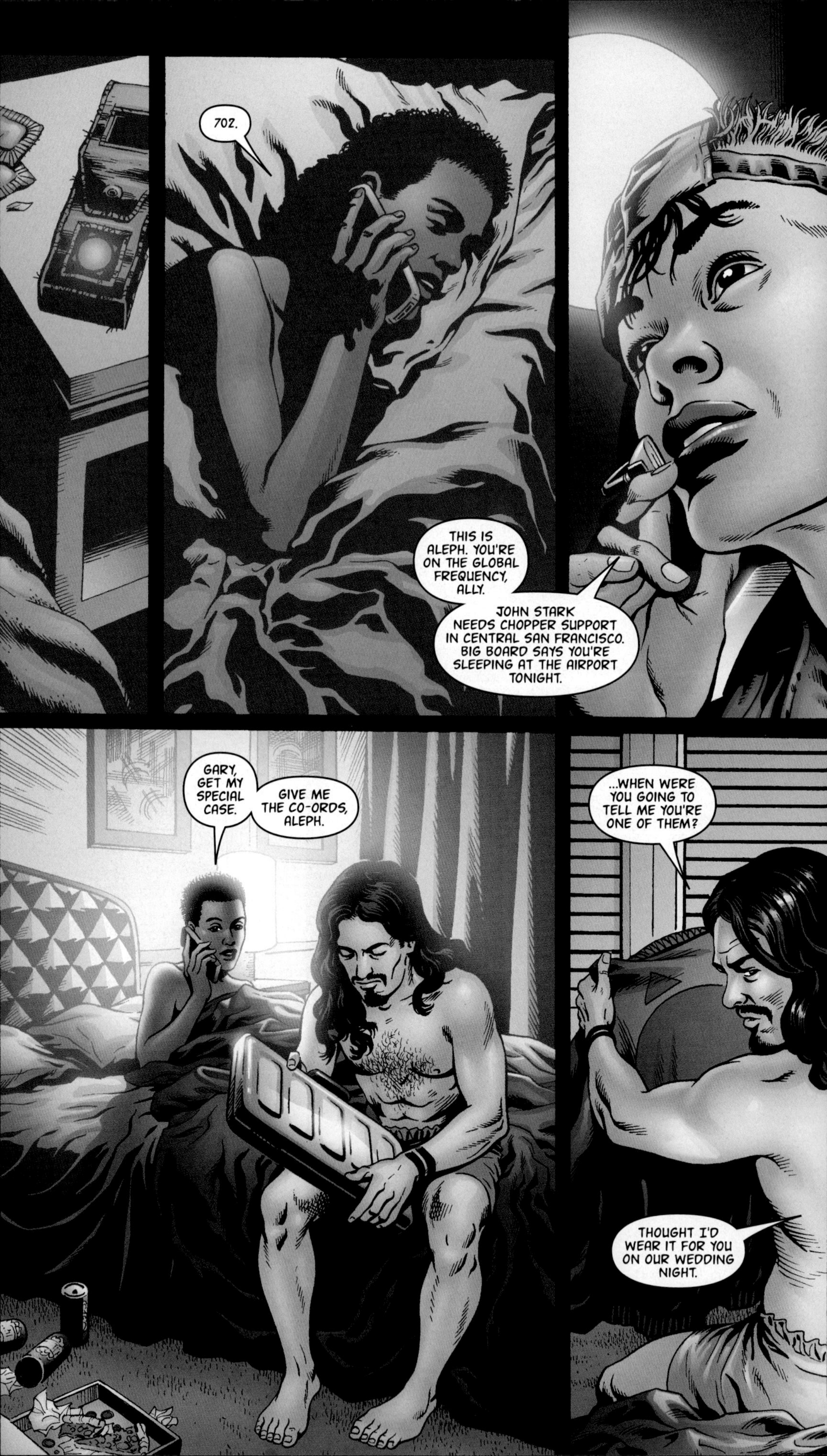
702.
THIS IS ALEPH. YOU'RE ON THE GLOBAL FREQUENCY, ALLY.
JOHN STARK NEEDS CHOPPER SUPPORT IN CENTRAL SAN FRANCISCO. BIG BOARD SAYS YOU'RE SLEEPING AT THE AIRPORT TONIGHT.
GARY, GET MY SPECIAL CASE.
GIVE ME THE CO-ORDS, ALEPH.
...WHEN WERE YOU GOING TO TELL ME YOU'RE ONE OF THEM?
THOUGHT I'D WEAR IT FOR YOU ON OUR WEDDING NIGHT.

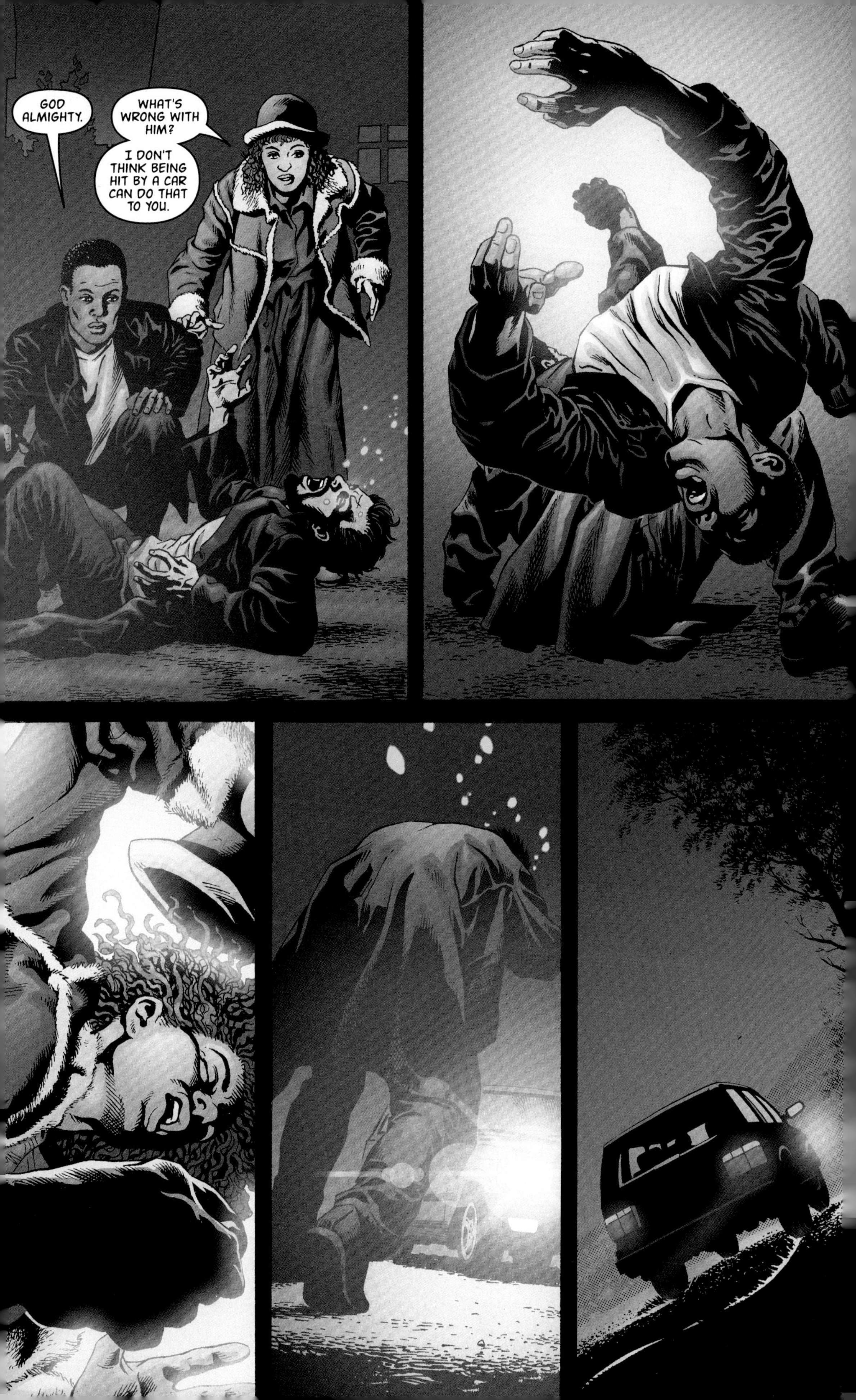
GOD ALMIGHTY.
WHAT'S WRONG WITH HIM?
I DON'T THINK BEING HIT BY A CAR CAN DO THAT TO YOU.

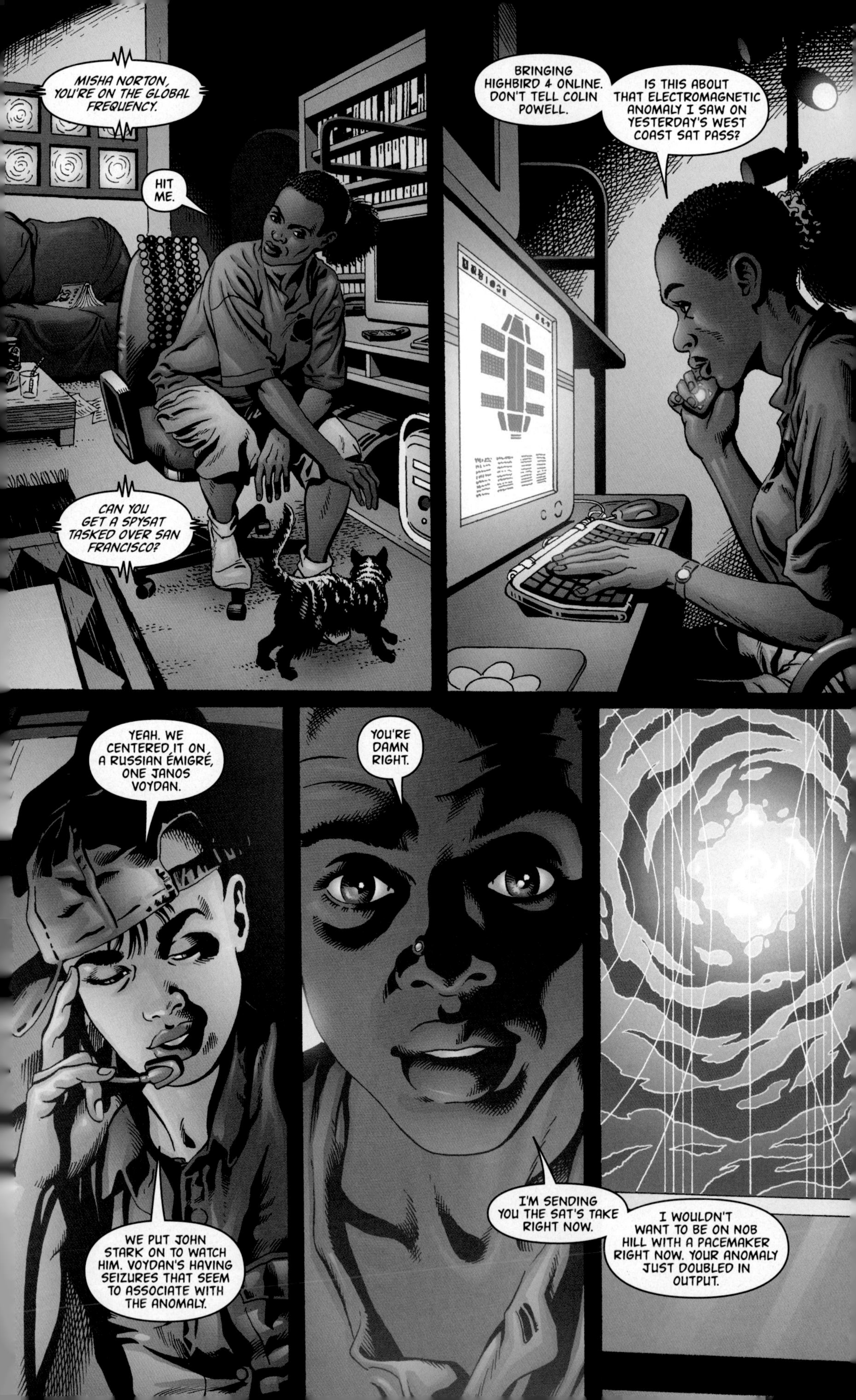
MISHA NORTON, YOU'RE ON THE GLOBAL FREQUENCY.
HIT ME.
CAN YOU GET A SPYSAT TASKED OVER SAN FRANCISCO?
BRINGING HIGHBIRD 4 ONLINE. DON'T TELL COLIN POWELL.
IS THIS ABOUT THAT ELECTROMAGNETIC ANOMALY I SAW ON YESTERDAY'S WEST COAST SAT PASS?
YEAH. WE CENTERED IT ON A RUSSIAN ÉMIGRÉ, ONE JANOS VOYDAN.
WE PUT JOHN STARK ON TO WATCH HIM. VOYDAN'S HAVING SEIZURES THAT SEEM TO ASSOCIATE WITH THE ANOMALY.
YOU'RE DAMN RIGHT.
I'M SENDING YOU THE SAT'S TAKE RIGHT NOW.
I WOULDN'T WANT TO BE ON NOB HILL WITH A PACEMAKER RIGHT NOW. YOUR ANOMALY JUST DOUBLED IN OUTPUT.

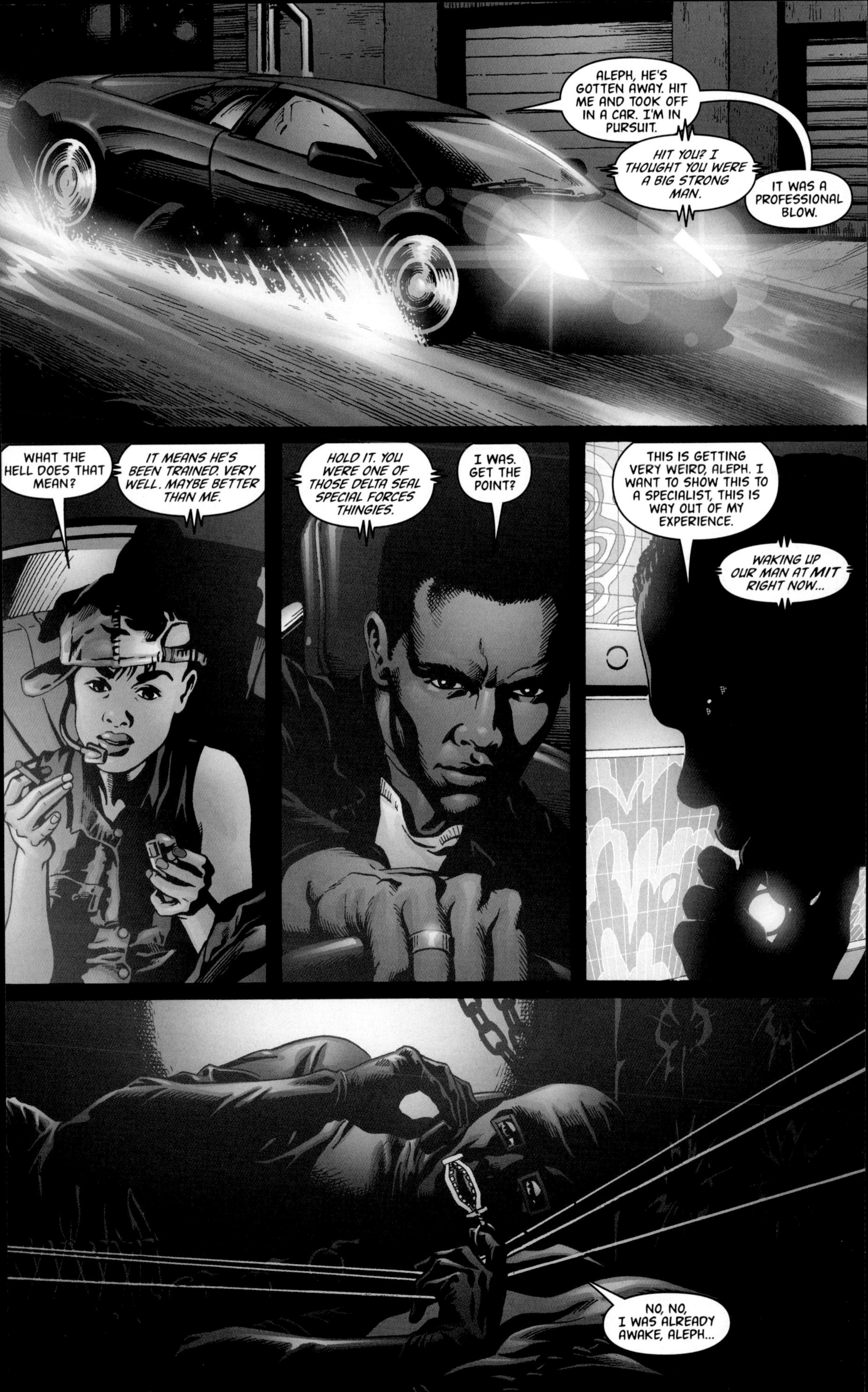
ALEPH, HE'S GOTTEN AWAY. HIT ME AND TOOK OFF IN A CAR. I'M IN PURSUIT.
HIT YOU? I THOUGHT YOU WERE A BIG STRONG MAN.
IT WAS A PROFESSIONAL BLOW.
WHAT THE HELL DOES THAT MEAN?
IT MEANS HE'S BEEN TRAINED. VERY WELL. MAYBE BETTER THAN ME.
HOLD IT. YOU WERE ONE OF THOSE DELTA SEAL SPECIAL FORCES THINGIES.
I WAS. GET THE POINT?
THIS IS GETTING VERY WEIRD, ALEPH. I WANT TO SHOW THIS TO A SPECIALIST, THIS IS WAY OUT OF MY EXPERIENCE.
WAKING UP OUR MAN AT MIT RIGHT NOW...
NO, NO, I WAS ALREADY AWAKE, ALEPH...

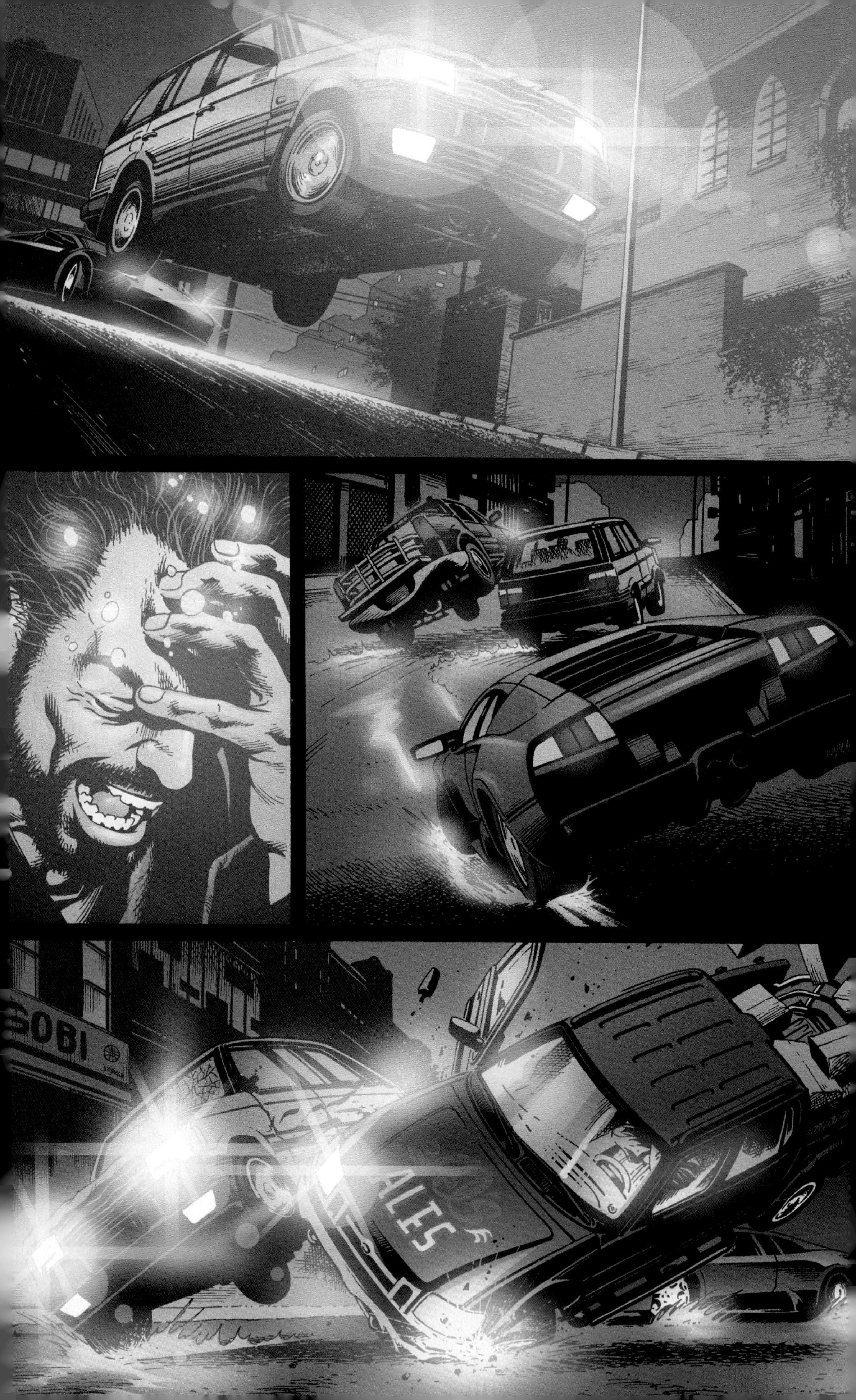
ALES

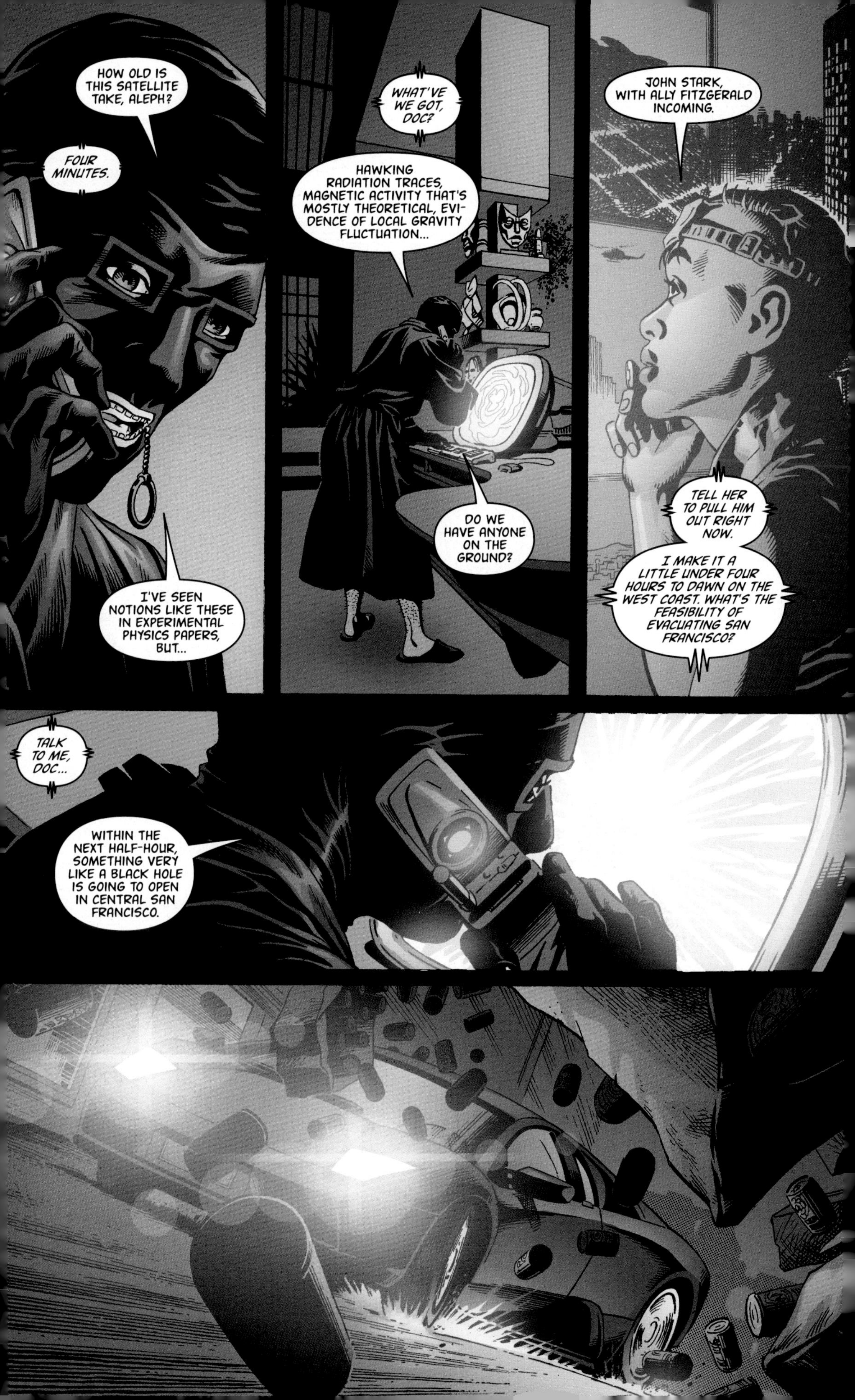
HOW OLD IS THIS SATELLITE TAKE, ALEPH?
FOUR MINUTES.
I'VE SEEN NOTIONS LIKE THESE IN EXPERIMENTAL PHYSICS PAPERS, BUT...
WHAT'VE WE GOT, DOC?
HAWKING RADIATION TRACES, MAGNETIC ACTIVITY THAT'S MOSTLY THEORETICAL, EVIDENCE OF LOCAL GRAVITY FLUCTUATION...
DO WE HAVE ANYONE ON THE GROUND?
JOHN STARK, WITH ALLY FITZGERALD INCOMING.
TELL HER TO PULL HIM OUT RIGHT NOW.
I MAKE IT A LITTLE UNDER FOUR HOURS TO DAWN ON THE WEST COAST. WHAT'S THE FEASIBILITY OF EVACUATING SAN FRANCISCO?
TALK TO ME, DOC...
WITHIN THE NEXT HALF-HOUR, SOMETHING VERY LIKE A BLACK HOLE IS GOING TO OPEN IN CENTRAL SAN FRANCISCO.

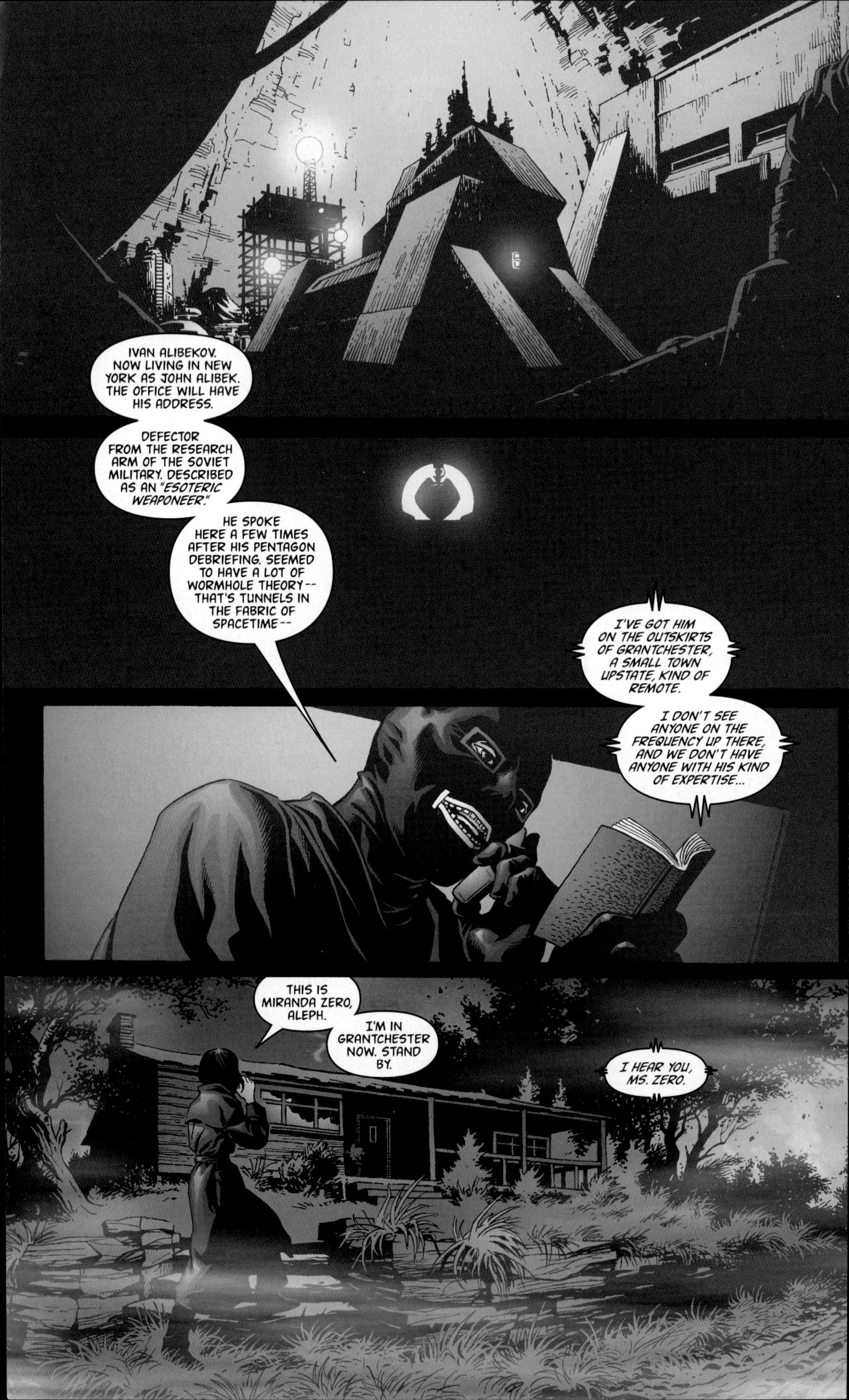
IVAN ALIBEKOV. NOW LIVING IN NEW YORK AS JOHN ALIBEK. THE OFFICE WILL HAVE HIS ADDRESS.
DEFECTOR FROM THE RESEARCH ARM OF THE SOVIET MILITARY. DESCRIBED AS AN "ESOTERIC WEAPONEER."
HE SPOKE HERE A FEW TIMES AFTER HIS PENTAGON DEBRIEFING. SEEMED TO HAVE A LOT OF WORMHOLE THEORY-- THAT'S TUNNELS IN THE FABRIC OF SPACETIME--
I'VE GOT HIM ON THE OUTSKIRTS OF GRANTCHESTER, A SMALL TOWN UPSTATE, KIND OF REMOTE.
I DON'T SEE ANYONE ON THE FREQUENCY UP THERE, AND WE DON'T HAVE ANYONE WITH HIS KIND OF EXPERTISE...
THIS IS MIRANDA ZERO, ALEPH.
I'M IN GRANTCHESTER NOW. STAND BY.
I HEAR YOU, MS. ZERO.

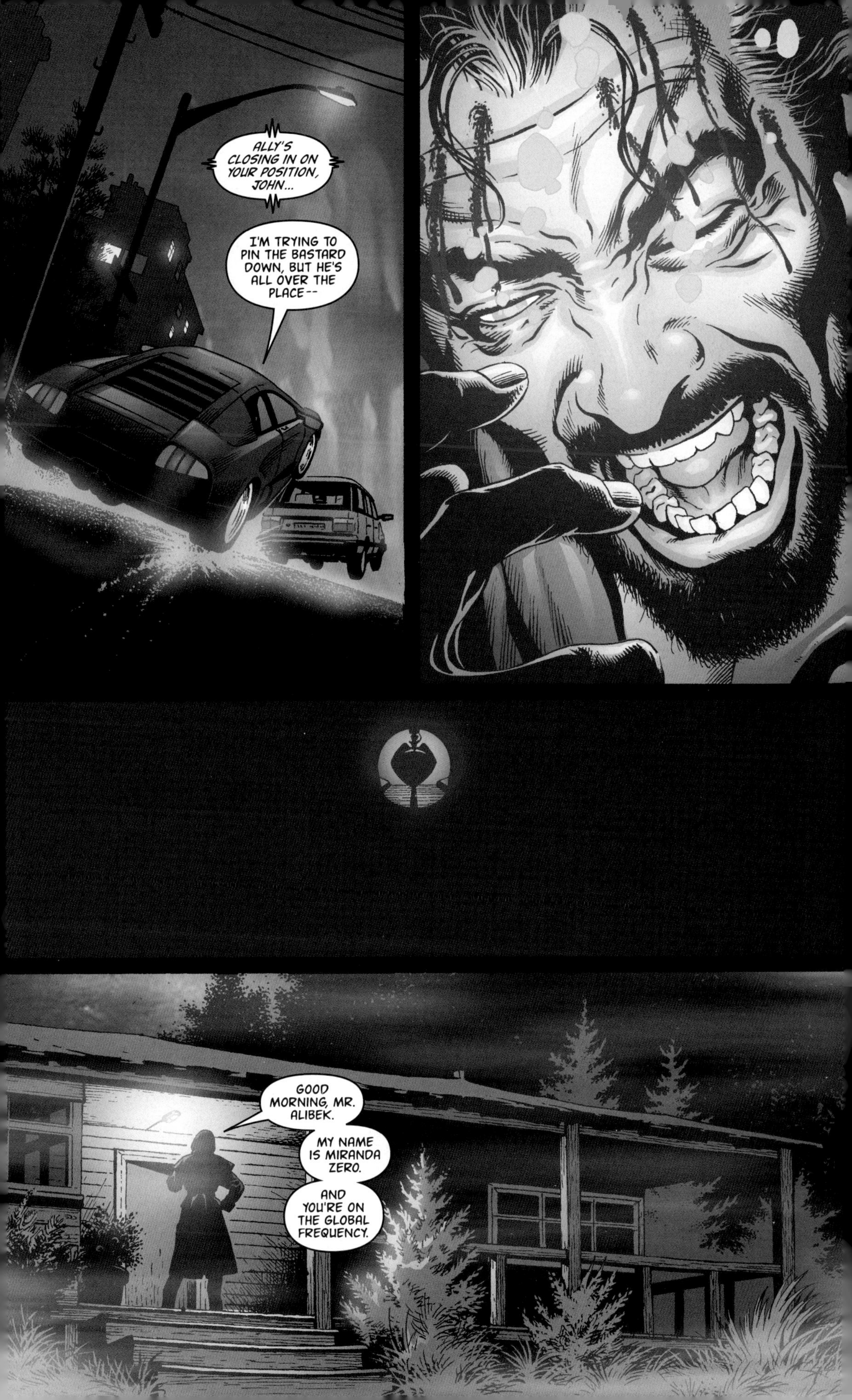
ALLY'S CLOSING IN ON YOUR POSITION, JOHN...
I'M TRYING TO PIN THE BASTARD DOWN, BUT HE'S ALL OVER THE PLACE--
GOOD MORNING, MR. ALIBEK.
MY NAME IS MIRANDA ZERO.
AND YOU'RE ON THE GLOBAL FREQUENCY.

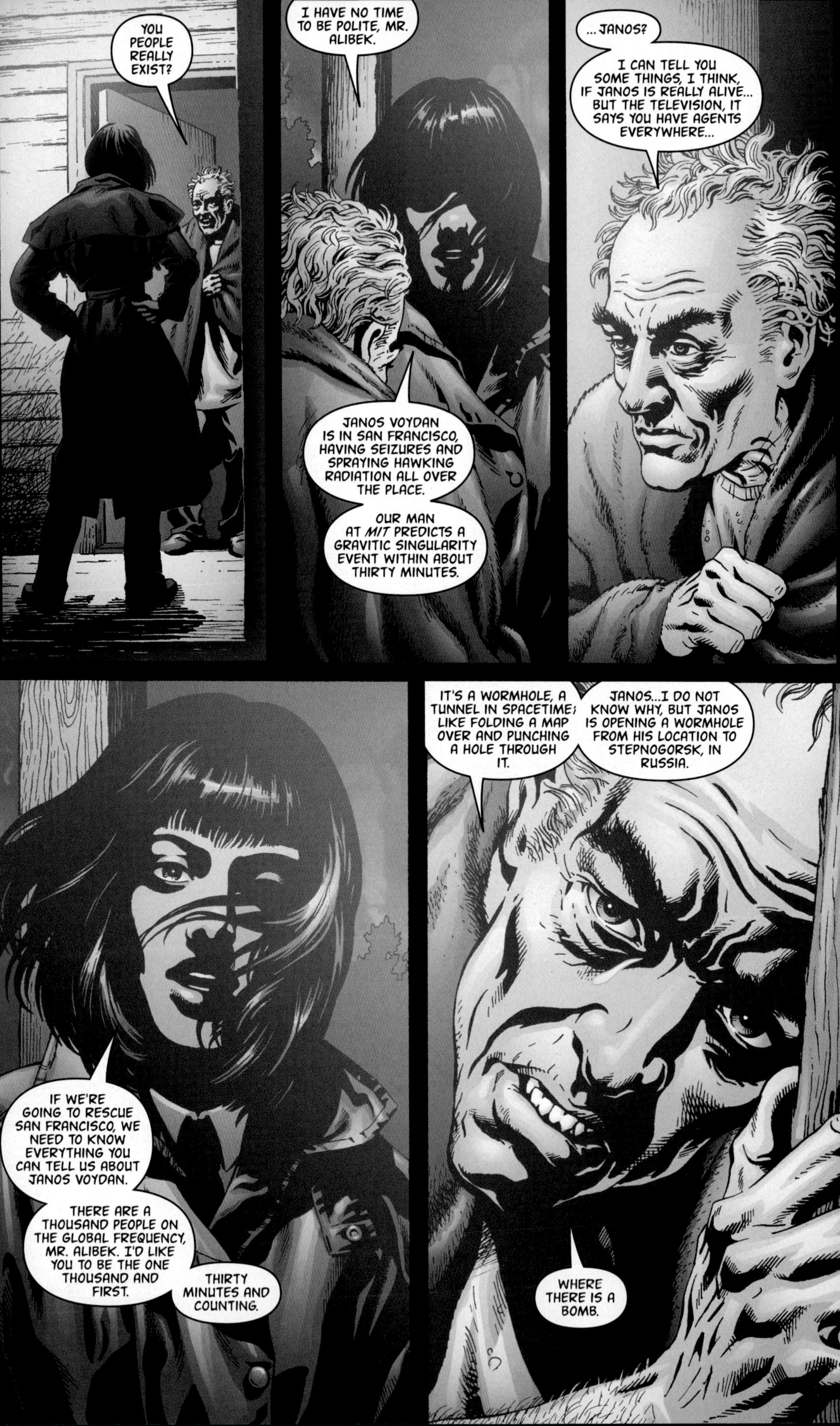
YOU PEOPLE REALLY EXIST?
I HAVE NO TIME TO BE POLITE, MR. ALIBEK.
JANOS VOYDAN IS IN SAN FRANCISCO, HAVING SEIZURES AND SPRAYING HAWKING RADIATION ALL OVER THE PLACE.
OUR MAN AT *MIT* PREDICTS A GRAVITIC SINGULARITY EVENT WITHIN ABOUT THIRTY MINUTES.
...JANOS?
I CAN TELL YOU SOME THINGS, I THINK, IF JANOS IS REALLY ALIVE... BUT THE TELEVISION, IT SAYS YOU HAVE AGENTS EVERYWHERE...
IF WE'RE GOING TO RESCUE SAN FRANCISCO, WE NEED TO KNOW EVERYTHING YOU CAN TELL US ABOUT JANOS VOYDAN.
THERE ARE A THOUSAND PEOPLE ON THE GLOBAL FREQUENCY, MR. ALIBEK. I'D LIKE YOU TO BE THE ONE THOUSAND AND FIRST.
THIRTY MINUTES AND COUNTING.
IT'S A WORMHOLE, A TUNNEL IN SPACETIME; LIKE FOLDING A MAP OVER AND PUNCHING A HOLE THROUGH IT.
JANOS...I DO NOT KNOW WHY, BUT JANOS IS OPENING A WORMHOLE FROM HIS LOCATION TO STEPNOGORSK, IN RUSSIA.
WHERE THERE IS A BOMB.

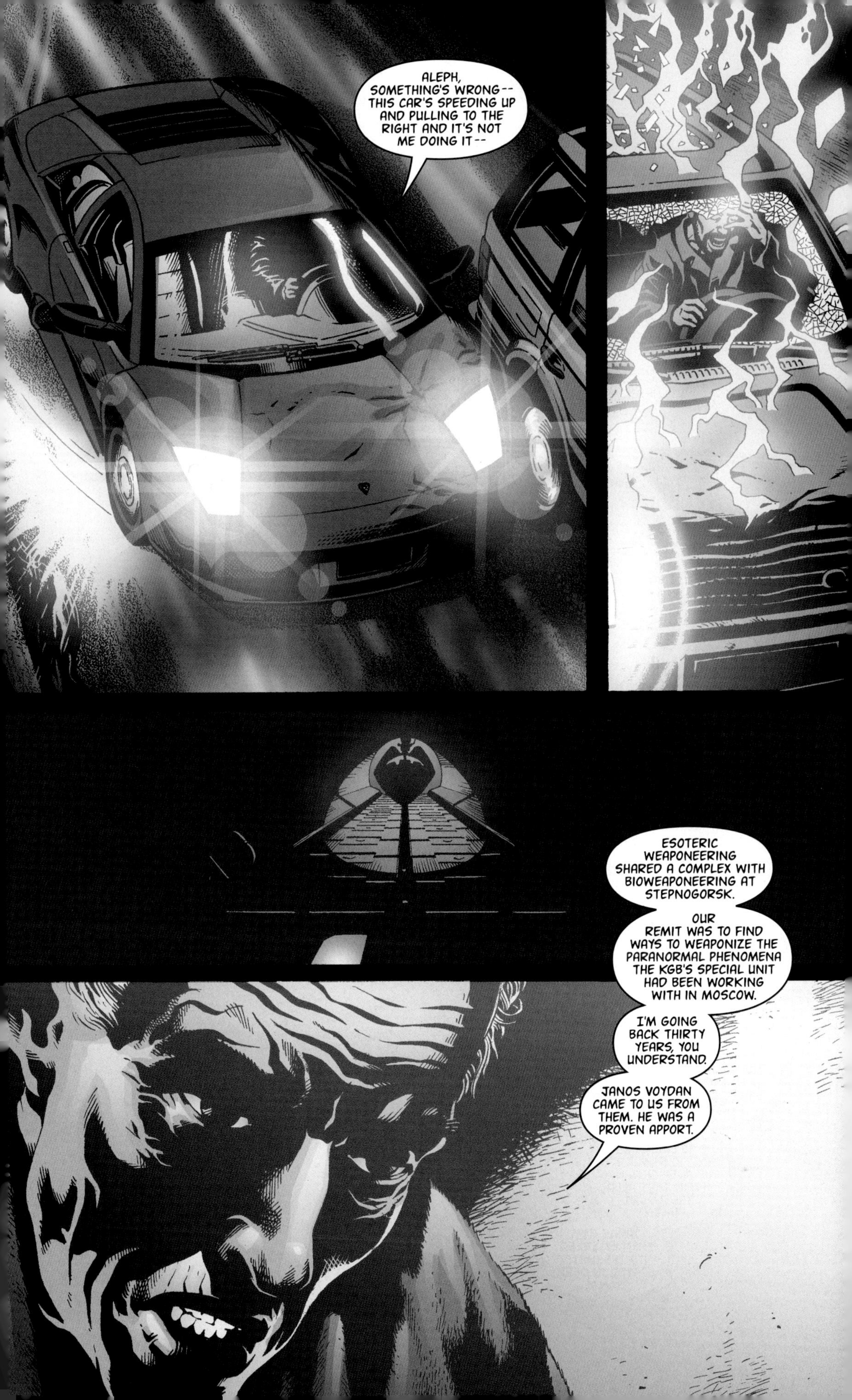
ALEPH, SOMETHING'S WRONG-- THIS CAR'S SPEEDING UP AND PULLING TO THE RIGHT AND IT'S NOT ME DOING IT--
ESOTERIC WEAPONEERING SHARED A COMPLEX WITH BIOWEAPONEERING AT STEPNOGORSK.
OUR REMIT WAS TO FIND WAYS TO WEAPONIZE THE PARANORMAL PHENOMENA THE KGB'S SPECIAL UNIT HAD BEEN WORKING WITH IN MOSCOW.
I'M GOING BACK THIRTY YEARS, YOU UNDERSTAND.
JANOS VOYDAN CAME TO US FROM THEM. HE WAS A PROVEN APPORT.

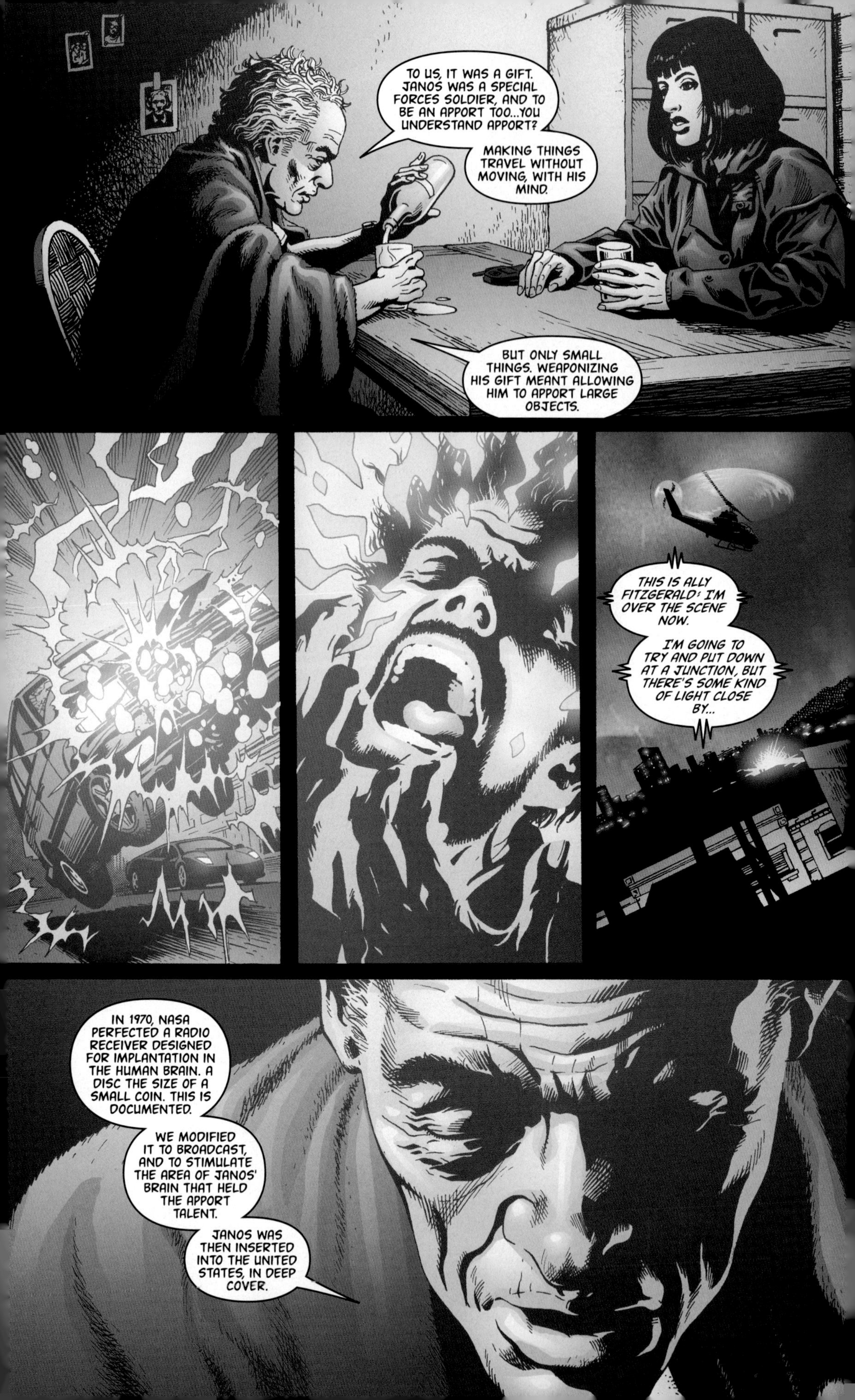
TO US, IT WAS A GIFT. JANOS WAS A SPECIAL FORCES SOLDIER, AND TO BE AN APPORT TOO...YOU UNDERSTAND APPORT?
MAKING THINGS TRAVEL WITHOUT MOVING, WITH HIS MIND.
BUT ONLY SMALL THINGS. WEAPONIZING HIS GIFT MEANT ALLOWING HIM TO APPORT LARGE OBJECTS.
THIS IS ALLY FITZGERALD: I'M OVER THE SCENE NOW.
I'M GOING TO TRY AND PUT DOWN AT A JUNCTION, BUT THERE'S SOME KIND OF LIGHT CLOSE BY...
IN 1970, NASA PERFECTED A RADIO RECEIVER DESIGNED FOR IMPLANTATION IN THE HUMAN BRAIN. A DISC THE SIZE OF A SMALL COIN. THIS IS DOCUMENTED.
WE MODIFIED IT TO BROADCAST, AND TO STIMULATE THE AREA OF JANOS' BRAIN THAT HELD THE APPORT TALENT.
JANOS WAS THEN INSERTED INTO THE UNITED STATES, IN DEEP COVER.

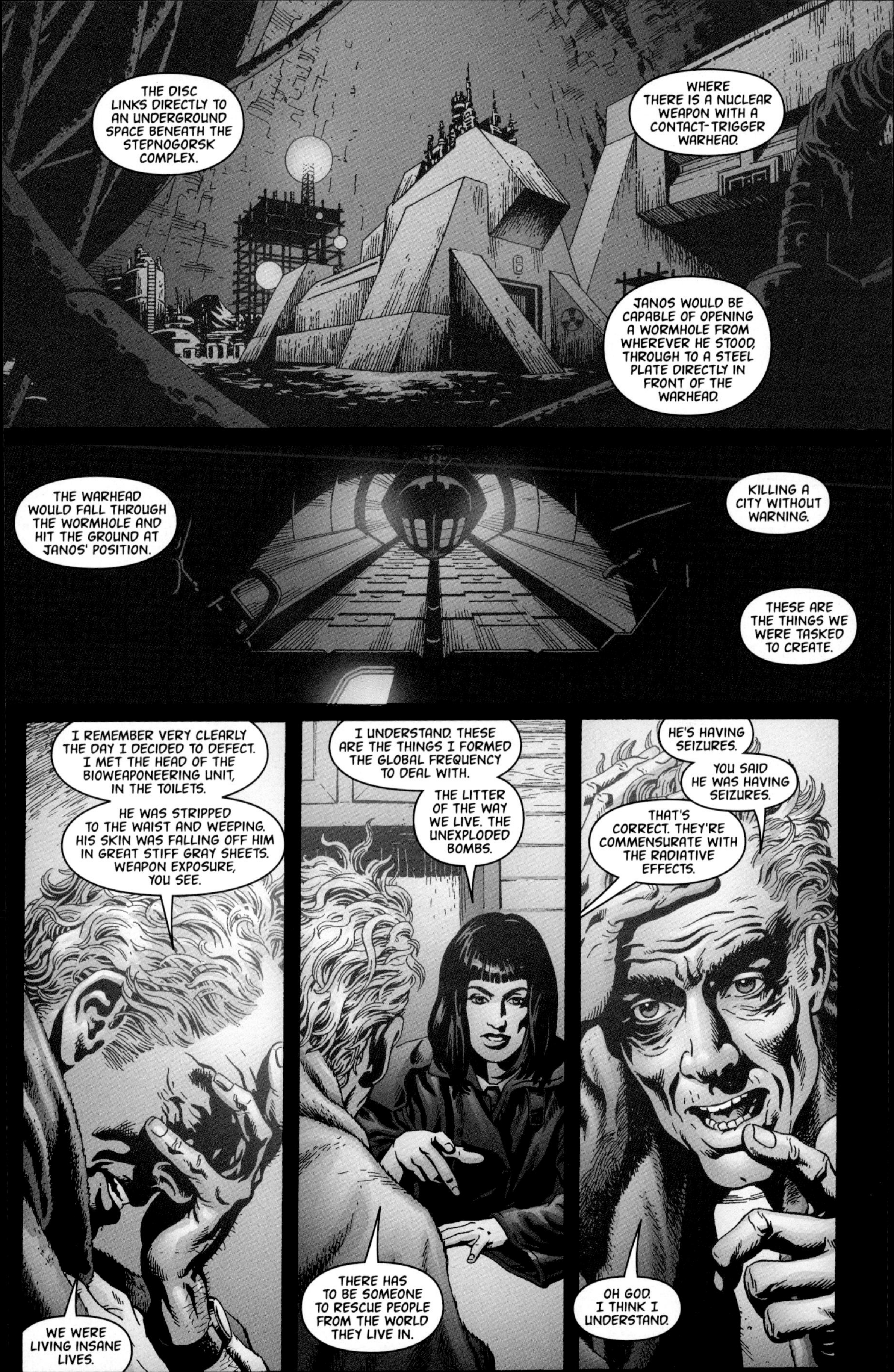
THE DISC LINKS DIRECTLY TO AN UNDERGROUND SPACE BENEATH THE STEPNOGORSK COMPLEX.
WHERE THERE IS A NUCLEAR WEAPON WITH A CONTACT-TRIGGER WARHEAD.
JANOS WOULD BE CAPABLE OF OPENING A WORMHOLE FROM WHEREVER HE STOOD, THROUGH TO A STEEL PLATE DIRECTLY IN FRONT OF THE WARHEAD.
THE WARHEAD WOULD FALL THROUGH THE WORMHOLE AND HIT THE GROUND AT JANOS' POSITION.
KILLING A CITY WITHOUT WARNING.
THESE ARE THE THINGS WE WERE TASKED TO CREATE.
I REMEMBER VERY CLEARLY THE DAY I DECIDED TO DEFECT. I MET THE HEAD OF THE BIOWEAPONEERING UNIT, IN THE TOILETS.
HE WAS STRIPPED TO THE WAIST AND WEEPING. HIS SKIN WAS FALLING OFF HIM IN GREAT STIFF GRAY SHEETS. WEAPON EXPOSURE, YOU SEE.
WE WERE LIVING INSANE LIVES.
I UNDERSTAND. THESE ARE THE THINGS I FORMED THE GLOBAL FREQUENCY TO DEAL WITH.
THE LITTER OF THE WAY WE LIVE. THE UNEXPLODED BOMBS.
THERE HAS TO BE SOMEONE TO RESCUE PEOPLE FROM THE WORLD THEY LIVE IN.
HE'S HAVING SEIZURES.
YOU SAID HE WAS HAVING SEIZURES.
THAT'S CORRECT. THEY'RE COMMENSURATE WITH THE RADIATIVE EFFECTS.
OH GOD. I THINK I UNDERSTAND.

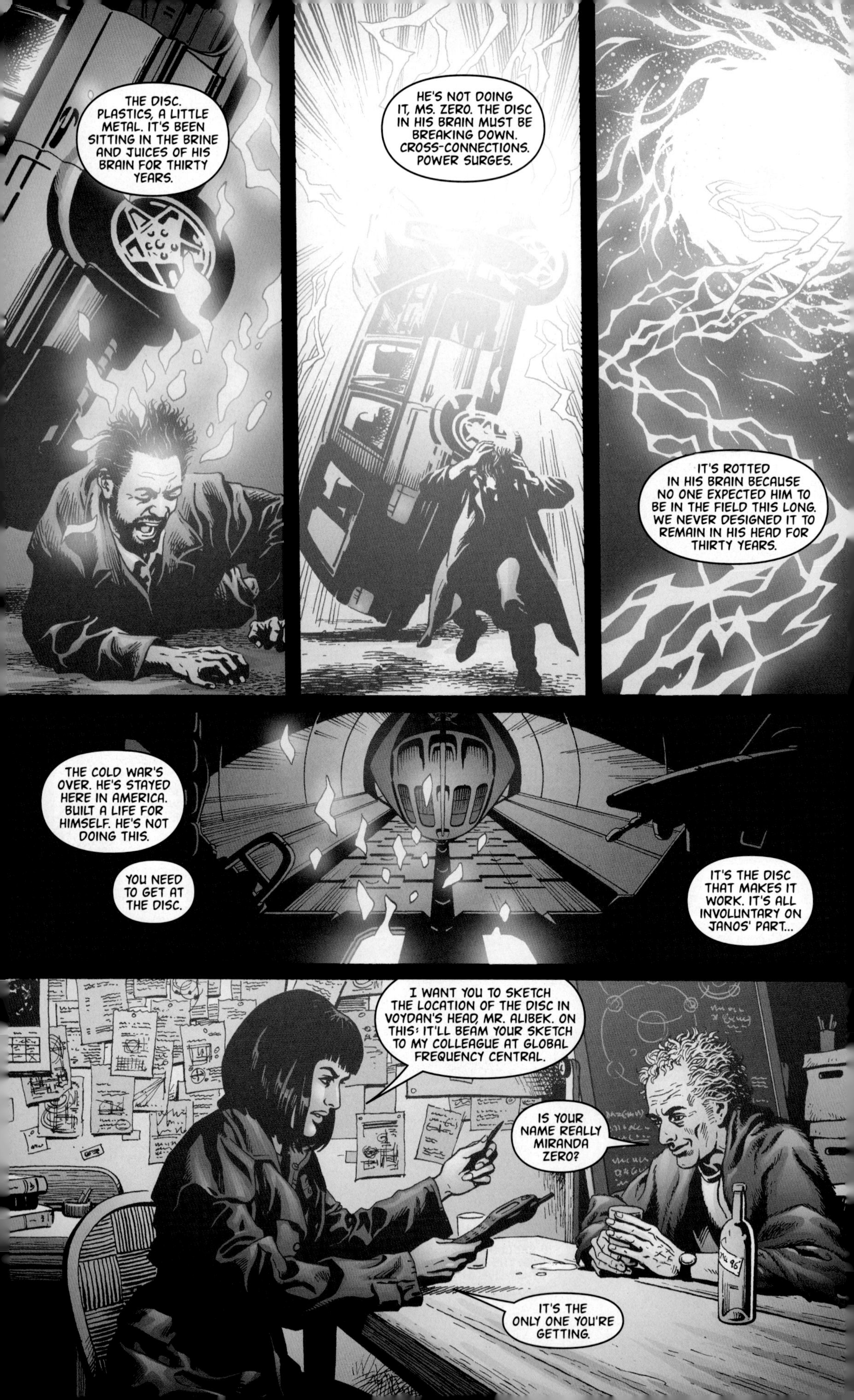
THE DISC. PLASTICS, A LITTLE METAL. IT'S BEEN SITTING IN THE BRINE AND JUICES OF HIS BRAIN FOR THIRTY YEARS.
HE'S NOT DOING IT, MS. ZERO. THE DISC IN HIS BRAIN MUST BE BREAKING DOWN. CROSS-CONNECTIONS. POWER SURGES.
IT'S ROTTED IN HIS BRAIN BECAUSE NO ONE EXPECTED HIM TO BE IN THE FIELD THIS LONG. WE NEVER DESIGNED IT TO REMAIN IN HIS HEAD FOR THIRTY YEARS.
THE COLD WAR'S OVER. HE'S STAYED HERE IN AMERICA. BUILT A LIFE FOR HIMSELF. HE'S NOT DOING THIS.
YOU NEED TO GET AT THE DISC.
IT'S THE DISC THAT MAKES IT WORK. IT'S ALL INVOLUNTARY ON JANOS' PART...
I WANT YOU TO SKETCH THE LOCATION OF THE DISC IN VOYDAN'S HEAD, MR. ALIBEK. ON THIS: IT'LL BEAM YOUR SKETCH TO MY COLLEAGUE AT GLOBAL FREQUENCY CENTRAL.
IS YOUR NAME REALLY MIRANDA ZERO?
IT'S THE ONLY ONE YOU'RE GETTING.

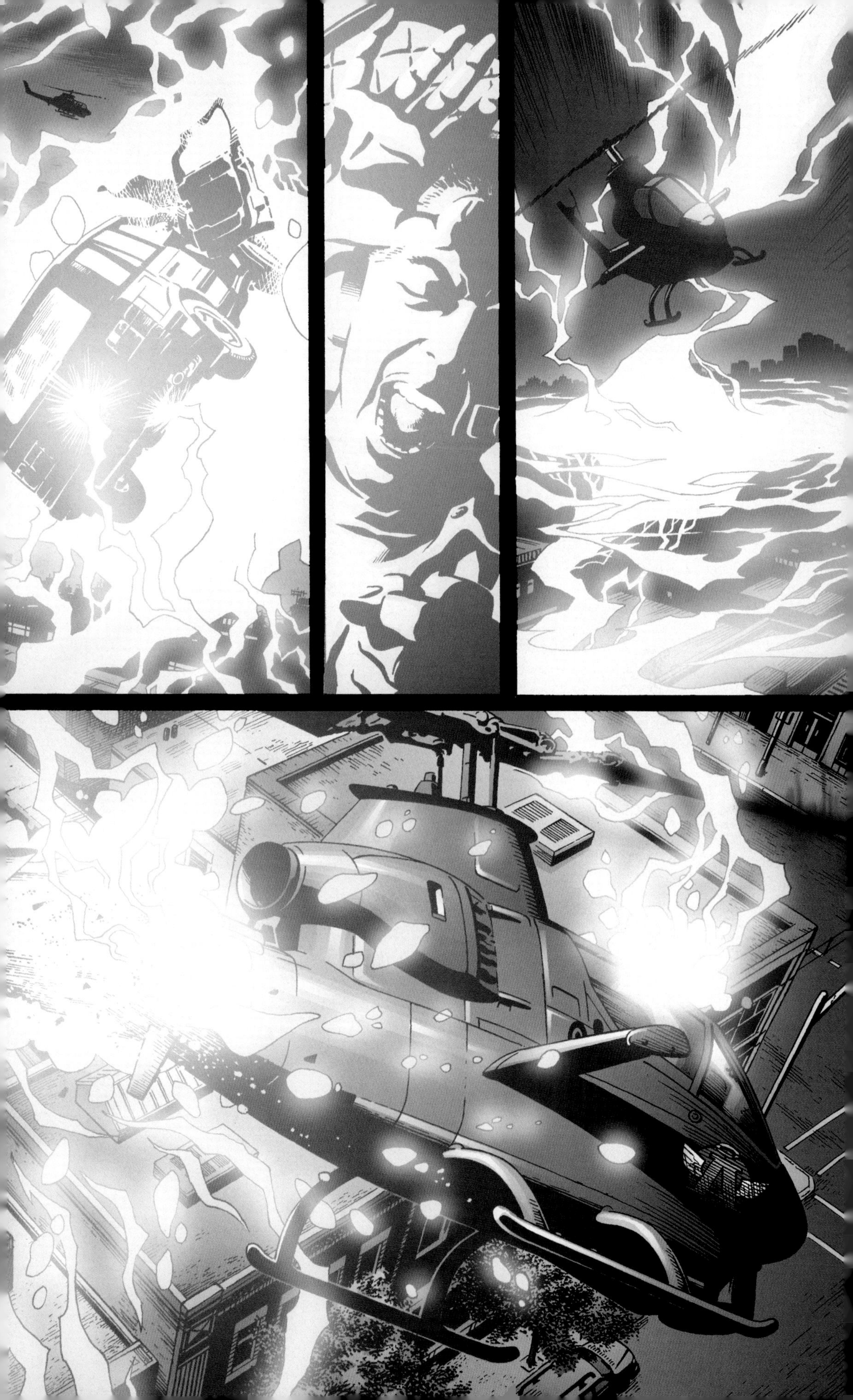

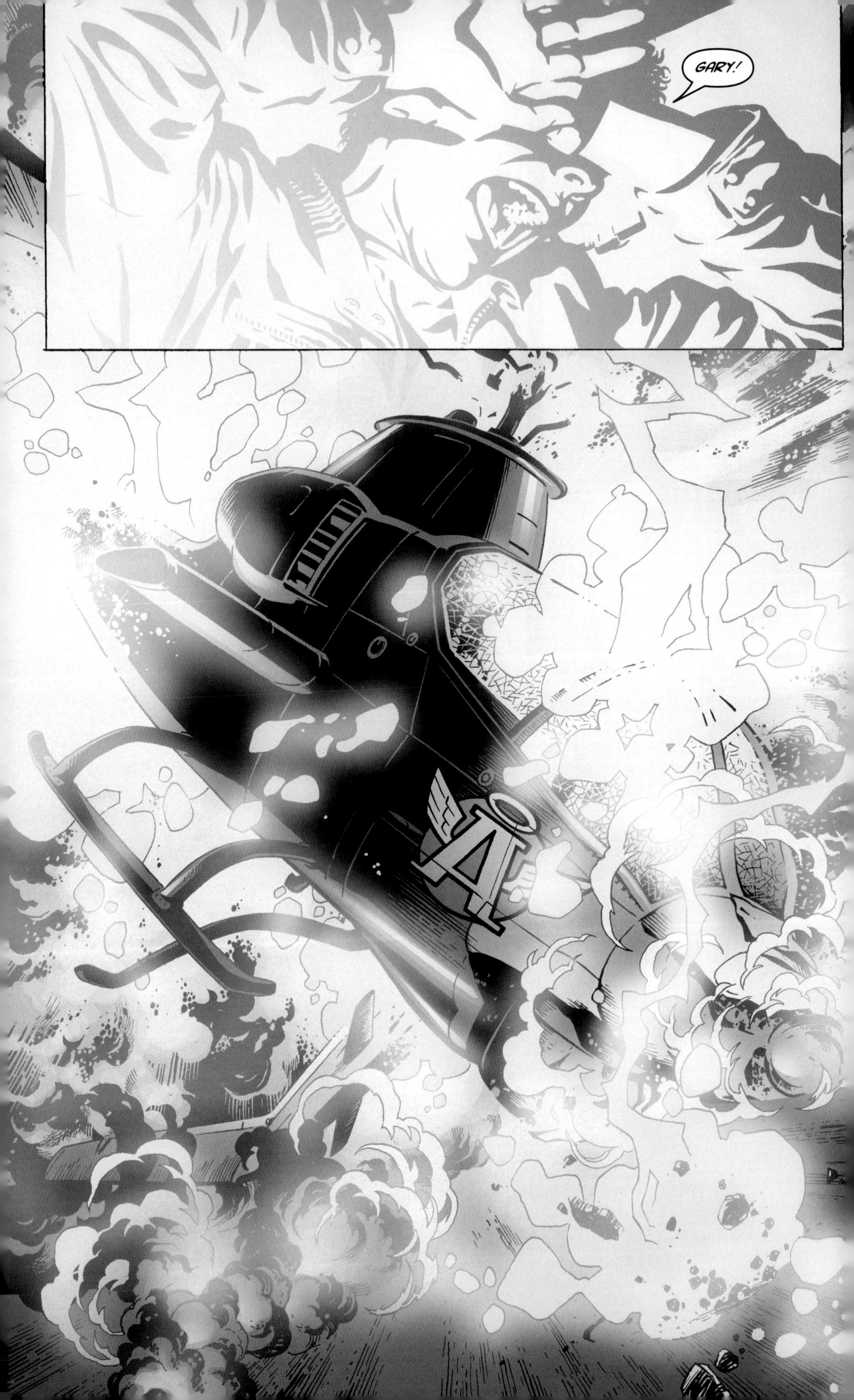
GARY!

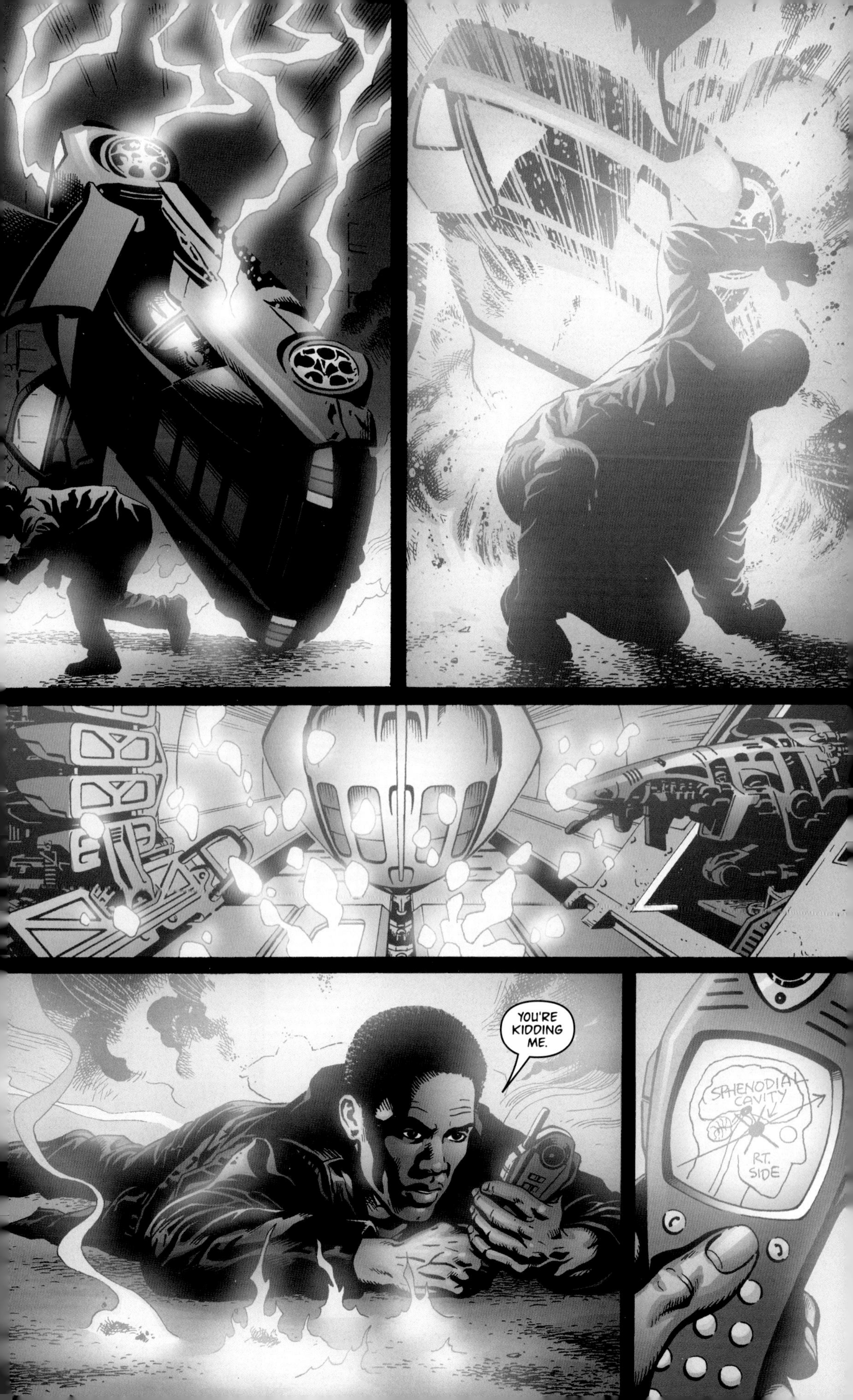
YOU'RE KIDDING ME.
SPHENODIAL CAVITY
RT. SIDE

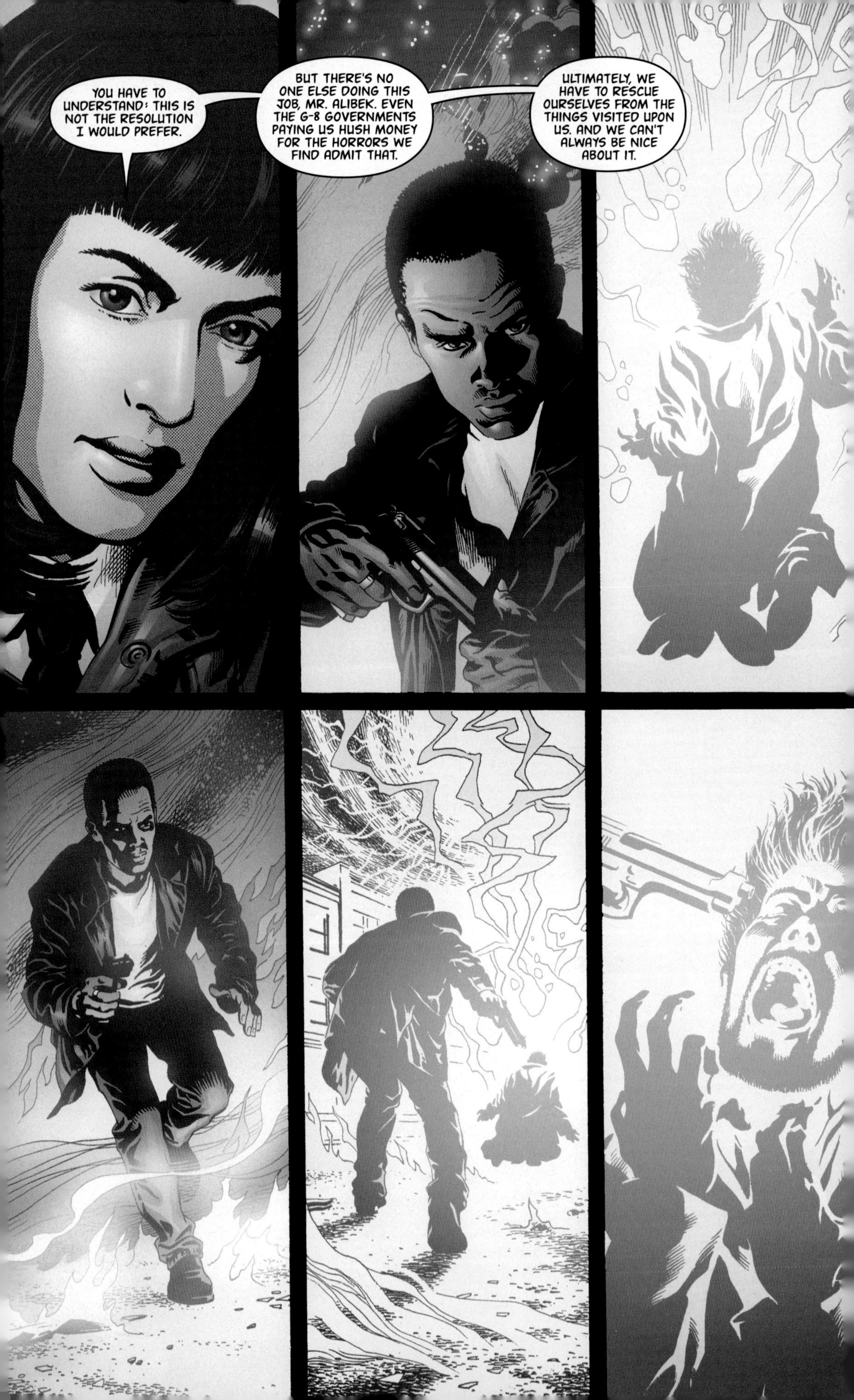
YOU HAVE TO UNDERSTAND: THIS IS NOT THE RESOLUTION I WOULD PREFER.
BUT THERE'S NO ONE ELSE DOING THIS JOB, MR. ALIBEK. EVEN THE G-8 GOVERNMENTS PAYING US HUSH MONEY FOR THE HORRORS WE FIND ADMIT THAT.
ULTIMATELY, WE HAVE TO RESCUE OURSELVES FROM THE THINGS VISITED UPON US. AND WE CAN'T ALWAYS BE NICE ABOUT IT.

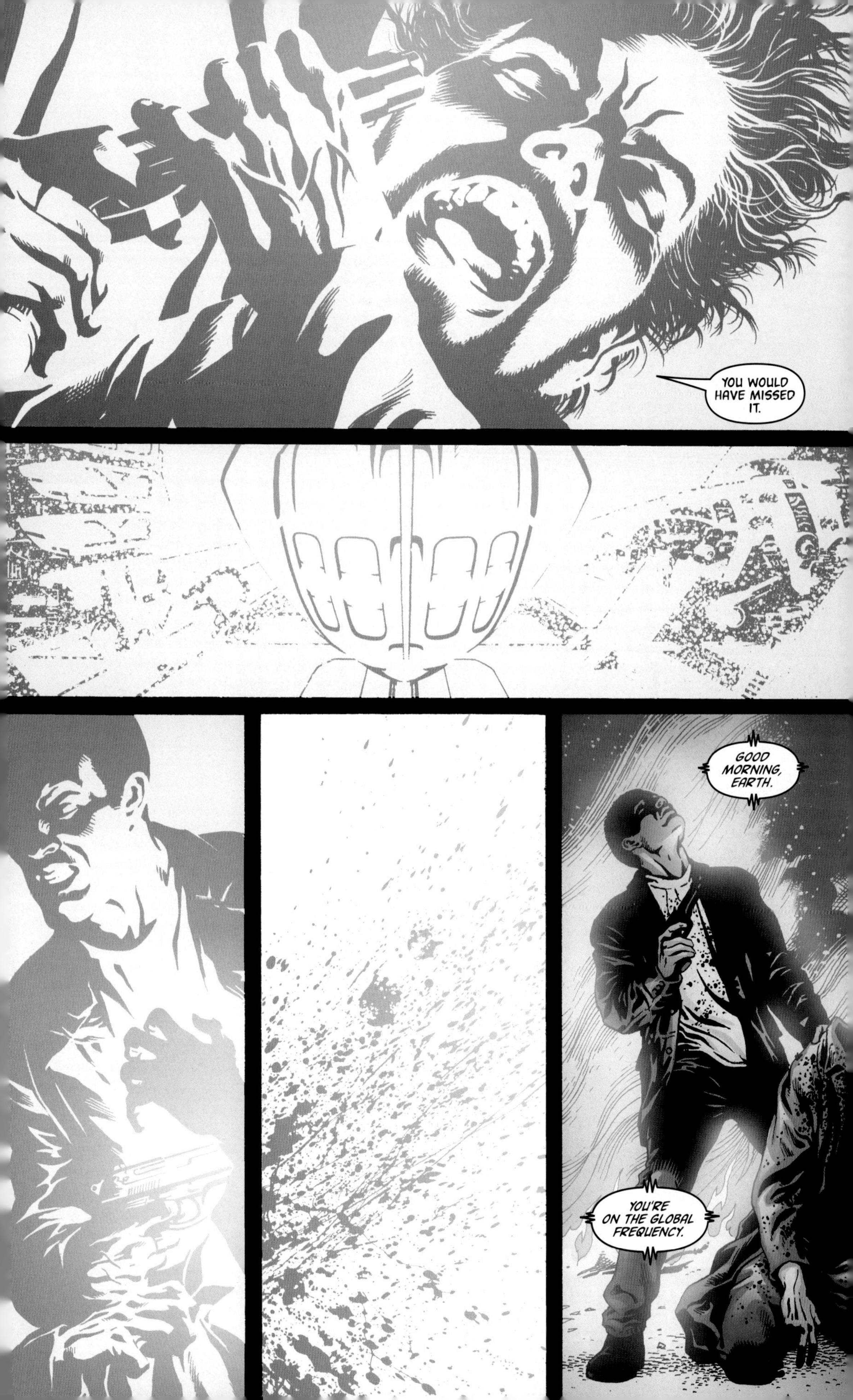

YOU WOULD HAVE MISSED IT.
GOOD MORNING, EARTH.
YOU'RE ON THE GLOBAL FREQUENCY.

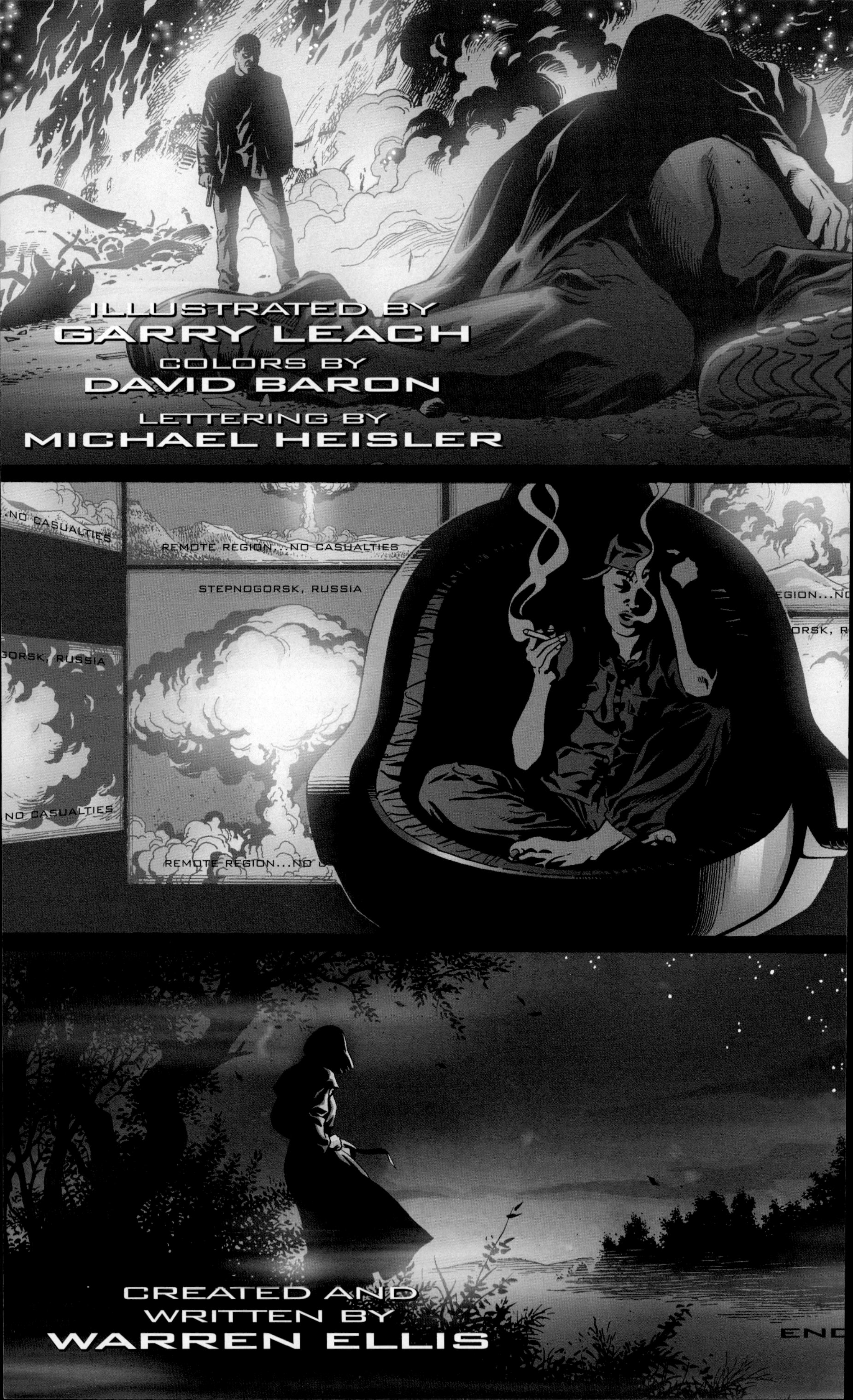
ILLUSTRATED BY
GARRY LEACH
COLORS BY
DAVID BARON
LETTERING BY
MICHAEL HEISLER
NO CASUALTIES
REMOTE REGION...NO CASUALTIES
STEPNOGORSK, RUSSIA
GORSK, RUSSIA
NO CASUALTIES
REMOTE REGION...NO
EGION...NO
ORSK,
CREATED AND
WRITTEN BY
WARREN ELLIS
END

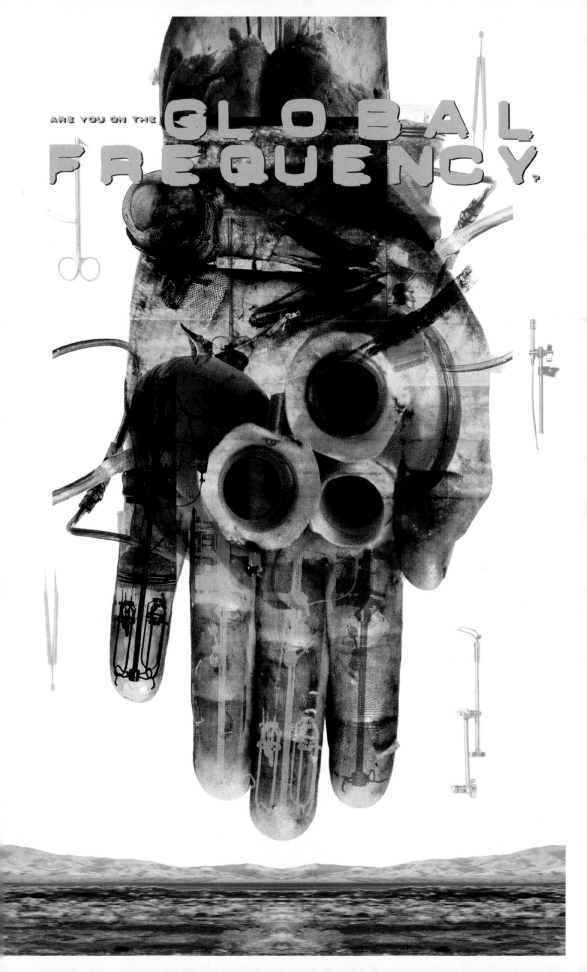

ARE YOU ON THE GLOBAL FREQUENCY?

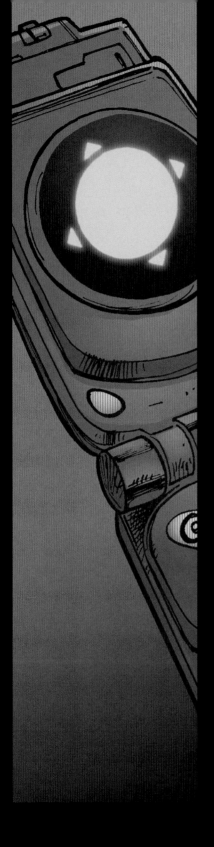

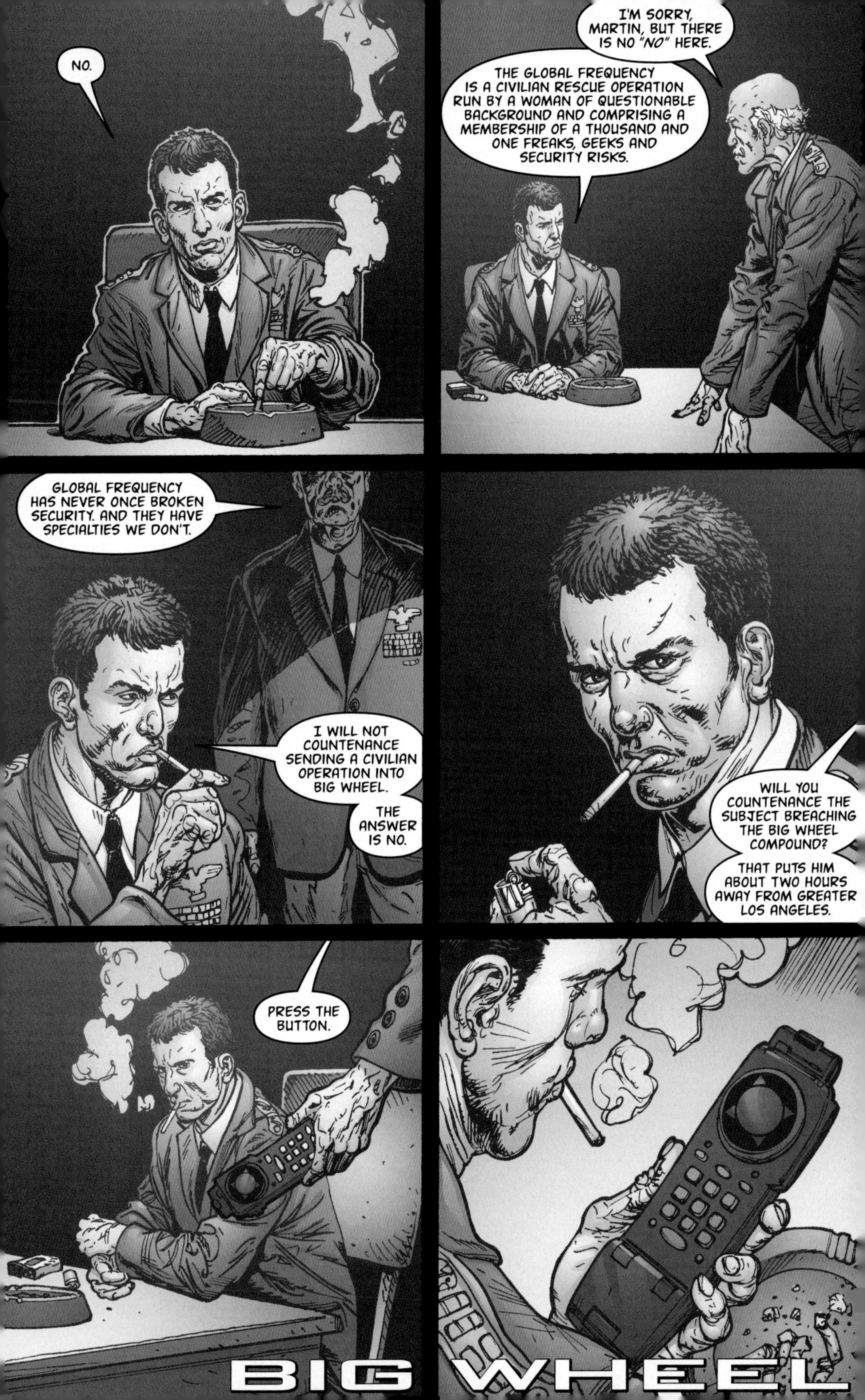
NO.
I'M SORRY, MARTIN, BUT THERE IS NO "NO" HERE.
THE GLOBAL FREQUENCY IS A CIVILIAN RESCUE OPERATION RUN BY A WOMAN OF QUESTIONABLE BACKGROUND AND COMPRISING A MEMBERSHIP OF A THOUSAND AND ONE FREAKS, GEEKS AND SECURITY RISKS.
GLOBAL FREQUENCY HAS NEVER ONCE BROKEN SECURITY. AND THEY HAVE SPECIALTIES WE DON'T.
I WILL NOT COUNTENANCE SENDING A CIVILIAN OPERATION INTO BIG WHEEL.
THE ANSWER IS NO.
WILL YOU COUNTENANCE THE SUBJECT BREACHING THE BIG WHEEL COMPOUND?
THAT PUTS HIM ABOUT TWO HOURS AWAY FROM GREATER LOS ANGELES.
PRESS THE BUTTON.
BIG WHEEL

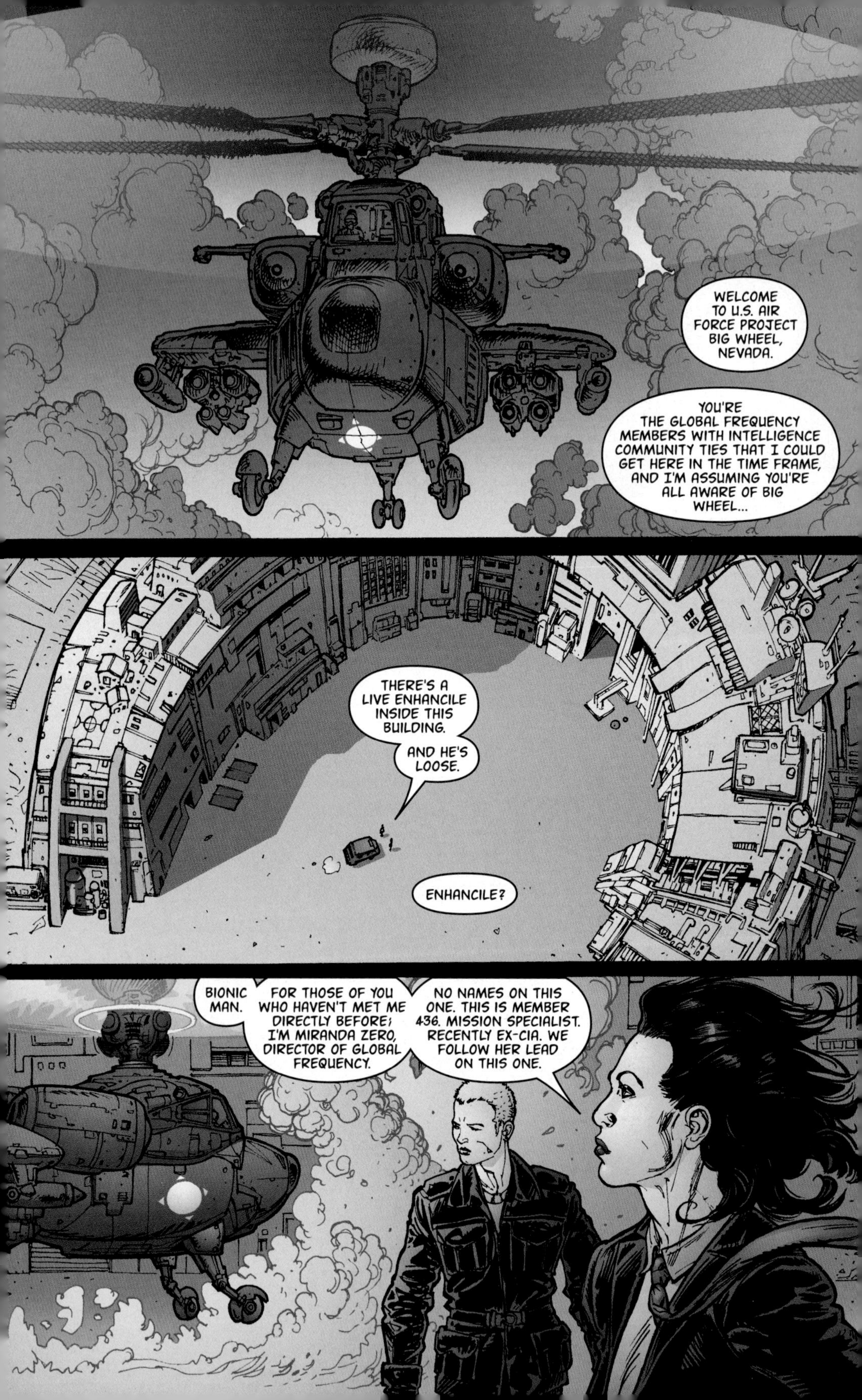
WELCOME TO U.S. AIR FORCE PROJECT BIG WHEEL, NEVADA.
YOU'RE THE GLOBAL FREQUENCY MEMBERS WITH INTELLIGENCE COMMUNITY TIES THAT I COULD GET HERE IN THE TIME FRAME, AND I'M ASSUMING YOU'RE ALL AWARE OF BIG WHEEL...
THERE'S A LIVE ENHANCILE INSIDE THIS BUILDING.
AND HE'S LOOSE.
ENHANCILE?
BIONIC MAN.
FOR THOSE OF YOU WHO HAVEN'T MET ME DIRECTLY BEFORE; I'M MIRANDA ZERO, DIRECTOR OF GLOBAL FREQUENCY.
NO NAMES ON THIS ONE. THIS IS MEMBER 436. MISSION SPECIALIST. RECENTLY EX-CIA. WE FOLLOW HER LEAD ON THIS ONE.

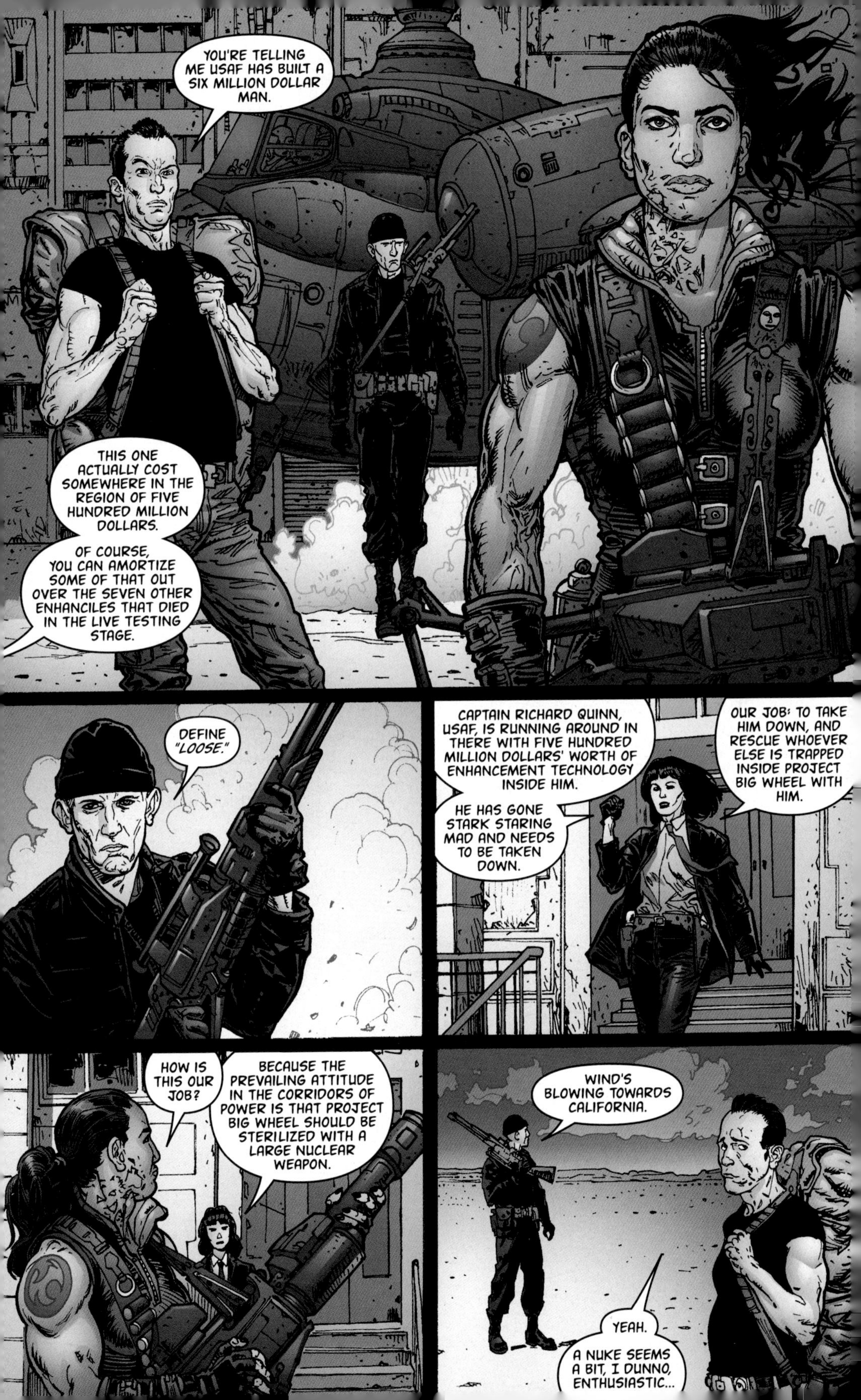
YOU'RE TELLING ME USAF HAS BUILT A SIX MILLION DOLLAR MAN.
THIS ONE ACTUALLY COST SOMEWHERE IN THE REGION OF FIVE HUNDRED MILLION DOLLARS.
OF COURSE, YOU CAN AMORTIZE SOME OF THAT OUT OVER THE SEVEN OTHER ENHANCILES THAT DIED IN THE LIVE TESTING STAGE.
DEFINE "LOOSE."
CAPTAIN RICHARD QUINN, USAF, IS RUNNING AROUND IN THERE WITH FIVE HUNDRED MILLION DOLLARS' WORTH OF ENHANCEMENT TECHNOLOGY INSIDE HIM.
HE HAS GONE STARK STARING MAD AND NEEDS TO BE TAKEN DOWN.
OUR JOB: TO TAKE HIM DOWN, AND RESCUE WHOEVER ELSE IS TRAPPED INSIDE PROJECT BIG WHEEL WITH HIM.
HOW IS THIS OUR JOB?
BECAUSE THE PREVAILING ATTITUDE IN THE CORRIDORS OF POWER IS THAT PROJECT BIG WHEEL SHOULD BE STERILIZED WITH A LARGE NUCLEAR WEAPON.
WIND'S BLOWING TOWARDS CALIFORNIA.
YEAH.
A NUKE SEEMS A BIT, I DUNNO, ENTHUSIASTIC...

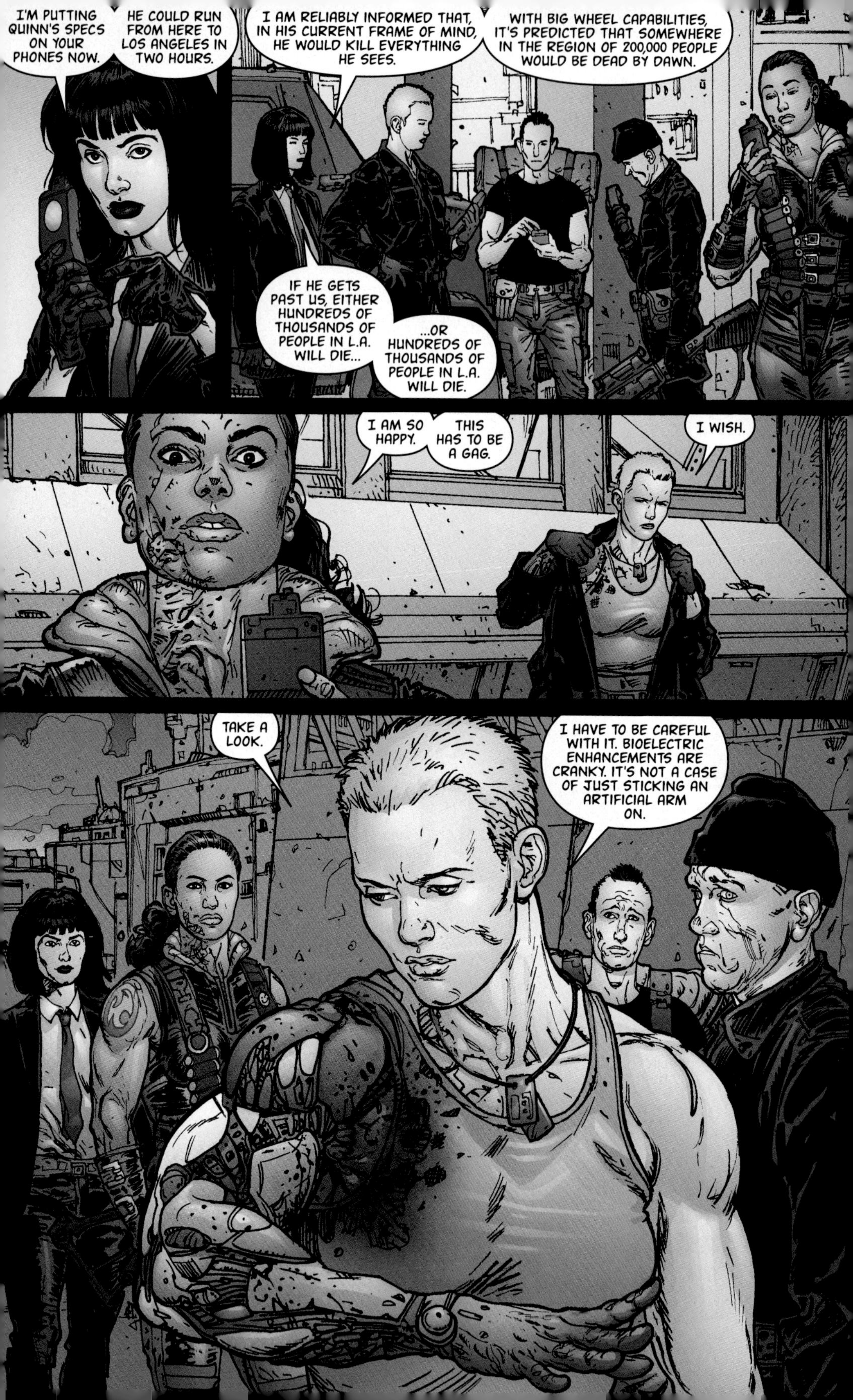
I'M PUTTING QUINN'S SPECS ON YOUR PHONES NOW.
HE COULD RUN FROM HERE TO LOS ANGELES IN TWO HOURS.
I AM RELIABLY INFORMED THAT, IN HIS CURRENT FRAME OF MIND, HE WOULD KILL EVERYTHING HE SEES.
WITH BIG WHEEL CAPABILITIES, IT'S PREDICTED THAT SOMEWHERE IN THE REGION OF 200,000 PEOPLE WOULD BE DEAD BY DAWN.
IF HE GETS PAST US, EITHER HUNDREDS OF THOUSANDS OF PEOPLE IN L.A. WILL DIE...
...OR HUNDREDS OF THOUSANDS OF PEOPLE IN L.A. WILL DIE.
I AM SO HAPPY.
THIS HAS TO BE A GAG.
I WISH.
TAKE A LOOK.
I HAVE TO BE CAREFUL WITH IT. BIOELECTRIC ENHANCEMENTS ARE CRANKY. IT'S NOT A CASE OF JUST STICKING AN ARTIFICIAL ARM ON.

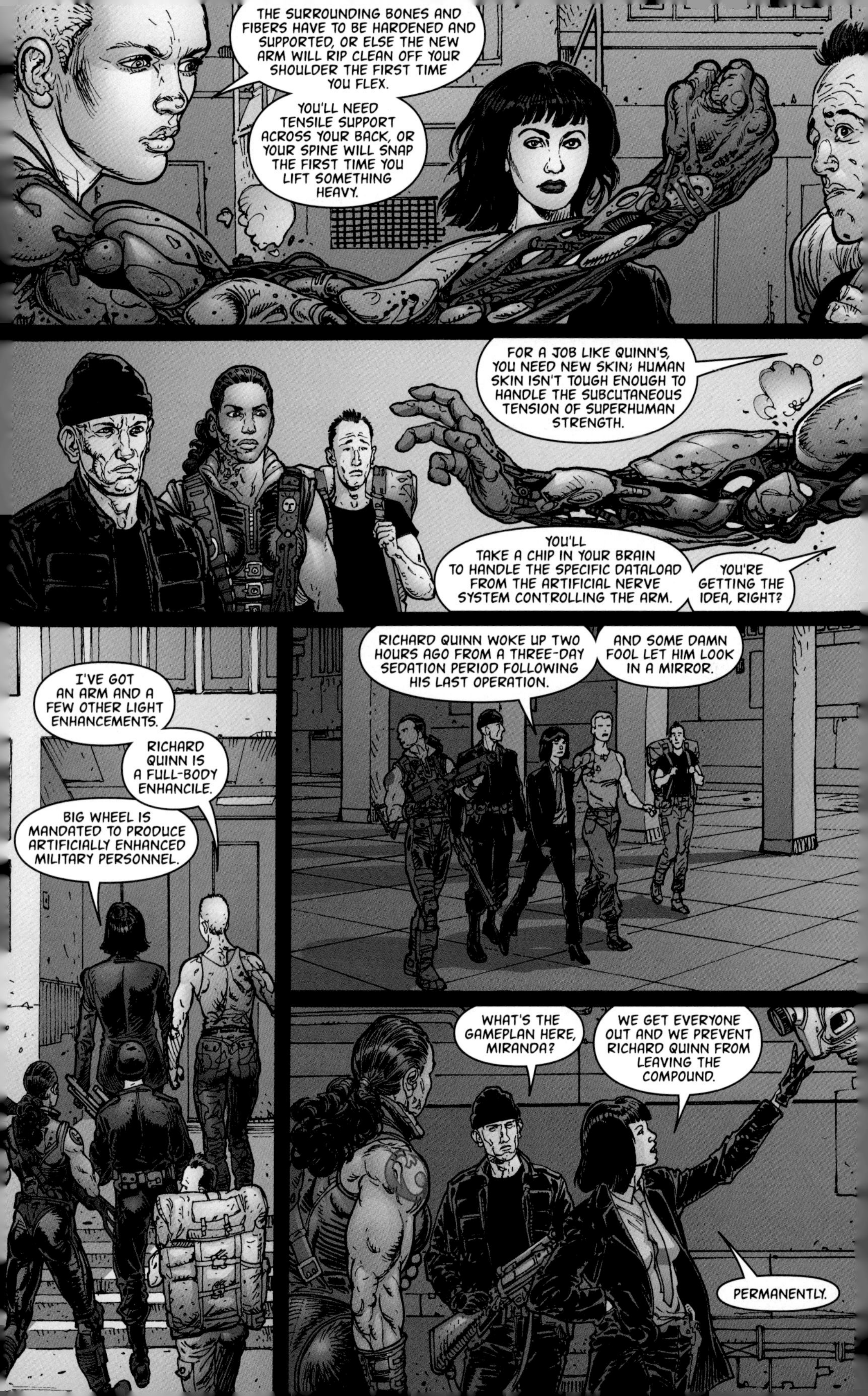
THE SURROUNDING BONES AND FIBERS HAVE TO BE HARDENED AND SUPPORTED, OR ELSE THE NEW ARM WILL RIP CLEAN OFF YOUR SHOULDER THE FIRST TIME YOU FLEX.
YOU'LL NEED TENSILE SUPPORT ACROSS YOUR BACK, OR YOUR SPINE WILL SNAP THE FIRST TIME YOU LIFT SOMETHING HEAVY.
FOR A JOB LIKE QUINN'S, YOU NEED NEW SKIN; HUMAN SKIN ISN'T TOUGH ENOUGH TO HANDLE THE SUBCUTANEOUS TENSION OF SUPERHUMAN STRENGTH.
YOU'LL TAKE A CHIP IN YOUR BRAIN TO HANDLE THE SPECIFIC DATALOAD FROM THE ARTIFICIAL NERVE SYSTEM CONTROLLING THE ARM.
YOU'RE GETTING THE IDEA, RIGHT?
I'VE GOT AN ARM AND A FEW OTHER LIGHT ENHANCEMENTS.
RICHARD QUINN IS A FULL-BODY ENHANCILE.
BIG WHEEL IS MANDATED TO PRODUCE ARTIFICIALLY ENHANCED MILITARY PERSONNEL.
RICHARD QUINN WOKE UP TWO HOURS AGO FROM A THREE-DAY SEDATION PERIOD FOLLOWING HIS LAST OPERATION.
AND SOME DAMN FOOL LET HIM LOOK IN A MIRROR.
WHAT'S THE GAMEPLAN HERE, MIRANDA?
WE GET EVERYONE OUT AND WE PREVENT RICHARD QUINN FROM LEAVING THE COMPOUND.
PERMANENTLY.

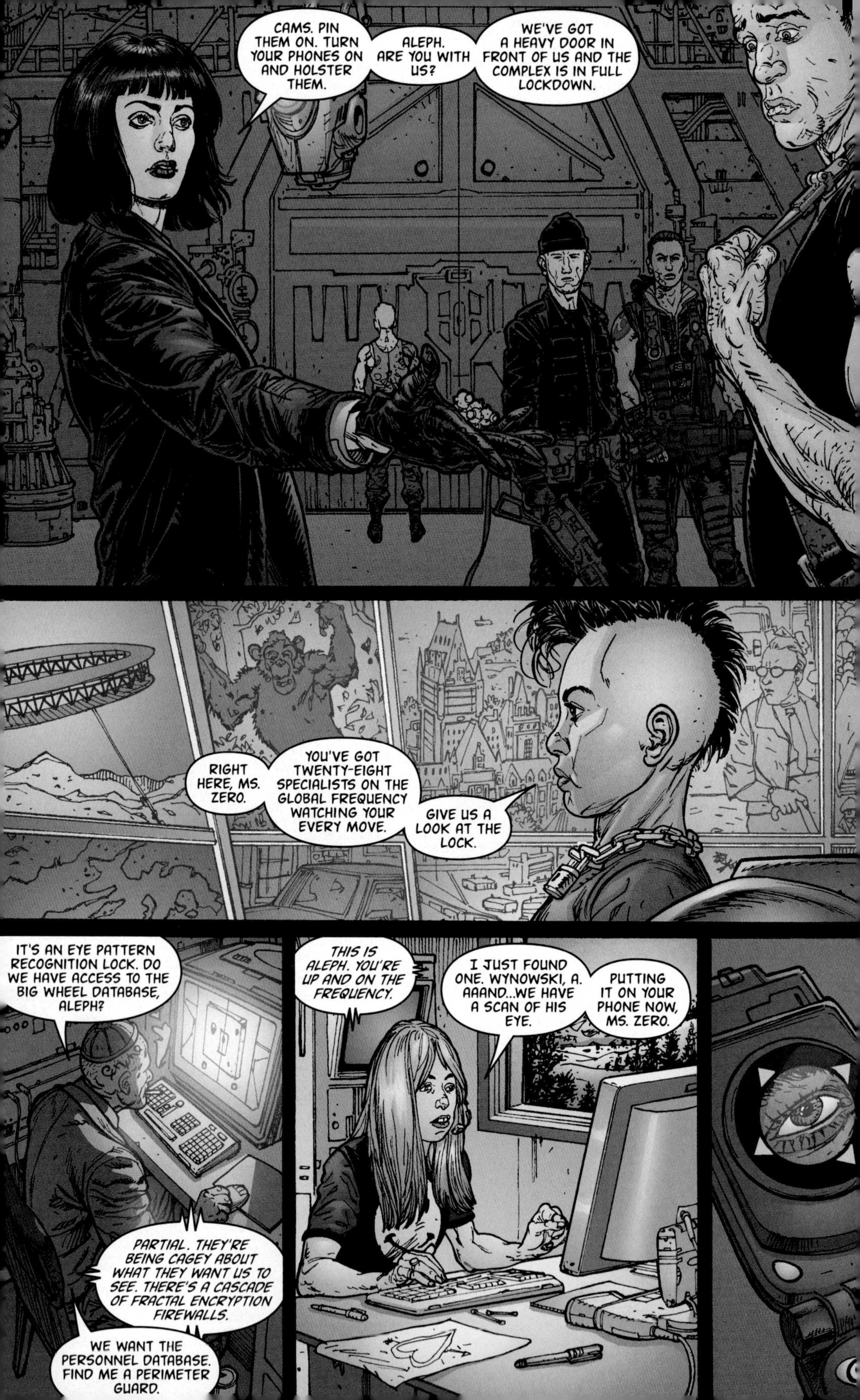
CAMS. PIN THEM ON. TURN YOUR PHONES ON AND HOLSTER THEM.
ALEPH. ARE YOU WITH US?
WE'VE GOT A HEAVY DOOR IN FRONT OF US AND THE COMPLEX IS IN FULL LOCKDOWN.
RIGHT HERE, MS. ZERO.
YOU'VE GOT TWENTY-EIGHT SPECIALISTS ON THE GLOBAL FREQUENCY WATCHING YOUR EVERY MOVE.
GIVE US A LOOK AT THE LOCK.
IT'S AN EYE PATTERN RECOGNITION LOCK. DO WE HAVE ACCESS TO THE BIG WHEEL DATABASE, ALEPH?
PARTIAL. THEY'RE BEING CAGEY ABOUT WHAT THEY WANT US TO SEE. THERE'S A CASCADE OF FRACTAL ENCRYPTION FIREWALLS.
WE WANT THE PERSONNEL DATABASE. FIND ME A PERIMETER GUARD.
THIS IS ALEPH. YOU'RE UP AND ON THE FREQUENCY.
I JUST FOUND ONE. WYNOWSKI, A. AAAND...WE HAVE A SCAN OF HIS EYE.
PUTTING IT ON YOUR PHONE NOW, MS. ZERO.

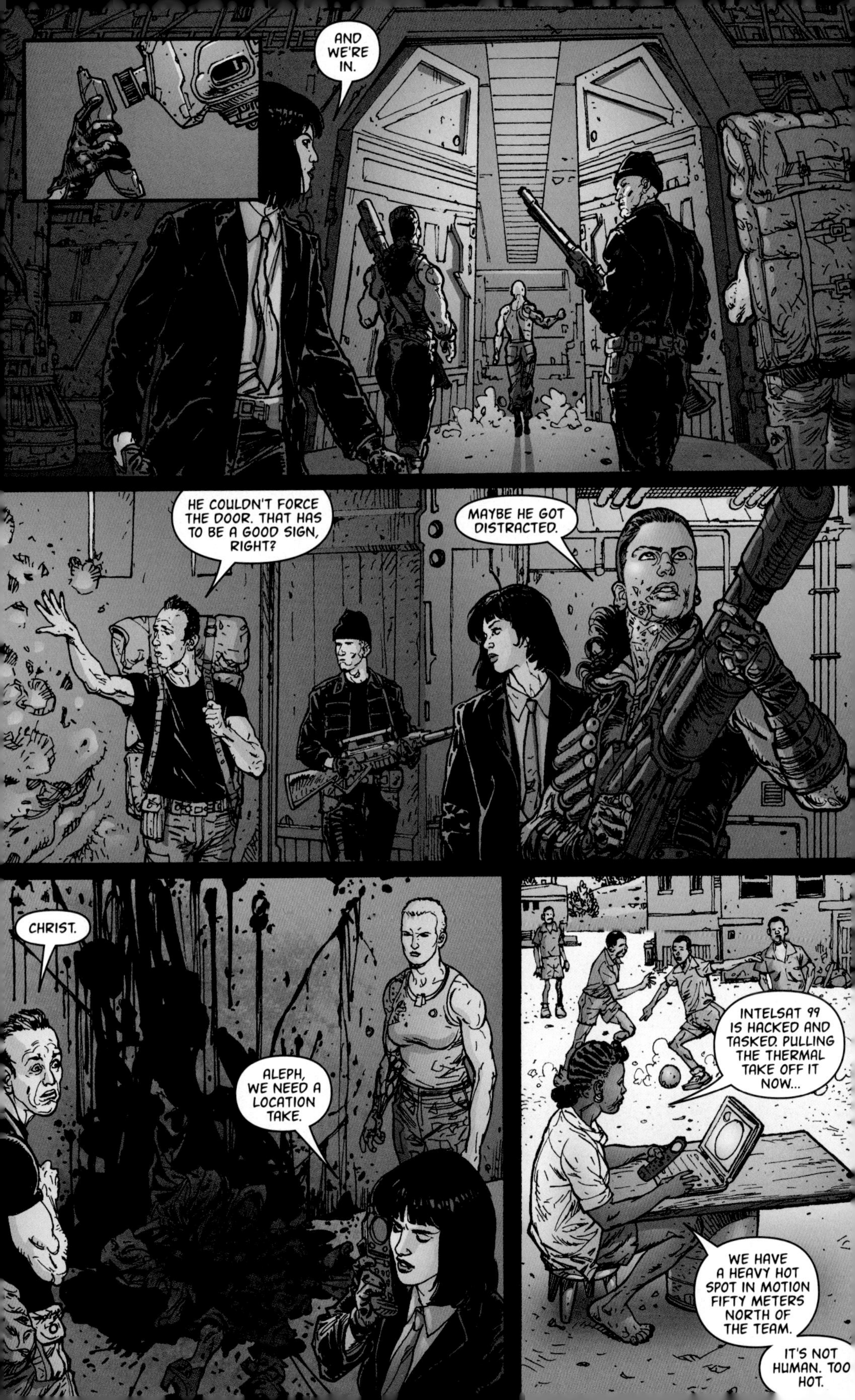
AND WE'RE IN.
HE COULDN'T FORCE THE DOOR. THAT HAS TO BE A GOOD SIGN, RIGHT?
MAYBE HE GOT DISTRACTED.
CHRIST.
ALEPH, WE NEED A LOCATION TAKE.
INTELSAT 99 IS HACKED AND TASKED. PULLING THE THERMAL TAKE OFF IT NOW...
WE HAVE A HEAVY HOT SPOT IN MOTION FIFTY METERS NORTH OF THE TEAM.
IT'S NOT HUMAN. TOO HOT.

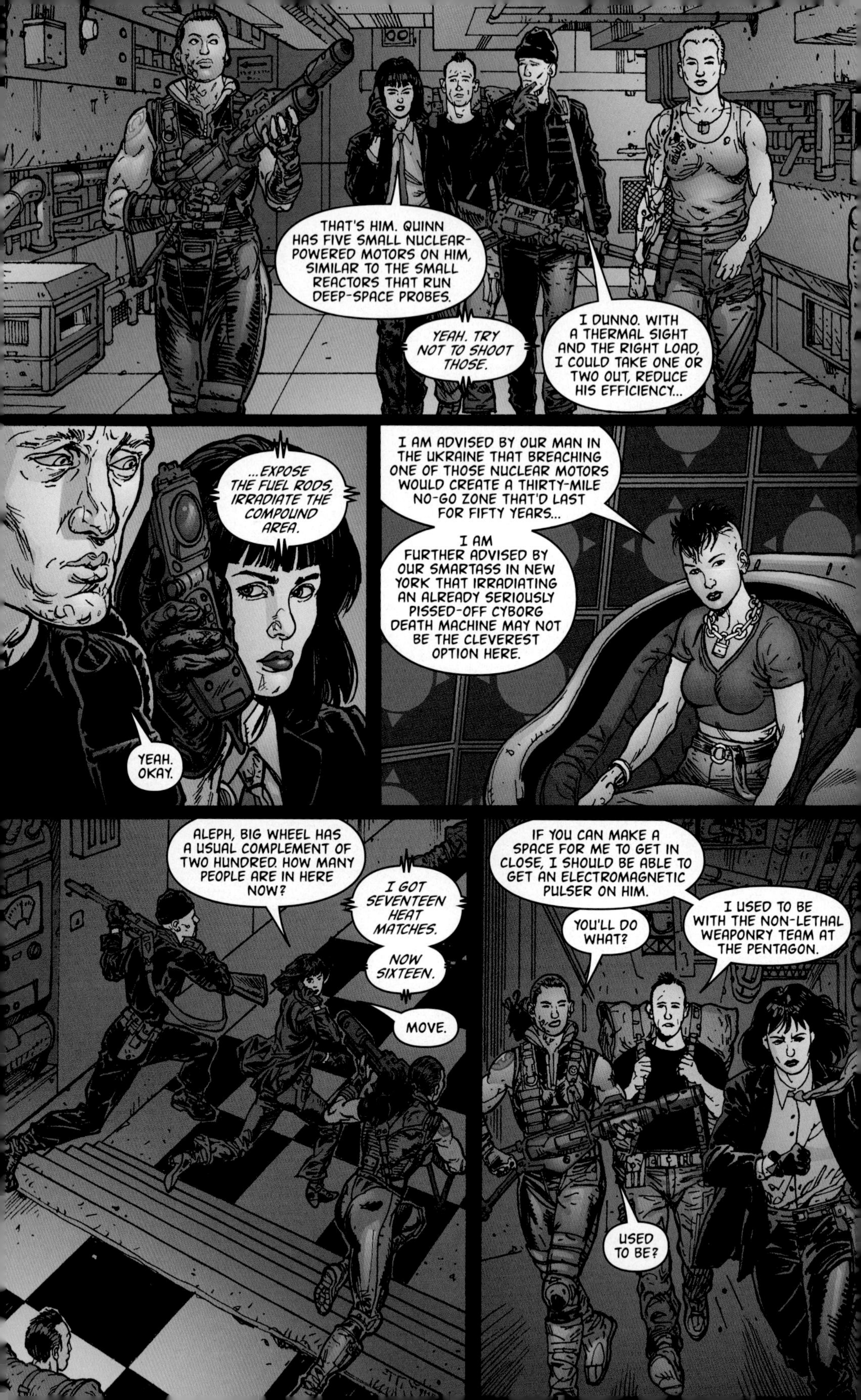
THAT'S HIM. QUINN HAS FIVE SMALL NUCLEAR-POWERED MOTORS ON HIM, SIMILAR TO THE SMALL REACTORS THAT RUN DEEP-SPACE PROBES.
YEAH. TRY NOT TO SHOOT THOSE.
I DUNNO. WITH A THERMAL SIGHT AND THE RIGHT LOAD, I COULD TAKE ONE OR TWO OUT, REDUCE HIS EFFICIENCY...
...EXPOSE THE FUEL RODS, IRRADIATE THE COMPOUND AREA.
YEAH. OKAY.
I AM ADVISED BY OUR MAN IN THE UKRAINE THAT BREACHING ONE OF THOSE NUCLEAR MOTORS WOULD CREATE A THIRTY-MILE NO-GO ZONE THAT'D LAST FOR FIFTY YEARS...
I AM FURTHER ADVISED BY OUR SMARTASS IN NEW YORK THAT IRRADIATING AN ALREADY SERIOUSLY PISSED-OFF CYBORG DEATH MACHINE MAY NOT BE THE CLEVEREST OPTION HERE.
ALEPH, BIG WHEEL HAS A USUAL COMPLEMENT OF TWO HUNDRED. HOW MANY PEOPLE ARE IN HERE NOW?
I GOT SEVENTEEN HEAT MATCHES.
NOW SIXTEEN.
MOVE.
IF YOU CAN MAKE A SPACE FOR ME TO GET IN CLOSE, I SHOULD BE ABLE TO GET AN ELECTROMAGNETIC PULSER ON HIM.
YOU'LL DO WHAT?
I USED TO BE WITH THE NON-LETHAL WEAPONRY TEAM AT THE PENTAGON.
USED TO BE?

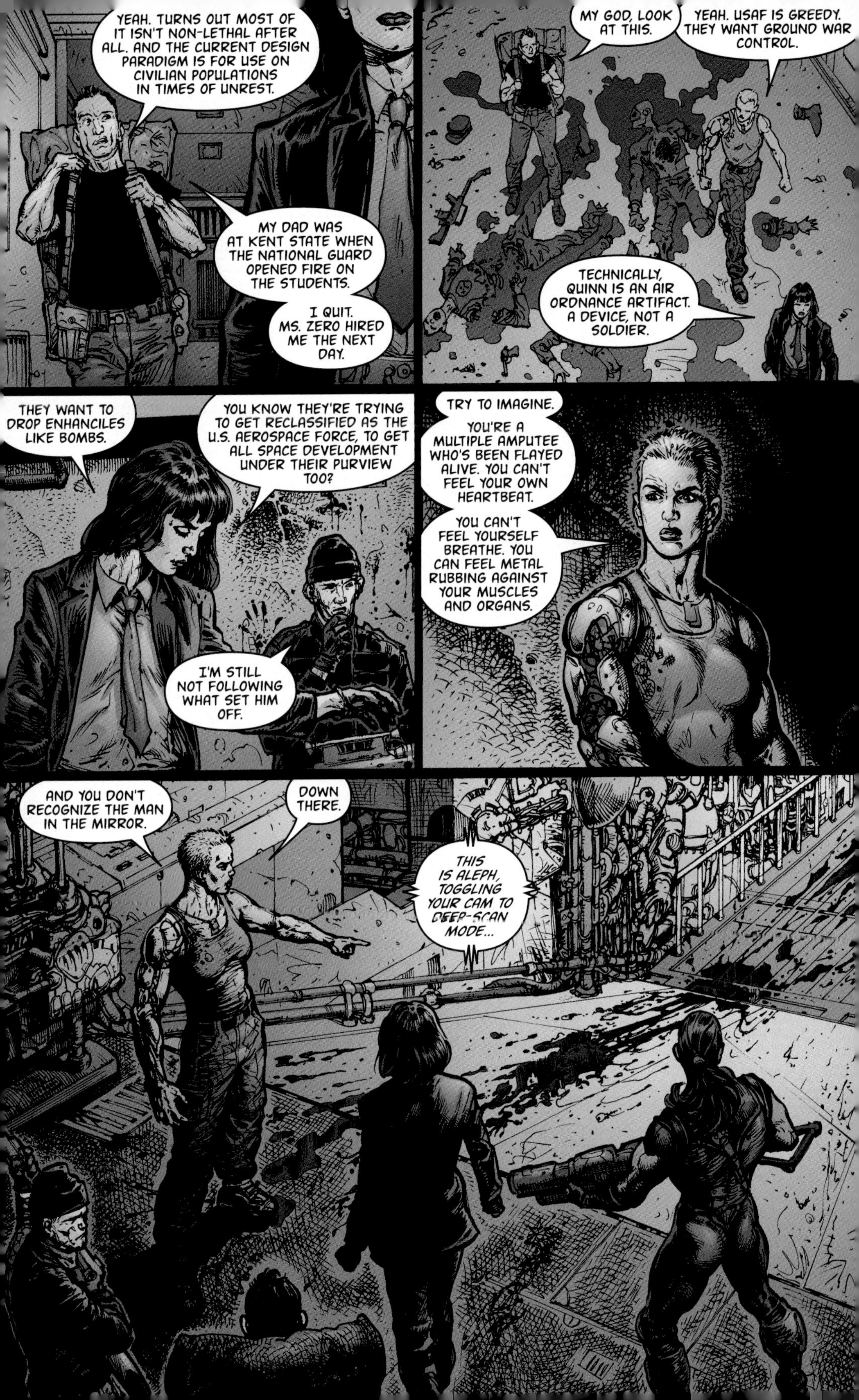
YEAH. TURNS OUT MOST OF IT ISN'T NON-LETHAL AFTER ALL. AND THE CURRENT DESIGN PARADIGM IS FOR USE ON CIVILIAN POPULATIONS IN TIMES OF UNREST.
MY DAD WAS AT KENT STATE WHEN THE NATIONAL GUARD OPENED FIRE ON THE STUDENTS.
I QUIT. MS. ZERO HIRED ME THE NEXT DAY.
MY GOD, LOOK AT THIS.
YEAH. USAF IS GREEDY. THEY WANT GROUND WAR CONTROL.
TECHNICALLY, QUINN IS AN AIR ORDNANCE ARTIFACT. A DEVICE, NOT A SOLDIER.
THEY WANT TO DROP ENHANCILES LIKE BOMBS.
YOU KNOW THEY'RE TRYING TO GET RECLASSIFIED AS THE U.S. AEROSPACE FORCE, TO GET ALL SPACE DEVELOPMENT UNDER THEIR PURVIEW TOO?
I'M STILL NOT FOLLOWING WHAT SET HIM OFF.
TRY TO IMAGINE.
YOU'RE A MULTIPLE AMPUTEE WHO'S BEEN FLAYED ALIVE. YOU CAN'T FEEL YOUR OWN HEARTBEAT.
YOU CAN'T FEEL YOURSELF BREATHE. YOU CAN FEEL METAL RUBBING AGAINST YOUR MUSCLES AND ORGANS.
AND YOU DON'T RECOGNIZE THE MAN IN THE MIRROR.
DOWN THERE.
THIS IS ALEPH, TOGGLING YOUR CAM TO DEEP-SCAN MODE...

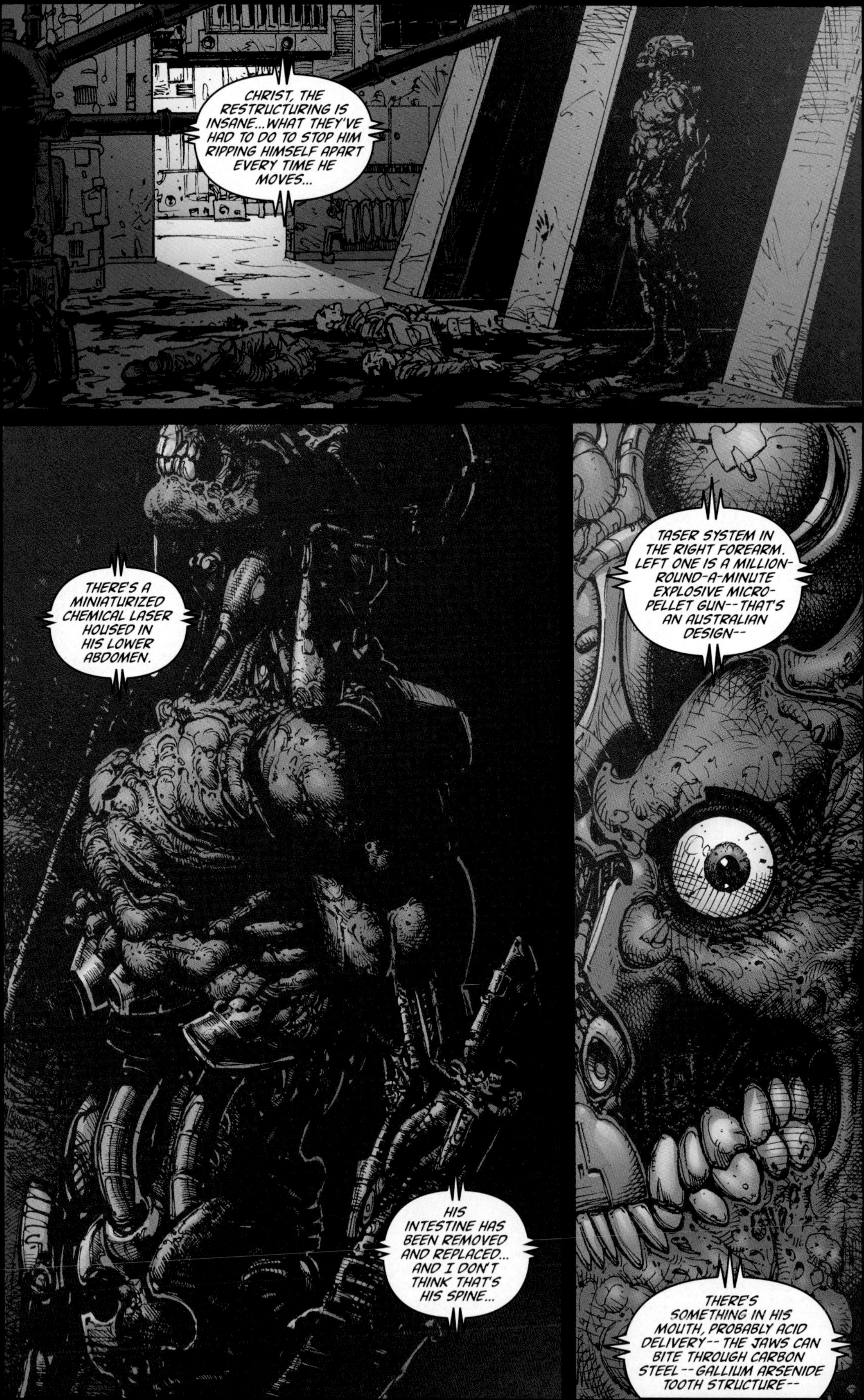
CHRIST, THE RESTRUCTURING IS INSANE...WHAT THEY'VE HAD TO DO TO STOP HIM RIPPING HIMSELF APART EVERY TIME HE MOVES...
THERE'S A MINIATURIZED CHEMICAL LASER HOUSED IN HIS LOWER ABDOMEN.
HIS INTESTINE HAS BEEN REMOVED AND REPLACED... AND I DON'T THINK THAT'S HIS SPINE...
TASER SYSTEM IN THE RIGHT FOREARM. LEFT ONE IS A MILLION-ROUND-A-MINUTE EXPLOSIVE MICRO-PELLET GUN--THAT'S AN AUSTRALIAN DESIGN--
THERE'S SOMETHING IN HIS MOUTH, PROBABLY ACID DELIVERY-- THE JAWS CAN BITE THROUGH CARBON STEEL--GALLIUM ARSENIDE TOOTH STRUCTURE--

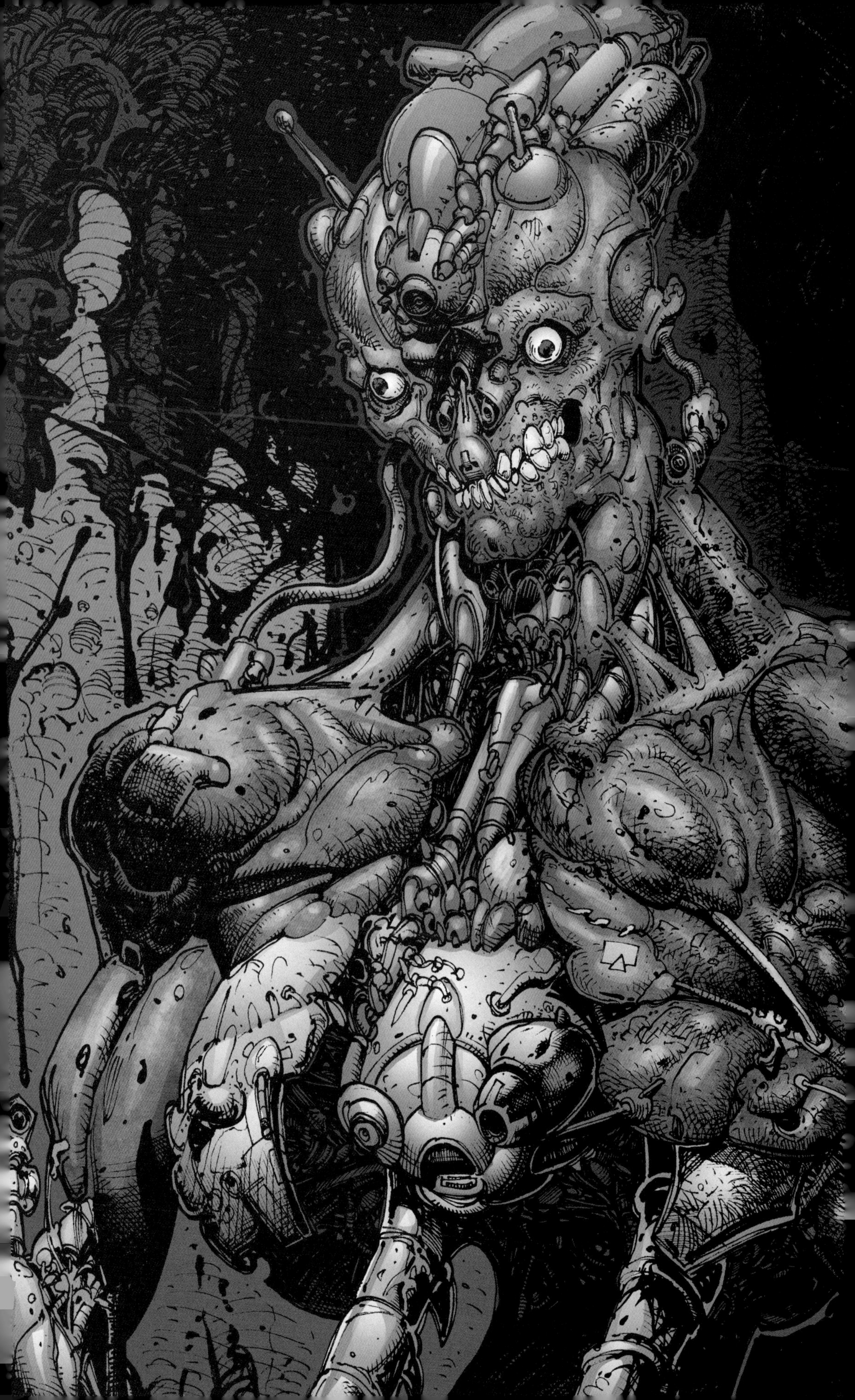

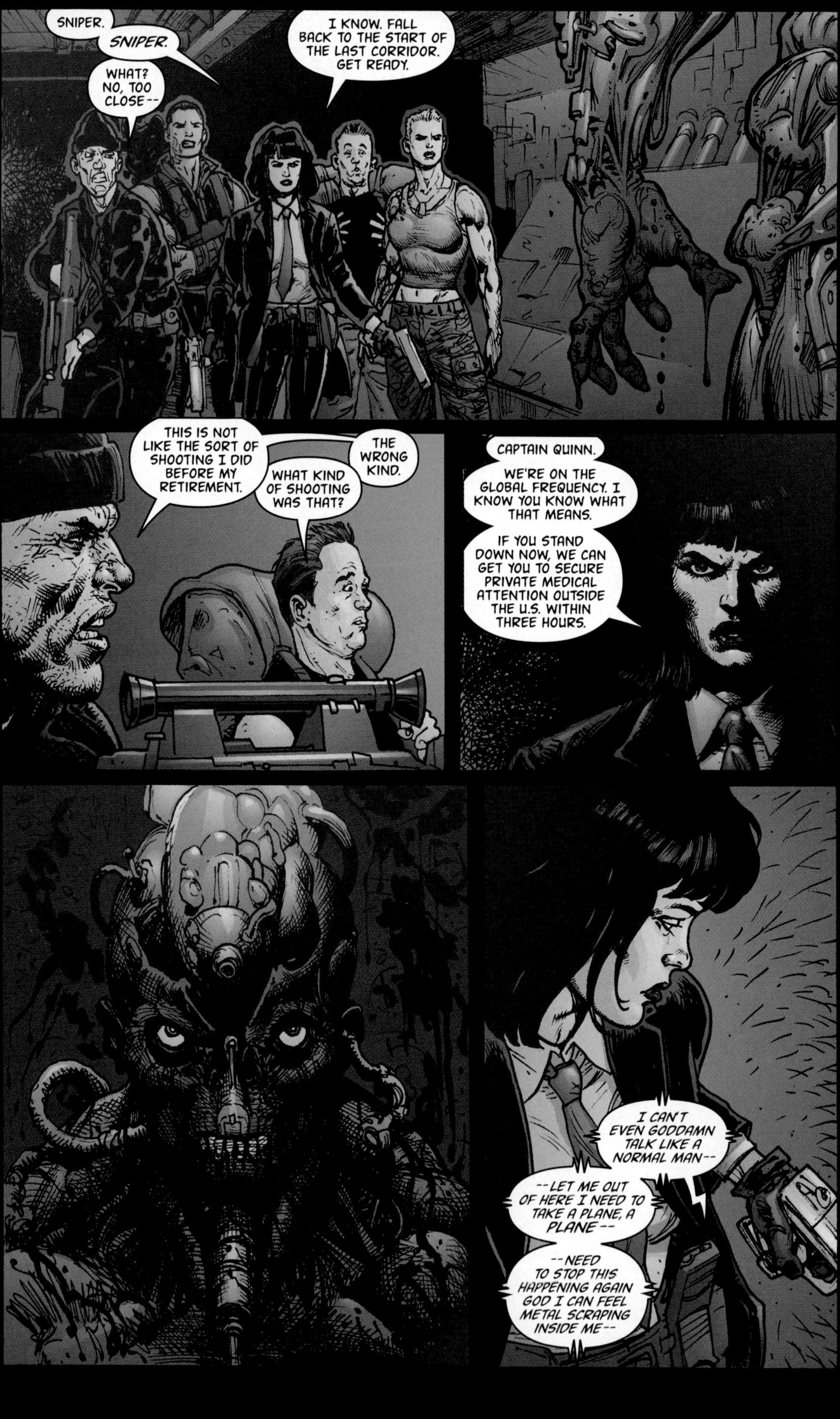
SNIPER.
SNIPER.
WHAT? NO, TOO CLOSE--
I KNOW. FALL BACK TO THE START OF THE LAST CORRIDOR. GET READY.
THIS IS NOT LIKE THE SORT OF SHOOTING I DID BEFORE MY RETIREMENT.
WHAT KIND OF SHOOTING WAS THAT?
THE WRONG KIND.
CAPTAIN QUINN.
WE'RE ON THE GLOBAL FREQUENCY. I KNOW YOU KNOW WHAT THAT MEANS.
IF YOU STAND DOWN NOW, WE CAN GET YOU TO SECURE PRIVATE MEDICAL ATTENTION OUTSIDE THE U.S. WITHIN THREE HOURS.
I CAN'T EVEN GODDAMN TALK LIKE A NORMAL MAN--
--LET ME OUT OF HERE I NEED TO TAKE A PLANE, A PLANE--
--NEED TO STOP THIS HAPPENING AGAIN GOD I CAN FEEL METAL SCRAPING INSIDE ME--

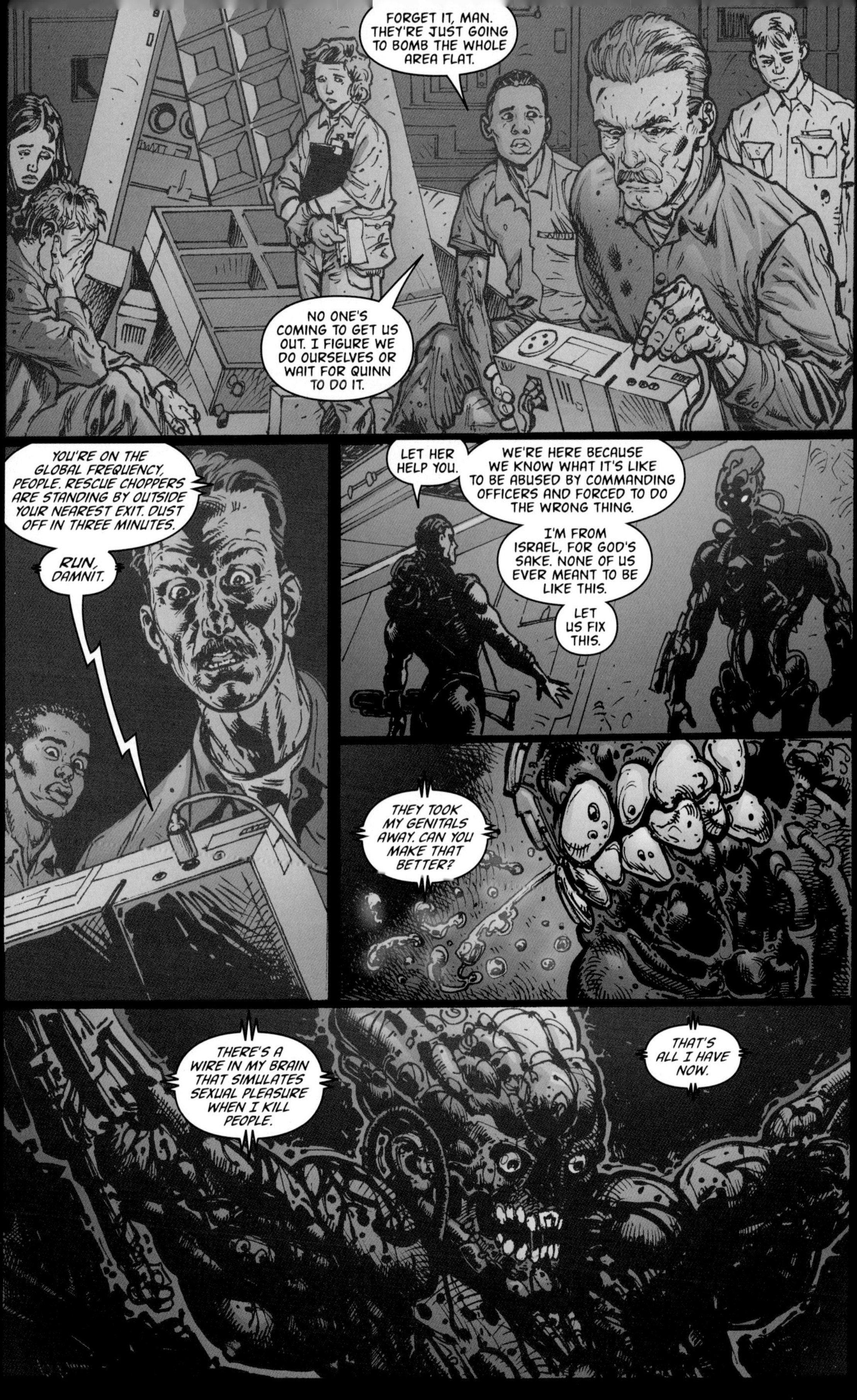
FORGET IT, MAN. THEY'RE JUST GOING TO BOMB THE WHOLE AREA FLAT.
NO ONE'S COMING TO GET US OUT. I FIGURE WE DO OURSELVES OR WAIT FOR QUINN TO DO IT.
YOU'RE ON THE GLOBAL FREQUENCY, PEOPLE. RESCUE CHOPPERS ARE STANDING BY OUTSIDE YOUR NEAREST EXIT. DUST OFF IN THREE MINUTES.
RUN, DAMNIT.
LET HER HELP YOU.
WE'RE HERE BECAUSE WE KNOW WHAT IT'S LIKE TO BE ABUSED BY COMMANDING OFFICERS AND FORCED TO DO THE WRONG THING.
I'M FROM ISRAEL, FOR GOD'S SAKE. NONE OF US EVER MEANT TO BE LIKE THIS.
LET US FIX THIS.
THEY TOOK MY GENITALS AWAY. CAN YOU MAKE THAT BETTER?
THERE'S A WIRE IN MY BRAIN THAT SIMULATES SEXUAL PLEASURE WHEN I KILL PEOPLE.
THAT'S ALL I HAVE NOW.

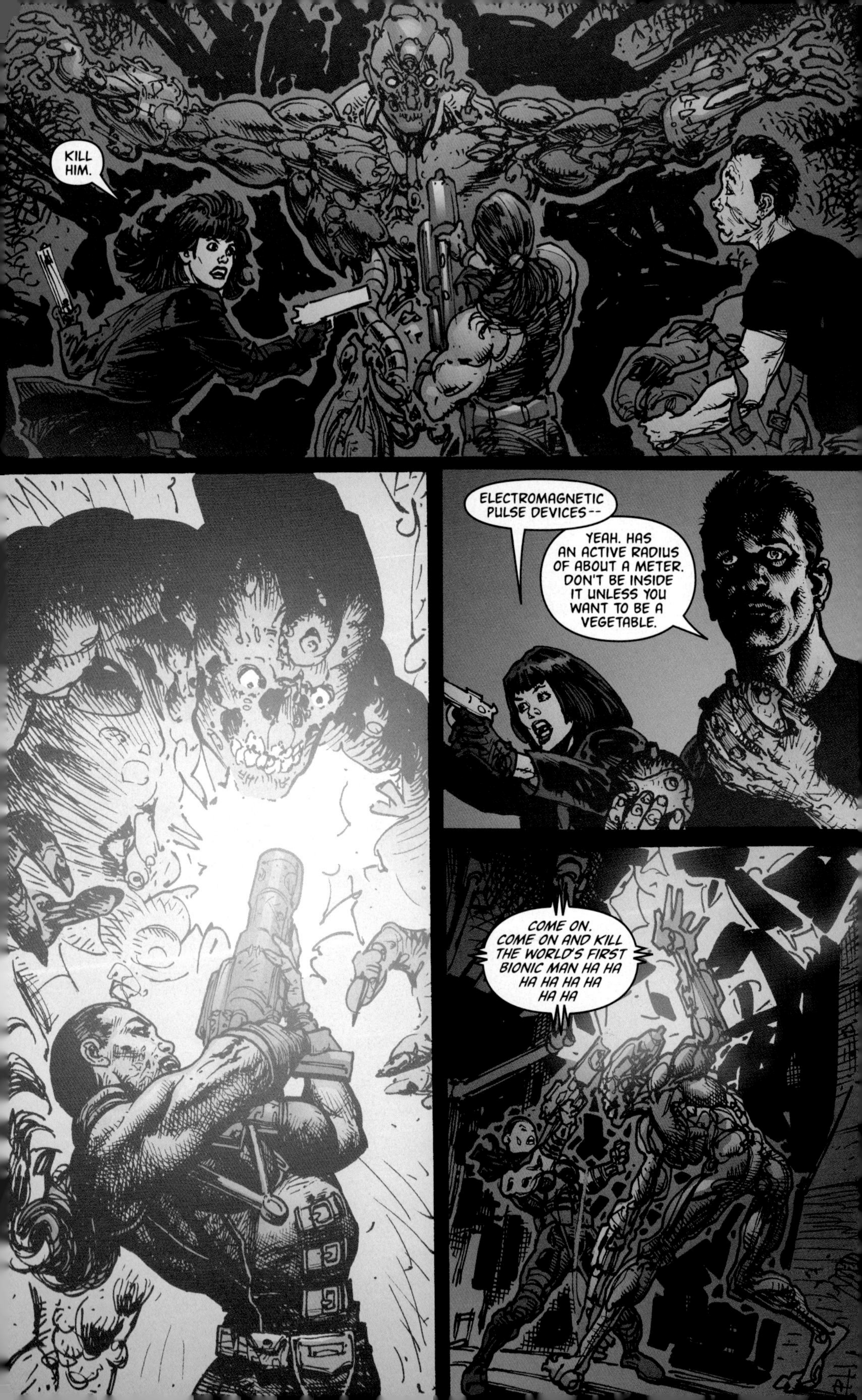
KILL HIM.
ELECTROMAGNETIC PULSE DEVICES--
YEAH. HAS AN ACTIVE RADIUS OF ABOUT A METER. DON'T BE INSIDE IT UNLESS YOU WANT TO BE A VEGETABLE.
COME ON. COME ON AND KILL THE WORLD'S FIRST BIONIC MAN HA HA HA HA HA HA HA HA

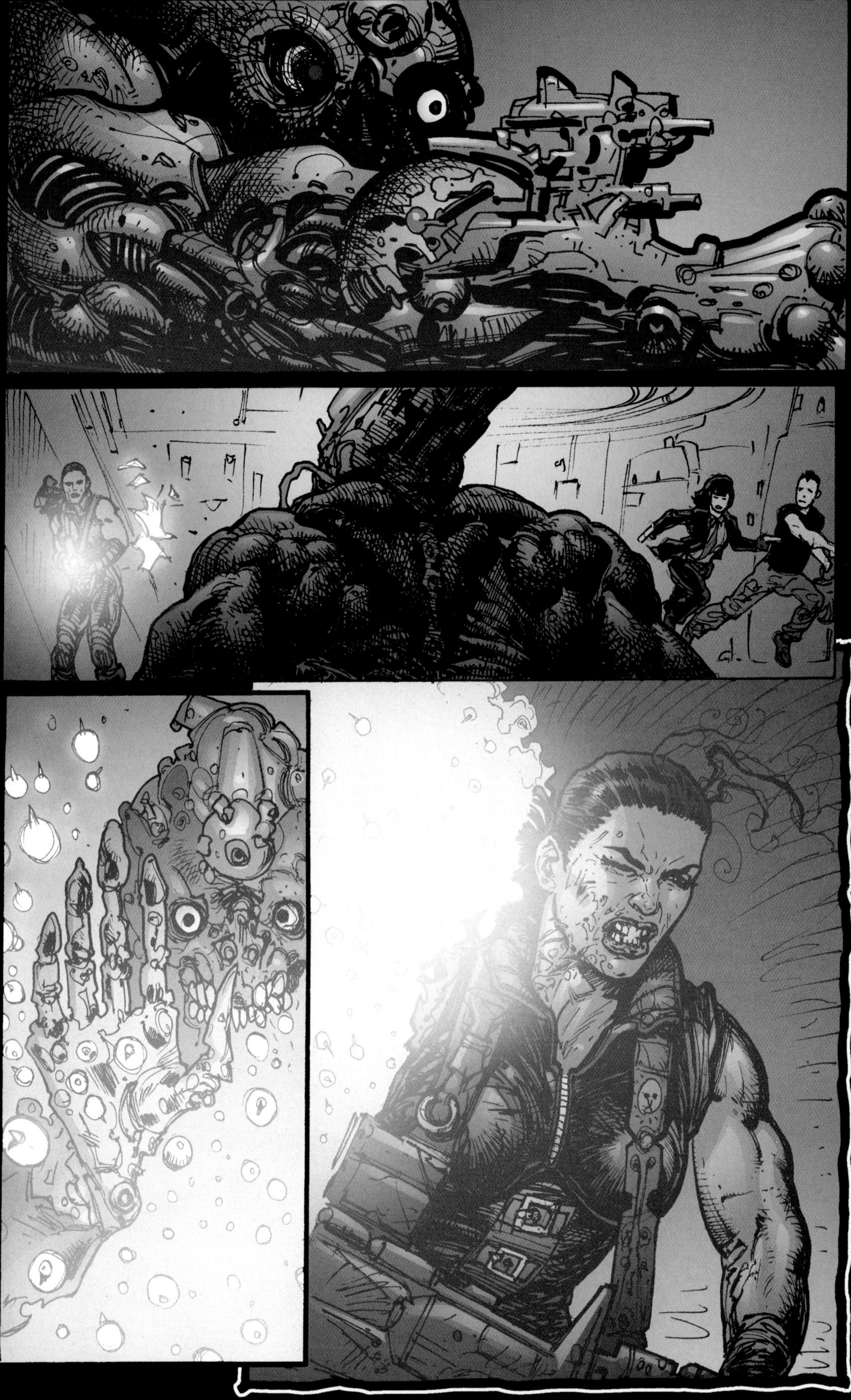

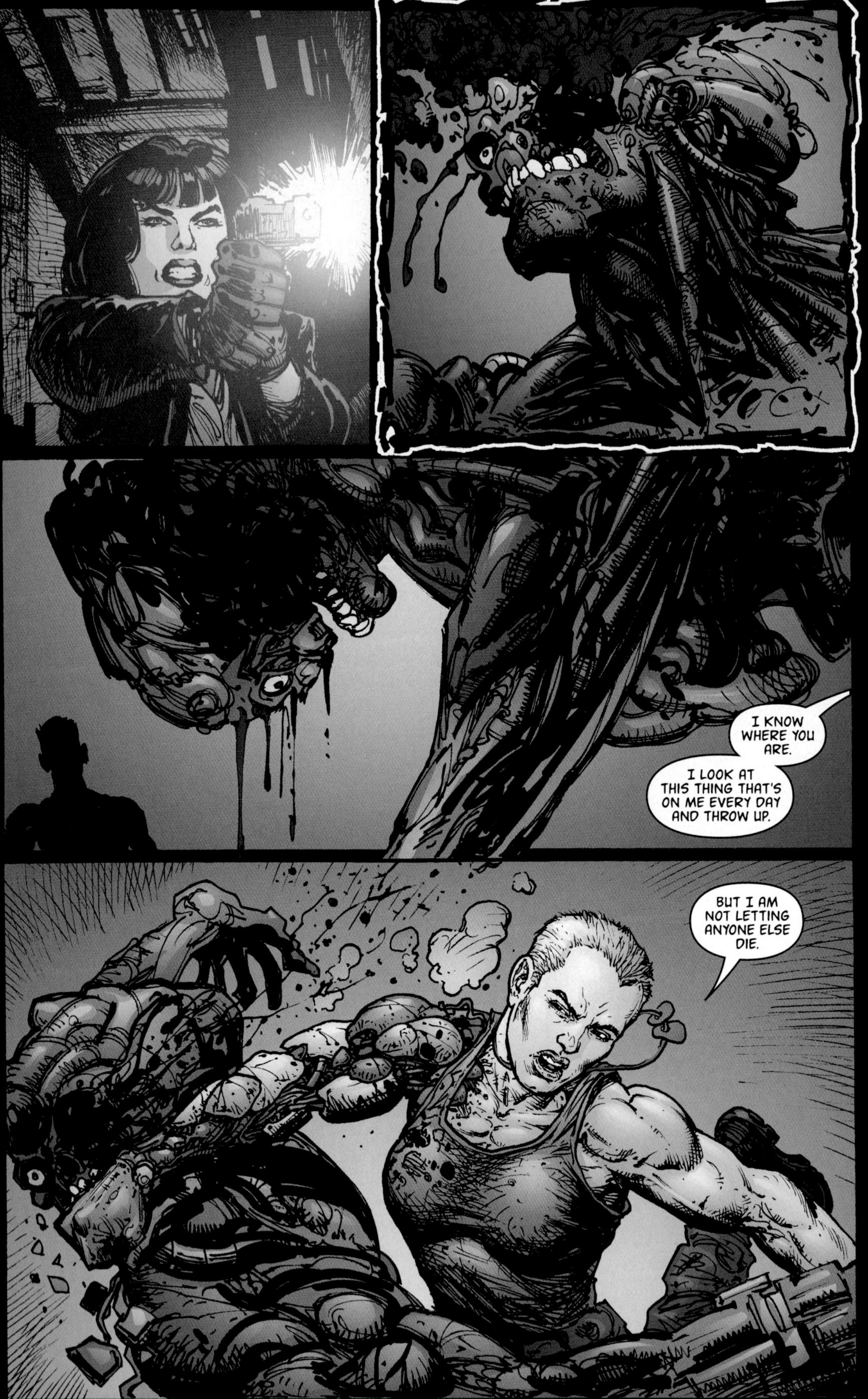
I KNOW WHERE YOU ARE.
I LOOK AT THIS THING THAT'S ON ME EVERY DAY AND THROW UP.
BUT I AM NOT LETTING ANYONE ELSE DIE.

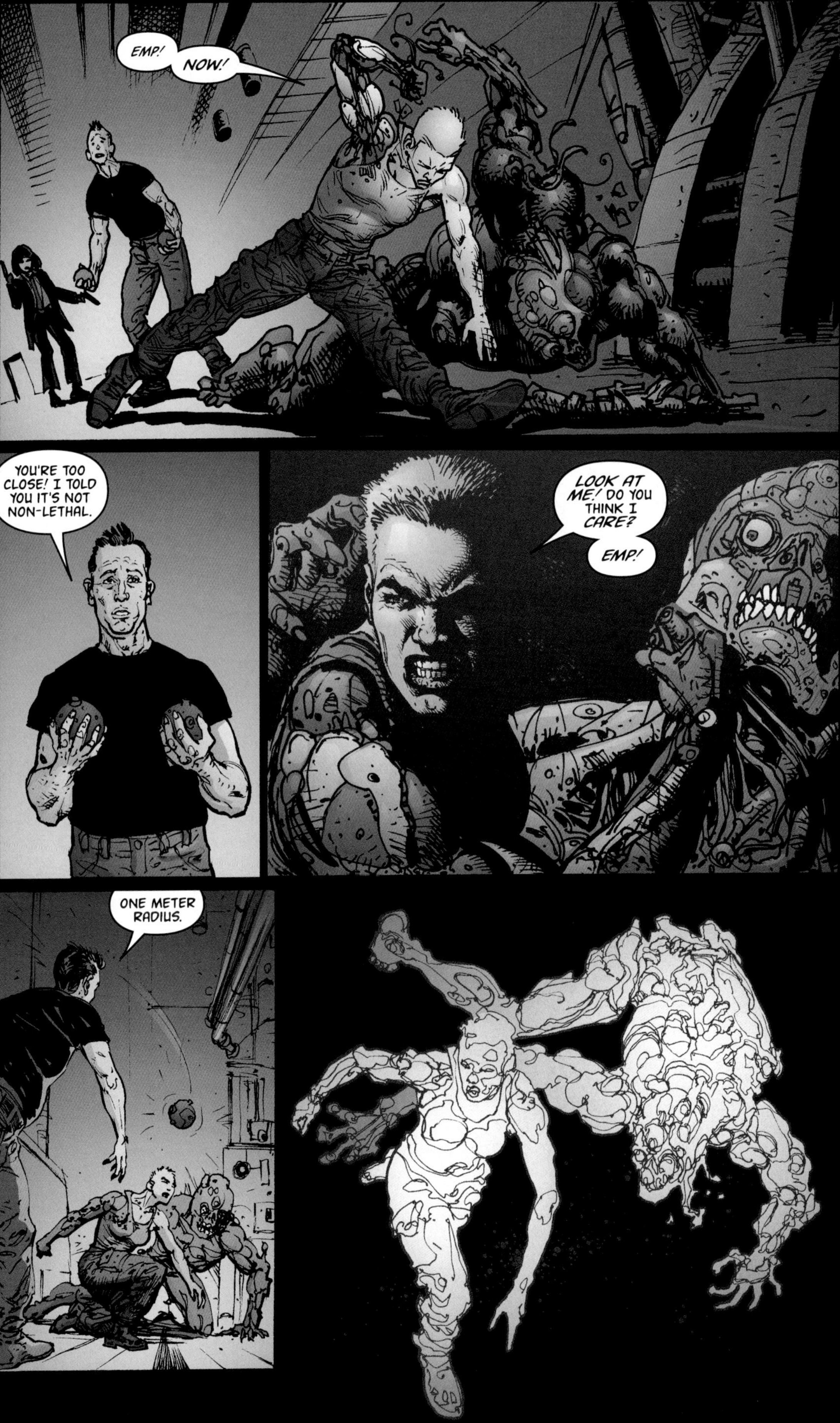
EMP!
NOW!
YOU'RE TOO CLOSE! I TOLD YOU IT'S NOT NON-LETHAL.
LOOK AT ME! DO YOU THINK I CARE?
EMP!
ONE METER RADIUS.

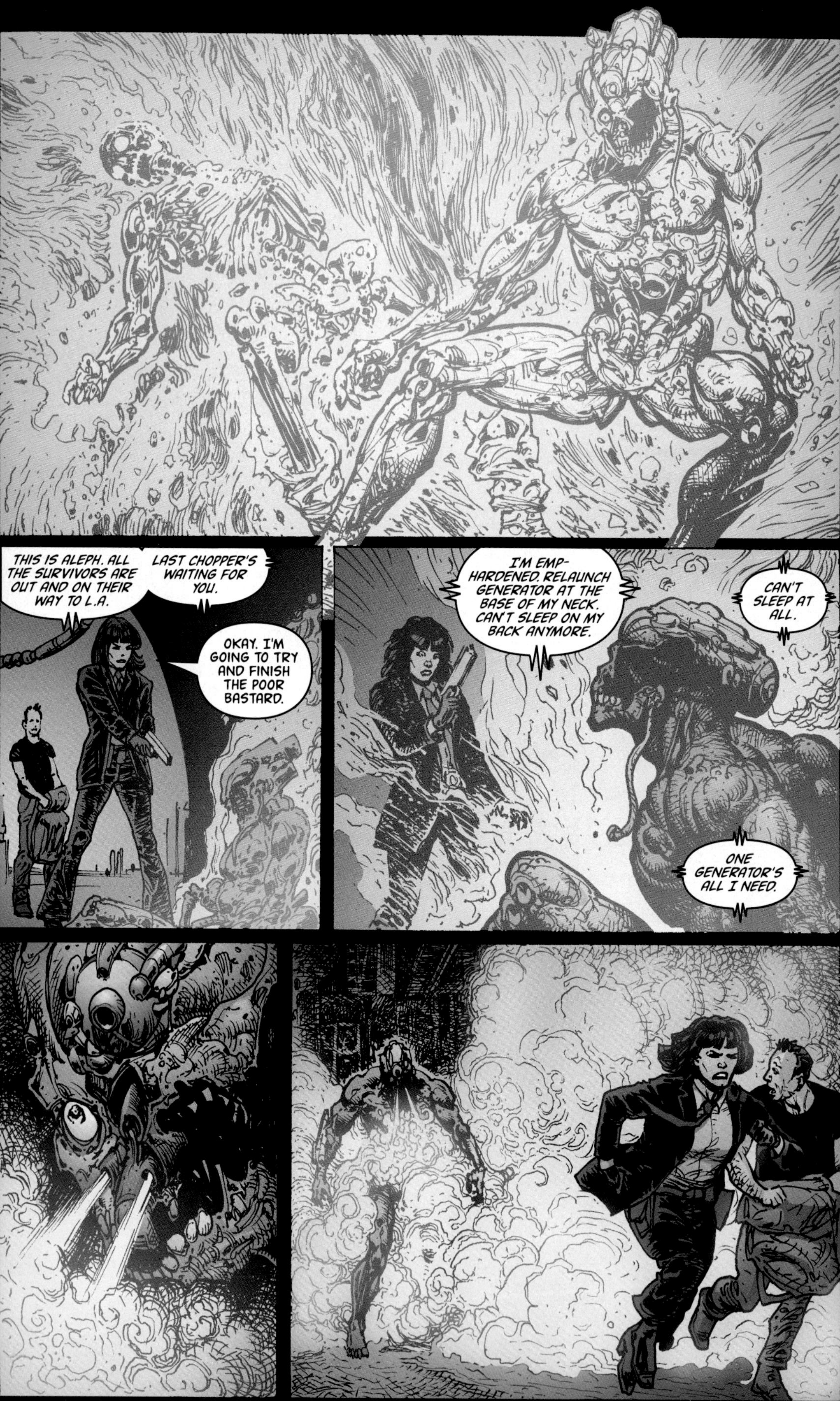
THIS IS ALEPH. ALL THE SURVIVORS ARE OUT AND ON THEIR WAY TO L.A.
LAST CHOPPER'S WAITING FOR YOU.
OKAY. I'M GOING TO TRY AND FINISH THE POOR BASTARD.
I'M EMP-HARDENED. RELAUNCH GENERATOR AT THE BASE OF MY NECK. CAN'T SLEEP ON MY BACK ANYMORE.
CAN'T SLEEP AT ALL.
ONE GENERATOR'S ALL I NEED.

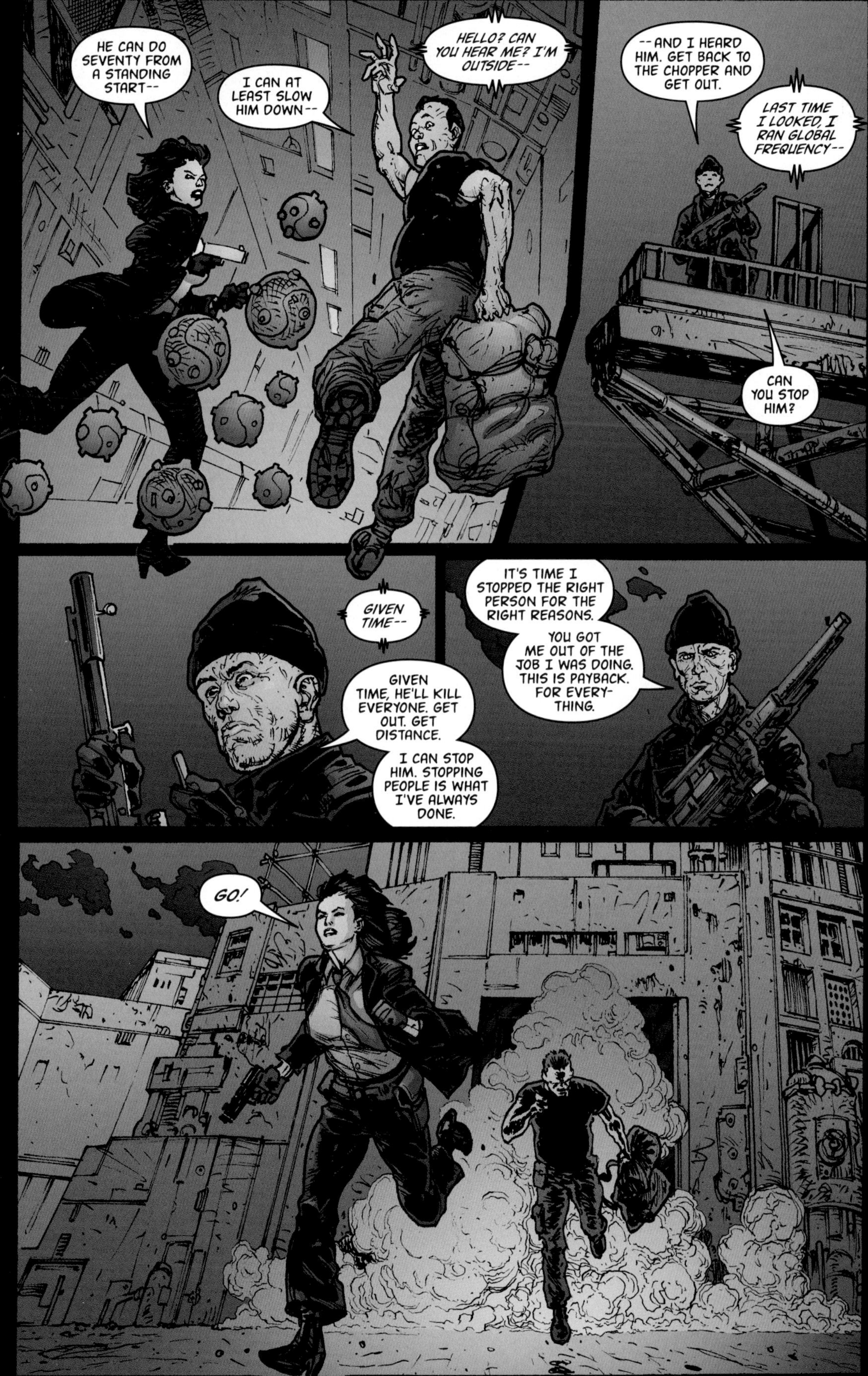
HE CAN DO SEVENTY FROM A STANDING START--
I CAN AT LEAST SLOW HIM DOWN--
HELLO? CAN YOU HEAR ME? I'M OUTSIDE--
--AND I HEARD HIM. GET BACK TO THE CHOPPER AND GET OUT.
LAST TIME I LOOKED, I RAN GLOBAL FREQUENCY--
CAN YOU STOP HIM?
GIVEN TIME--
GIVEN TIME, HE'LL KILL EVERYONE. GET OUT. GET DISTANCE.
I CAN STOP HIM. STOPPING PEOPLE IS WHAT I'VE ALWAYS DONE.
IT'S TIME I STOPPED THE RIGHT PERSON FOR THE RIGHT REASONS.
YOU GOT ME OUT OF THE JOB I WAS DOING. THIS IS PAYBACK. FOR EVERY-THING.
GO!

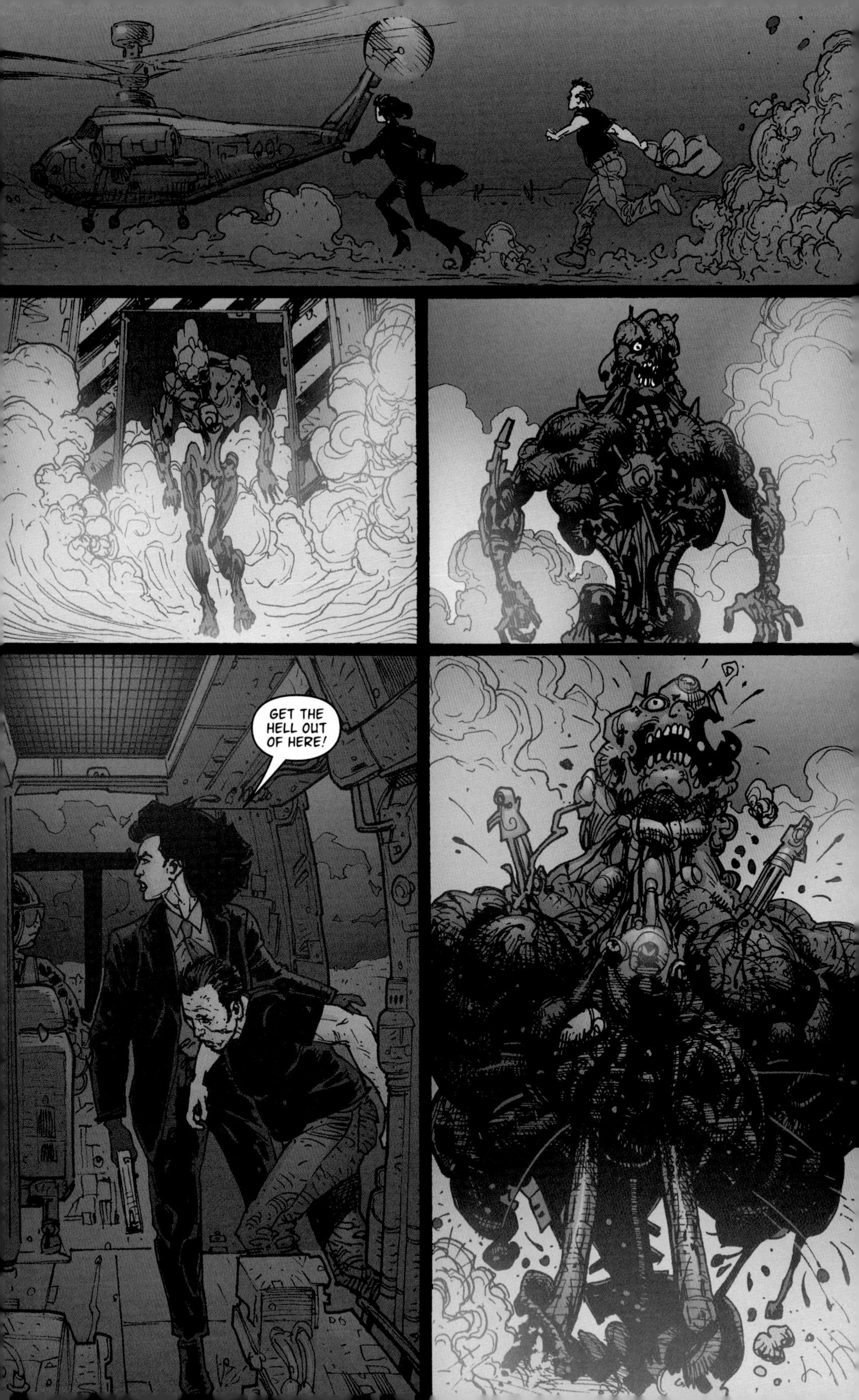
GET THE HELL OUT OF HERE!

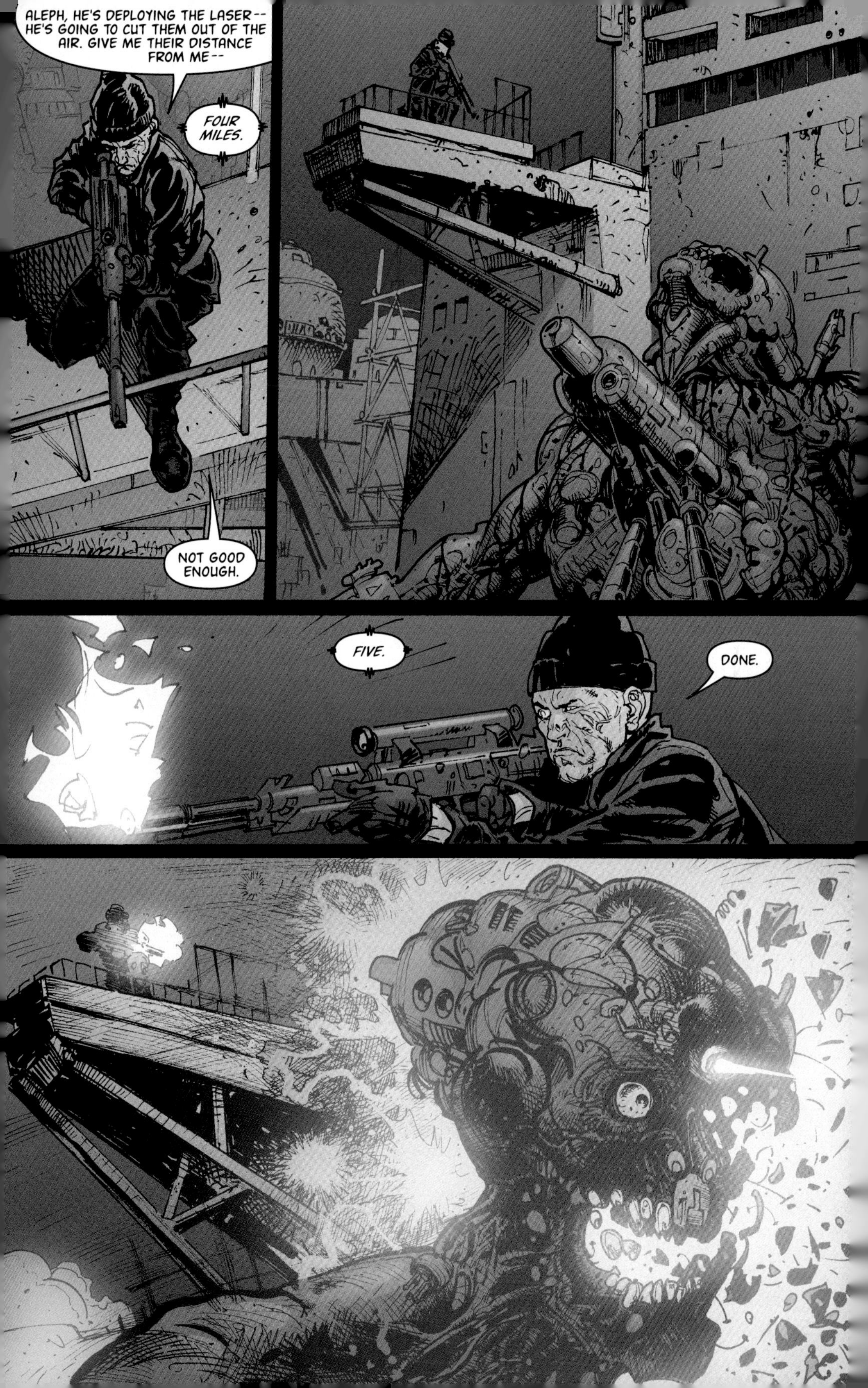
ALEPH, HE'S DEPLOYING THE LASER--
HE'S GOING TO CUT THEM OUT OF THE AIR. GIVE ME THEIR DISTANCE FROM ME--
FOUR MILES.
NOT GOOD ENOUGH.
FIVE.
DONE.

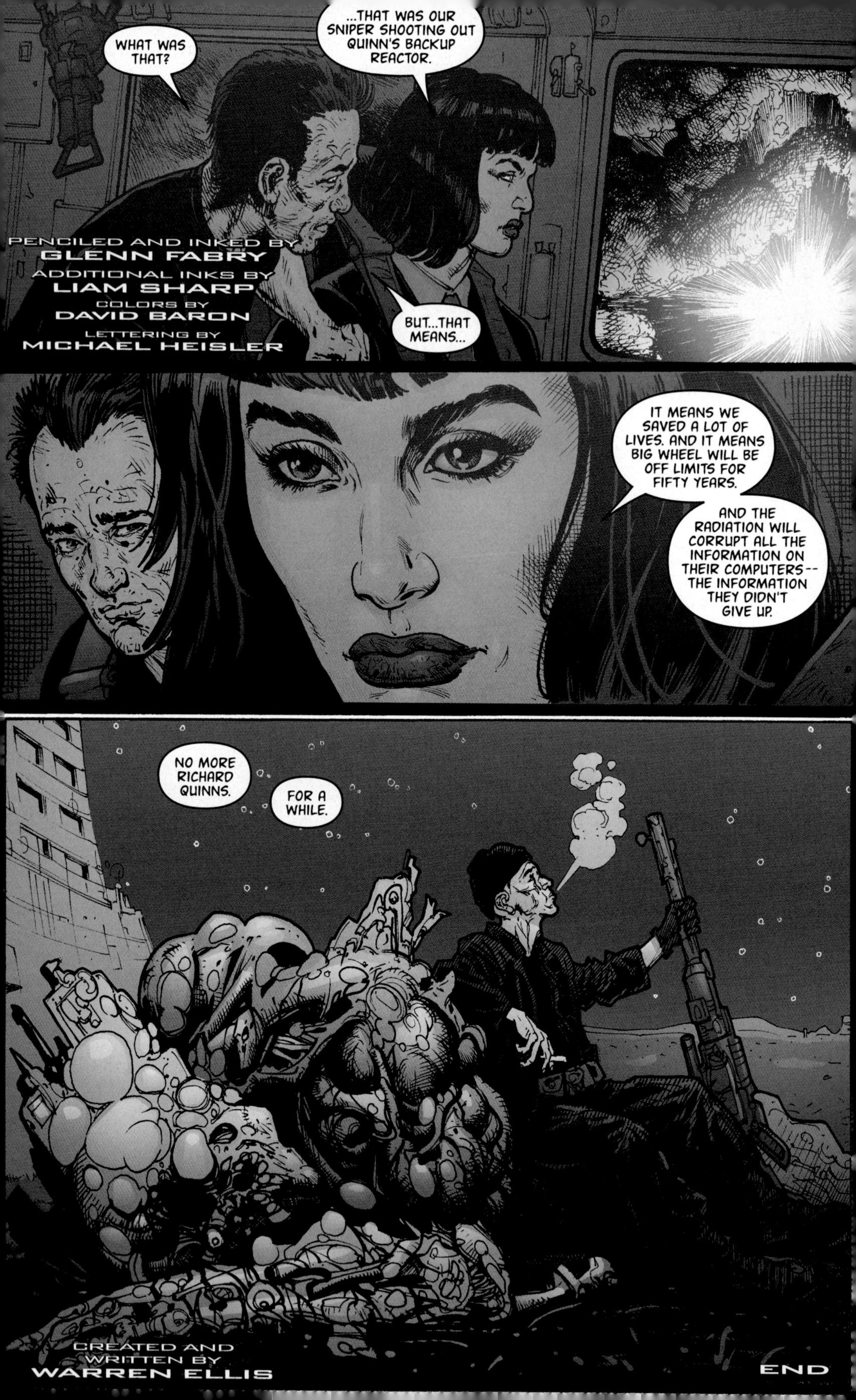
WHAT WAS THAT?
...THAT WAS OUR SNIPER SHOOTING OUT QUINN'S BACKUP REACTOR.
PENCILED AND INKED BY GLENN FABRY
ADDITIONAL INKS BY LIAM SHARP
COLORS BY DAVID BARON
LETTERING BY MICHAEL HEISLER
BUT...THAT MEANS...
IT MEANS WE SAVED A LOT OF LIVES. AND IT MEANS BIG WHEEL WILL BE OFF LIMITS FOR FIFTY YEARS.
AND THE RADIATION WILL CORRUPT ALL THE INFORMATION ON THEIR COMPUTERS-- THE INFORMATION THEY DIDN'T GIVE UP.
NO MORE RICHARD QUINNS.
FOR A WHILE.
CREATED AND WRITTEN BY WARREN ELLIS
END

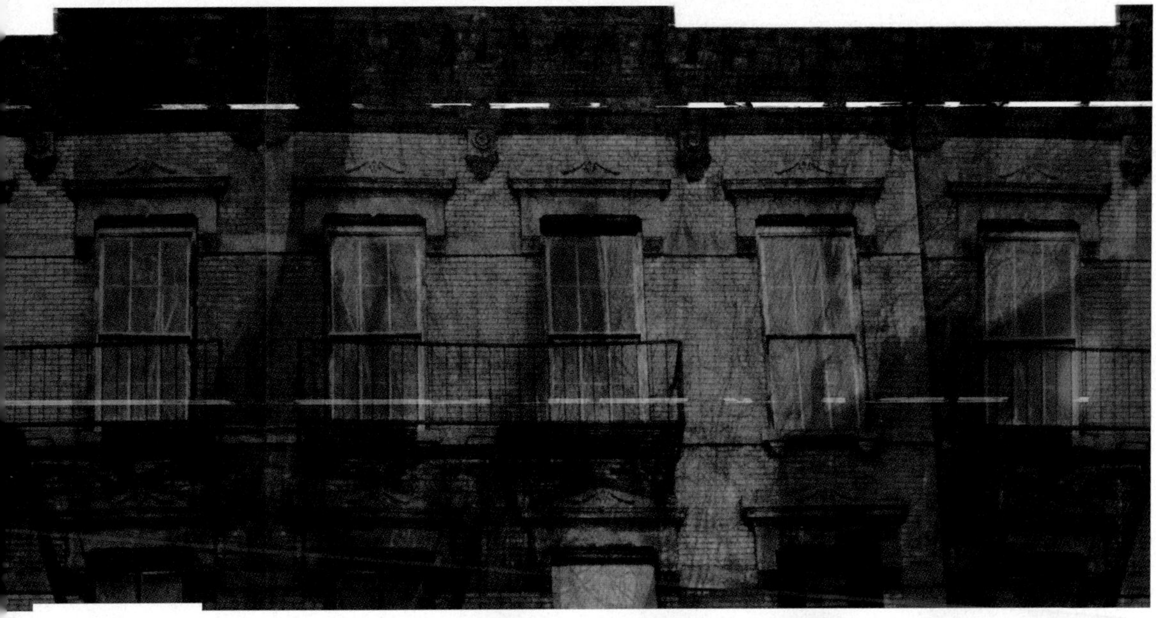

ARE YOU ON THE GLOBAL FREQUENCY?

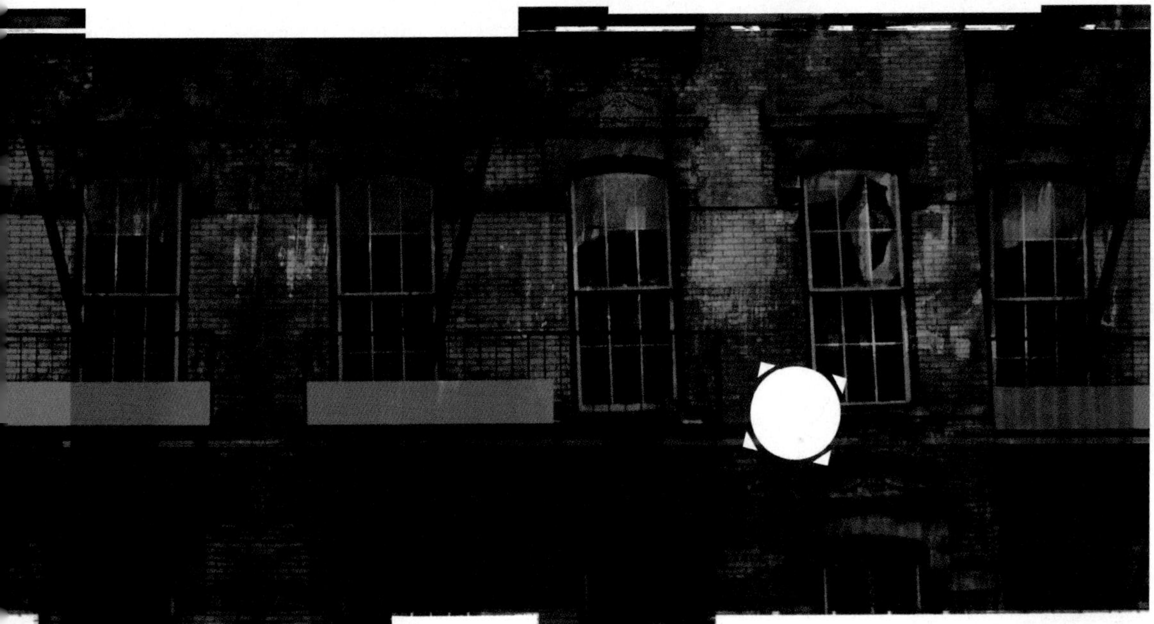

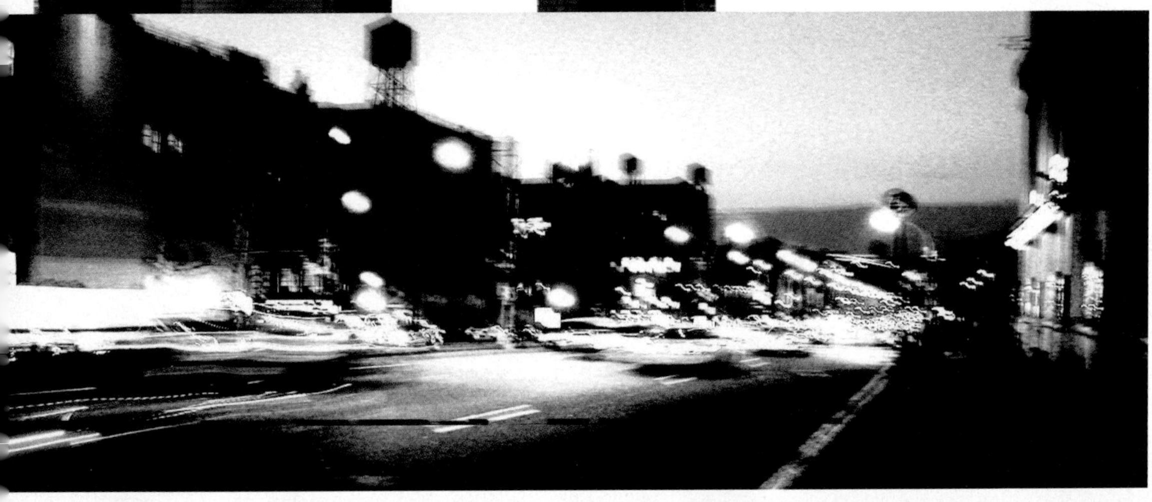

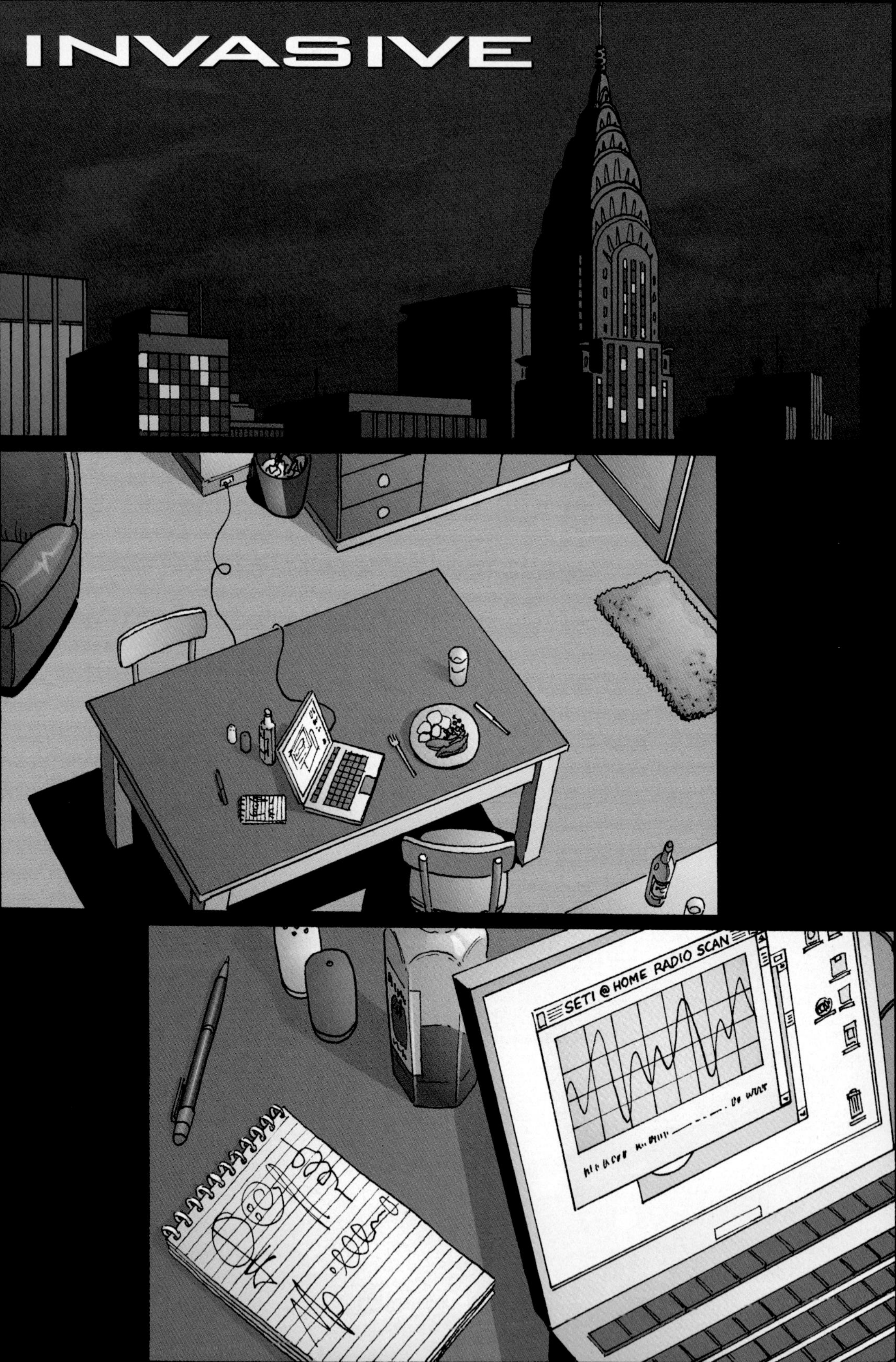
INVASIVE
SETI @ HOME RADIO SCAN

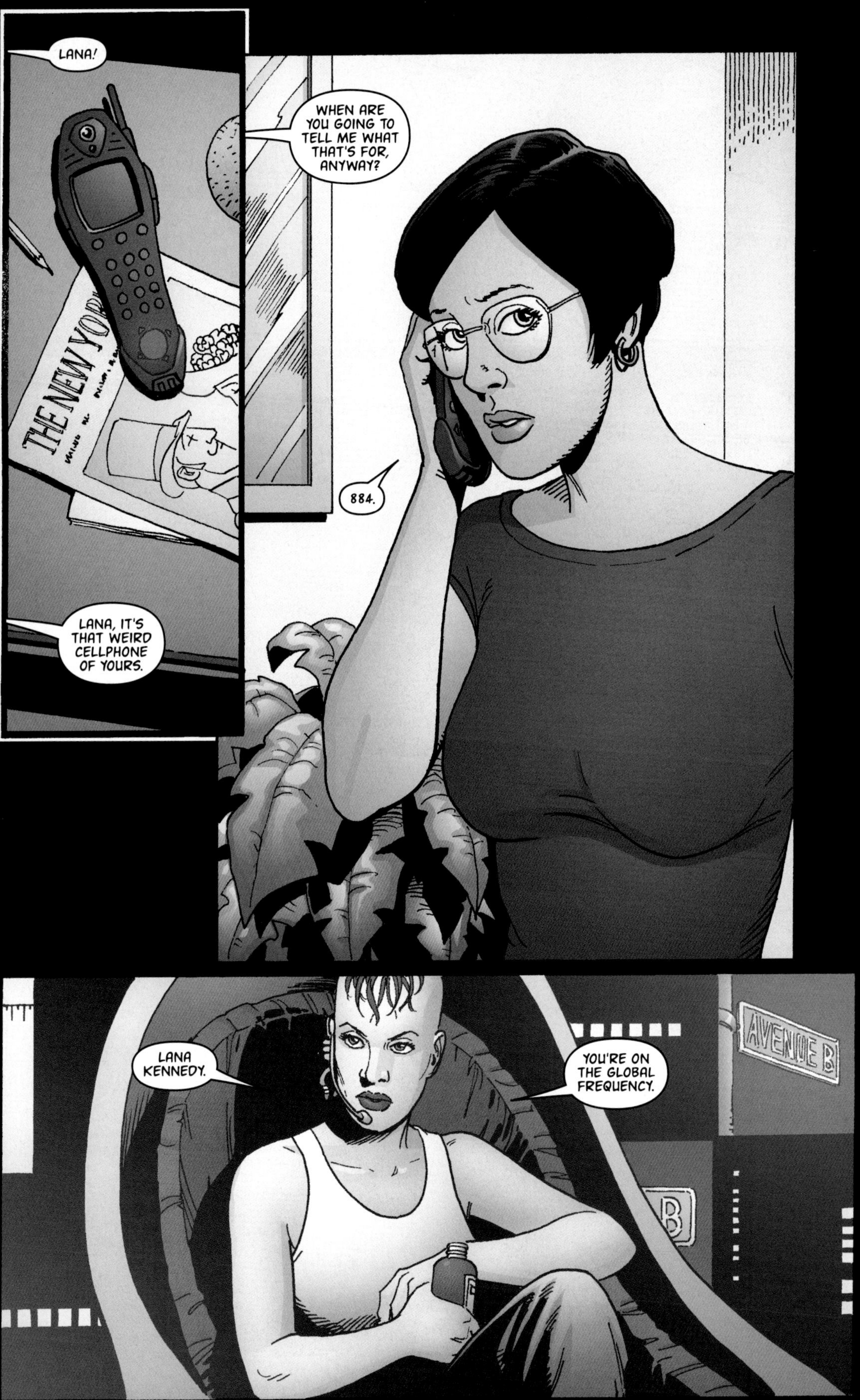
LANA!
WHEN ARE YOU GOING TO TELL ME WHAT THAT'S FOR, ANYWAY?
LANA, IT'S THAT WEIRD CELLPHONE OF YOURS.
884.
LANA KENNEDY.
YOU'RE ON THE GLOBAL FREQUENCY.
AVENUE B

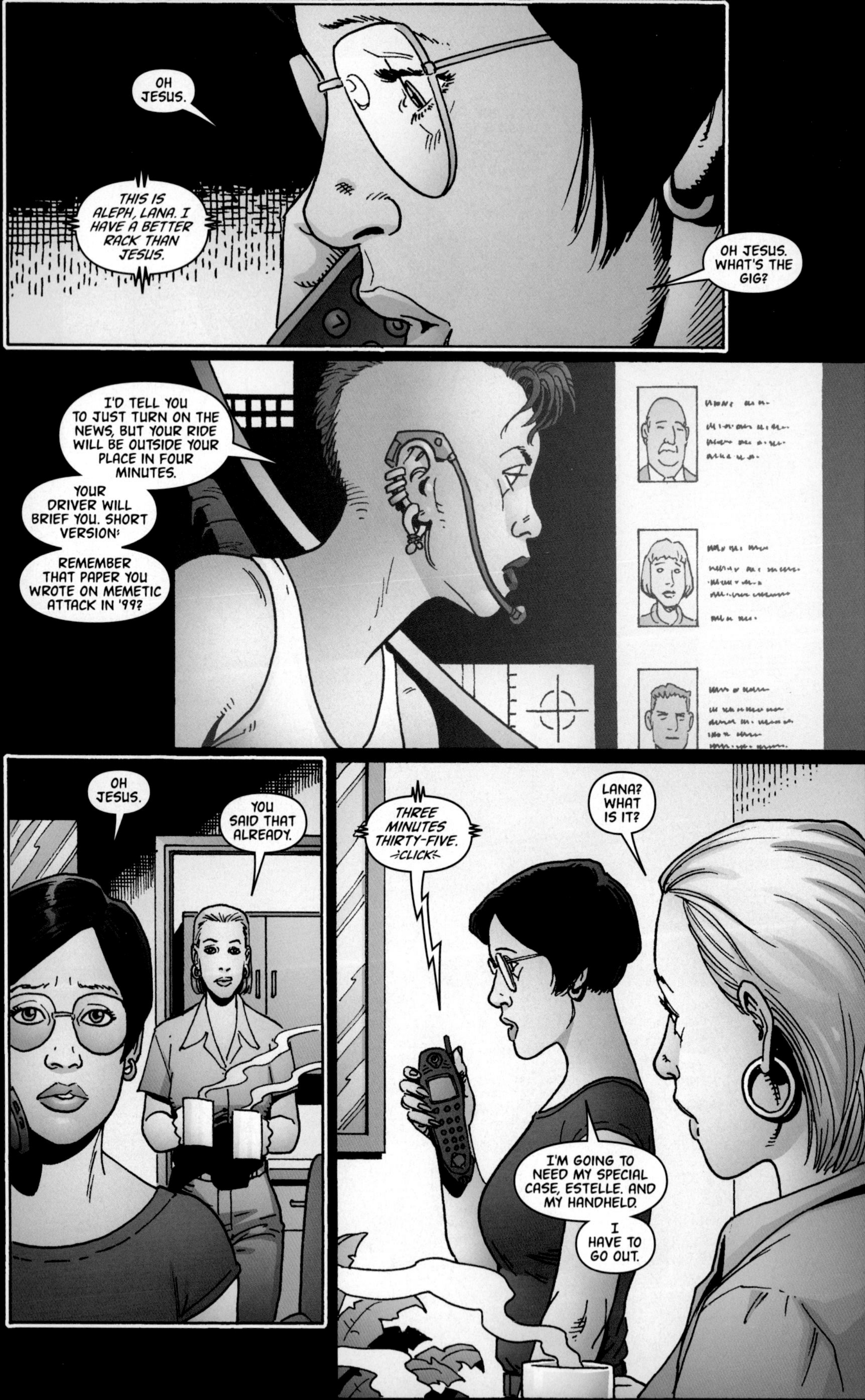

OH JESUS.
THIS IS ALEPH, LANA. I HAVE A BETTER RACK THAN JESUS.
OH JESUS. WHAT'S THE GIG?
I'D TELL YOU TO JUST TURN ON THE NEWS, BUT YOUR RIDE WILL BE OUTSIDE YOUR PLACE IN FOUR MINUTES.
YOUR DRIVER WILL BRIEF YOU. SHORT VERSION:
REMEMBER THAT PAPER YOU WROTE ON MEMETIC ATTACK IN '99?
OH JESUS.
YOU SAID THAT ALREADY.
THREE MINUTES THIRTY-FIVE.
CLICK
LANA? WHAT IS IT?
I'M GOING TO NEED MY SPECIAL CASE, ESTELLE. AND MY HANDHELD.
I HAVE TO GO OUT.

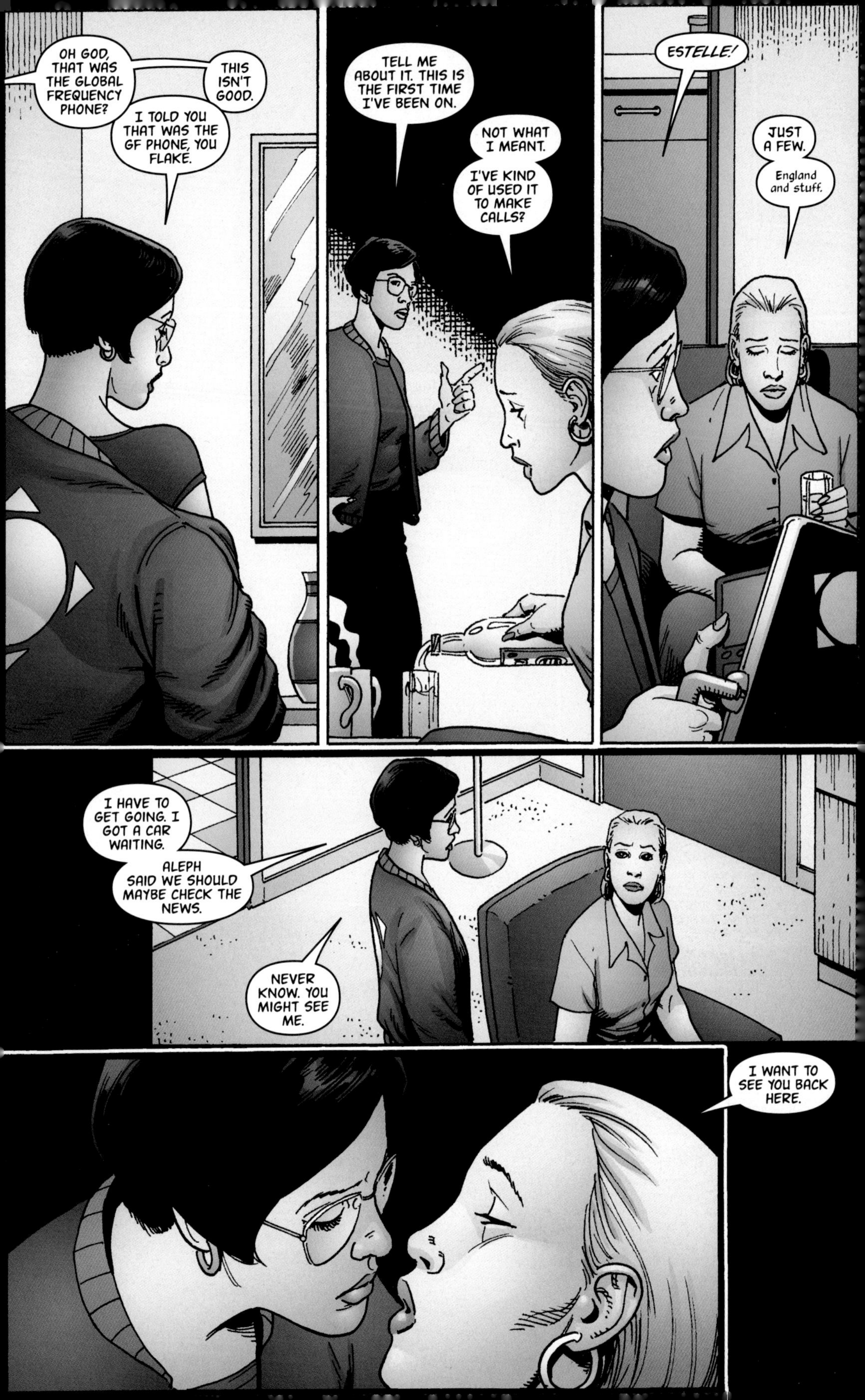
OH GOD, THAT WAS THE GLOBAL FREQUENCY PHONE?
THIS ISN'T GOOD.
I TOLD YOU THAT WAS THE GF PHONE, YOU FLAKE.
TELL ME ABOUT IT. THIS IS THE FIRST TIME I'VE BEEN ON.
NOT WHAT I MEANT.
I'VE KIND OF USED IT TO MAKE CALLS?
ESTELLE!
JUST A FEW.
England and stuff.
I HAVE TO GET GOING. I GOT A CAR WAITING.
ALEPH SAID WE SHOULD MAYBE CHECK THE NEWS.
NEVER KNOW. YOU MIGHT SEE ME.
I WANT TO SEE YOU BACK HERE.

I'M NICK CHO, ON THE FREQUENCY.

LET'S RIDE.

MIRANDA ZERO? REALLY? EXTREMELY COOL! ONLY MET HER ONCE. YOU?

JUST THE ONCE. LISTEN, SHOULD YOU HAVE YOUR FOOT DOWN IN--

ALEPH, I GOT LANA KENNEDY AND WE'RE EN ROUTE.

WE'RE GOING TO SEE IF WE CAN GET YOU THERE A LITTLE FASTER. MS. ZERO IS ALREADY ON THE SCENE.

HA! CHECK THIS OUT!

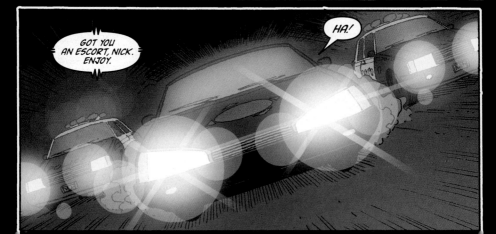

GOT YOU AN ESCORT, NICK. ENJOY.

HA!

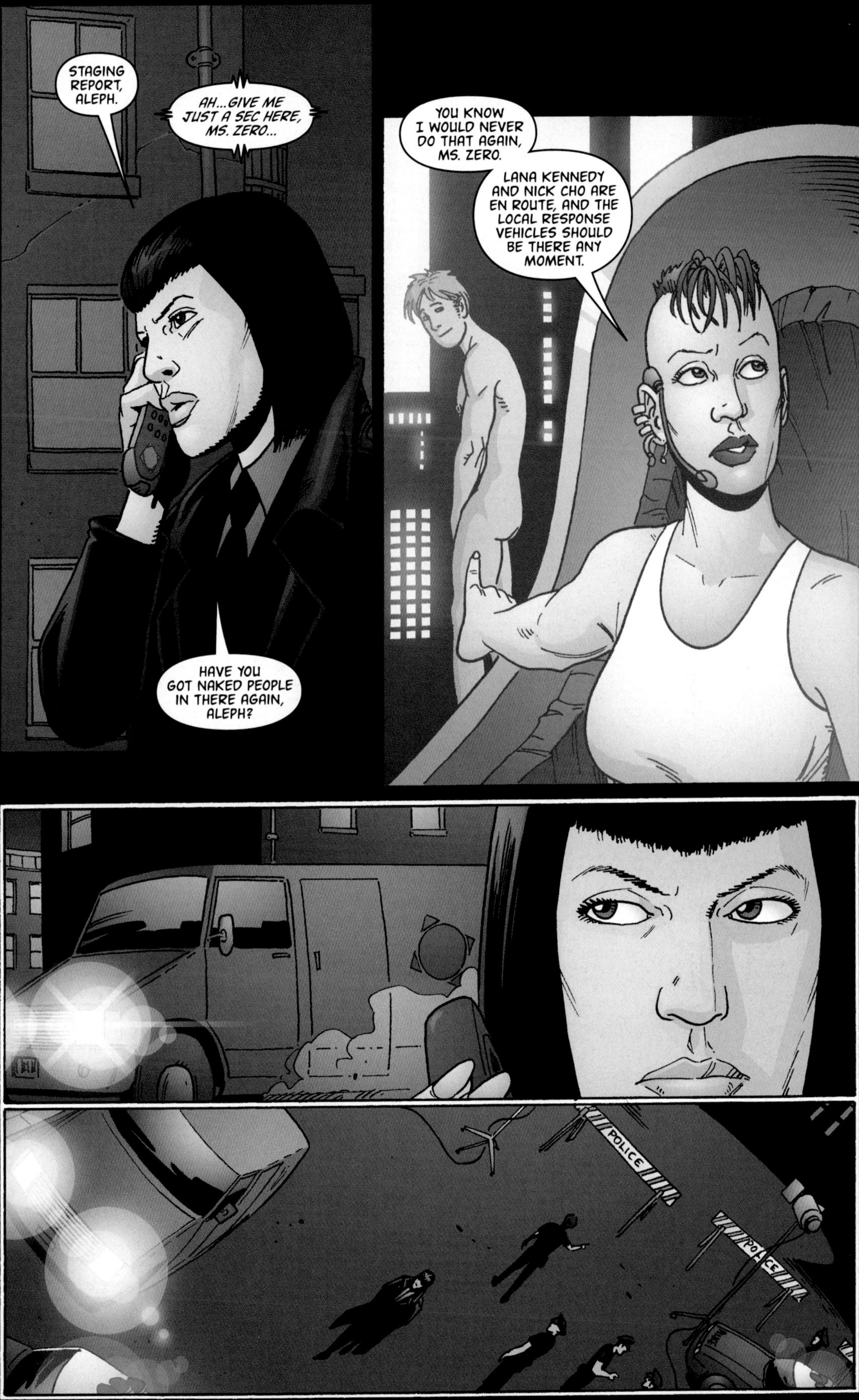
STAGING REPORT, ALEPH.
AH...GIVE ME JUST A SEC HERE, MS. ZERO...
HAVE YOU GOT NAKED PEOPLE IN THERE AGAIN, ALEPH?
YOU KNOW I WOULD NEVER DO THAT AGAIN, MS. ZERO.
LANA KENNEDY AND NICK CHO ARE EN ROUTE, AND THE LOCAL RESPONSE VEHICLES SHOULD BE THERE ANY MOMENT.
POLICE
POLICE

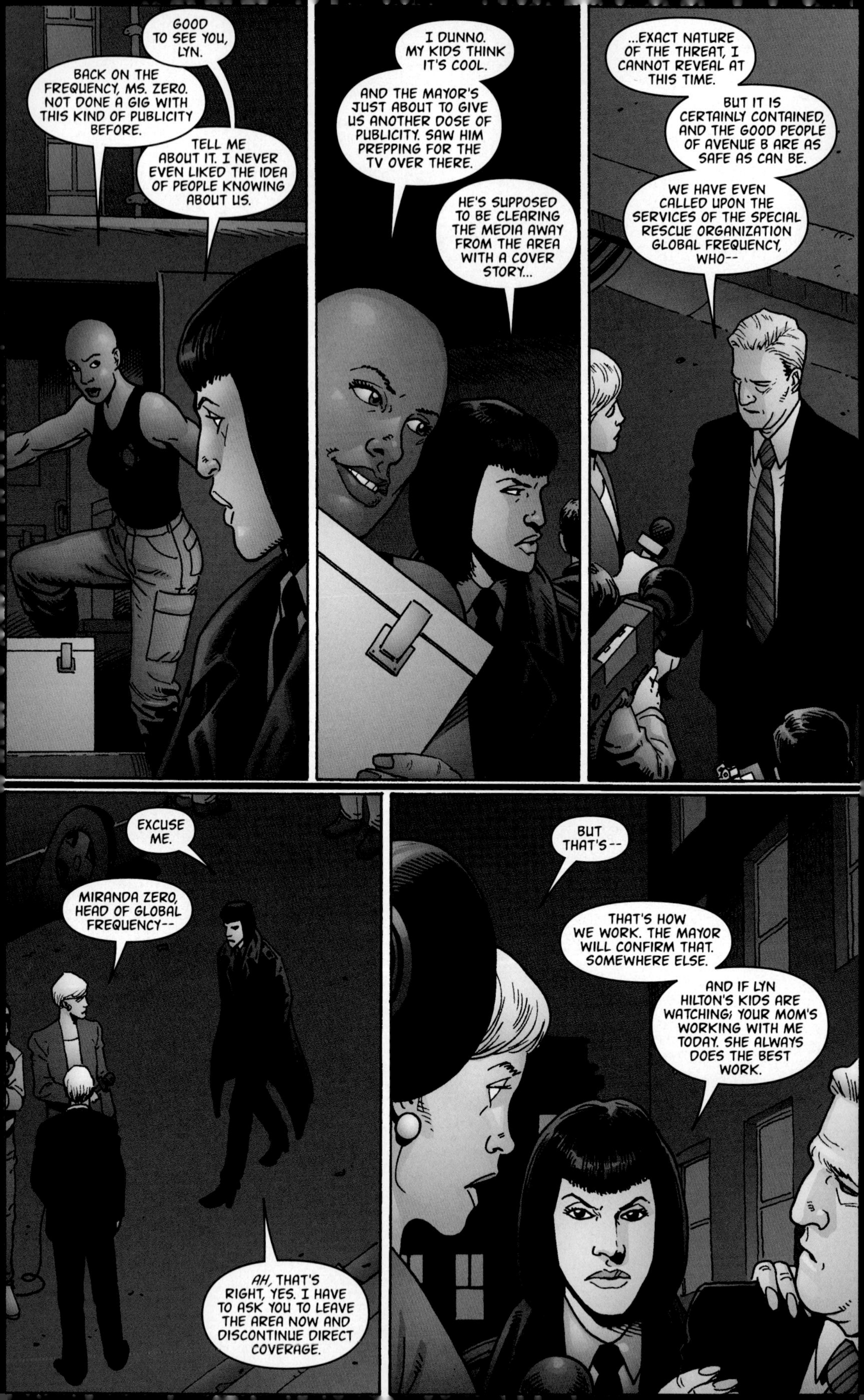
BACK ON THE FREQUENCY, MS. ZERO. NOT DONE A GIG WITH THIS KIND OF PUBLICITY BEFORE.
GOOD TO SEE YOU, LYN.
TELL ME ABOUT IT. I NEVER EVEN LIKED THE IDEA OF PEOPLE KNOWING ABOUT US.
I DUNNO. MY KIDS THINK IT'S COOL.
AND THE MAYOR'S JUST ABOUT TO GIVE US ANOTHER DOSE OF PUBLICITY. SAW HIM PREPPING FOR THE TV OVER THERE.
HE'S SUPPOSED TO BE CLEARING THE MEDIA AWAY FROM THE AREA WITH A COVER STORY...
...EXACT NATURE OF THE THREAT, I CANNOT REVEAL AT THIS TIME.
BUT IT IS CERTAINLY CONTAINED, AND THE GOOD PEOPLE OF AVENUE B ARE AS SAFE AS CAN BE.
WE HAVE EVEN CALLED UPON THE SERVICES OF THE SPECIAL RESCUE ORGANIZATION GLOBAL FREQUENCY, WHO--
EXCUSE ME.
MIRANDA ZERO, HEAD OF GLOBAL FREQUENCY--
AH, THAT'S RIGHT, YES. I HAVE TO ASK YOU TO LEAVE THE AREA NOW AND DISCONTINUE DIRECT COVERAGE.
BUT THAT'S--
THAT'S HOW WE WORK. THE MAYOR WILL CONFIRM THAT. SOMEWHERE ELSE.
AND IF LYN HILTON'S KIDS ARE WATCHING; YOUR MOM'S WORKING WITH ME TODAY. SHE ALWAYS DOES THE BEST WORK.

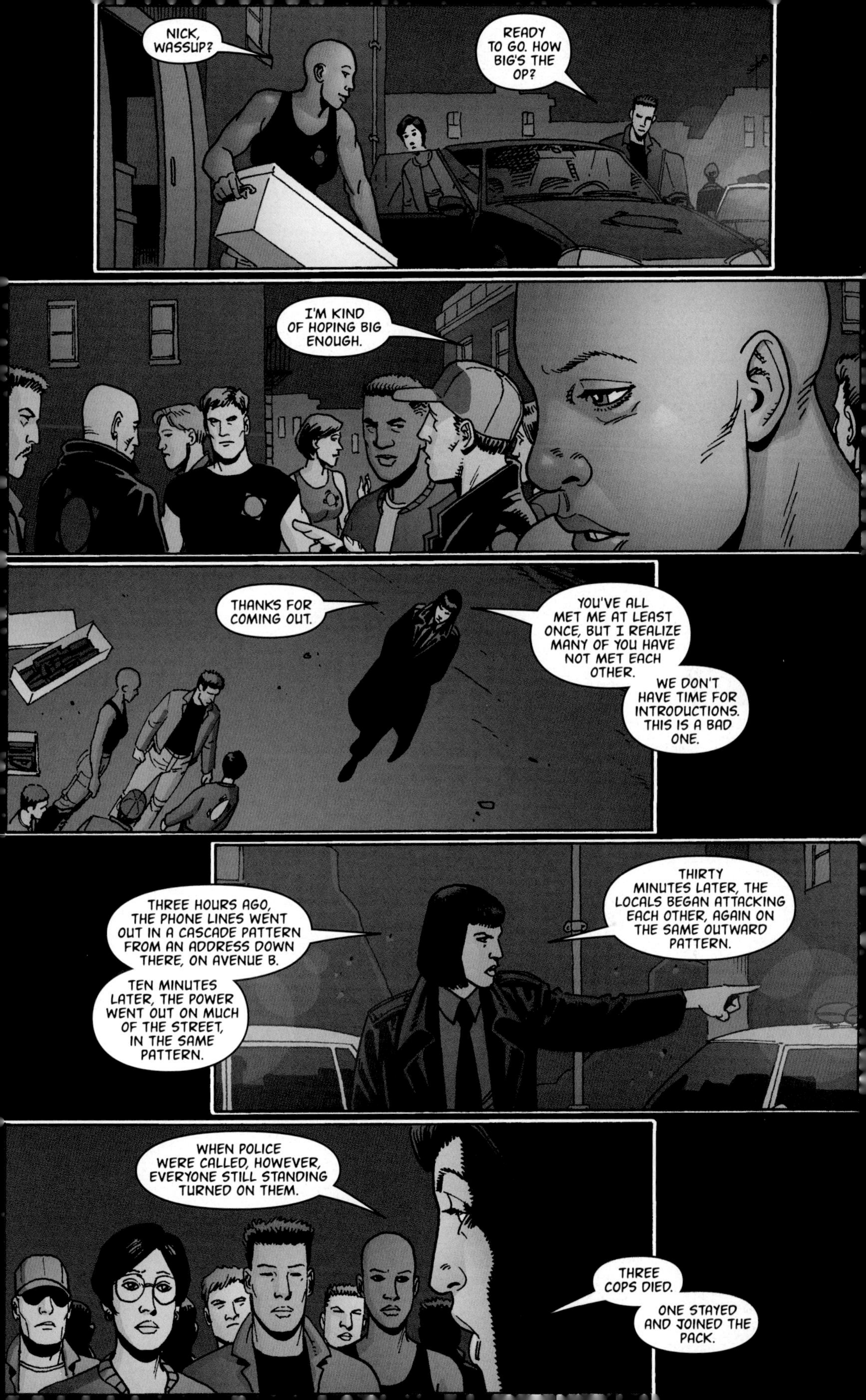
NICK, WASSUP?
READY TO GO. HOW BIG'S THE OP?
I'M KIND OF HOPING BIG ENOUGH.
THANKS FOR COMING OUT.
YOU'VE ALL MET ME AT LEAST ONCE, BUT I REALIZE MANY OF YOU HAVE NOT MET EACH OTHER.
WE DON'T HAVE TIME FOR INTRODUCTIONS. THIS IS A BAD ONE.
THREE HOURS AGO, THE PHONE LINES WENT OUT IN A CASCADE PATTERN FROM AN ADDRESS DOWN THERE, ON AVENUE B.
TEN MINUTES LATER, THE POWER WENT OUT ON MUCH OF THE STREET, IN THE SAME PATTERN.
THIRTY MINUTES LATER, THE LOCALS BEGAN ATTACKING EACH OTHER, AGAIN ON THE SAME OUTWARD PATTERN.
WHEN POLICE WERE CALLED, HOWEVER, EVERYONE STILL STANDING TURNED ON THEM.
THREE COPS DIED.
ONE STAYED AND JOINED THE PACK.

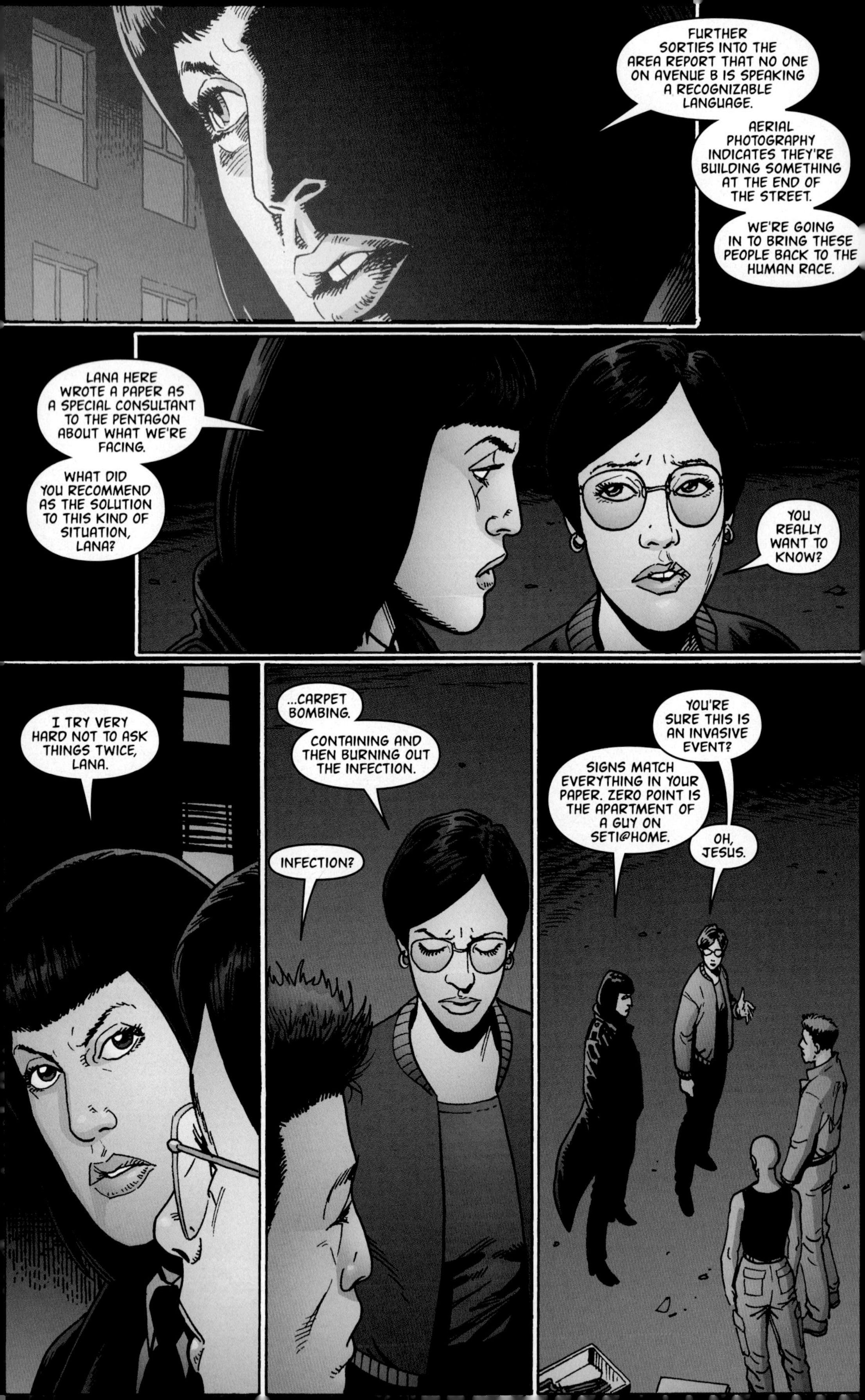
FURTHER SORTIES INTO THE AREA REPORT THAT NO ONE ON AVENUE B IS SPEAKING A RECOGNIZABLE LANGUAGE.
AERIAL PHOTOGRAPHY INDICATES THEY'RE BUILDING SOMETHING AT THE END OF THE STREET.
WE'RE GOING IN TO BRING THESE PEOPLE BACK TO THE HUMAN RACE.
LANA HERE WROTE A PAPER AS A SPECIAL CONSULTANT TO THE PENTAGON ABOUT WHAT WE'RE FACING.
WHAT DID YOU RECOMMEND AS THE SOLUTION TO THIS KIND OF SITUATION, LANA?
YOU REALLY WANT TO KNOW?
I TRY VERY HARD NOT TO ASK THINGS TWICE, LANA.
...CARPET BOMBING.
CONTAINING AND THEN BURNING OUT THE INFECTION.
INFECTION?
YOU'RE SURE THIS IS AN INVASIVE EVENT?
SIGNS MATCH EVERYTHING IN YOUR PAPER. ZERO POINT IS THE APARTMENT OF A GUY ON SETI@HOME.
OH, JESUS.

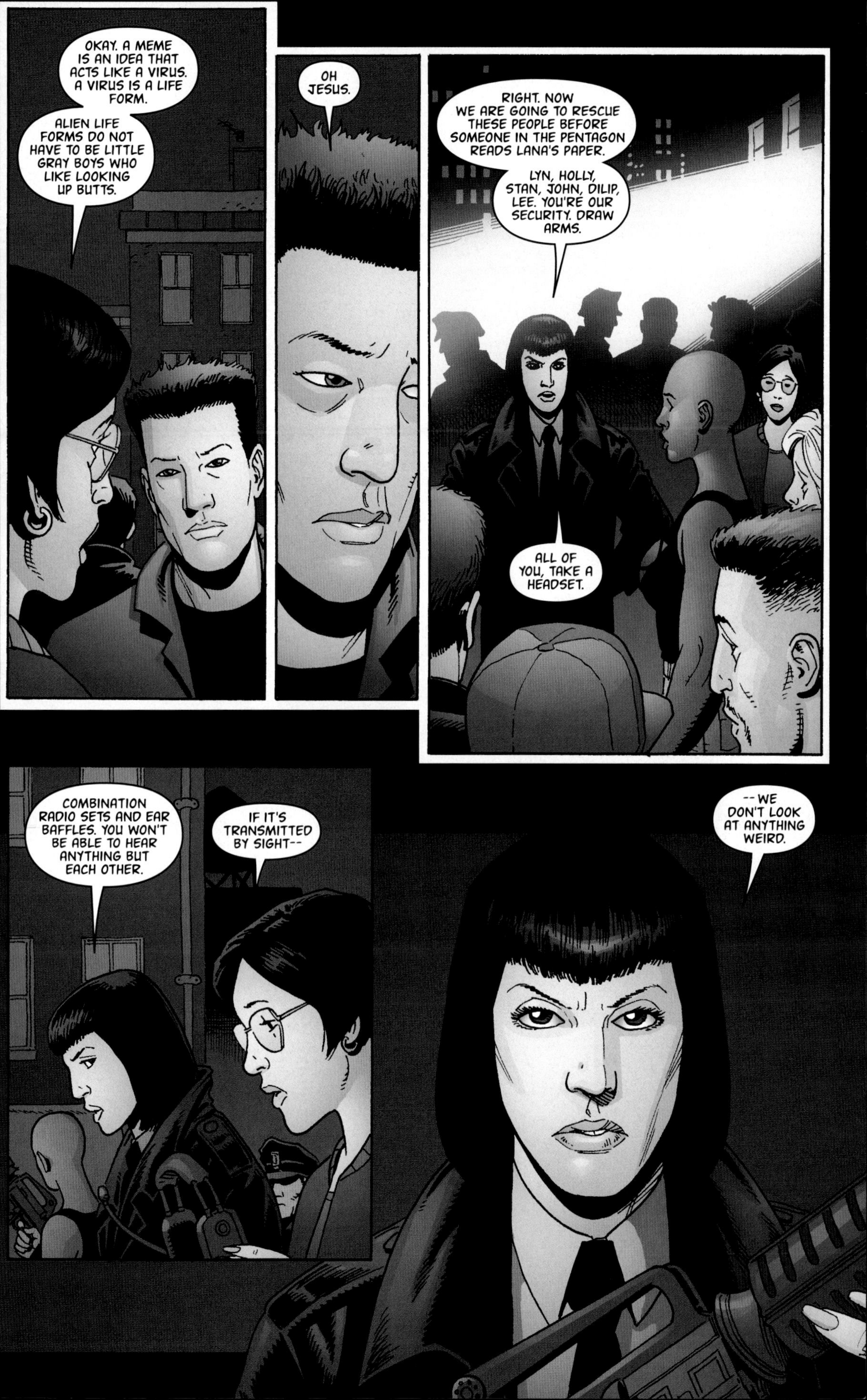
OKAY. A MEME IS AN IDEA THAT ACTS LIKE A VIRUS. A VIRUS IS A LIFE FORM.
ALIEN LIFE FORMS DO NOT HAVE TO BE LITTLE GRAY BOYS WHO LIKE LOOKING UP BUTTS.
OH JESUS.
RIGHT. NOW WE ARE GOING TO RESCUE THESE PEOPLE BEFORE SOMEONE IN THE PENTAGON READS LANA'S PAPER.
LYN, HOLLY, STAN, JOHN, DILIP, LEE. YOU'RE OUR SECURITY. DRAW ARMS.
ALL OF YOU, TAKE A HEADSET.
COMBINATION RADIO SETS AND EAR BAFFLES. YOU WON'T BE ABLE TO HEAR ANYTHING BUT EACH OTHER.
IF IT'S TRANSMITTED BY SIGHT--
--WE DON'T LOOK AT ANYTHING WEIRD.

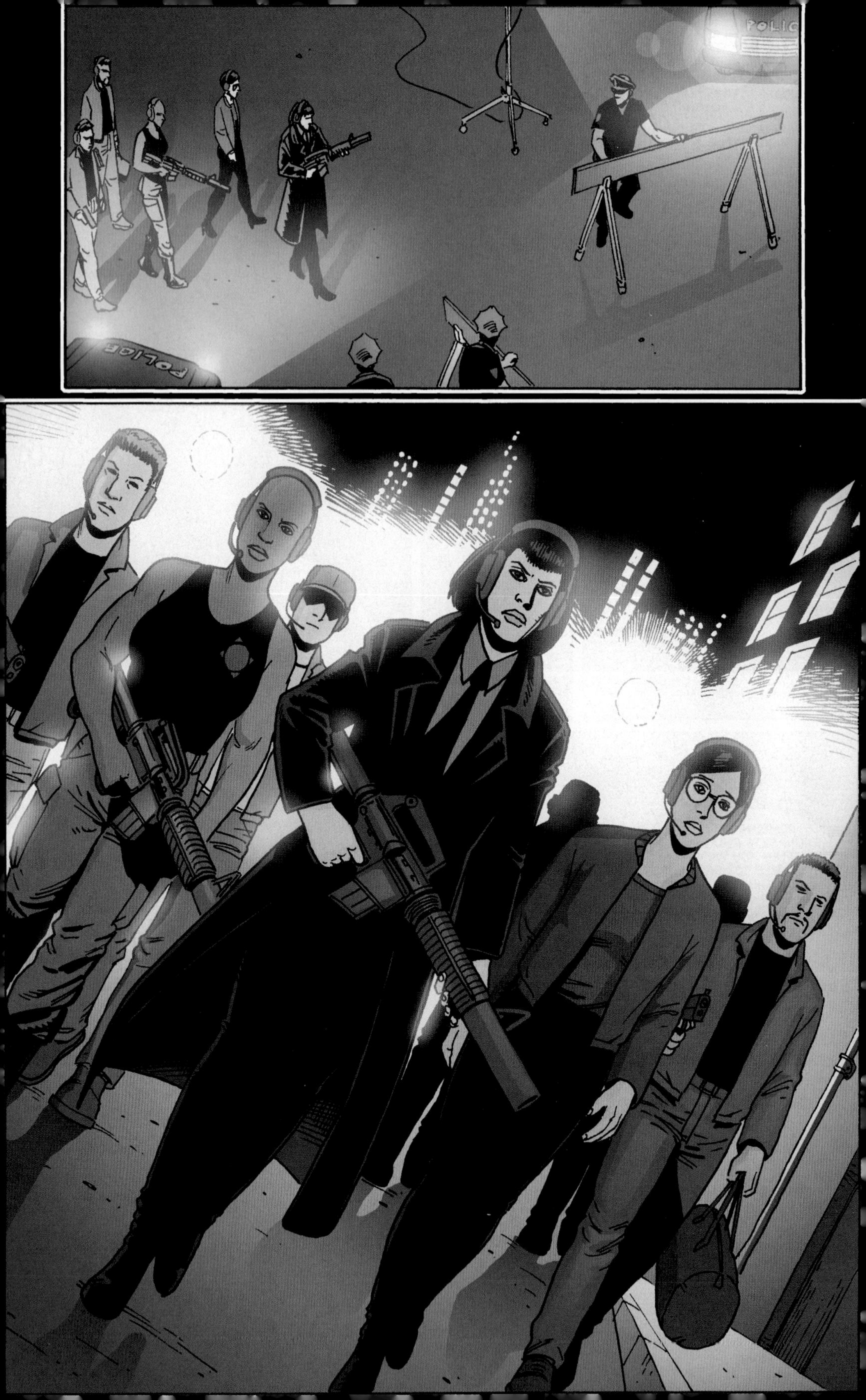

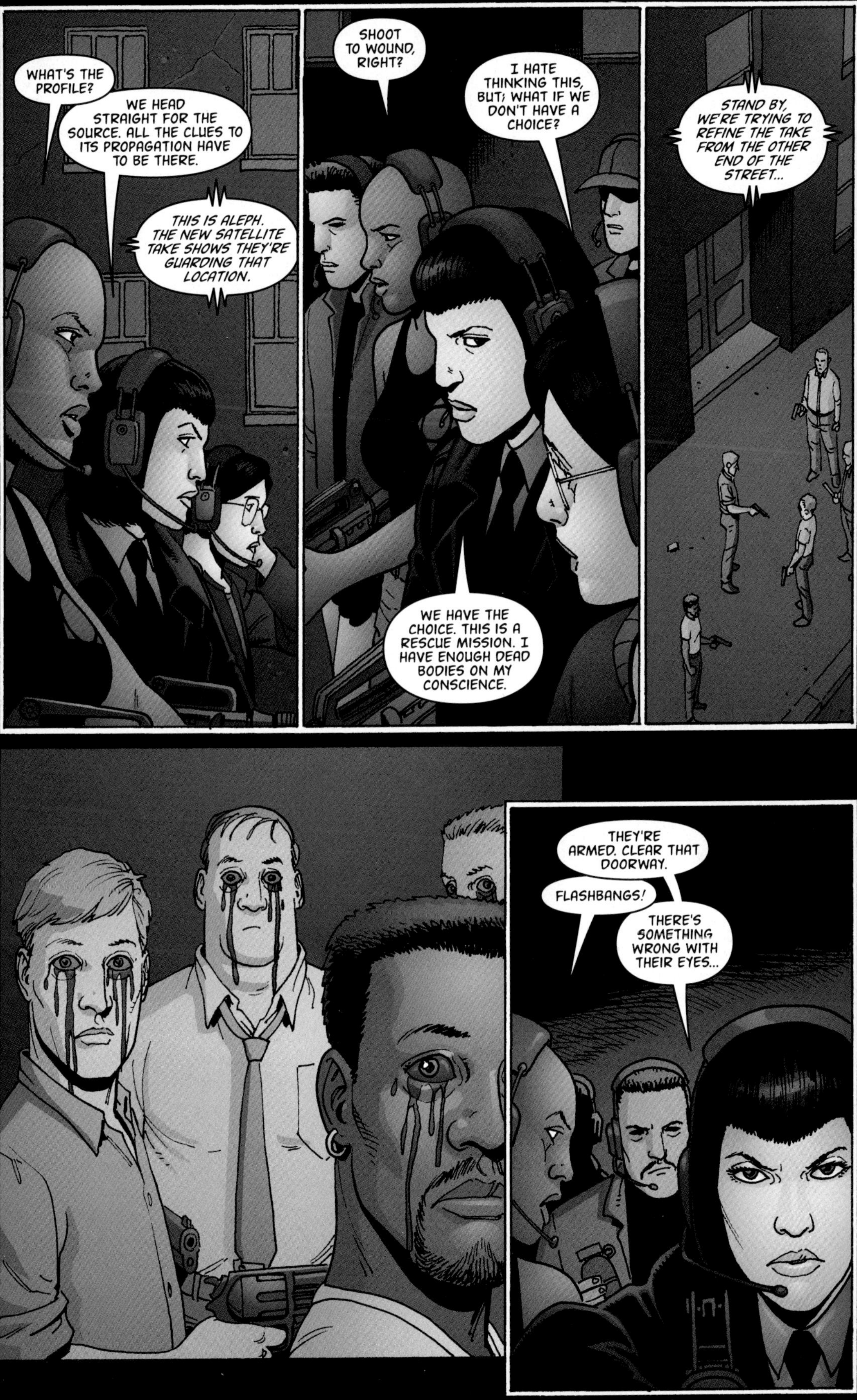
WHAT'S THE PROFILE?
WE HEAD STRAIGHT FOR THE SOURCE. ALL THE CLUES TO ITS PROPAGATION HAVE TO BE THERE.
THIS IS ALEPH. THE NEW SATELLITE TAKE SHOWS THEY'RE GUARDING THAT LOCATION.
SHOOT TO WOUND, RIGHT?
I HATE THINKING THIS, BUT; WHAT IF WE DON'T HAVE A CHOICE?
WE HAVE THE CHOICE. THIS IS A RESCUE MISSION. I HAVE ENOUGH DEAD BODIES ON MY CONSCIENCE.
STAND BY, WE'RE TRYING TO REFINE THE TAKE FROM THE OTHER END OF THE STREET...
THEY'RE ARMED. CLEAR THAT DOORWAY.
FLASHBANGS!
THERE'S SOMETHING WRONG WITH THEIR EYES...

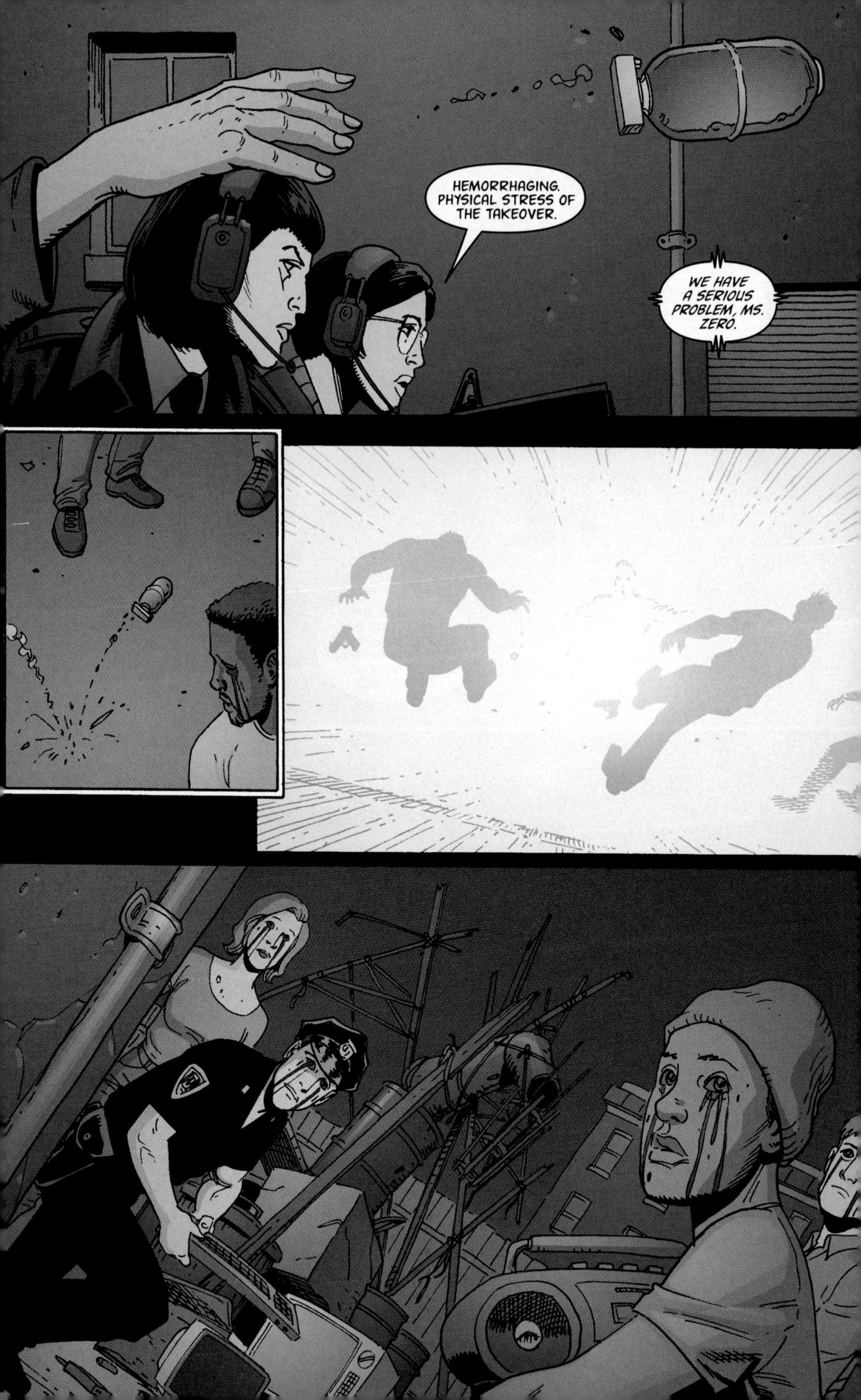
HEMORRHAGING. PHYSICAL STRESS OF THE TAKEOVER.
WE HAVE A SERIOUS PROBLEM, MS. ZERO.

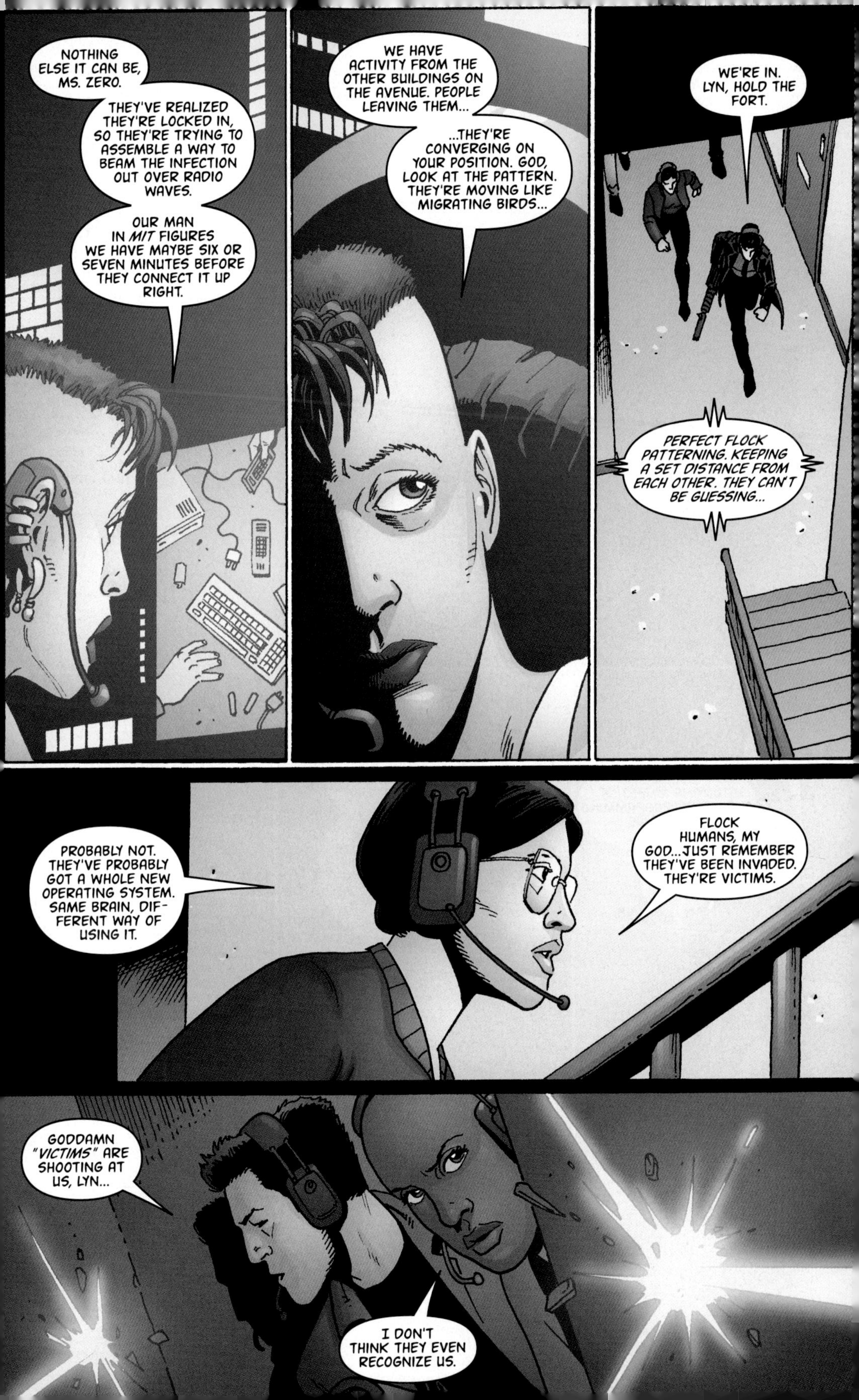
NOTHING ELSE IT CAN BE, MS. ZERO.
THEY'VE REALIZED THEY'RE LOCKED IN, SO THEY'RE TRYING TO ASSEMBLE A WAY TO BEAM THE INFECTION OUT OVER RADIO WAVES.
OUR MAN IN *MIT* FIGURES WE HAVE MAYBE SIX OR SEVEN MINUTES BEFORE THEY CONNECT IT UP RIGHT.
WE HAVE ACTIVITY FROM THE OTHER BUILDINGS ON THE AVENUE. PEOPLE LEAVING THEM...
...THEY'RE CONVERGING ON YOUR POSITION. GOD, LOOK AT THE PATTERN. THEY'RE MOVING LIKE MIGRATING BIRDS...
WE'RE IN. LYN, HOLD THE FORT.
PERFECT FLOCK PATTERNING. KEEPING A SET DISTANCE FROM EACH OTHER. THEY CAN'T BE GUESSING...
PROBABLY NOT. THEY'VE PROBABLY GOT A WHOLE NEW OPERATING SYSTEM. SAME BRAIN, DIF-FERENT WAY OF USING IT.
FLOCK HUMANS, MY GOD...JUST REMEMBER THEY'VE BEEN INVADED. THEY'RE VICTIMS.
GODDAMN "*VICTIMS*" ARE SHOOTING AT US, LYN...
I DON'T THINK THEY EVEN RECOGNIZE US.

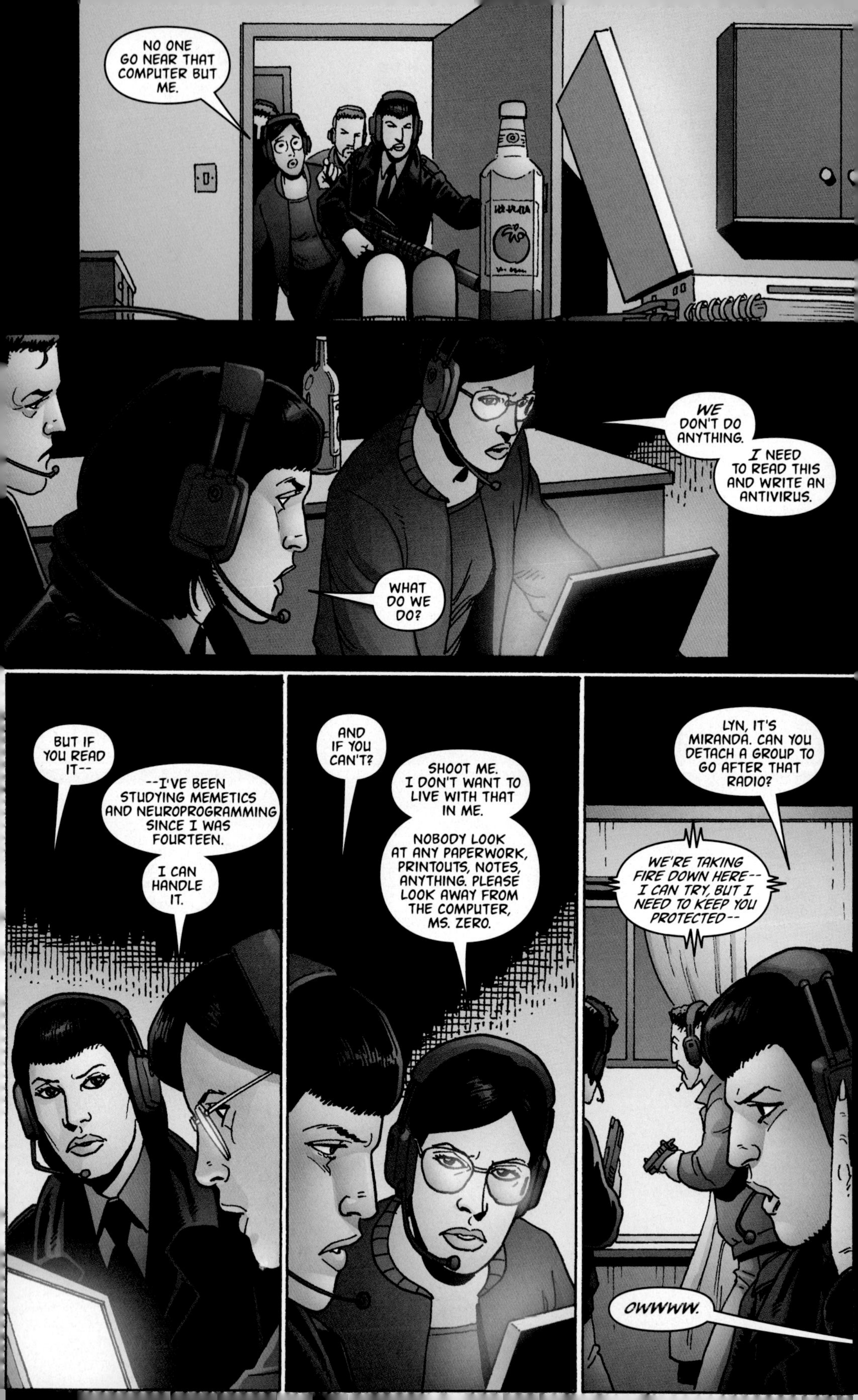
NO ONE GO NEAR THAT COMPUTER BUT ME.
WE DON'T DO ANYTHING.
I NEED TO READ THIS AND WRITE AN ANTIVIRUS.
WHAT DO WE DO?
BUT IF YOU READ IT--
--I'VE BEEN STUDYING MEMETICS AND NEUROPROGRAMMING SINCE I WAS FOURTEEN.
I CAN HANDLE IT.
AND IF YOU CAN'T?
SHOOT ME. I DON'T WANT TO LIVE WITH THAT IN ME.
NOBODY LOOK AT ANY PAPERWORK, PRINTOUTS, NOTES, ANYTHING. PLEASE LOOK AWAY FROM THE COMPUTER, MS. ZERO.
LYN, IT'S MIRANDA. CAN YOU DETACH A GROUP TO GO AFTER THAT RADIO?
WE'RE TAKING FIRE DOWN HERE-- I CAN TRY, BUT I NEED TO KEEP YOU PROTECTED--
OWWWW.

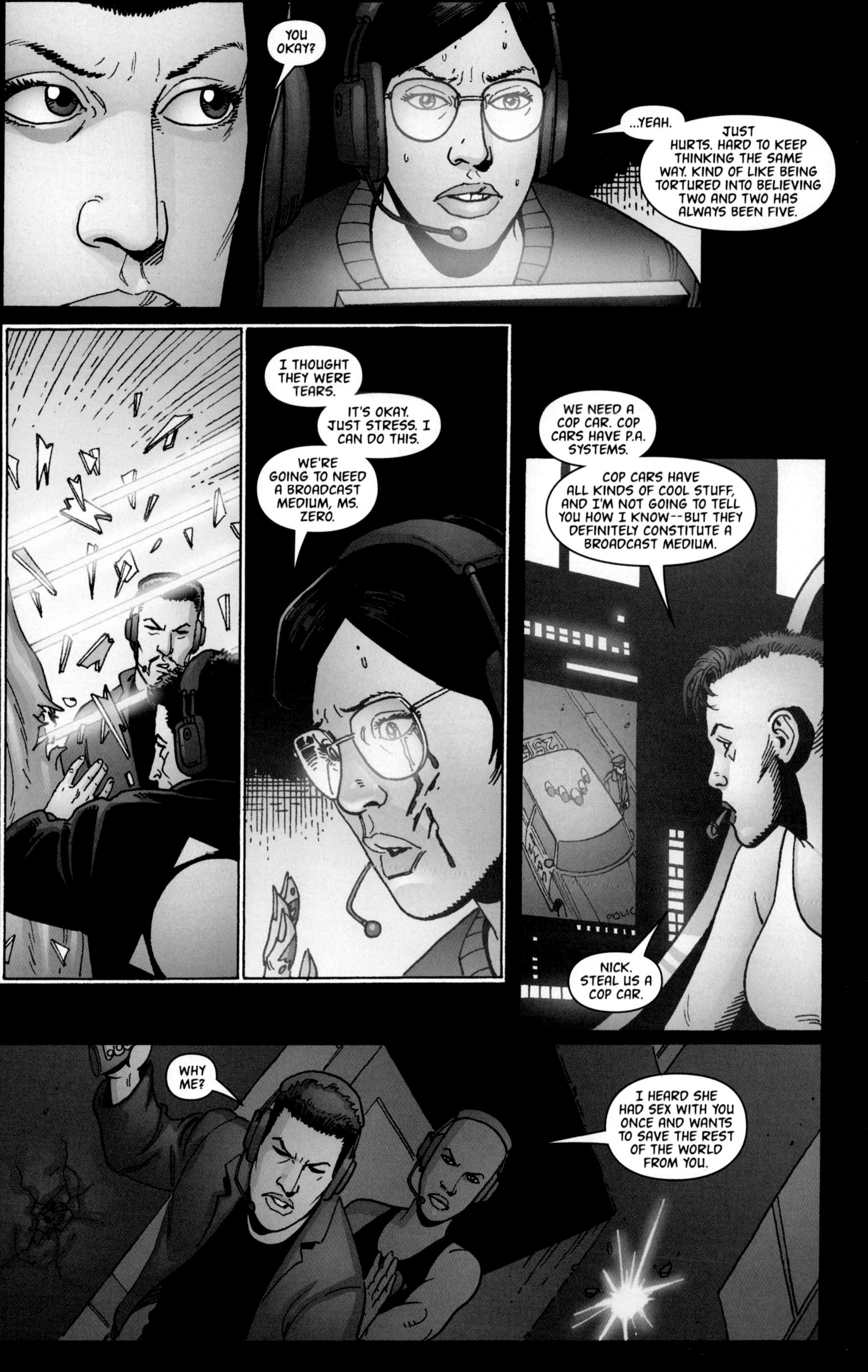
YOU OKAY?
...YEAH.
JUST HURTS. HARD TO KEEP THINKING THE SAME WAY. KIND OF LIKE BEING TORTURED INTO BELIEVING TWO AND TWO HAS ALWAYS BEEN FIVE.
I THOUGHT THEY WERE TEARS.
IT'S OKAY. JUST STRESS. I CAN DO THIS.
WE'RE GOING TO NEED A BROADCAST MEDIUM, MS. ZERO.
WE NEED A COP CAR. COP CARS HAVE P.A. SYSTEMS.
COP CARS HAVE ALL KINDS OF COOL STUFF, AND I'M NOT GOING TO TELL YOU HOW I KNOW--BUT THEY DEFINITELY CONSTITUTE A BROADCAST MEDIUM.
NICK. STEAL US A COP CAR.
WHY ME?
I HEARD SHE HAD SEX WITH YOU ONCE AND WANTS TO SAVE THE REST OF THE WORLD FROM YOU.

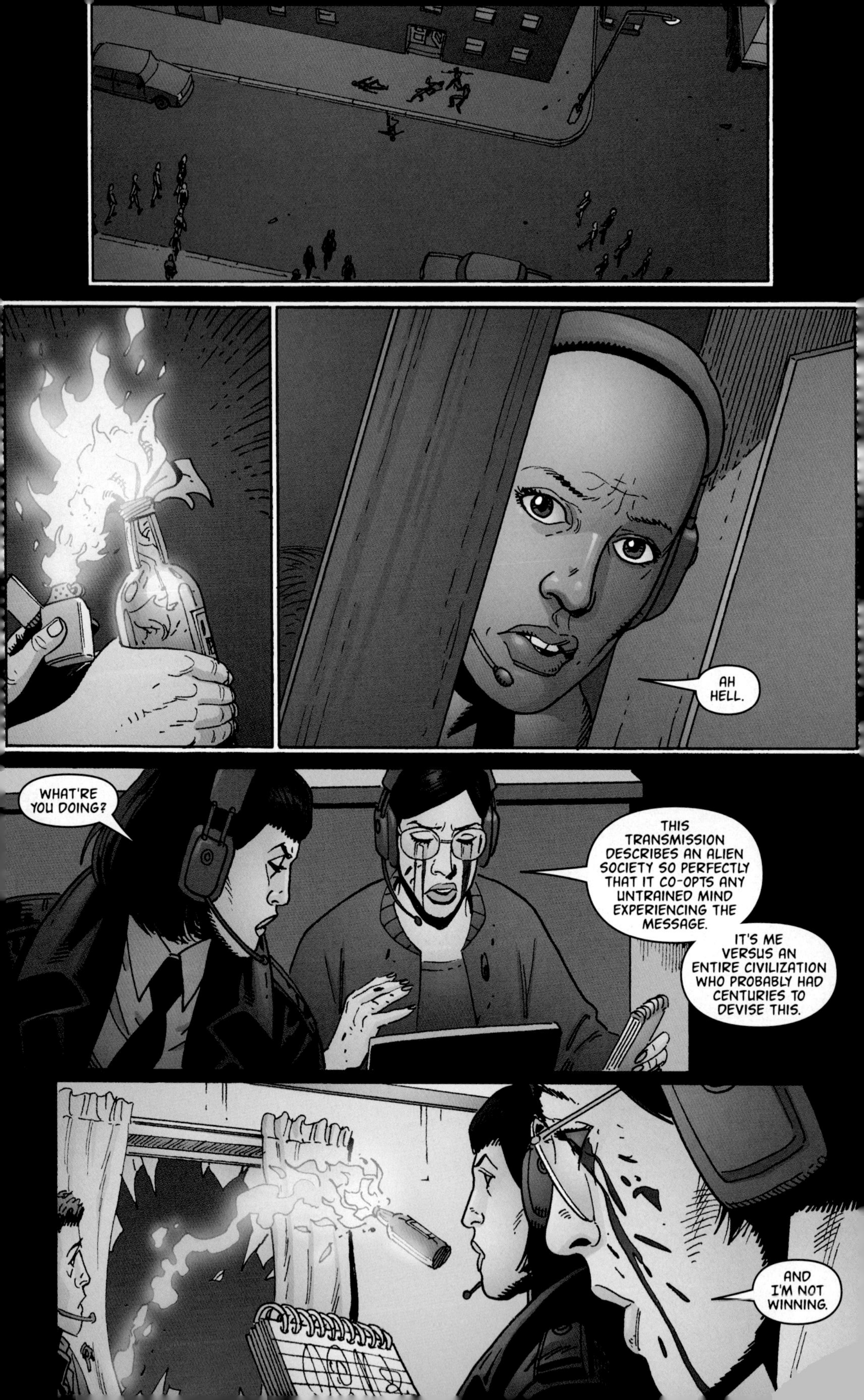
AH HELL.
WHAT'RE YOU DOING?
THIS TRANSMISSION DESCRIBES AN ALIEN SOCIETY SO PERFECTLY THAT IT CO-OPTS ANY UNTRAINED MIND EXPERIENCING THE MESSAGE.
IT'S ME VERSUS AN ENTIRE CIVILIZATION WHO PROBABLY HAD CENTURIES TO DEVISE THIS.
AND I'M NOT WINNING.

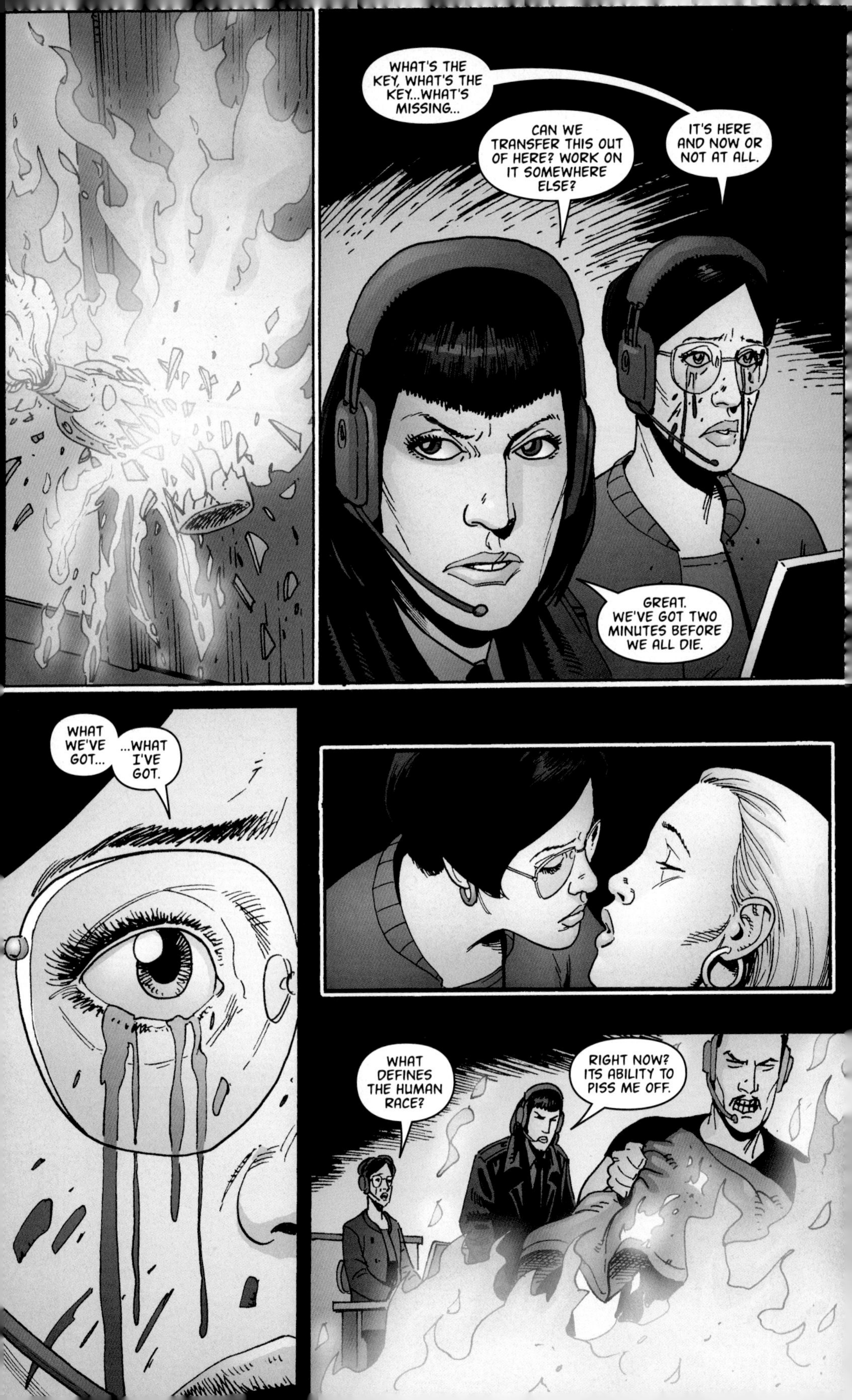
WHAT'S THE KEY, WHAT'S THE KEY...WHAT'S MISSING...
CAN WE TRANSFER THIS OUT OF HERE? WORK ON IT SOMEWHERE ELSE?
IT'S HERE AND NOW OR NOT AT ALL.
GREAT. WE'VE GOT TWO MINUTES BEFORE WE ALL DIE.
WHAT WE'VE GOT...
...WHAT I'VE GOT.
WHAT DEFINES THE HUMAN RACE?
RIGHT NOW? ITS ABILITY TO PISS ME OFF.

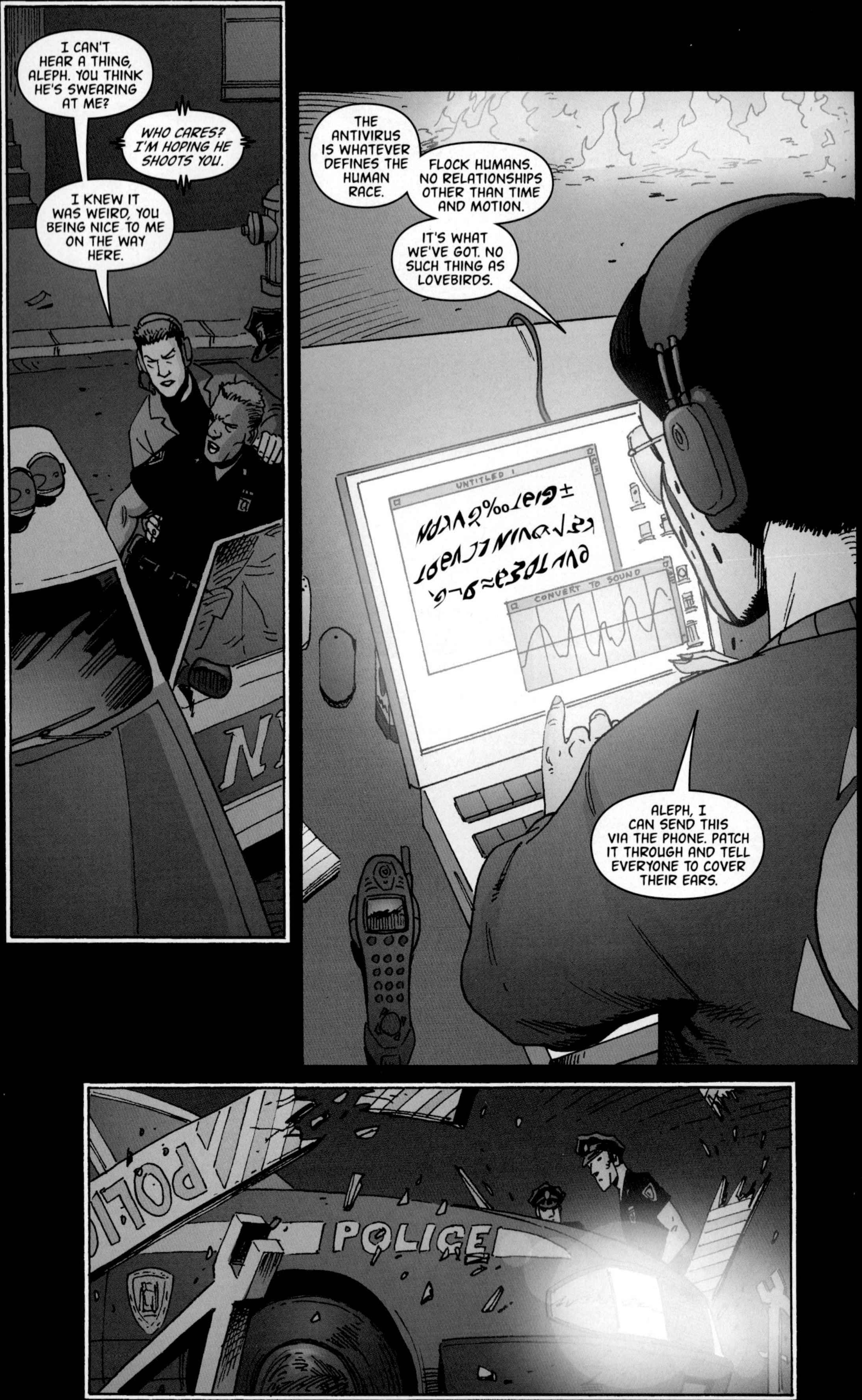
I CAN'T HEAR A THING, ALEPH. YOU THINK HE'S SWEARING AT ME?
WHO CARES? I'M HOPING HE SHOOTS YOU.
I KNEW IT WAS WEIRD, YOU BEING NICE TO ME ON THE WAY HERE.
THE ANTIVIRUS IS WHATEVER DEFINES THE HUMAN RACE.
FLOCK HUMANS. NO RELATIONSHIPS OTHER THAN TIME AND MOTION.
IT'S WHAT WE'VE GOT. NO SUCH THING AS LOVEBIRDS.
ALEPH, I CAN SEND THIS VIA THE PHONE. PATCH IT THROUGH AND TELL EVERYONE TO COVER THEIR EARS.
POLICE

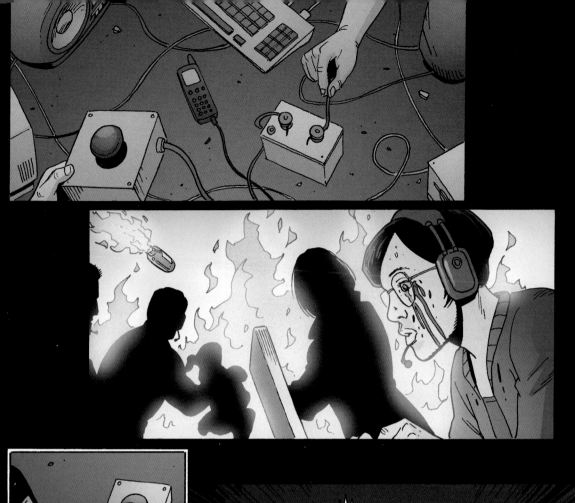

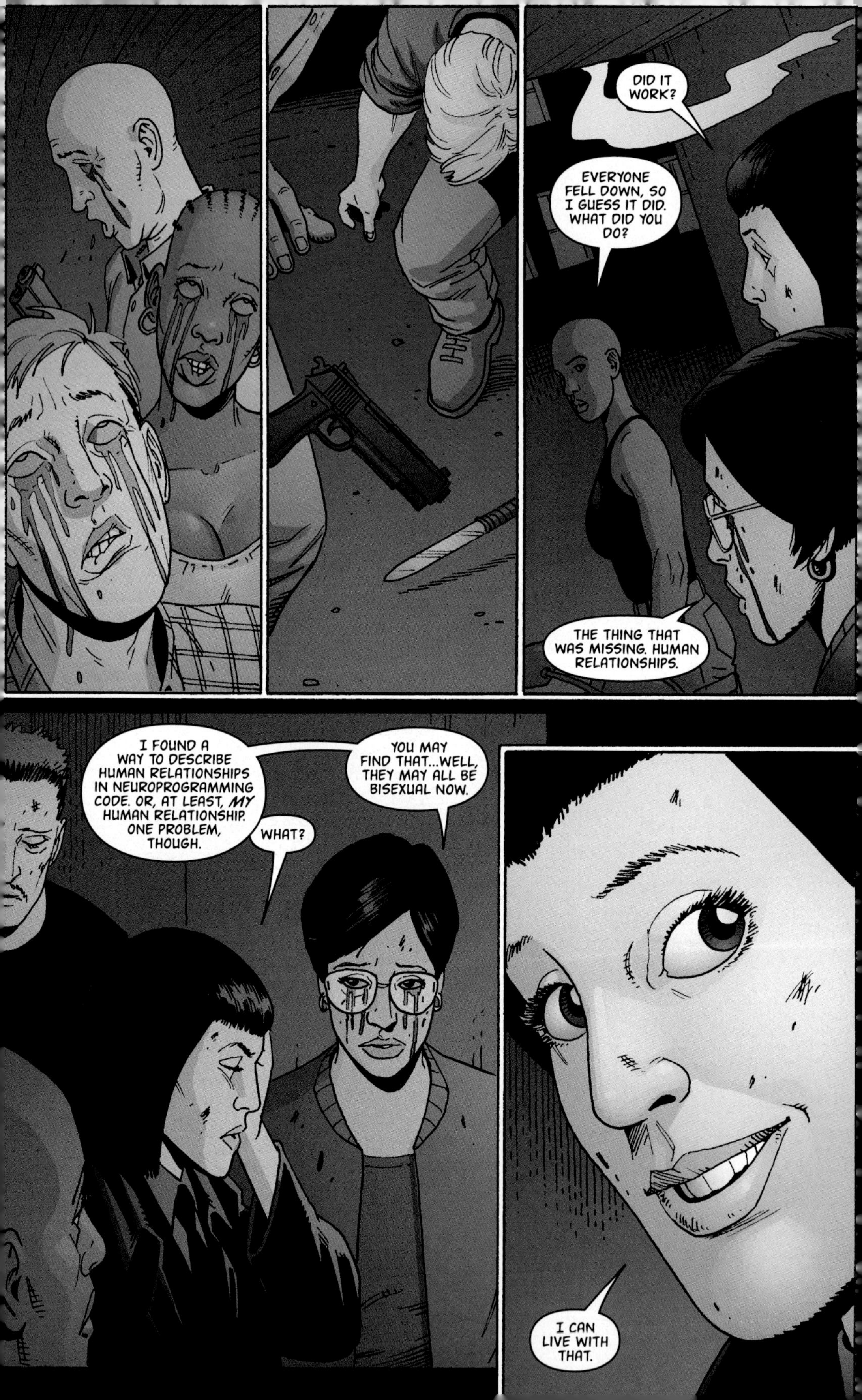
DID IT WORK?
EVERYONE FELL DOWN, SO I GUESS IT DID. WHAT DID YOU DO?
THE THING THAT WAS MISSING. HUMAN RELATIONSHIPS.
I FOUND A WAY TO DESCRIBE HUMAN RELATIONSHIPS IN NEUROPROGRAMMING CODE. OR, AT LEAST, MY HUMAN RELATIONSHIP. ONE PROBLEM, THOUGH.
WHAT?
YOU MAY FIND THAT...WELL, THEY MAY ALL BE BISEXUAL NOW.
I CAN LIVE WITH THAT.

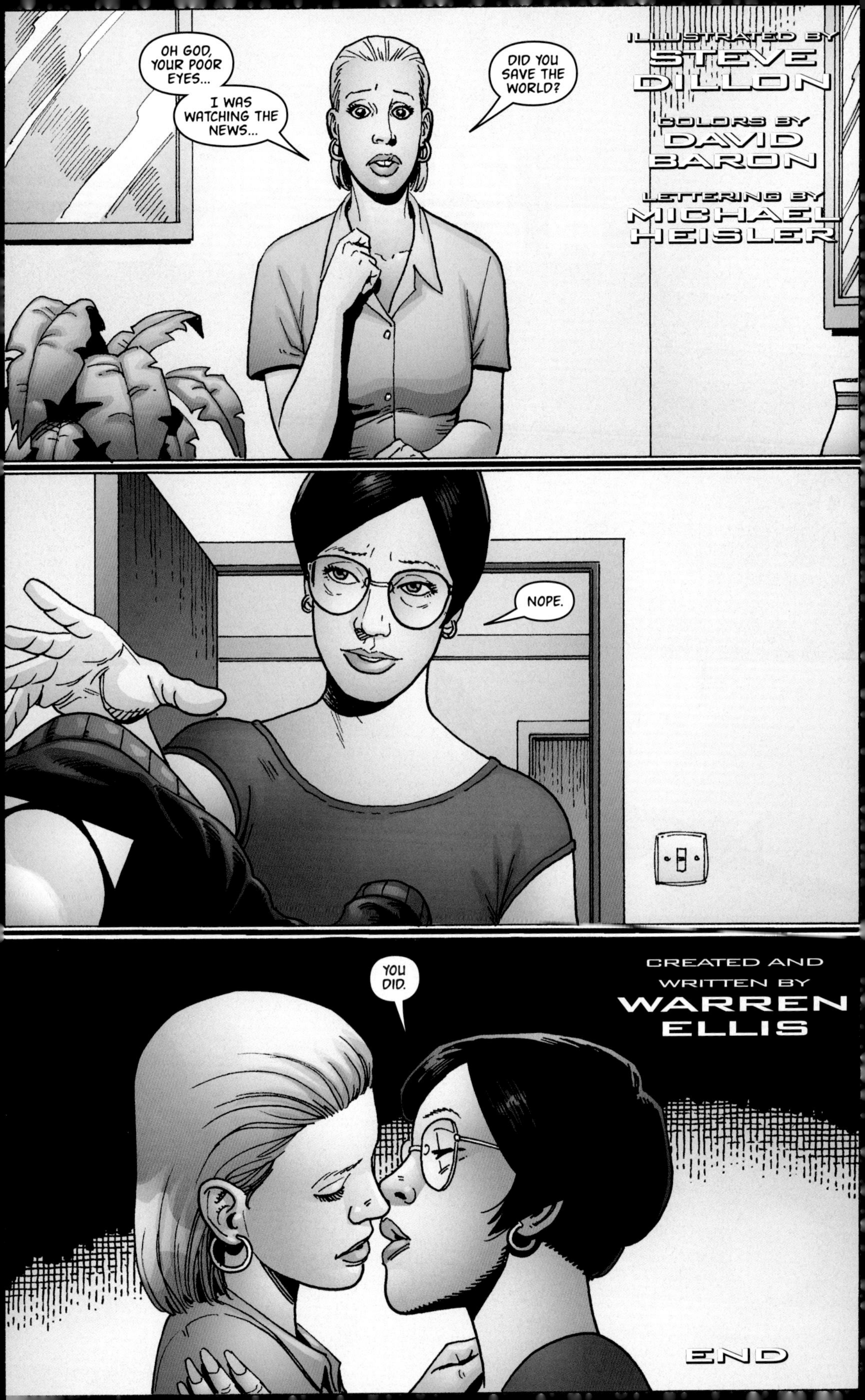
OH GOD, YOUR POOR EYES...
I WAS WATCHING THE NEWS...
DID YOU SAVE THE WORLD?
ILLUSTRATED BY STEVE DILLON
COLORS BY DAVID BARON
LETTERING BY MICHAEL HEISLER
NOPE.
YOU DID.
CREATED AND WRITTEN BY WARREN ELLIS
END

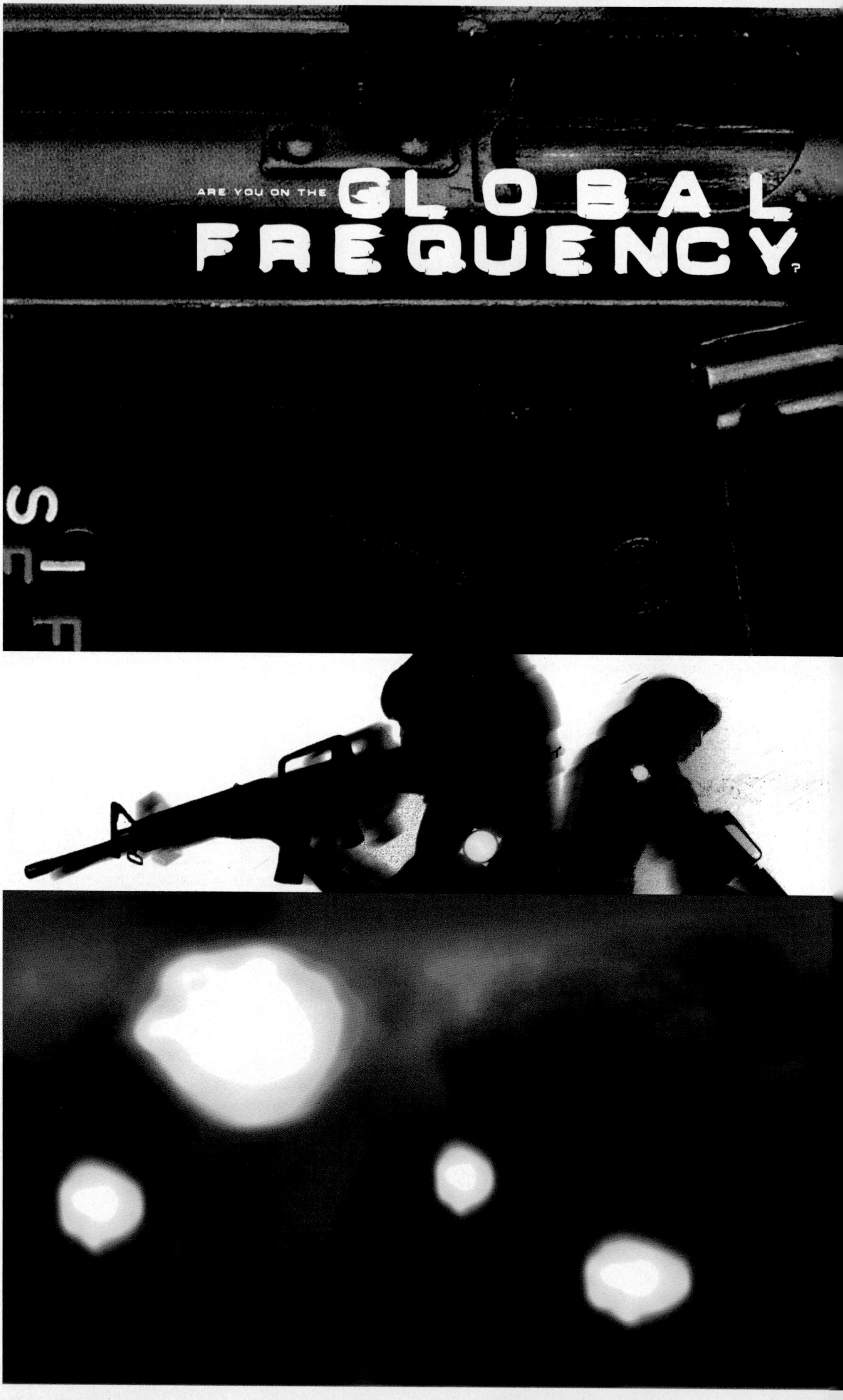
ARE YOU ON THE GLOBAL FREQUENCY?

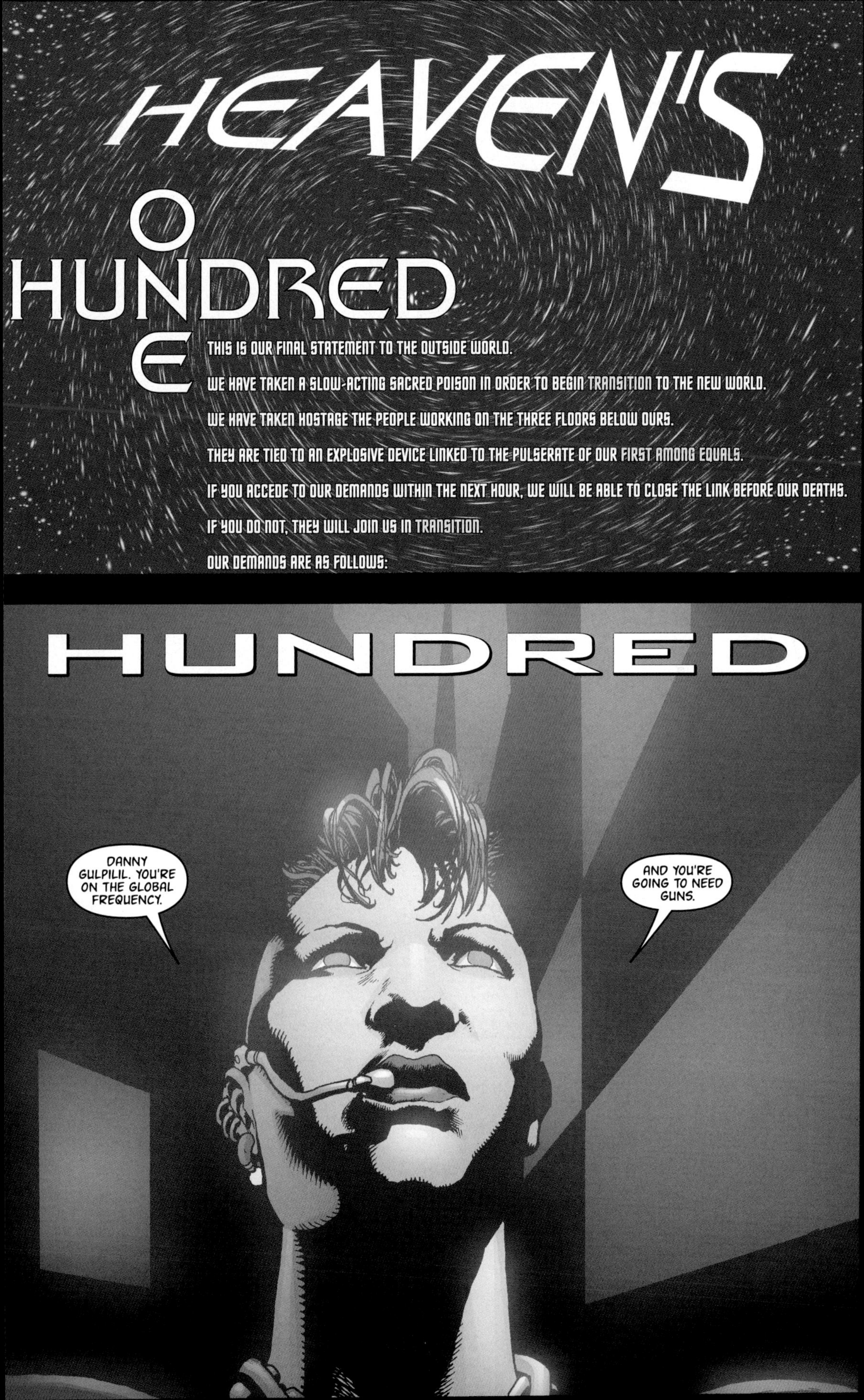
HEAVEN'S
ONE HUNDRED
THIS IS OUR FINAL STATEMENT TO THE OUTSIDE WORLD.
WE HAVE TAKEN A SLOW-ACTING SACRED POISON IN ORDER TO BEGIN TRANSITION TO THE NEW WORLD.
WE HAVE TAKEN HOSTAGE THE PEOPLE WORKING ON THE THREE FLOORS BELOW OURS.
THEY ARE TIED TO AN EXPLOSIVE DEVICE LINKED TO THE PULSERATE OF OUR FIRST AMONG EQUALS.
IF YOU ACCEDE TO OUR DEMANDS WITHIN THE NEXT HOUR, WE WILL BE ABLE TO CLOSE THE LINK BEFORE OUR DEATHS.
IF YOU DO NOT, THEY WILL JOIN US IN TRANSITION.
OUR DEMANDS ARE AS FOLLOWS:
HUNDRED
DANNY GULPILIL. YOU'RE ON THE GLOBAL FREQUENCY.
AND YOU'RE GOING TO NEED GUNS.

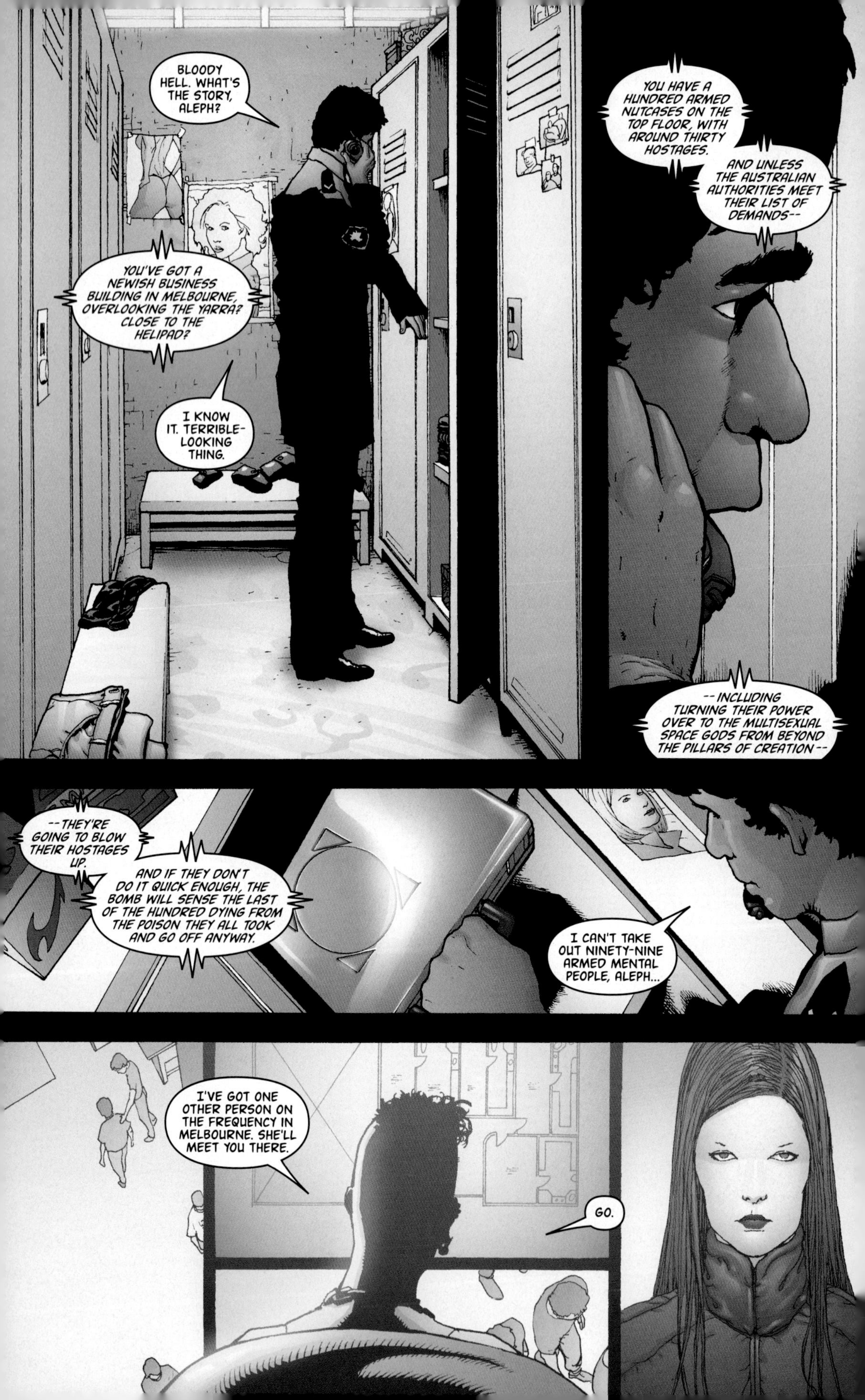
BLOODY HELL. WHAT'S THE STORY, ALEPH?
YOU HAVE A HUNDRED ARMED NUTCASES ON THE TOP FLOOR, WITH AROUND THIRTY HOSTAGES.
AND UNLESS THE AUSTRALIAN AUTHORITIES MEET THEIR LIST OF DEMANDS--
YOU'VE GOT A NEWISH BUSINESS BUILDING IN MELBOURNE, OVERLOOKING THE YARRA? CLOSE TO THE HELIPAD?
I KNOW IT. TERRIBLE-LOOKING THING.
--INCLUDING TURNING THEIR POWER OVER TO THE MULTISEXUAL SPACE GODS FROM BEYOND THE PILLARS OF CREATION--
--THEY'RE GOING TO BLOW THEIR HOSTAGES UP.
AND IF THEY DON'T DO IT QUICK ENOUGH, THE BOMB WILL SENSE THE LAST OF THE HUNDRED DYING FROM THE POISON THEY ALL TOOK AND GO OFF ANYWAY.
I CAN'T TAKE OUT NINETY-NINE ARMED MENTAL PEOPLE, ALEPH...
I'VE GOT ONE OTHER PERSON ON THE FREQUENCY IN MELBOURNE. SHE'LL MEET YOU THERE.
GO.

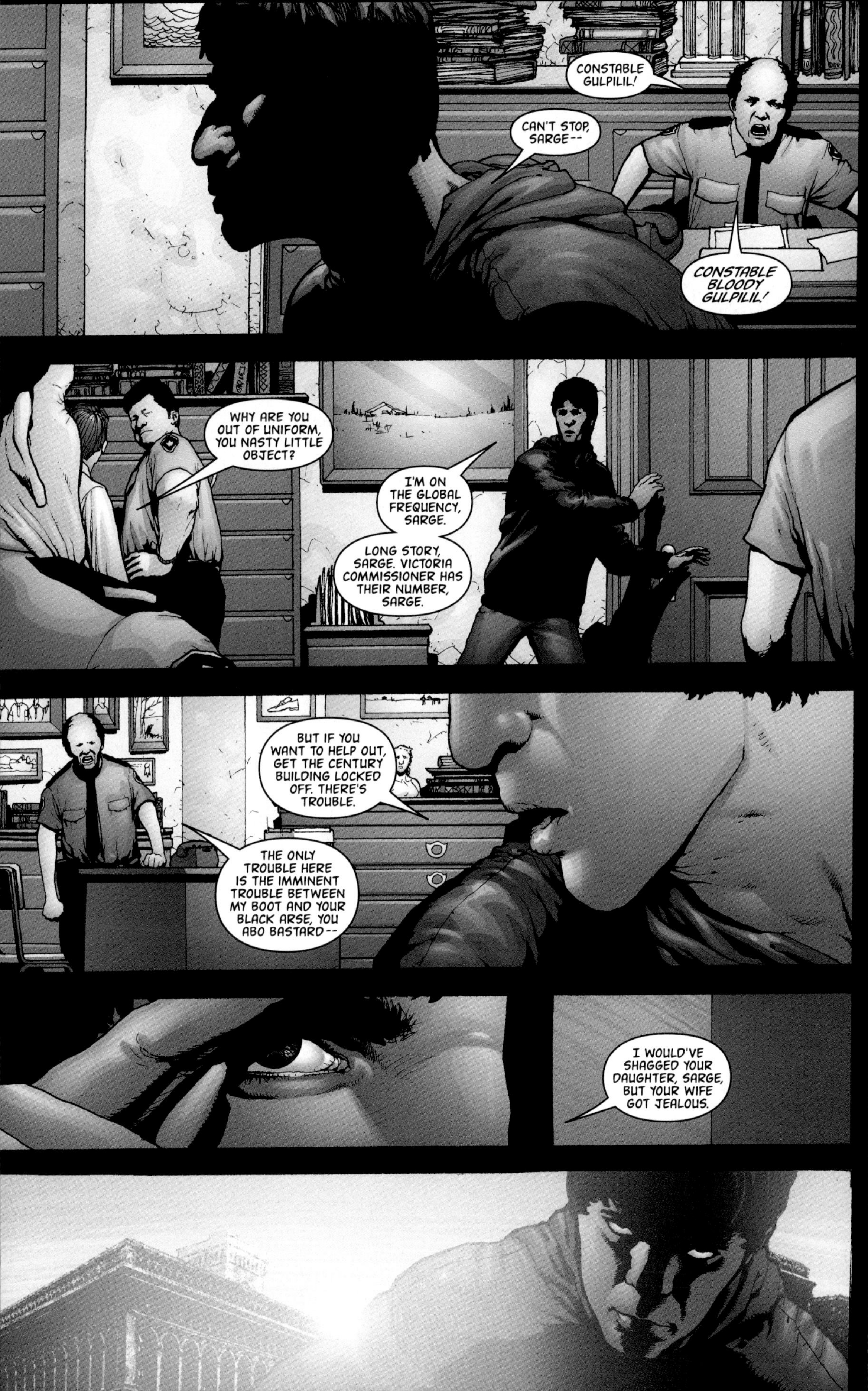
CONSTABLE GULPILIL!
CAN'T STOP, SARGE--
CONSTABLE BLOODY GULPILIL!
WHY ARE YOU OUT OF UNIFORM, YOU NASTY LITTLE OBJECT?
I'M ON THE GLOBAL FREQUENCY, SARGE.
LONG STORY, SARGE. VICTORIA COMMISSIONER HAS THEIR NUMBER, SARGE.
BUT IF YOU WANT TO HELP OUT, GET THE CENTURY BUILDING LOCKED OFF. THERE'S TROUBLE.
THE ONLY TROUBLE HERE IS THE IMMINENT TROUBLE BETWEEN MY BOOT AND YOUR BLACK ARSE, YOU ABO BASTARD--
I WOULD'VE SHAGGED YOUR DAUGHTER, SARGE, BUT YOUR WIFE GOT JEALOUS.

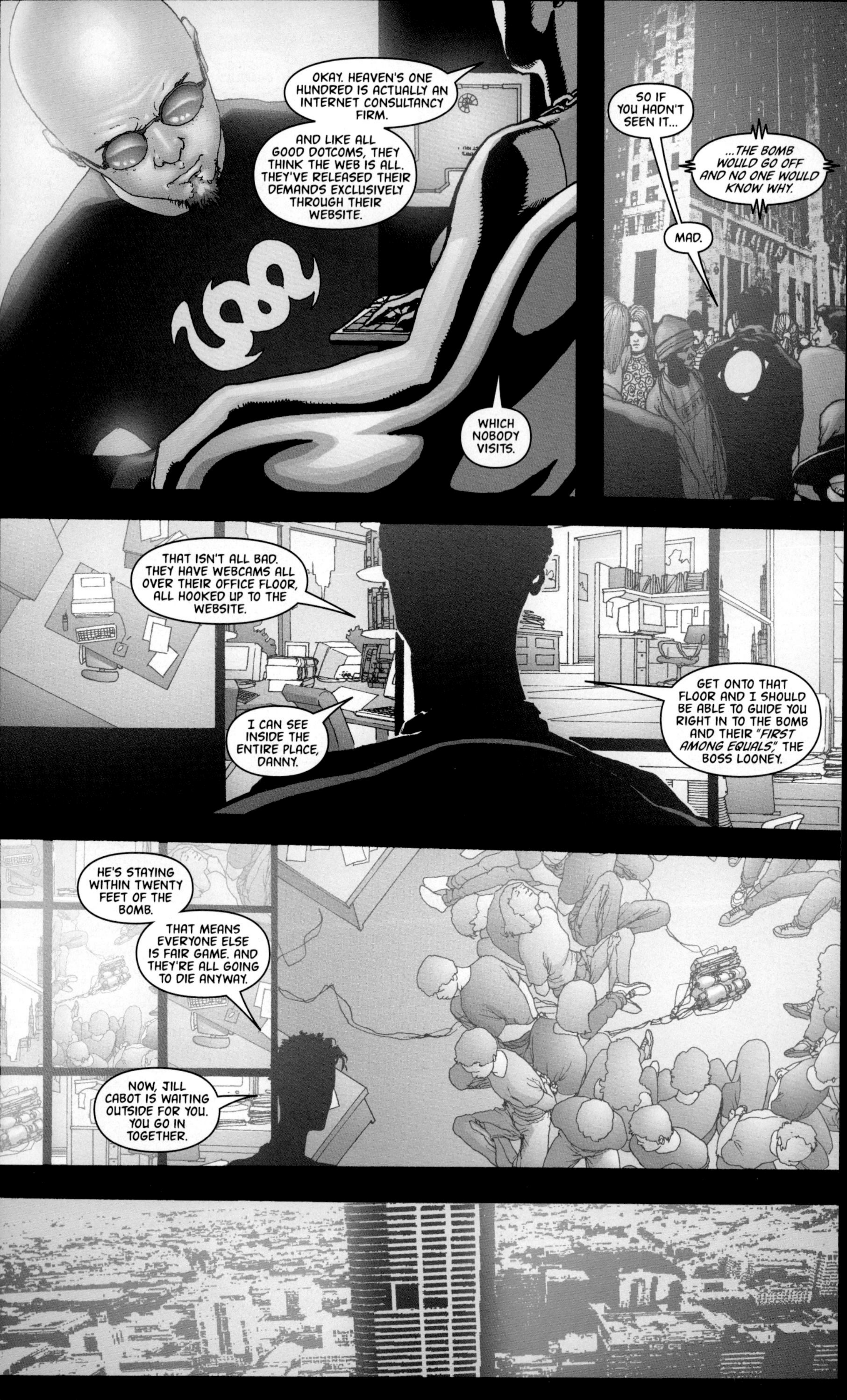
OKAY. HEAVEN'S ONE HUNDRED IS ACTUALLY AN INTERNET CONSULTANCY FIRM.
AND LIKE ALL GOOD DOTCOMS, THEY THINK THE WEB IS ALL. THEY'VE RELEASED THEIR DEMANDS EXCLUSIVELY THROUGH THEIR WEBSITE.
WHICH NOBODY VISITS.
SO IF YOU HADN'T SEEN IT...
...THE BOMB WOULD GO OFF AND NO ONE WOULD KNOW WHY.
MAD.
THAT ISN'T ALL BAD. THEY HAVE WEBCAMS ALL OVER THEIR OFFICE FLOOR, ALL HOOKED UP TO THE WEBSITE.
I CAN SEE INSIDE THE ENTIRE PLACE, DANNY.
GET ONTO THAT FLOOR AND I SHOULD BE ABLE TO GUIDE YOU RIGHT IN TO THE BOMB AND THEIR "FIRST AMONG EQUALS," THE BOSS LOONEY.
HE'S STAYING WITHIN TWENTY FEET OF THE BOMB.
THAT MEANS EVERYONE ELSE IS FAIR GAME. AND THEY'RE ALL GOING TO DIE ANYWAY.
NOW, JILL CABOT IS WAITING OUTSIDE FOR YOU. YOU GO IN TOGETHER.

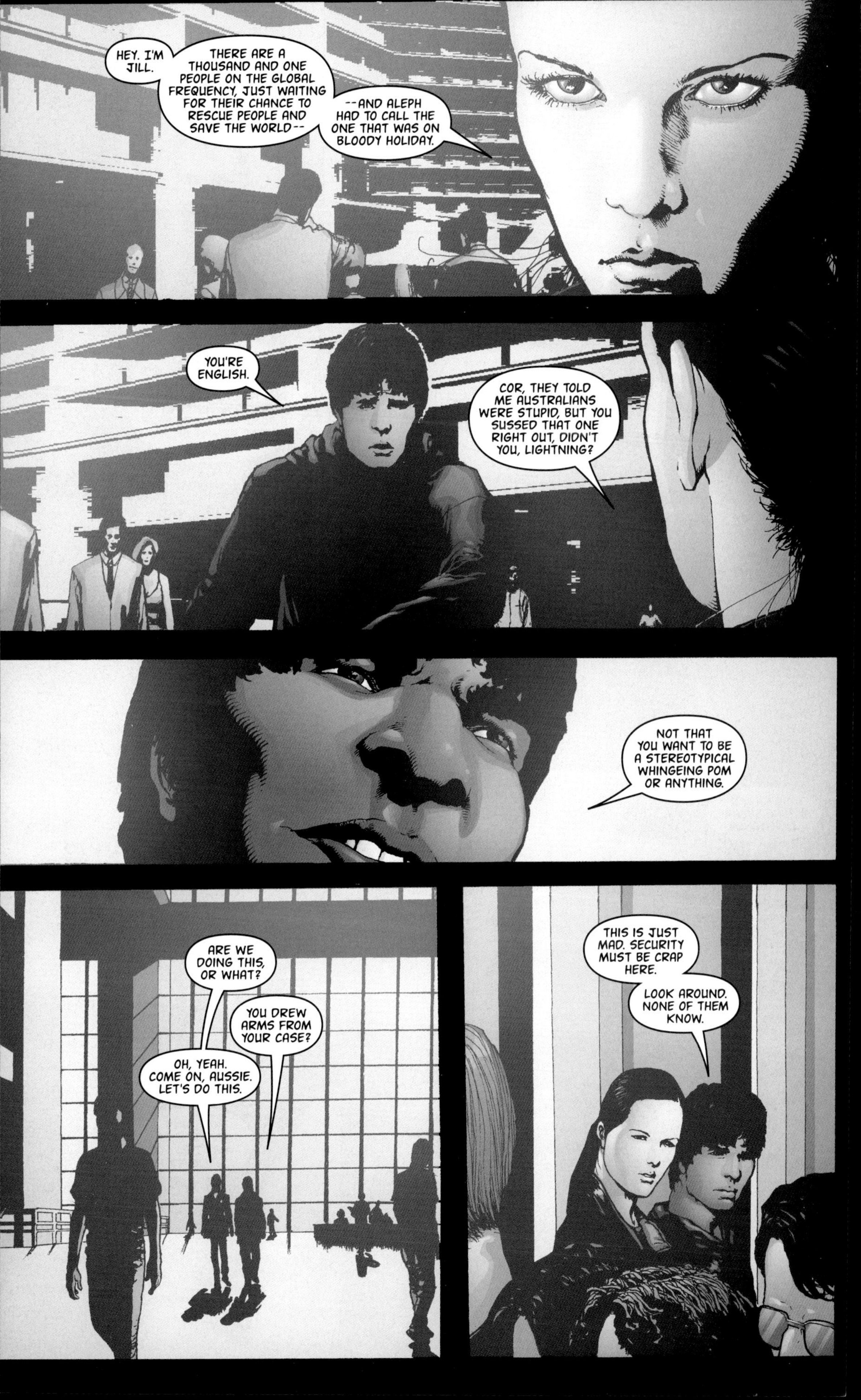
HEY. I'M JILL.
THERE ARE A THOUSAND AND ONE PEOPLE ON THE GLOBAL FREQUENCY, JUST WAITING FOR THEIR CHANCE TO RESCUE PEOPLE AND SAVE THE WORLD--
--AND ALEPH HAD TO CALL THE ONE THAT WAS ON BLOODY HOLIDAY.
YOU'RE ENGLISH.
COR, THEY TOLD ME AUSTRALIANS WERE STUPID, BUT YOU SUSSED THAT ONE RIGHT OUT, DIDN'T YOU, LIGHTNING?
NOT THAT YOU WANT TO BE A STEREOTYPICAL WHINGEING POM OR ANYTHING.
ARE WE DOING THIS, OR WHAT?
YOU DREW ARMS FROM YOUR CASE?
OH, YEAH. COME ON, AUSSIE. LET'S DO THIS.
THIS IS JUST MAD. SECURITY MUST BE CRAP HERE.
LOOK AROUND. NONE OF THEM KNOW.

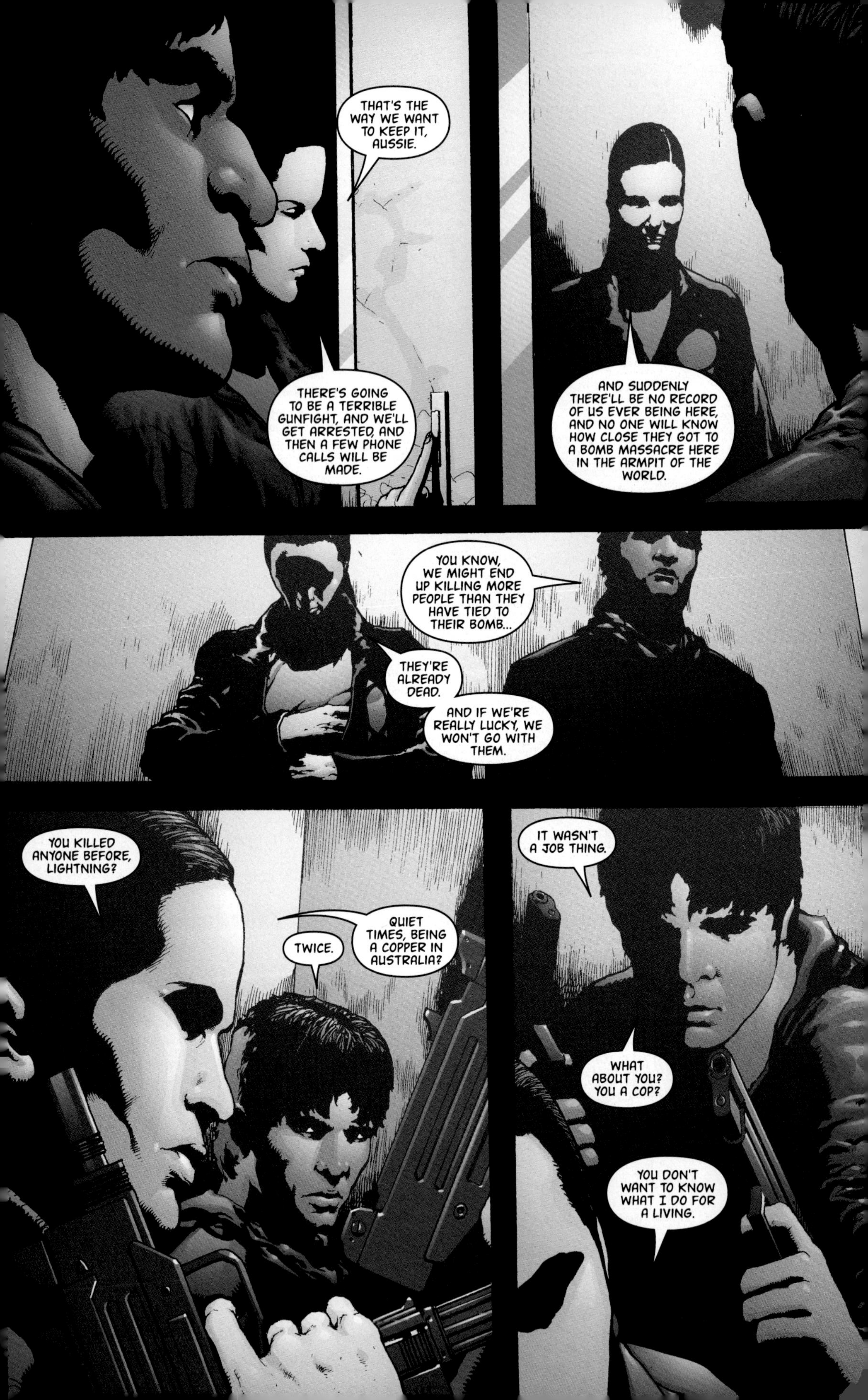
THAT'S THE WAY WE WANT TO KEEP IT, AUSSIE.
THERE'S GOING TO BE A TERRIBLE GUNFIGHT, AND WE'LL GET ARRESTED, AND THEN A FEW PHONE CALLS WILL BE MADE.
AND SUDDENLY THERE'LL BE NO RECORD OF US EVER BEING HERE, AND NO ONE WILL KNOW HOW CLOSE THEY GOT TO A BOMB MASSACRE HERE IN THE ARMPIT OF THE WORLD.
YOU KNOW, WE MIGHT END UP KILLING MORE PEOPLE THAN THEY HAVE TIED TO THEIR BOMB...
THEY'RE ALREADY DEAD.
AND IF WE'RE REALLY LUCKY, WE WON'T GO WITH THEM.
YOU KILLED ANYONE BEFORE, LIGHTNING?
TWICE.
QUIET TIMES, BEING A COPPER IN AUSTRALIA?
IT WASN'T A JOB THING.
WHAT ABOUT YOU? YOU A COP?
YOU DON'T WANT TO KNOW WHAT I DO FOR A LIVING.

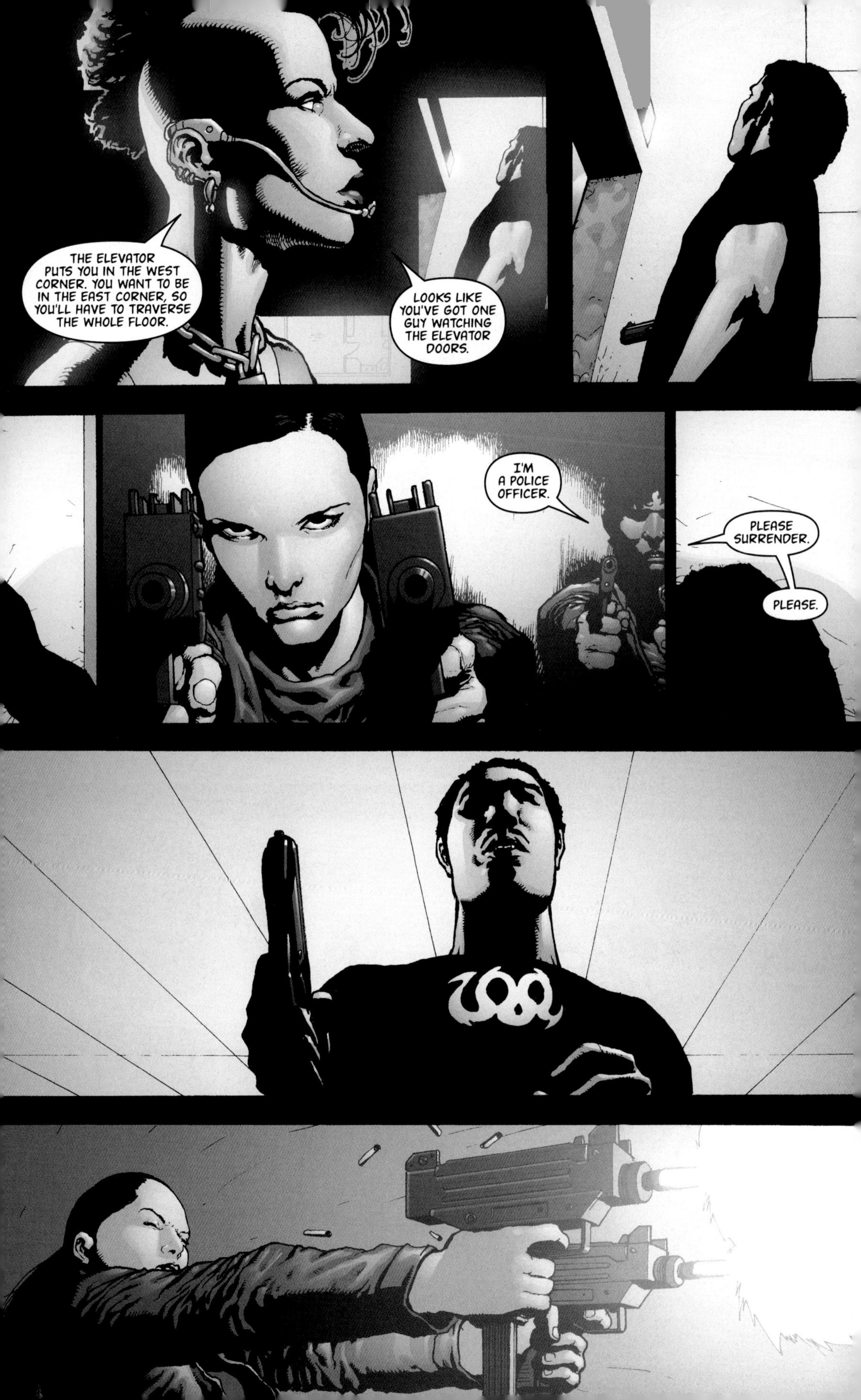
THE ELEVATOR PUTS YOU IN THE WEST CORNER. YOU WANT TO BE IN THE EAST CORNER, SO YOU'LL HAVE TO TRAVERSE THE WHOLE FLOOR.
LOOKS LIKE YOU'VE GOT ONE GUY WATCHING THE ELEVATOR DOORS.
I'M A POLICE OFFICER.
PLEASE SURRENDER.
PLEASE.

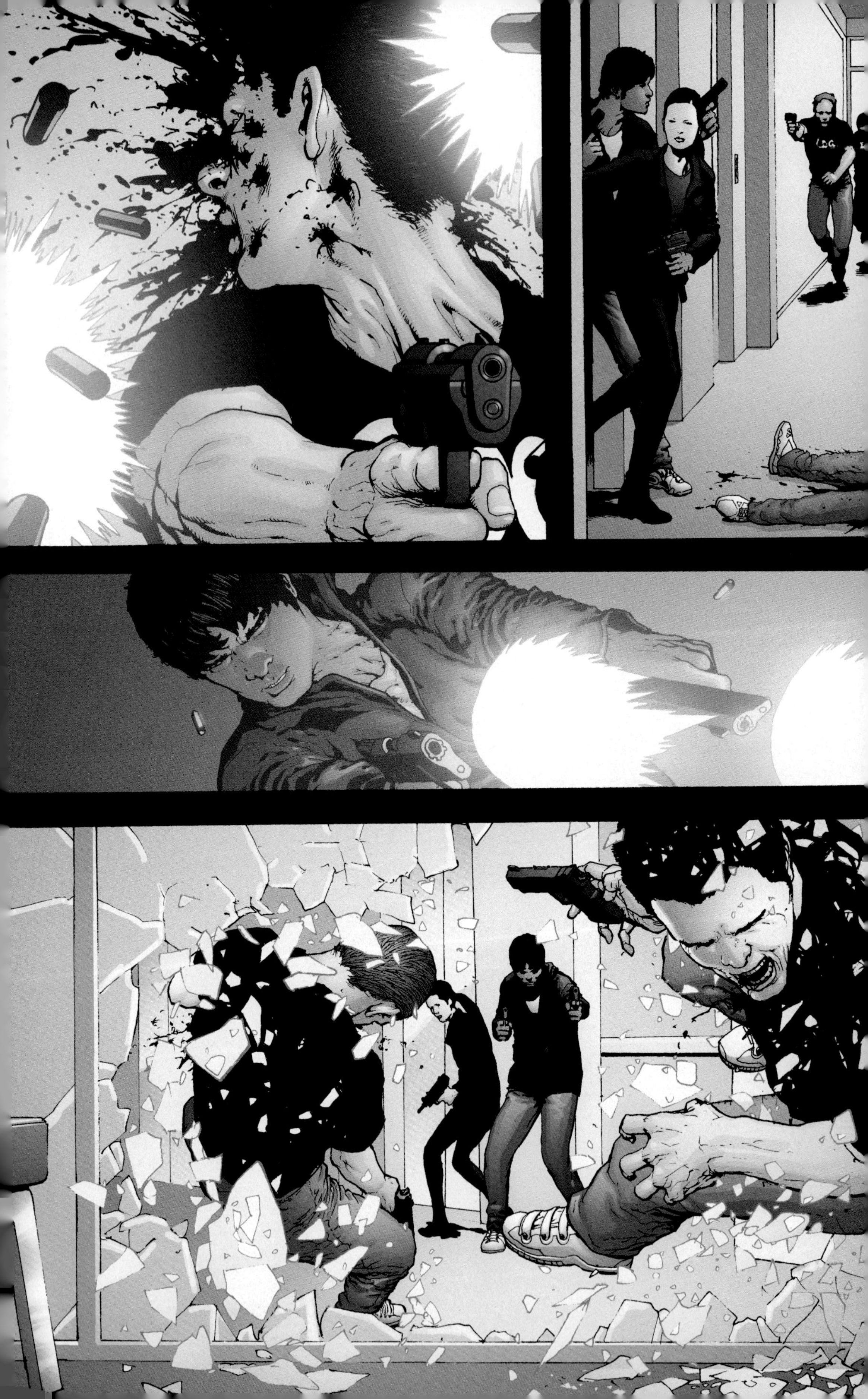

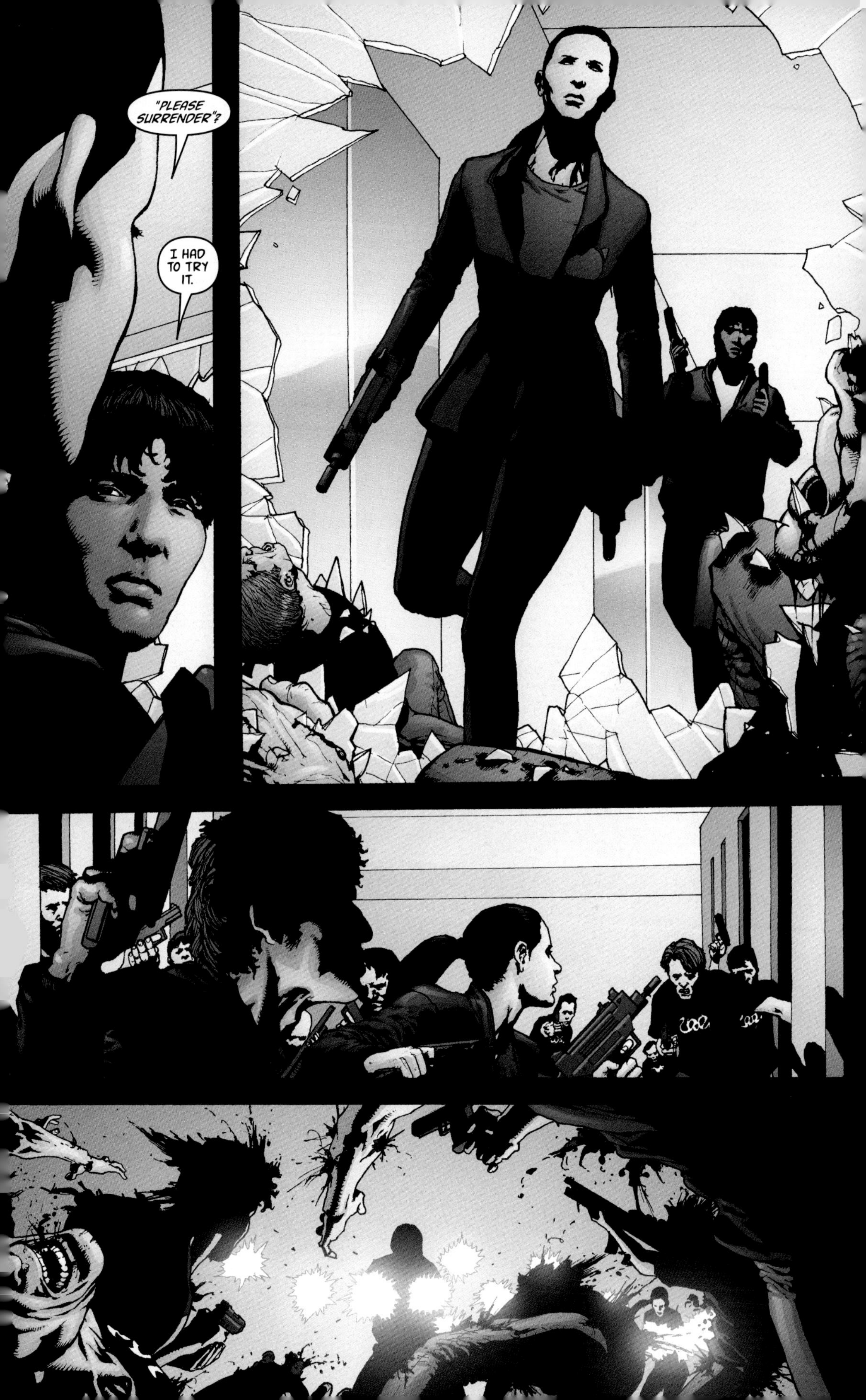
"PLEASE SURRENDER"?
I HAD TO TRY IT.

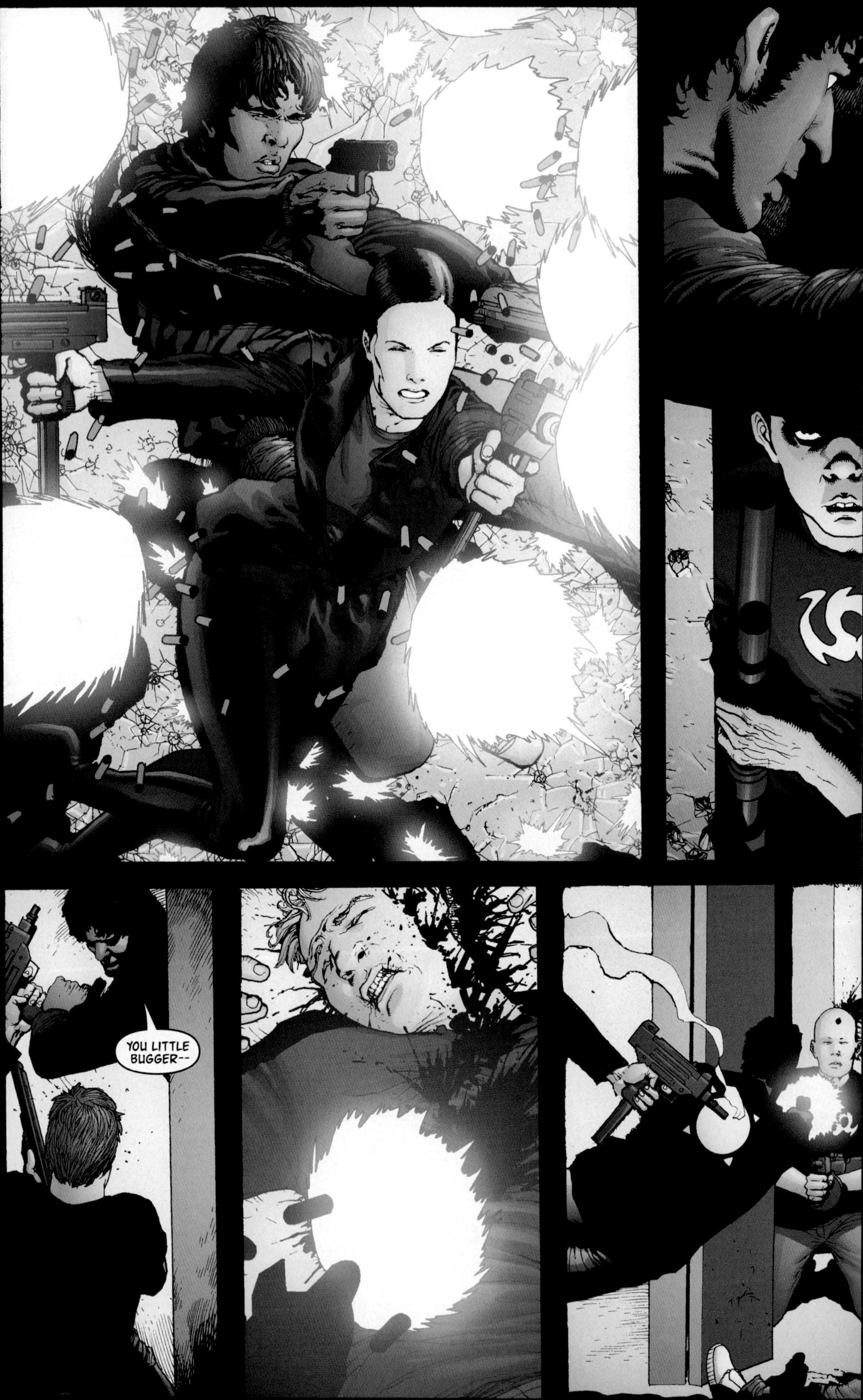
YOU LITTLE BUGGER--

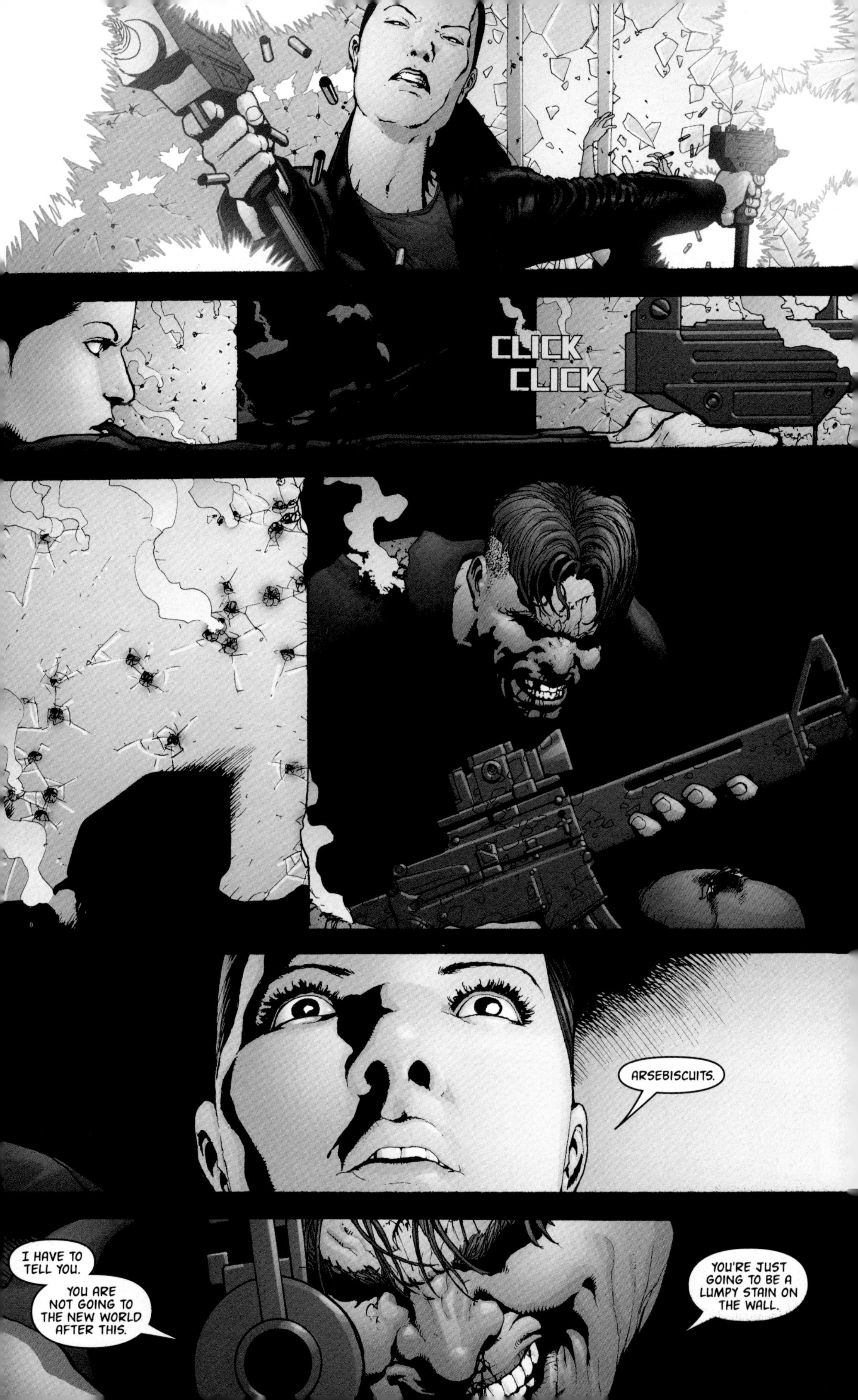
CLICK
CLICK
ARSEBISCUITS.
I HAVE TO TELL YOU.
YOU ARE NOT GOING TO THE NEW WORLD AFTER THIS.
YOU'RE JUST GOING TO BE A LUMPY STAIN ON THE WALL.

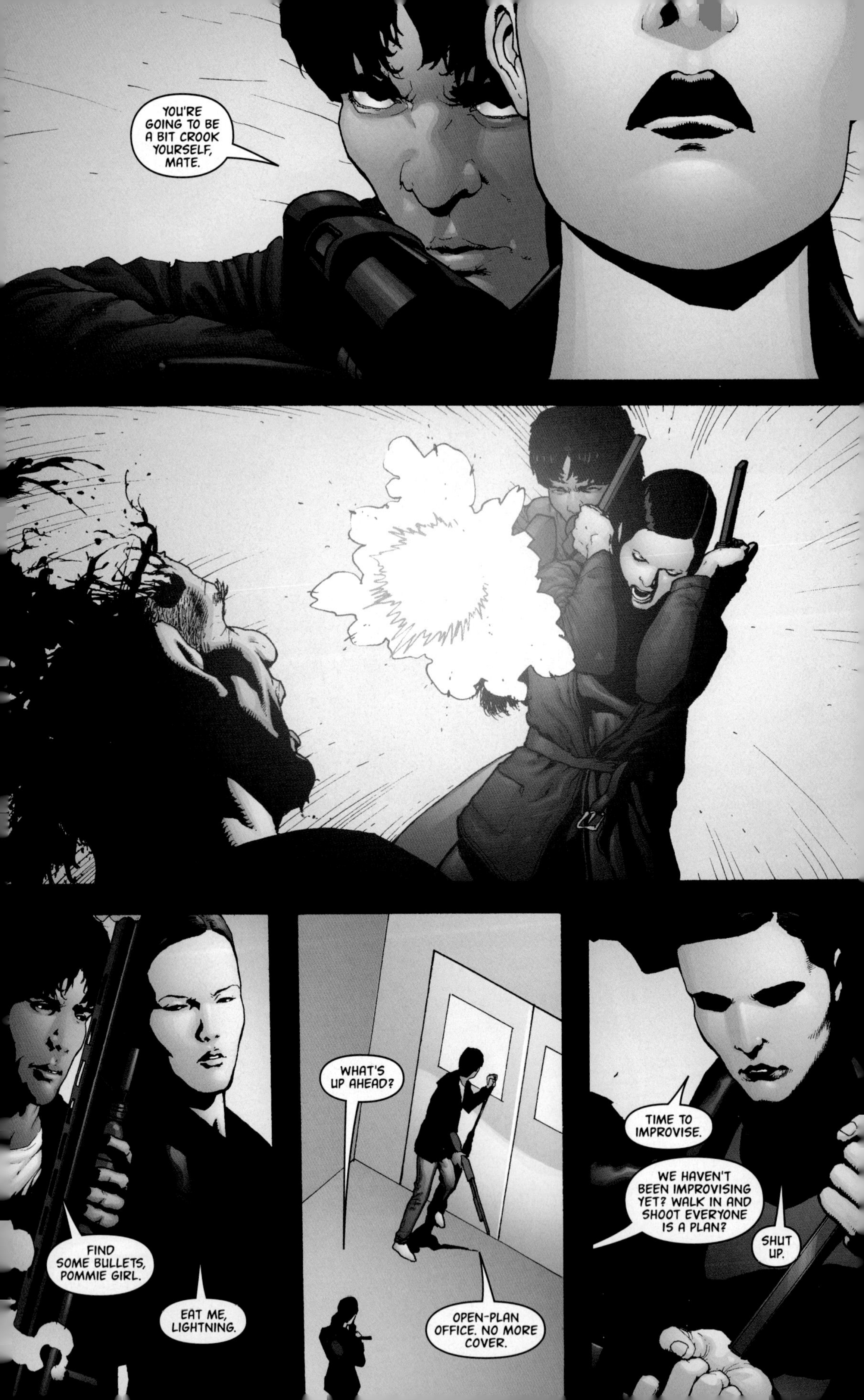
YOU'RE GOING TO BE A BIT CROOK YOURSELF, MATE.
FIND SOME BULLETS, POMMIE GIRL.
EAT ME, LIGHTNING.
WHAT'S UP AHEAD?
OPEN-PLAN OFFICE. NO MORE COVER.
TIME TO IMPROVISE.
WE HAVEN'T BEEN IMPROVISING YET? WALK IN AND SHOOT EVERYONE IS A PLAN?
SHUT UP.

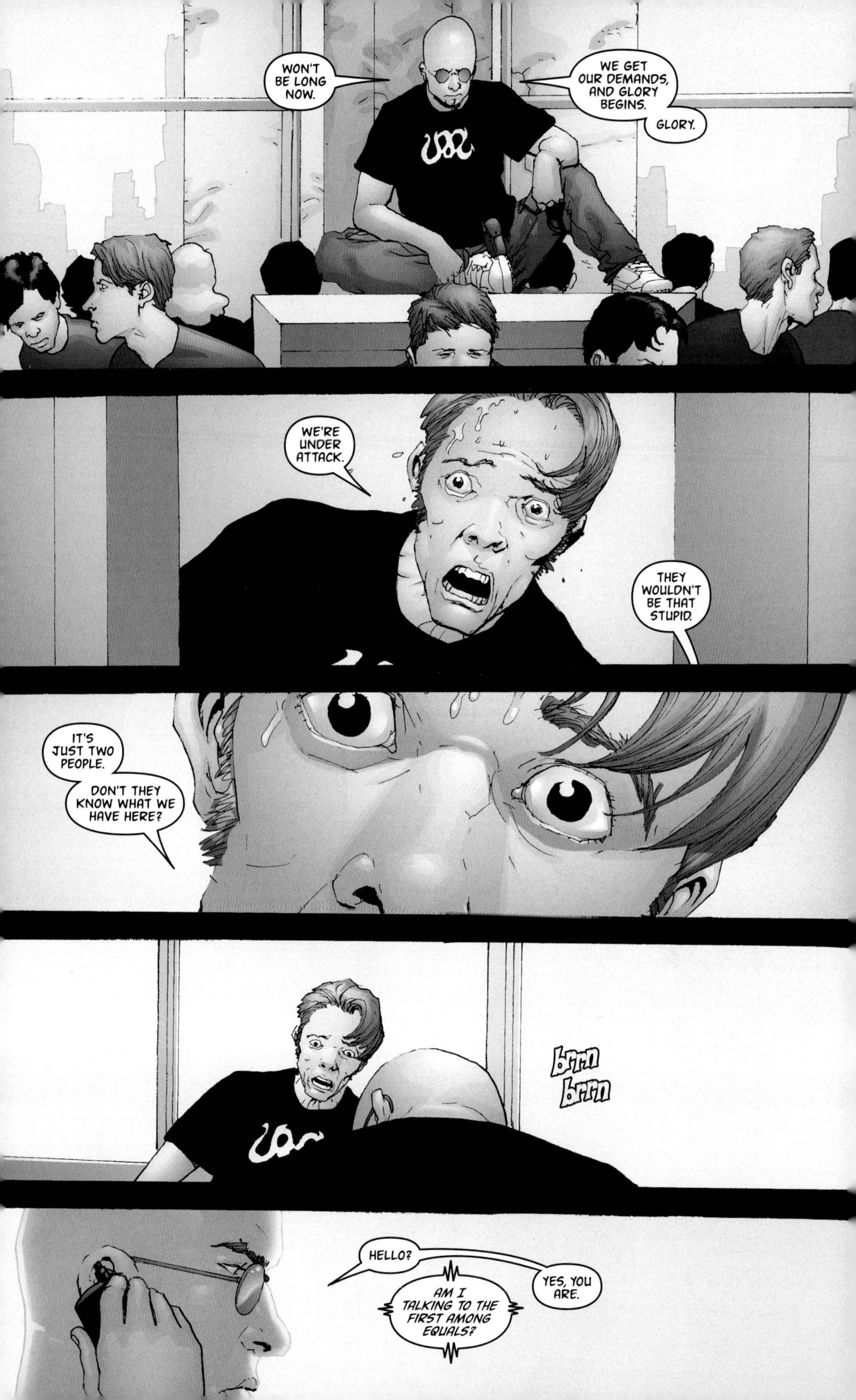
WON'T BE LONG NOW.
WE GET OUR DEMANDS, AND GLORY BEGINS.
GLORY.
WE'RE UNDER ATTACK.
THEY WOULDN'T BE THAT STUPID.
IT'S JUST TWO PEOPLE.
DON'T THEY KNOW WHAT WE HAVE HERE?
brrn brrn
HELLO?
AM I TALKING TO THE FIRST AMONG EQUALS?
YES, YOU ARE.

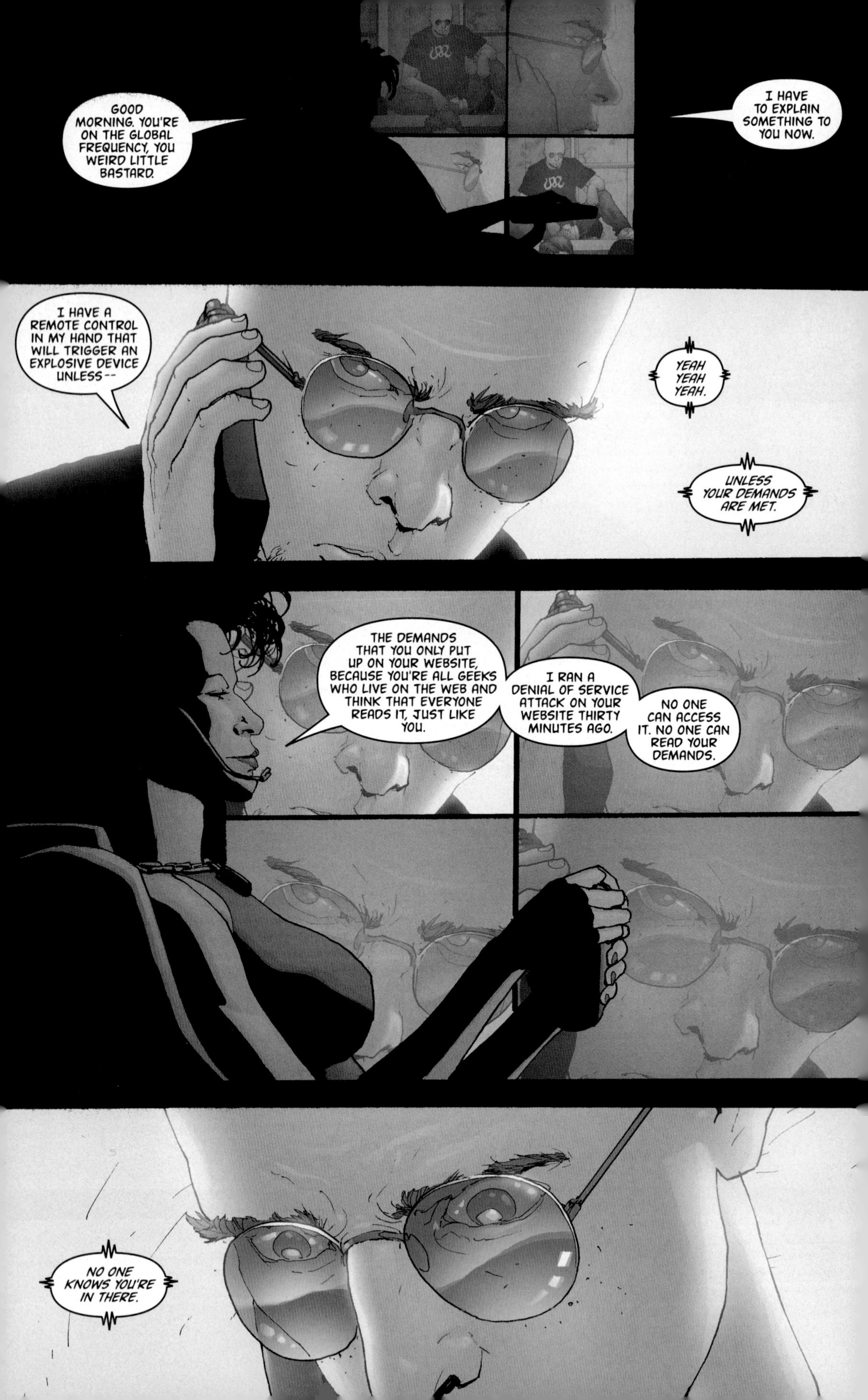

GOOD MORNING. YOU'RE ON THE GLOBAL FREQUENCY, YOU WEIRD LITTLE BASTARD.
I HAVE TO EXPLAIN SOMETHING TO YOU NOW.
I HAVE A REMOTE CONTROL IN MY HAND THAT WILL TRIGGER AN EXPLOSIVE DEVICE UNLESS--
YEAH YEAH YEAH.
UNLESS YOUR DEMANDS ARE MET.
THE DEMANDS THAT YOU ONLY PUT UP ON YOUR WEBSITE, BECAUSE YOU'RE ALL GEEKS WHO LIVE ON THE WEB AND THINK THAT EVERYONE READS IT, JUST LIKE YOU.
I RAN A DENIAL OF SERVICE ATTACK ON YOUR WEBSITE THIRTY MINUTES AGO.
NO ONE CAN ACCESS IT. NO ONE CAN READ YOUR DEMANDS.
NO ONE KNOWS YOU'RE IN THERE.

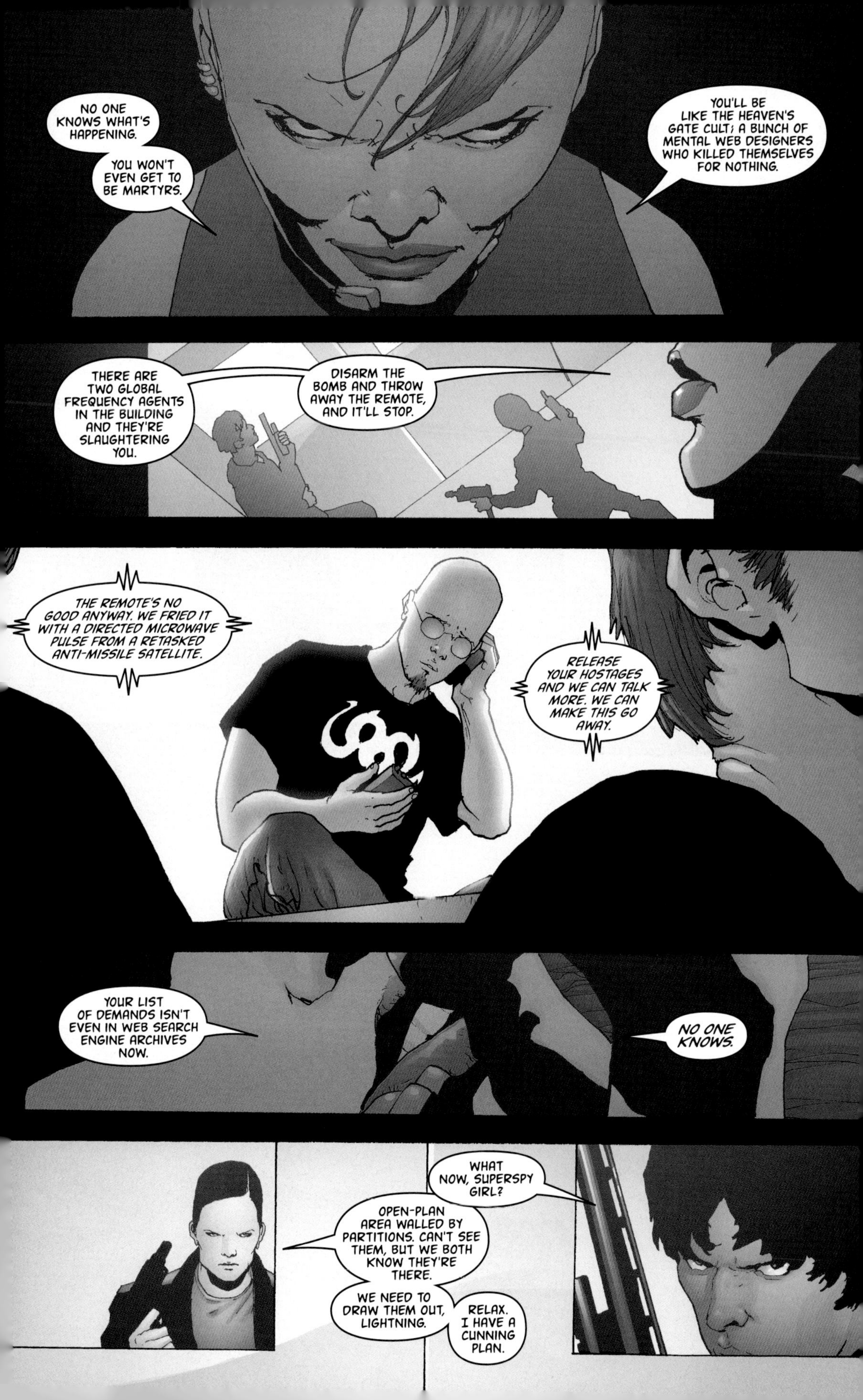

NO ONE KNOWS WHAT'S HAPPENING.
YOU WON'T EVEN GET TO BE MARTYRS.
YOU'LL BE LIKE THE HEAVEN'S GATE CULT; A BUNCH OF MENTAL WEB DESIGNERS WHO KILLED THEMSELVES FOR NOTHING.
THERE ARE TWO GLOBAL FREQUENCY AGENTS IN THE BUILDING AND THEY'RE SLAUGHTERING YOU.
DISARM THE BOMB AND THROW AWAY THE REMOTE, AND IT'LL STOP.
THE REMOTE'S NO GOOD ANYWAY. WE FRIED IT WITH A DIRECTED MICROWAVE PULSE FROM A RETASKED ANTI-MISSILE SATELLITE.
RELEASE YOUR HOSTAGES AND WE CAN TALK MORE. WE CAN MAKE THIS GO AWAY.
YOUR LIST OF DEMANDS ISN'T EVEN IN WEB SEARCH ENGINE ARCHIVES NOW.
NO ONE KNOWS.
WHAT NOW, SUPERSPY GIRL?
OPEN-PLAN AREA WALLED BY PARTITIONS. CAN'T SEE THEM, BUT WE BOTH KNOW THEY'RE THERE.
WE NEED TO DRAW THEM OUT, LIGHTNING.
RELAX. I HAVE A CUNNING PLAN.

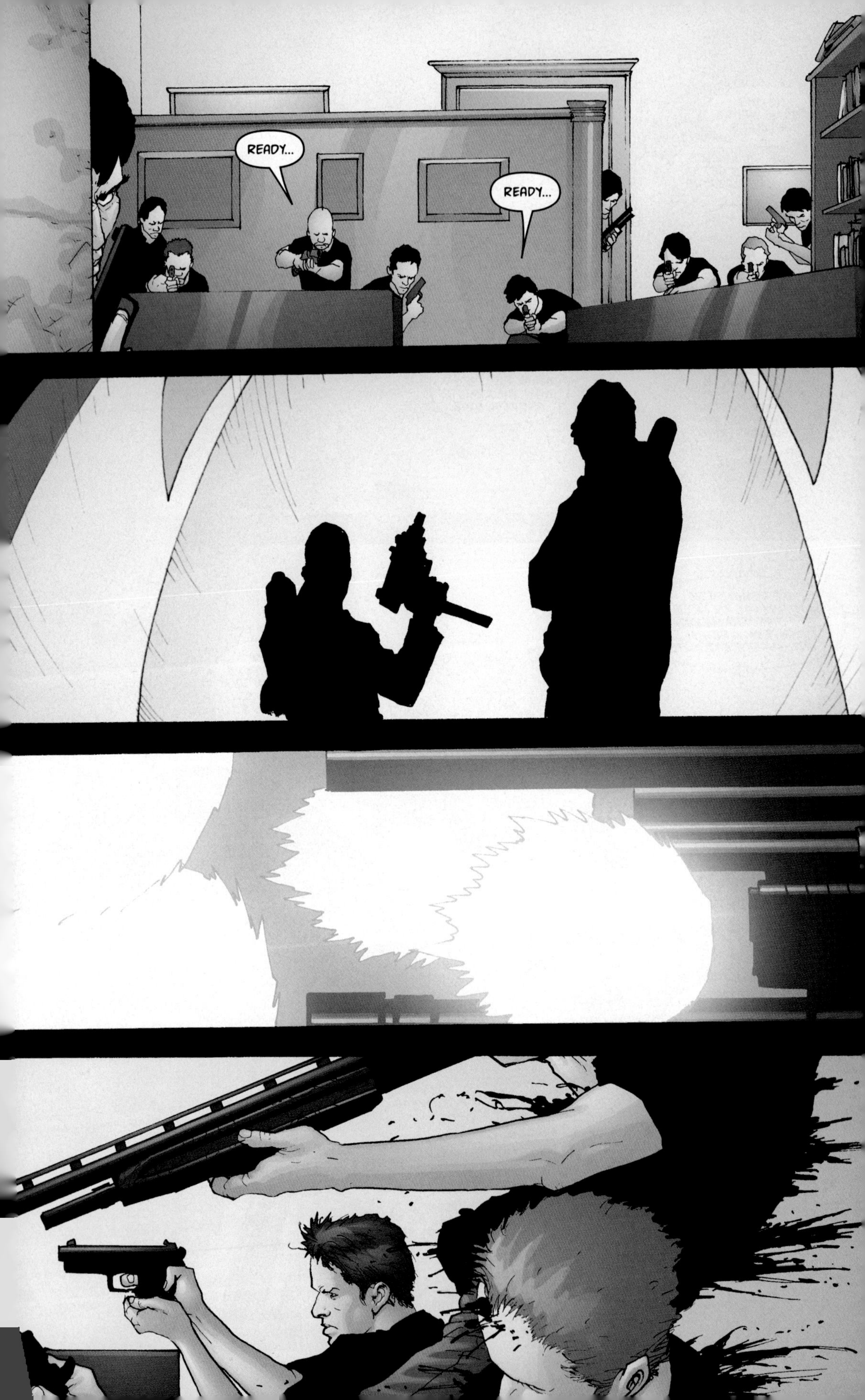
READY...
READY...

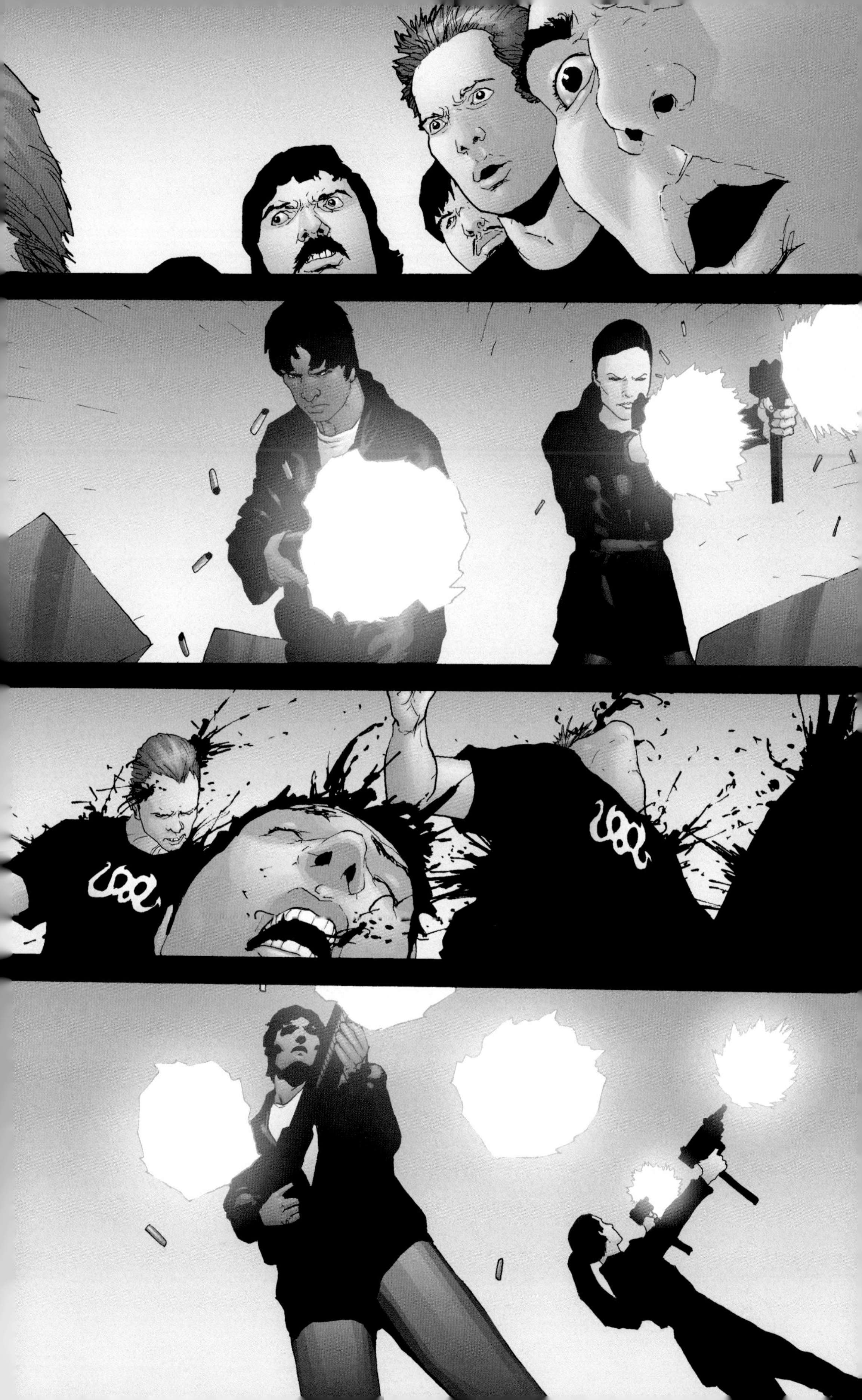

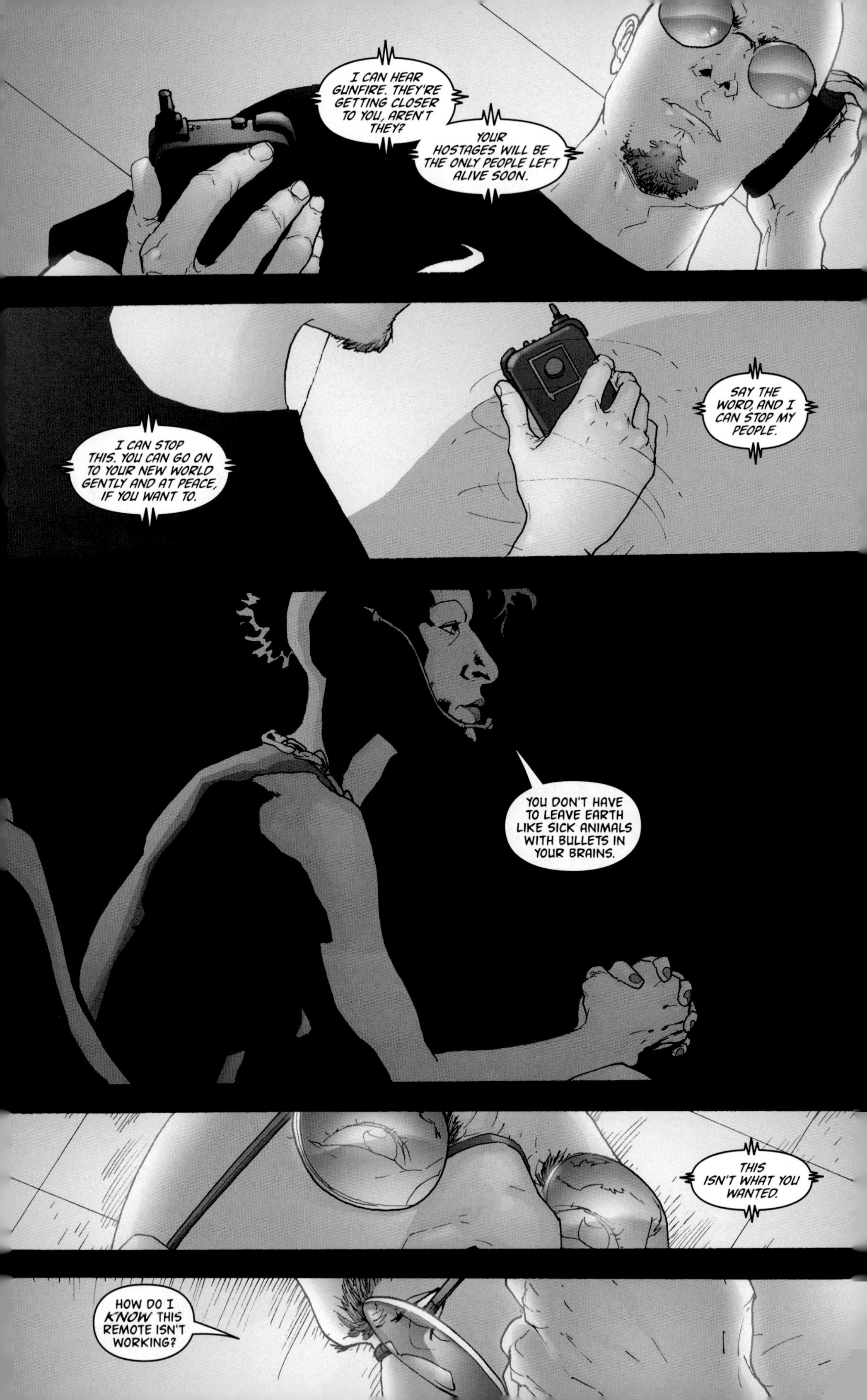

I CAN HEAR GUNFIRE. THEY'RE GETTING CLOSER TO YOU, AREN'T THEY?
YOUR HOSTAGES WILL BE THE ONLY PEOPLE LEFT ALIVE SOON.
I CAN STOP THIS. YOU CAN GO ON TO YOUR NEW WORLD GENTLY AND AT PEACE, IF YOU WANT TO.
SAY THE WORD, AND I CAN STOP MY PEOPLE.
YOU DON'T HAVE TO LEAVE EARTH LIKE SICK ANIMALS WITH BULLETS IN YOUR BRAINS.
THIS ISN'T WHAT YOU WANTED.
HOW DO I *KNOW* THIS REMOTE ISN'T WORKING?

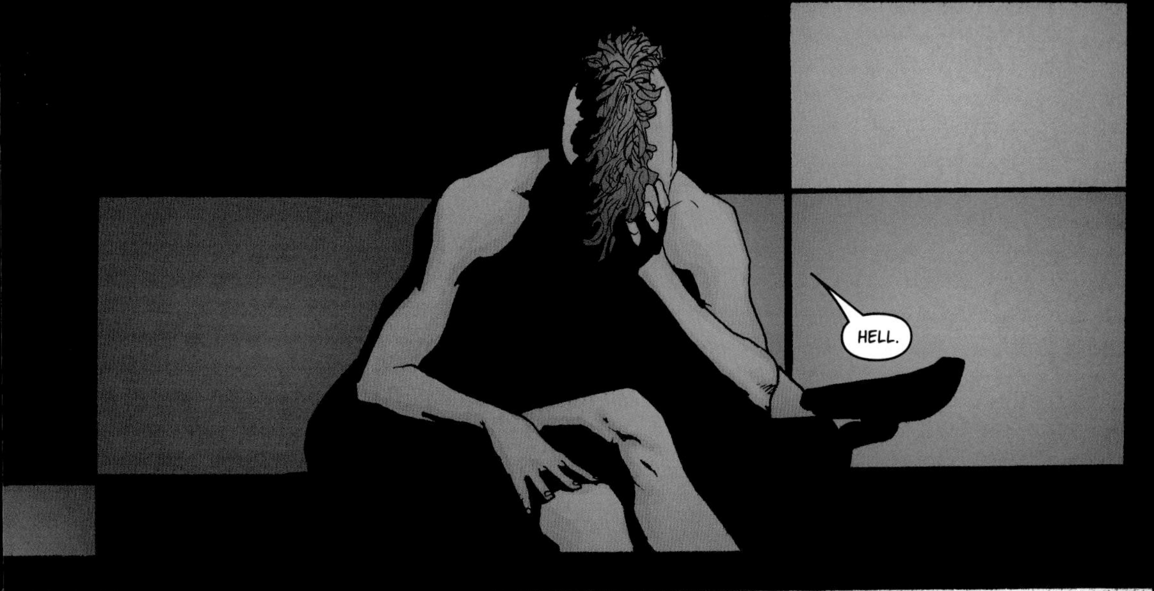
HELL.

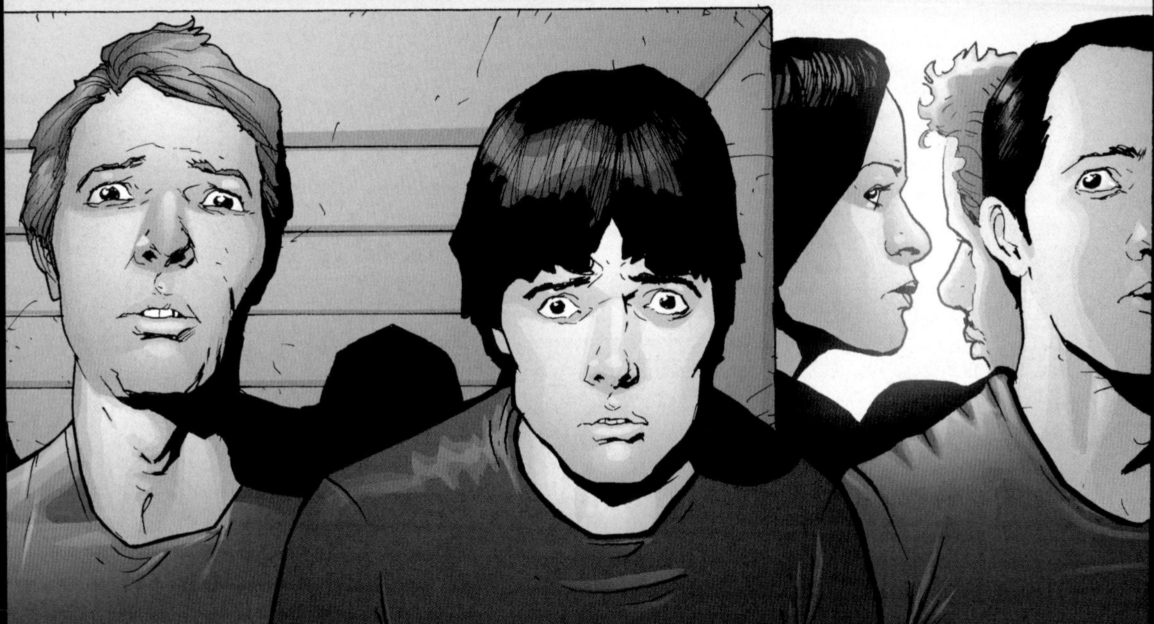

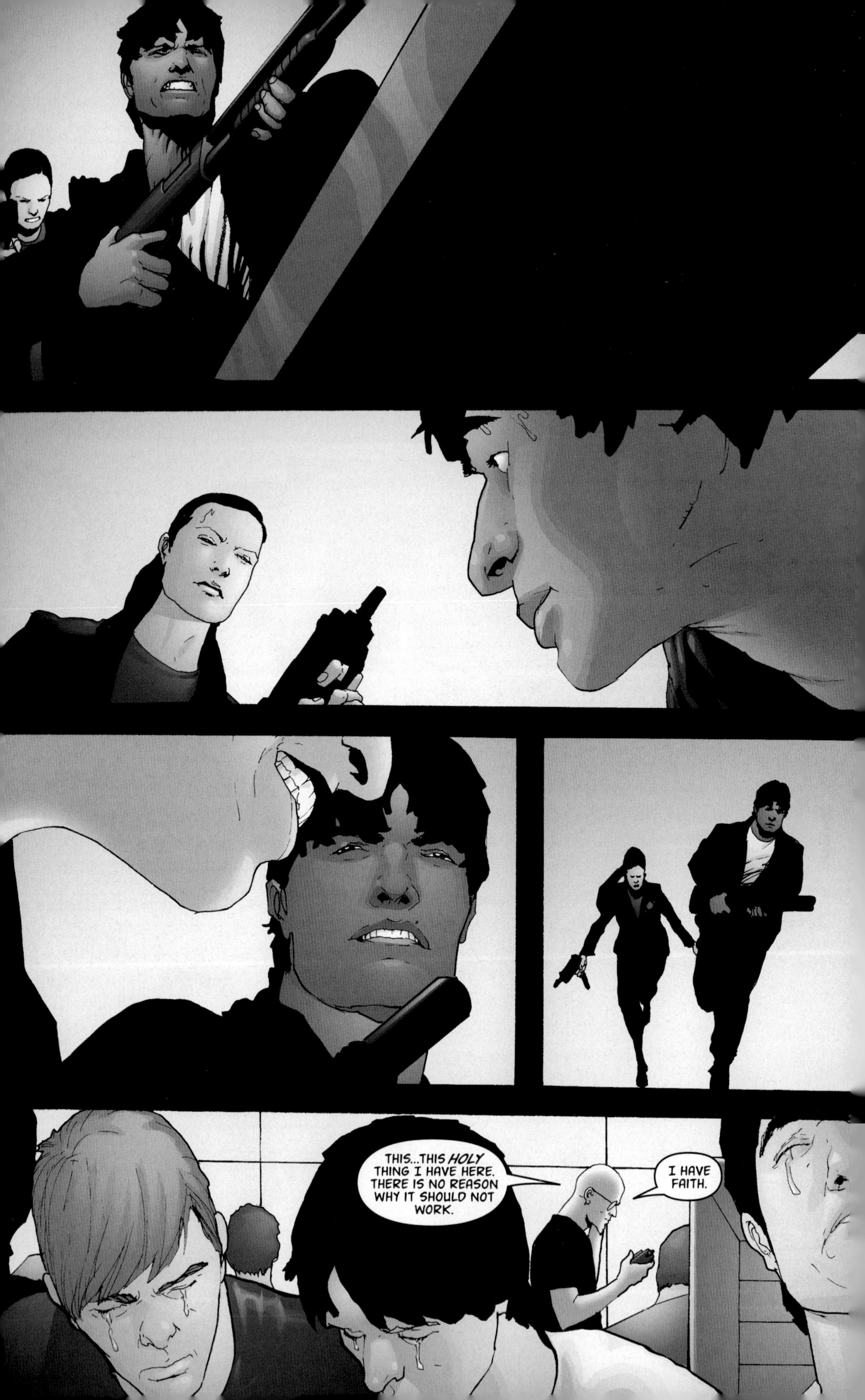
THIS...THIS *HOLY* THING I HAVE HERE. THERE IS NO REASON WHY IT SHOULD NOT WORK.
I HAVE FAITH.

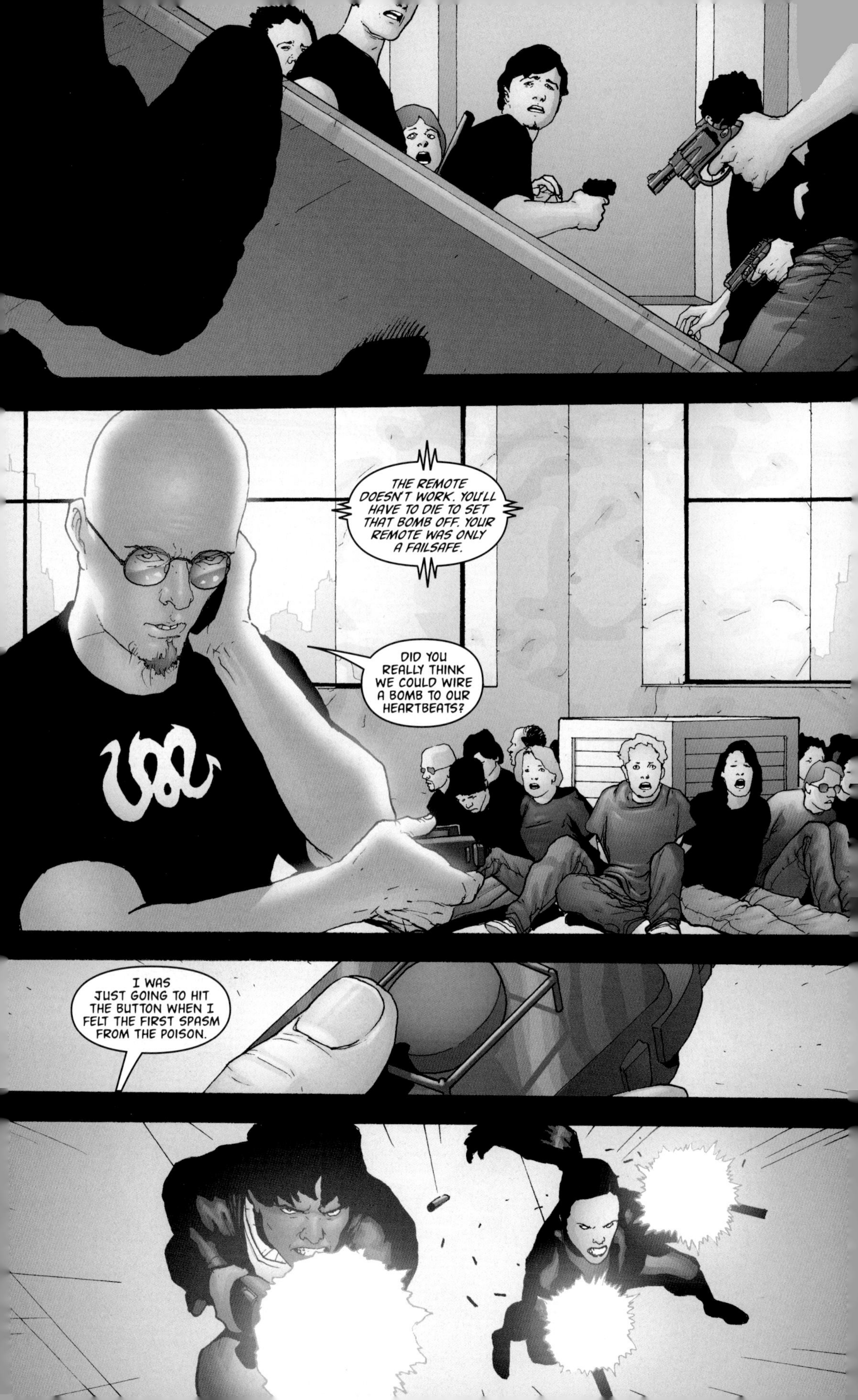
THE REMOTE DOESN'T WORK. YOU'LL HAVE TO DIE TO SET THAT BOMB OFF. YOUR REMOTE WAS ONLY A FAILSAFE.
DID YOU REALLY THINK WE COULD WIRE A BOMB TO OUR HEARTBEATS?
I WAS JUST GOING TO HIT THE BUTTON WHEN I FELT THE FIRST SPASM FROM THE POISON.

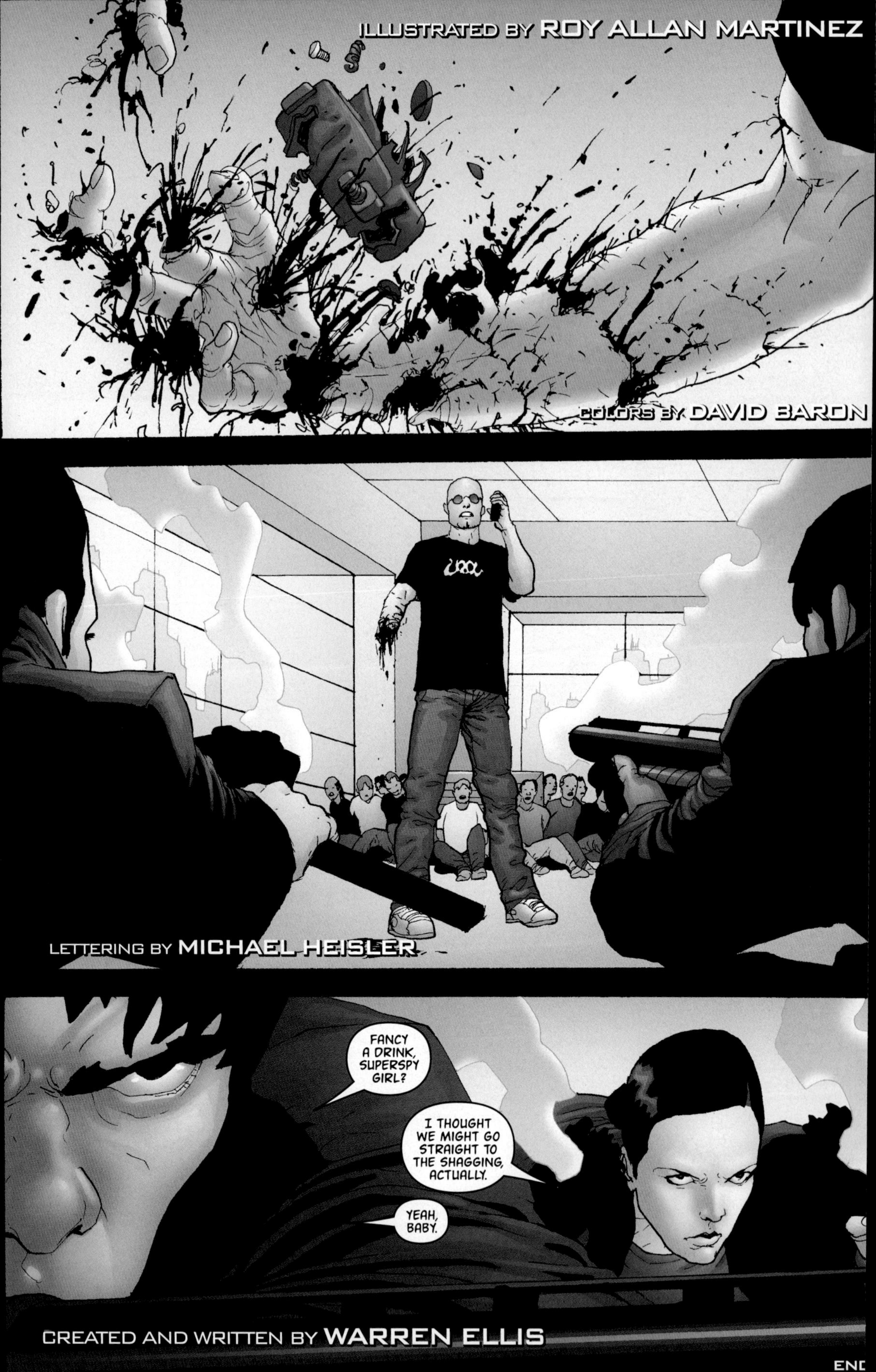
ILLUSTRATED BY ROY ALLAN MARTINEZ
COLORS BY DAVID BARON
LETTERING BY MICHAEL HEISLER
FANCY A DRINK, SUPERSPY GIRL?
I THOUGHT WE MIGHT GO STRAIGHT TO THE SHAGGING, ACTUALLY.
YEAH, BABY.
CREATED AND WRITTEN BY WARREN ELLIS
END

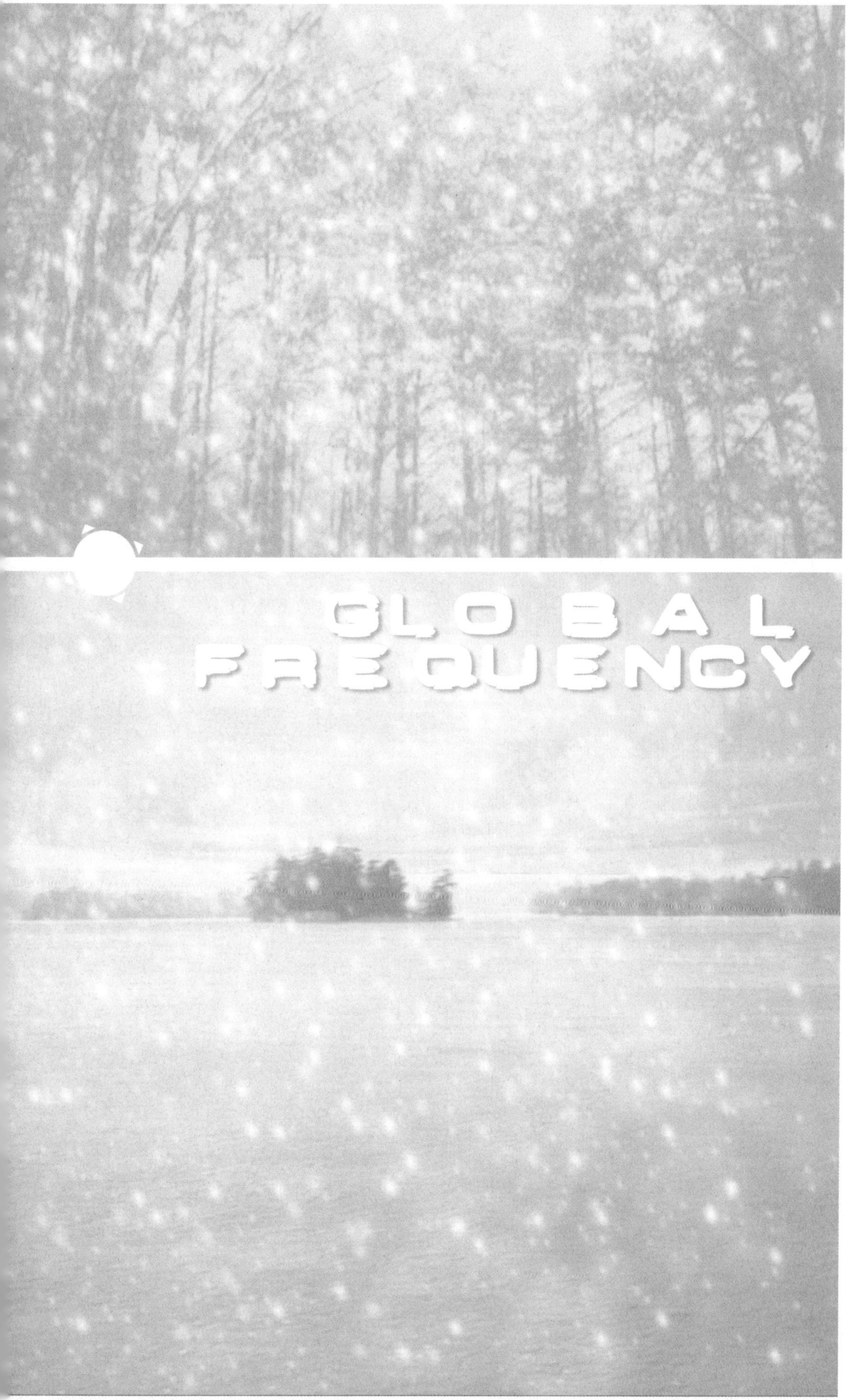
GLOBAL
FREQUENCY

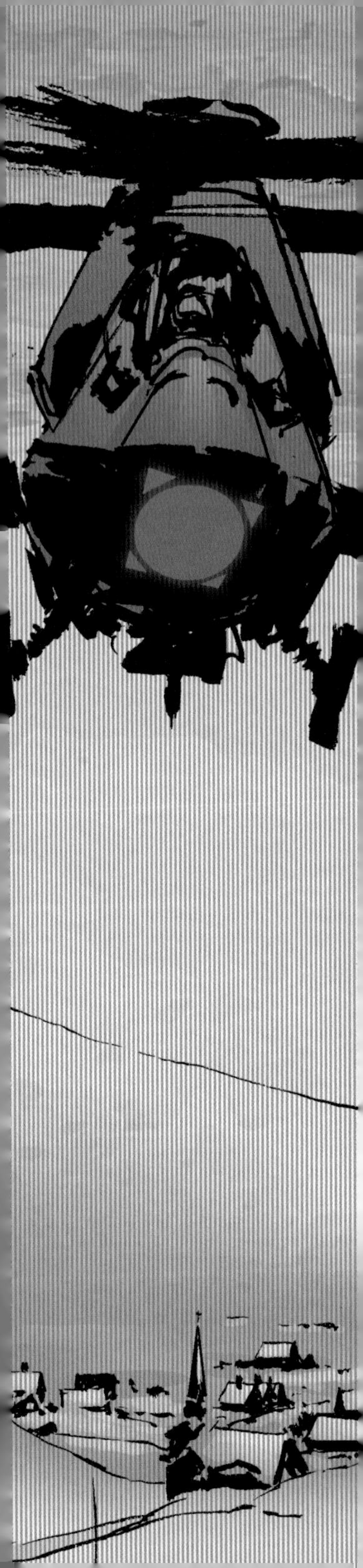

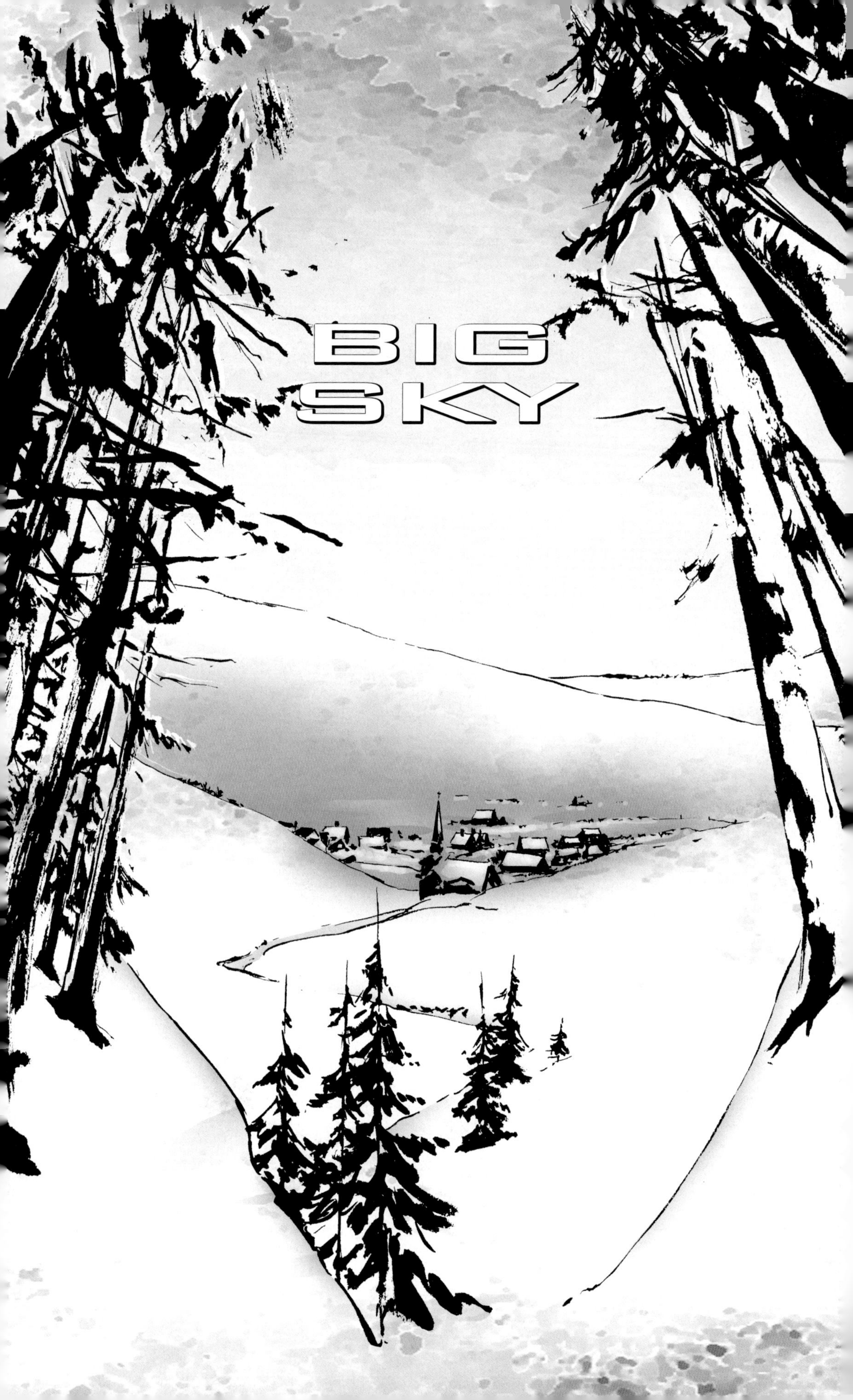
BIG
SKY

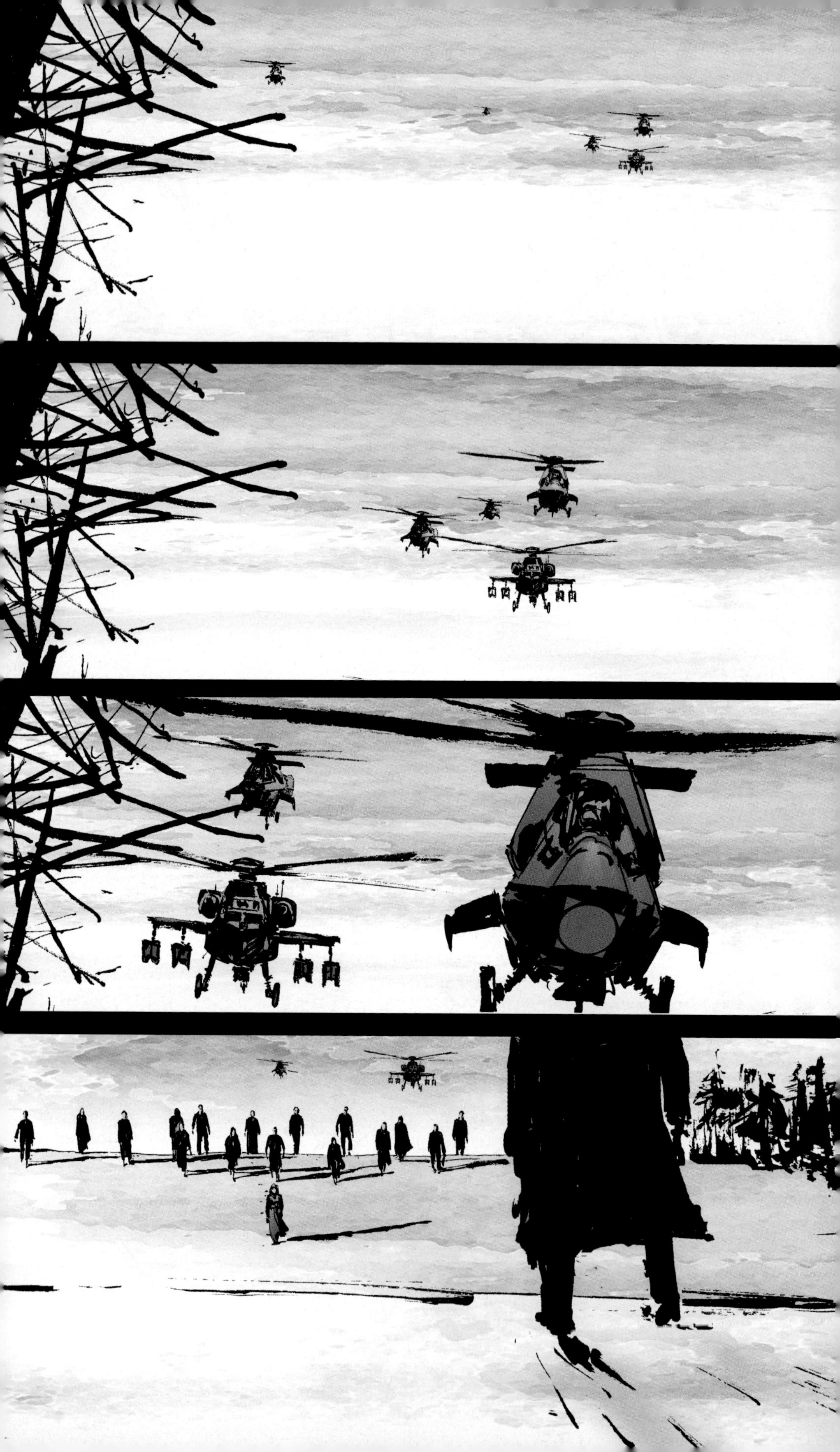

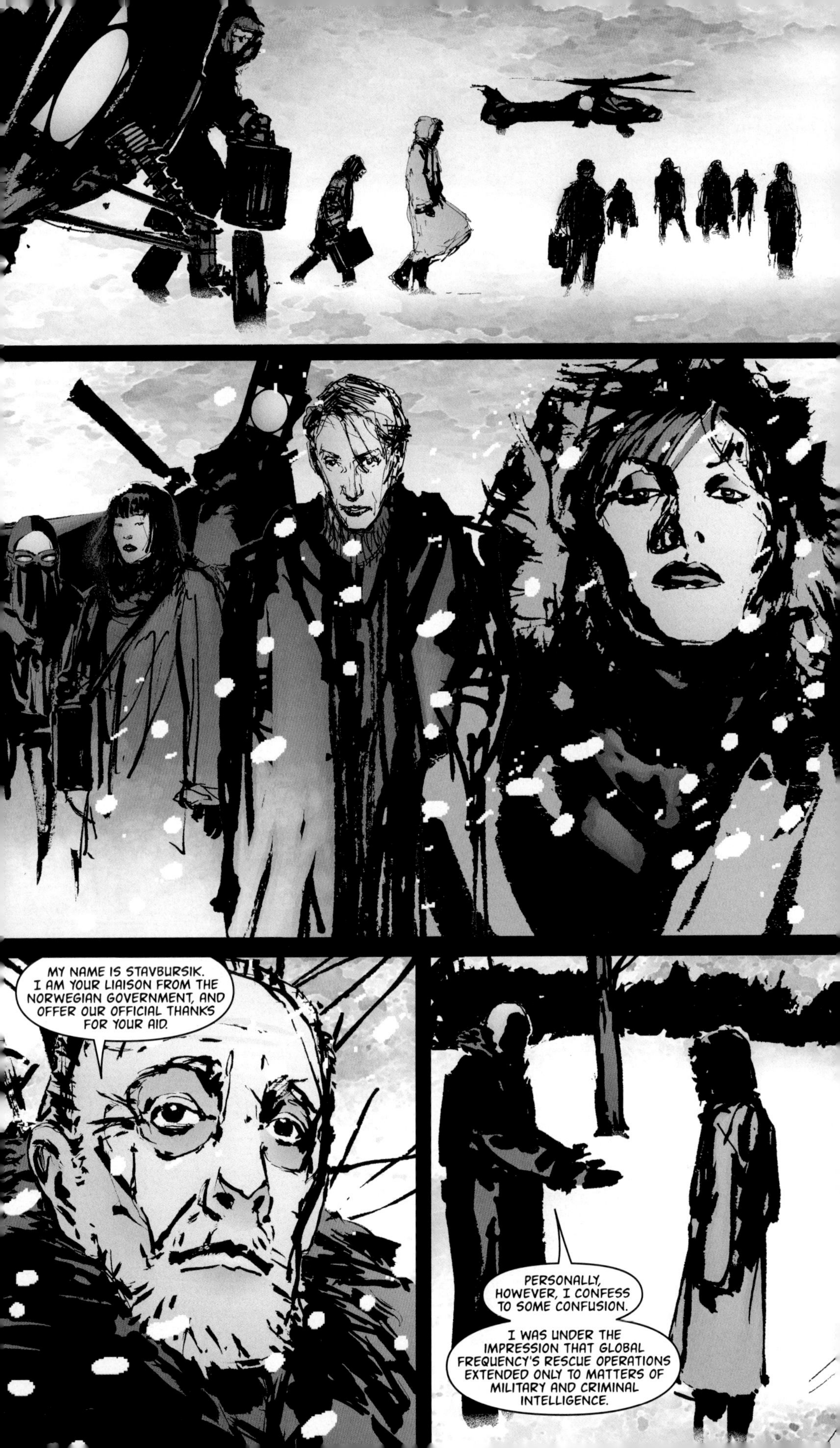
MY NAME IS STAVBURSIK. I AM YOUR LIAISON FROM THE NORWEGIAN GOVERNMENT, AND OFFER OUR OFFICIAL THANKS FOR YOUR AID.
PERSONALLY, HOWEVER, I CONFESS TO SOME CONFUSION.
I WAS UNDER THE IMPRESSION THAT GLOBAL FREQUENCY'S RESCUE OPERATIONS EXTENDED ONLY TO MATTERS OF MILITARY AND CRIMINAL INTELLIGENCE.

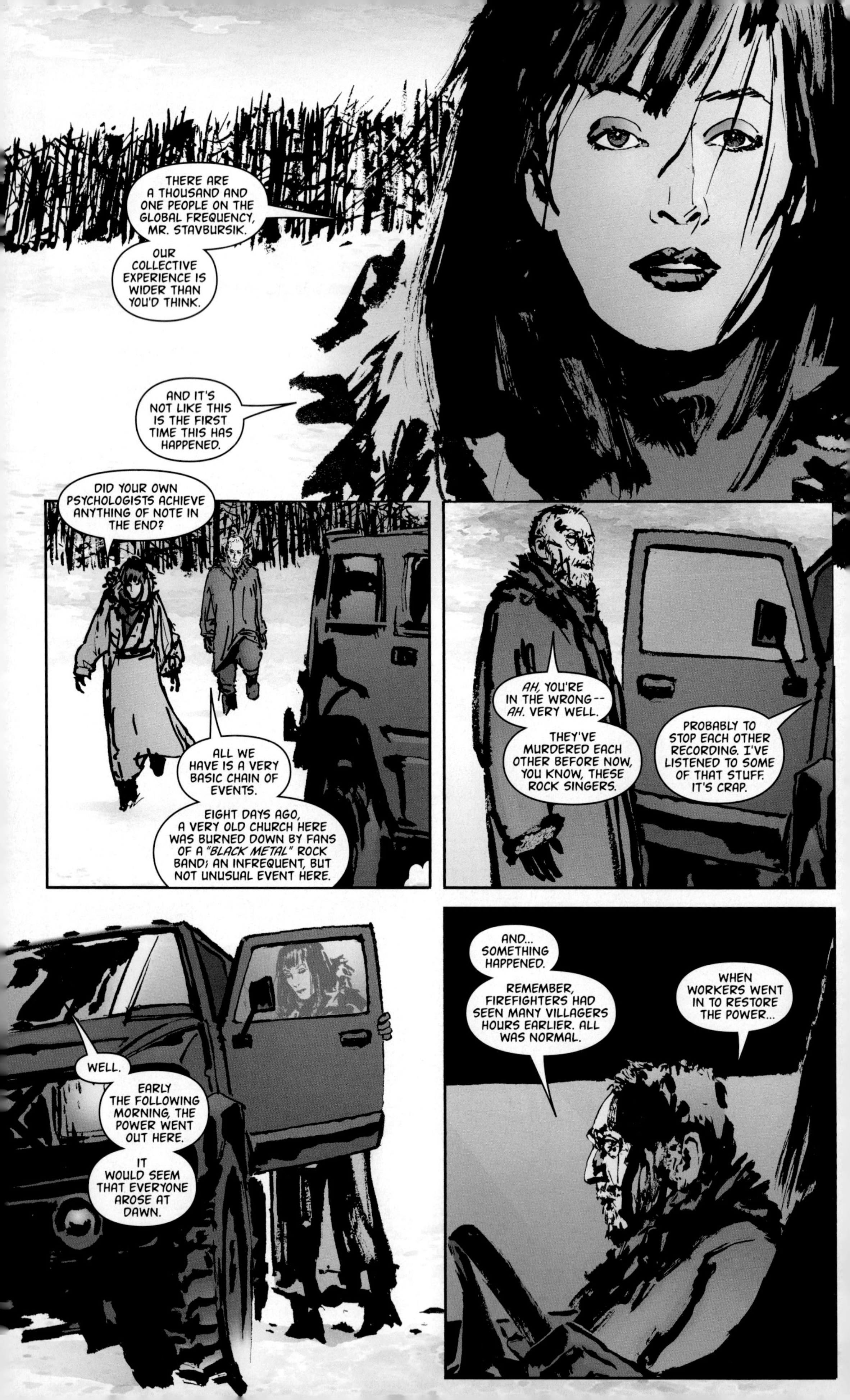
THERE ARE A THOUSAND AND ONE PEOPLE ON THE GLOBAL FREQUENCY, MR. STAVBURSIK.
OUR COLLECTIVE EXPERIENCE IS WIDER THAN YOU'D THINK.
AND IT'S NOT LIKE THIS IS THE FIRST TIME THIS HAS HAPPENED.
DID YOUR OWN PSYCHOLOGISTS ACHIEVE ANYTHING OF NOTE IN THE END?
ALL WE HAVE IS A VERY BASIC CHAIN OF EVENTS.
EIGHT DAYS AGO, A VERY OLD CHURCH HERE WAS BURNED DOWN BY FANS OF A "BLACK METAL" ROCK BAND; AN INFREQUENT, BUT NOT UNUSUAL EVENT HERE.
AH, YOU'RE IN THE WRONG-- AH. VERY WELL.
THEY'VE MURDERED EACH OTHER BEFORE NOW, YOU KNOW, THESE ROCK SINGERS.
PROBABLY TO STOP EACH OTHER RECORDING. I'VE LISTENED TO SOME OF THAT STUFF. IT'S CRAP.
WELL.
EARLY THE FOLLOWING MORNING, THE POWER WENT OUT HERE.
IT WOULD SEEM THAT EVERYONE AROSE AT DAWN.
AND... SOMETHING HAPPENED.
REMEMBER, FIREFIGHTERS HAD SEEN MANY VILLAGERS HOURS EARLIER. ALL WAS NORMAL.
WHEN WORKERS WENT IN TO RESTORE THE POWER...

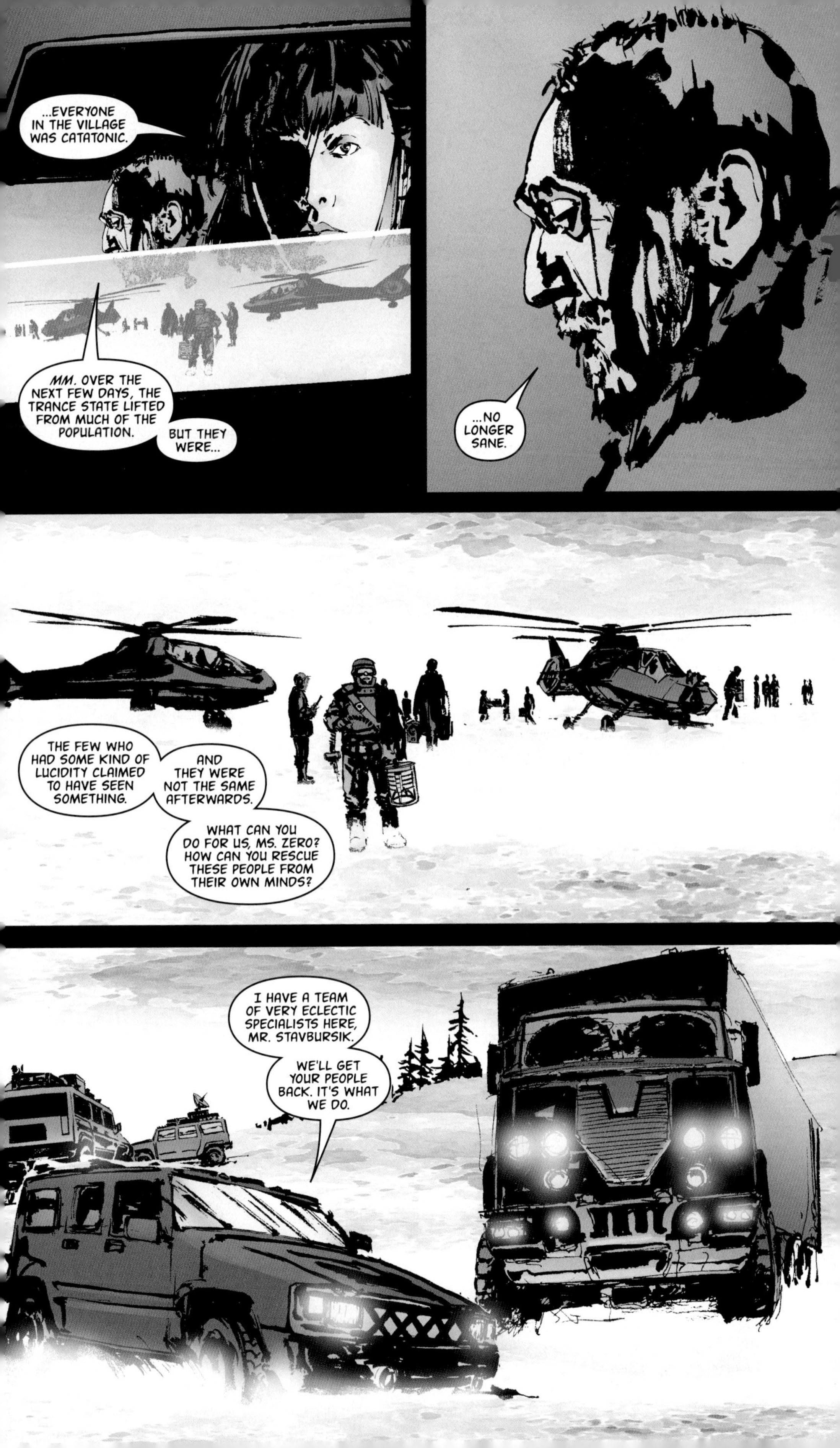
...EVERYONE IN THE VILLAGE WAS CATATONIC.
MM. OVER THE NEXT FEW DAYS, THE TRANCE STATE LIFTED FROM MUCH OF THE POPULATION.
BUT THEY WERE...
...NO LONGER SANE.
THE FEW WHO HAD SOME KIND OF LUCIDITY CLAIMED TO HAVE SEEN SOMETHING.
AND THEY WERE NOT THE SAME AFTERWARDS.
WHAT CAN YOU DO FOR US, MS. ZERO? HOW CAN YOU RESCUE THESE PEOPLE FROM THEIR OWN MINDS?
I HAVE A TEAM OF VERY ECLECTIC SPECIALISTS HERE, MR. STAVBURSIK.
WE'LL GET YOUR PEOPLE BACK. IT'S WHAT WE DO.

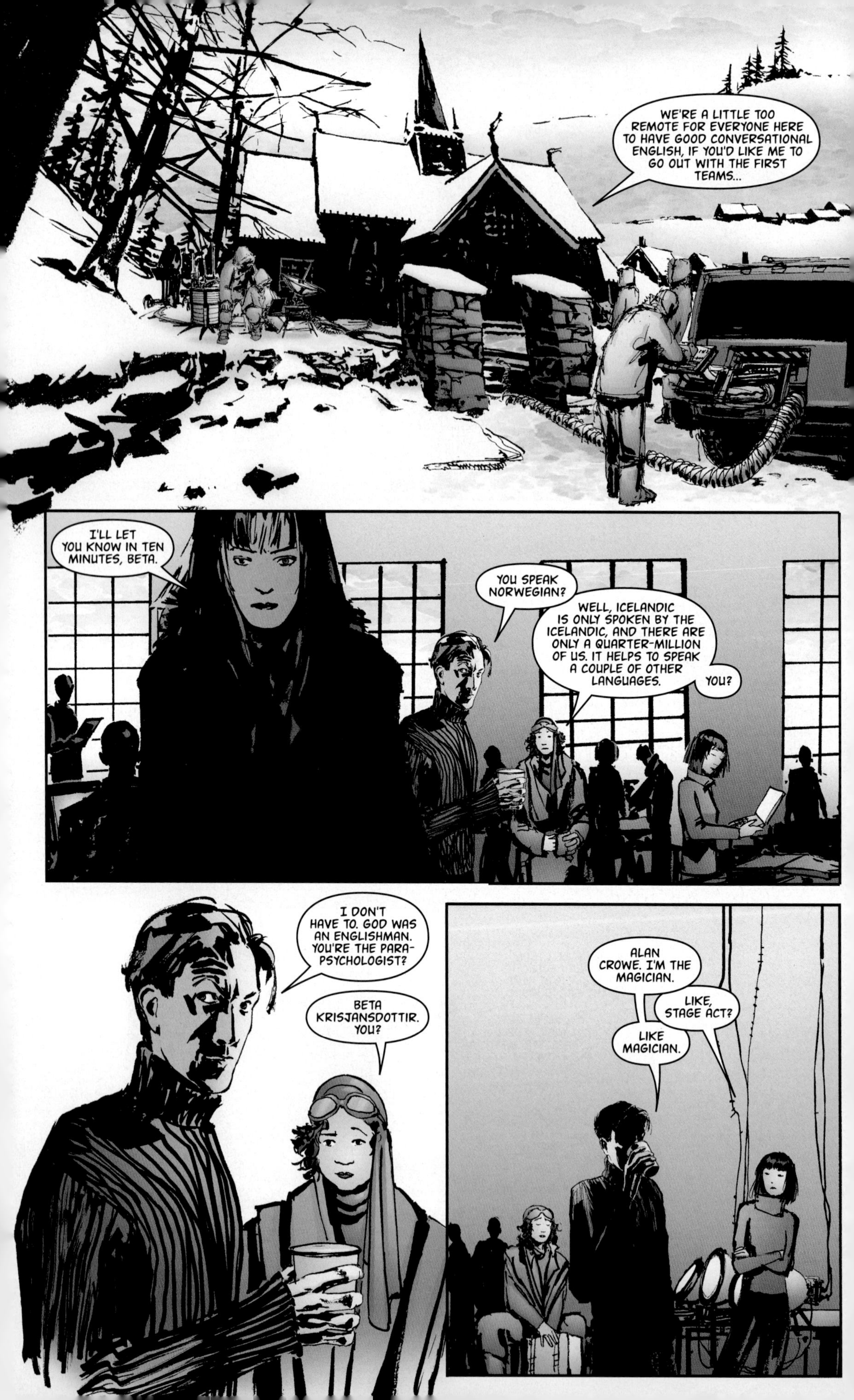
WE'RE A LITTLE TOO REMOTE FOR EVERYONE HERE TO HAVE GOOD CONVERSATIONAL ENGLISH, IF YOU'D LIKE ME TO GO OUT WITH THE FIRST TEAMS...
I'LL LET YOU KNOW IN TEN MINUTES, BETA.
YOU SPEAK NORWEGIAN?
WELL, ICELANDIC IS ONLY SPOKEN BY THE ICELANDIC, AND THERE ARE ONLY A QUARTER-MILLION OF US. IT HELPS TO SPEAK A COUPLE OF OTHER LANGUAGES.
YOU?
I DON'T HAVE TO. GOD WAS AN ENGLISHMAN. YOU'RE THE PARA-PSYCHOLOGIST?
BETA KRISJANSDOTTIR. YOU?
ALAN CROWE. I'M THE MAGICIAN.
LIKE, STAGE ACT?
LIKE MAGICIAN.

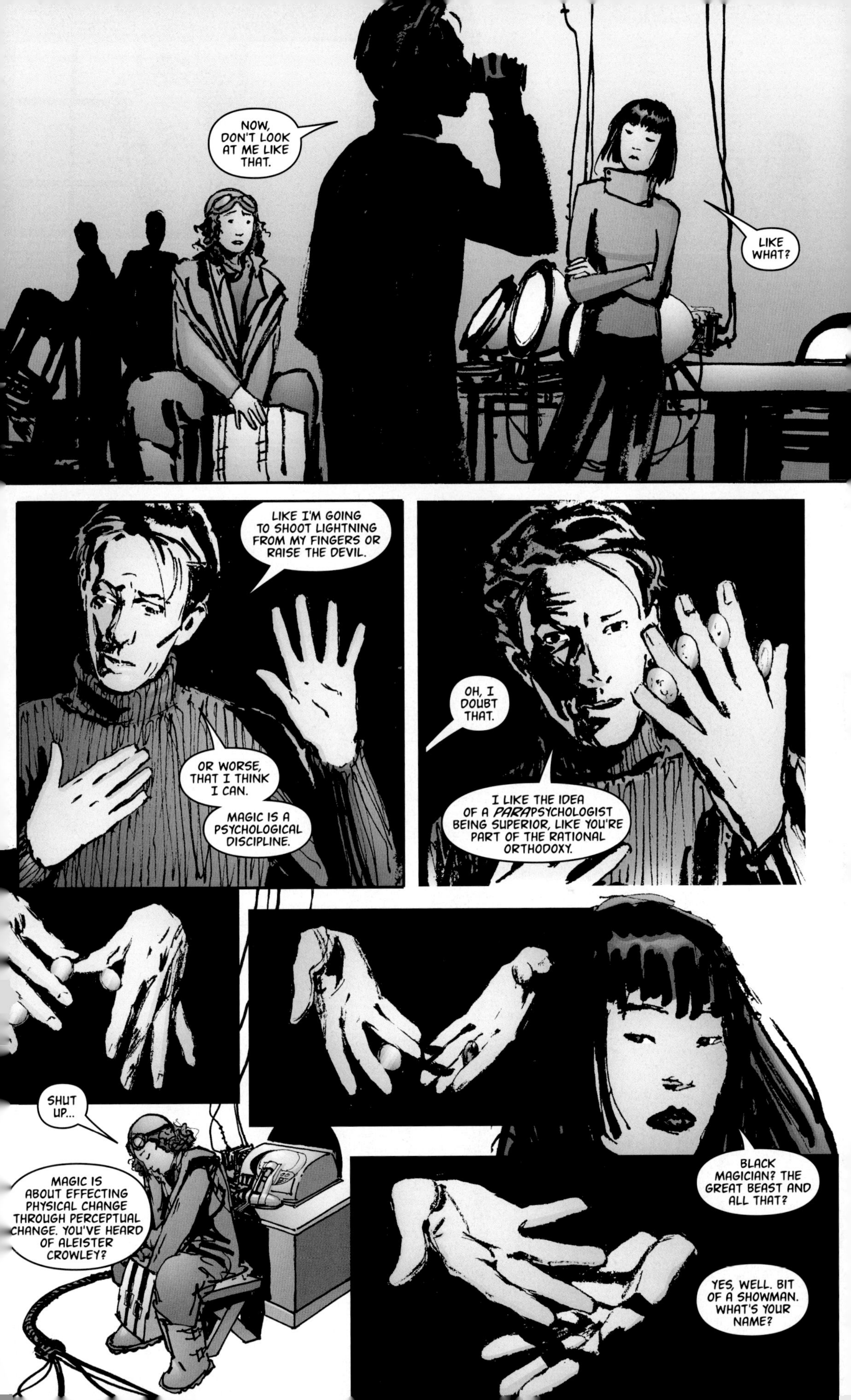

NOW, DON'T LOOK AT ME LIKE THAT.
LIKE WHAT?
LIKE I'M GOING TO SHOOT LIGHTNING FROM MY FINGERS OR RAISE THE DEVIL.
OR WORSE, THAT I THINK I CAN.
MAGIC IS A PSYCHOLOGICAL DISCIPLINE.
OH, I DOUBT THAT.
I LIKE THE IDEA OF A *PARA*PSYCHOLOGIST BEING SUPERIOR, LIKE YOU'RE PART OF THE RATIONAL ORTHODOXY.
SHUT UP...
MAGIC IS ABOUT EFFECTING PHYSICAL CHANGE THROUGH PERCEPTUAL CHANGE. YOU'VE HEARD OF ALEISTER CROWLEY?
BLACK MAGICIAN? THE GREAT BEAST AND ALL THAT?
YES, WELL. BIT OF A SHOWMAN. WHAT'S YOUR NAME?

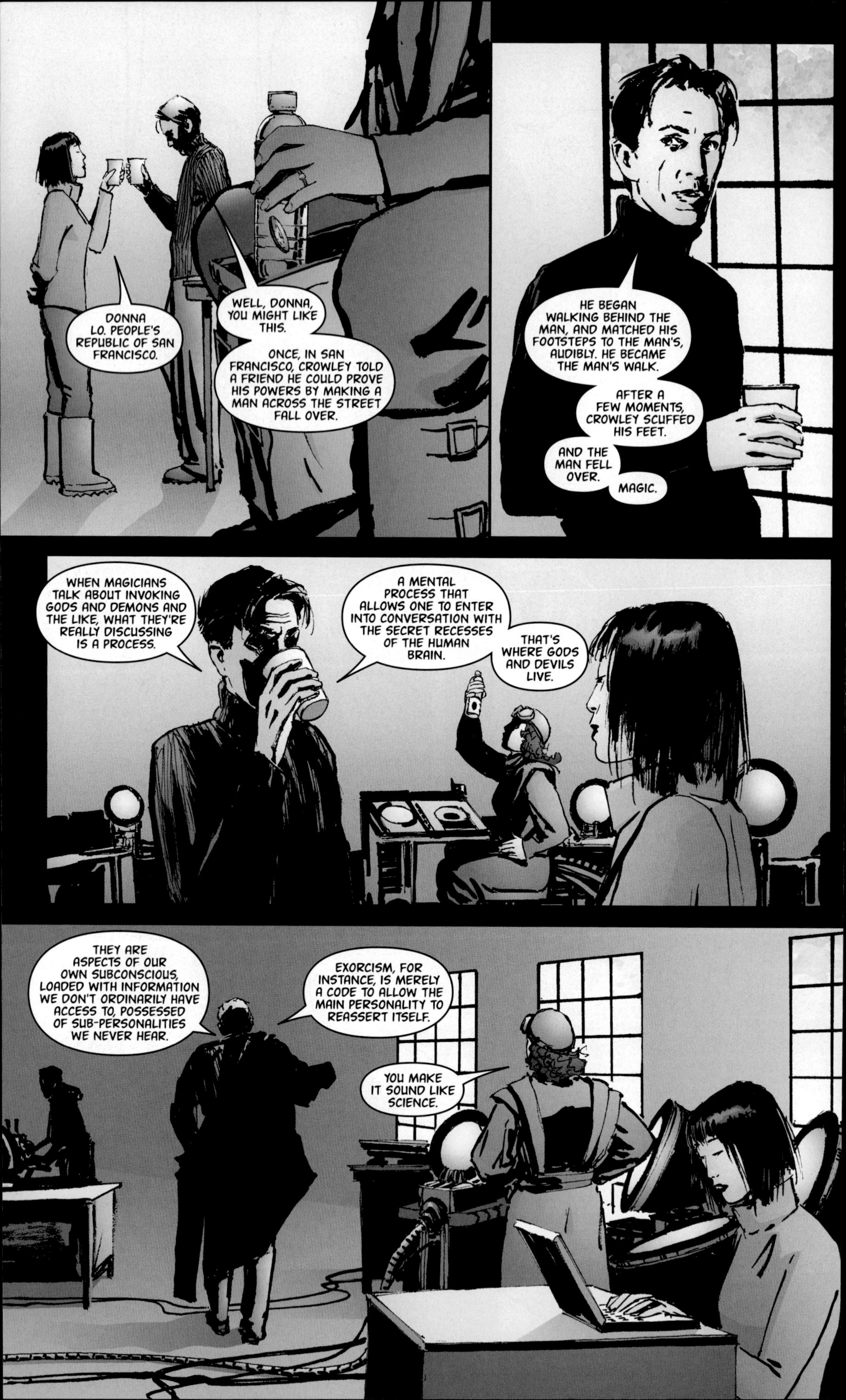
DONNA LO. PEOPLE'S REPUBLIC OF SAN FRANCISCO.
WELL, DONNA, YOU MIGHT LIKE THIS.
ONCE, IN SAN FRANCISCO, CROWLEY TOLD A FRIEND HE COULD PROVE HIS POWERS BY MAKING A MAN ACROSS THE STREET FALL OVER.
HE BEGAN WALKING BEHIND THE MAN, AND MATCHED HIS FOOTSTEPS TO THE MAN'S, AUDIBLY. HE BECAME THE MAN'S WALK.
AFTER A FEW MOMENTS, CROWLEY SCUFFED HIS FEET.
AND THE MAN FELL OVER.
MAGIC.
WHEN MAGICIANS TALK ABOUT INVOKING GODS AND DEMONS AND THE LIKE, WHAT THEY'RE REALLY DISCUSSING IS A PROCESS.
A MENTAL PROCESS THAT ALLOWS ONE TO ENTER INTO CONVERSATION WITH THE SECRET RECESSES OF THE HUMAN BRAIN.
THAT'S WHERE GODS AND DEVILS LIVE.
THEY ARE ASPECTS OF OUR OWN SUBCONSCIOUS, LOADED WITH INFORMATION WE DON'T ORDINARILY HAVE ACCESS TO, POSSESSED OF SUB-PERSONALITIES WE NEVER HEAR.
EXORCISM, FOR INSTANCE, IS MERELY A CODE TO ALLOW THE MAIN PERSONALITY TO REASSERT ITSELF.
YOU MAKE IT SOUND LIKE SCIENCE.

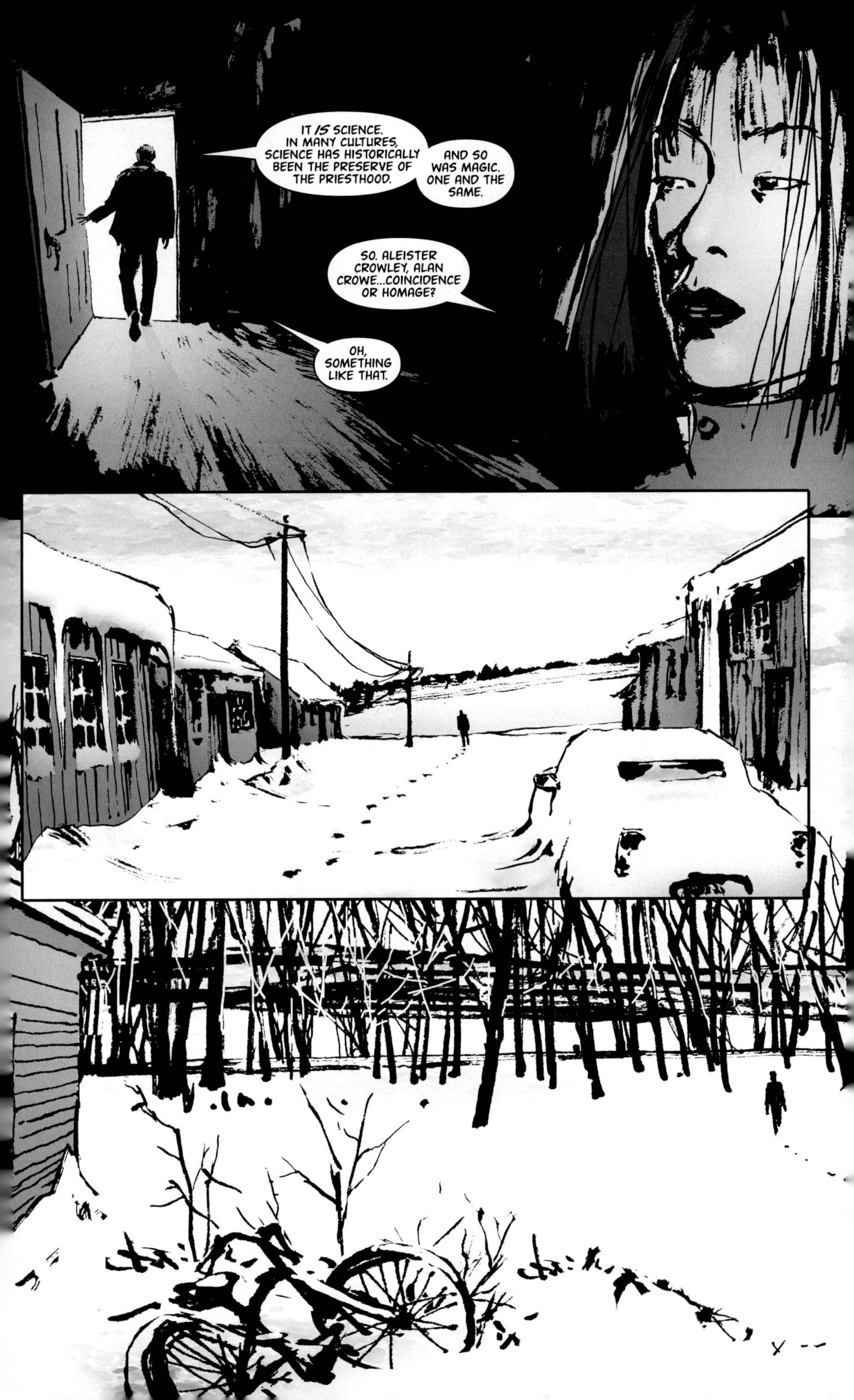
IT IS SCIENCE. IN MANY CULTURES, SCIENCE HAS HISTORICALLY BEEN THE PRESERVE OF THE PRIESTHOOD.
AND SO WAS MAGIC. ONE AND THE SAME.
SO. ALEISTER CROWLEY, ALAN CROWE...COINCIDENCE OR HOMAGE?
OH, SOMETHING LIKE THAT.

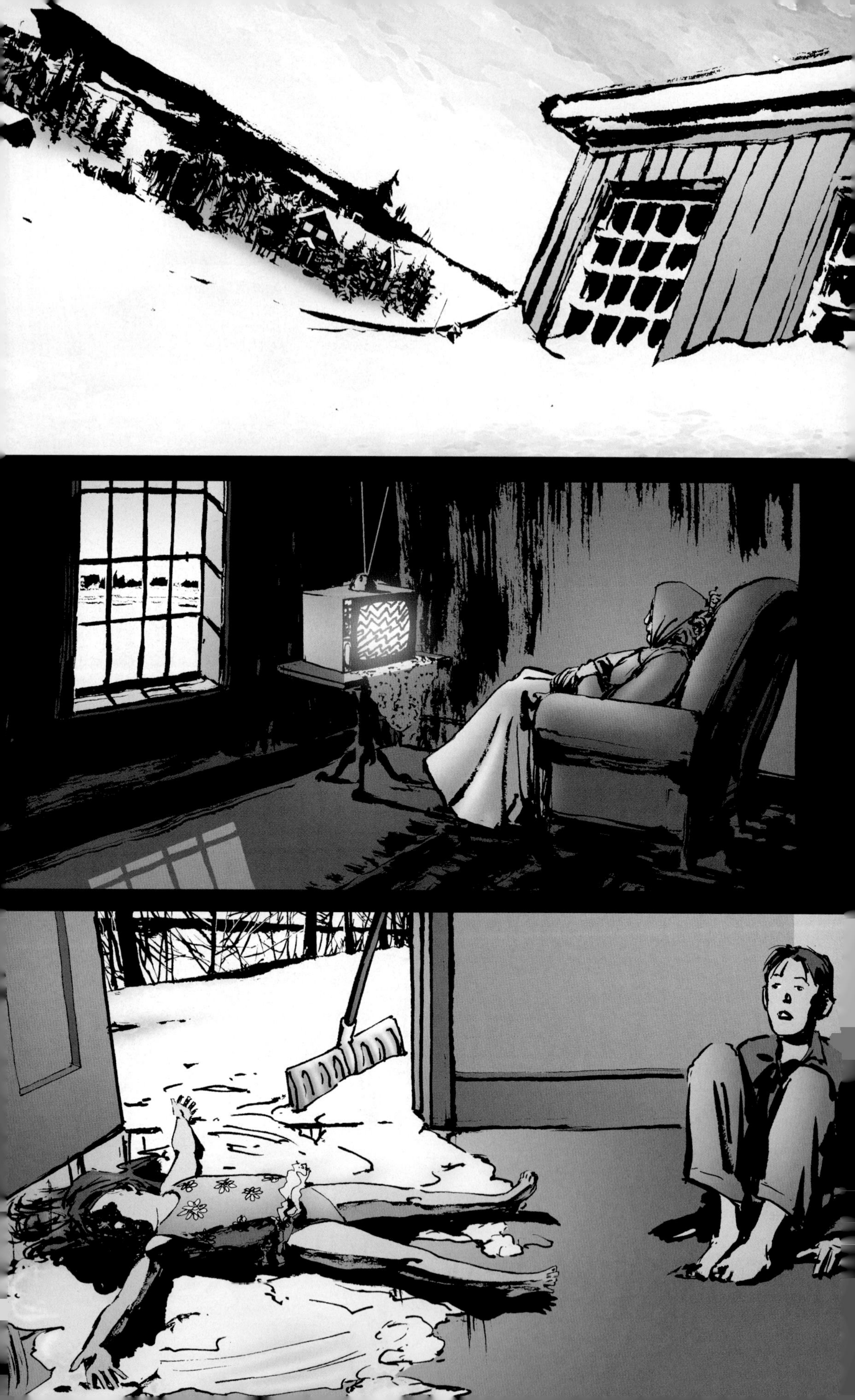

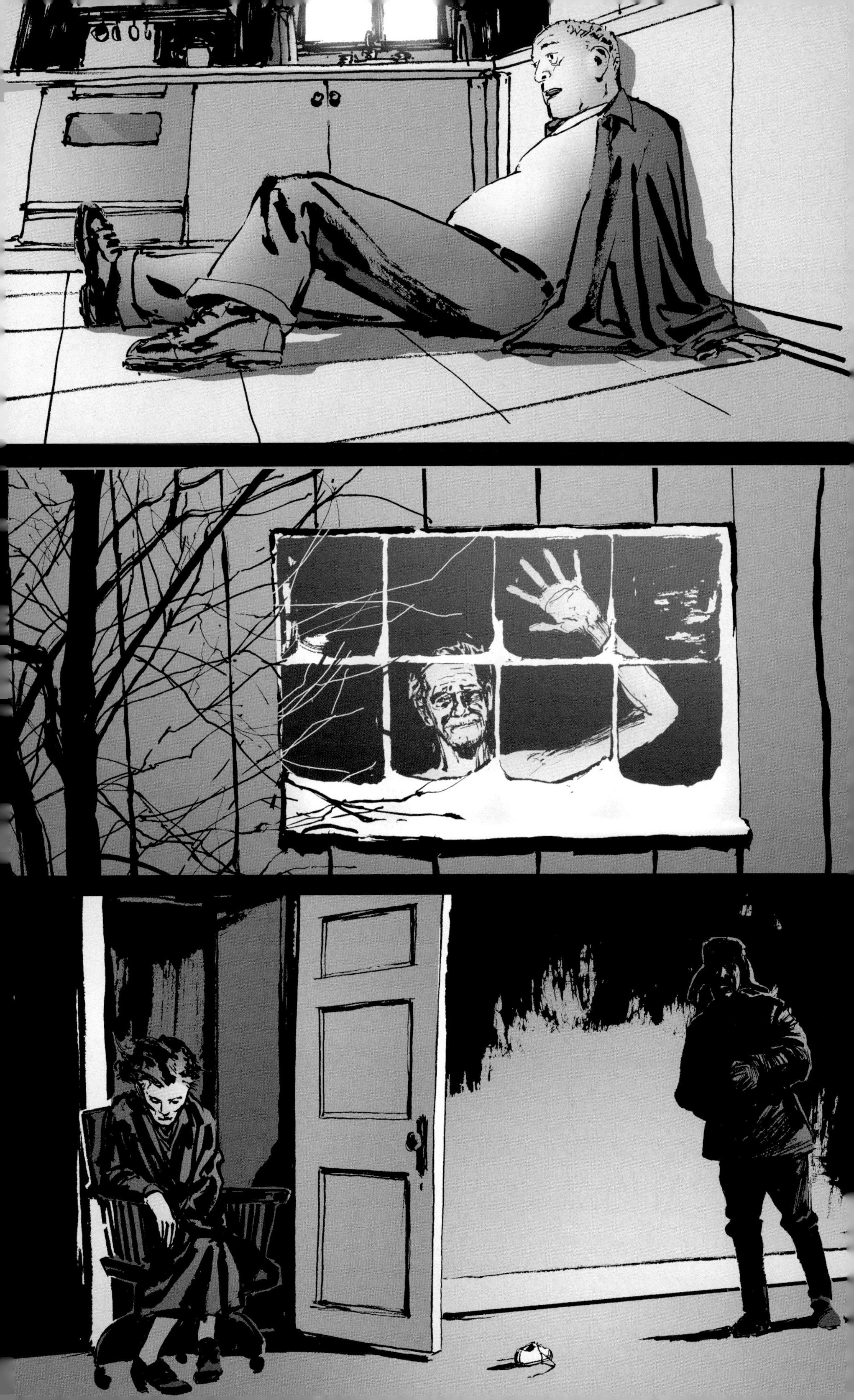

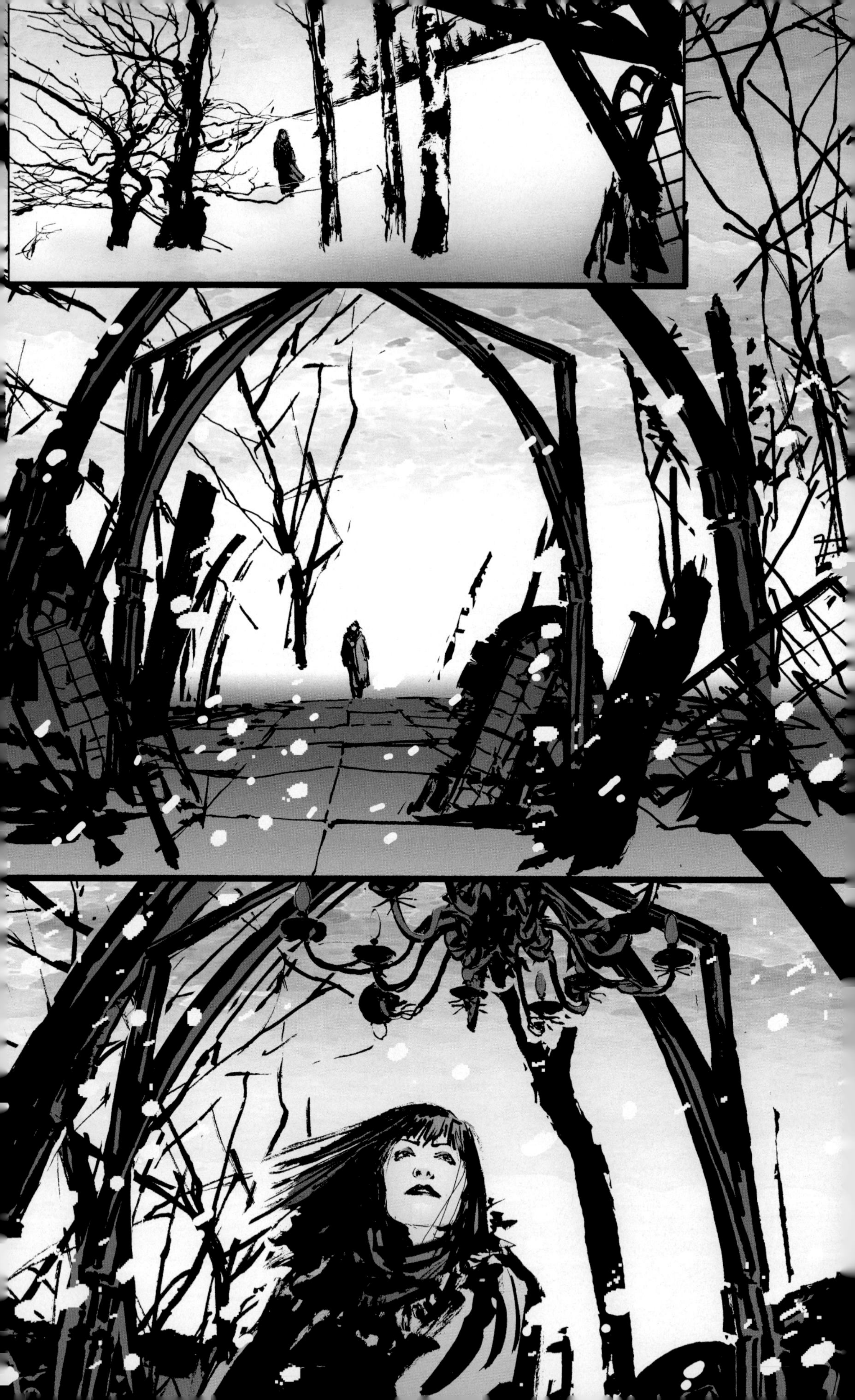

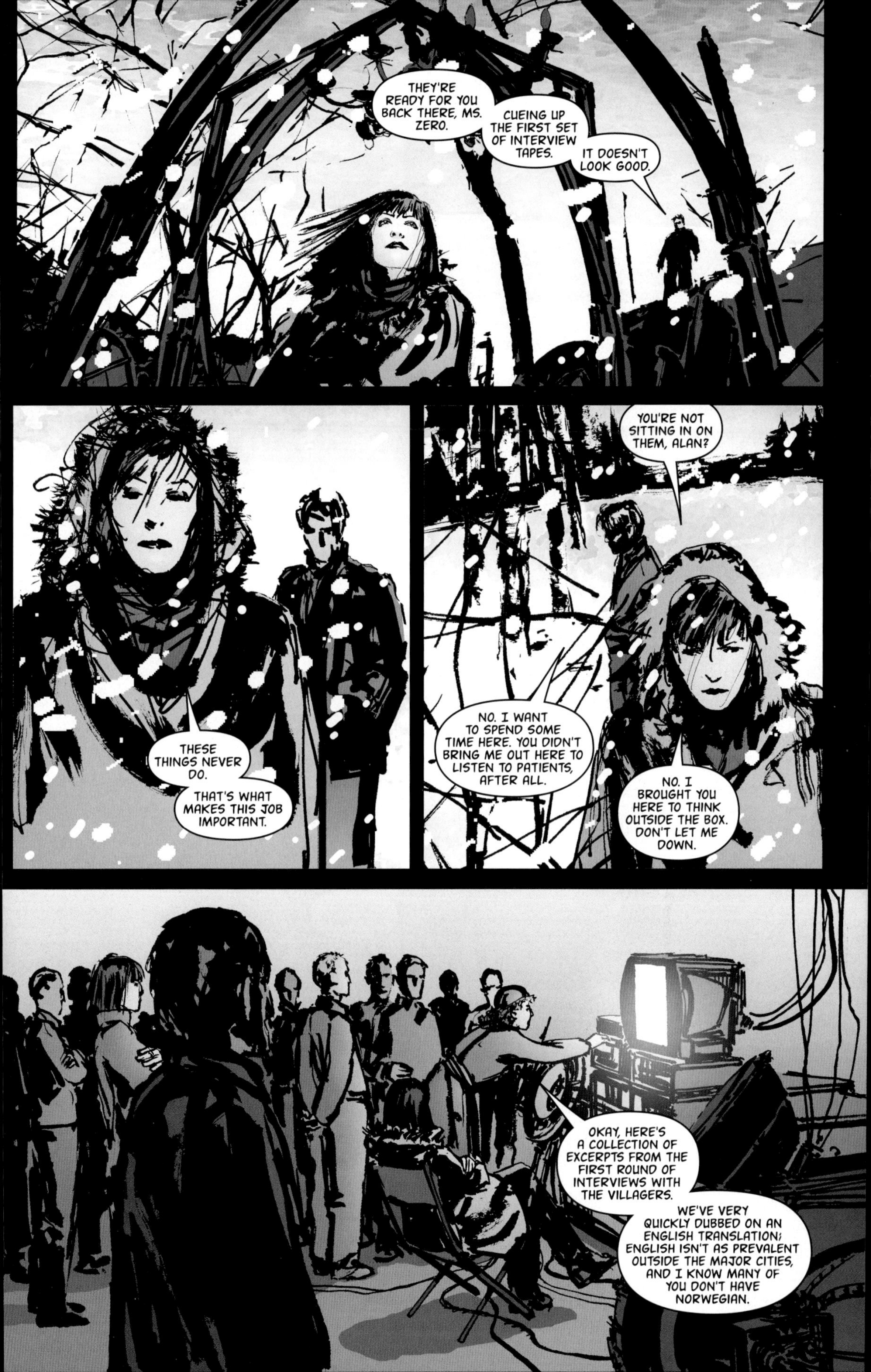
THEY'RE READY FOR YOU BACK THERE, MS. ZERO.
CUEING UP THE FIRST SET OF INTERVIEW TAPES.
IT DOESN'T LOOK GOOD.
THESE THINGS NEVER DO.
THAT'S WHAT MAKES THIS JOB IMPORTANT.
YOU'RE NOT SITTING IN ON THEM, ALAN?
NO. I WANT TO SPEND SOME TIME HERE. YOU DIDN'T BRING ME OUT HERE TO LISTEN TO PATIENTS, AFTER ALL.
NO. I BROUGHT YOU HERE TO THINK OUTSIDE THE BOX. DON'T LET ME DOWN.
OKAY, HERE'S A COLLECTION OF EXCERPTS FROM THE FIRST ROUND OF INTERVIEWS WITH THE VILLAGERS.
WE'VE VERY QUICKLY DUBBED ON AN ENGLISH TRANSLATION; ENGLISH ISN'T AS PREVALENT OUTSIDE THE MAJOR CITIES, AND I KNOW MANY OF YOU DON'T HAVE NORWEGIAN.

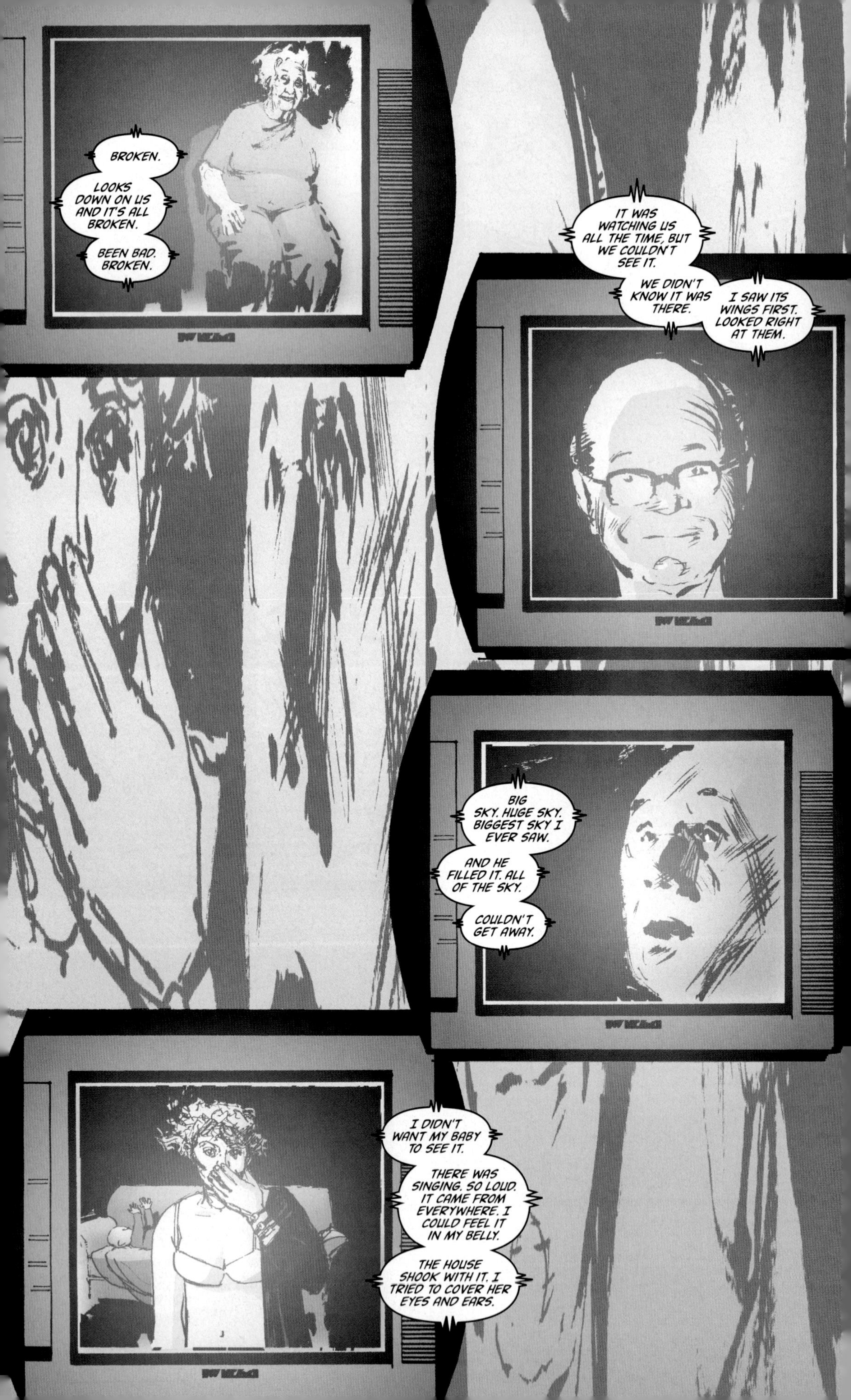

BROKEN.
LOOKS DOWN ON US AND IT'S ALL BROKEN.
BEEN BAD. BROKEN.
IT WAS WATCHING US ALL THE TIME, BUT WE COULDN'T SEE IT.
WE DIDN'T KNOW IT WAS THERE.
I SAW ITS WINGS FIRST. LOOKED RIGHT AT THEM.
BIG SKY. HUGE SKY. BIGGEST SKY I EVER SAW.
AND HE FILLED IT. ALL OF THE SKY.
COULDN'T GET AWAY.
I DIDN'T WANT MY BABY TO SEE IT.
THERE WAS SINGING. SO LOUD. IT CAME FROM EVERYWHERE. I COULD FEEL IT IN MY BELLY.
THE HOUSE SHOOK WITH IT. I TRIED TO COVER HER EYES AND EARS.

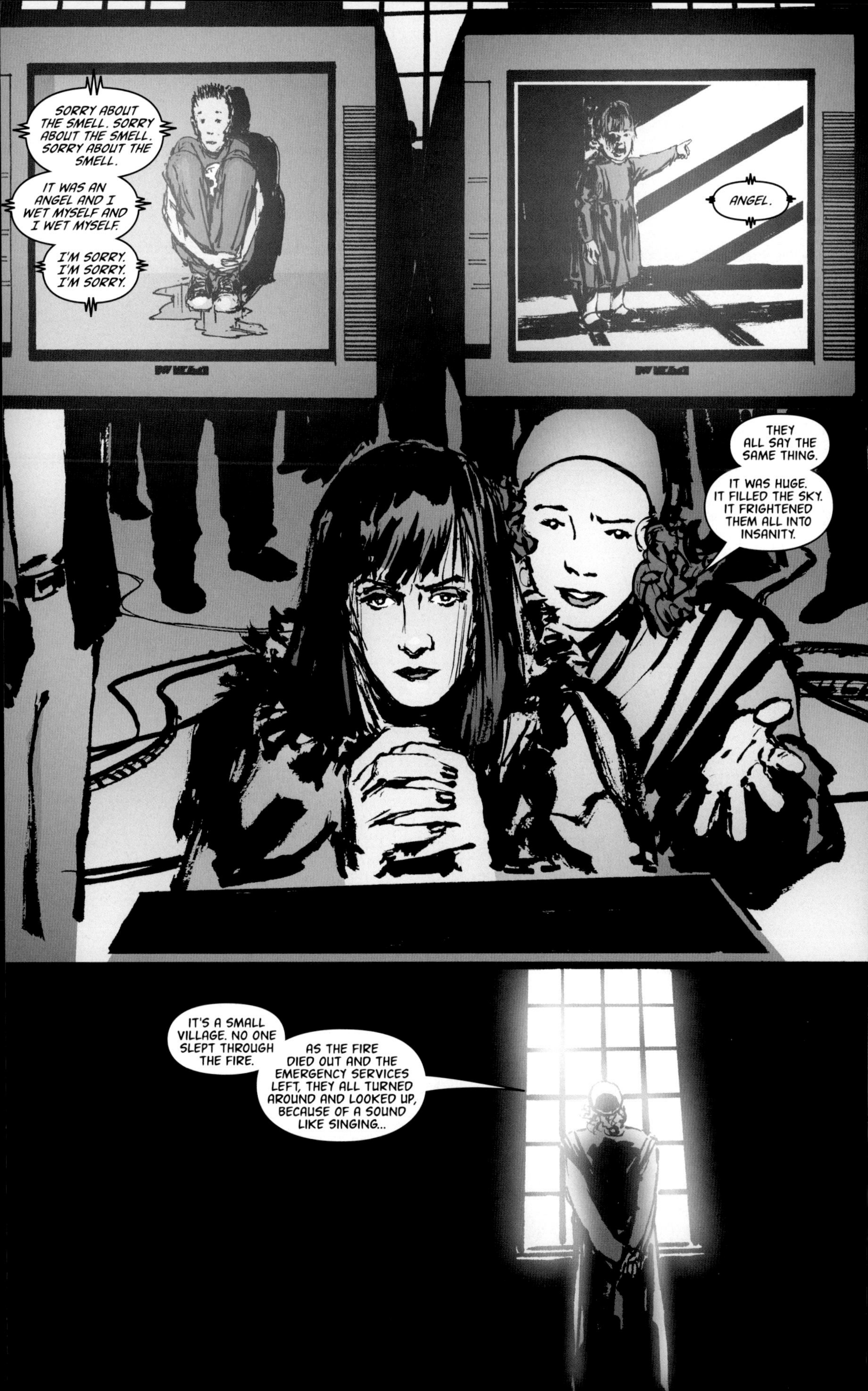
SORRY ABOUT THE SMELL. SORRY ABOUT THE SMELL. SORRY ABOUT THE SMELL.
IT WAS AN ANGEL AND I WET MYSELF AND I WET MYSELF.
I'M SORRY. I'M SORRY. I'M SORRY.
ANGEL.
THEY ALL SAY THE SAME THING.
IT WAS HUGE. IT FILLED THE SKY. IT FRIGHTENED THEM ALL INTO INSANITY.
IT'S A SMALL VILLAGE. NO ONE SLEPT THROUGH THE FIRE.
AS THE FIRE DIED OUT AND THE EMERGENCY SERVICES LEFT, THEY ALL TURNED AROUND AND LOOKED UP, BECAUSE OF A SOUND LIKE SINGING...

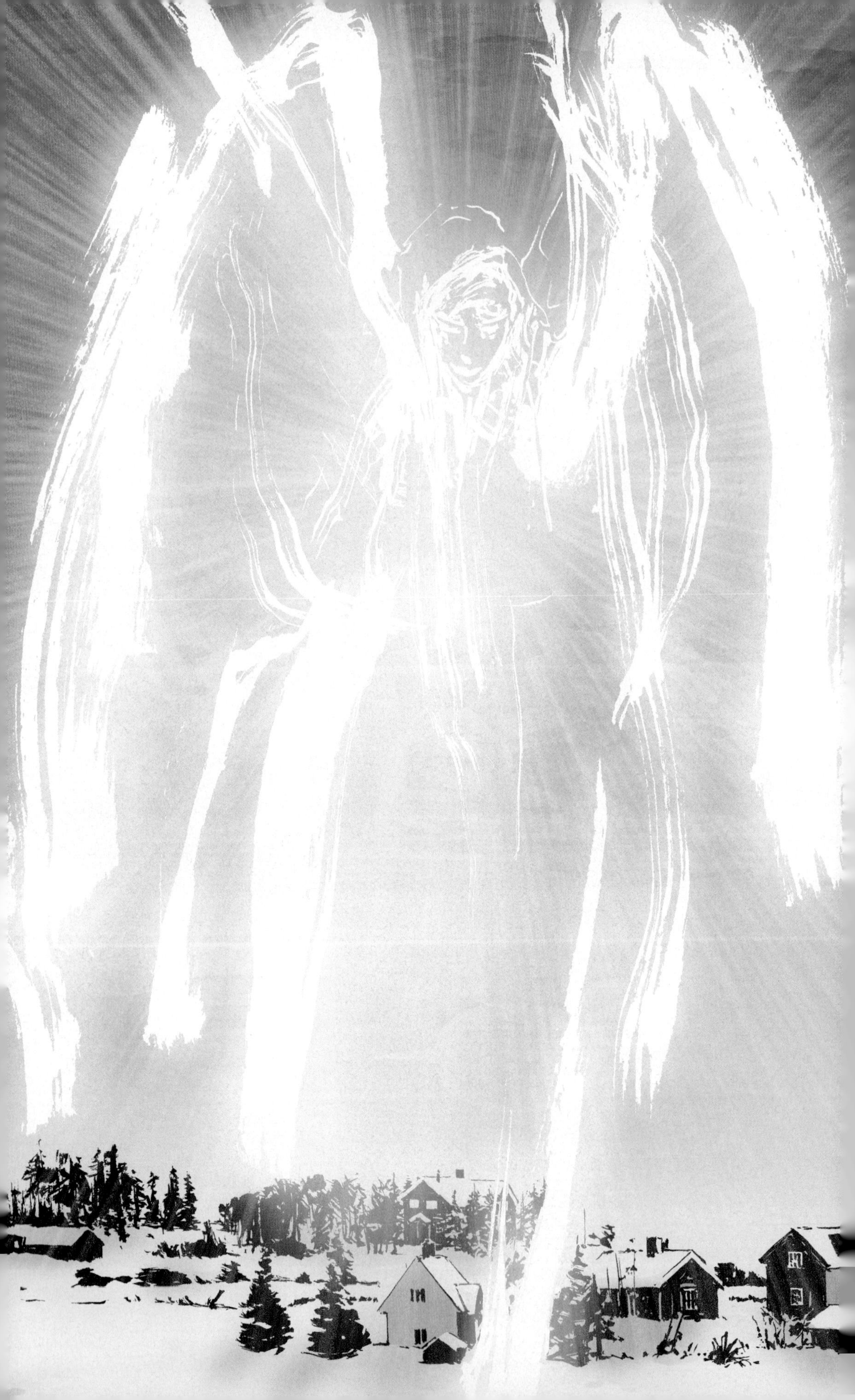

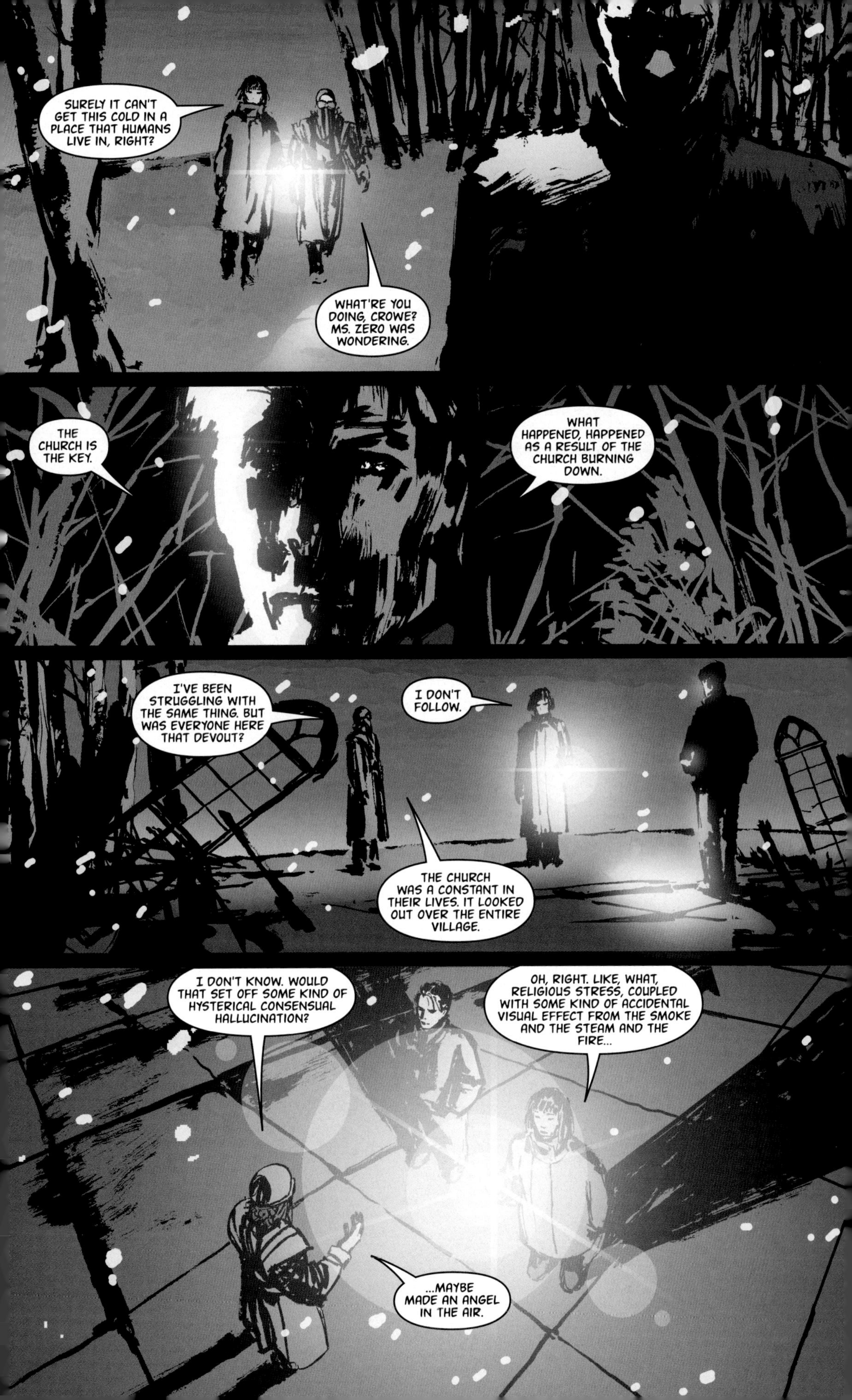
SURELY IT CAN'T GET THIS COLD IN A PLACE THAT HUMANS LIVE IN, RIGHT?
WHAT'RE YOU DOING, CROWE? MS. ZERO WAS WONDERING.
THE CHURCH IS THE KEY.
WHAT HAPPENED, HAPPENED AS A RESULT OF THE CHURCH BURNING DOWN.
I'VE BEEN STRUGGLING WITH THE SAME THING. BUT WAS EVERYONE HERE THAT DEVOUT?
I DON'T FOLLOW.
THE CHURCH WAS A CONSTANT IN THEIR LIVES. IT LOOKED OUT OVER THE ENTIRE VILLAGE.
I DON'T KNOW. WOULD THAT SET OFF SOME KIND OF HYSTERICAL CONSENSUAL HALLUCINATION?
OH, RIGHT. LIKE, WHAT, RELIGIOUS STRESS, COUPLED WITH SOME KIND OF ACCIDENTAL VISUAL EFFECT FROM THE SMOKE AND THE STEAM AND THE FIRE...
...MAYBE MADE AN ANGEL IN THE AIR.

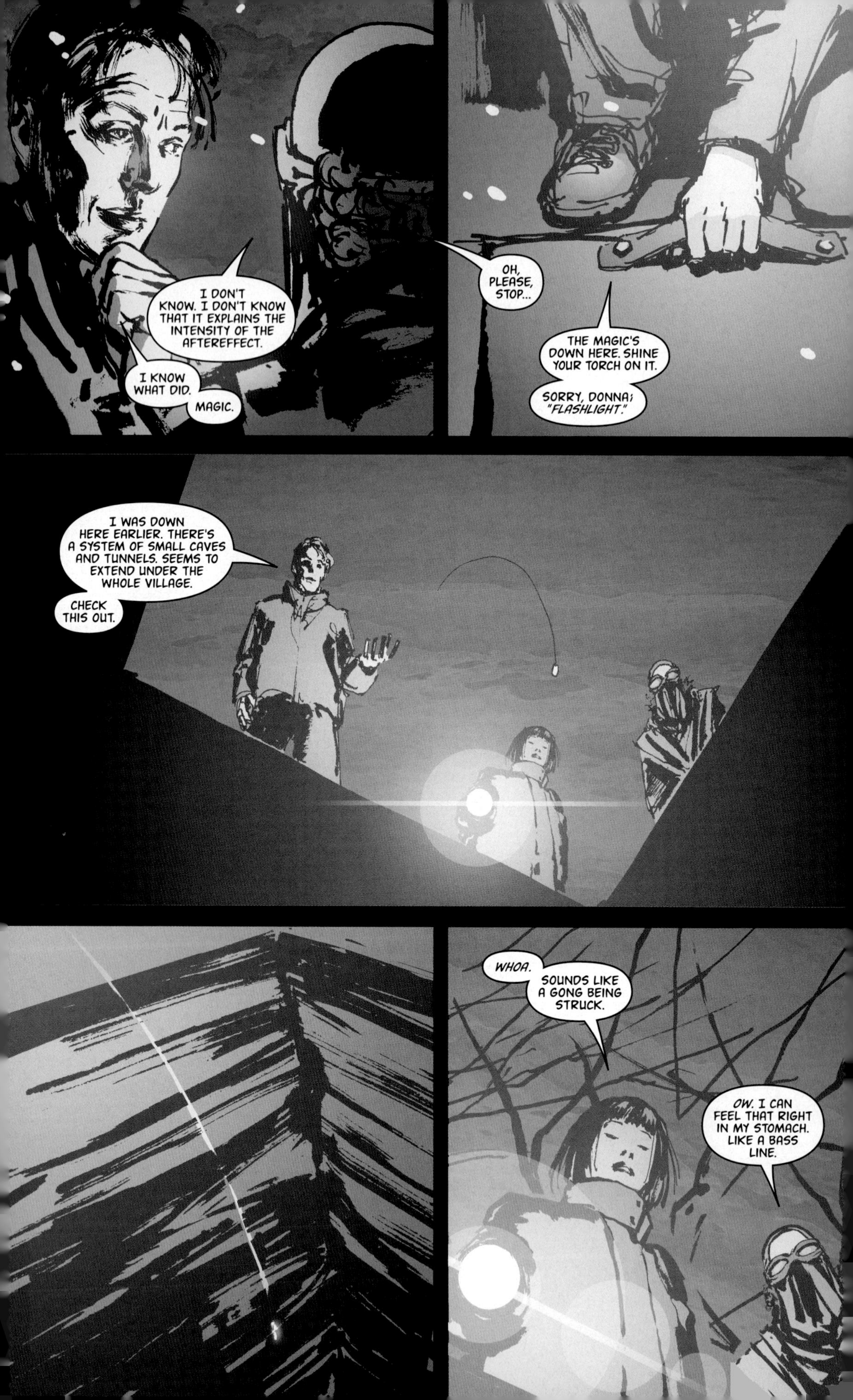
I DON'T KNOW. I DON'T KNOW THAT IT EXPLAINS THE INTENSITY OF THE AFTEREFFECT.
I KNOW WHAT DID.
MAGIC.
OH, PLEASE, STOP...
THE MAGIC'S DOWN HERE. SHINE YOUR TORCH ON IT.
SORRY, DONNA; "FLASHLIGHT."
I WAS DOWN HERE EARLIER. THERE'S A SYSTEM OF SMALL CAVES AND TUNNELS. SEEMS TO EXTEND UNDER THE WHOLE VILLAGE.
CHECK THIS OUT.
WHOA.
SOUNDS LIKE A GONG BEING STRUCK.
OW. I CAN FEEL THAT RIGHT IN MY STOMACH. LIKE A BASS LINE.

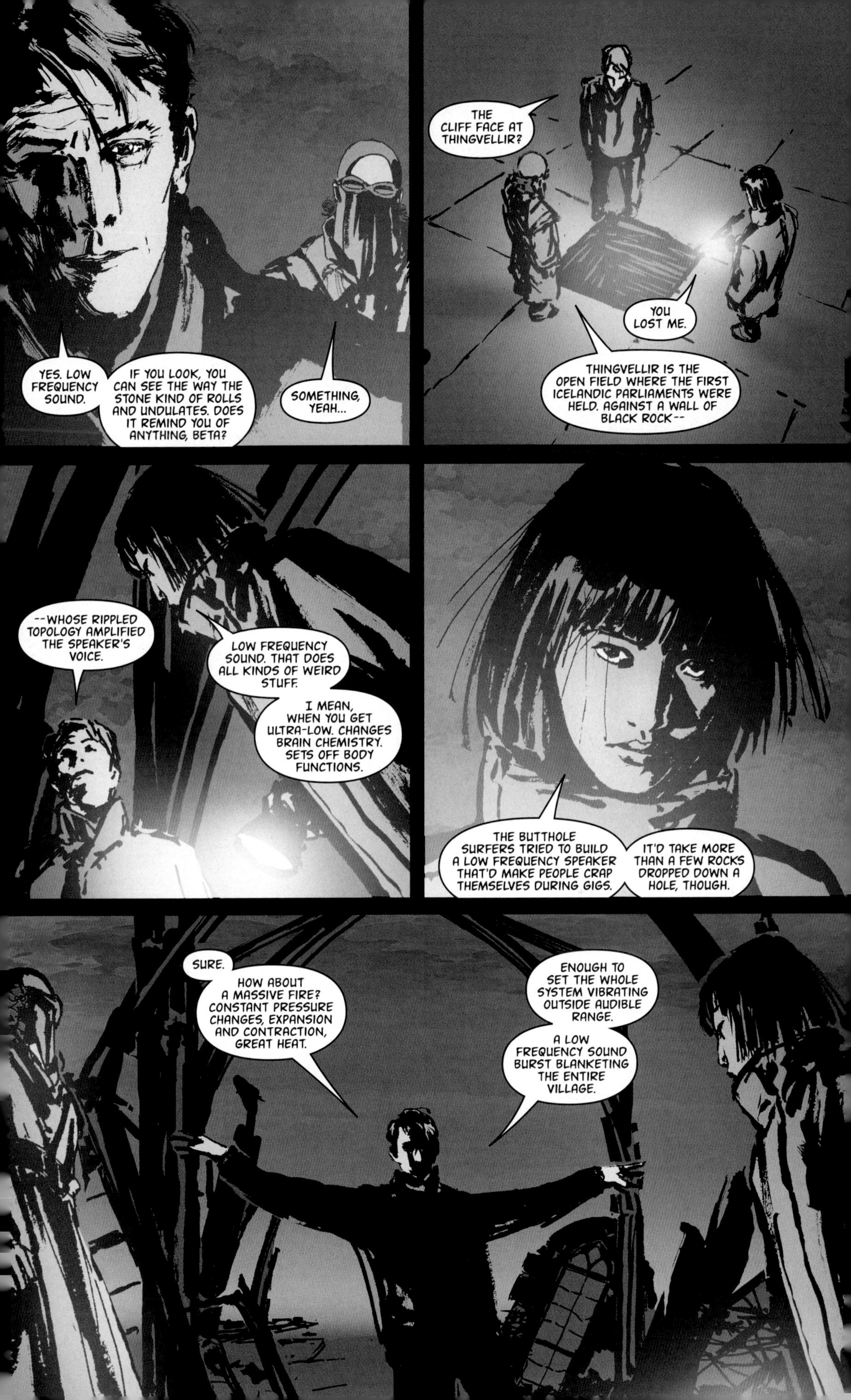
YES. LOW FREQUENCY SOUND.
IF YOU LOOK, YOU CAN SEE THE WAY THE STONE KIND OF ROLLS AND UNDULATES. DOES IT REMIND YOU OF ANYTHING, BETA?
SOMETHING, YEAH...
THE CLIFF FACE AT THINGVELLIR?
YOU LOST ME.
THINGVELLIR IS THE OPEN FIELD WHERE THE FIRST ICELANDIC PARLIAMENTS WERE HELD. AGAINST A WALL OF BLACK ROCK--
--WHOSE RIPPLED TOPOLOGY AMPLIFIED THE SPEAKER'S VOICE.
LOW FREQUENCY SOUND. THAT DOES ALL KINDS OF WEIRD STUFF.
I MEAN, WHEN YOU GET ULTRA-LOW. CHANGES BRAIN CHEMISTRY. SETS OFF BODY FUNCTIONS.
THE BUTTHOLE SURFERS TRIED TO BUILD A LOW FREQUENCY SPEAKER THAT'D MAKE PEOPLE CRAP THEMSELVES DURING GIGS.
IT'D TAKE MORE THAN A FEW ROCKS DROPPED DOWN A HOLE, THOUGH.
SURE.
HOW ABOUT A MASSIVE FIRE? CONSTANT PRESSURE CHANGES, EXPANSION AND CONTRACTION, GREAT HEAT.
ENOUGH TO SET THE WHOLE SYSTEM VIBRATING OUTSIDE AUDIBLE RANGE.
A LOW FREQUENCY SOUND BURST BLANKETING THE ENTIRE VILLAGE.

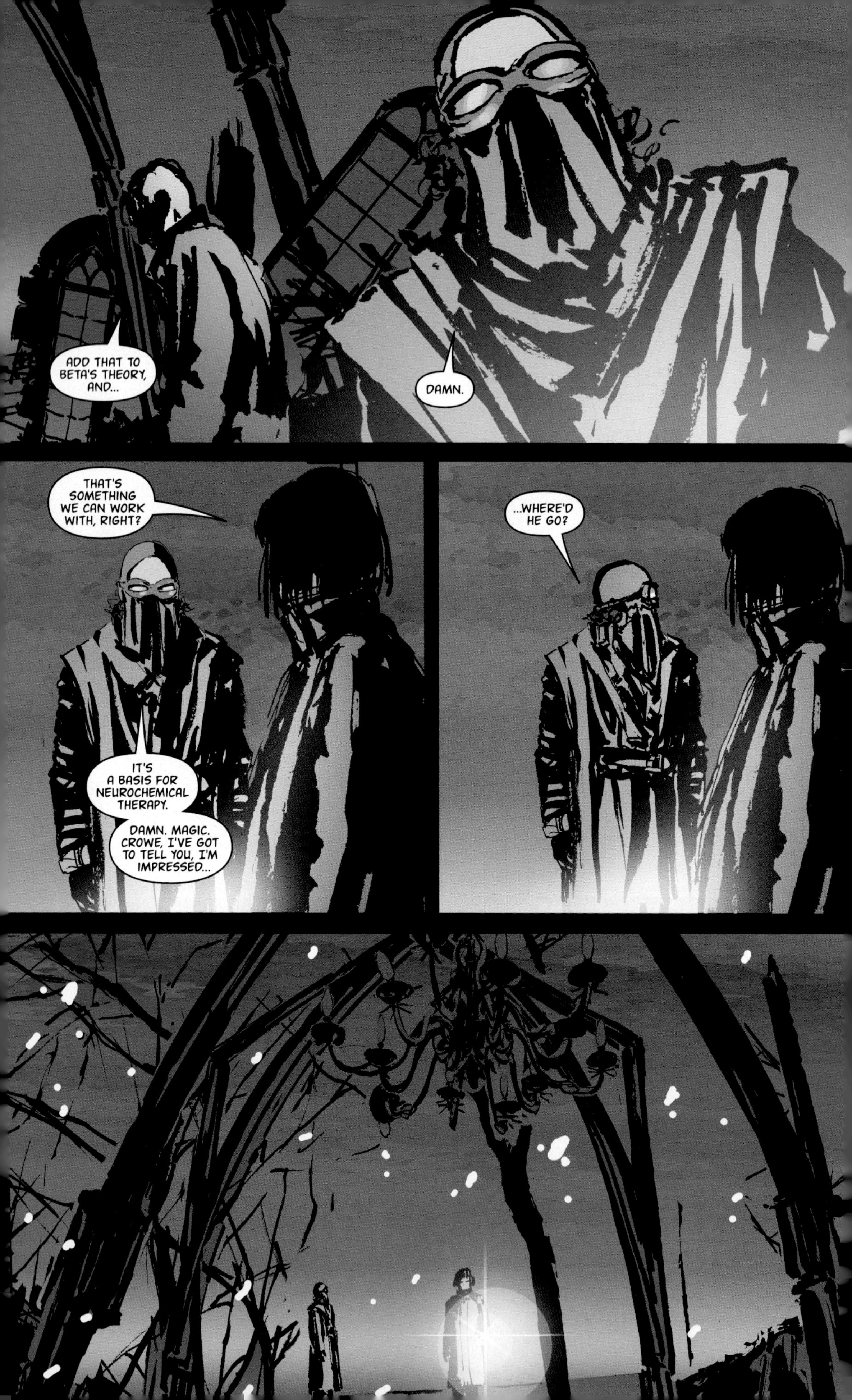
ADD THAT TO BETA'S THEORY, AND...
DAMN.
THAT'S SOMETHING WE CAN WORK WITH, RIGHT?
IT'S A BASIS FOR NEUROCHEMICAL THERAPY.
DAMN. MAGIC. CROWE, I'VE GOT TO TELL YOU, I'M IMPRESSED...
...WHERE'D HE GO?

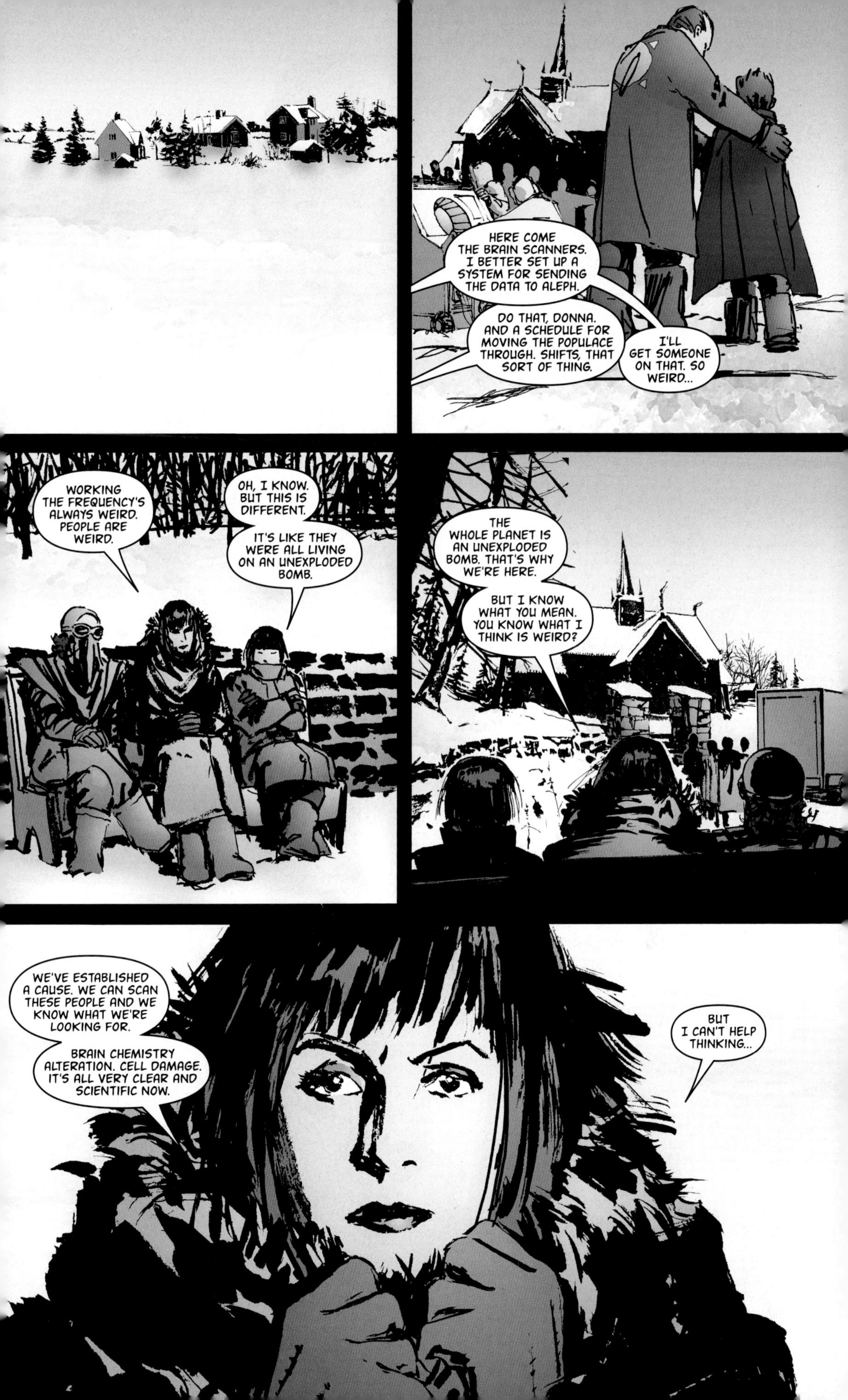
HERE COME THE BRAIN SCANNERS. I BETTER SET UP A SYSTEM FOR SENDING THE DATA TO ALEPH.
DO THAT, DONNA. AND A SCHEDULE FOR MOVING THE POPULACE THROUGH. SHIFTS, THAT SORT OF THING.
I'LL GET SOMEONE ON THAT. SO WEIRD...
WORKING THE FREQUENCY'S ALWAYS WEIRD. PEOPLE ARE WEIRD.
OH, I KNOW. BUT THIS IS DIFFERENT.
IT'S LIKE THEY WERE ALL LIVING ON AN UNEXPLODED BOMB.
THE WHOLE PLANET IS AN UNEXPLODED BOMB. THAT'S WHY WE'RE HERE.
BUT I KNOW WHAT YOU MEAN. YOU KNOW WHAT I THINK IS WEIRD?
WE'VE ESTABLISHED A CAUSE. WE CAN SCAN THESE PEOPLE AND WE KNOW WHAT WE'RE LOOKING FOR.
BRAIN CHEMISTRY ALTERATION. CELL DAMAGE. IT'S ALL VERY CLEAR AND SCIENTIFIC NOW.
BUT I CAN'T HELP THINKING...

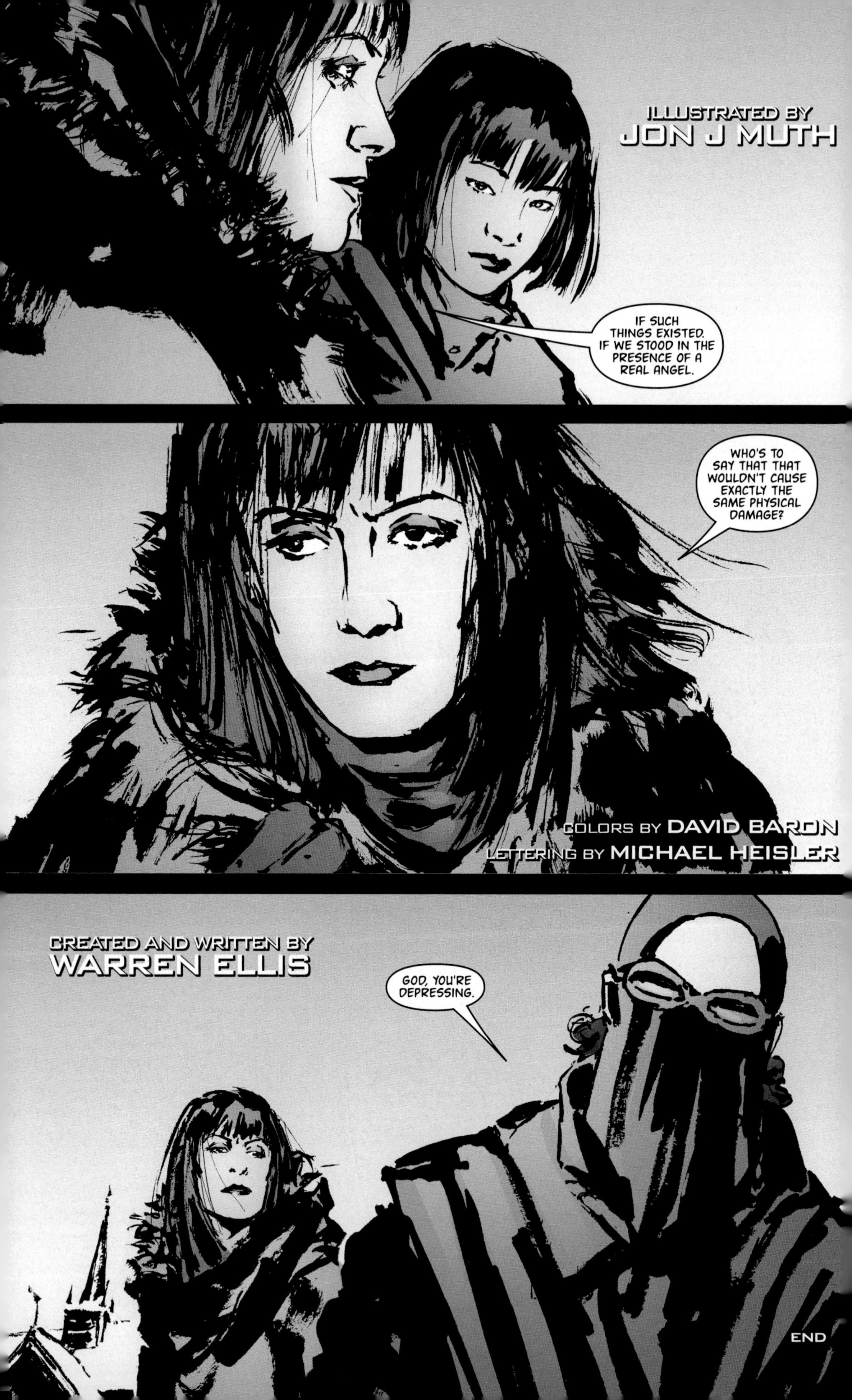
ILLUSTRATED BY
JON J MUTH
IF SUCH THINGS EXISTED. IF WE STOOD IN THE PRESENCE OF A REAL ANGEL.
WHO'S TO SAY THAT THAT WOULDN'T CAUSE EXACTLY THE SAME PHYSICAL DAMAGE?
COLORS BY DAVID BARON
LETTERING BY MICHAEL HEISLER
CREATED AND WRITTEN BY
WARREN ELLIS
GOD, YOU'RE DEPRESSING.
END

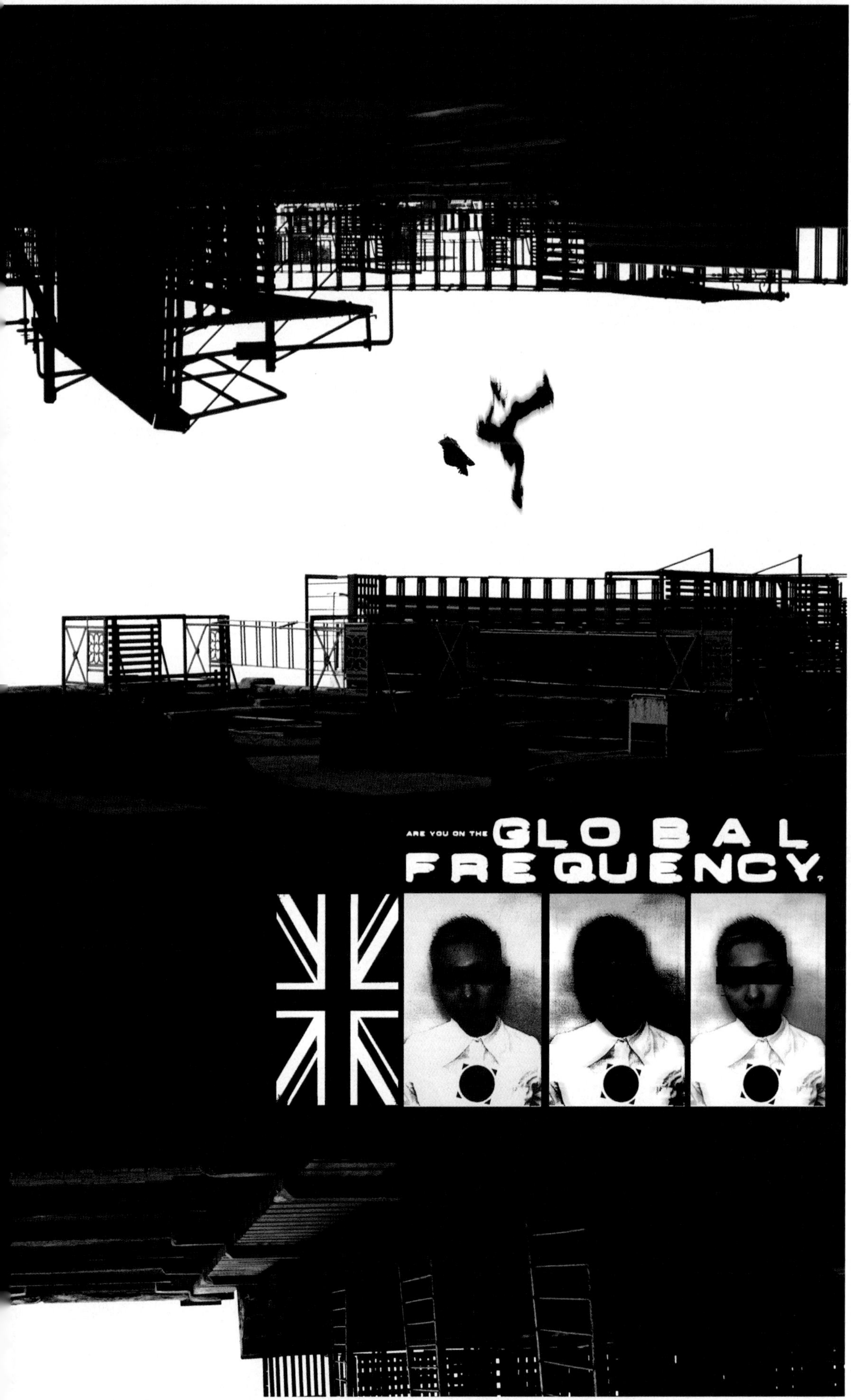
ARE YOU ON THE GLOBAL FREQUENCY?

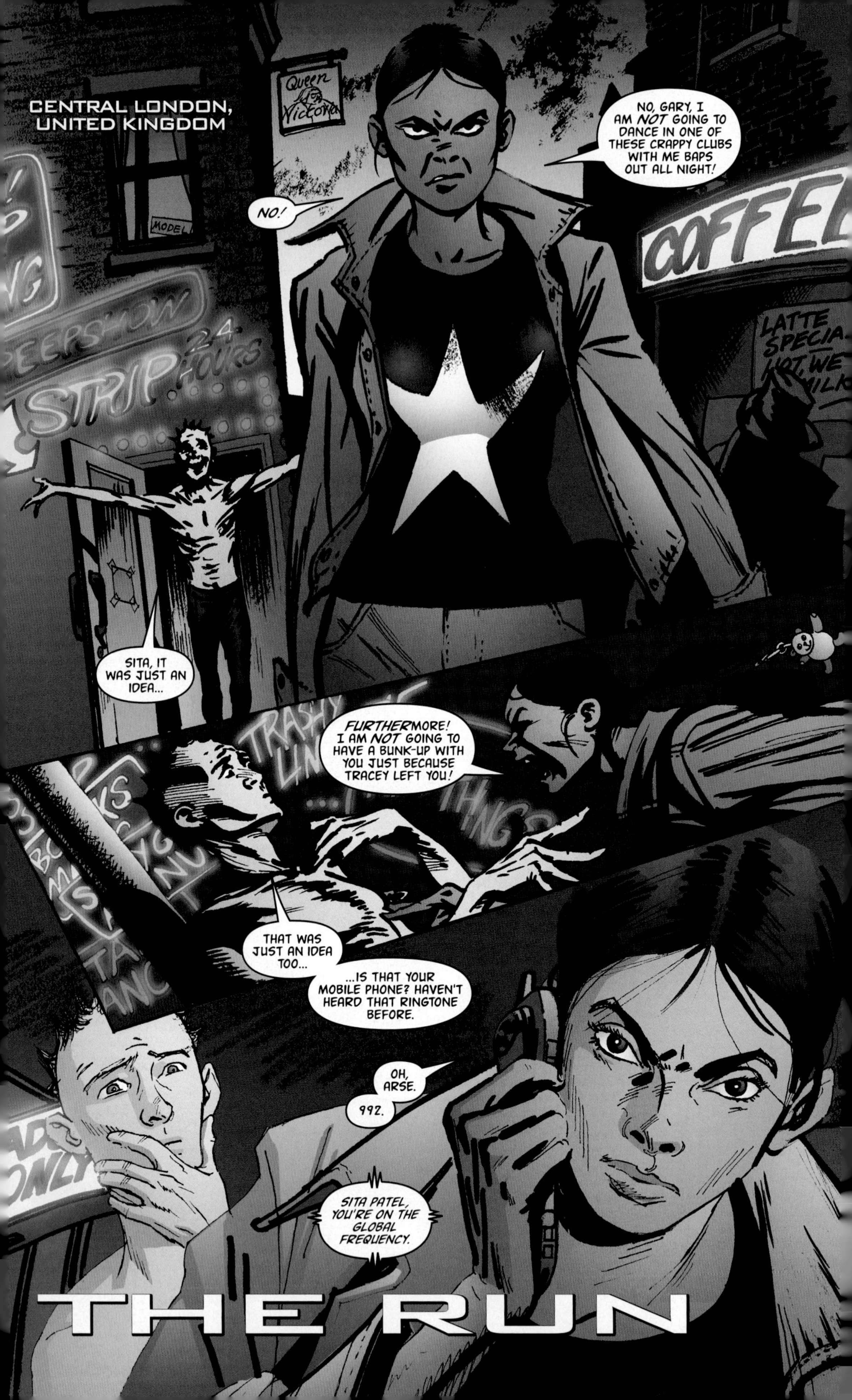
CENTRAL LONDON, UNITED KINGDOM
NO, GARY, I AM NOT GOING TO DANCE IN ONE OF THESE CRAPPY CLUBS WITH ME BAPS OUT ALL NIGHT!
NO!
SITA, IT WAS JUST AN IDEA...
FURTHERMORE! I AM NOT GOING TO HAVE A BUNK-UP WITH YOU JUST BECAUSE TRACEY LEFT YOU!
THAT WAS JUST AN IDEA TOO...
...IS THAT YOUR MOBILE PHONE? HAVEN'T HEARD THAT RINGTONE BEFORE.
OH, ARSE.
992.
SITA PATEL, YOU'RE ON THE GLOBAL FREQUENCY.
THE RUN

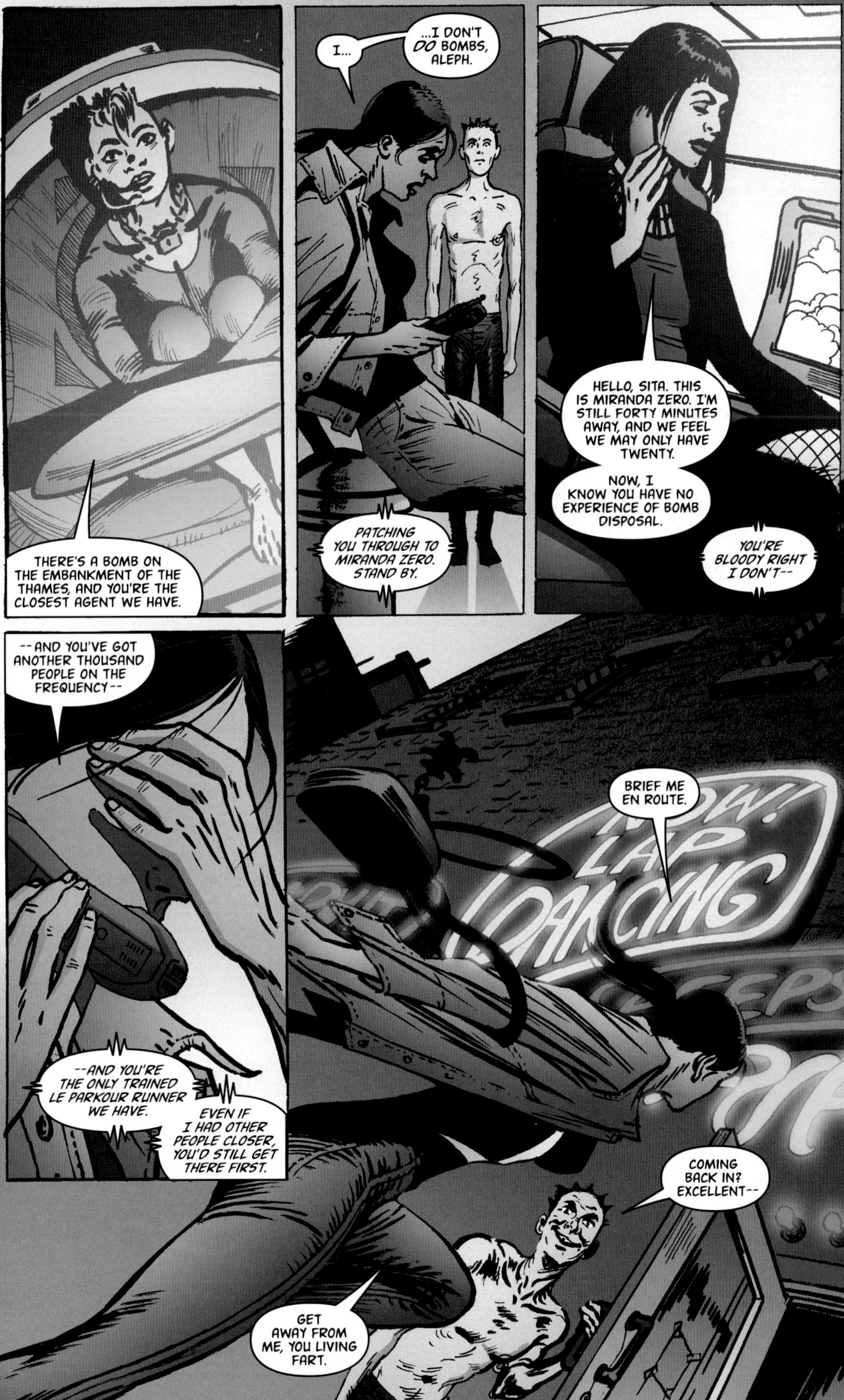
THERE'S A BOMB ON THE EMBANKMENT OF THE THAMES, AND YOU'RE THE CLOSEST AGENT WE HAVE.
I...
...I DON'T DO BOMBS, ALEPH.
PATCHING YOU THROUGH TO MIRANDA ZERO. STAND BY.
HELLO, SITA. THIS IS MIRANDA ZERO. I'M STILL FORTY MINUTES AWAY, AND WE FEEL WE MAY ONLY HAVE TWENTY.
NOW, I KNOW YOU HAVE NO EXPERIENCE OF BOMB DISPOSAL.
YOU'RE BLOODY RIGHT I DON'T--
--AND YOU'VE GOT ANOTHER THOUSAND PEOPLE ON THE FREQUENCY--
--AND YOU'RE THE ONLY TRAINED LE PARKOUR RUNNER WE HAVE.
EVEN IF I HAD OTHER PEOPLE CLOSER, YOU'D STILL GET THERE FIRST.
BRIEF ME EN ROUTE.
LAP DANCING
COMING BACK IN? EXCELLENT--
GET AWAY FROM ME, YOU LIVING FART.

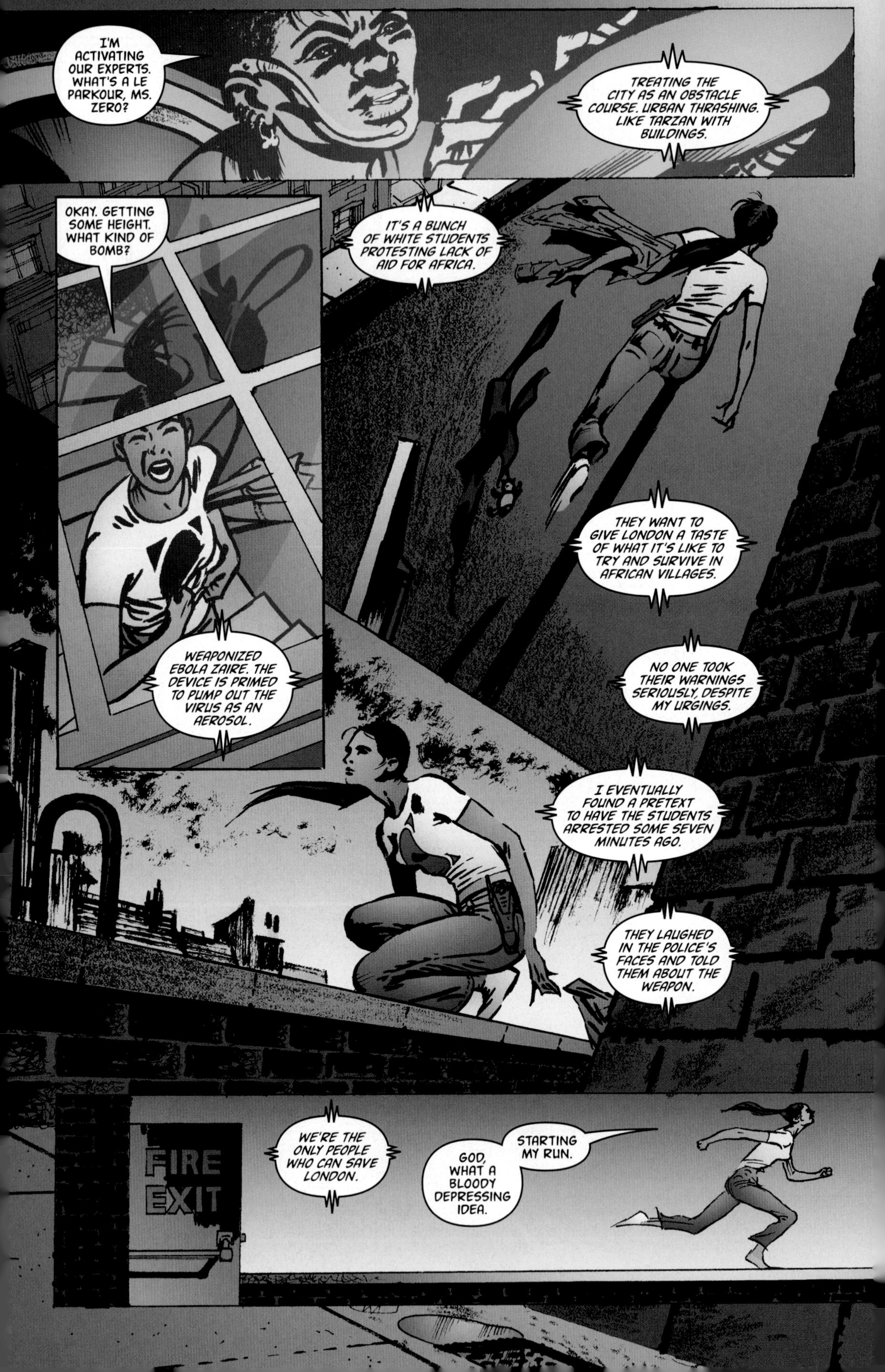
I'M ACTIVATING OUR EXPERTS. WHAT'S A LE PARKOUR, MS. ZERO?
TREATING THE CITY AS AN OBSTACLE COURSE. URBAN THRASHING. LIKE TARZAN WITH BUILDINGS.
OKAY. GETTING SOME HEIGHT. WHAT KIND OF BOMB?
IT'S A BUNCH OF WHITE STUDENTS PROTESTING LACK OF AID FOR AFRICA.
THEY WANT TO GIVE LONDON A TASTE OF WHAT IT'S LIKE TO TRY AND SURVIVE IN AFRICAN VILLAGES.
WEAPONIZED EBOLA ZAIRE. THE DEVICE IS PRIMED TO PUMP OUT THE VIRUS AS AN AEROSOL.
NO ONE TOOK THEIR WARNINGS SERIOUSLY, DESPITE MY URGINGS.
I EVENTUALLY FOUND A PRETEXT TO HAVE THE STUDENTS ARRESTED SOME SEVEN MINUTES AGO.
THEY LAUGHED IN THE POLICE'S FACES AND TOLD THEM ABOUT THE WEAPON.
FIRE EXIT
WE'RE THE ONLY PEOPLE WHO CAN SAVE LONDON.
STARTING MY RUN.
GOD, WHAT A BLOODY DEPRESSING IDEA.

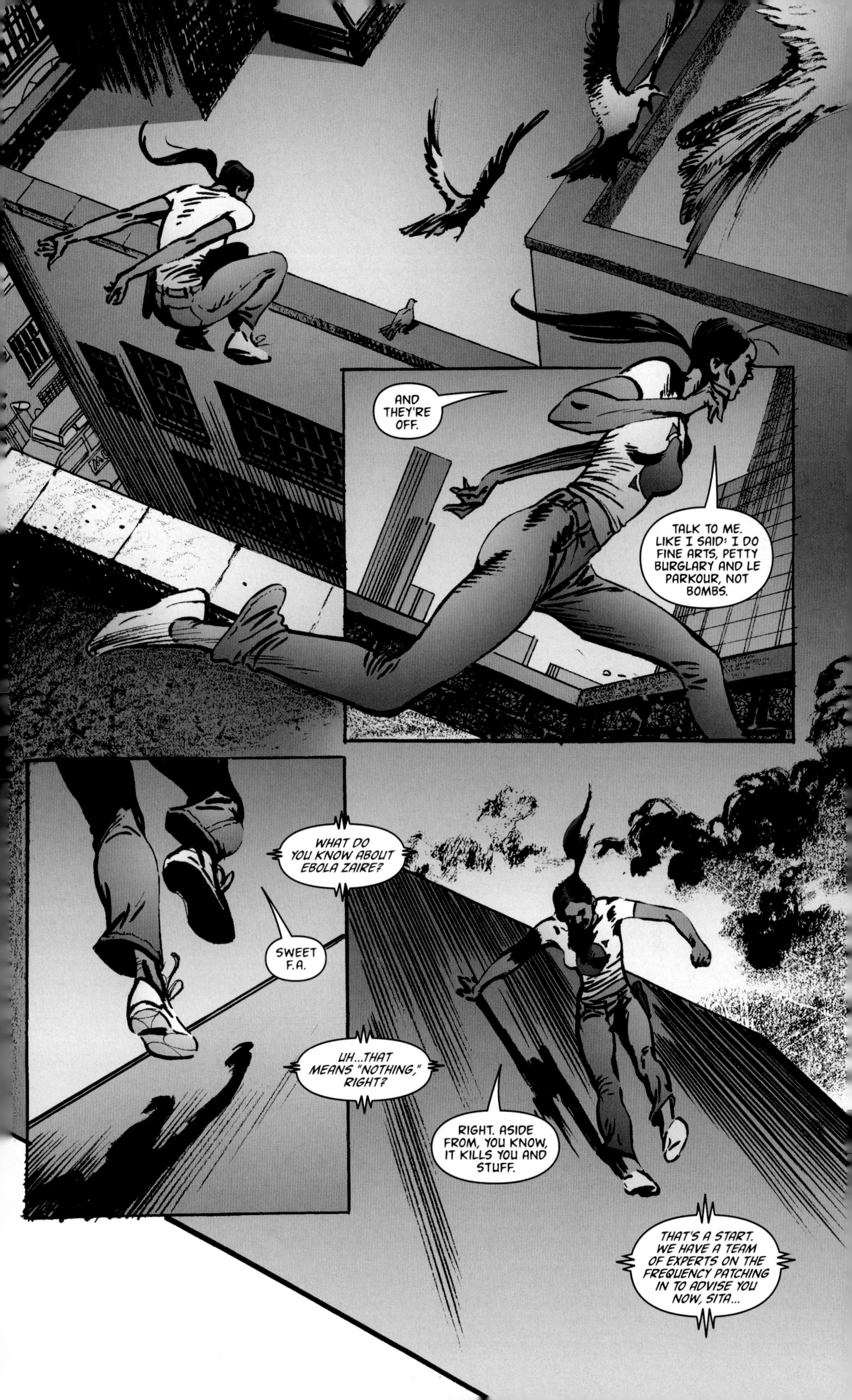
AND THEY'RE OFF.
TALK TO ME. LIKE I SAID: I DO FINE ARTS, PETTY BURGLARY AND LE PARKOUR, NOT BOMBS.
WHAT DO YOU KNOW ABOUT EBOLA ZAIRE?
SWEET F.A.
UH...THAT MEANS "NOTHING," RIGHT?
RIGHT. ASIDE FROM, YOU KNOW, IT KILLS YOU AND STUFF.
THAT'S A START. WE HAVE A TEAM OF EXPERTS ON THE FREQUENCY PATCHING IN TO ADVISE YOU NOW, SITA...

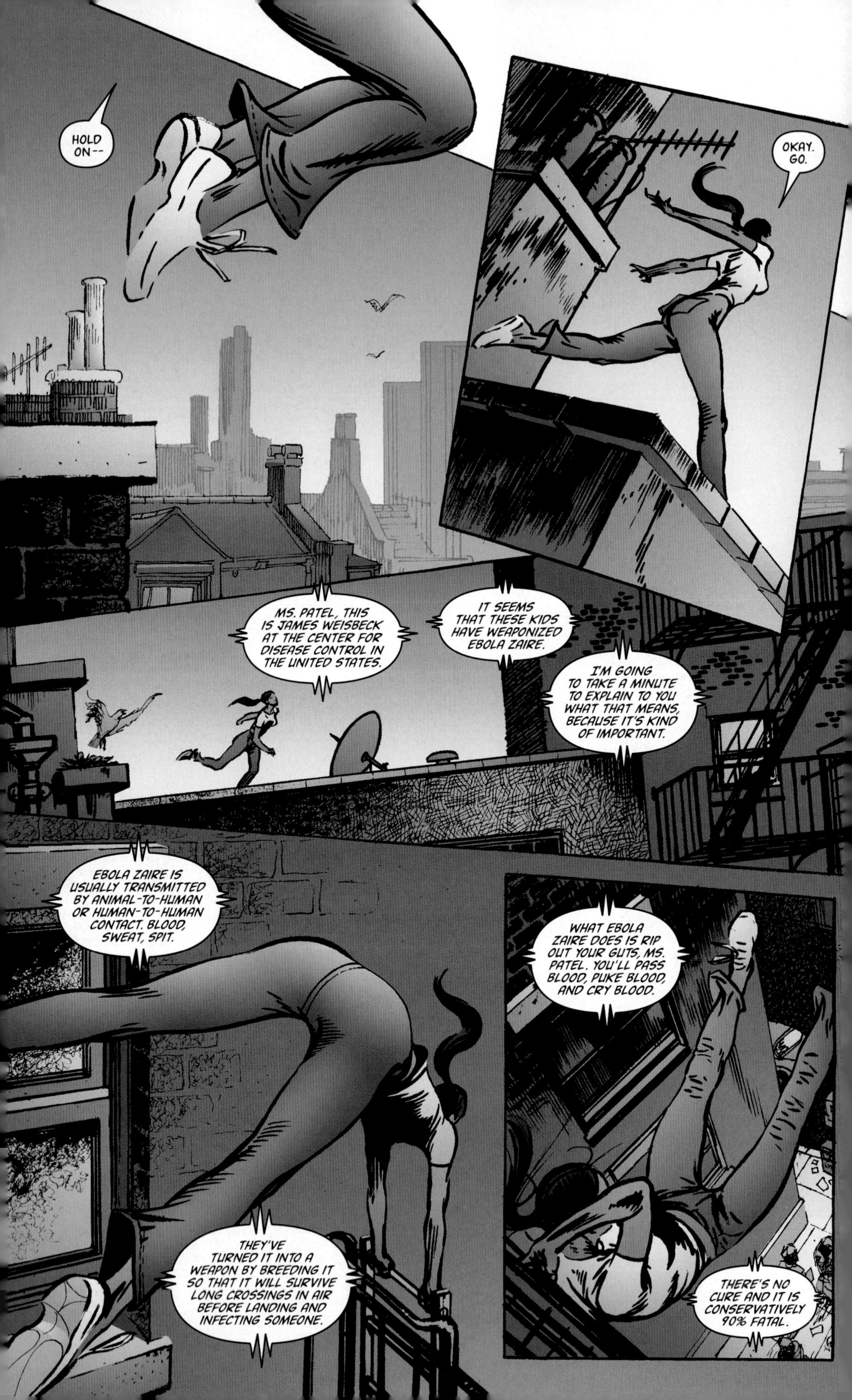
HOLD ON--
OKAY. GO.
MS. PATEL, THIS IS JAMES WEISBECK AT THE CENTER FOR DISEASE CONTROL IN THE UNITED STATES.
IT SEEMS THAT THESE KIDS HAVE WEAPONIZED EBOLA ZAIRE.
I'M GOING TO TAKE A MINUTE TO EXPLAIN TO YOU WHAT THAT MEANS, BECAUSE IT'S KIND OF IMPORTANT.
EBOLA ZAIRE IS USUALLY TRANSMITTED BY ANIMAL-TO-HUMAN OR HUMAN-TO-HUMAN CONTACT. BLOOD, SWEAT, SPIT.
THEY'VE TURNED IT INTO A WEAPON BY BREEDING IT SO THAT IT WILL SURVIVE LONG CROSSINGS IN AIR BEFORE LANDING AND INFECTING SOMEONE.
WHAT EBOLA ZAIRE DOES IS RIP OUT YOUR GUTS, MS. PATEL. YOU'LL PASS BLOOD, PUKE BLOOD, AND CRY BLOOD.
THERE'S NO CURE AND IT IS CONSERVATIVELY 90% FATAL.

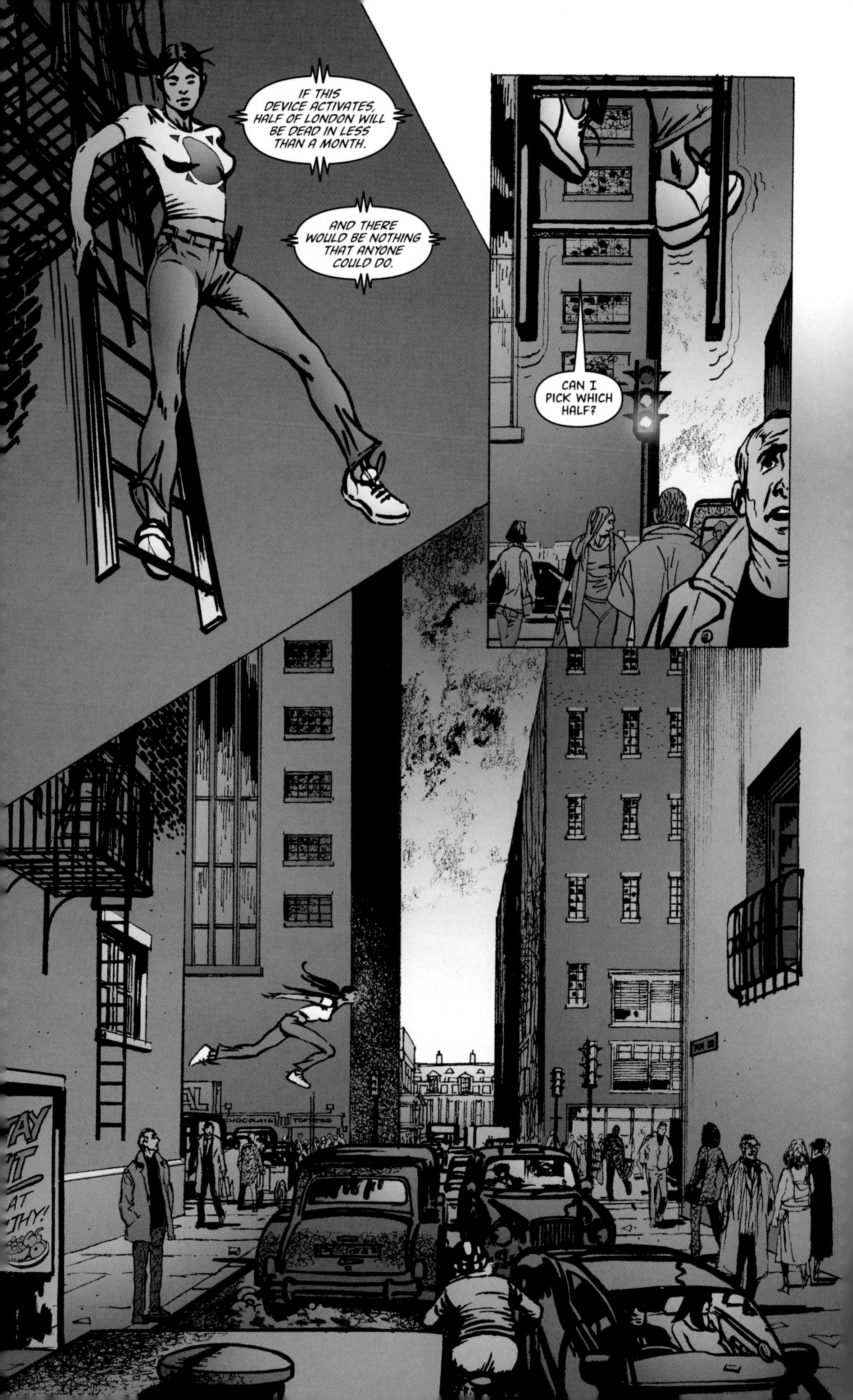
IF THIS DEVICE ACTIVATES, HALF OF LONDON WILL BE DEAD IN LESS THAN A MONTH.
AND THERE WOULD BE NOTHING THAT ANYONE COULD DO.
CAN I PICK WHICH HALF?

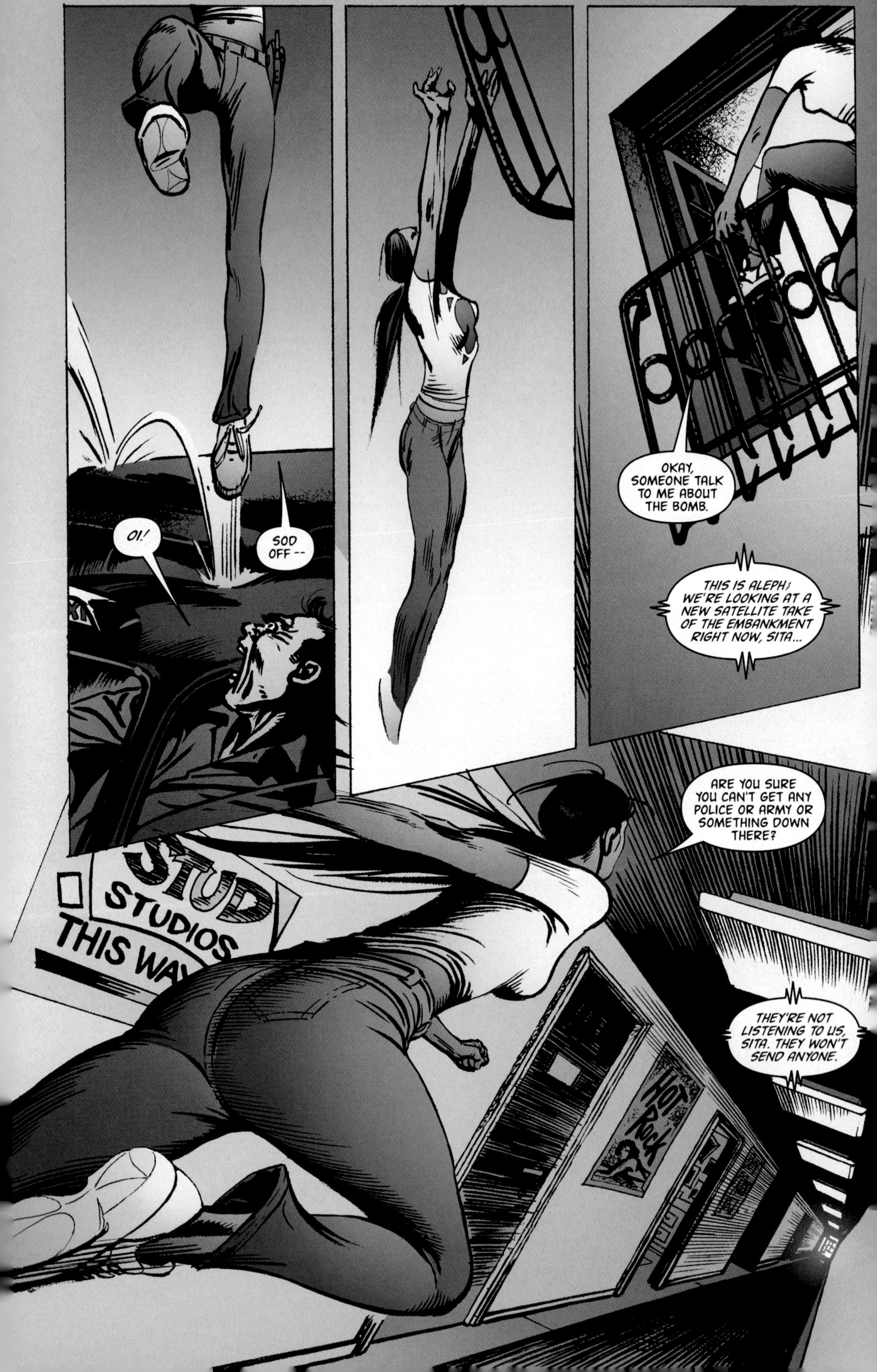
OI!
SOD OFF --
OKAY, SOMEONE TALK TO ME ABOUT THE BOMB.
THIS IS ALEPH; WE'RE LOOKING AT A NEW SATELLITE TAKE OF THE EMBANKMENT RIGHT NOW, SITA...
STUD STUDIOS THIS WA
ARE YOU SURE YOU CAN'T GET ANY POLICE OR ARMY OR SOMETHING DOWN THERE?
THEY'RE NOT LISTENING TO US, SITA. THEY WON'T SEND ANYONE.
HOT ROCK

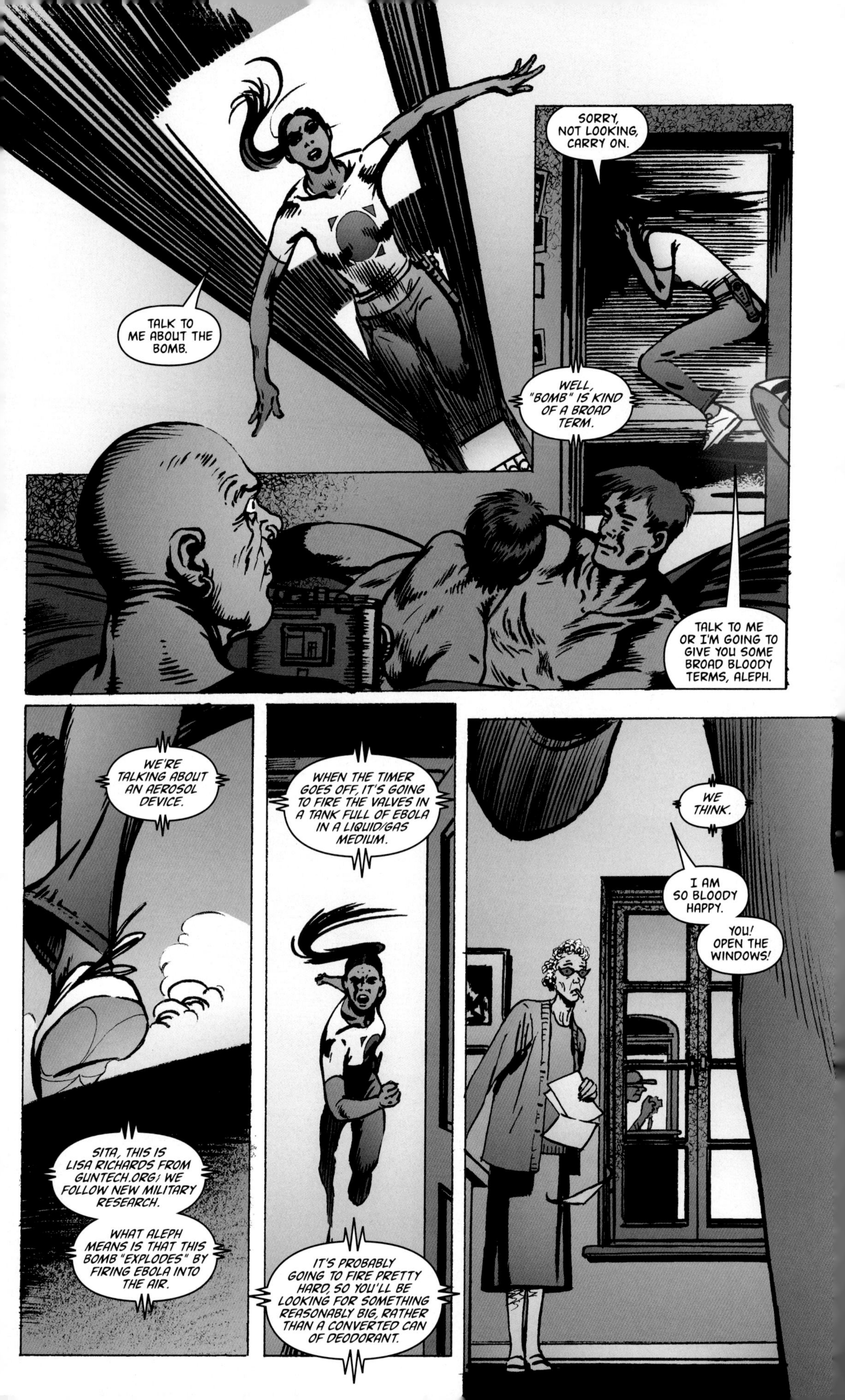
TALK TO ME ABOUT THE BOMB.
SORRY, NOT LOOKING, CARRY ON.
WELL, "BOMB" IS KIND OF A BROAD TERM.
TALK TO ME OR I'M GOING TO GIVE YOU SOME BROAD BLOODY TERMS, ALEPH.
WE'RE TALKING ABOUT AN AEROSOL DEVICE.
SITA, THIS IS LISA RICHARDS FROM GUNTECH.ORG; WE FOLLOW NEW MILITARY RESEARCH.
WHAT ALEPH MEANS IS THAT THIS BOMB "EXPLODES" BY FIRING EBOLA INTO THE AIR.
WHEN THE TIMER GOES OFF, IT'S GOING TO FIRE THE VALVES IN A TANK FULL OF EBOLA IN A LIQUID/GAS MEDIUM.
IT'S PROBABLY GOING TO FIRE PRETTY HARD, SO YOU'LL BE LOOKING FOR SOMETHING REASONABLY BIG, RATHER THAN A CONVERTED CAN OF DEODORANT.
WE THINK.
I AM SO BLOODY HAPPY.
YOU! OPEN THE WINDOWS!

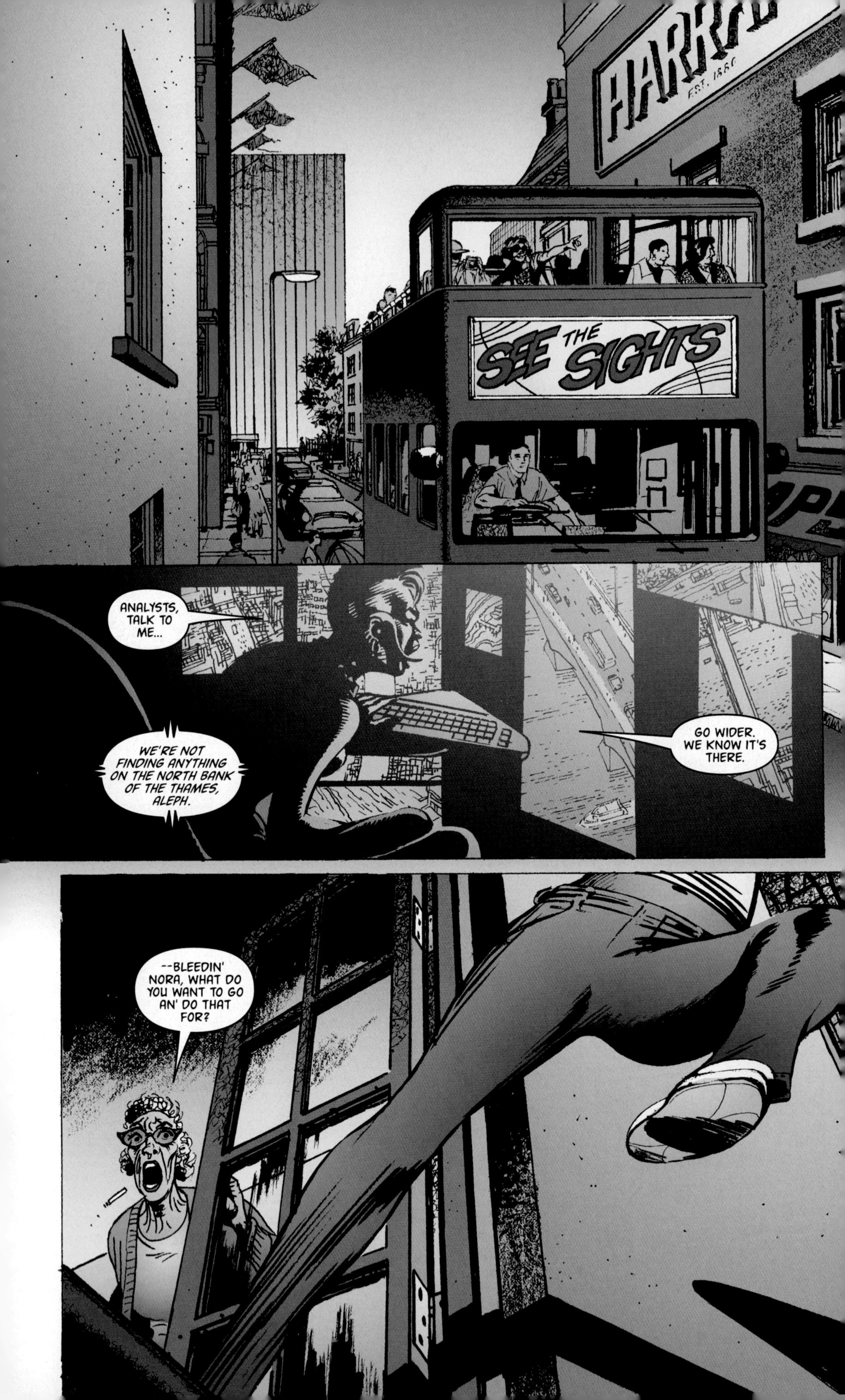
HARROD
EST. 1880
SEE THE SIGHTS
ANALYSTS, TALK TO ME...
WE'RE NOT FINDING ANYTHING ON THE NORTH BANK OF THE THAMES, ALEPH.
GO WIDER. WE KNOW IT'S THERE.
--BLEEDIN' NORA, WHAT DO YOU WANT TO GO AN' DO THAT FOR?

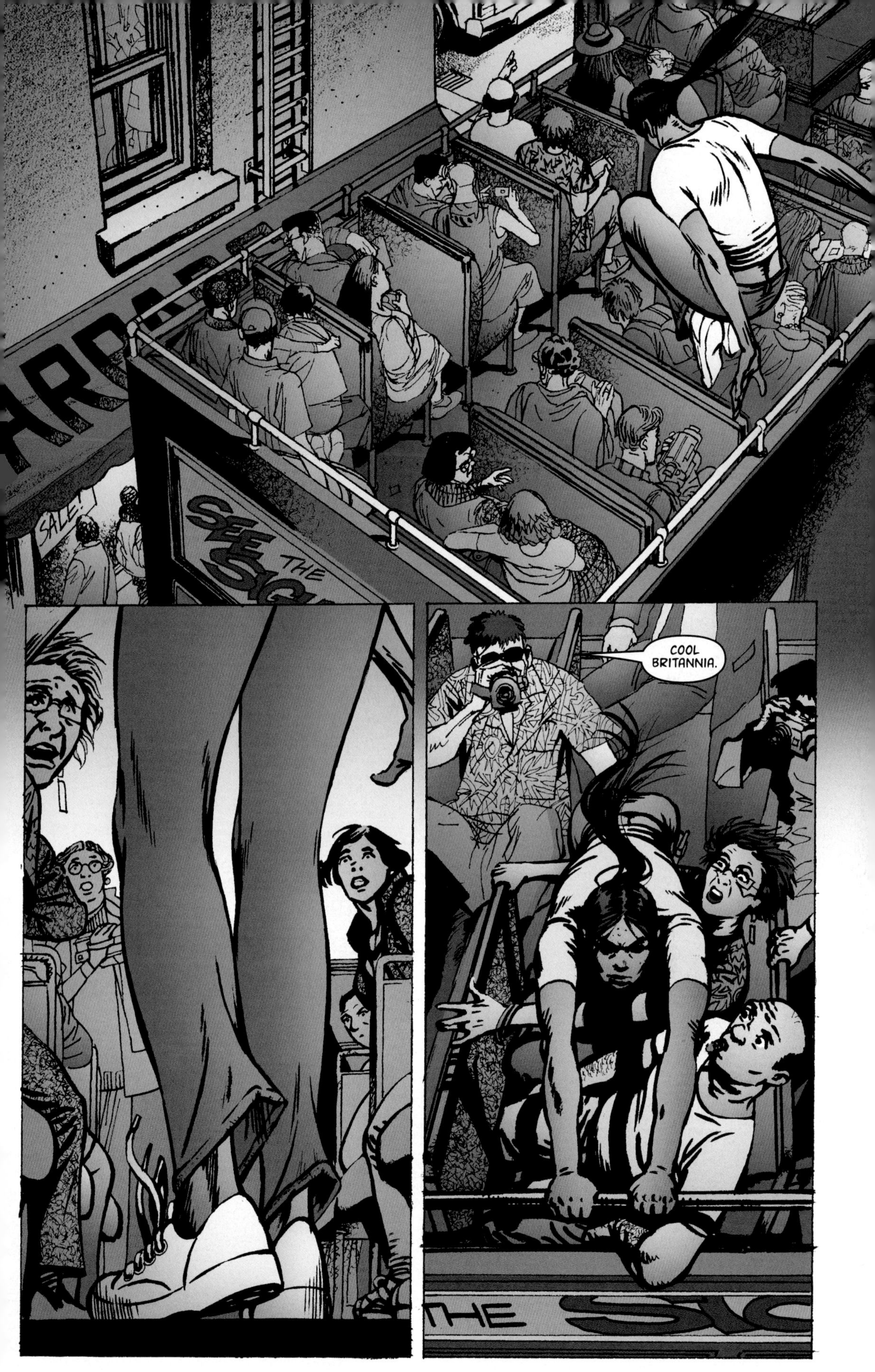
SEE THE
SALE!
COOL BRITANNIA.

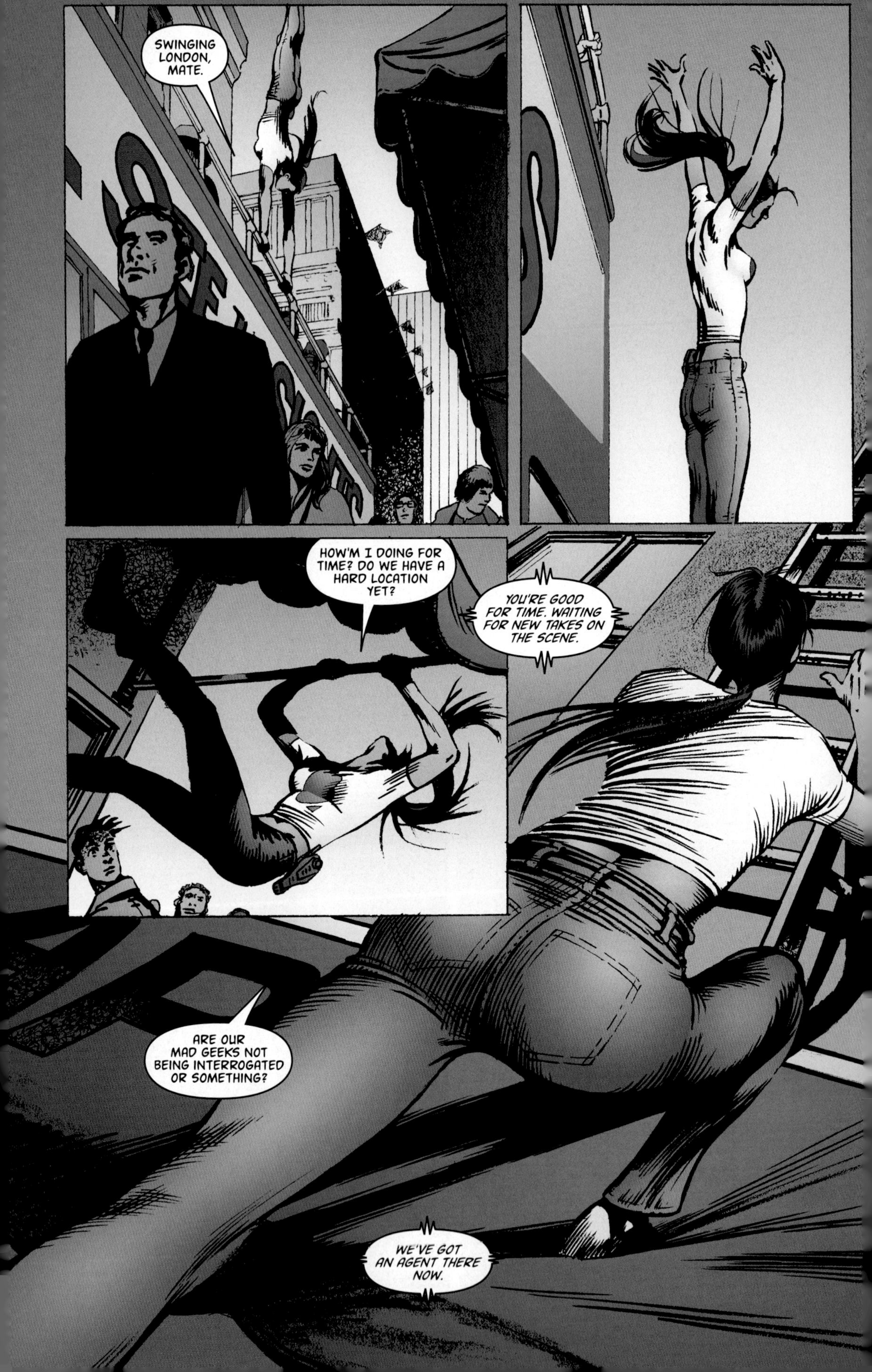
SWINGING LONDON, MATE.
HOW'M I DOING FOR TIME? DO WE HAVE A HARD LOCATION YET?
YOU'RE GOOD FOR TIME. WAITING FOR NEW TAKES ON THE SCENE.
ARE OUR MAD GEEKS NOT BEING INTERROGATED OR SOMETHING?
WE'VE GOT AN AGENT THERE NOW.

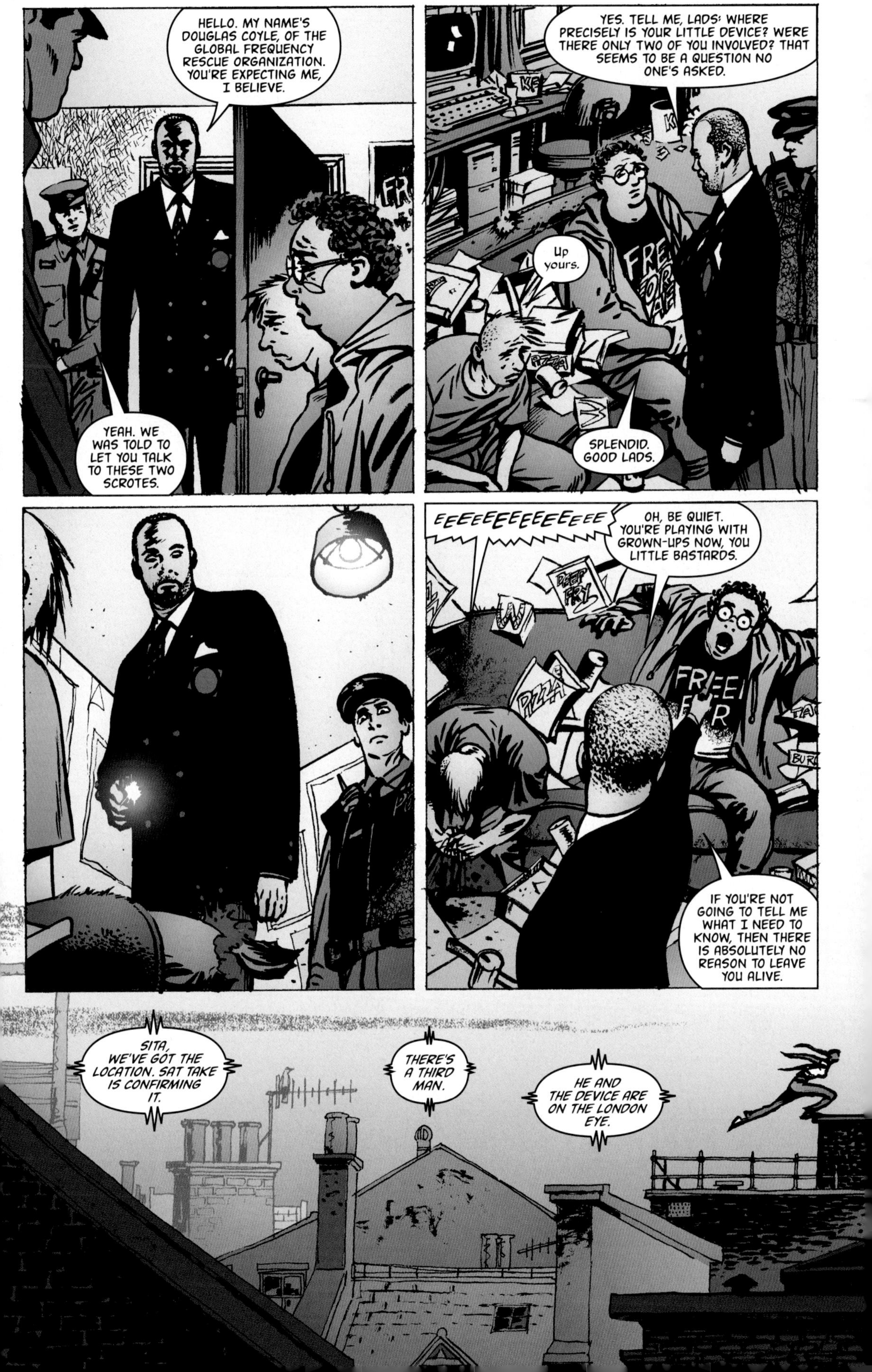
HELLO. MY NAME'S DOUGLAS COYLE, OF THE GLOBAL FREQUENCY RESCUE ORGANIZATION. YOU'RE EXPECTING ME, I BELIEVE.
YEAH. WE WAS TOLD TO LET YOU TALK TO THESE TWO SCROTES.
YES. TELL ME, LADS: WHERE PRECISELY IS YOUR LITTLE DEVICE? WERE THERE ONLY TWO OF YOU INVOLVED? THAT SEEMS TO BE A QUESTION NO ONE'S ASKED.
Up yours.
SPLENDID. GOOD LADS.
EEEEEEEEEEEEEE
OH, BE QUIET. YOU'RE PLAYING WITH GROWN-UPS NOW, YOU LITTLE BASTARDS.
IF YOU'RE NOT GOING TO TELL ME WHAT I NEED TO KNOW, THEN THERE IS ABSOLUTELY NO REASON TO LEAVE YOU ALIVE.
SITA, WE'VE GOT THE LOCATION. SAT TAKE IS CONFIRMING IT.
THERE'S A THIRD MAN.
HE AND THE DEVICE ARE ON THE LONDON EYE.

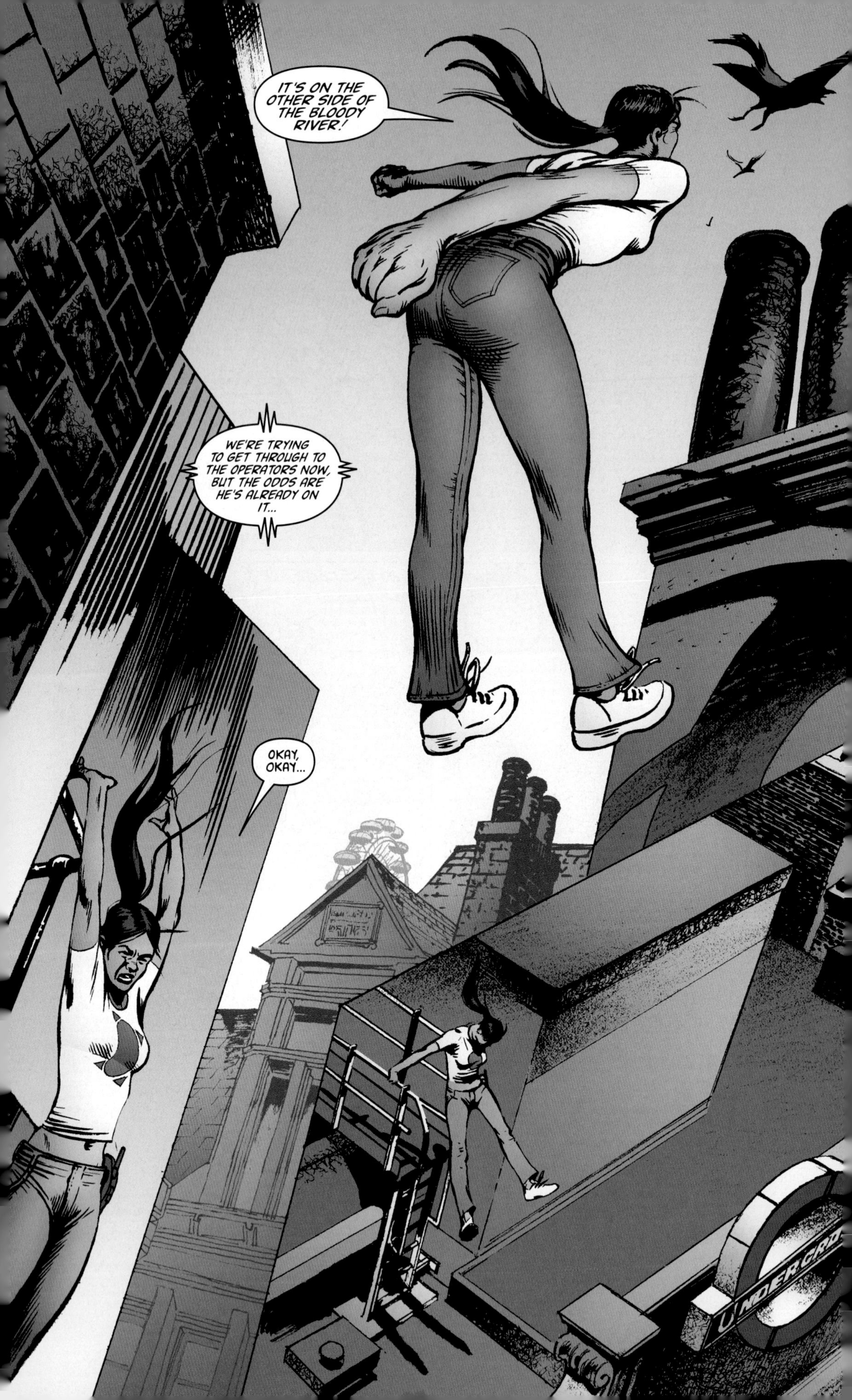
IT'S ON THE OTHER SIDE OF THE BLOODY RIVER!
WE'RE TRYING TO GET THROUGH TO THE OPERATORS NOW, BUT THE ODDS ARE HE'S ALREADY ON IT...
OKAY, OKAY...

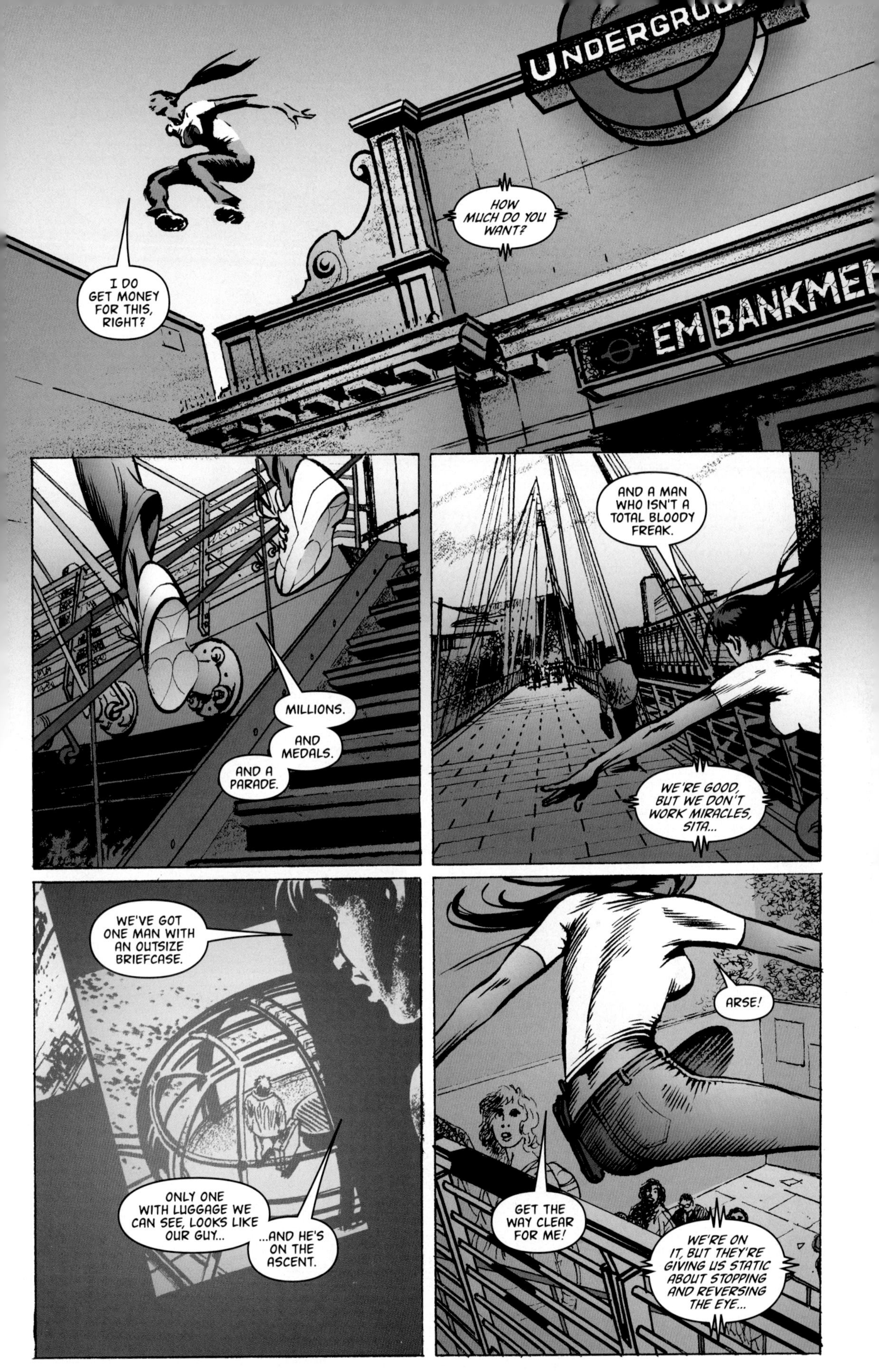
UNDERGROU
EMBANKME
I DO GET MONEY FOR THIS, RIGHT?
HOW MUCH DO YOU WANT?
MILLIONS.
AND MEDALS.
AND A PARADE.
AND A MAN WHO ISN'T A TOTAL BLOODY FREAK.
WE'RE GOOD, BUT WE DON'T WORK MIRACLES, SITA...
WE'VE GOT ONE MAN WITH AN OUTSIZE BRIEFCASE.
ONLY ONE WITH LUGGAGE WE CAN SEE, LOOKS LIKE OUR GUY...
...AND HE'S ON THE ASCENT.
ARSE!
GET THE WAY CLEAR FOR ME!
WE'RE ON IT, BUT THEY'RE GIVING US STATIC ABOUT STOPPING AND REVERSING THE EYE...

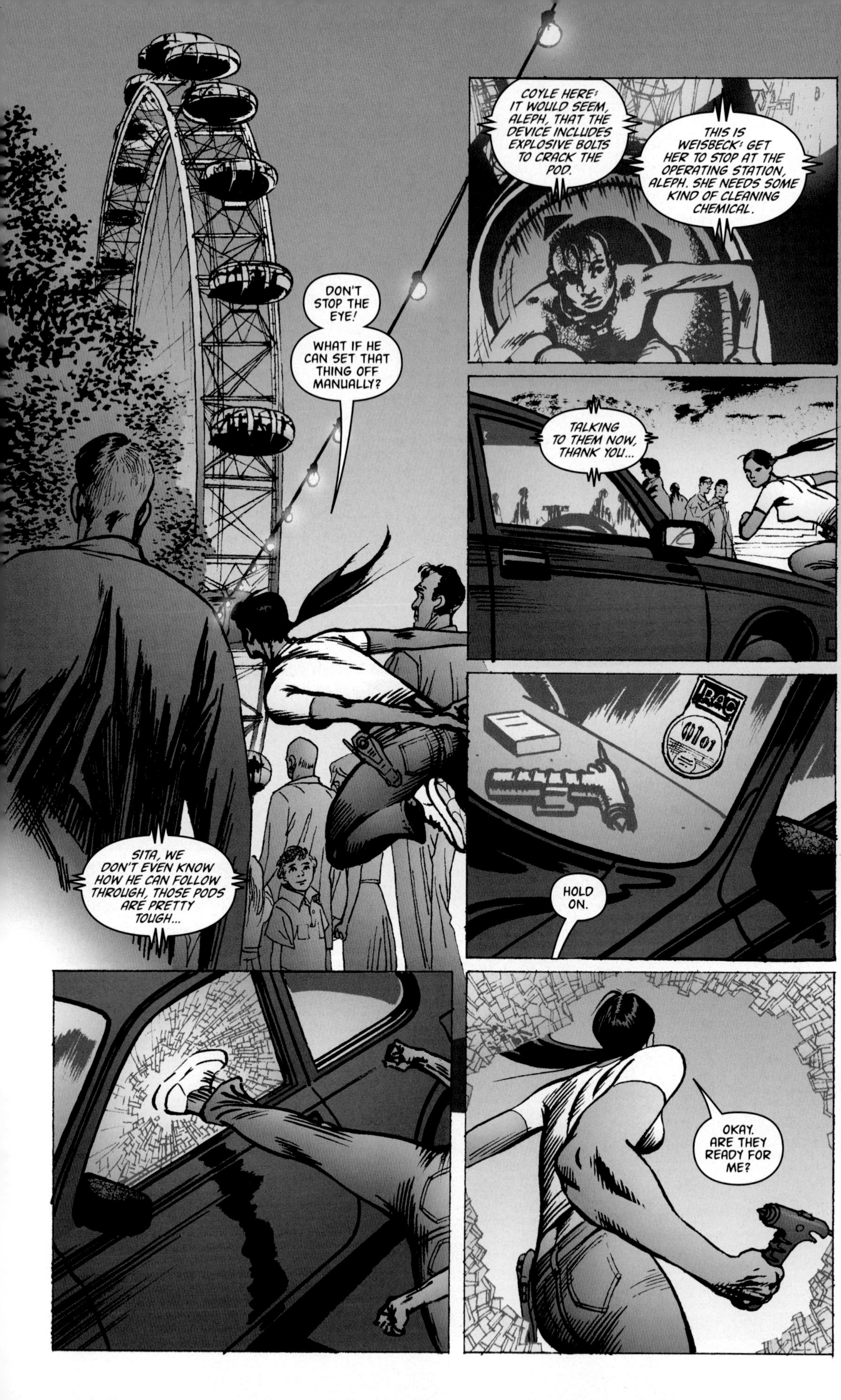

DON'T STOP THE EYE!
WHAT IF HE CAN SET THAT THING OFF MANUALLY?
SITA, WE DON'T EVEN KNOW HOW HE CAN FOLLOW THROUGH, THOSE PODS ARE PRETTY TOUGH...
COYLE HERE: IT WOULD SEEM, ALEPH, THAT THE DEVICE INCLUDES EXPLOSIVE BOLTS TO CRACK THE POD.
THIS IS WEISBECK: GET HER TO STOP AT THE OPERATING STATION, ALEPH. SHE NEEDS SOME KIND OF CLEANING CHEMICAL.
TALKING TO THEM NOW, THANK YOU...
RAC
HOLD ON.
OKAY. ARE THEY READY FOR ME?

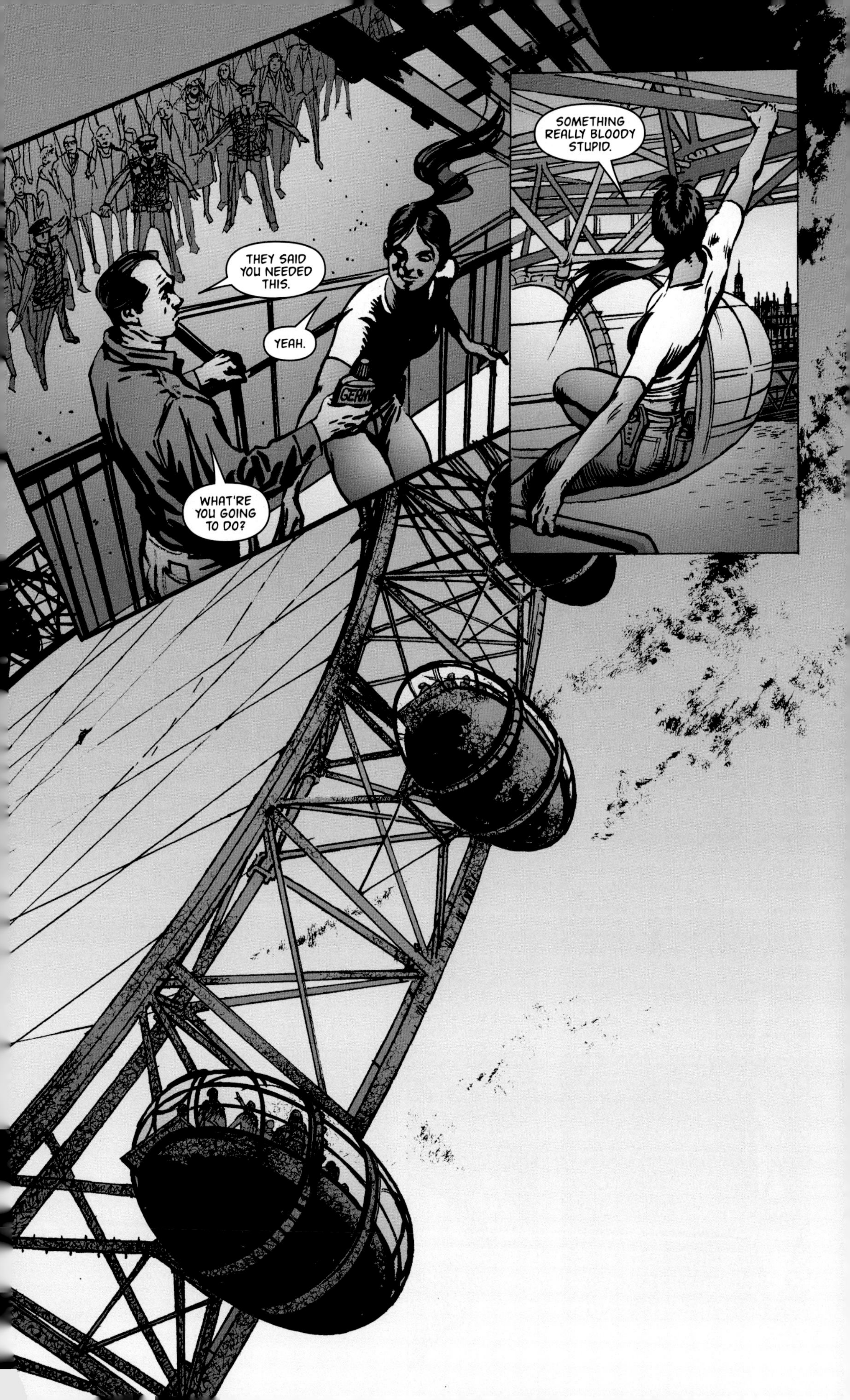
THEY SAID YOU NEEDED THIS.
YEAH.
WHAT'RE YOU GOING TO DO?
SOMETHING REALLY BLOODY STUPID.

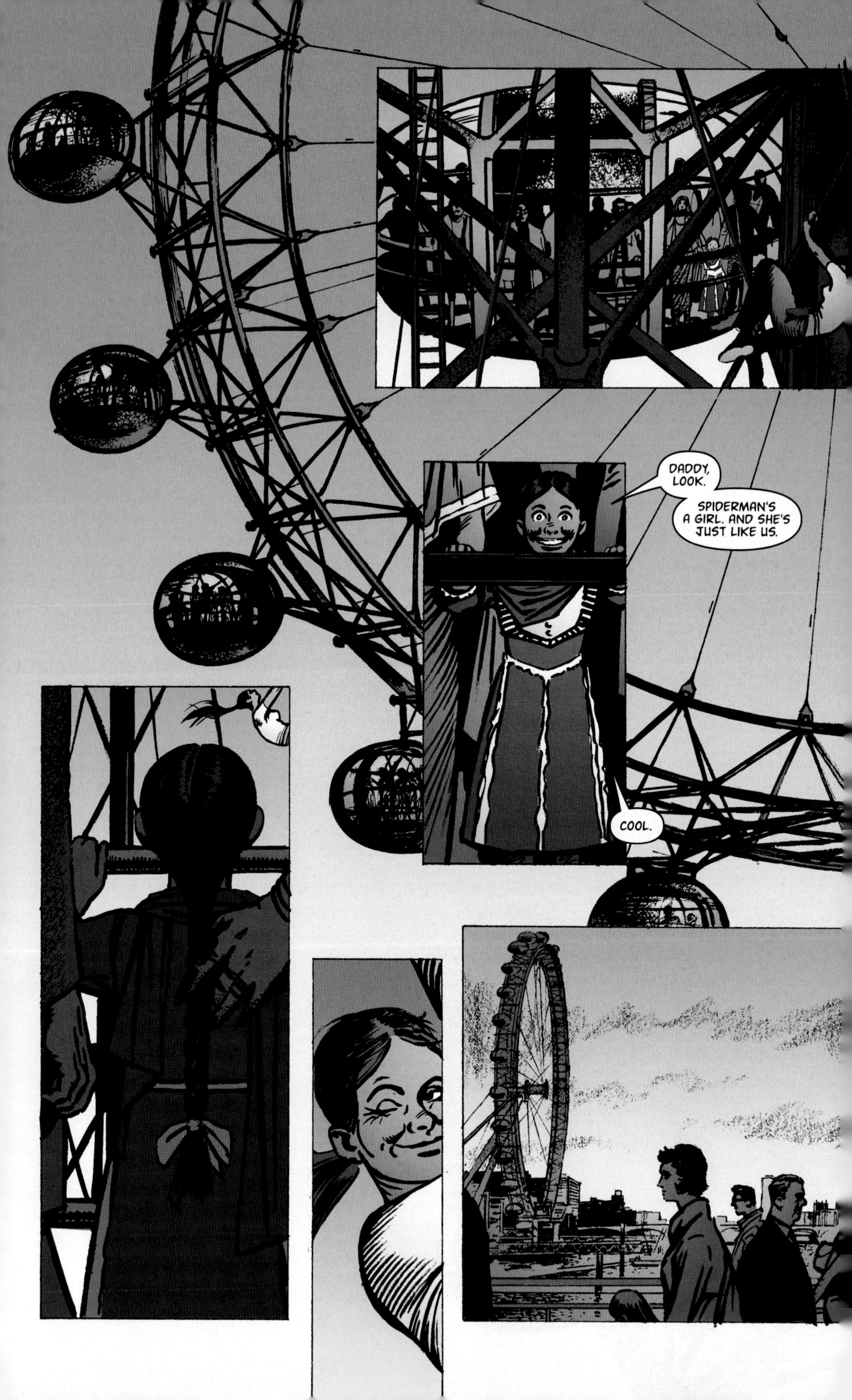
DADDY, LOOK.
SPIDERMAN'S A GIRL. AND SHE'S JUST LIKE US.
COOL.

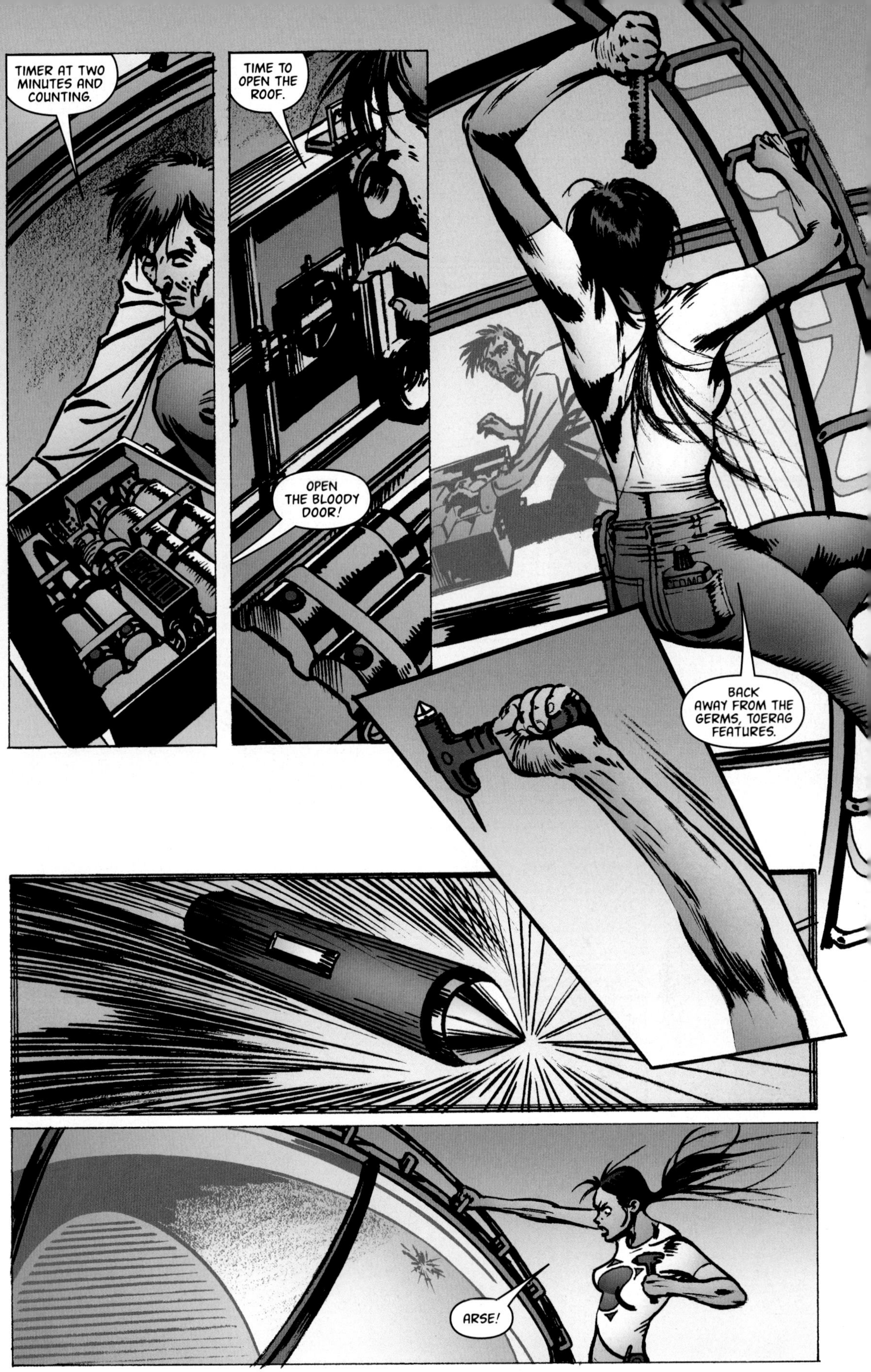

TIMER AT TWO MINUTES AND COUNTING.
TIME TO OPEN THE ROOF.
OPEN THE BLOODY DOOR!
BACK AWAY FROM THE GERMS, TOERAG FEATURES.
ARSE!

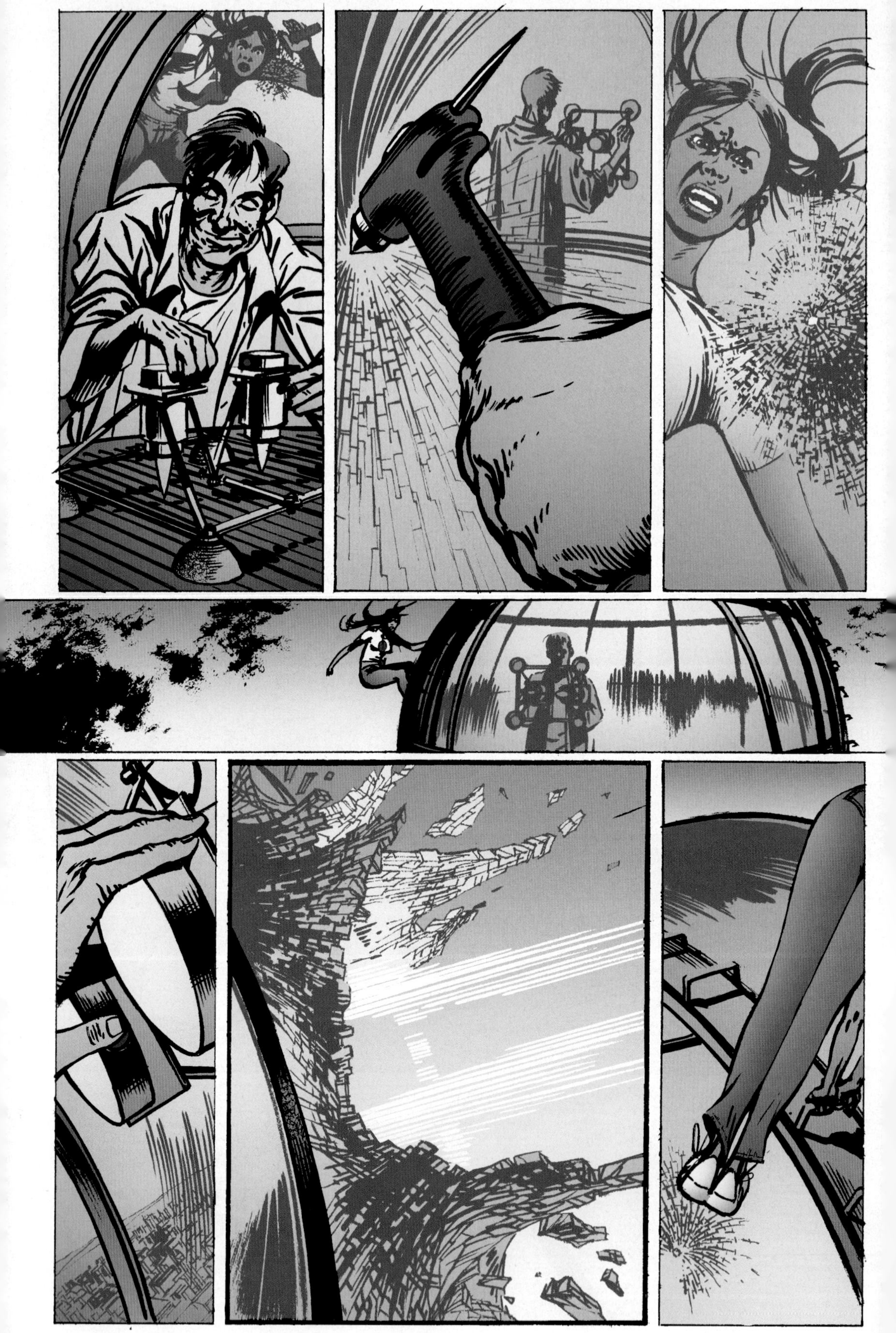

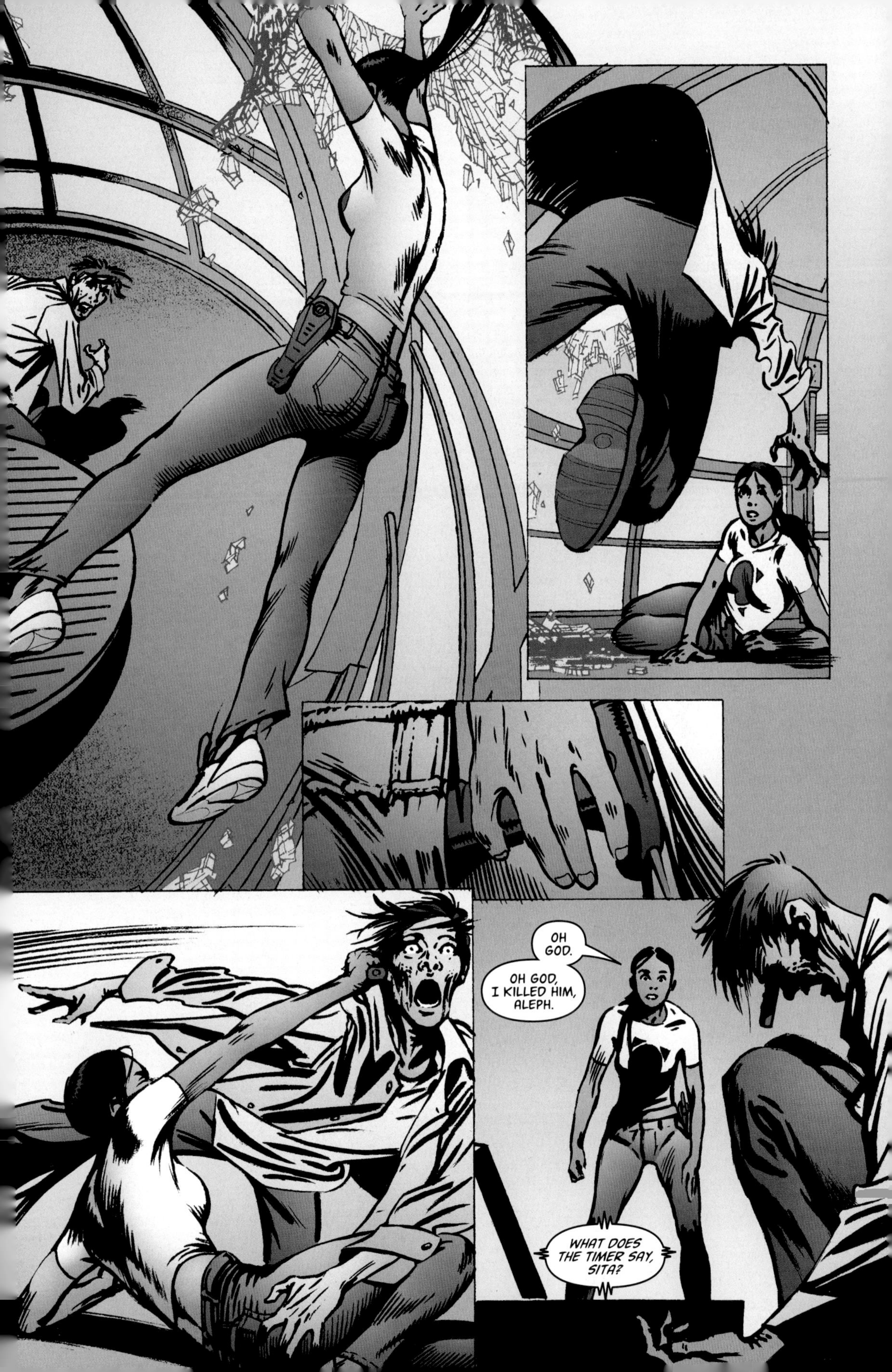
OH GOD.
OH GOD, I KILLED HIM, ALEPH.
WHAT DOES THE TIMER SAY, SITA?

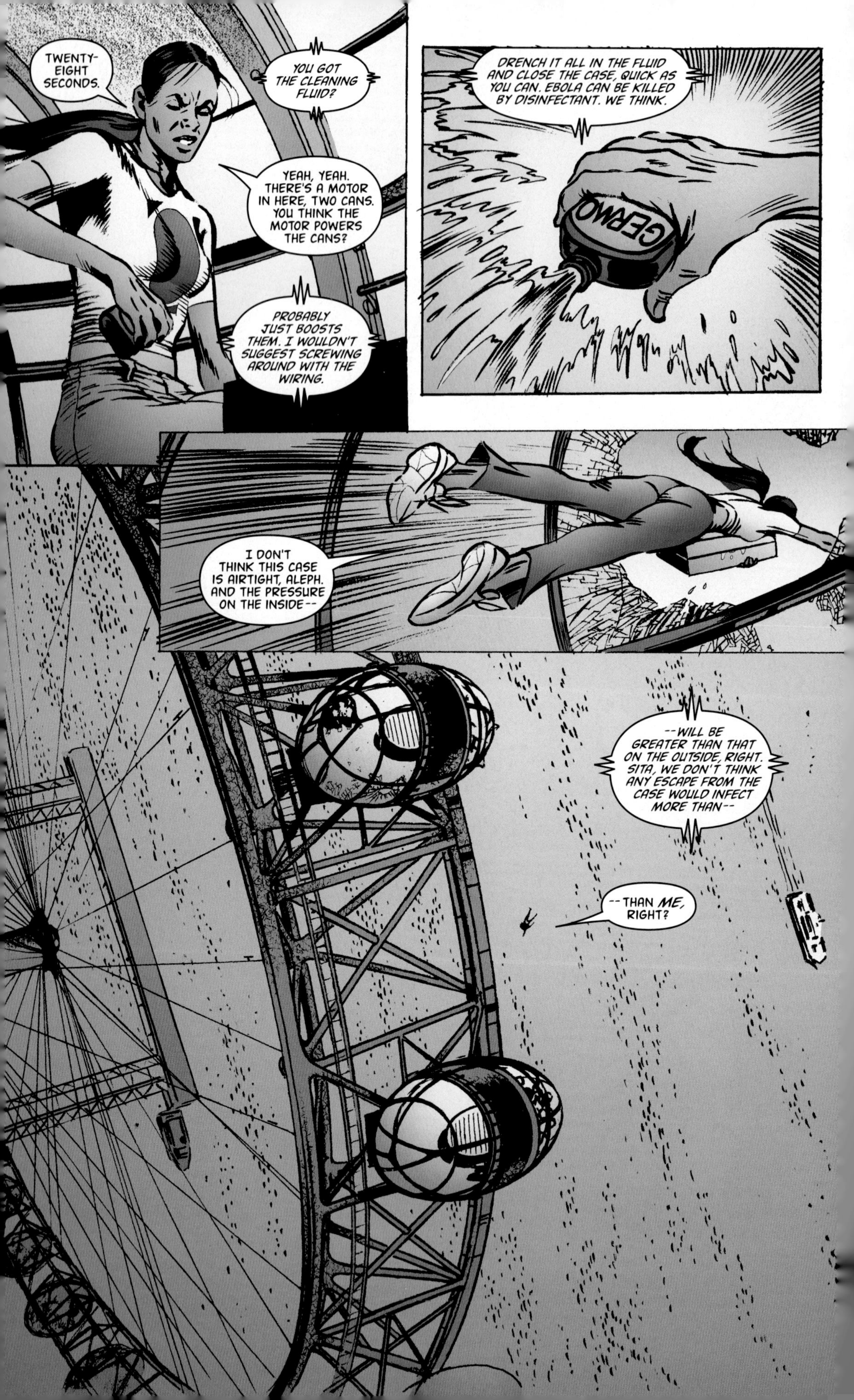
TWENTY-EIGHT SECONDS.
YOU GOT THE CLEANING FLUID?
YEAH, YEAH. THERE'S A MOTOR IN HERE, TWO CANS. YOU THINK THE MOTOR POWERS THE CANS?
PROBABLY JUST BOOSTS THEM. I WOULDN'T SUGGEST SCREWING AROUND WITH THE WIRING.
DRENCH IT ALL IN THE FLUID AND CLOSE THE CASE, QUICK AS YOU CAN. EBOLA CAN BE KILLED BY DISINFECTANT. WE THINK.
GERMO
I DON'T THINK THIS CASE IS AIRTIGHT, ALEPH. AND THE PRESSURE ON THE INSIDE--
--WILL BE GREATER THAN THAT ON THE OUTSIDE, RIGHT. SITA, WE DON'T THINK ANY ESCAPE FROM THE CASE WOULD INFECT MORE THAN--
--THAN ME, RIGHT?

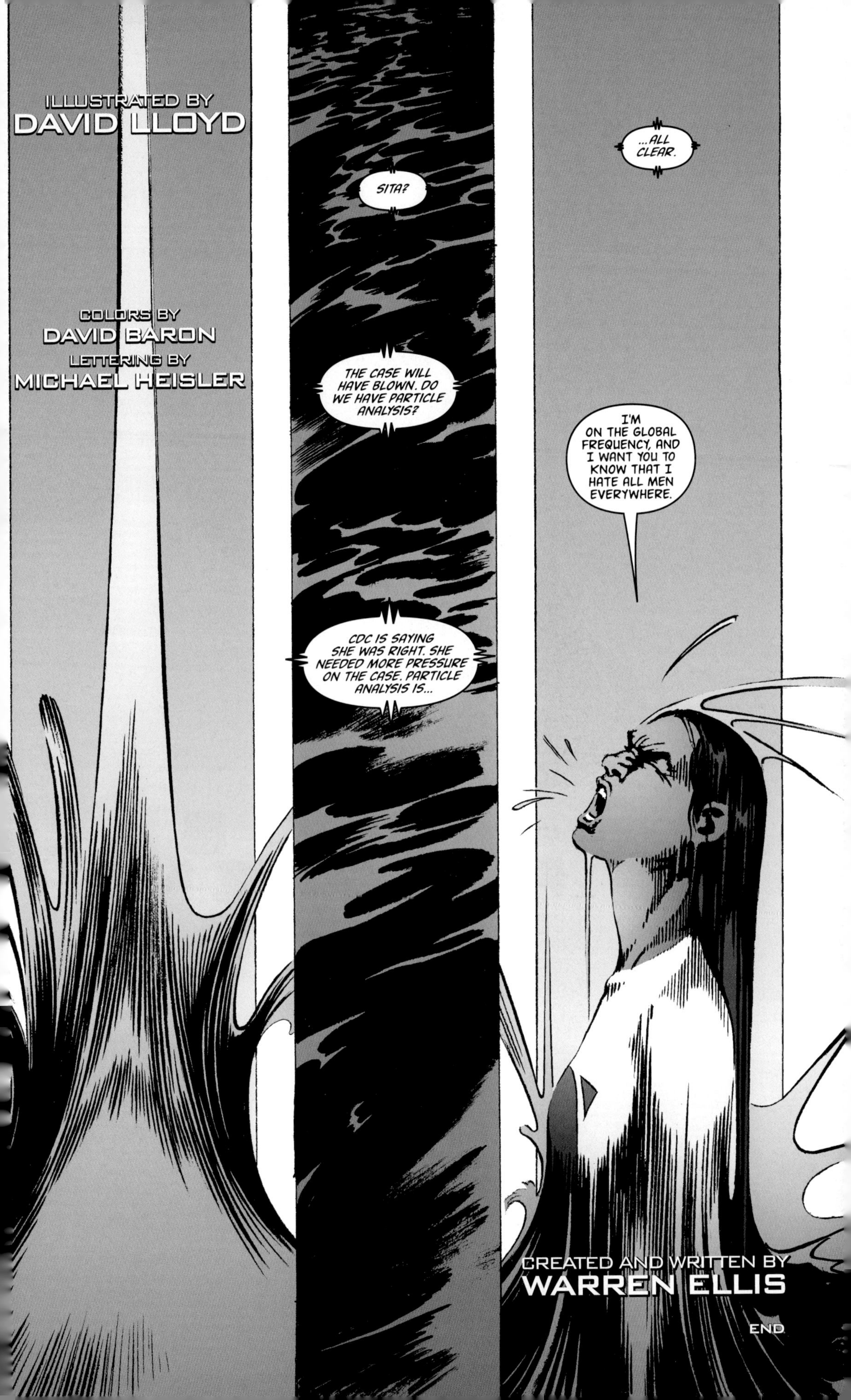
ILLUSTRATED BY
DAVID LLOYD
COLORS BY
DAVID BARON
LETTERING BY
MICHAEL HEISLER
SITA?
THE CASE WILL HAVE BLOWN. DO WE HAVE PARTICLE ANALYSIS?
CDC IS SAYING SHE WAS RIGHT. SHE NEEDED MORE PRESSURE ON THE CASE. PARTICLE ANALYSIS IS...
...ALL CLEAR.
I'M ON THE GLOBAL FREQUENCY, AND I WANT YOU TO KNOW THAT I HATE ALL MEN EVERYWHERE.
CREATED AND WRITTEN BY
WARREN ELLIS
END

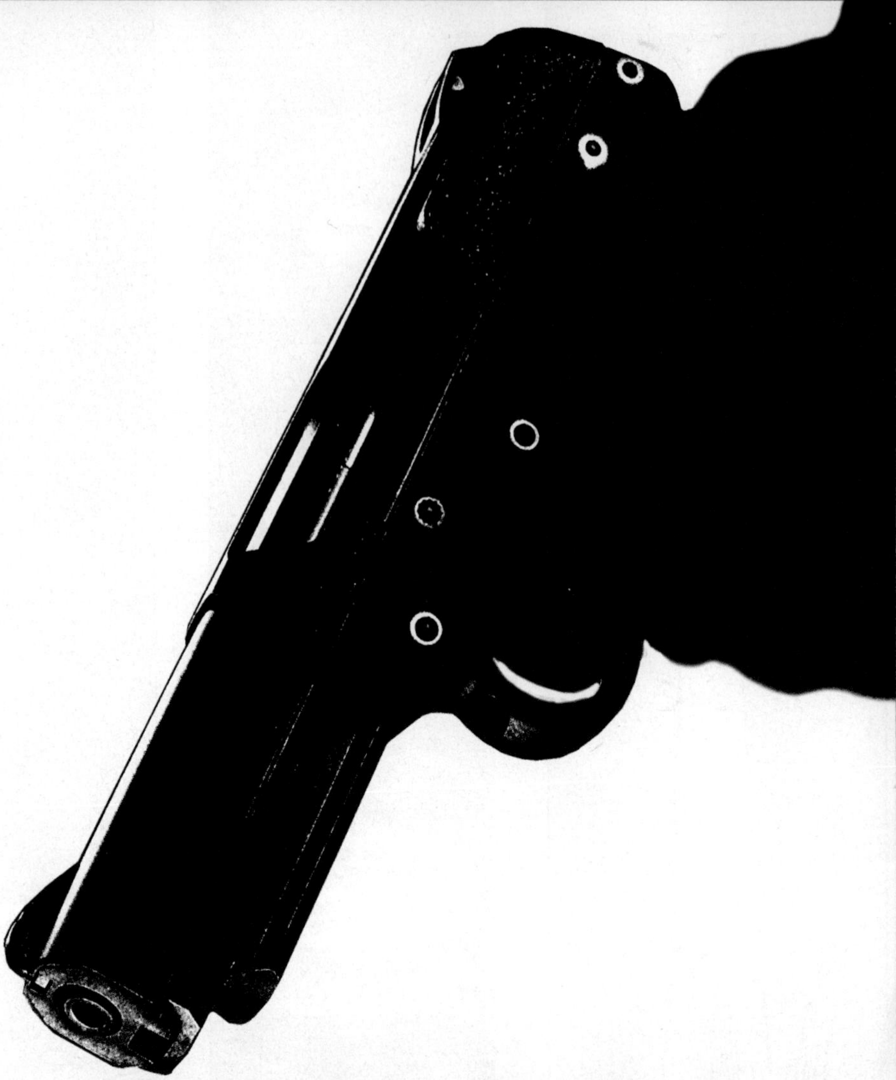

ARE YOU ON THE **GLOBAL FREQUENCY?**

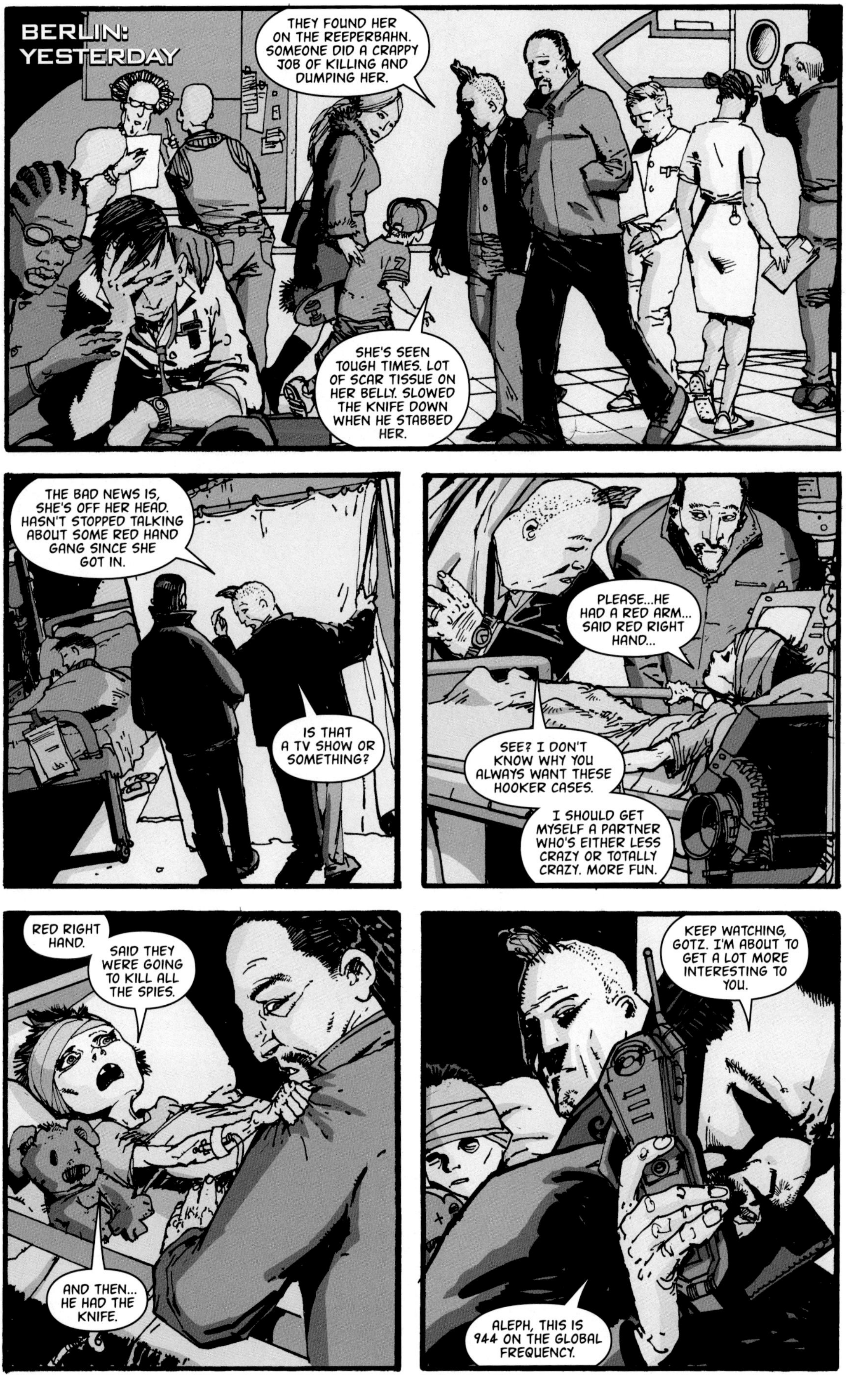
BERLIN: YESTERDAY
THEY FOUND HER ON THE REEPERBAHN. SOMEONE DID A CRAPPY JOB OF KILLING AND DUMPING HER.
SHE'S SEEN TOUGH TIMES. LOT OF SCAR TISSUE ON HER BELLY. SLOWED THE KNIFE DOWN WHEN HE STABBED HER.
THE BAD NEWS IS, SHE'S OFF HER HEAD. HASN'T STOPPED TALKING ABOUT SOME RED HAND GANG SINCE SHE GOT IN.
IS THAT A TV SHOW OR SOMETHING?
PLEASE...HE HAD A RED ARM... SAID RED RIGHT HAND...
SEE? I DON'T KNOW WHY YOU ALWAYS WANT THESE HOOKER CASES.
I SHOULD GET MYSELF A PARTNER WHO'S EITHER LESS CRAZY OR TOTALLY CRAZY. MORE FUN.
RED RIGHT HAND.
SAID THEY WERE GOING TO KILL ALL THE SPIES.
AND THEN... HE HAD THE KNIFE.
KEEP WATCHING, GOTZ. I'M ABOUT TO GET A LOT MORE INTERESTING TO YOU.
ALEPH, THIS IS 944 ON THE GLOBAL FREQUENCY.

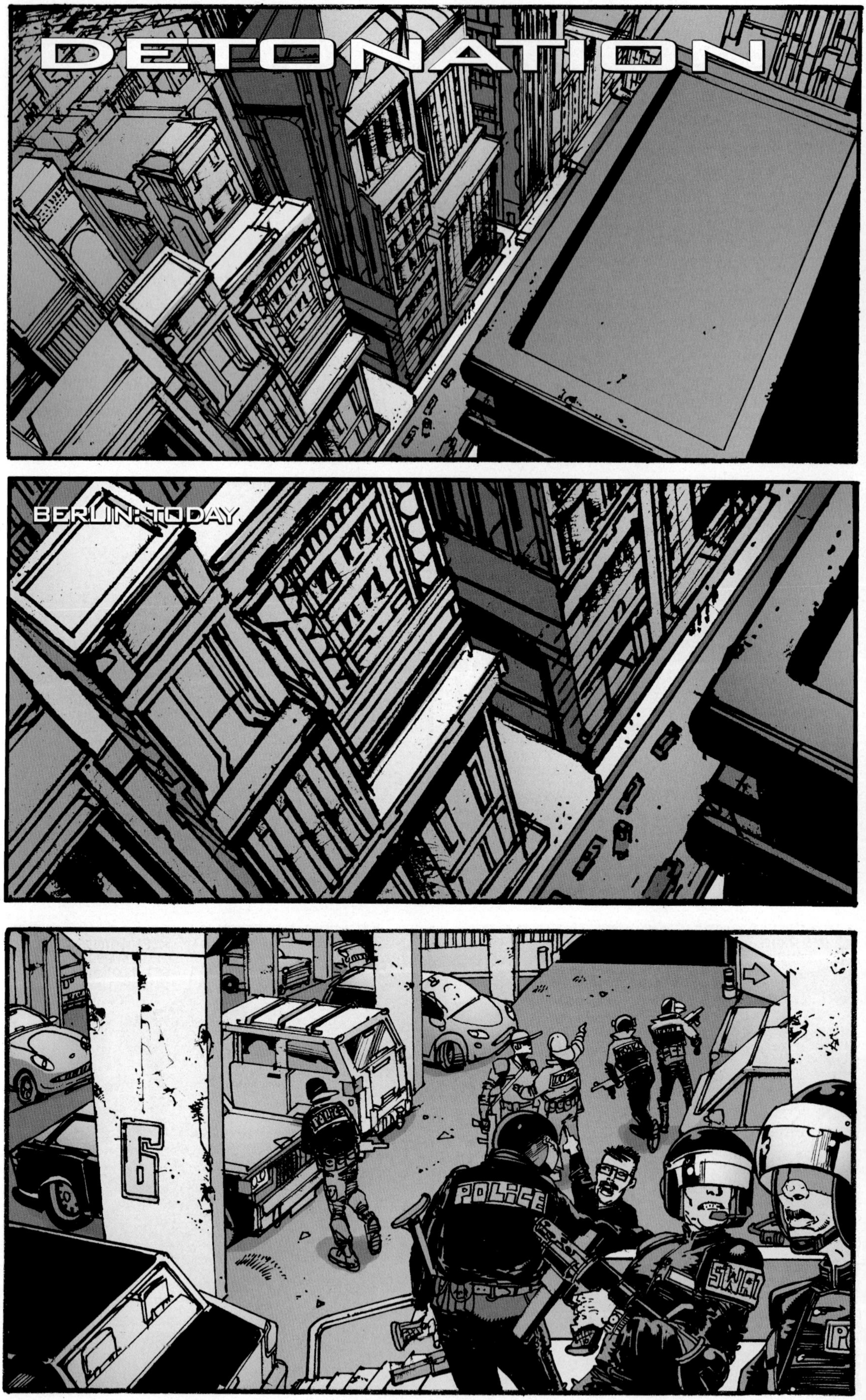
DETONATION
BERLIN: TODAY
6
POLICE
SWAT

MR. GERRARD.

MY NAME IS MIRANDA ZERO. AND YOU'RE ON THE GLOBAL FREQUENCY.

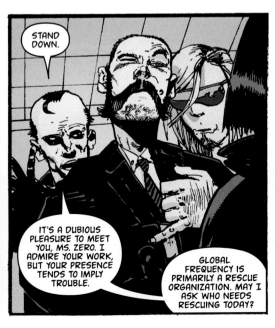

STAND DOWN.

IT'S A DUBIOUS PLEASURE TO MEET YOU, MS. ZERO. I ADMIRE YOUR WORK, BUT YOUR PRESENCE TENDS TO IMPLY TROUBLE.

GLOBAL FREQUENCY IS PRIMARILY A RESCUE ORGANIZATION. MAY I ASK WHO NEEDS RESCUING TODAY?

YOU.

YOU'VE BEEN MEETING HERE TODAY, IN YOUR ROLE AS DIRECTOR OF MI6, WITH THE GERMAN AND RUSSIAN SECRET SERVICES.

THE MEETING WAS REGARDING SUPPOSED INTELLIGENCE INCURSIONS BY CHINA AND NORTH KOREA.

THESE INCURSIONS WERE FALSIFIED. YOU WERE BROUGHT HERE SO THAT YOU CAN ALL BE KILLED.

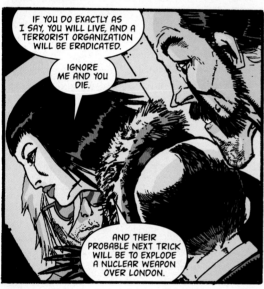

IF YOU DO EXACTLY AS I SAY, YOU WILL LIVE, AND A TERRORIST ORGANIZATION WILL BE ERADICATED.

IGNORE ME AND YOU DIE.

AND THEIR PROBABLE NEXT TRICK WILL BE TO EXPLODE A NUCLEAR WEAPON OVER LONDON.

HOW MANY OF YOUR TEAM ARE HERE? THEY ALWAYS SAY THAT THERE ARE A THOUSAND AND ONE AGENTS ON THE GLOBAL FREQUENCY.

WE HAVE... ENOUGH. TWO OF THEM HAVE BEEN WATCHING YOUR ENTIRE PROTECTION OPERATION DOWN HERE.

COME ON IN.

MR. GRUSHKO IS A SPECIALIST FROM RUSSIA. MS. LAU IS A SPECIALIST FROM CHINA.

I'M AWARE OF THE YOUNG LADY. THE LAM CASE IN KOWLOON. BUT YOU, MR. GRUSHKO...?

DID YOU EVER HAVE A NIGHTMARE ABOUT A LARGE MAN WHO KILLED YOUR PARENTS, AND YOUR SIBLINGS, AND THEN YOUR LOVER, AND THEN EVERYONE YOU KNOW?

AND THEN BURNED YOUR HOUSE DOWN AND DESTROYED EVERYTHING PRECIOUS YOU EVER CONCEIVED OF?

THAT WAS ME.

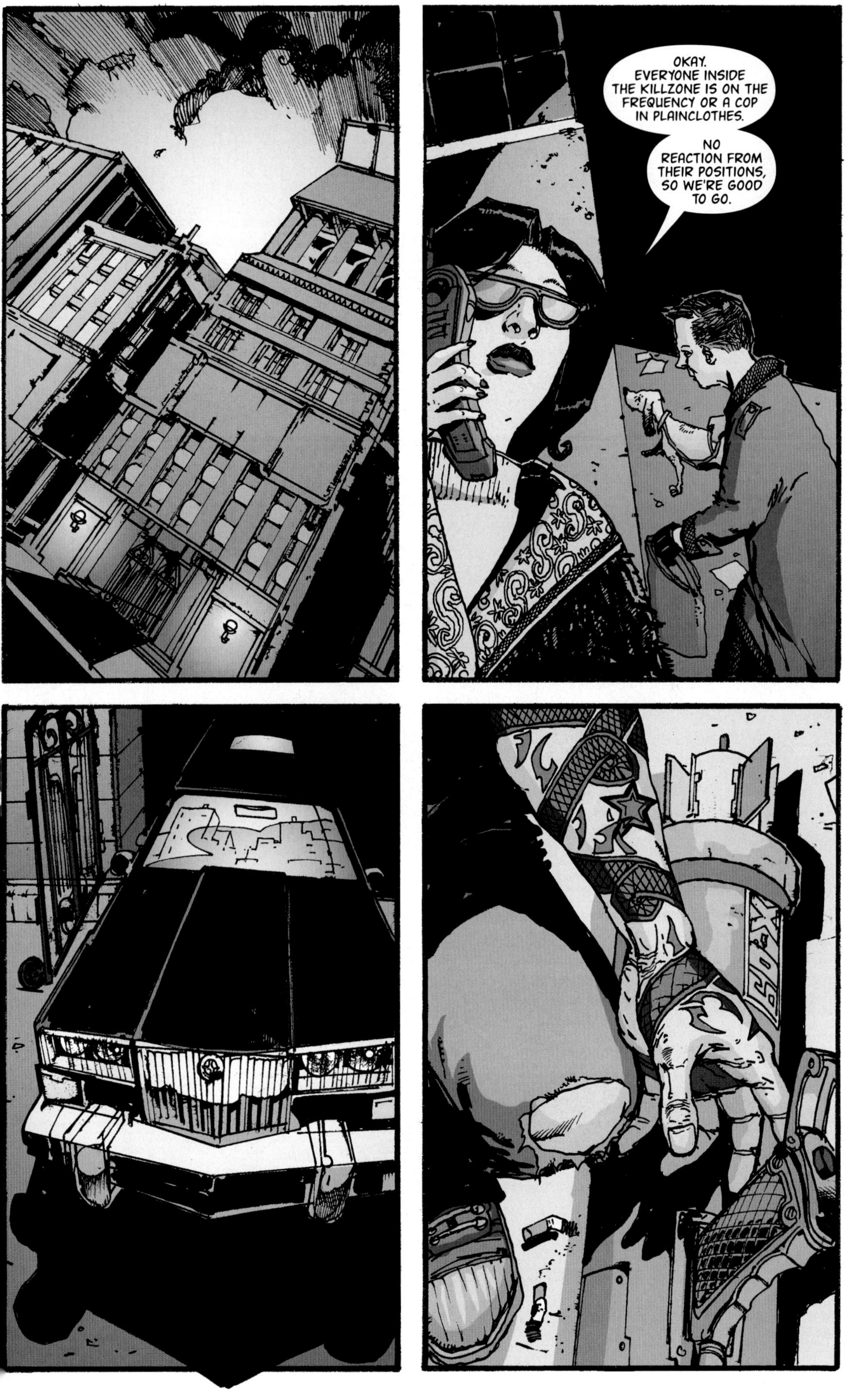
OKAY. EVERYONE INSIDE THE KILLZONE IS ON THE FREQUENCY OR A COP IN PLAINCLOTHES.
NO REACTION FROM THEIR POSITIONS, SO WE'RE GOOD TO GO.

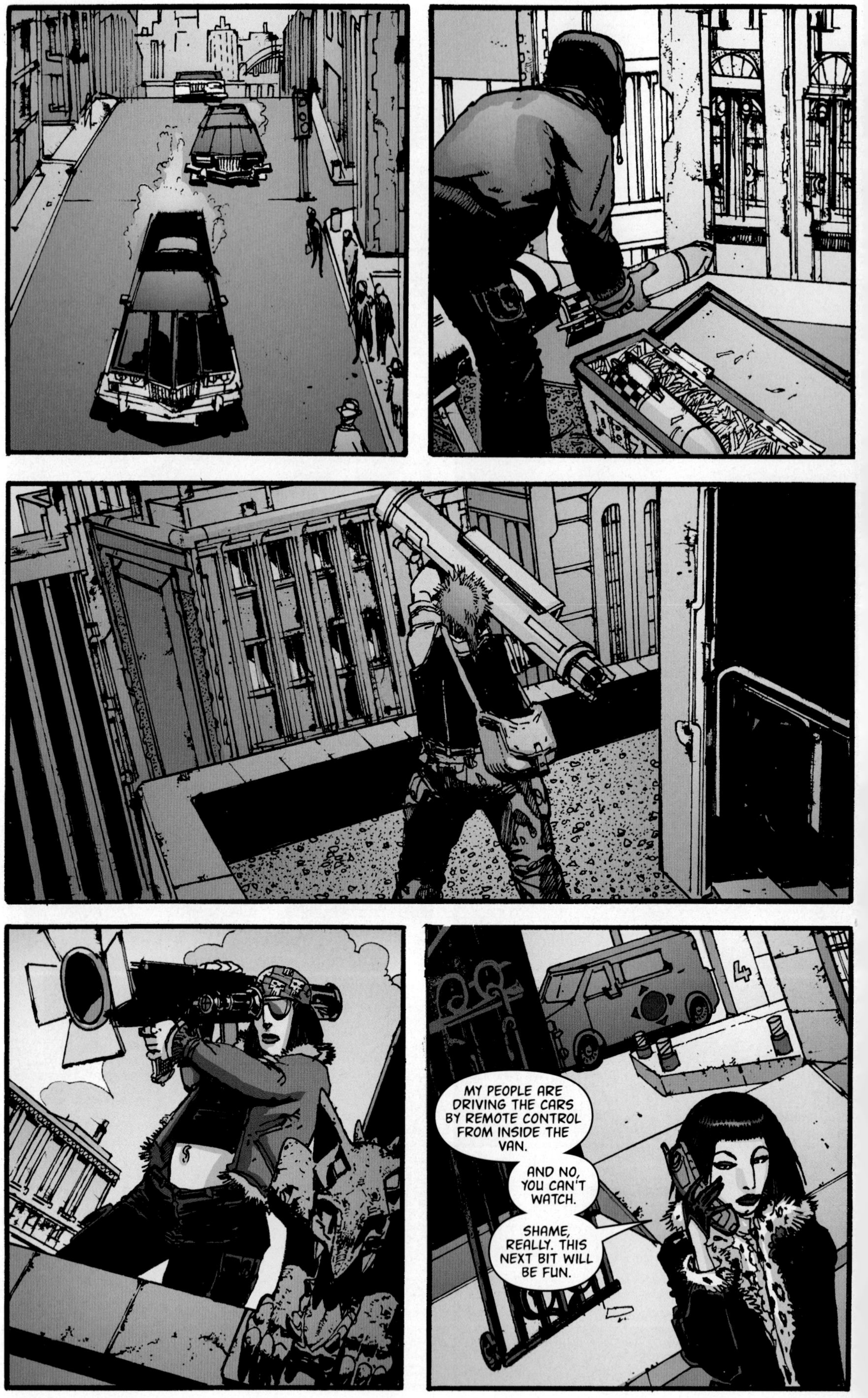
MY PEOPLE ARE DRIVING THE CARS BY REMOTE CONTROL FROM INSIDE THE VAN.
AND NO, YOU CAN'T WATCH.
SHAME, REALLY. THIS NEXT BIT WILL BE FUN.

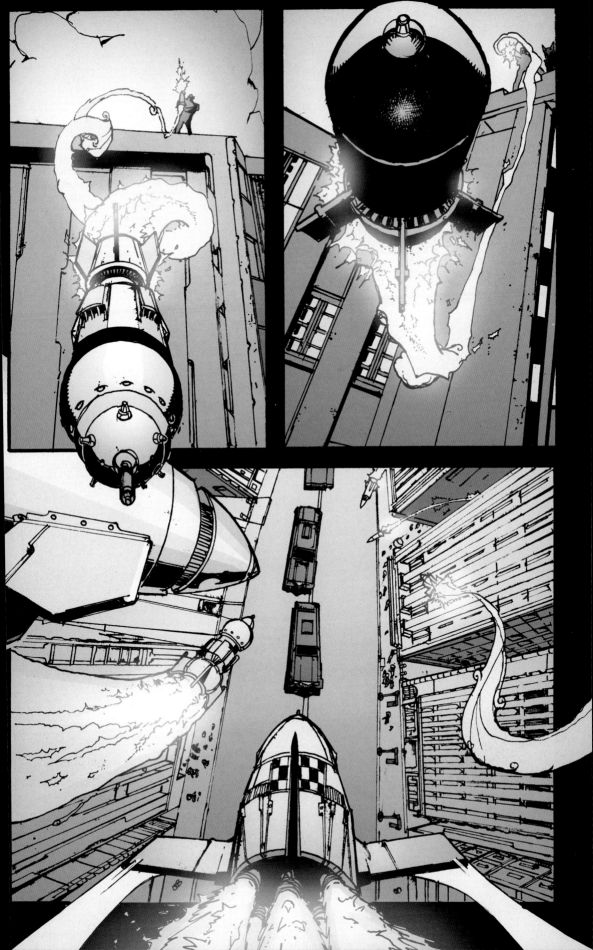

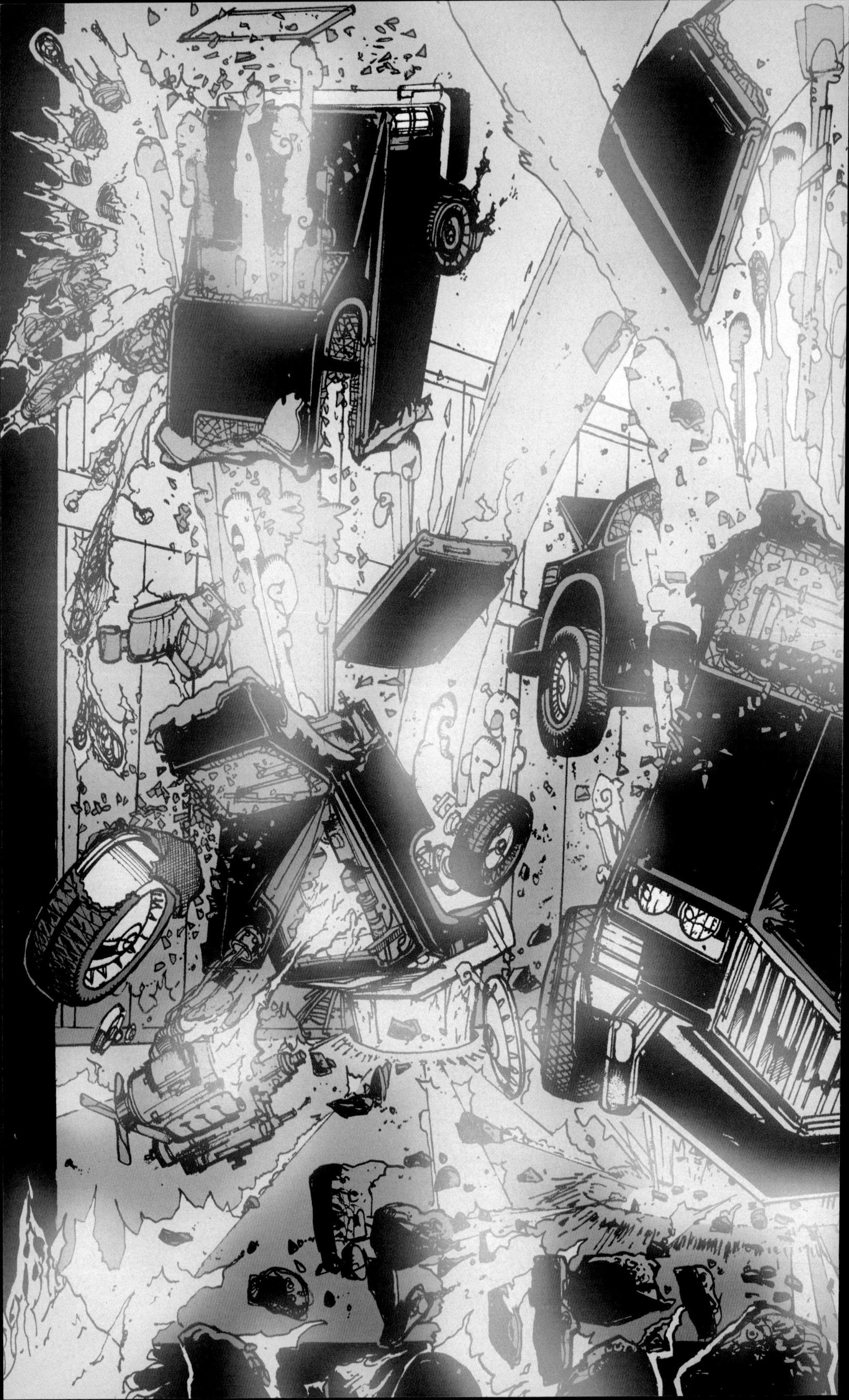

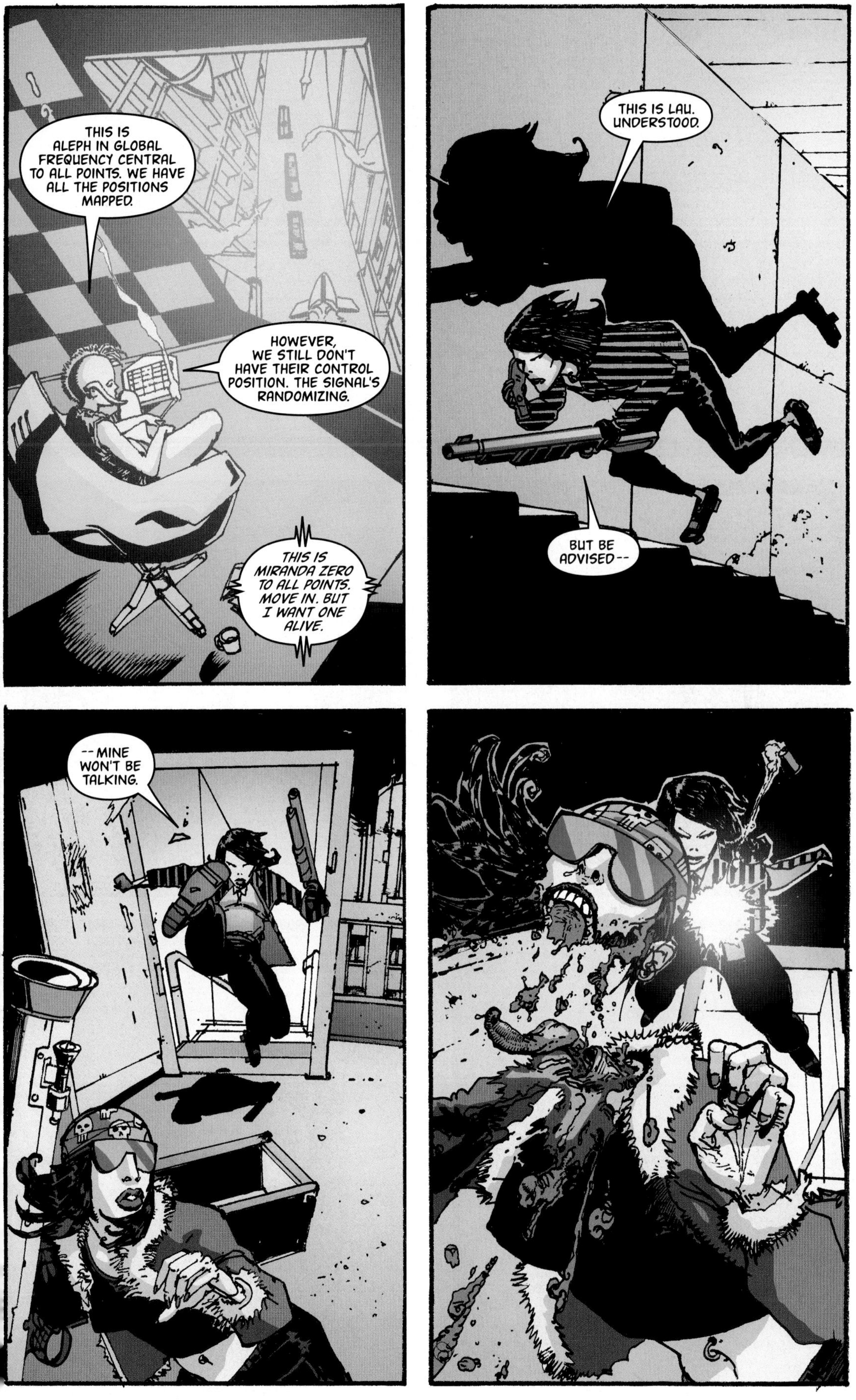
THIS IS ALEPH IN GLOBAL FREQUENCY CENTRAL TO ALL POINTS. WE HAVE ALL THE POSITIONS MAPPED.
HOWEVER, WE STILL DON'T HAVE THEIR CONTROL POSITION. THE SIGNAL'S RANDOMIZING.
THIS IS MIRANDA ZERO TO ALL POINTS. MOVE IN. BUT I WANT ONE ALIVE.
THIS IS LAU. UNDERSTOOD.
BUT BE ADVISED--
--MINE WON'T BE TALKING.

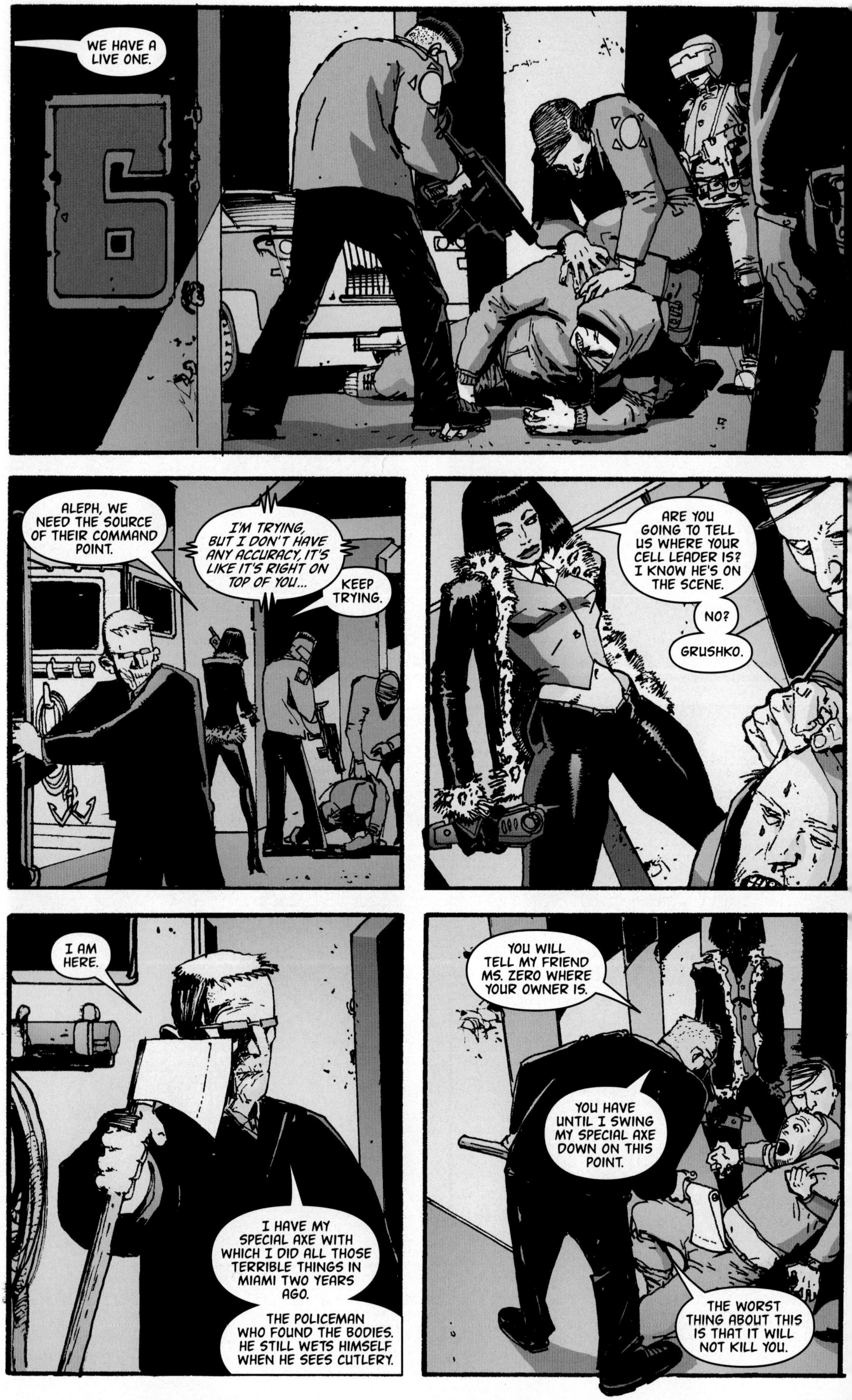
WE HAVE A LIVE ONE.
ALEPH, WE NEED THE SOURCE OF THEIR COMMAND POINT.
I'M TRYING, BUT I DON'T HAVE ANY ACCURACY, IT'S LIKE IT'S RIGHT ON TOP OF YOU...
KEEP TRYING.
ARE YOU GOING TO TELL US WHERE YOUR CELL LEADER IS? I KNOW HE'S ON THE SCENE.
NO?
GRUSHKO.
I AM HERE.
I HAVE MY SPECIAL AXE WITH WHICH I DID ALL THOSE TERRIBLE THINGS IN MIAMI TWO YEARS AGO.
THE POLICEMAN WHO FOUND THE BODIES. HE STILL WETS HIMSELF WHEN HE SEES CUTLERY.
YOU WILL TELL MY FRIEND MS. ZERO WHERE YOUR OWNER IS.
YOU HAVE UNTIL I SWING MY SPECIAL AXE DOWN ON THIS POINT.
THE WORST THING ABOUT THIS IS THAT IT WILL NOT KILL YOU.

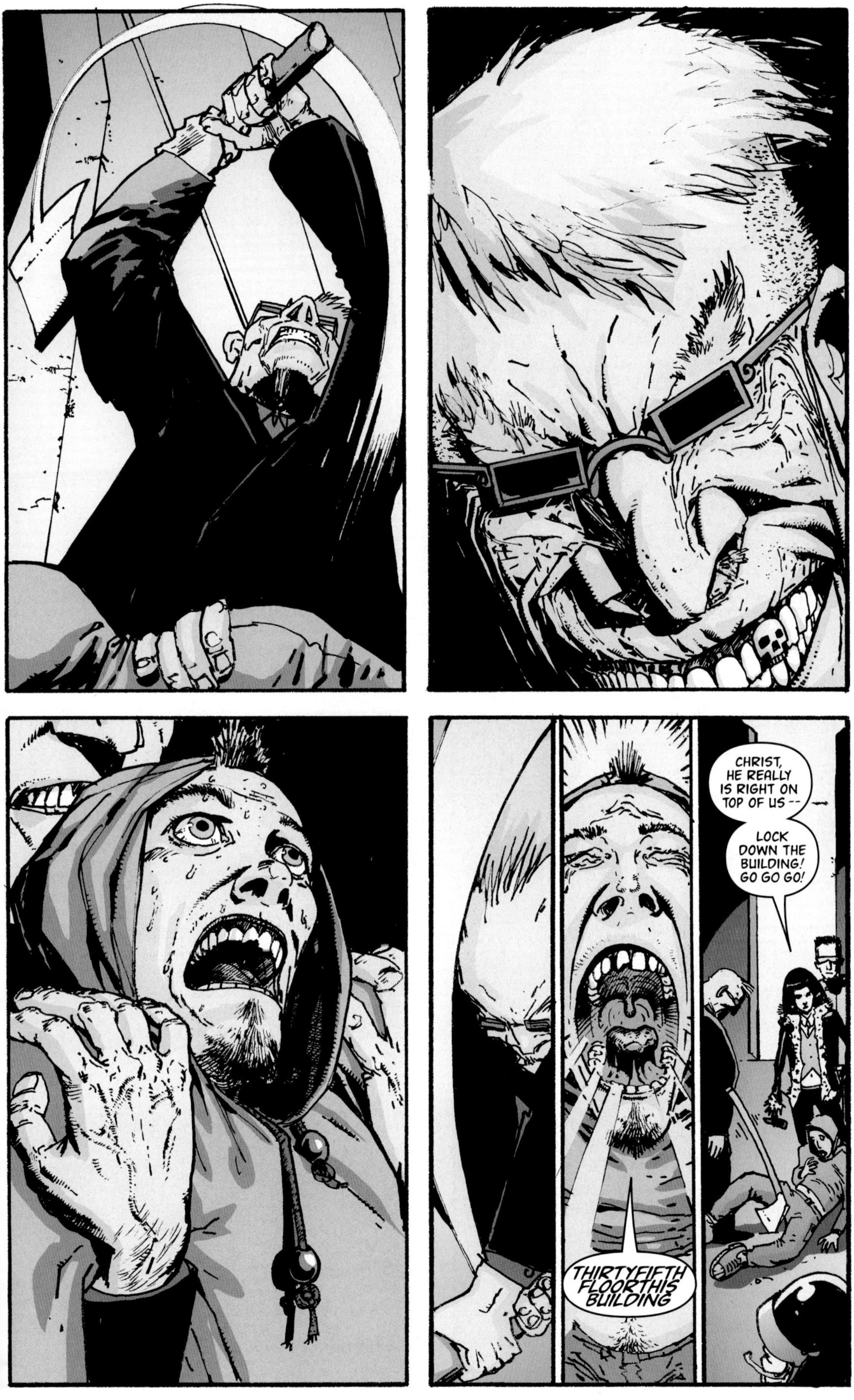
CHRIST, HE REALLY IS RIGHT ON TOP OF US --
LOCK DOWN THE BUILDING! GO GO GO!
THIRTYFIFTH FLOORTHIS BUILDING

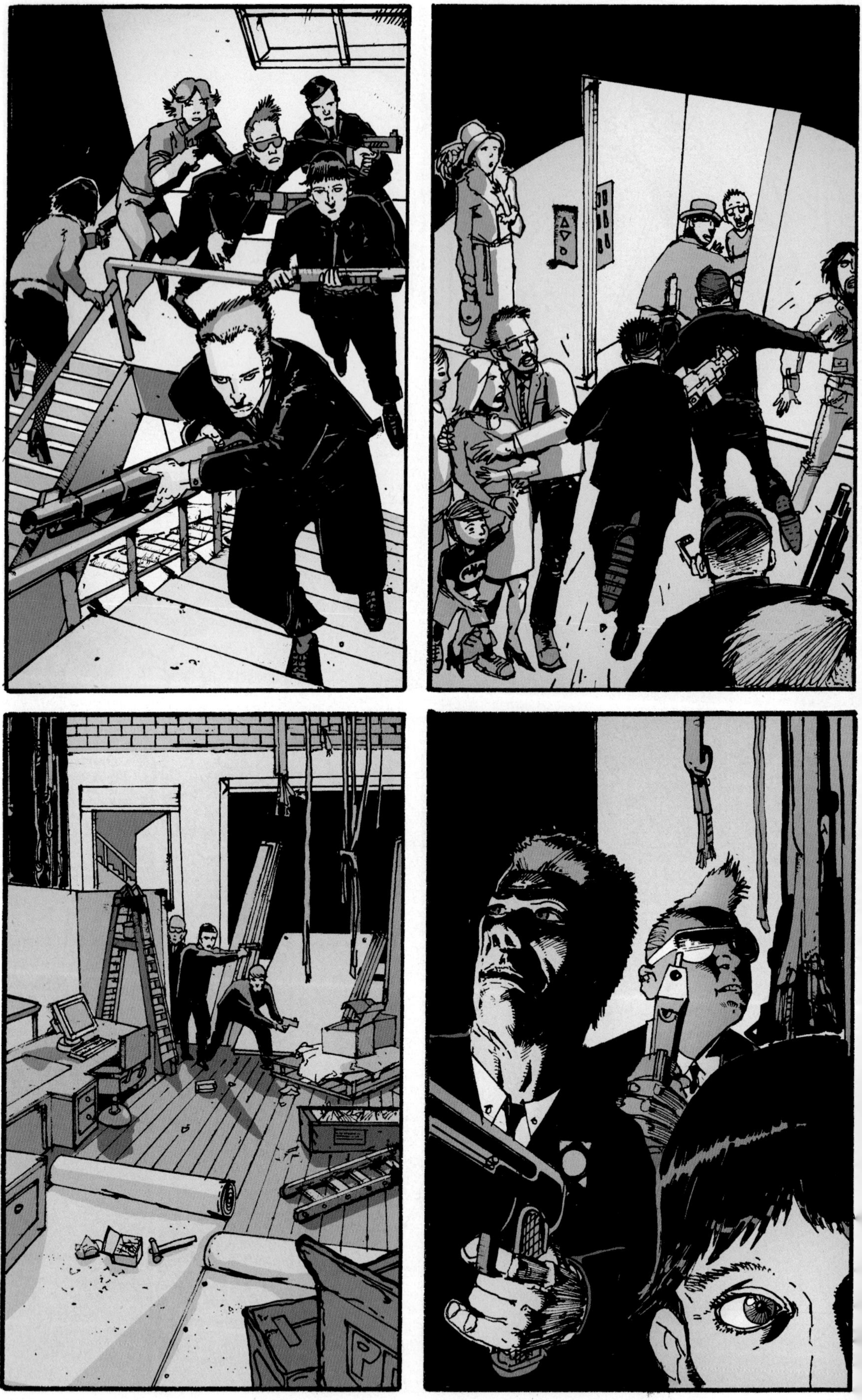

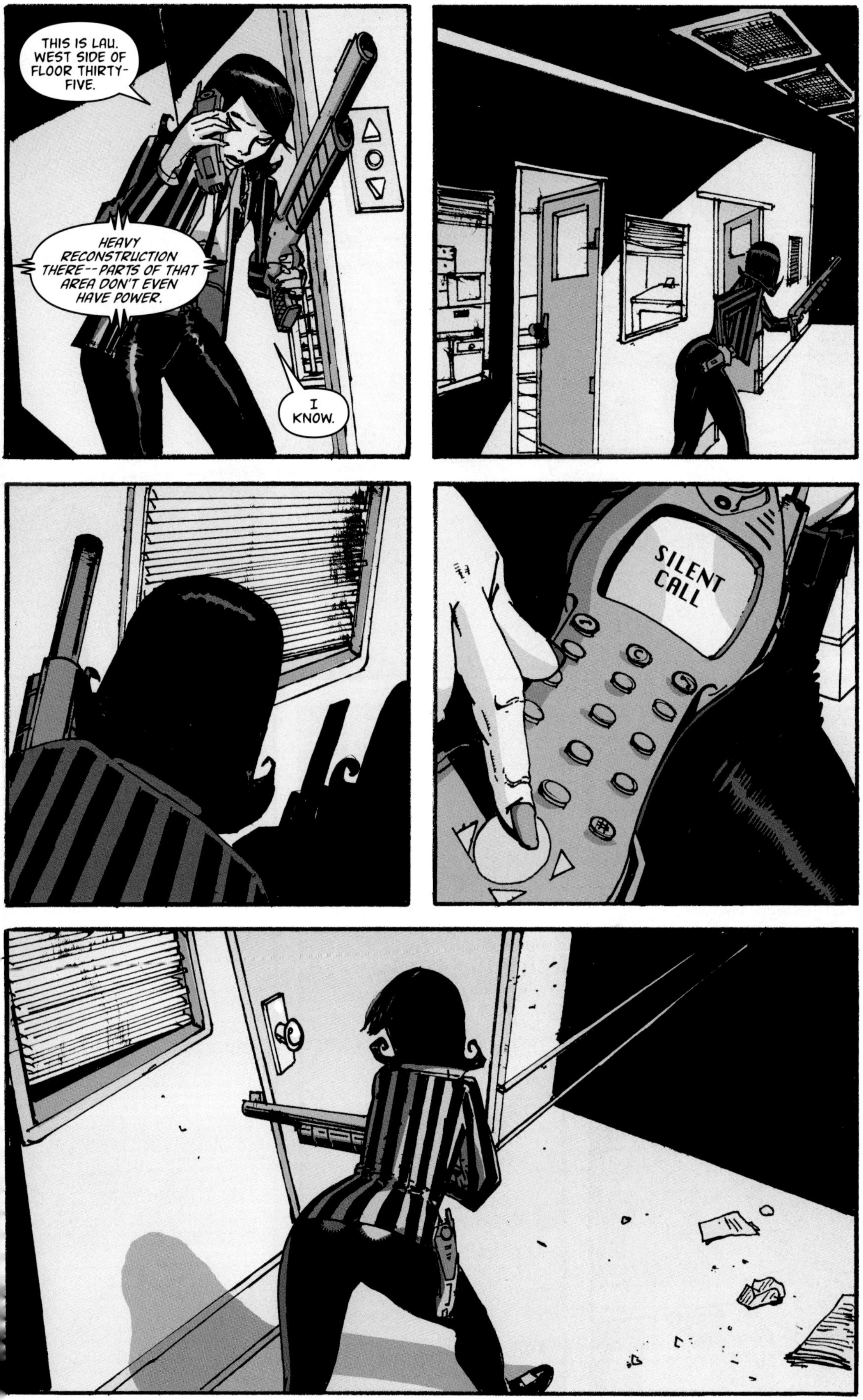
THIS IS LAU. WEST SIDE OF FLOOR THIRTY-FIVE.
HEAVY RECONSTRUCTION THERE--PARTS OF THAT AREA DON'T EVEN HAVE POWER.
I KNOW.
SILENT CALL

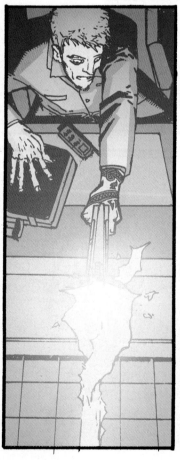

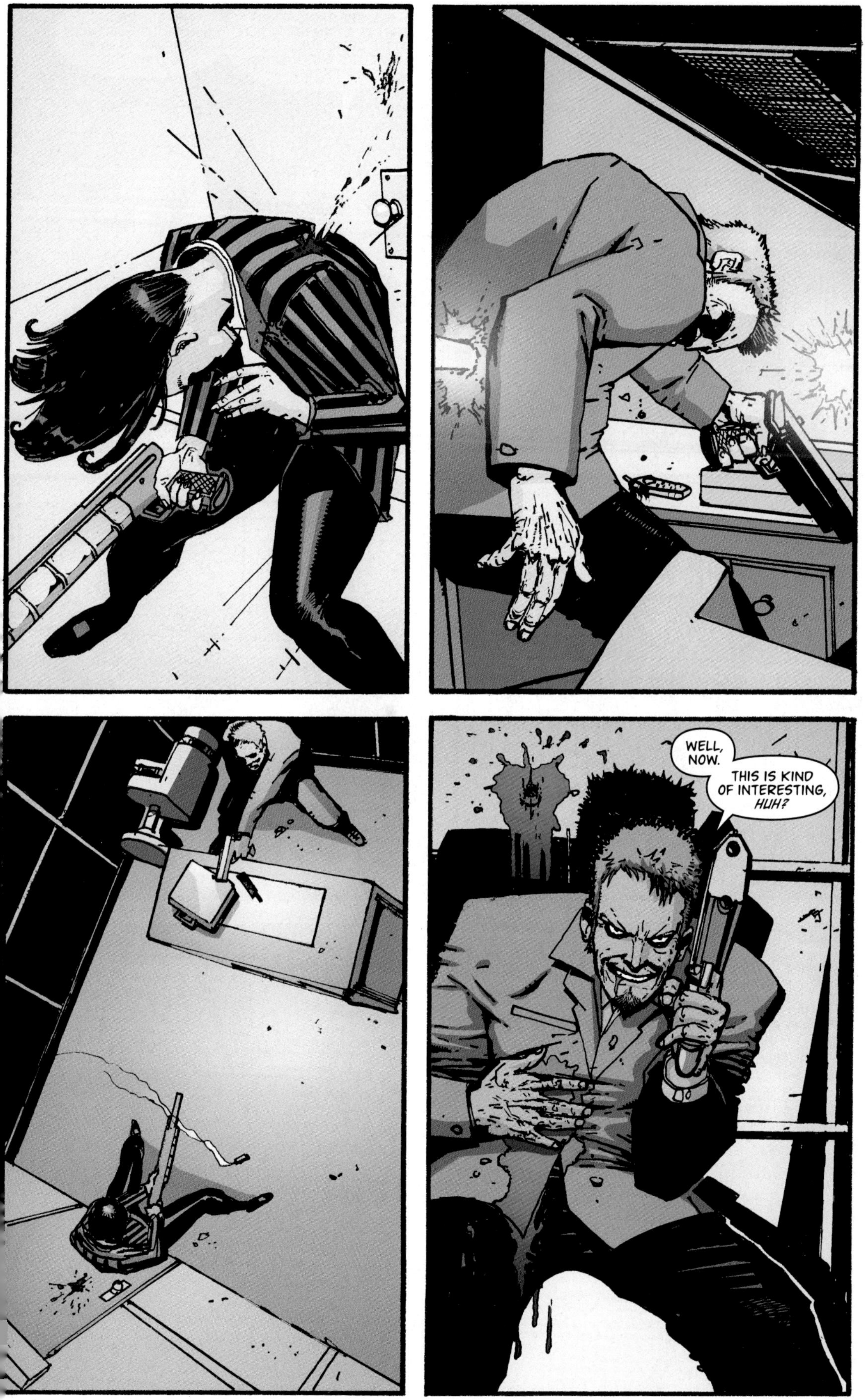
WELL, NOW.
THIS IS KIND OF INTERESTING, HUH?

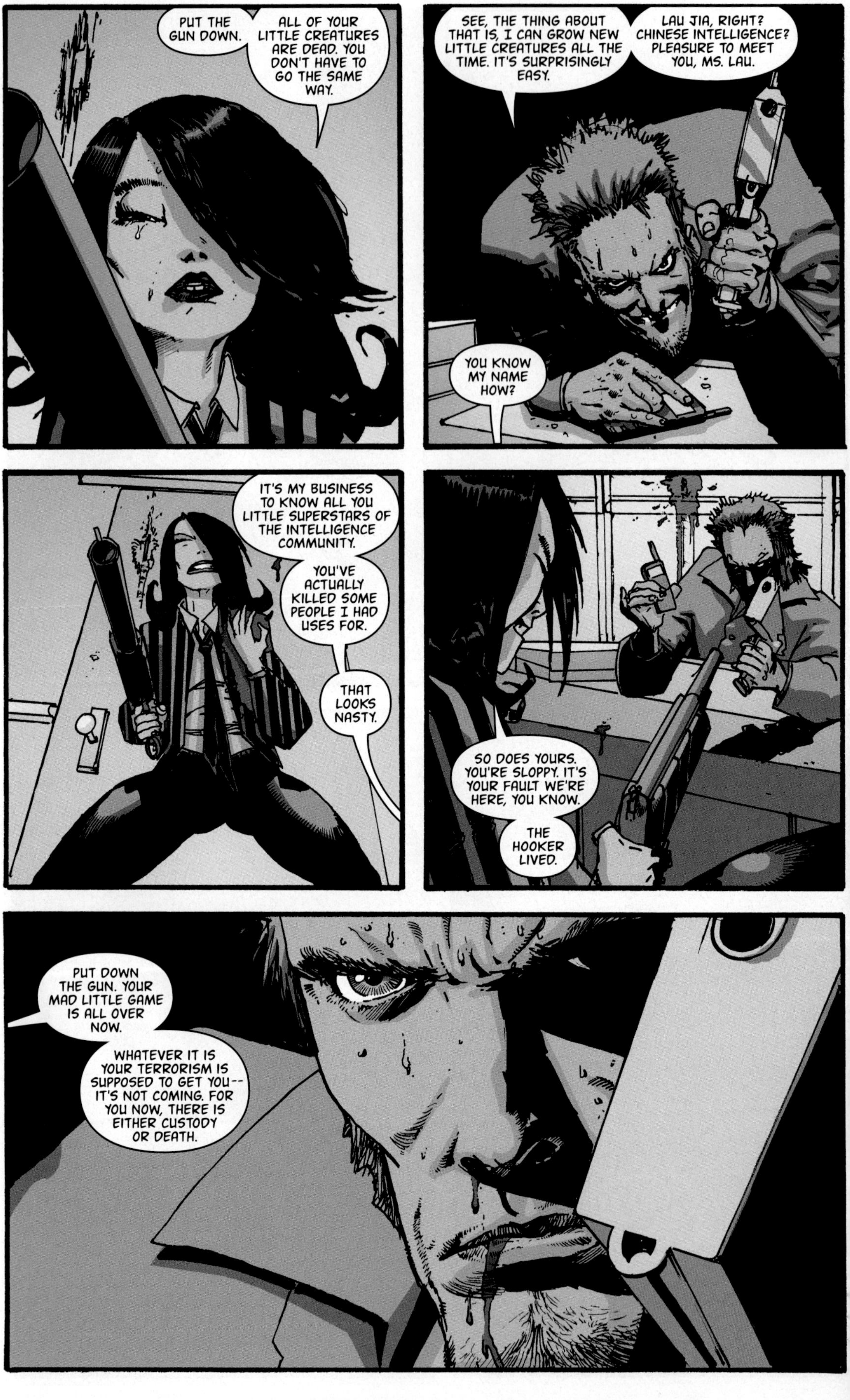
PUT THE GUN DOWN.
ALL OF YOUR LITTLE CREATURES ARE DEAD. YOU DON'T HAVE TO GO THE SAME WAY.
SEE, THE THING ABOUT THAT IS, I CAN GROW NEW LITTLE CREATURES ALL THE TIME. IT'S SURPRISINGLY EASY.
LAU JIA, RIGHT? CHINESE INTELLIGENCE? PLEASURE TO MEET YOU, MS. LAU.
YOU KNOW MY NAME HOW?
IT'S MY BUSINESS TO KNOW ALL YOU LITTLE SUPERSTARS OF THE INTELLIGENCE COMMUNITY.
YOU'VE ACTUALLY KILLED SOME PEOPLE I HAD USES FOR.
THAT LOOKS NASTY.
SO DOES YOURS. YOU'RE SLOPPY. IT'S YOUR FAULT WE'RE HERE, YOU KNOW.
THE HOOKER LIVED.
PUT DOWN THE GUN. YOUR MAD LITTLE GAME IS ALL OVER NOW.
WHATEVER IT IS YOUR TERRORISM IS SUPPOSED TO GET YOU-- IT'S NOT COMING. FOR YOU NOW, THERE IS EITHER CUSTODY OR DEATH.

WE EVEN KNOW ABOUT THE NUCLEAR DEVICE YOU INTENDED TO EXPLODE OVER LONDON, PARKED AT HAMBURG AIRPORT.

PUT THE GUN DOWN. MIRANDA ZERO IS EAGER TO MEET WITH YOU. SHE'S EVEN READ YOUR E-BOOK.

YOU KNOW ABOUT THE DEVICE? NO, YOU DON'T.

IF YOU KNEW ABOUT THE DEVICE, YOU'D KNOW IT'S ON A PLANE THAT'S ALREADY IN THE AIR.

AND THE DEVICE IS TRIGGERED BY A CODE TEXTED TO IT FROM A SATELLITE-ENABLED MOBILE PHONE.

IT'LL STILL BE OVER GERMAN SOIL, RIGHT NOW.

IT'S A DIRTY DEVICE. IMAGINE WHAT IT'D RAIN DOWN ON GERMANY.

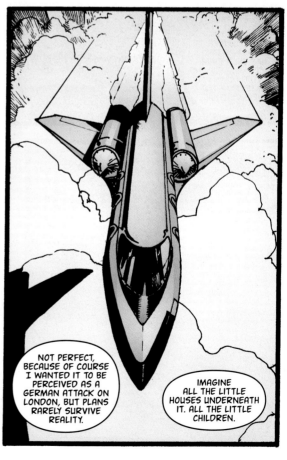

NOT PERFECT, BECAUSE OF COURSE I WANTED IT TO BE PERCEIVED AS A GERMAN ATTACK ON LONDON, BUT PLANS RARELY SURVIVE REALITY.

IMAGINE ALL THE LITTLE HOUSES UNDERNEATH IT. ALL THE LITTLE CHILDREN.

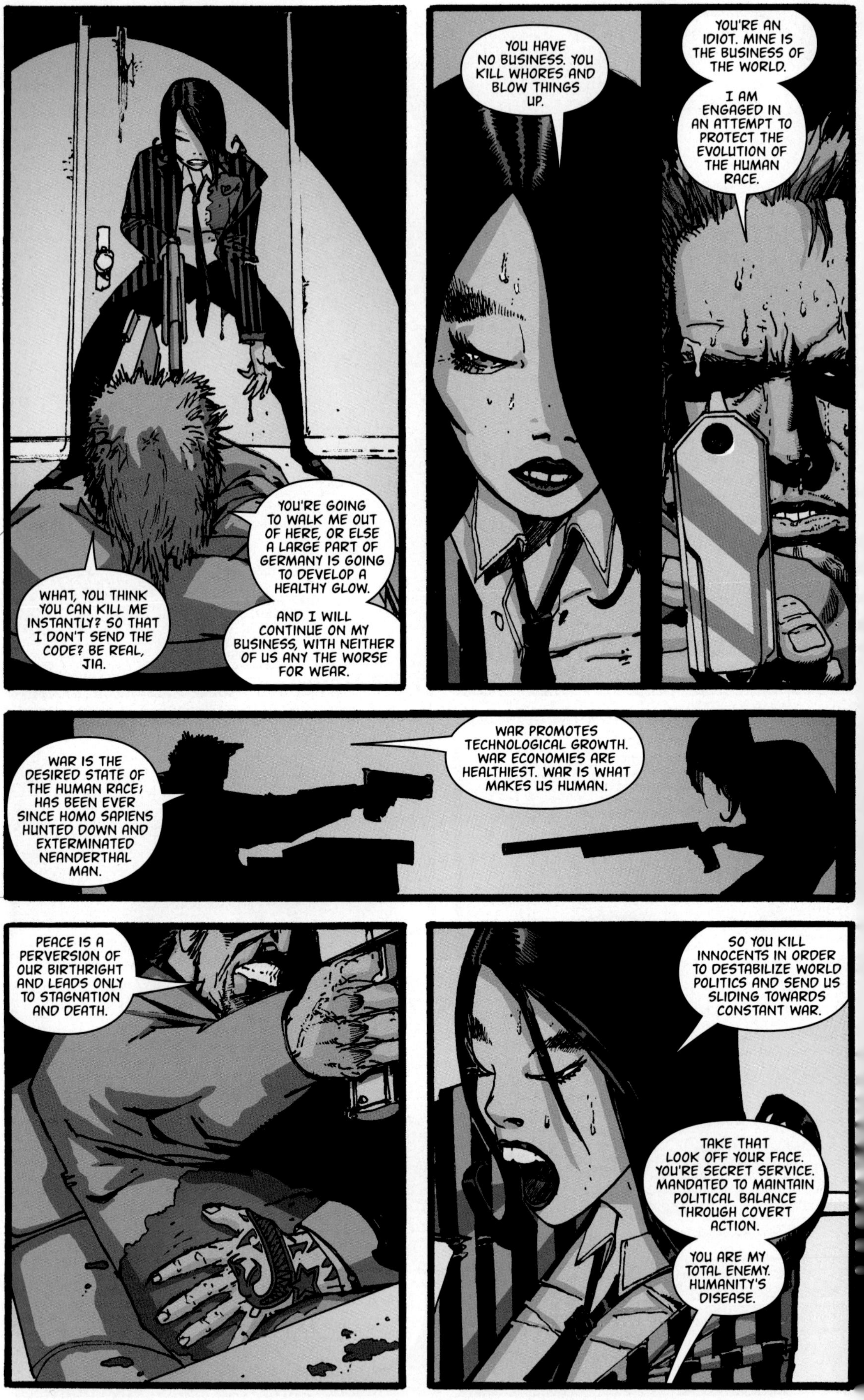

YOU'RE GOING TO WALK ME OUT OF HERE, OR ELSE A LARGE PART OF GERMANY IS GOING TO DEVELOP A HEALTHY GLOW.
AND I WILL CONTINUE ON MY BUSINESS, WITH NEITHER OF US ANY THE WORSE FOR WEAR.
WHAT, YOU THINK YOU CAN KILL ME INSTANTLY? SO THAT I DON'T SEND THE CODE? BE REAL, JIA.
YOU HAVE NO BUSINESS. YOU KILL WHORES AND BLOW THINGS UP.
YOU'RE AN IDIOT. MINE IS THE BUSINESS OF THE WORLD.
I AM ENGAGED IN AN ATTEMPT TO PROTECT THE EVOLUTION OF THE HUMAN RACE.
WAR IS THE DESIRED STATE OF THE HUMAN RACE; HAS BEEN EVER SINCE HOMO SAPIENS HUNTED DOWN AND EXTERMINATED NEANDERTHAL MAN.
WAR PROMOTES TECHNOLOGICAL GROWTH. WAR ECONOMIES ARE HEALTHIEST. WAR IS WHAT MAKES US HUMAN.
PEACE IS A PERVERSION OF OUR BIRTHRIGHT AND LEADS ONLY TO STAGNATION AND DEATH.
SO YOU KILL INNOCENTS IN ORDER TO DESTABILIZE WORLD POLITICS AND SEND US SLIDING TOWARDS CONSTANT WAR.
TAKE THAT LOOK OFF YOUR FACE. YOU'RE SECRET SERVICE. MANDATED TO MAINTAIN POLITICAL BALANCE THROUGH COVERT ACTION.
YOU ARE MY TOTAL ENEMY. HUMANITY'S DISEASE.

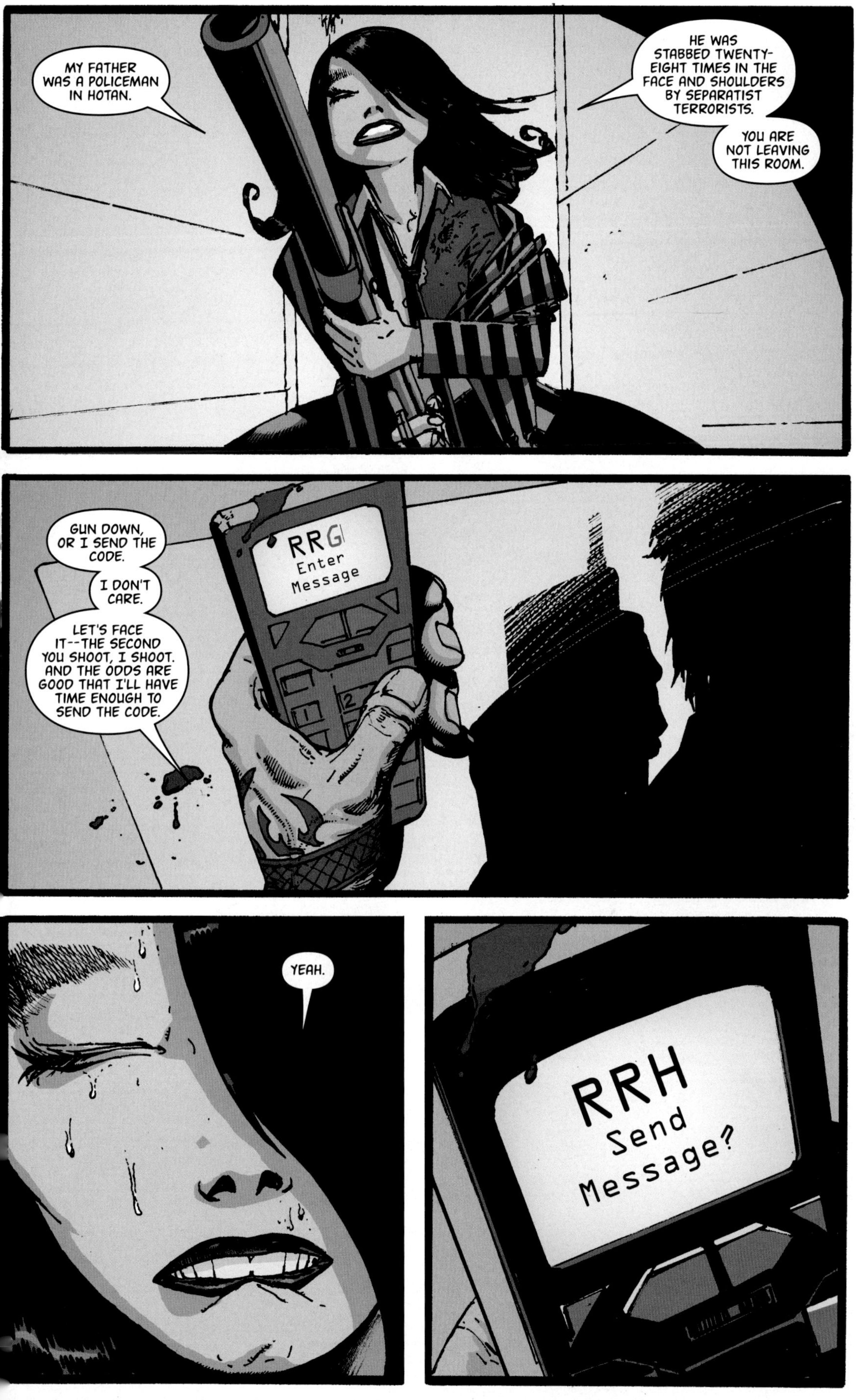

MY FATHER WAS A POLICEMAN IN HOTAN.
HE WAS STABBED TWENTY-EIGHT TIMES IN THE FACE AND SHOULDERS BY SEPARATIST TERRORISTS.
YOU ARE NOT LEAVING THIS ROOM.
GUN DOWN, OR I SEND THE CODE.
RRG
Enter Message
I DON'T CARE.
LET'S FACE IT--THE SECOND YOU SHOOT, I SHOOT. AND THE ODDS ARE GOOD THAT I'LL HAVE TIME ENOUGH TO SEND THE CODE.
YEAH.
RRH
Send Message?

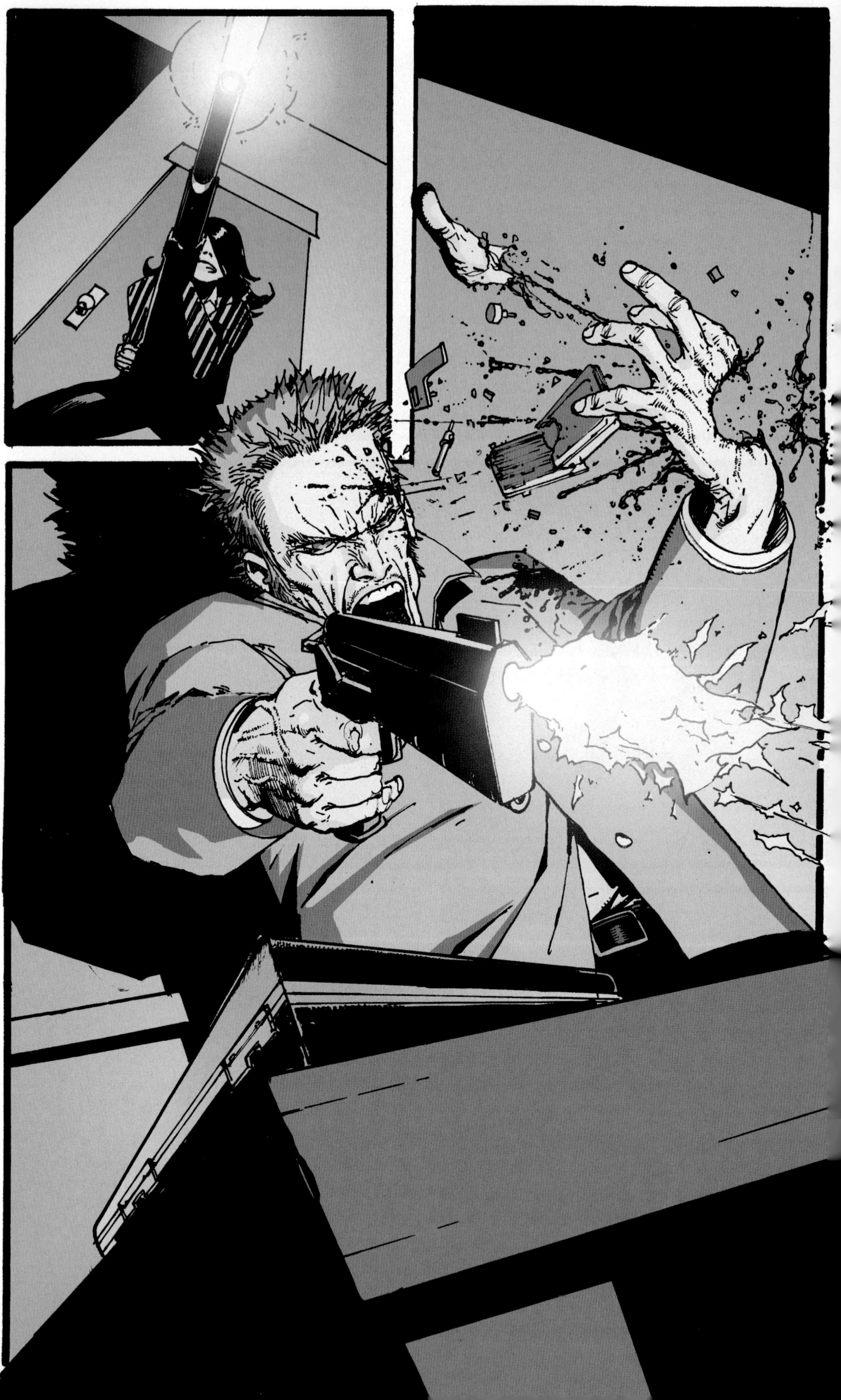

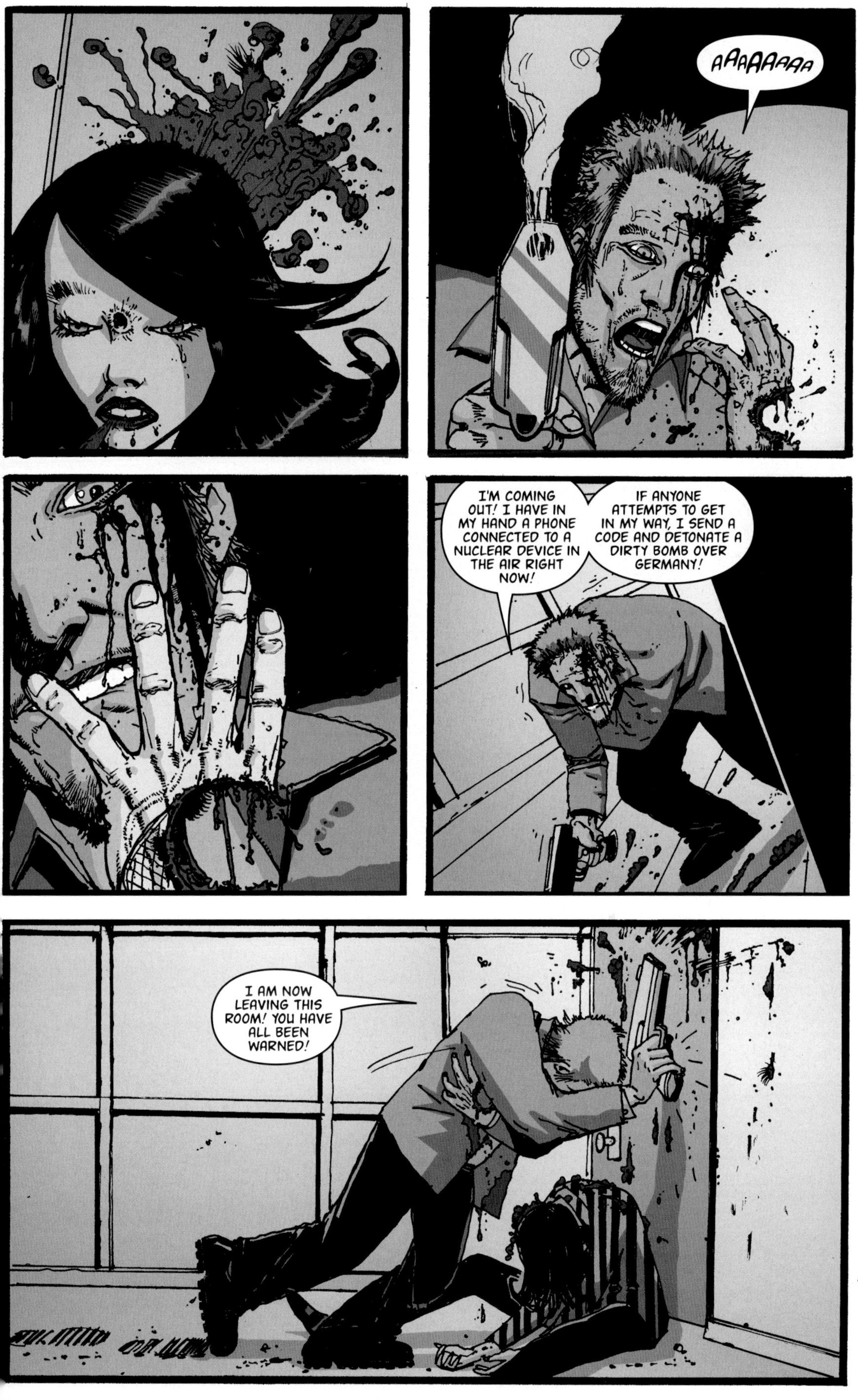
AAAAAAAA
I'M COMING OUT! I HAVE IN MY HAND A PHONE CONNECTED TO A NUCLEAR DEVICE IN THE AIR RIGHT NOW!
IF ANYONE ATTEMPTS TO GET IN MY WAY, I SEND A CODE AND DETONATE A DIRTY BOMB OVER GERMANY!
I AM NOW LEAVING THIS ROOM! YOU HAVE ALL BEEN WARNED!

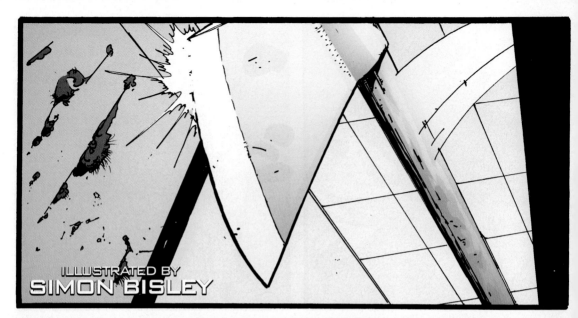

ILLUSTRATED BY
SIMON BISLEY

COLORS BY
DAVID BARON

LETTERING BY
MICHAEL HEISLER

LAU HAD HER PHONE ON THE ENTIRE TIME. ALEPH HEARD YOUR MOBILE PHONE EXPLODE.

AND SHE TOLD YOU THAT YOU WERE NOT LEAVING THE ROOM.

CREATED AND WRITTEN BY
WARREN ELLIS

the
End

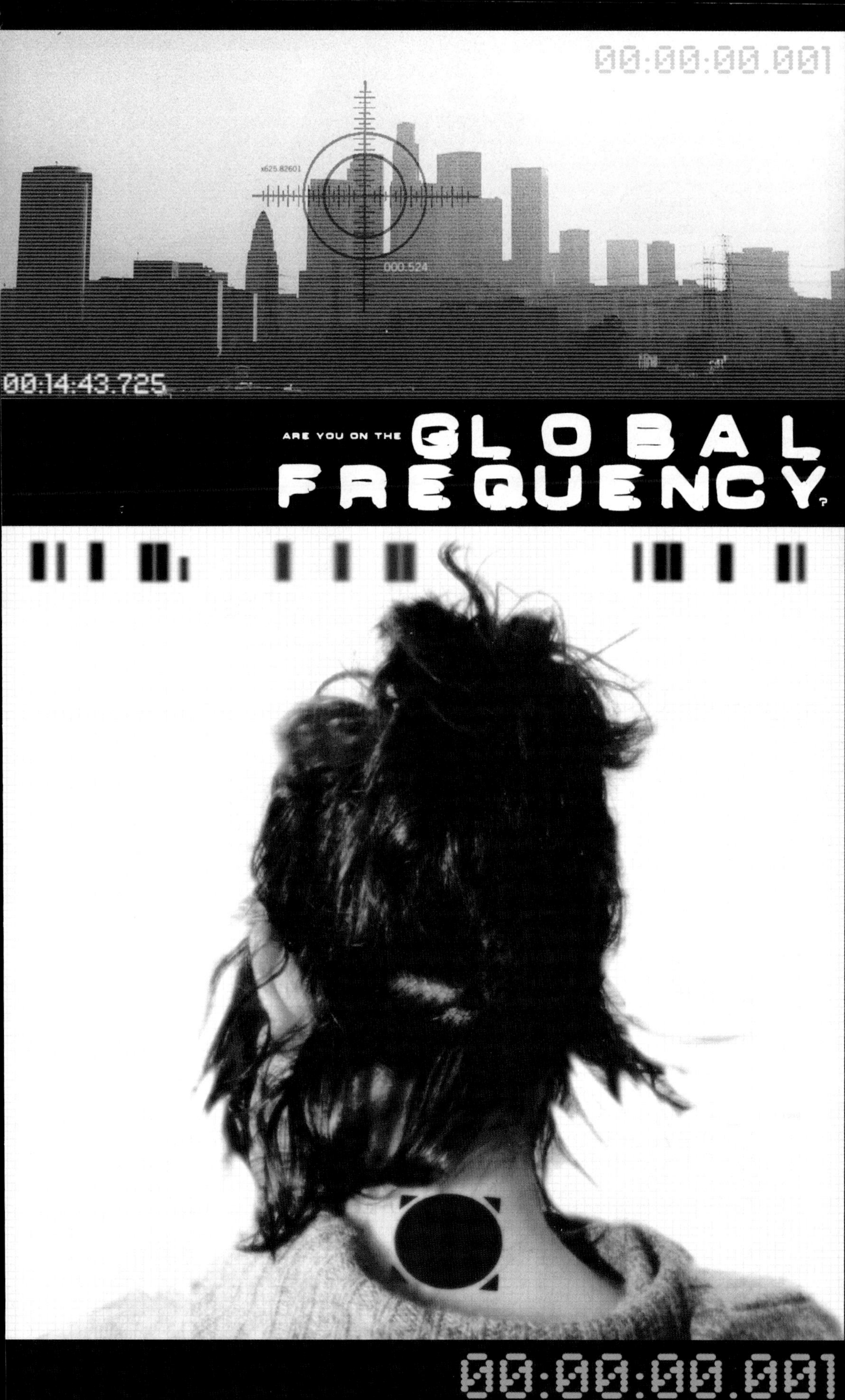
00:00:00.001
x625.82601
000.524
00:14:43.725
ARE YOU ON THE GLOBAL FREQUENCY?
00:00:00.001

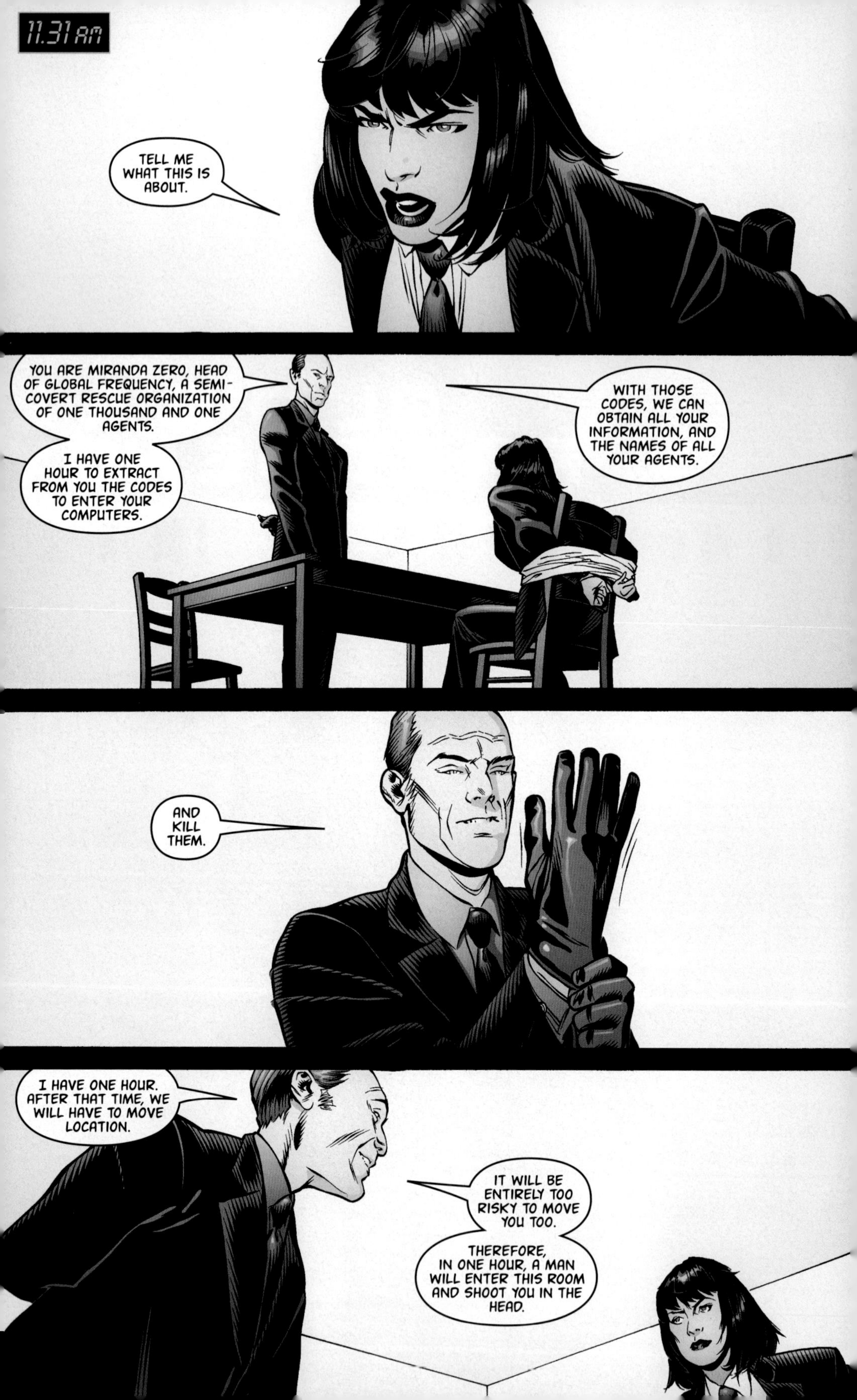
11.31 AM
TELL ME WHAT THIS IS ABOUT.
YOU ARE MIRANDA ZERO, HEAD OF GLOBAL FREQUENCY, A SEMI-COVERT RESCUE ORGANIZATION OF ONE THOUSAND AND ONE AGENTS.
I HAVE ONE HOUR TO EXTRACT FROM YOU THE CODES TO ENTER YOUR COMPUTERS.
WITH THOSE CODES, WE CAN OBTAIN ALL YOUR INFORMATION, AND THE NAMES OF ALL YOUR AGENTS.
AND KILL THEM.
I HAVE ONE HOUR. AFTER THAT TIME, WE WILL HAVE TO MOVE LOCATION.
IT WILL BE ENTIRELY TOO RISKY TO MOVE YOU TOO.
THEREFORE, IN ONE HOUR, A MAN WILL ENTER THIS ROOM AND SHOOT YOU IN THE HEAD.

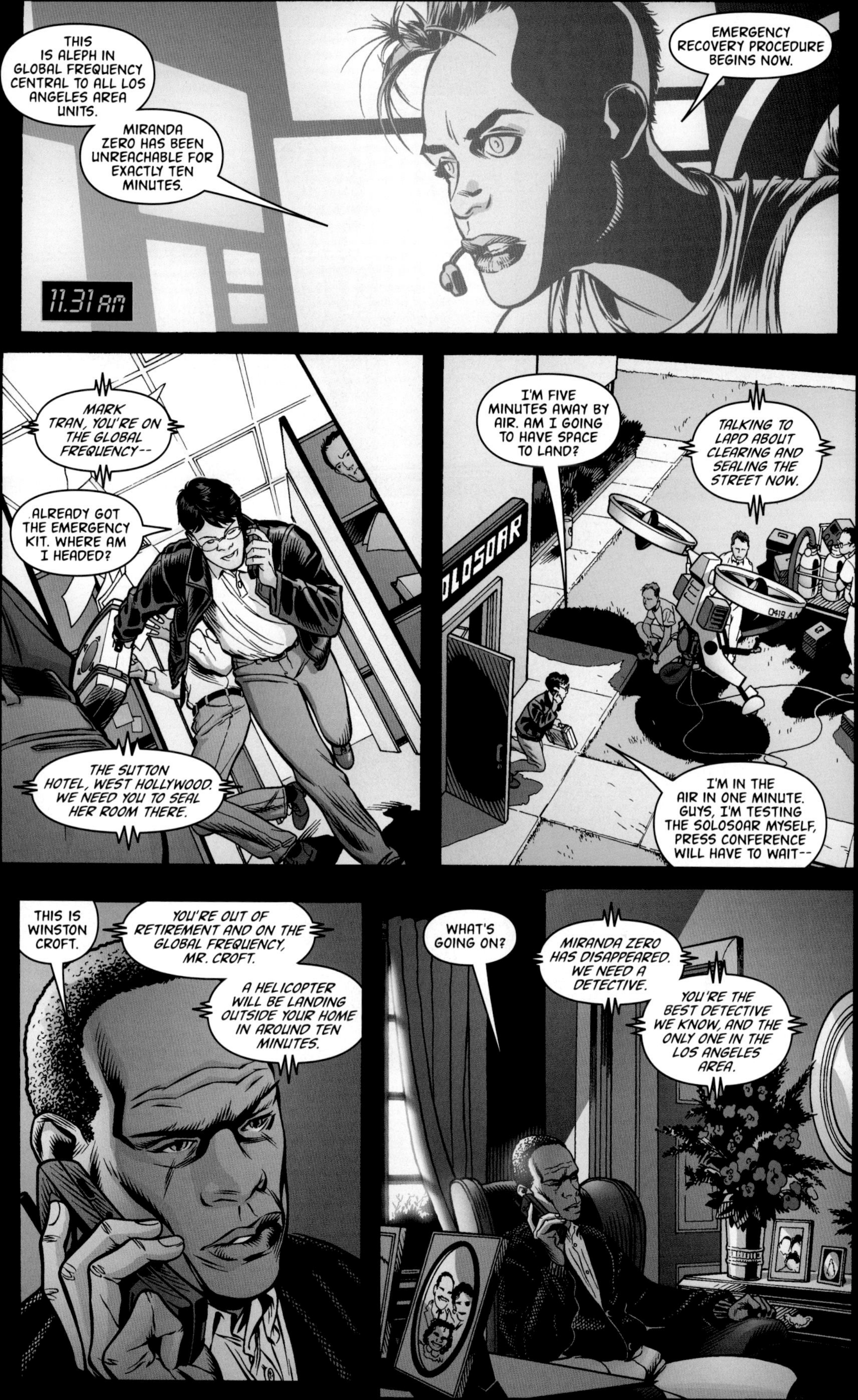
THIS IS ALEPH IN GLOBAL FREQUENCY CENTRAL TO ALL LOS ANGELES AREA UNITS.
MIRANDA ZERO HAS BEEN UNREACHABLE FOR EXACTLY TEN MINUTES.
EMERGENCY RECOVERY PROCEDURE BEGINS NOW.
11.31 AM
MARK TRAN, YOU'RE ON THE GLOBAL FREQUENCY--
...ALREADY GOT THE EMERGENCY KIT. WHERE AM I HEADED?
THE SUTTON HOTEL, WEST HOLLYWOOD. WE NEED YOU TO SEAL HER ROOM THERE.
I'M FIVE MINUTES AWAY BY AIR. AM I GOING TO HAVE SPACE TO LAND?
TALKING TO LAPD ABOUT CLEARING AND SEALING THE STREET NOW.
SOLOSOAR
I'M IN THE AIR IN ONE MINUTE. GUYS, I'M TESTING THE SOLOSOAR MYSELF, PRESS CONFERENCE WILL HAVE TO WAIT--
THIS IS WINSTON CROFT.
YOU'RE OUT OF RETIREMENT AND ON THE GLOBAL FREQUENCY, MR. CROFT.
A HELICOPTER WILL BE LANDING OUTSIDE YOUR HOME IN AROUND TEN MINUTES.
WHAT'S GOING ON?
MIRANDA ZERO HAS DISAPPEARED. WE NEED A DETECTIVE.
YOU'RE THE BEST DETECTIVE WE KNOW, AND THE ONLY ONE IN THE LOS ANGELES AREA.

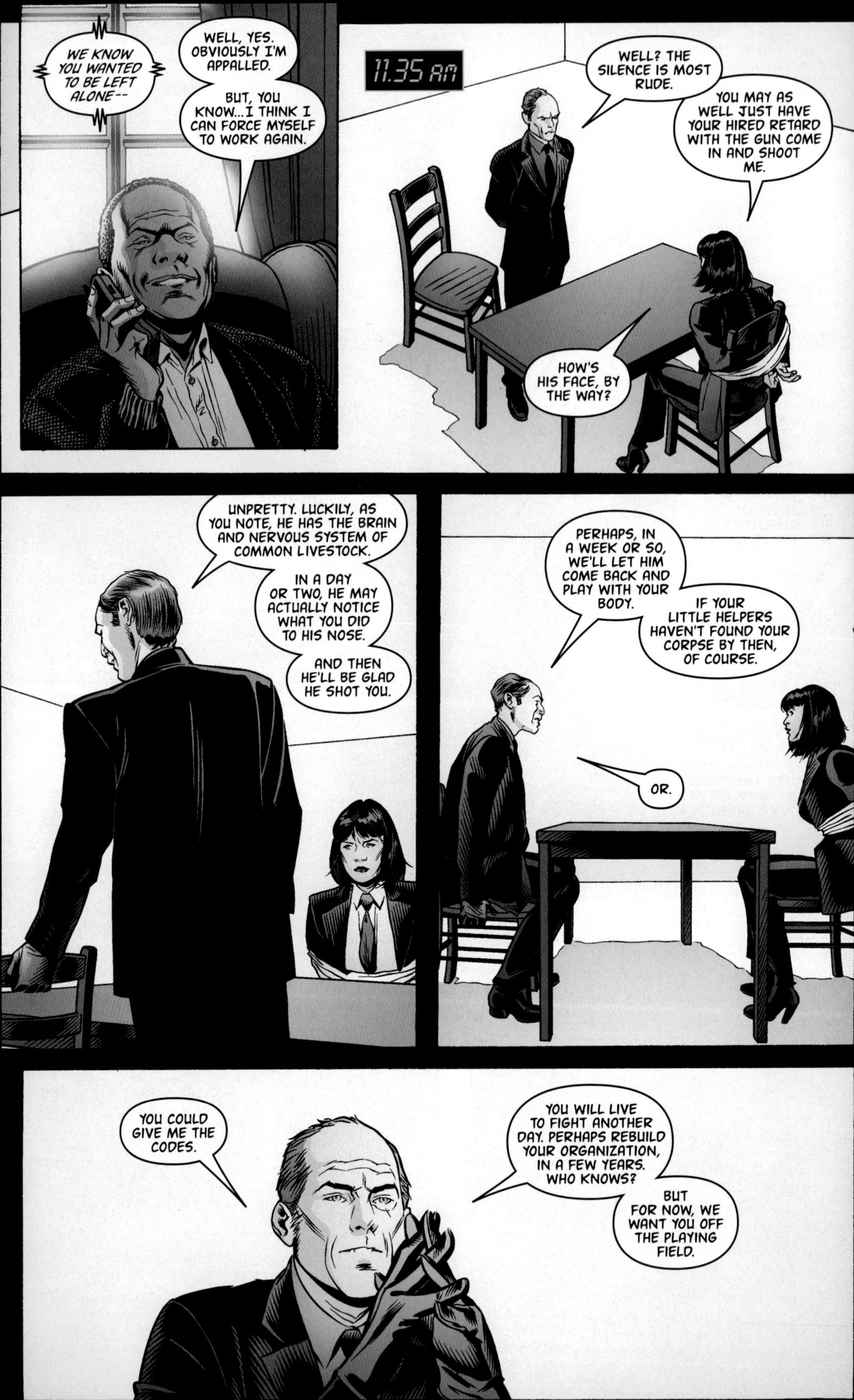
WE KNOW YOU WANTED TO BE LEFT ALONE--
WELL, YES. OBVIOUSLY I'M APPALLED.
BUT, YOU KNOW...I THINK I CAN FORCE MYSELF TO WORK AGAIN.
11:35 AM
WELL? THE SILENCE IS MOST RUDE.
YOU MAY AS WELL JUST HAVE YOUR HIRED RETARD WITH THE GUN COME IN AND SHOOT ME.
HOW'S HIS FACE, BY THE WAY?
UNPRETTY. LUCKILY, AS YOU NOTE, HE HAS THE BRAIN AND NERVOUS SYSTEM OF COMMON LIVESTOCK.
IN A DAY OR TWO, HE MAY ACTUALLY NOTICE WHAT YOU DID TO HIS NOSE.
AND THEN HE'LL BE GLAD HE SHOT YOU.
PERHAPS, IN A WEEK OR SO, WE'LL LET HIM COME BACK AND PLAY WITH YOUR BODY.
IF YOUR LITTLE HELPERS HAVEN'T FOUND YOUR CORPSE BY THEN, OF COURSE.
OR.
YOU COULD GIVE ME THE CODES.
YOU WILL LIVE TO FIGHT ANOTHER DAY. PERHAPS REBUILD YOUR ORGANIZATION, IN A FEW YEARS. WHO KNOWS?
BUT FOR NOW, WE WANT YOU OFF THE PLAYING FIELD.

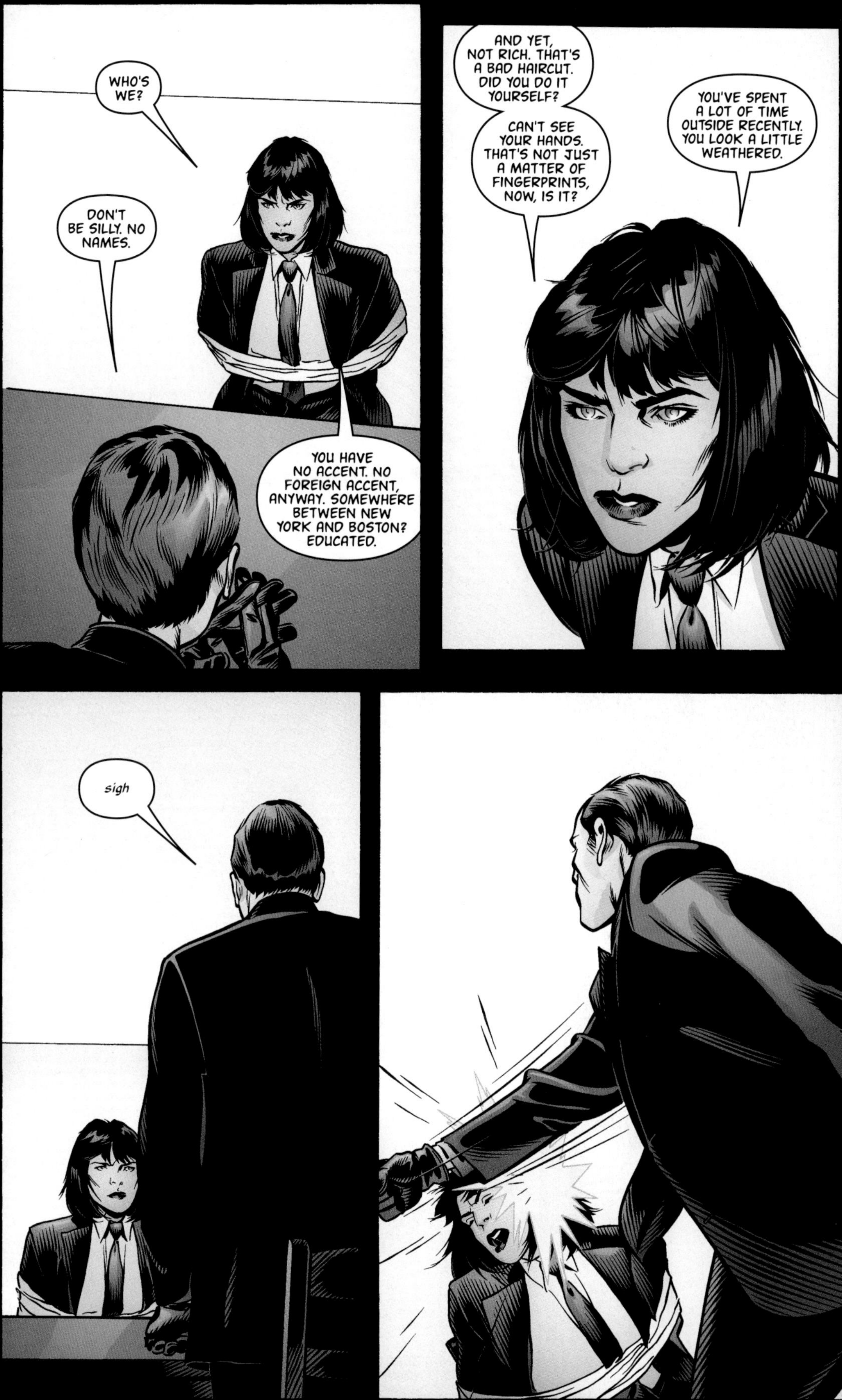
WHO'S WE?
DON'T BE SILLY. NO NAMES.
YOU HAVE NO ACCENT. NO FOREIGN ACCENT, ANYWAY. SOMEWHERE BETWEEN NEW YORK AND BOSTON? EDUCATED.
AND YET, NOT RICH. THAT'S A BAD HAIRCUT. DID YOU DO IT YOURSELF?
CAN'T SEE YOUR HANDS. THAT'S NOT JUST A MATTER OF FINGERPRINTS, NOW, IS IT?
YOU'VE SPENT A LOT OF TIME OUTSIDE RECENTLY. YOU LOOK A LITTLE WEATHERED.
sigh

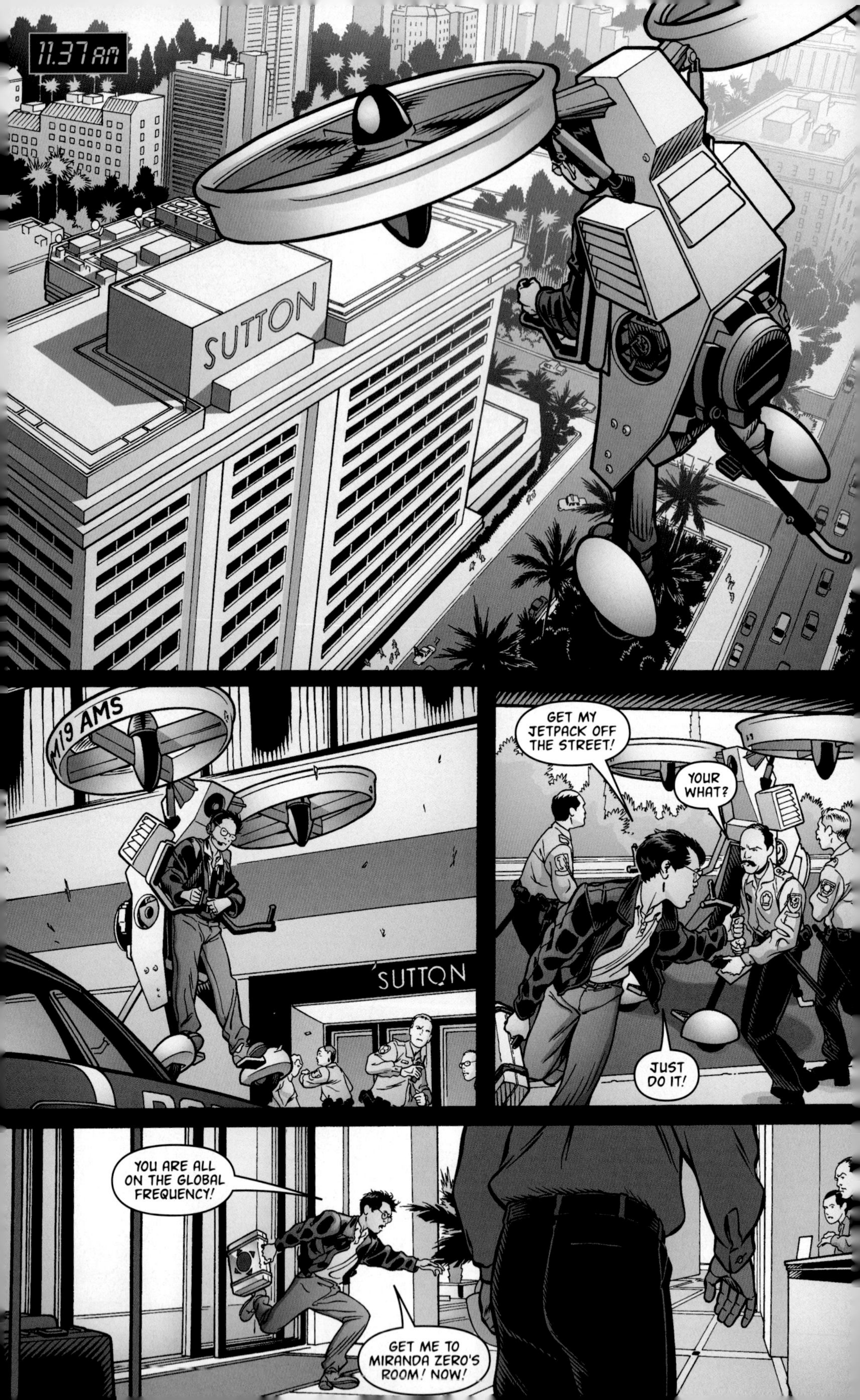
11.37AM
SUTTON
M19 AMS
SUTTON
GET MY JETPACK OFF THE STREET!
YOUR WHAT?
JUST DO IT!
YOU ARE ALL ON THE GLOBAL FREQUENCY!
GET ME TO MIRANDA ZERO'S ROOM! NOW!

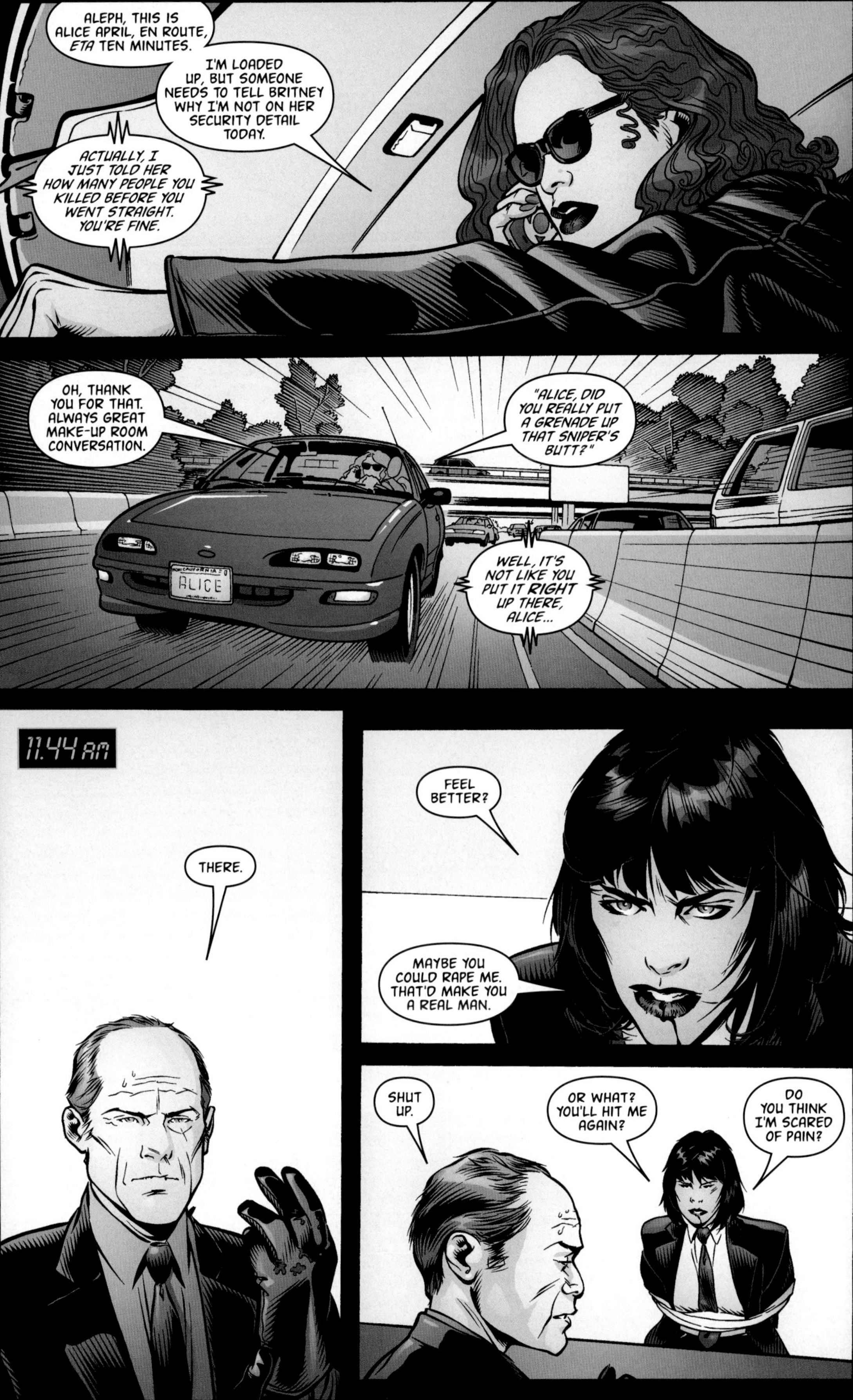
ALEPH, THIS IS ALICE APRIL, EN ROUTE, ETA TEN MINUTES.
I'M LOADED UP, BUT SOMEONE NEEDS TO TELL BRITNEY WHY I'M NOT ON HER SECURITY DETAIL TODAY.
ACTUALLY, I JUST TOLD HER HOW MANY PEOPLE YOU KILLED BEFORE YOU WENT STRAIGHT. YOU'RE FINE.
OH, THANK YOU FOR THAT. ALWAYS GREAT MAKE-UP ROOM CONVERSATION.
"ALICE, DID YOU REALLY PUT A GRENADE UP THAT SNIPER'S BUTT?"
WELL, IT'S NOT LIKE YOU PUT IT RIGHT UP THERE, ALICE...
ALICE
11.44 AM
THERE.
FEEL BETTER?
MAYBE YOU COULD RAPE ME. THAT'D MAKE YOU A REAL MAN.
SHUT UP.
OR WHAT? YOU'LL HIT ME AGAIN?
DO YOU THINK I'M SCARED OF PAIN?

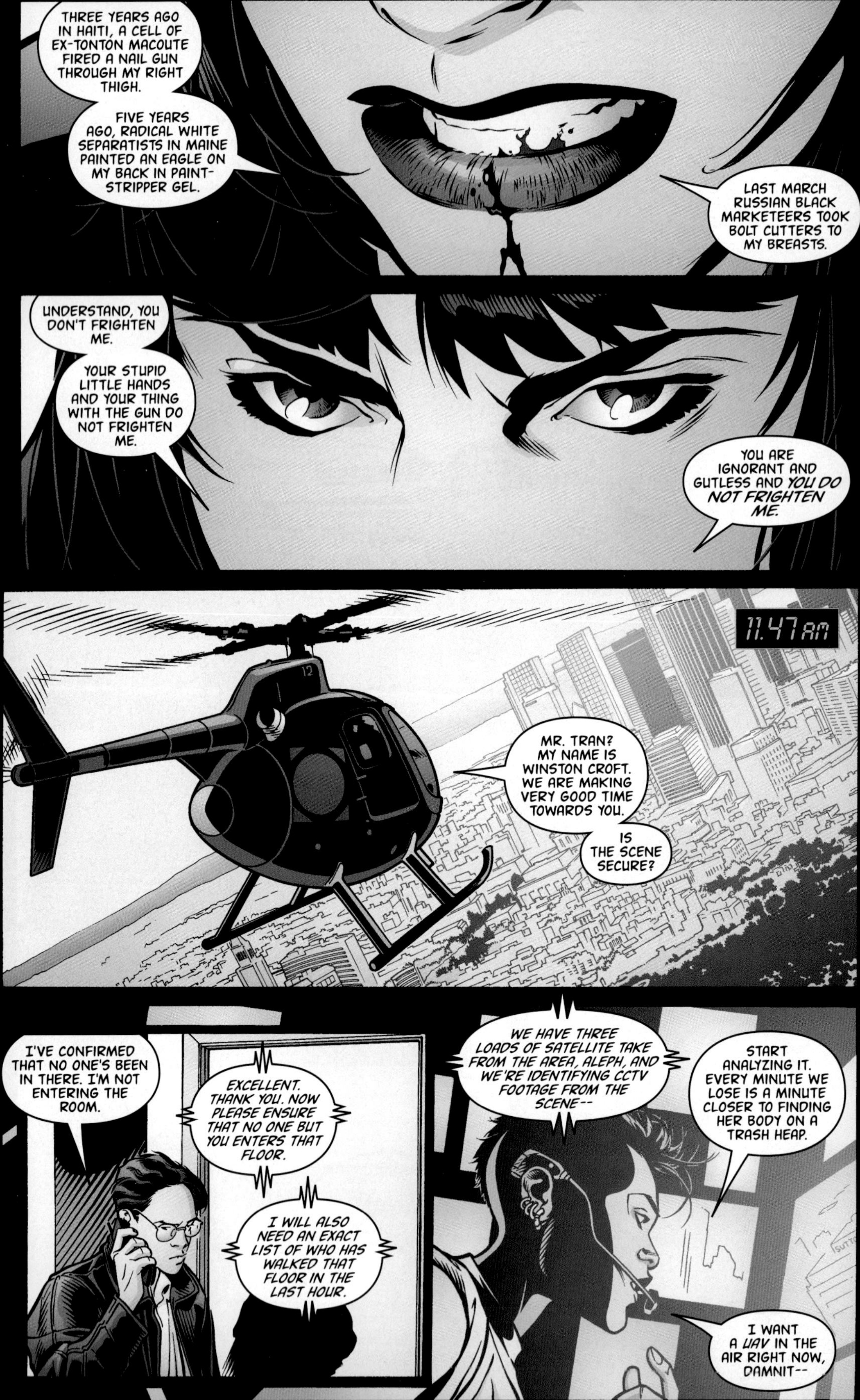
THREE YEARS AGO IN HAITI, A CELL OF EX-TONTON MACOUTE FIRED A NAIL GUN THROUGH MY RIGHT THIGH.
FIVE YEARS AGO, RADICAL WHITE SEPARATISTS IN MAINE PAINTED AN EAGLE ON MY BACK IN PAINT-STRIPPER GEL.
LAST MARCH RUSSIAN BLACK MARKETEERS TOOK BOLT CUTTERS TO MY BREASTS.
UNDERSTAND, YOU DON'T FRIGHTEN ME.
YOUR STUPID LITTLE HANDS AND YOUR THING WITH THE GUN DO NOT FRIGHTEN ME.
YOU ARE IGNORANT AND GUTLESS AND *YOU DO NOT FRIGHTEN ME.*
11.47 AM
12
MR. TRAN? MY NAME IS WINSTON CROFT. WE ARE MAKING VERY GOOD TIME TOWARDS YOU.
IS THE SCENE SECURE?
I'VE CONFIRMED THAT NO ONE'S BEEN IN THERE. I'M NOT ENTERING THE ROOM.
EXCELLENT. THANK YOU. NOW PLEASE ENSURE THAT NO ONE BUT YOU ENTERS THAT FLOOR.
I WILL ALSO NEED AN EXACT LIST OF WHO HAS WALKED THAT FLOOR IN THE LAST HOUR.
WE HAVE THREE LOADS OF SATELLITE TAKE FROM THE AREA, ALEPH, AND WE'RE IDENTIFYING CCTV FOOTAGE FROM THE SCENE--
START ANALYZING IT. EVERY MINUTE WE LOSE IS A MINUTE CLOSER TO FINDING HER BODY ON A TRASH HEAP.
I WANT A *UAV* IN THE AIR RIGHT NOW, DAMNIT--

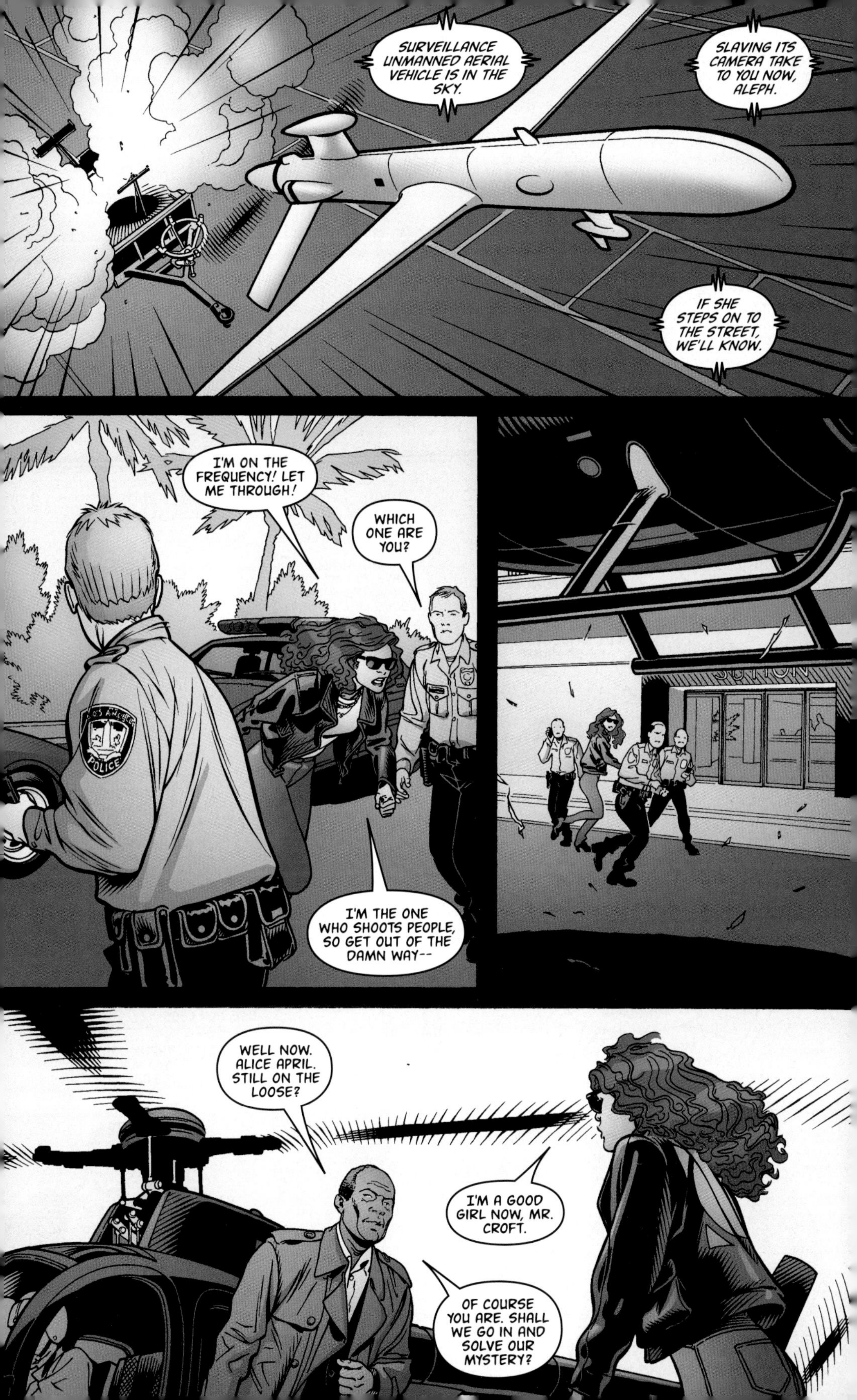
SURVEILLANCE UNMANNED AERIAL VEHICLE IS IN THE SKY.
SLAVING ITS CAMERA TAKE TO YOU NOW, ALEPH.
IF SHE STEPS ON TO THE STREET, WE'LL KNOW.
I'M ON THE FREQUENCY! LET ME THROUGH!
WHICH ONE ARE YOU?
I'M THE ONE WHO SHOOTS PEOPLE, SO GET OUT OF THE DAMN WAY--
POLICE
WELL NOW. ALICE APRIL. STILL ON THE LOOSE?
I'M A GOOD GIRL NOW, MR. CROFT.
OF COURSE YOU ARE. SHALL WE GO IN AND SOLVE OUR MYSTERY?

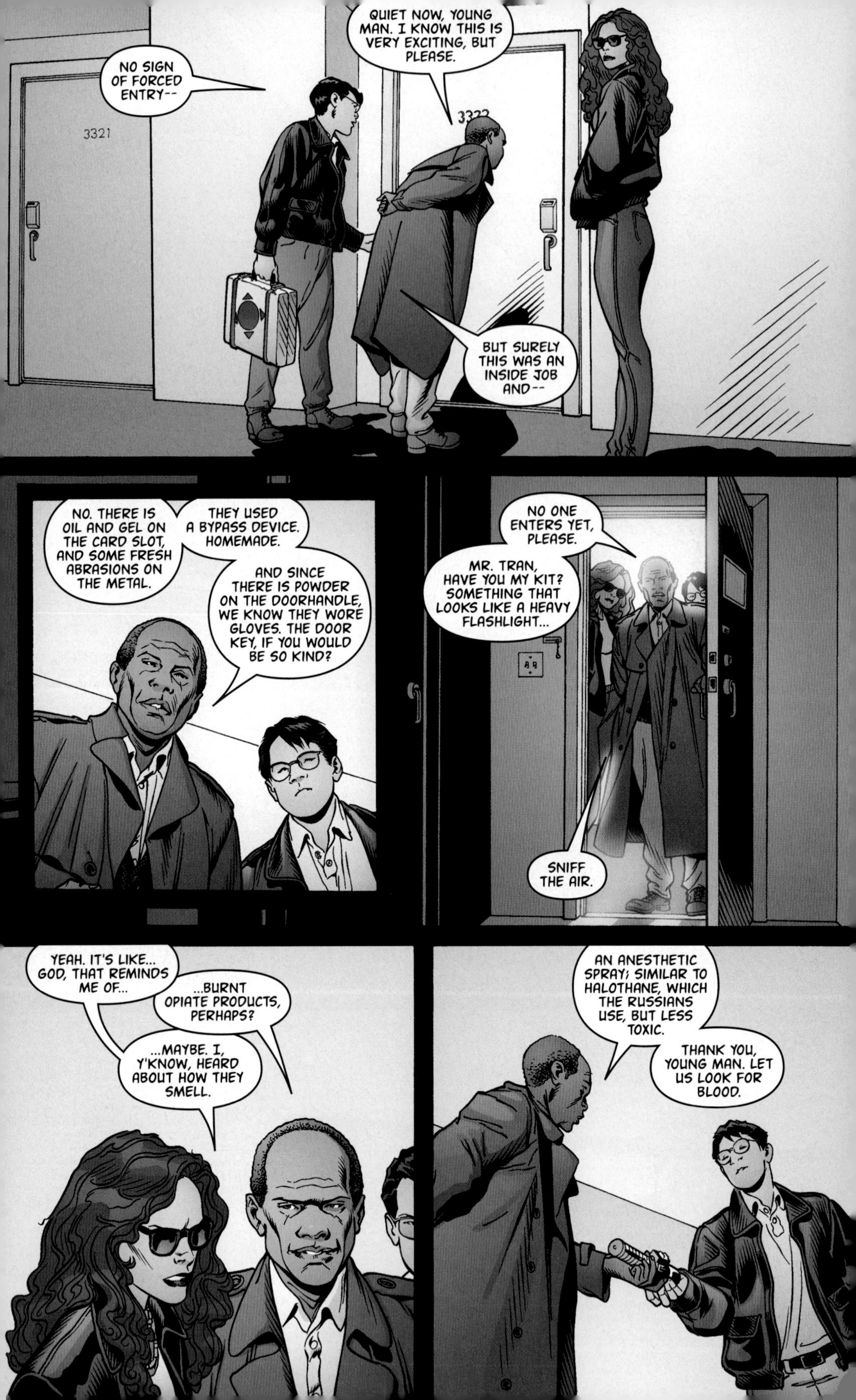
NO SIGN OF FORCED ENTRY--
QUIET NOW, YOUNG MAN. I KNOW THIS IS VERY EXCITING, BUT PLEASE.
3321
BUT SURELY THIS WAS AN INSIDE JOB AND--
NO. THERE IS OIL AND GEL ON THE CARD SLOT, AND SOME FRESH ABRASIONS ON THE METAL.
THEY USED A BYPASS DEVICE. HOMEMADE.
AND SINCE THERE IS POWDER ON THE DOORHANDLE, WE KNOW THEY WORE GLOVES. THE DOOR KEY, IF YOU WOULD BE SO KIND?
NO ONE ENTERS YET, PLEASE.
MR. TRAN, HAVE YOU MY KIT? SOMETHING THAT LOOKS LIKE A HEAVY FLASHLIGHT...
SNIFF THE AIR.
YEAH. IT'S LIKE... GOD, THAT REMINDS ME OF...
...BURNT OPIATE PRODUCTS, PERHAPS?
...MAYBE. I, Y'KNOW, HEARD ABOUT HOW THEY SMELL.
AN ANESTHETIC SPRAY; SIMILAR TO HALOTHANE, WHICH THE RUSSIANS USE, BUT LESS TOXIC.
THANK YOU, YOUNG MAN. LET US LOOK FOR BLOOD.

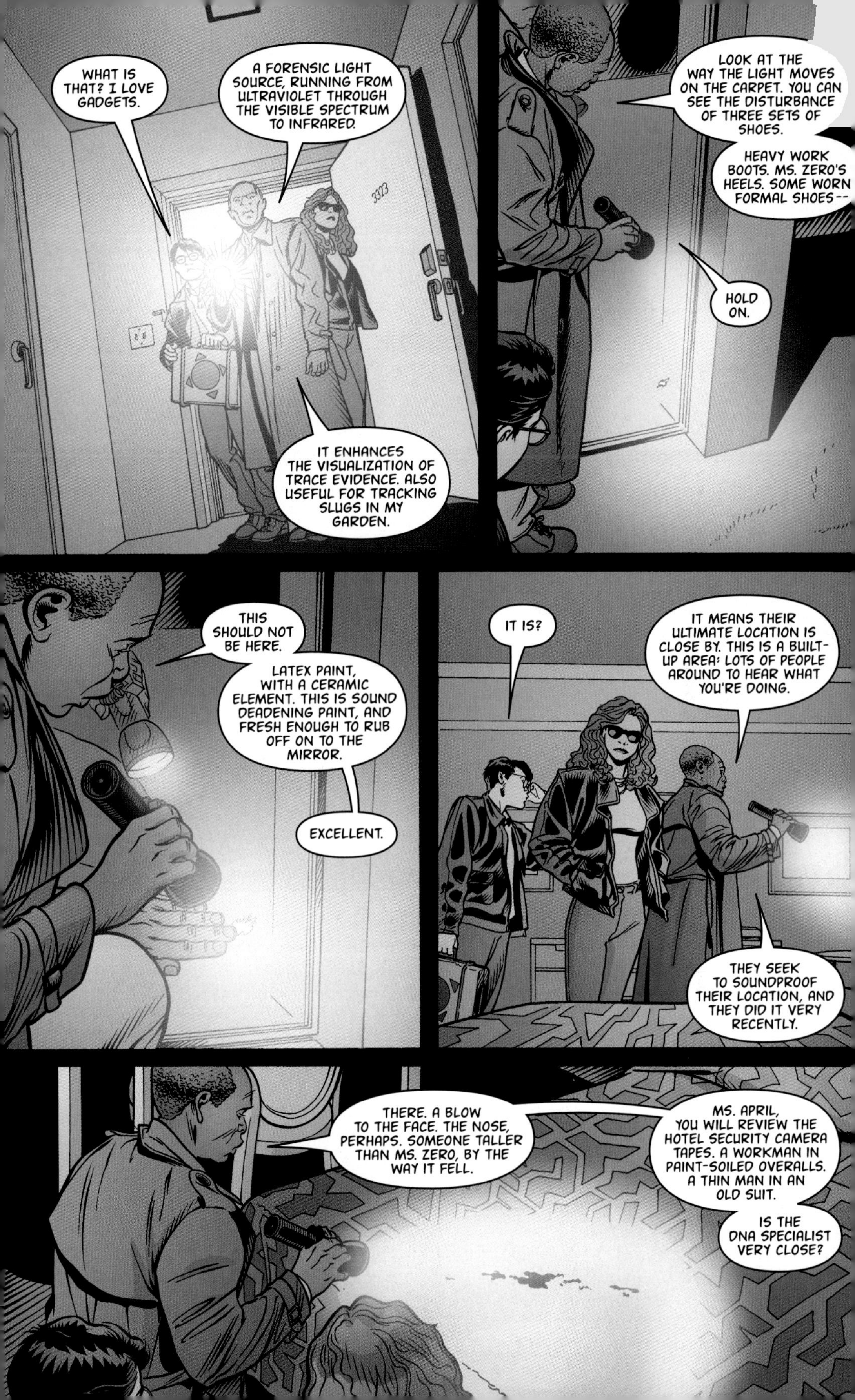
WHAT IS THAT? I LOVE GADGETS.
A FORENSIC LIGHT SOURCE, RUNNING FROM ULTRAVIOLET THROUGH THE VISIBLE SPECTRUM TO INFRARED.
3323
IT ENHANCES THE VISUALIZATION OF TRACE EVIDENCE. ALSO USEFUL FOR TRACKING SLUGS IN MY GARDEN.
LOOK AT THE WAY THE LIGHT MOVES ON THE CARPET. YOU CAN SEE THE DISTURBANCE OF THREE SETS OF SHOES.
HEAVY WORK BOOTS. MS. ZERO'S HEELS. SOME WORN FORMAL SHOES--
HOLD ON.
THIS SHOULD NOT BE HERE.
LATEX PAINT, WITH A CERAMIC ELEMENT. THIS IS SOUND DEADENING PAINT, AND FRESH ENOUGH TO RUB OFF ON TO THE MIRROR.
EXCELLENT.
IT IS?
IT MEANS THEIR ULTIMATE LOCATION IS CLOSE BY. THIS IS A BUILT-UP AREA: LOTS OF PEOPLE AROUND TO HEAR WHAT YOU'RE DOING.
THEY SEEK TO SOUNDPROOF THEIR LOCATION, AND THEY DID IT VERY RECENTLY.
THERE. A BLOW TO THE FACE. THE NOSE, PERHAPS. SOMEONE TALLER THAN MS. ZERO, BY THE WAY IT FELL.
MS. APRIL, YOU WILL REVIEW THE HOTEL SECURITY CAMERA TAPES. A WORKMAN IN PAINT-SOILED OVERALLS. A THIN MAN IN AN OLD SUIT.
IS THE DNA SPECIALIST VERY CLOSE?

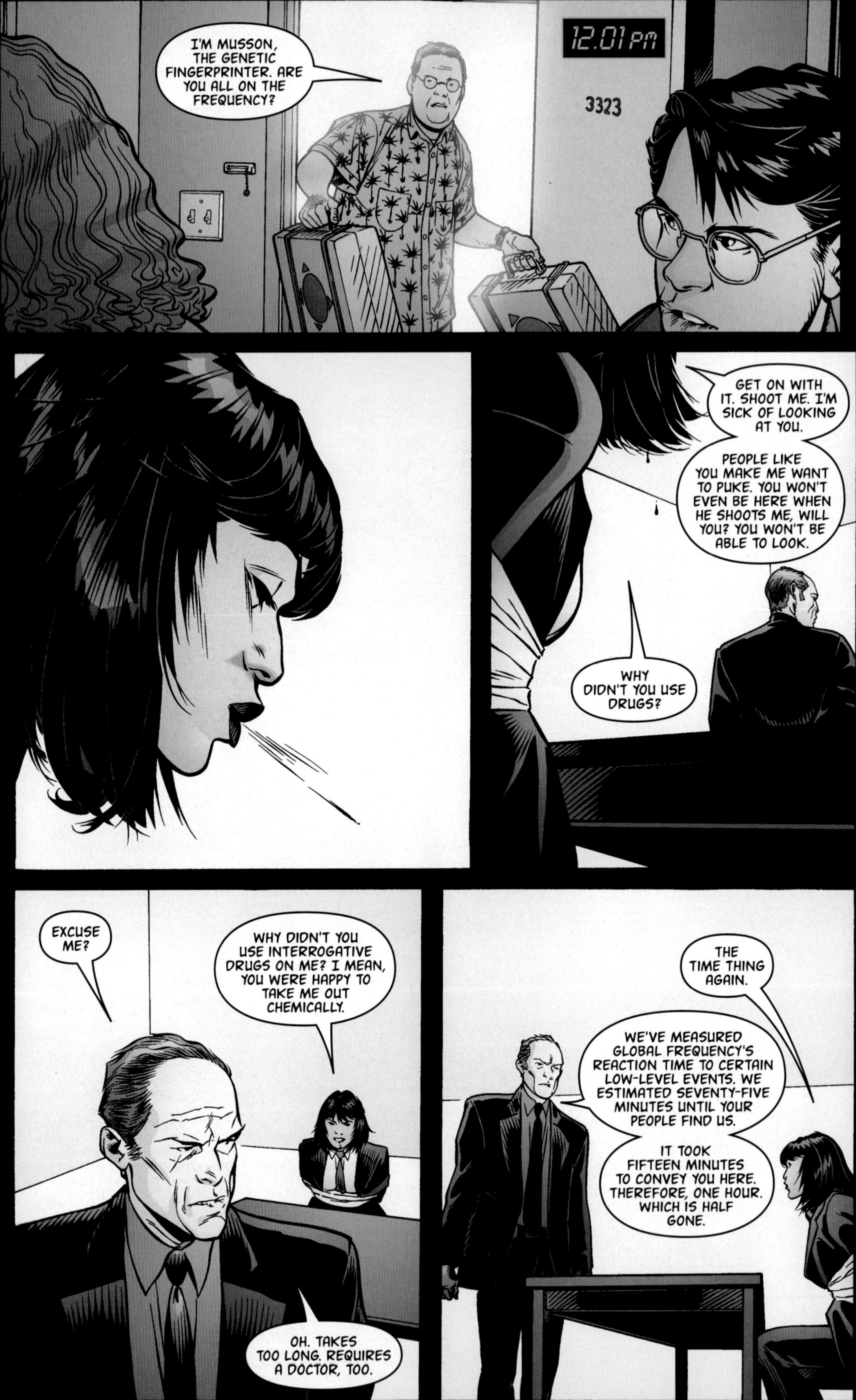
I'M MUSSON, THE GENETIC FINGERPRINTER. ARE YOU ALL ON THE FREQUENCY?
12.01 PM
3323
GET ON WITH IT. SHOOT ME. I'M SICK OF LOOKING AT YOU.
PEOPLE LIKE YOU MAKE ME WANT TO PUKE. YOU WON'T EVEN BE HERE WHEN HE SHOOTS ME, WILL YOU? YOU WON'T BE ABLE TO LOOK.
WHY DIDN'T YOU USE DRUGS?
EXCUSE ME?
WHY DIDN'T YOU USE INTERROGATIVE DRUGS ON ME? I MEAN, YOU WERE HAPPY TO TAKE ME OUT CHEMICALLY.
OH. TAKES TOO LONG. REQUIRES A DOCTOR, TOO.
THE TIME THING AGAIN.
WE'VE MEASURED GLOBAL FREQUENCY'S REACTION TIME TO CERTAIN LOW-LEVEL EVENTS. WE ESTIMATED SEVENTY-FIVE MINUTES UNTIL YOUR PEOPLE FIND US.
IT TOOK FIFTEEN MINUTES TO CONVEY YOU HERE. THEREFORE, ONE HOUR. WHICH IS HALF GONE.

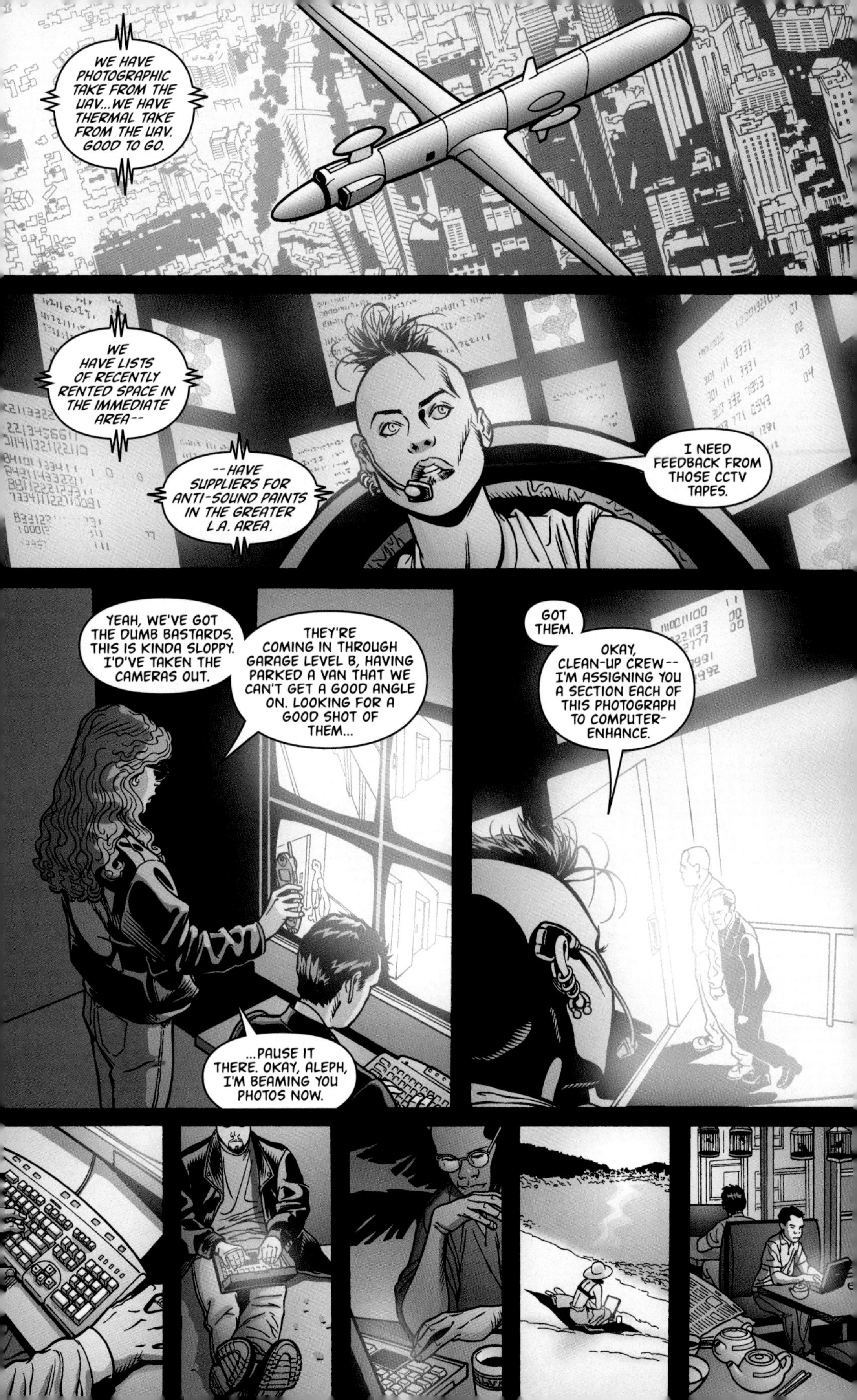
WE HAVE PHOTOGRAPHIC TAKE FROM THE UAV...WE HAVE THERMAL TAKE FROM THE UAV. GOOD TO GO.
WE HAVE LISTS OF RECENTLY RENTED SPACE IN THE IMMEDIATE AREA--
--HAVE SUPPLIERS FOR ANTI-SOUND PAINTS IN THE GREATER L.A. AREA.
I NEED FEEDBACK FROM THOSE CCTV TAPES.
YEAH, WE'VE GOT THE DUMB BASTARDS. THIS IS KINDA SLOPPY. I'D'VE TAKEN THE CAMERAS OUT.
THEY'RE COMING IN THROUGH GARAGE LEVEL B, HAVING PARKED A VAN THAT WE CAN'T GET A GOOD ANGLE ON. LOOKING FOR A GOOD SHOT OF THEM...
...PAUSE IT THERE. OKAY, ALEPH, I'M BEAMING YOU PHOTOS NOW.
GOT THEM.
OKAY, CLEAN-UP CREW-- I'M ASSIGNING YOU A SECTION EACH OF THIS PHOTOGRAPH TO COMPUTER-ENHANCE.

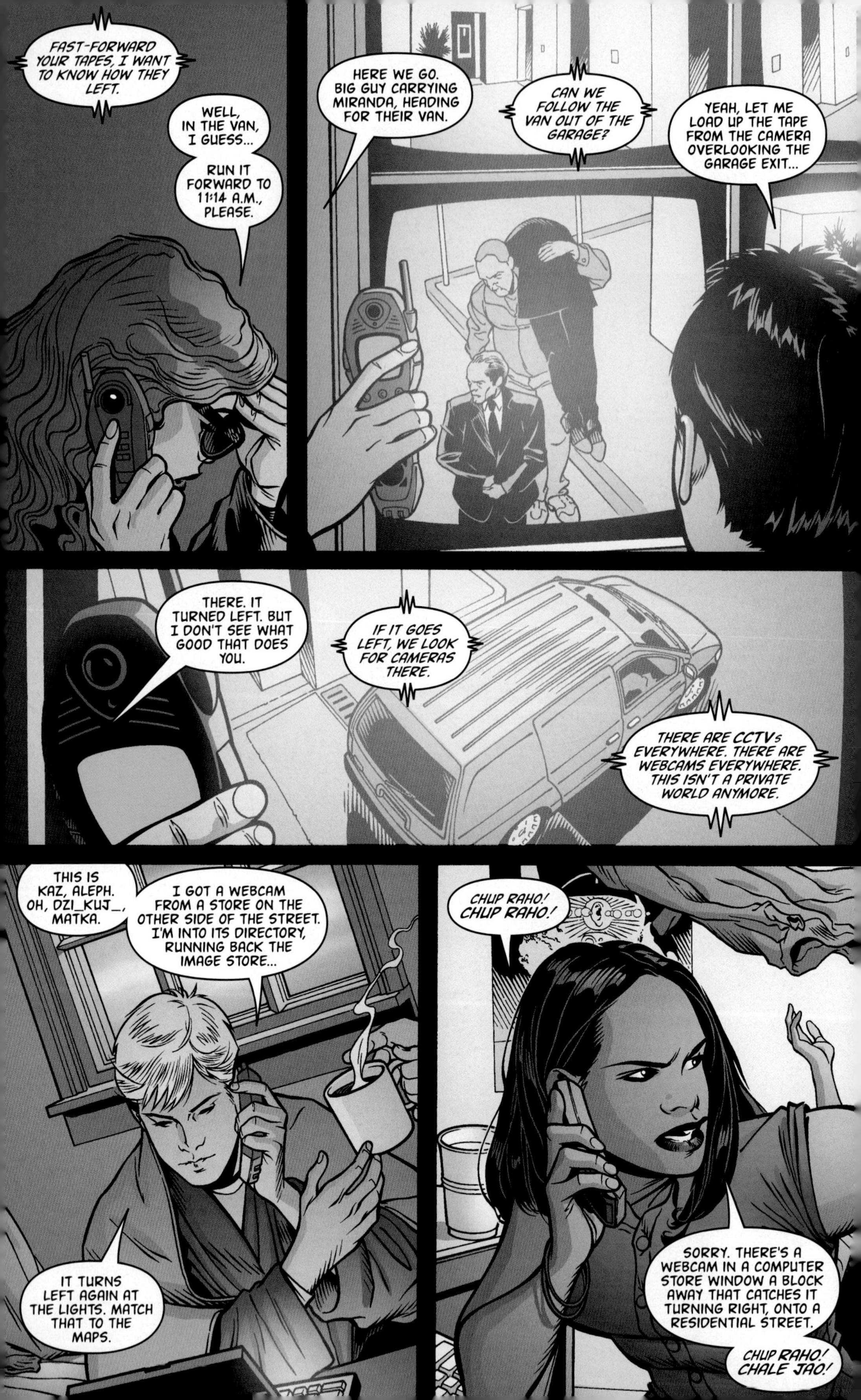
FAST-FORWARD YOUR TAPES, I WANT TO KNOW HOW THEY LEFT.
WELL, IN THE VAN, I GUESS...
RUN IT FORWARD TO 11:14 A.M., PLEASE.
HERE WE GO. BIG GUY CARRYING MIRANDA, HEADING FOR THEIR VAN.
CAN WE FOLLOW THE VAN OUT OF THE GARAGE?
YEAH, LET ME LOAD UP THE TAPE FROM THE CAMERA OVERLOOKING THE GARAGE EXIT...
THERE. IT TURNED LEFT. BUT I DON'T SEE WHAT GOOD THAT DOES YOU.
IF IT GOES LEFT, WE LOOK FOR CAMERAS THERE.
THERE ARE CCTVs EVERYWHERE. THERE ARE WEBCAMS EVERYWHERE. THIS ISN'T A PRIVATE WORLD ANYMORE.
THIS IS KAZ, ALEPH. OH, DZI_KUJ_, MATKA.
I GOT A WEBCAM FROM A STORE ON THE OTHER SIDE OF THE STREET. I'M INTO ITS DIRECTORY, RUNNING BACK THE IMAGE STORE...
IT TURNS LEFT AGAIN AT THE LIGHTS. MATCH THAT TO THE MAPS.
CHUP RAHO! CHUP RAHO!
SORRY. THERE'S A WEBCAM IN A COMPUTER STORE WINDOW A BLOCK AWAY THAT CATCHES IT TURNING RIGHT, ONTO A RESIDENTIAL STREET.
CHUP RAHO! CHALE JAO!

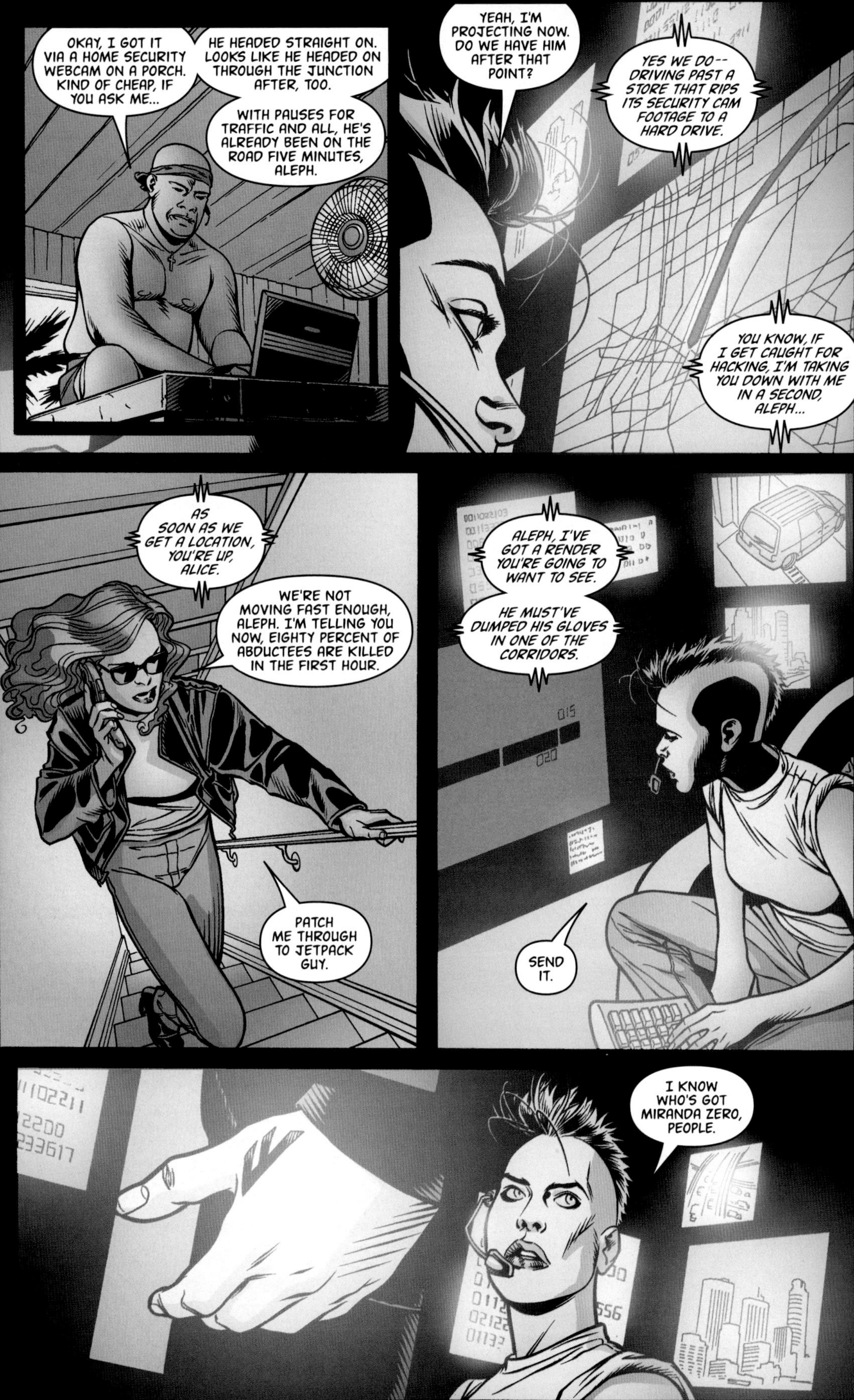
OKAY, I GOT IT VIA A HOME SECURITY WEBCAM ON A PORCH. KIND OF CHEAP, IF YOU ASK ME...
HE HEADED STRAIGHT ON. LOOKS LIKE HE HEADED ON THROUGH THE JUNCTION AFTER, TOO.
WITH PAUSES FOR TRAFFIC AND ALL, HE'S ALREADY BEEN ON THE ROAD FIVE MINUTES, ALEPH.
YEAH, I'M PROJECTING NOW. DO WE HAVE HIM AFTER THAT POINT?
YES WE DO-- DRIVING PAST A STORE THAT RIPS ITS SECURITY CAM FOOTAGE TO A HARD DRIVE.
YOU KNOW, IF I GET CAUGHT FOR HACKING, I'M TAKING YOU DOWN WITH ME IN A SECOND, ALEPH...
AS SOON AS WE GET A LOCATION, YOU'RE UP, ALICE.
WE'RE NOT MOVING FAST ENOUGH, ALEPH. I'M TELLING YOU NOW, EIGHTY PERCENT OF ABDUCTEES ARE KILLED IN THE FIRST HOUR.
PATCH ME THROUGH TO JETPACK GUY.
ALEPH, I'VE GOT A RENDER YOU'RE GOING TO WANT TO SEE.
HE MUST'VE DUMPED HIS GLOVES IN ONE OF THE CORRIDORS.
SEND IT.
I KNOW WHO'S GOT MIRANDA ZERO, PEOPLE.

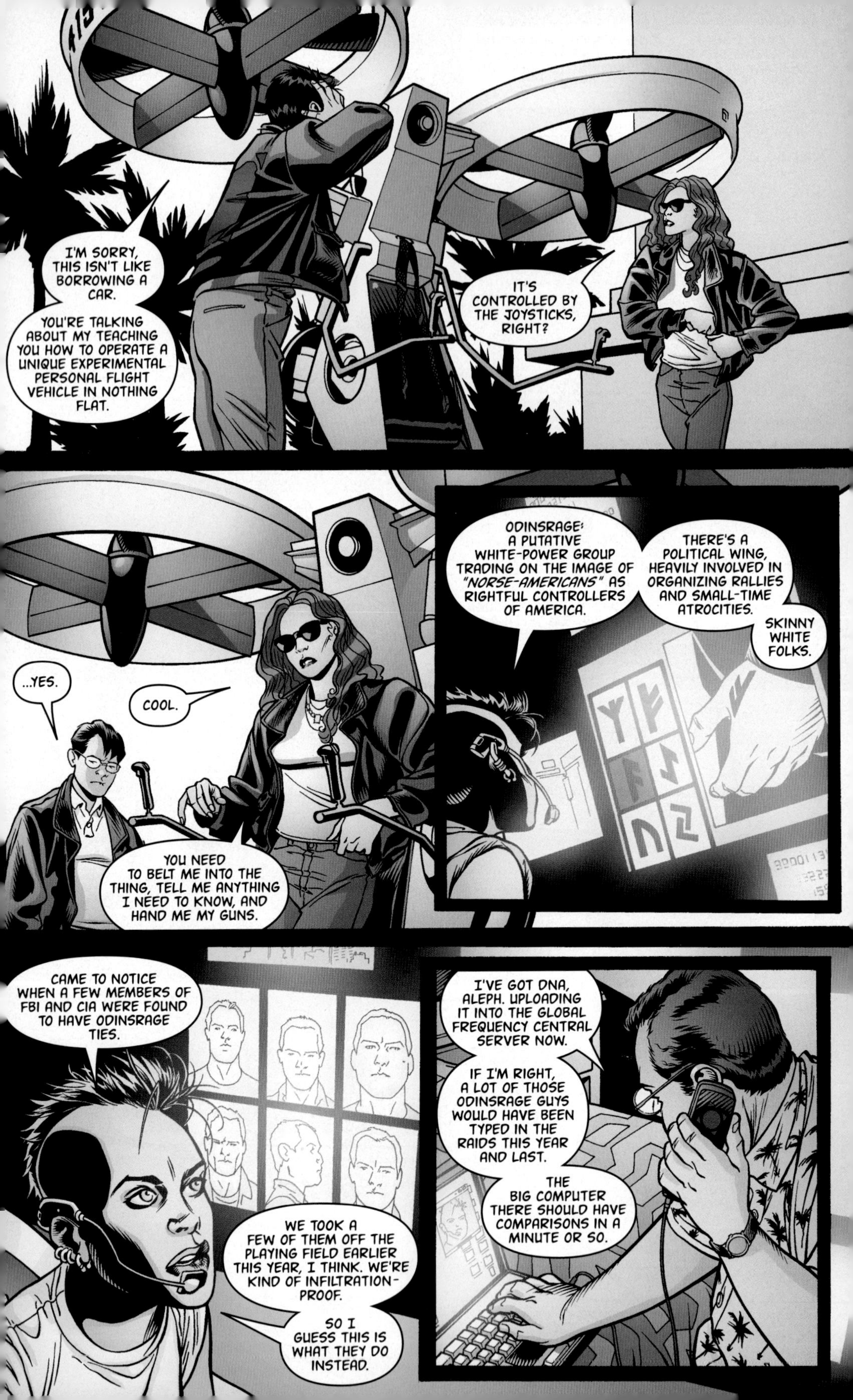
I'M SORRY, THIS ISN'T LIKE BORROWING A CAR.
YOU'RE TALKING ABOUT MY TEACHING YOU HOW TO OPERATE A UNIQUE EXPERIMENTAL PERSONAL FLIGHT VEHICLE IN NOTHING FLAT.
IT'S CONTROLLED BY THE JOYSTICKS, RIGHT?
...YES.
COOL.
YOU NEED TO BELT ME INTO THE THING, TELL ME ANYTHING I NEED TO KNOW, AND HAND ME MY GUNS.
ODINSRAGE: A PUTATIVE WHITE-POWER GROUP TRADING ON THE IMAGE OF "NORSE-AMERICANS" AS RIGHTFUL CONTROLLERS OF AMERICA.
THERE'S A POLITICAL WING, HEAVILY INVOLVED IN ORGANIZING RALLIES AND SMALL-TIME ATROCITIES.
SKINNY WHITE FOLKS.
CAME TO NOTICE WHEN A FEW MEMBERS OF FBI AND CIA WERE FOUND TO HAVE ODINSRAGE TIES.
WE TOOK A FEW OF THEM OFF THE PLAYING FIELD EARLIER THIS YEAR, I THINK. WE'RE KIND OF INFILTRATION-PROOF.
SO I GUESS THIS IS WHAT THEY DO INSTEAD.
I'VE GOT DNA, ALEPH. UPLOADING IT INTO THE GLOBAL FREQUENCY CENTRAL SERVER NOW.
IF I'M RIGHT, A LOT OF THOSE ODINSRAGE GUYS WOULD HAVE BEEN TYPED IN THE RAIDS THIS YEAR AND LAST.
THE BIG COMPUTER THERE SHOULD HAVE COMPARISONS IN A MINUTE OR SO.

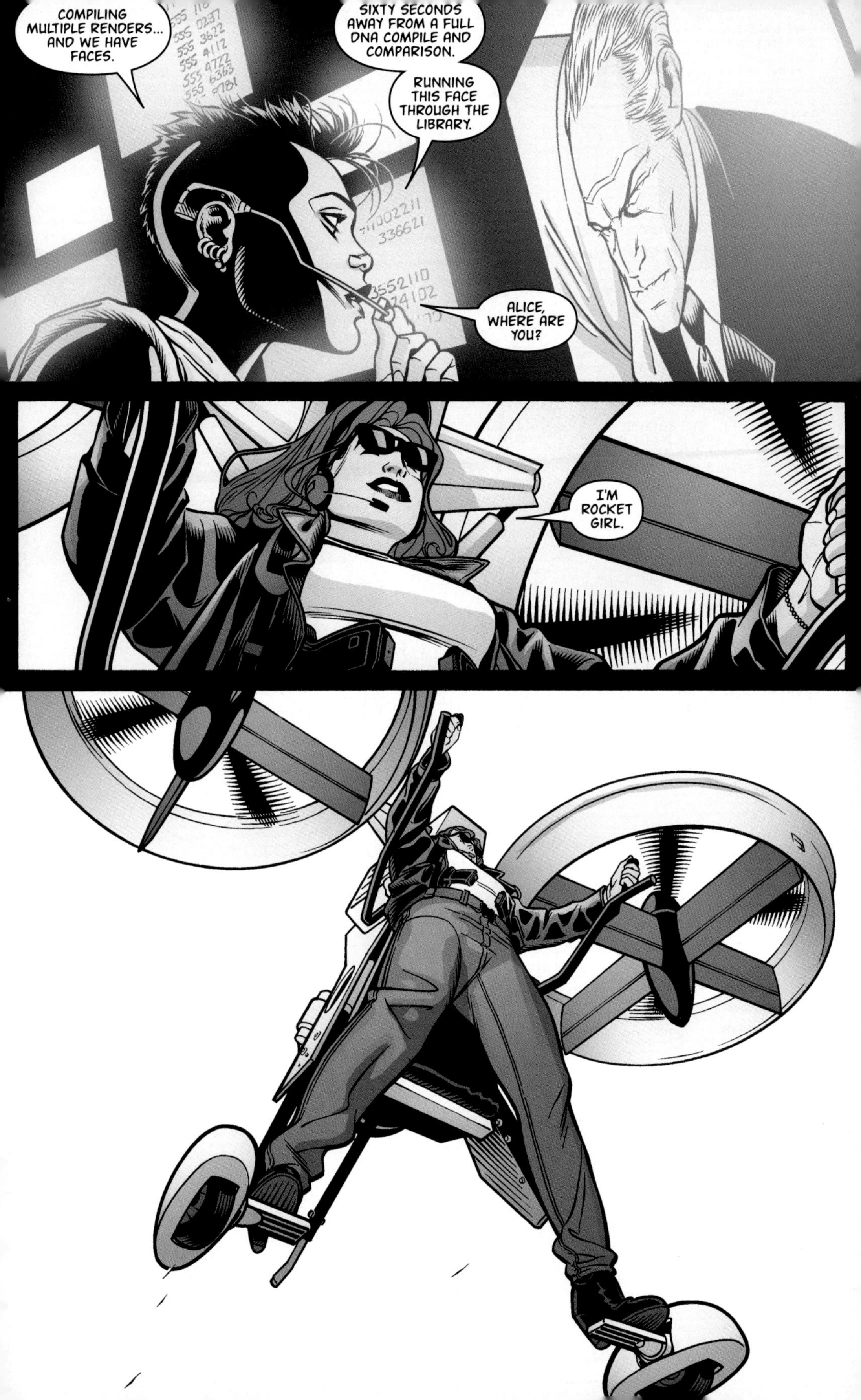
COMPILING MULTIPLE RENDERS... AND WE HAVE FACES.
SIXTY SECONDS AWAY FROM A FULL DNA COMPILE AND COMPARISON.
RUNNING THIS FACE THROUGH THE LIBRARY.
ALICE, WHERE ARE YOU?
I'M ROCKET GIRL.

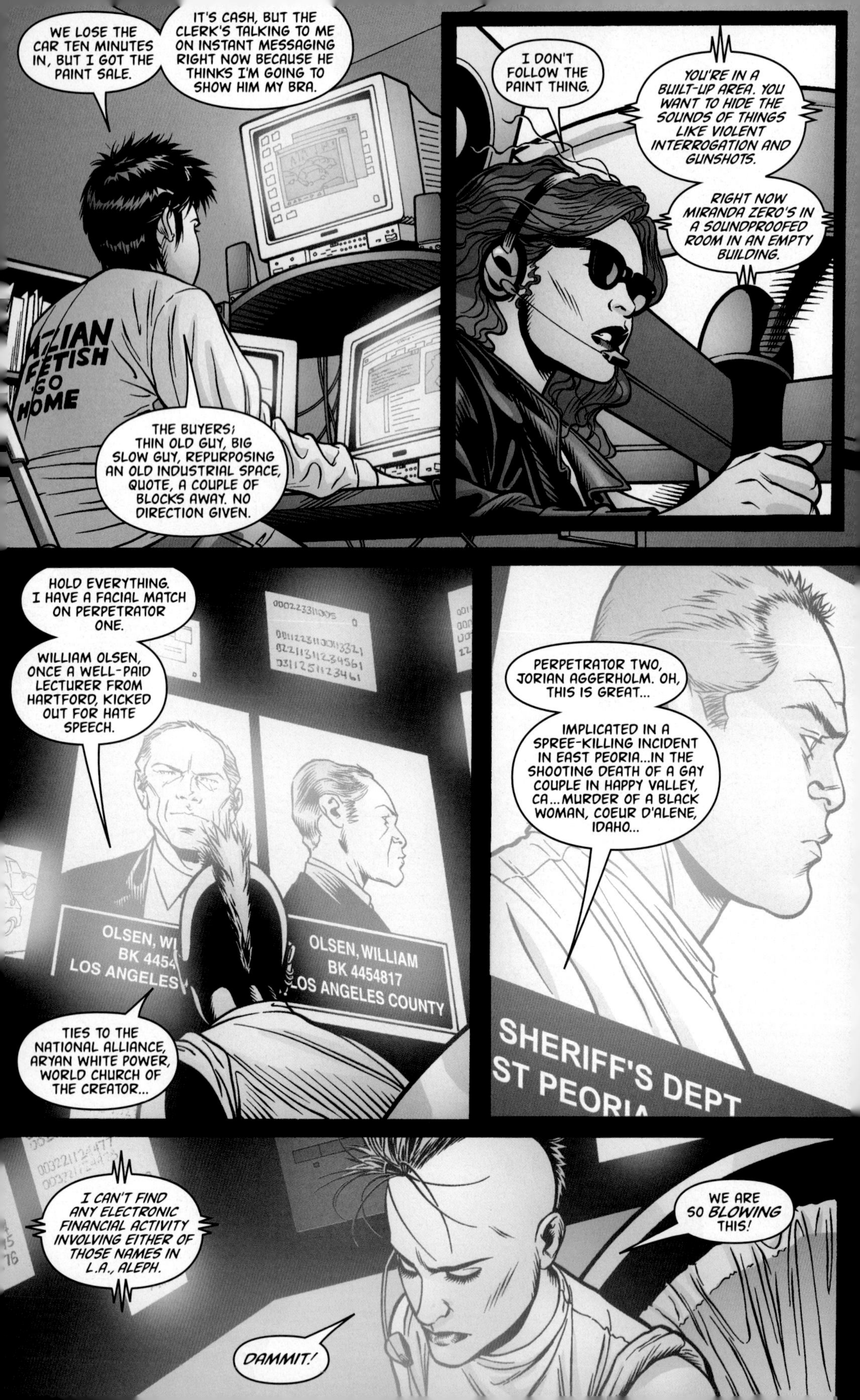
WE LOSE THE CAR TEN MINUTES IN, BUT I GOT THE PAINT SALE.
IT'S CASH, BUT THE CLERK'S TALKING TO ME ON INSTANT MESSAGING RIGHT NOW BECAUSE HE THINKS I'M GOING TO SHOW HIM MY BRA.
ALIAN FETISH GO HOME
THE BUYERS; THIN OLD GUY, BIG SLOW GUY, REPURPOSING AN OLD INDUSTRIAL SPACE, QUOTE, A COUPLE OF BLOCKS AWAY. NO DIRECTION GIVEN.
I DON'T FOLLOW THE PAINT THING.
YOU'RE IN A BUILT-UP AREA. YOU WANT TO HIDE THE SOUNDS OF THINGS LIKE VIOLENT INTERROGATION AND GUNSHOTS.
RIGHT NOW MIRANDA ZERO'S IN A SOUNDPROOFED ROOM IN AN EMPTY BUILDING.
HOLD EVERYTHING. I HAVE A FACIAL MATCH ON PERPETRATOR ONE.
WILLIAM OLSEN, ONCE A WELL-PAID LECTURER FROM HARTFORD, KICKED OUT FOR HATE SPEECH.
OLSEN, WILLIAM
BK 4454817
LOS ANGELES COUNTY
TIES TO THE NATIONAL ALLIANCE, ARYAN WHITE POWER, WORLD CHURCH OF THE CREATOR...
PERPETRATOR TWO, JORIAN AGGERHOLM. OH, THIS IS GREAT...
IMPLICATED IN A SPREE-KILLING INCIDENT IN EAST PEORIA...IN THE SHOOTING DEATH OF A GAY COUPLE IN HAPPY VALLEY, CA...MURDER OF A BLACK WOMAN, COEUR D'ALENE, IDAHO...
SHERIFF'S DEPT
ST PEORIA
I CAN'T FIND ANY ELECTRONIC FINANCIAL ACTIVITY INVOLVING EITHER OF THOSE NAMES IN L.A., ALEPH.
WE ARE SO BLOWING THIS!
DAMMIT!

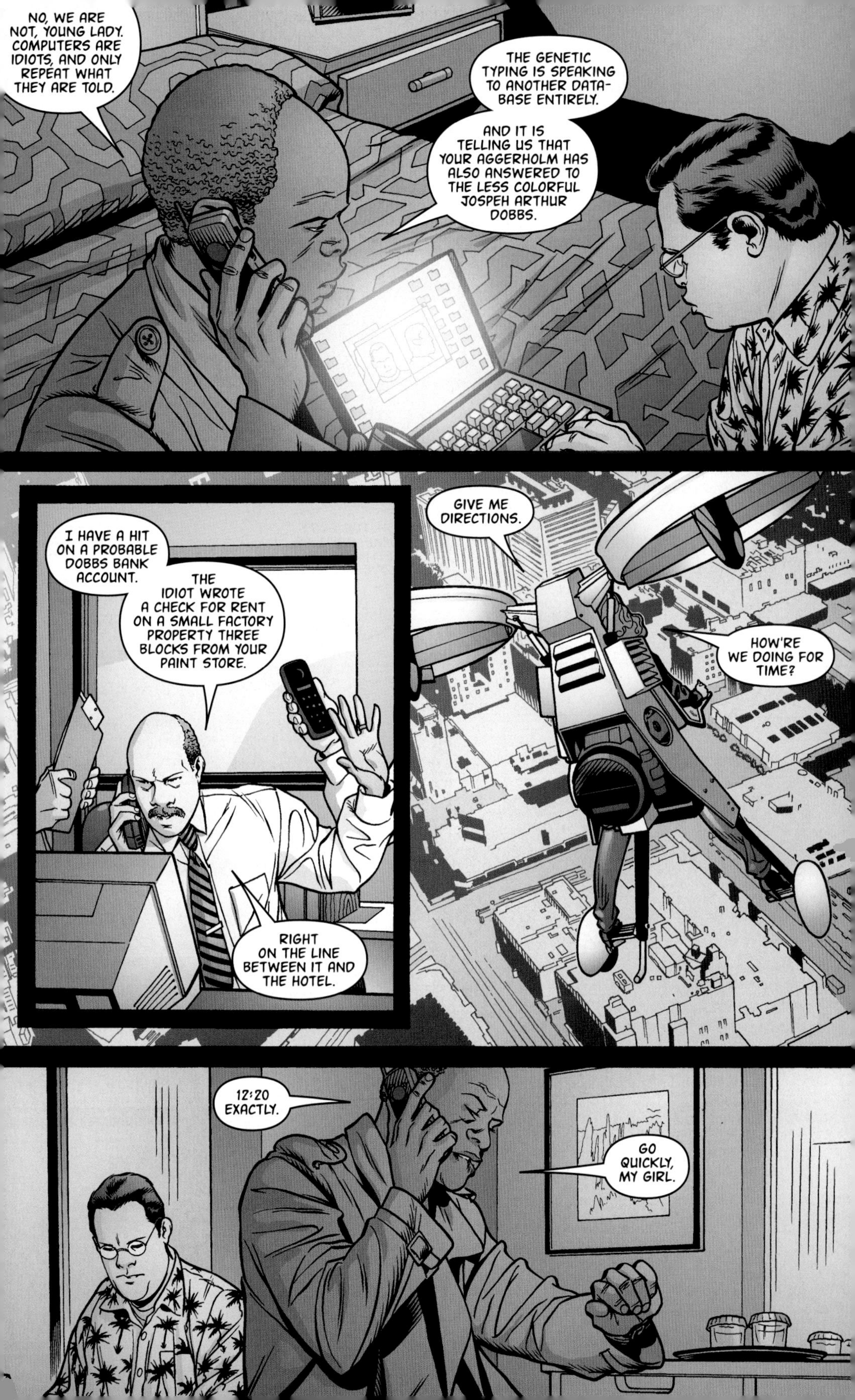
NO, WE ARE NOT, YOUNG LADY. COMPUTERS ARE IDIOTS, AND ONLY REPEAT WHAT THEY ARE TOLD.
THE GENETIC TYPING IS SPEAKING TO ANOTHER DATA-BASE ENTIRELY.
AND IT IS TELLING US THAT YOUR AGGERHOLM HAS ALSO ANSWERED TO THE LESS COLORFUL JOSPEH ARTHUR DOBBS.
I HAVE A HIT ON A PROBABLE DOBBS BANK ACCOUNT.
THE IDIOT WROTE A CHECK FOR RENT ON A SMALL FACTORY PROPERTY THREE BLOCKS FROM YOUR PAINT STORE.
RIGHT ON THE LINE BETWEEN IT AND THE HOTEL.
GIVE ME DIRECTIONS.
HOW'RE WE DOING FOR TIME?
12:20 EXACTLY.
GO QUICKLY, MY GIRL.

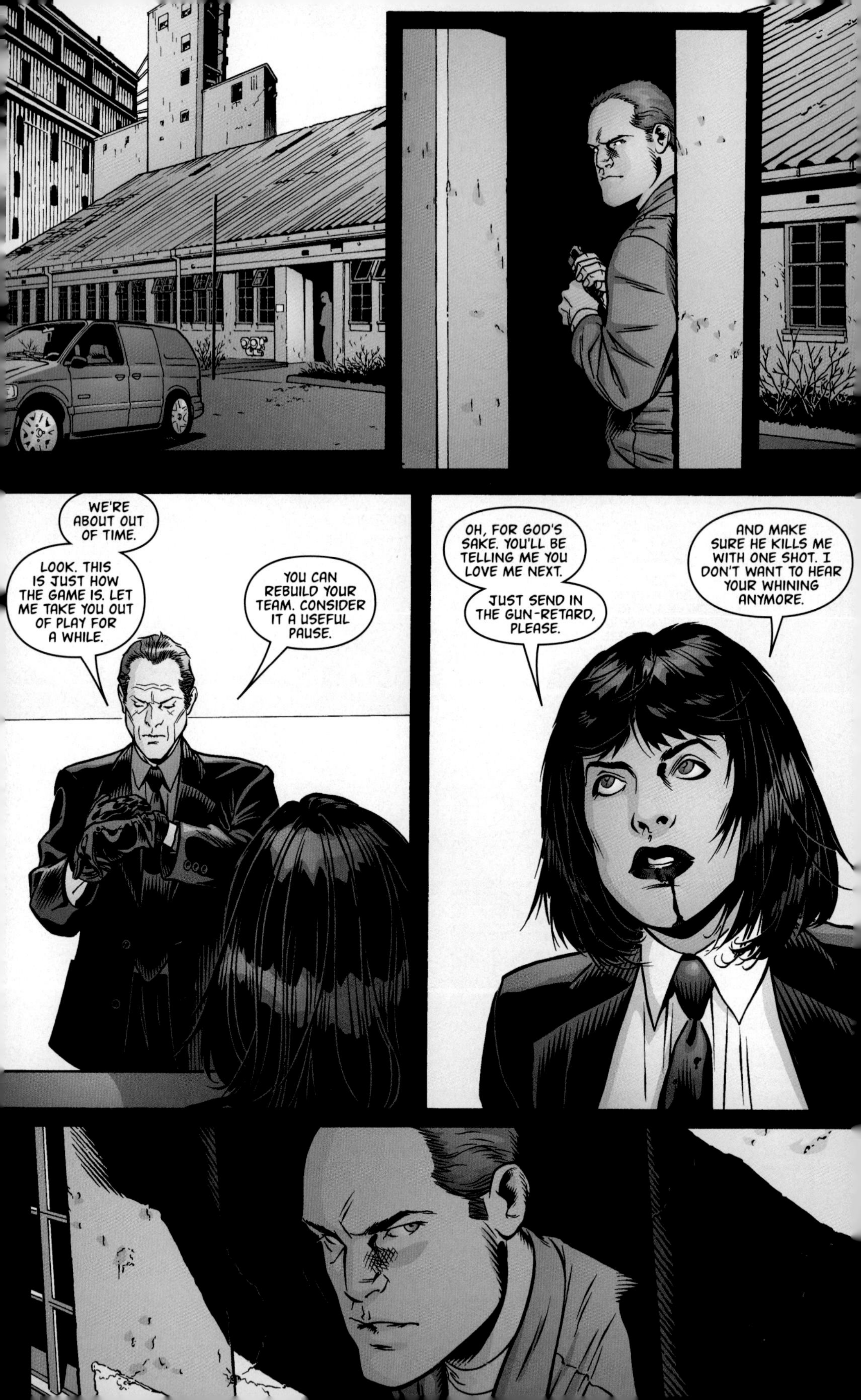
WE'RE ABOUT OUT OF TIME.
LOOK. THIS IS JUST HOW THE GAME IS. LET ME TAKE YOU OUT OF PLAY FOR A WHILE.
YOU CAN REBUILD YOUR TEAM. CONSIDER IT A USEFUL PAUSE.
OH, FOR GOD'S SAKE. YOU'LL BE TELLING ME YOU LOVE ME NEXT.
JUST SEND IN THE GUN-RETARD, PLEASE.
AND MAKE SURE HE KILLS ME WITH ONE SHOT. I DON'T WANT TO HEAR YOUR WHINING ANYMORE.

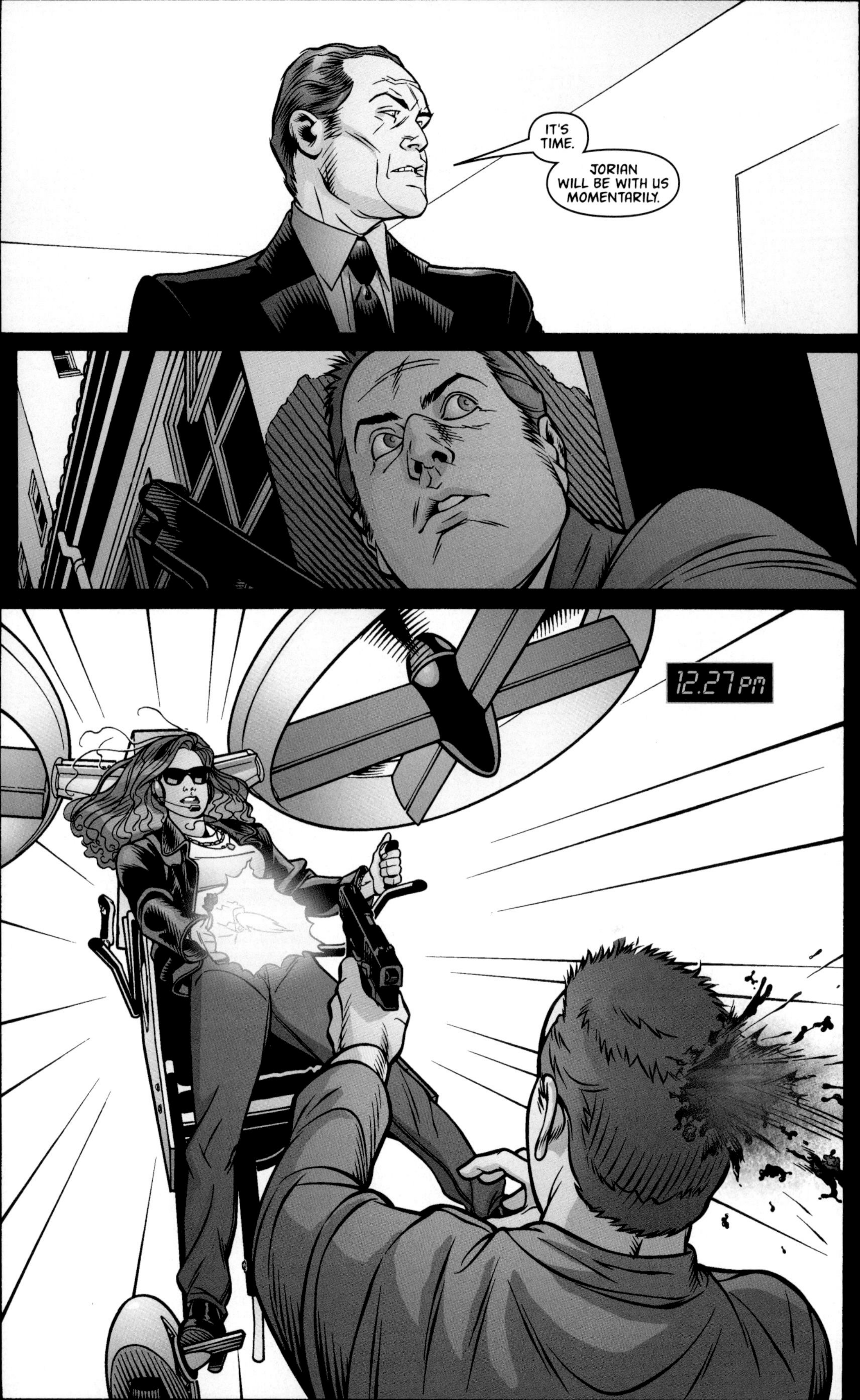
IT'S TIME.
JORIAN WILL BE WITH US MOMENTARILY.
12:27 PM

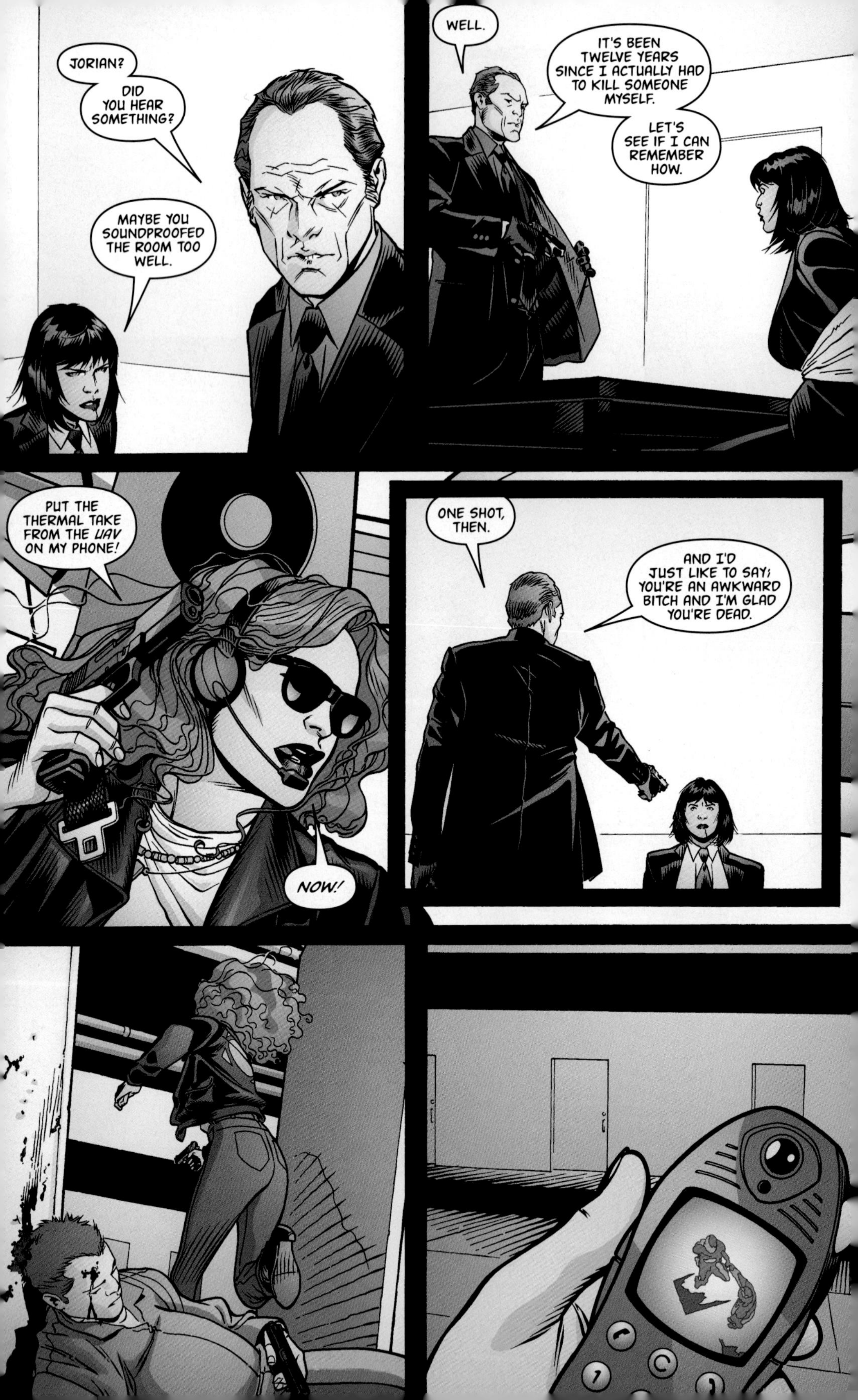
JORIAN?
DID YOU HEAR SOMETHING?
MAYBE YOU SOUNDPROOFED THE ROOM TOO WELL.
WELL.
IT'S BEEN TWELVE YEARS SINCE I ACTUALLY HAD TO KILL SOMEONE MYSELF.
LET'S SEE IF I CAN REMEMBER HOW.
PUT THE THERMAL TAKE FROM THE *UAV* ON MY PHONE!
NOW!
ONE SHOT, THEN.
AND I'D JUST LIKE TO SAY; YOU'RE AN AWKWARD BITCH AND I'M GLAD YOU'RE DEAD.

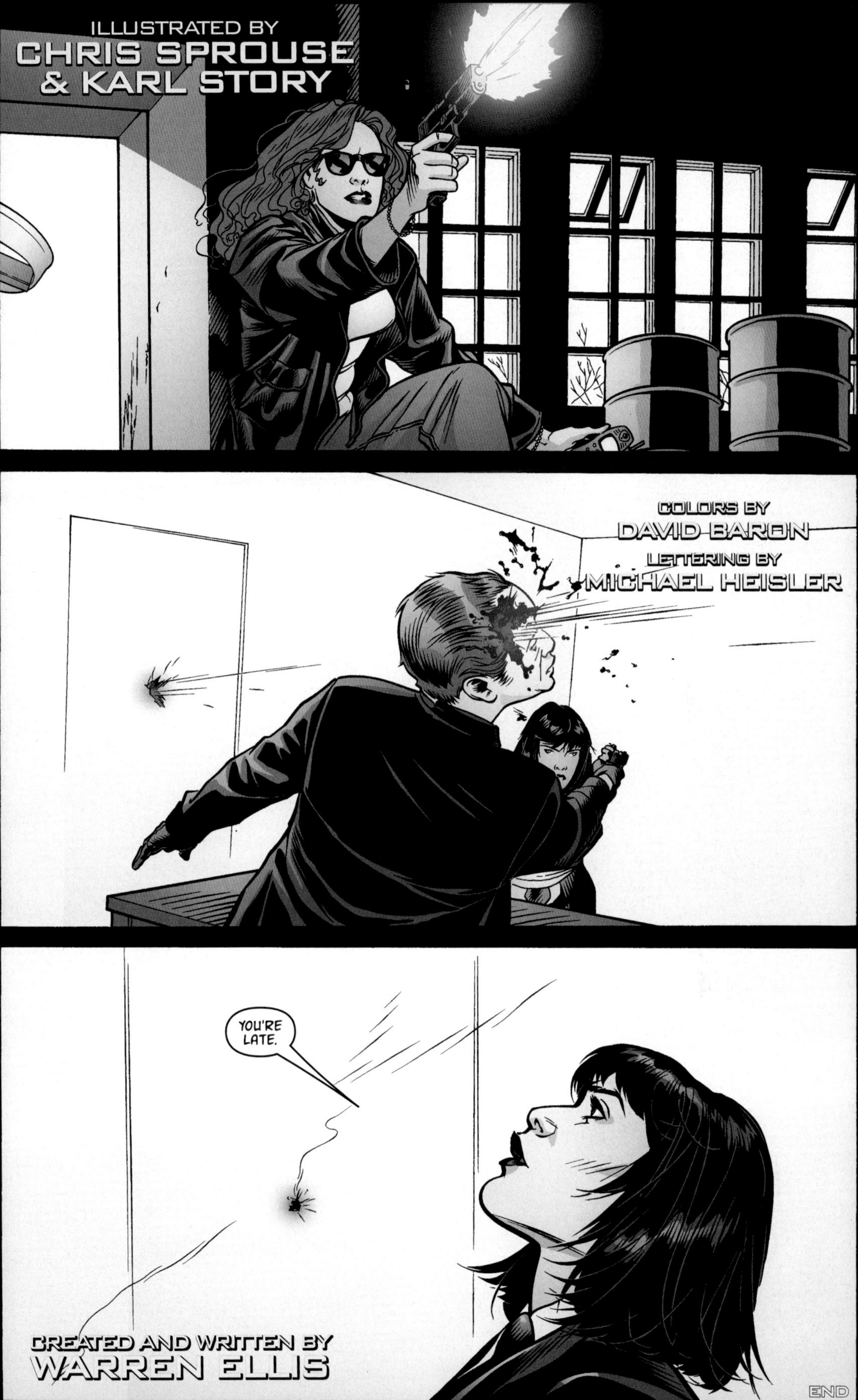
ILLUSTRATED BY
CHRIS SPROUSE
& KARL STORY
COLORS BY
DAVID BARON
LETTERING BY
MICHAEL HEISLER
YOU'RE LATE.
CREATED AND WRITTEN BY
WARREN ELLIS
END

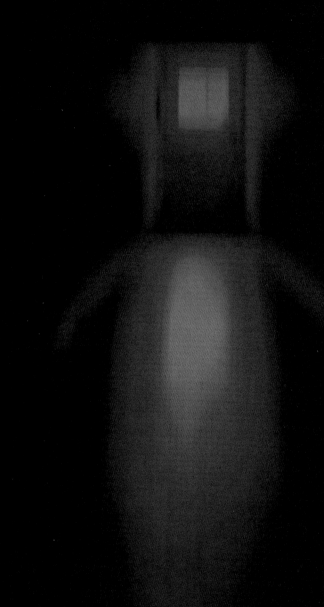

GLOBAL
FREQUENCY

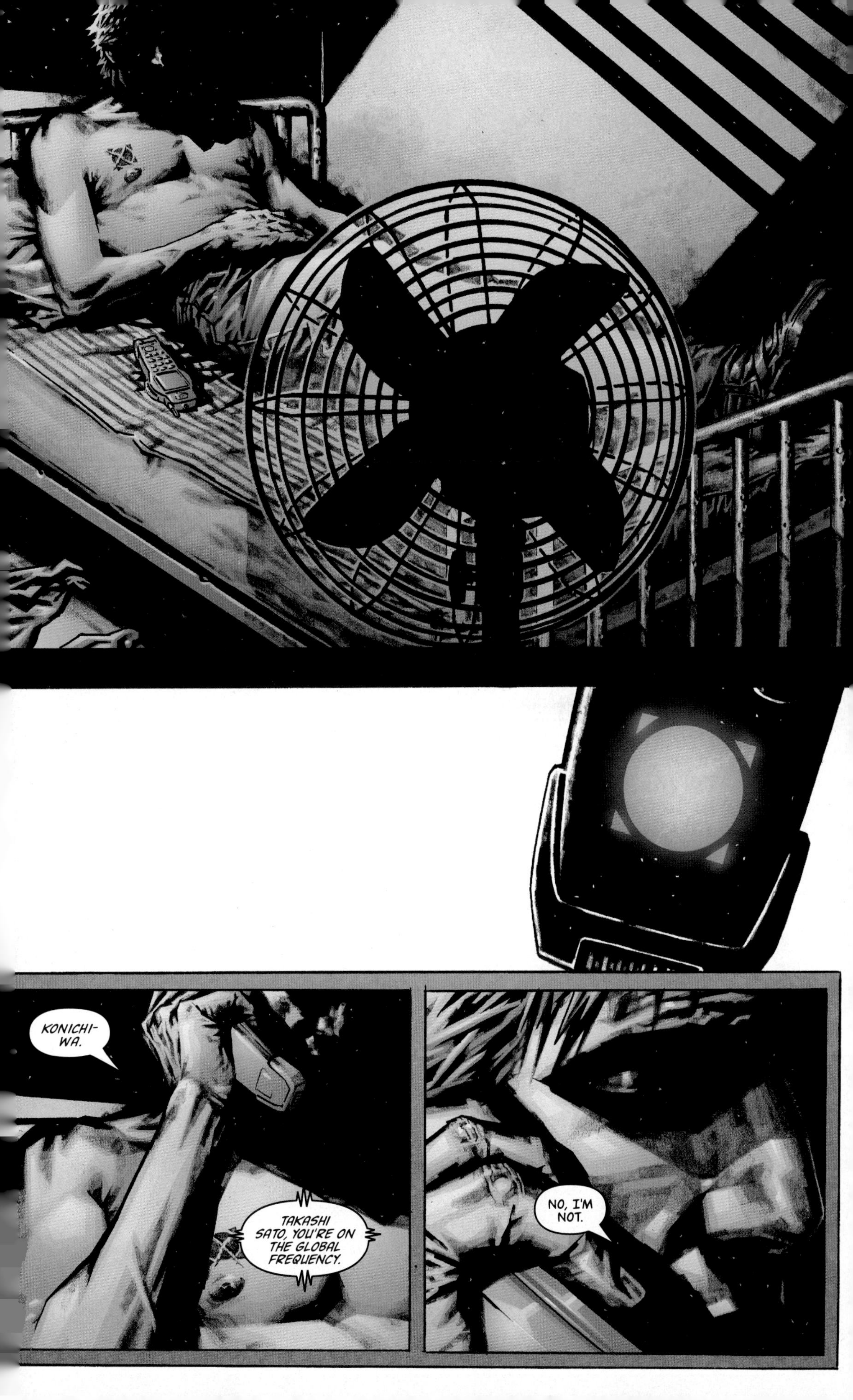
KONICHI-
WA.
TAKASHI
SATO, YOU'RE ON
THE GLOBAL
FREQUENCY.
NO, I'M
NOT.

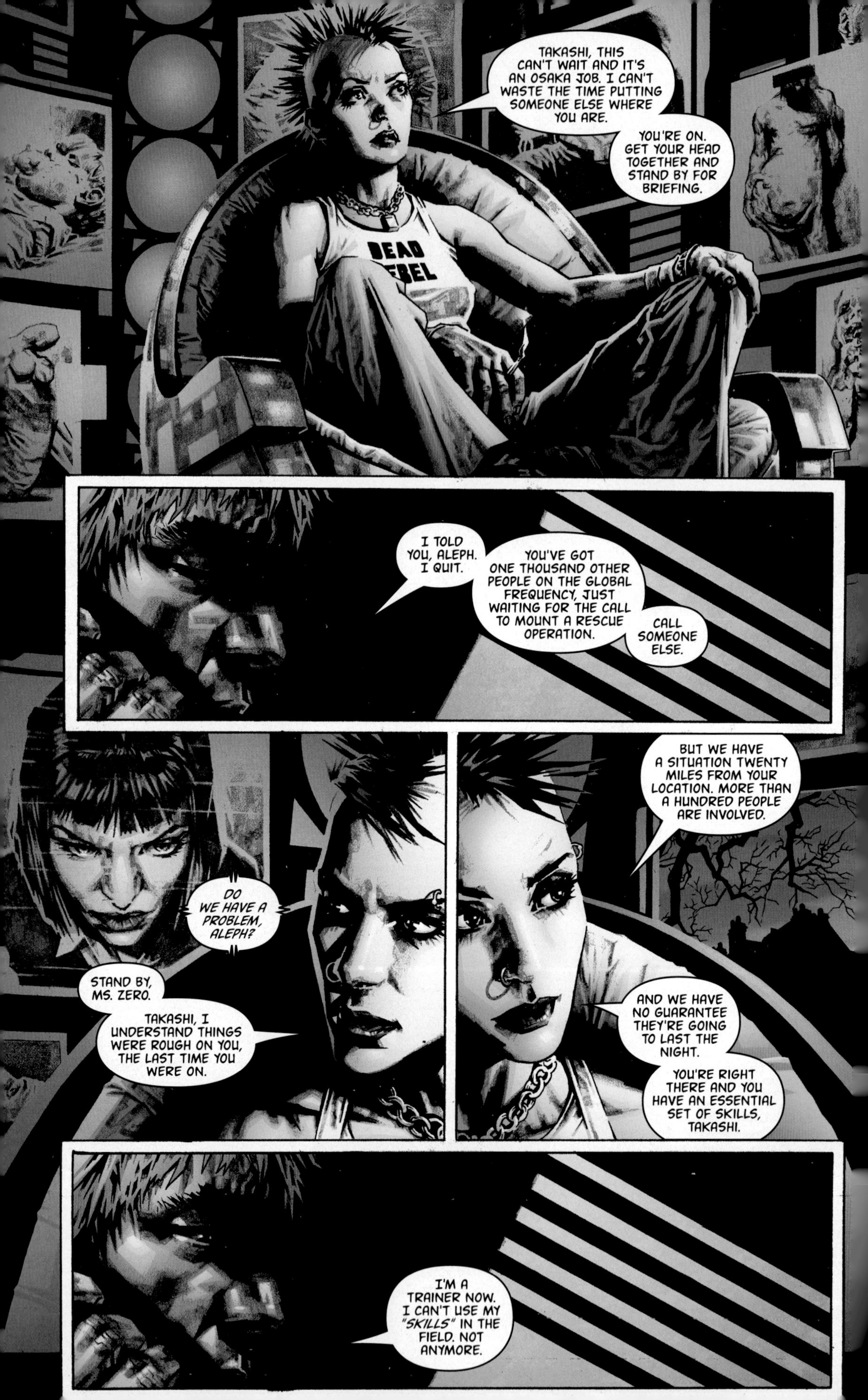
TAKASHI, THIS CAN'T WAIT AND IT'S AN OSAKA JOB. I CAN'T WASTE THE TIME PUTTING SOMEONE ELSE WHERE YOU ARE.
YOU'RE ON. GET YOUR HEAD TOGETHER AND STAND BY FOR BRIEFING.
DEAD REBEL
I TOLD YOU, ALEPH. I QUIT.
YOU'VE GOT ONE THOUSAND OTHER PEOPLE ON THE GLOBAL FREQUENCY, JUST WAITING FOR THE CALL TO MOUNT A RESCUE OPERATION.
CALL SOMEONE ELSE.
DO WE HAVE A PROBLEM, ALEPH?
STAND BY, MS. ZERO.
TAKASHI, I UNDERSTAND THINGS WERE ROUGH ON YOU, THE LAST TIME YOU WERE ON.
BUT WE HAVE A SITUATION TWENTY MILES FROM YOUR LOCATION. MORE THAN A HUNDRED PEOPLE ARE INVOLVED.
AND WE HAVE NO GUARANTEE THEY'RE GOING TO LAST THE NIGHT.
YOU'RE RIGHT THERE AND YOU HAVE AN ESSENTIAL SET OF SKILLS, TAKASHI.
I'M A TRAINER NOW. I CAN'T USE MY "SKILLS" IN THE FIELD. NOT ANYMORE.

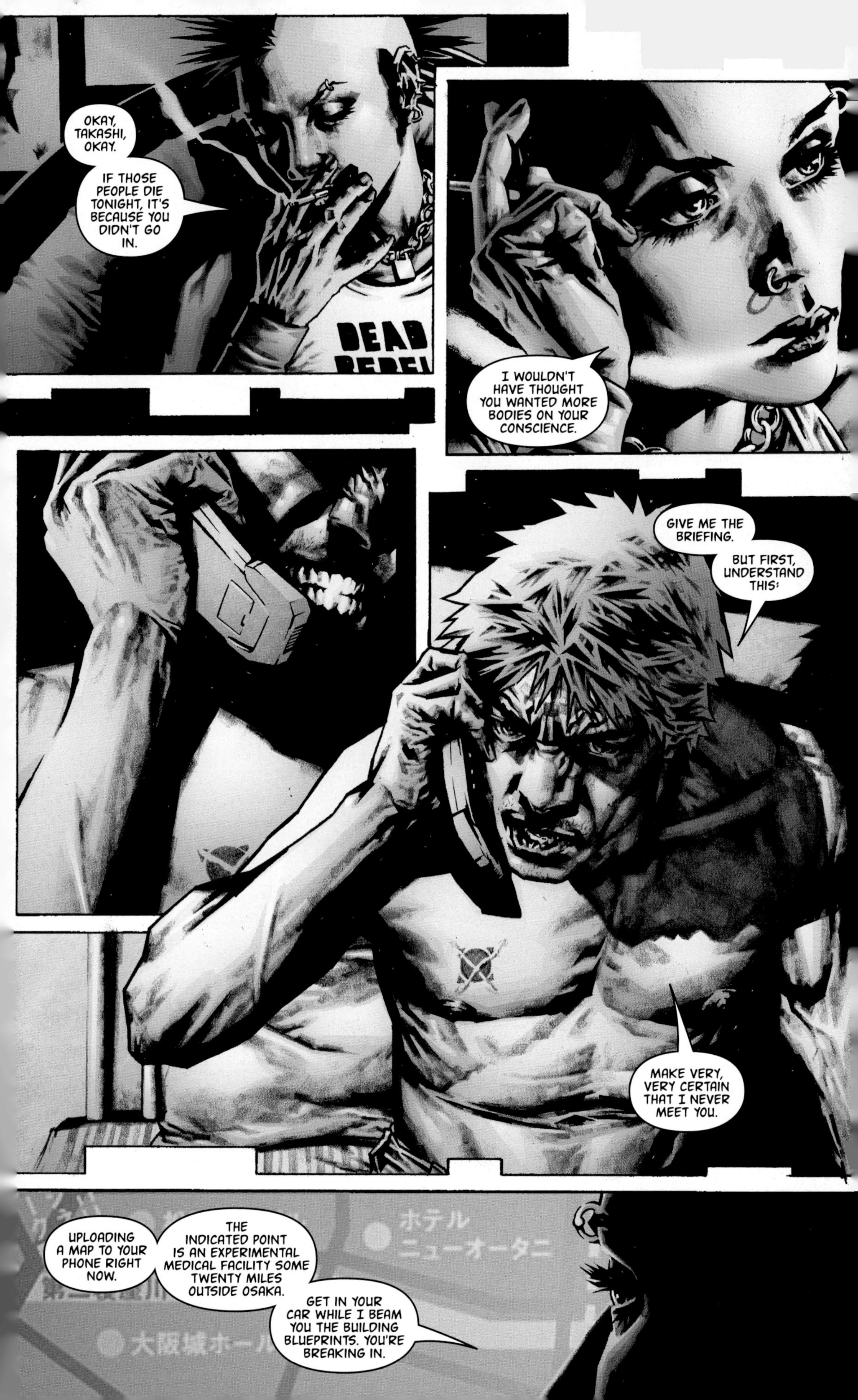
OKAY, TAKASHI, OKAY.
IF THOSE PEOPLE DIE TONIGHT, IT'S BECAUSE YOU DIDN'T GO IN.
DEAD
I WOULDN'T HAVE THOUGHT YOU WANTED MORE BODIES ON YOUR CONSCIENCE.
GIVE ME THE BRIEFING.
BUT FIRST, UNDERSTAND THIS:
MAKE VERY, VERY CERTAIN THAT I NEVER MEET YOU.
ホテル
ニューオータニ
大阪城ホール
UPLOADING A MAP TO YOUR PHONE RIGHT NOW.
THE INDICATED POINT IS AN EXPERIMENTAL MEDICAL FACILITY SOME TWENTY MILES OUTSIDE OSAKA.
GET IN YOUR CAR WHILE I BEAM YOU THE BUILDING BLUEPRINTS. YOU'RE BREAKING IN.

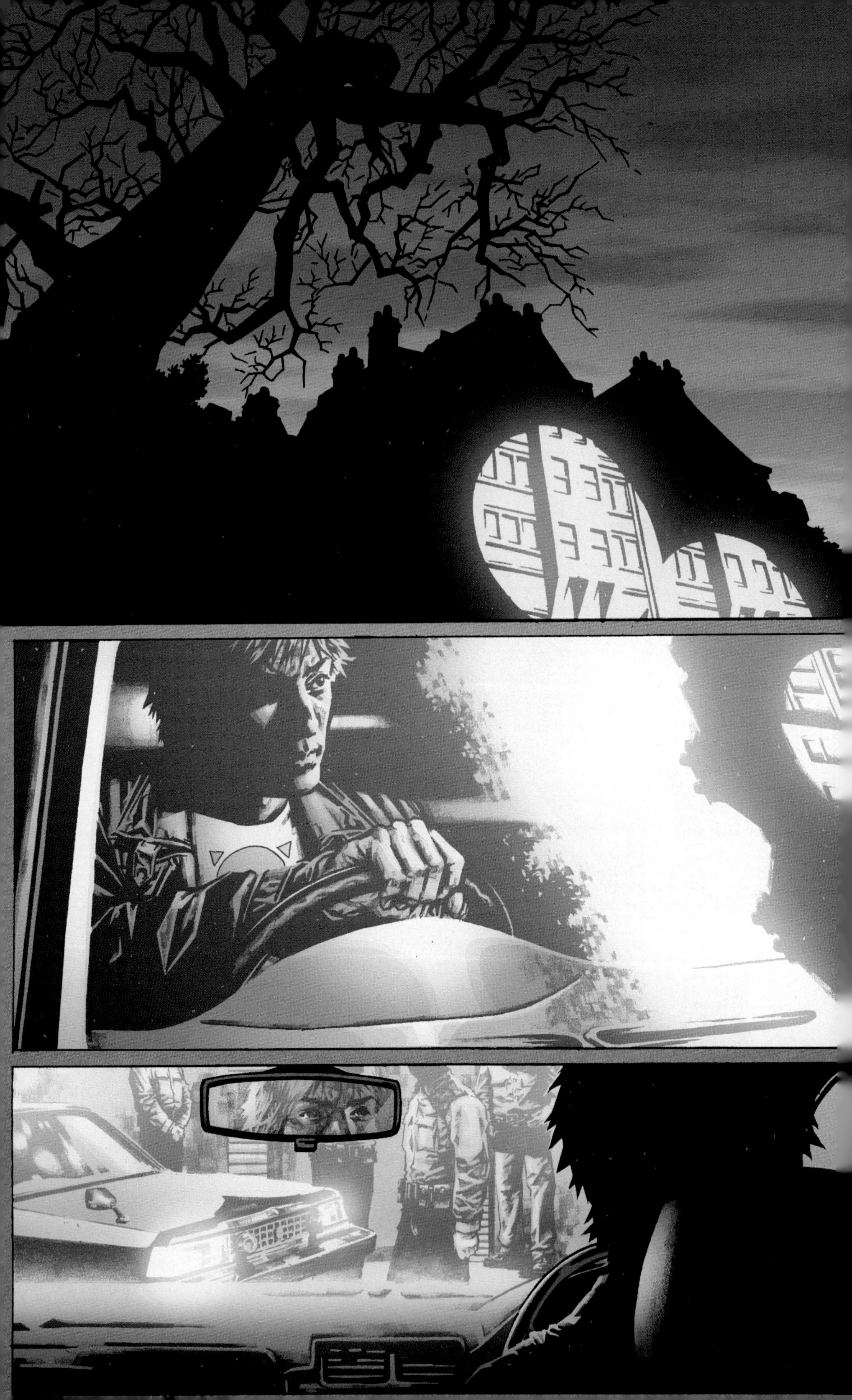

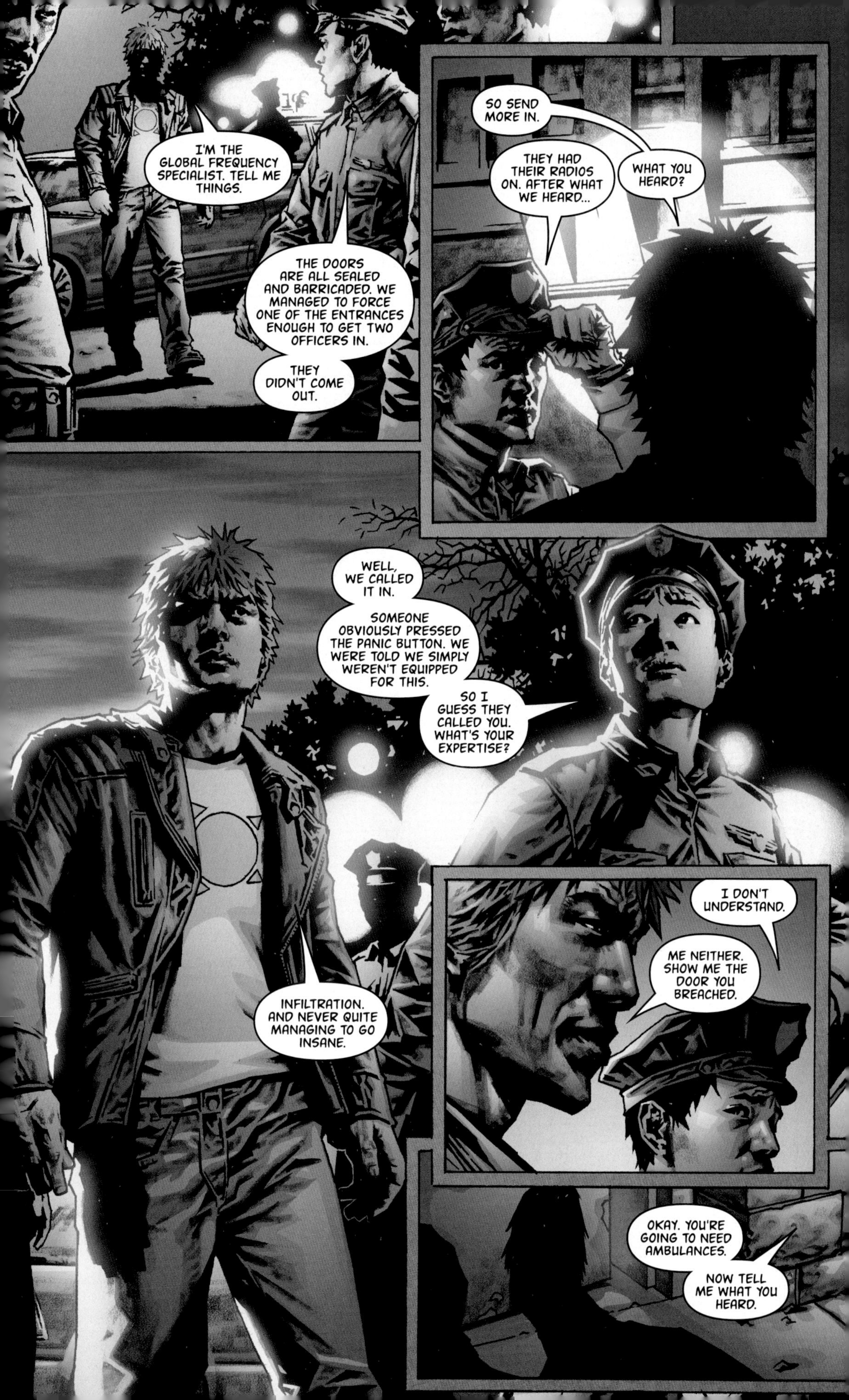
I'M THE GLOBAL FREQUENCY SPECIALIST. TELL ME THINGS.
THE DOORS ARE ALL SEALED AND BARRICADED. WE MANAGED TO FORCE ONE OF THE ENTRANCES ENOUGH TO GET TWO OFFICERS IN.
THEY DIDN'T COME OUT.
SO SEND MORE IN.
THEY HAD THEIR RADIOS ON. AFTER WHAT WE HEARD...
WHAT YOU HEARD?
WELL, WE CALLED IT IN.
SOMEONE OBVIOUSLY PRESSED THE PANIC BUTTON. WE WERE TOLD WE SIMPLY WEREN'T EQUIPPED FOR THIS.
SO I GUESS THEY CALLED YOU. WHAT'S YOUR EXPERTISE?
INFILTRATION. AND NEVER QUITE MANAGING TO GO INSANE.
I DON'T UNDERSTAND.
ME NEITHER. SHOW ME THE DOOR YOU BREACHED.
OKAY. YOU'RE GOING TO NEED AMBULANCES.
NOW TELL ME WHAT YOU HEARD.

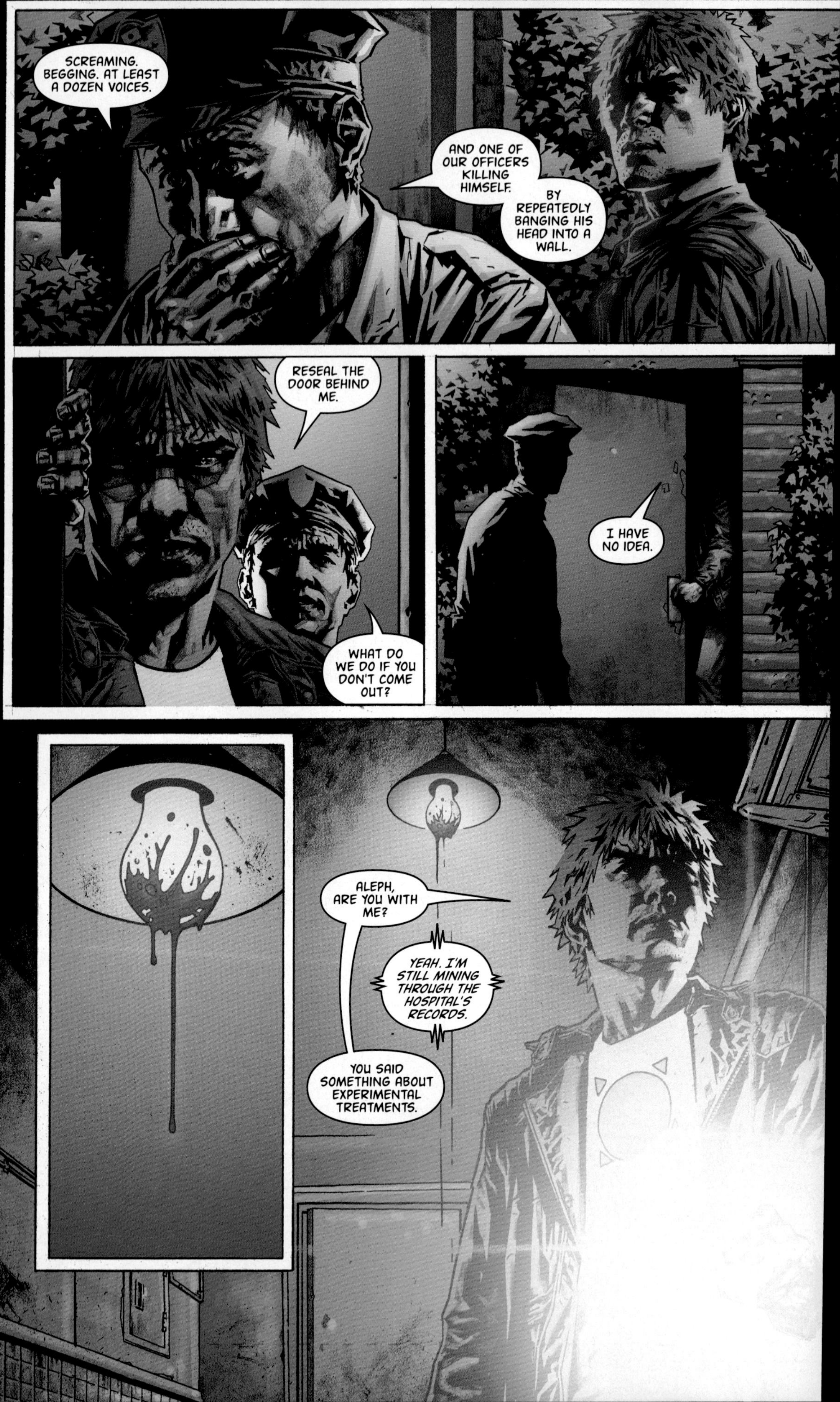
SCREAMING. BEGGING. AT LEAST A DOZEN VOICES.
AND ONE OF OUR OFFICERS KILLING HIMSELF.
BY REPEATEDLY BANGING HIS HEAD INTO A WALL.
RESEAL THE DOOR BEHIND ME.
WHAT DO WE DO IF YOU DON'T COME OUT?
I HAVE NO IDEA.
ALEPH, ARE YOU WITH ME?
YEAH. I'M STILL MINING THROUGH THE HOSPITAL'S RECORDS.
YOU SAID SOMETHING ABOUT EXPERIMENTAL TREATMENTS.

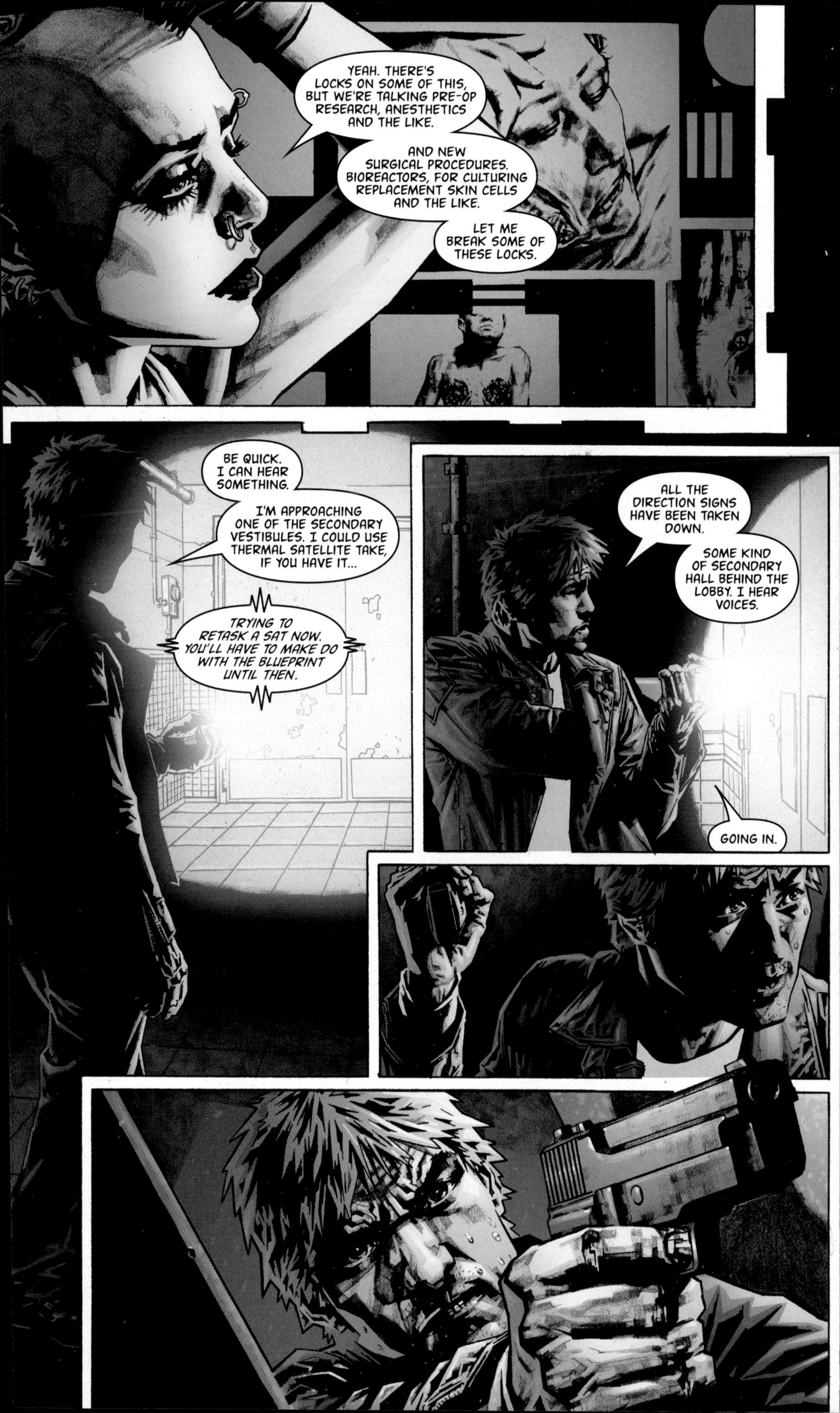

YEAH. THERE'S LOCKS ON SOME OF THIS, BUT WE'RE TALKING PRE-OP RESEARCH, ANESTHETICS AND THE LIKE.
AND NEW SURGICAL PROCEDURES. BIOREACTORS, FOR CULTURING REPLACEMENT SKIN CELLS AND THE LIKE.
LET ME BREAK SOME OF THESE LOCKS.
BE QUICK. I CAN HEAR SOMETHING.
I'M APPROACHING ONE OF THE SECONDARY VESTIBULES. I COULD USE THERMAL SATELLITE TAKE, IF YOU HAVE IT...
TRYING TO RETASK A SAT NOW. YOU'LL HAVE TO MAKE DO WITH THE BLUEPRINT UNTIL THEN.
ALL THE DIRECTION SIGNS HAVE BEEN TAKEN DOWN.
SOME KIND OF SECONDARY HALL BEHIND THE LOBBY. I HEAR VOICES.
GOING IN.

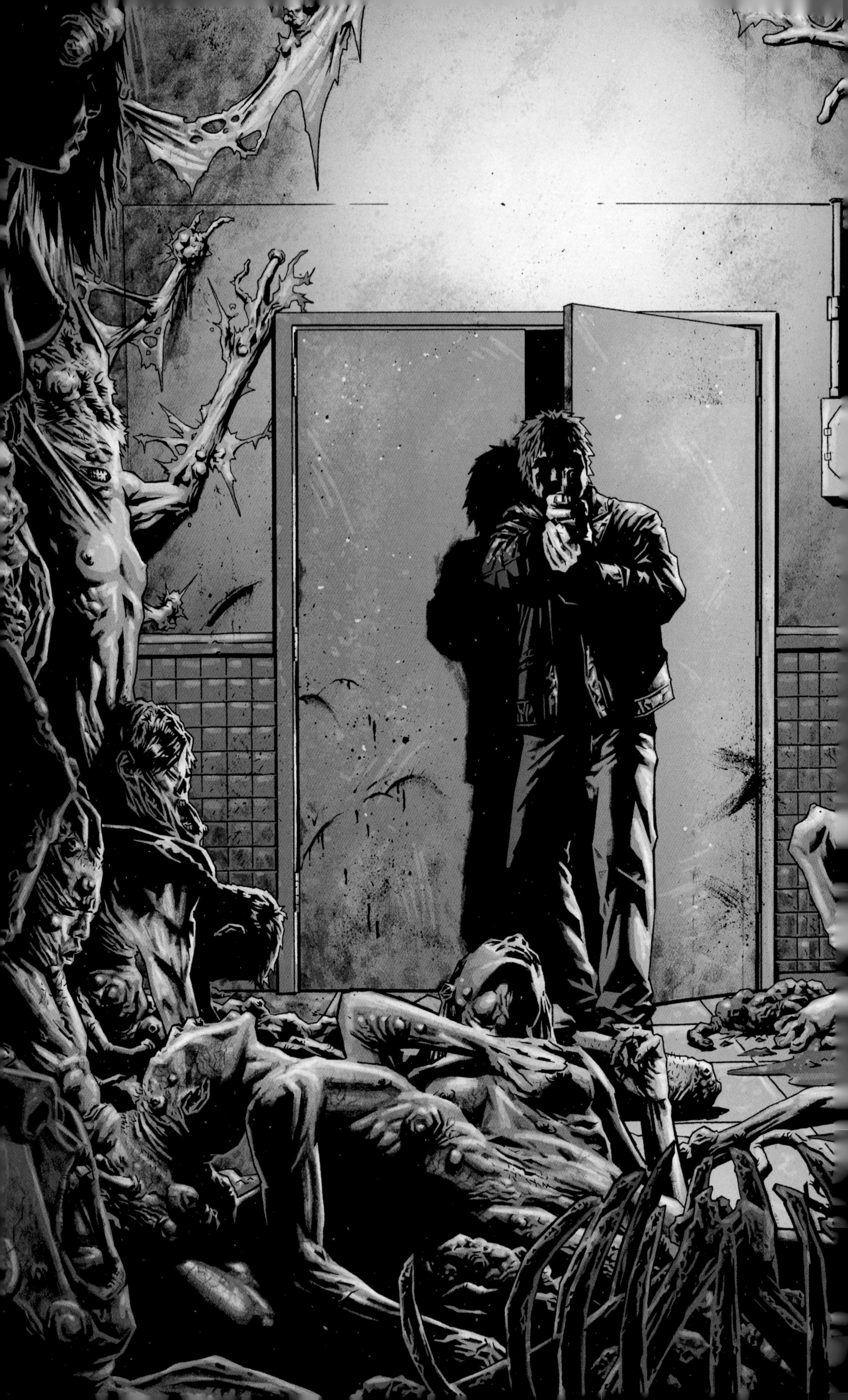

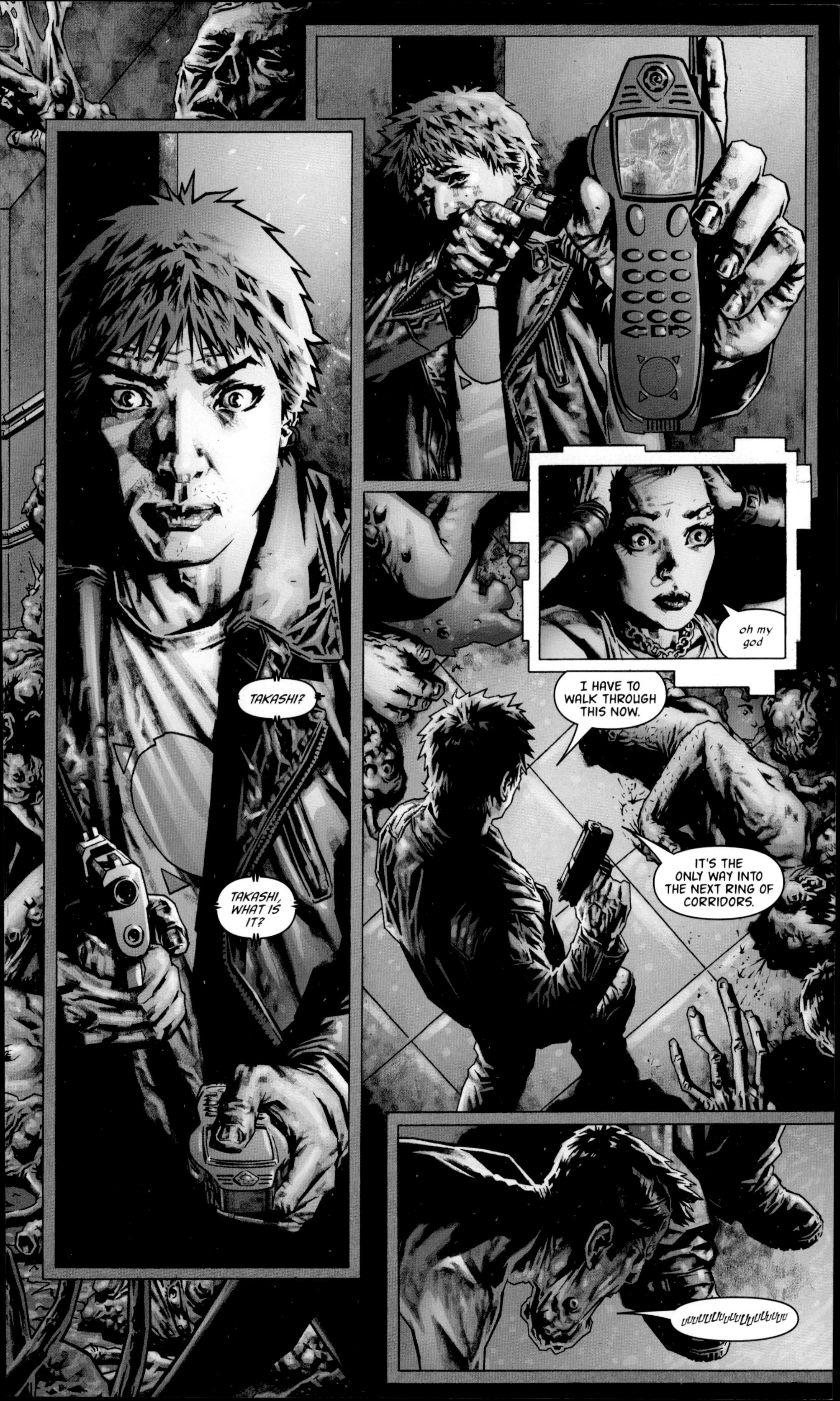
TAKASHI?
TAKASHI, WHAT IS IT?
oh my god
I HAVE TO WALK THROUGH THIS NOW.
IT'S THE ONLY WAY INTO THE NEXT RING OF CORRIDORS.
uuuuuuuuuuuuuuu

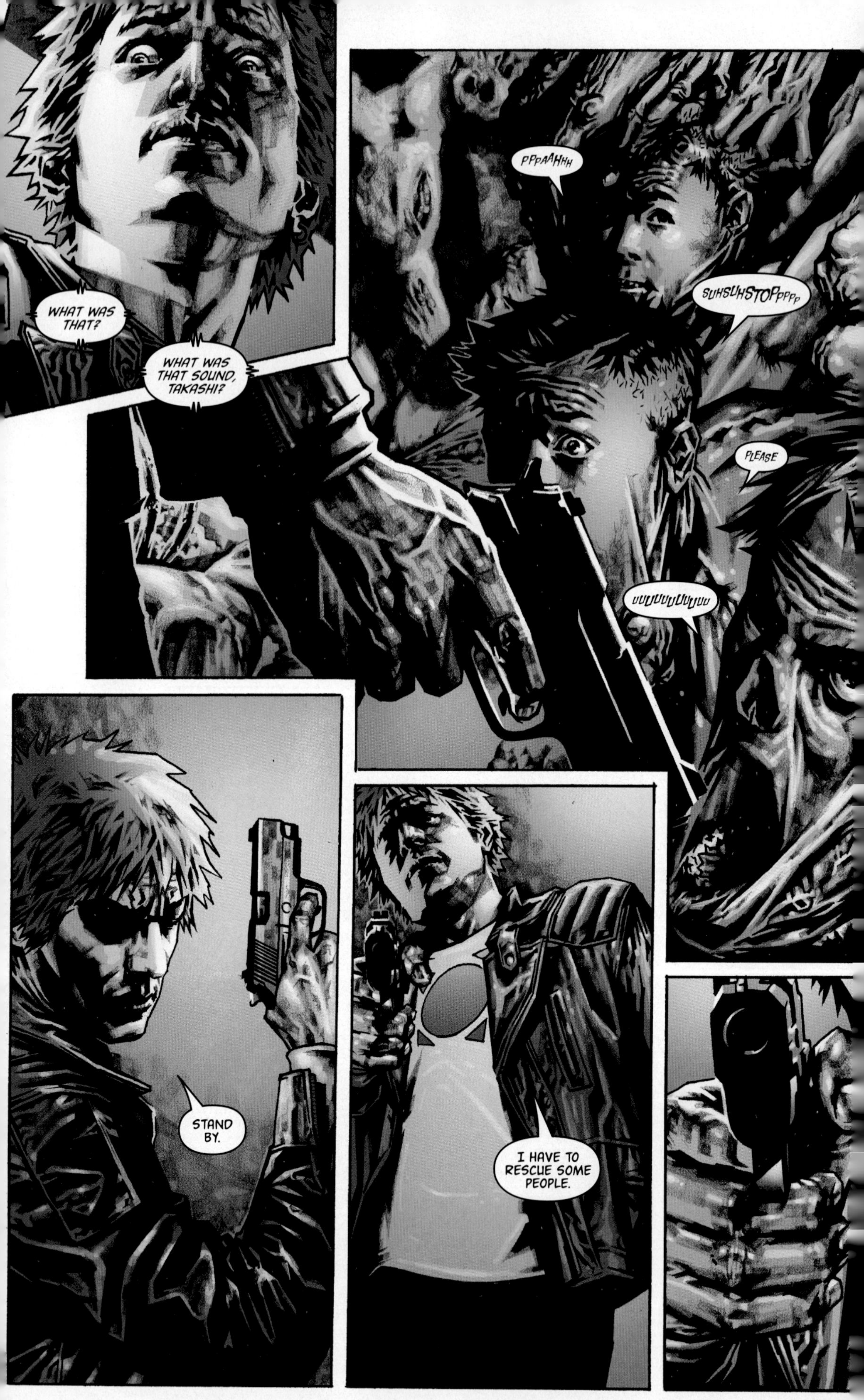
WHAT WAS THAT?
WHAT WAS THAT SOUND, TAKASHI?
PPPAAHHH
SUHSUHSTOPPPPP
PLEASE
UUUUUUUUUUU
STAND BY.
I HAVE TO RESCUE SOME PEOPLE.

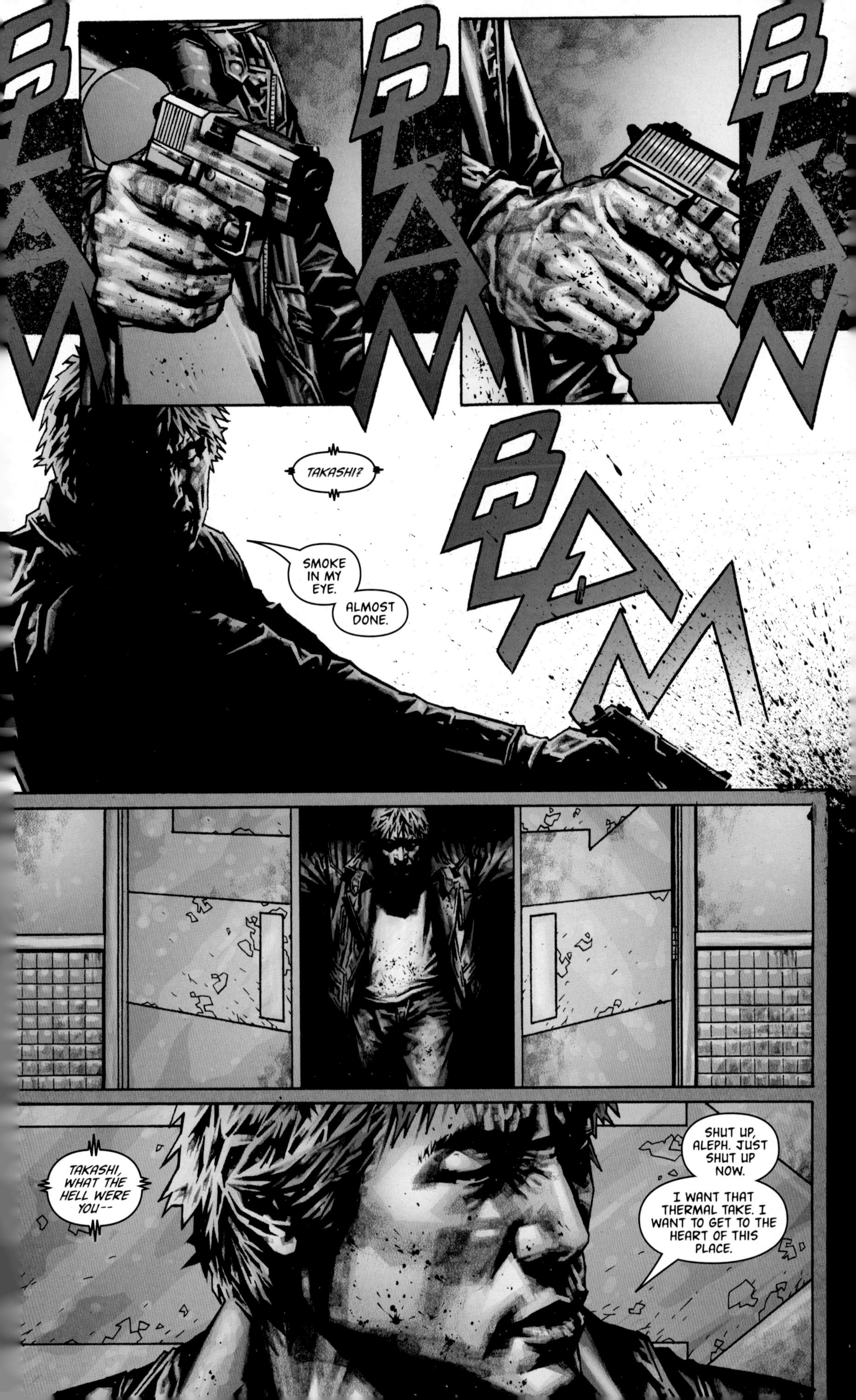
BLAM
BLAM
BLAM
BLAM
TAKASHI?
SMOKE IN MY EYE.
ALMOST DONE.
TAKASHI, WHAT THE HELL WERE YOU--
SHUT UP, ALEPH. JUST SHUT UP NOW.
I WANT THAT THERMAL TAKE. I WANT TO GET TO THE HEART OF THIS PLACE.

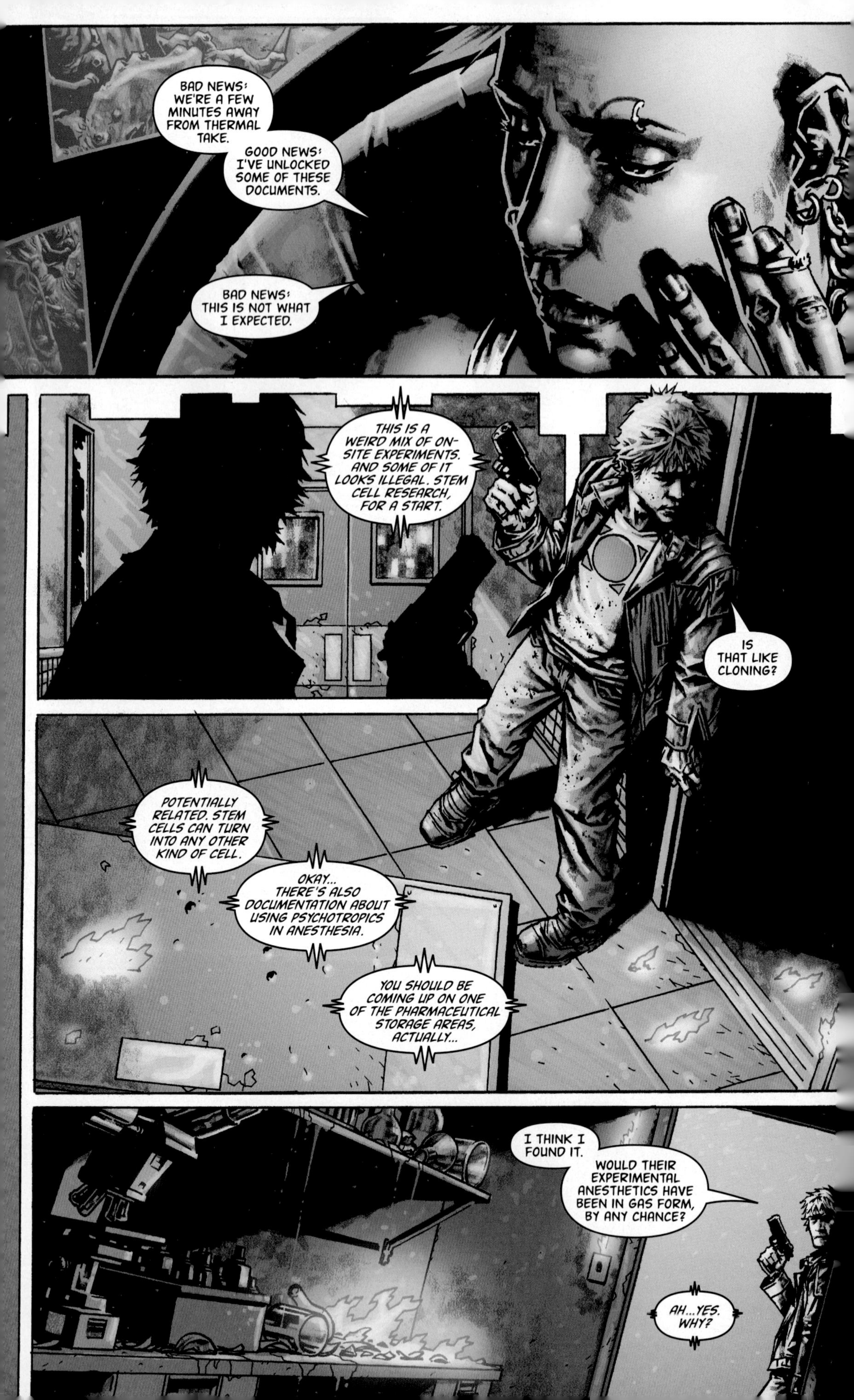
BAD NEWS: WE'RE A FEW MINUTES AWAY FROM THERMAL TAKE.
GOOD NEWS: I'VE UNLOCKED SOME OF THESE DOCUMENTS.
BAD NEWS: THIS IS NOT WHAT I EXPECTED.
THIS IS A WEIRD MIX OF ON-SITE EXPERIMENTS. AND SOME OF IT LOOKS ILLEGAL. STEM CELL RESEARCH, FOR A START.
IS THAT LIKE CLONING?
POTENTIALLY RELATED. STEM CELLS CAN TURN INTO ANY OTHER KIND OF CELL.
OKAY... THERE'S ALSO DOCUMENTATION ABOUT USING PSYCHOTROPICS IN ANESTHESIA.
YOU SHOULD BE COMING UP ON ONE OF THE PHARMACEUTICAL STORAGE AREAS, ACTUALLY...
I THINK I FOUND IT.
WOULD THEIR EXPERIMENTAL ANESTHETICS HAVE BEEN IN GAS FORM, BY ANY CHANCE?
AH...YES. WHY?

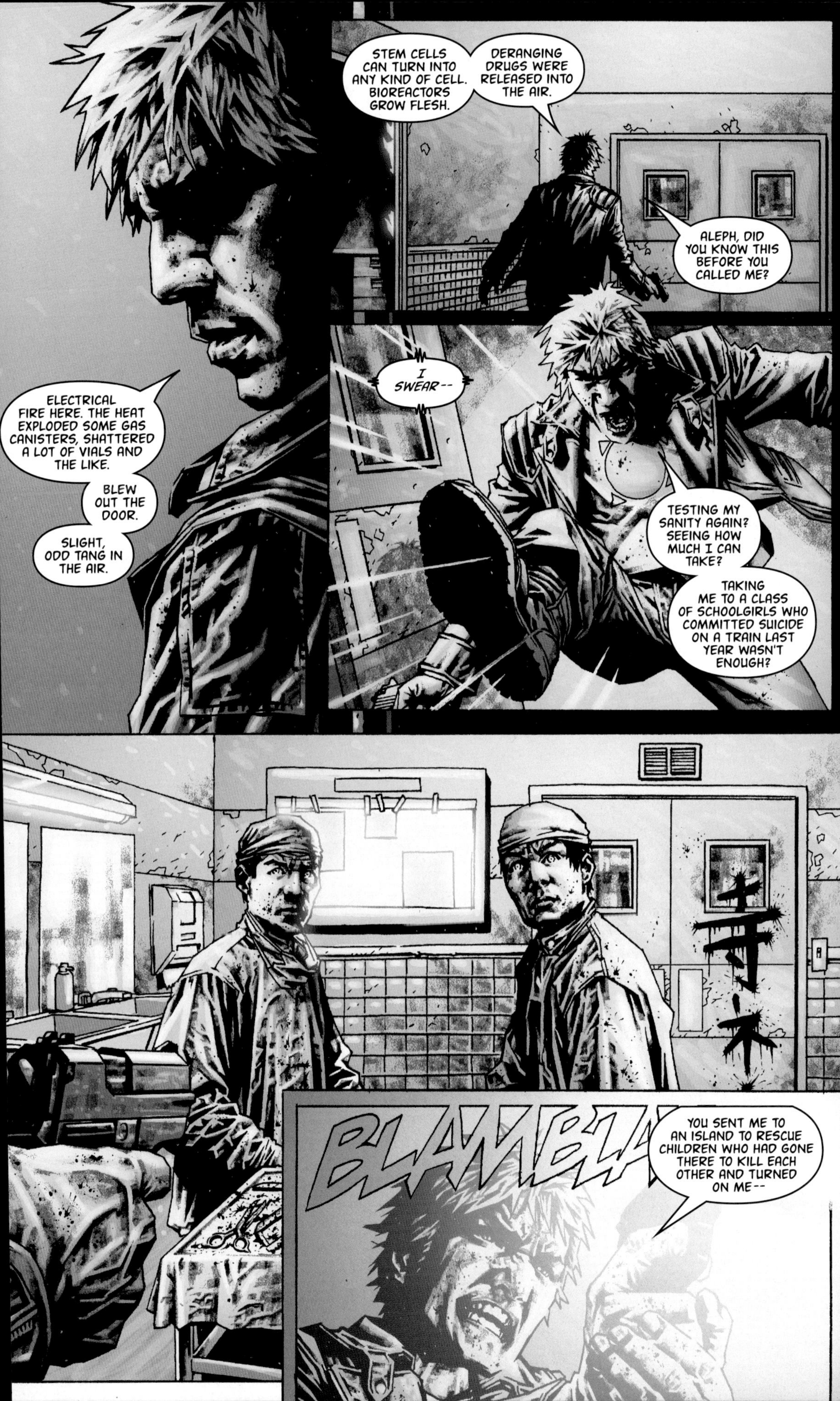
ELECTRICAL FIRE HERE. THE HEAT EXPLODED SOME GAS CANISTERS, SHATTERED A LOT OF VIALS AND THE LIKE.
BLEW OUT THE DOOR.
SLIGHT, ODD TANG IN THE AIR.
STEM CELLS CAN TURN INTO ANY KIND OF CELL. BIOREACTORS GROW FLESH.
DERANGING DRUGS WERE RELEASED INTO THE AIR.
ALEPH, DID YOU KNOW THIS BEFORE YOU CALLED ME?
I SWEAR--
TESTING MY SANITY AGAIN? SEEING HOW MUCH I CAN TAKE?
TAKING ME TO A CLASS OF SCHOOLGIRLS WHO COMMITTED SUICIDE ON A TRAIN LAST YEAR WASN'T ENOUGH?
BLAMBLA
YOU SENT ME TO AN ISLAND TO RESCUE CHILDREN WHO HAD GONE THERE TO KILL EACH OTHER AND TURNED ON ME--

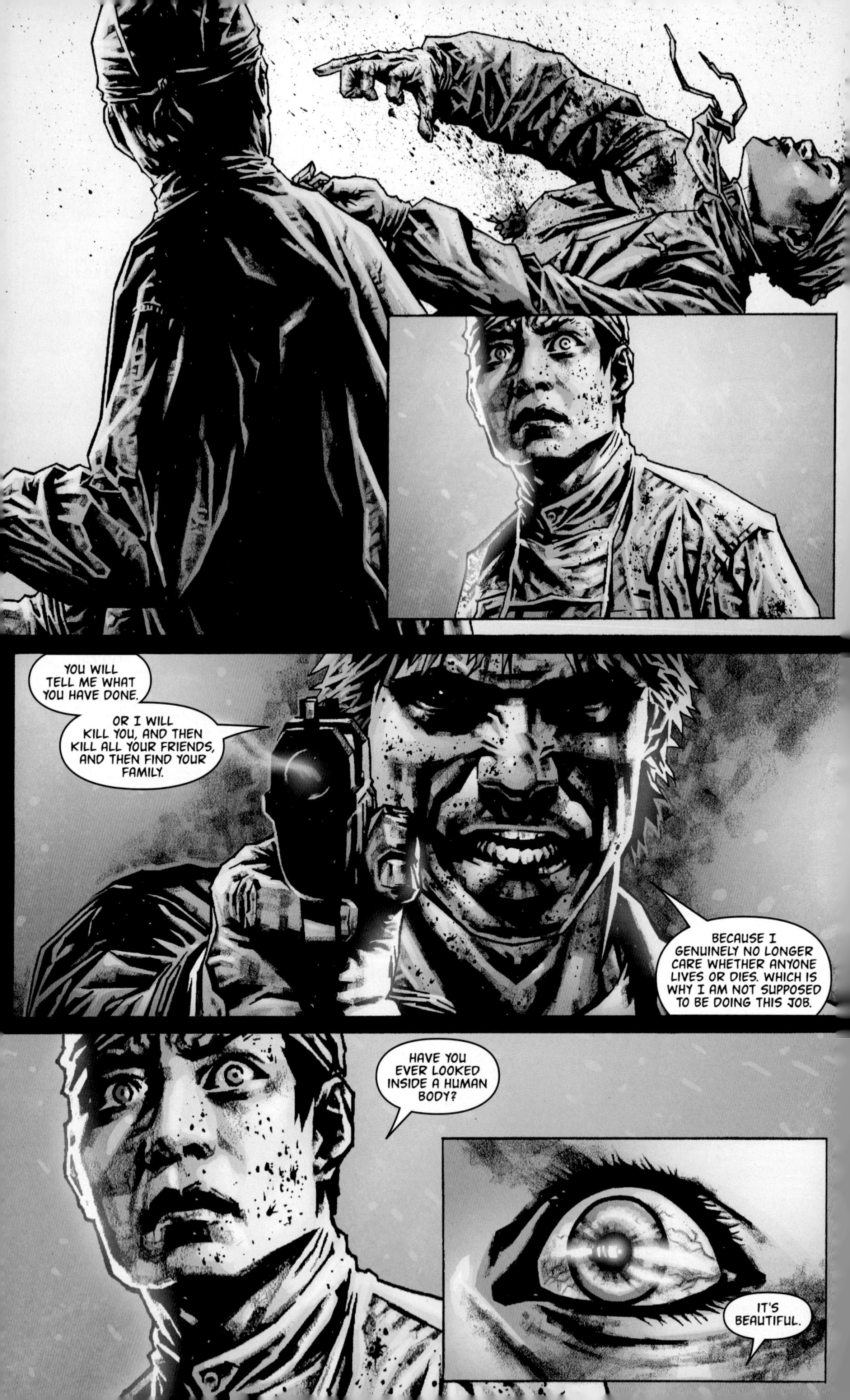
YOU WILL TELL ME WHAT YOU HAVE DONE.
OR I WILL KILL YOU, AND THEN KILL ALL YOUR FRIENDS, AND THEN FIND YOUR FAMILY.
BECAUSE I GENUINELY NO LONGER CARE WHETHER ANYONE LIVES OR DIES. WHICH IS WHY I AM NOT SUPPOSED TO BE DOING THIS JOB.
HAVE YOU EVER LOOKED INSIDE A HUMAN BODY?
IT'S BEAUTIFUL.

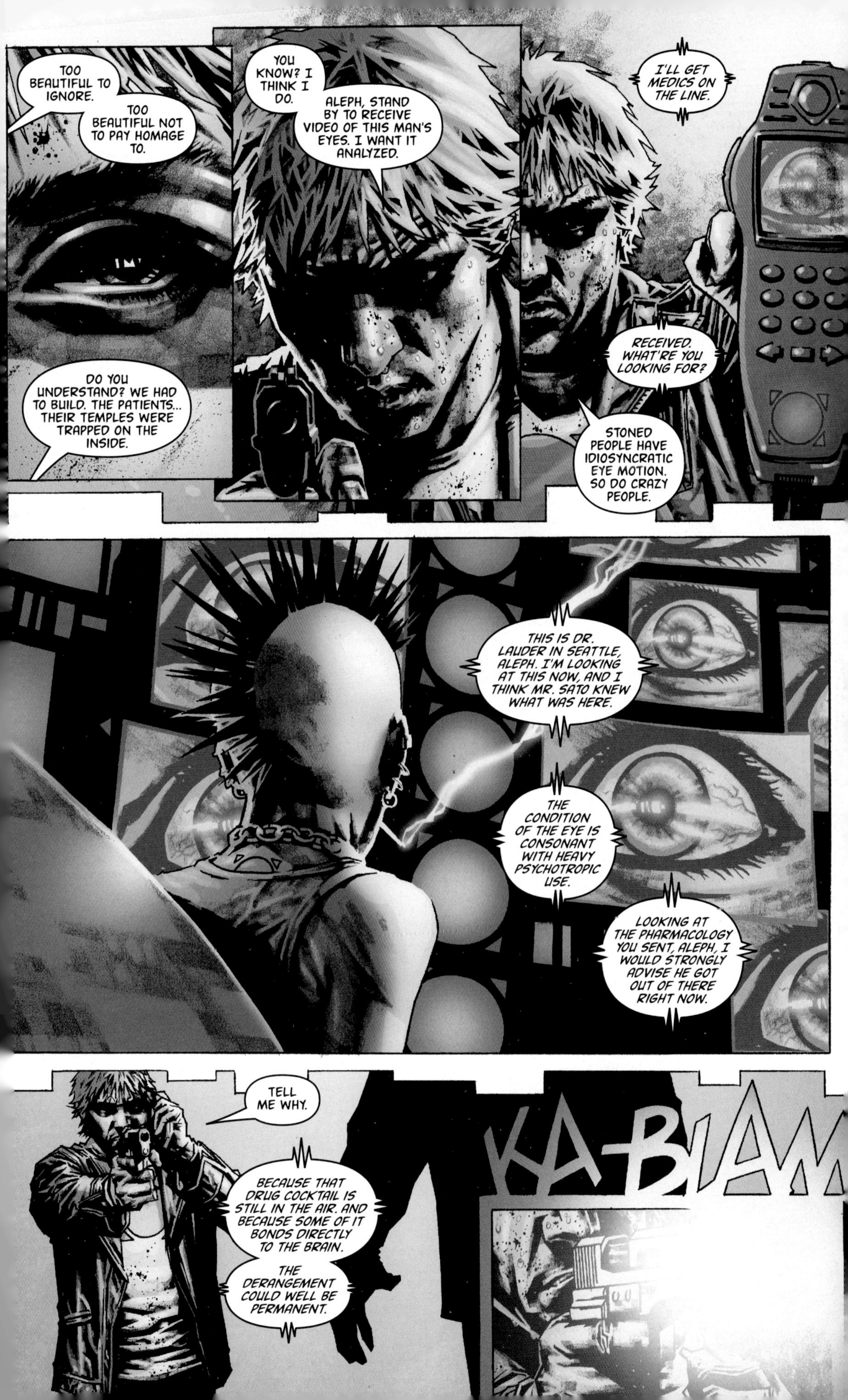
TOO BEAUTIFUL TO IGNORE.
TOO BEAUTIFUL NOT TO PAY HOMAGE TO.
DO YOU UNDERSTAND? WE HAD TO BUILD. THE PATIENTS... THEIR TEMPLES WERE TRAPPED ON THE INSIDE.
YOU KNOW? I THINK I DO.
ALEPH, STAND BY TO RECEIVE VIDEO OF THIS MAN'S EYES. I WANT IT ANALYZED.
I'LL GET MEDICS ON THE LINE.
RECEIVED. WHAT'RE YOU LOOKING FOR?
STONED PEOPLE HAVE IDIOSYNCRATIC EYE MOTION. SO DO CRAZY PEOPLE.
THIS IS DR. LAUDER IN SEATTLE, ALEPH. I'M LOOKING AT THIS NOW, AND I THINK MR. SATO KNEW WHAT WAS HERE.
THE CONDITION OF THE EYE IS CONSONANT WITH HEAVY PSYCHOTROPIC USE.
LOOKING AT THE PHARMACOLOGY YOU SENT, ALEPH, I WOULD STRONGLY ADVISE HE GOT OUT OF THERE RIGHT NOW.
TELL ME WHY.
BECAUSE THAT DRUG COCKTAIL IS STILL IN THE AIR. AND BECAUSE SOME OF IT BONDS DIRECTLY TO THE BRAIN.
THE DERANGEMENT COULD WELL BE PERMANENT.
KA-BLAM

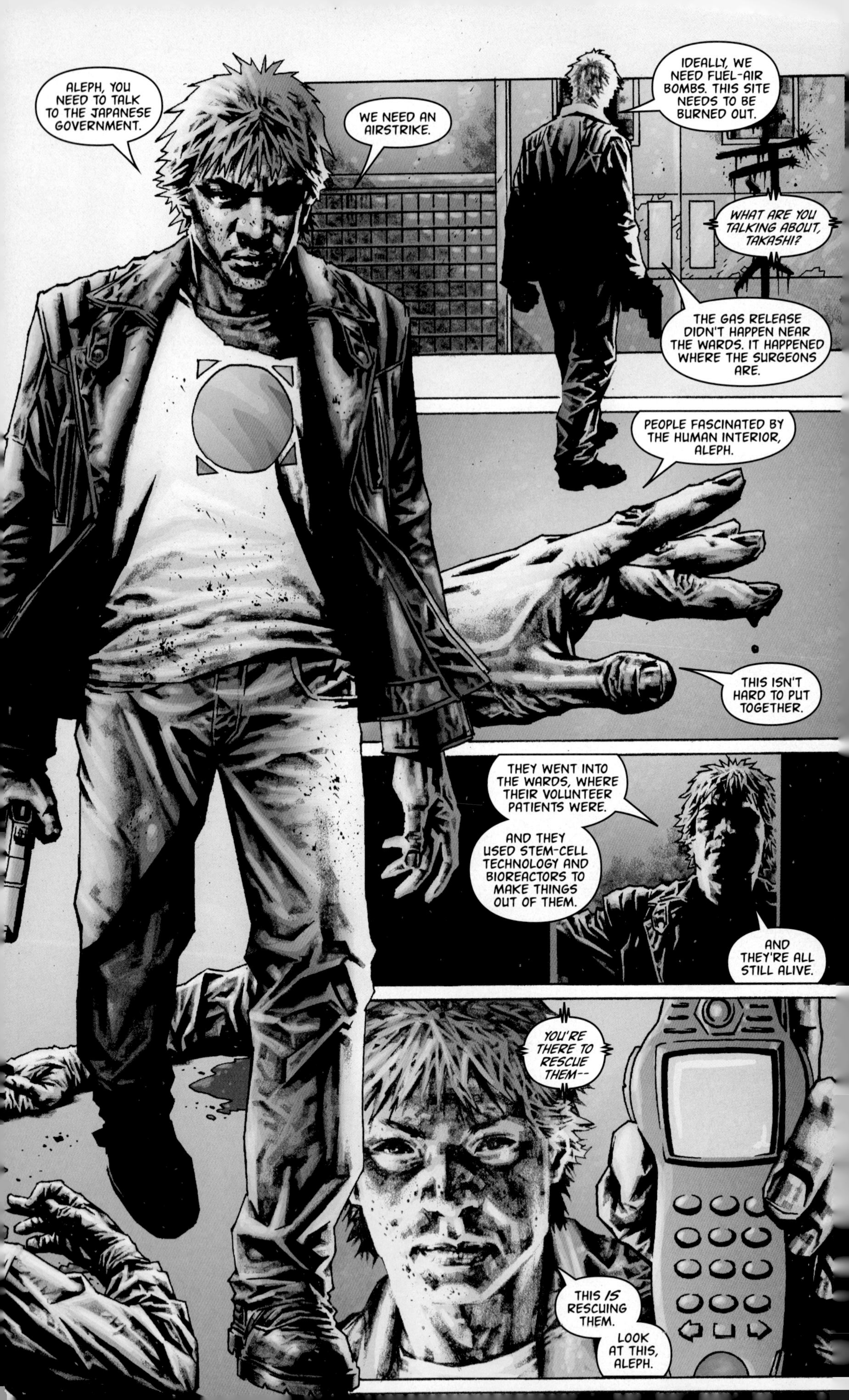
ALEPH, YOU NEED TO TALK TO THE JAPANESE GOVERNMENT.
WE NEED AN AIRSTRIKE.
IDEALLY, WE NEED FUEL-AIR BOMBS. THIS SITE NEEDS TO BE BURNED OUT.
WHAT ARE YOU TALKING ABOUT, TAKASHI?
THE GAS RELEASE DIDN'T HAPPEN NEAR THE WARDS. IT HAPPENED WHERE THE SURGEONS ARE.
PEOPLE FASCINATED BY THE HUMAN INTERIOR, ALEPH.
THIS ISN'T HARD TO PUT TOGETHER.
THEY WENT INTO THE WARDS, WHERE THEIR VOLUNTEER PATIENTS WERE.
AND THEY USED STEM-CELL TECHNOLOGY AND BIOREACTORS TO MAKE THINGS OUT OF THEM.
AND THEY'RE ALL STILL ALIVE.
YOU'RE THERE TO RESCUE THEM--
THIS IS RESCUING THEM.
LOOK AT THIS, ALEPH.

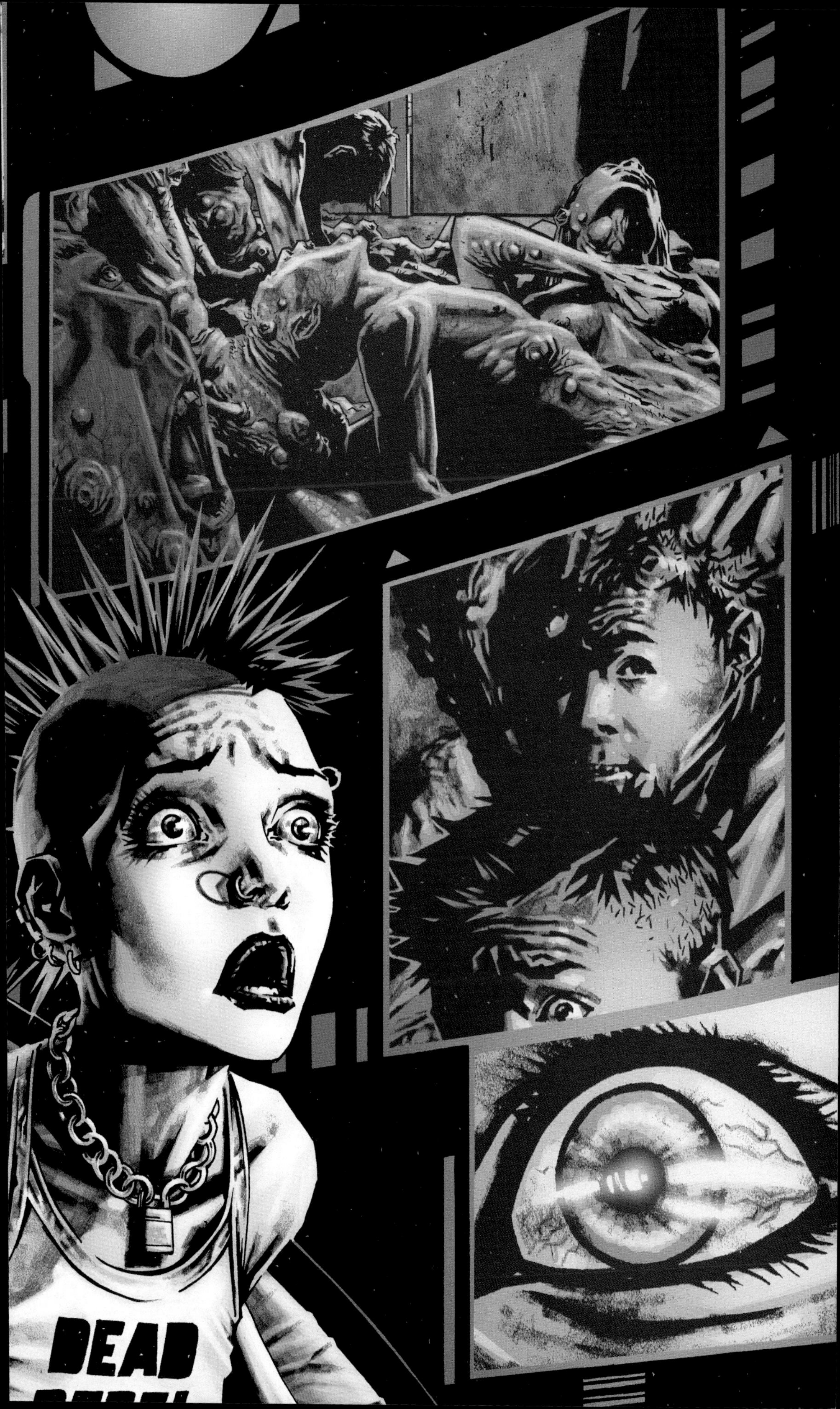
DEAD

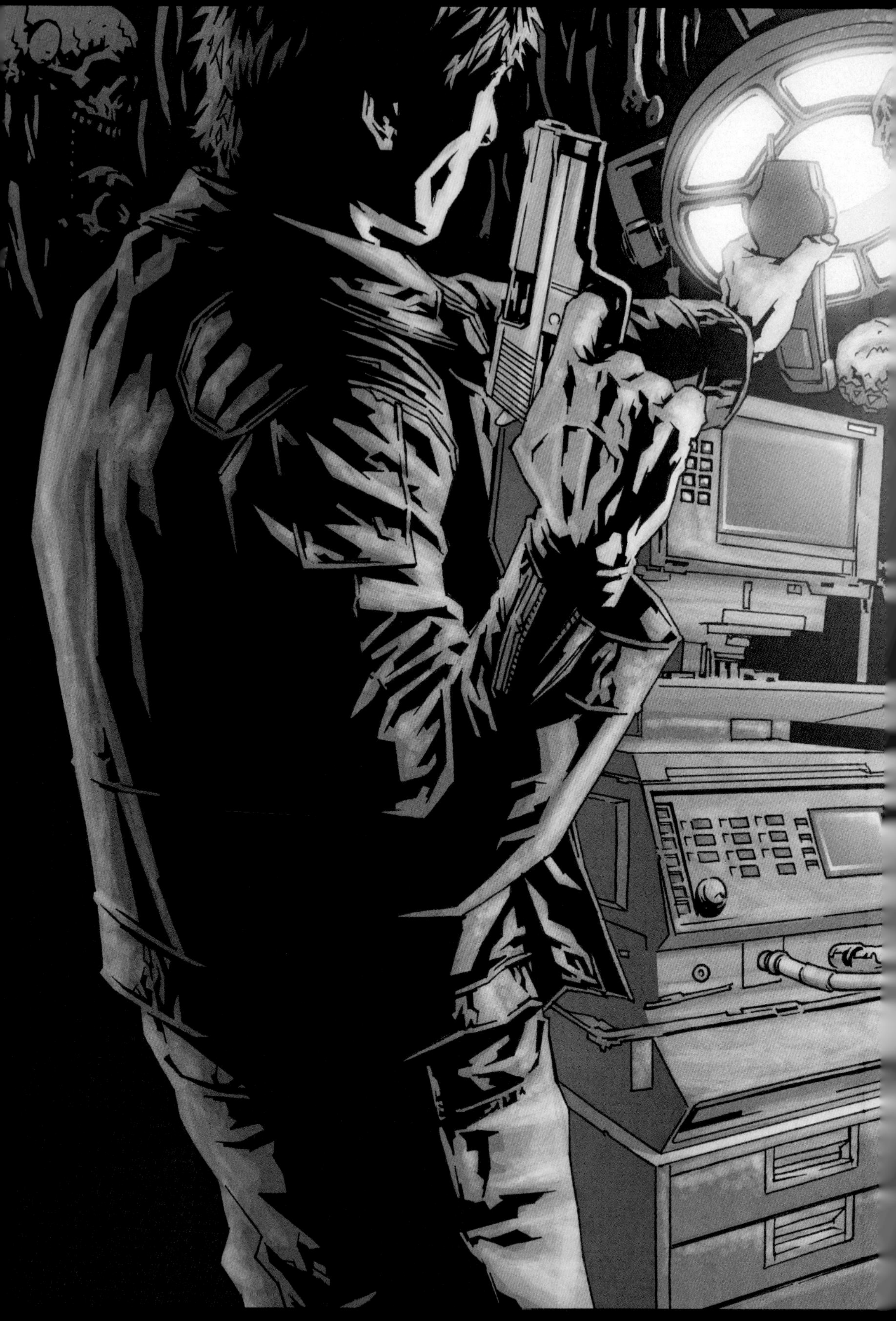

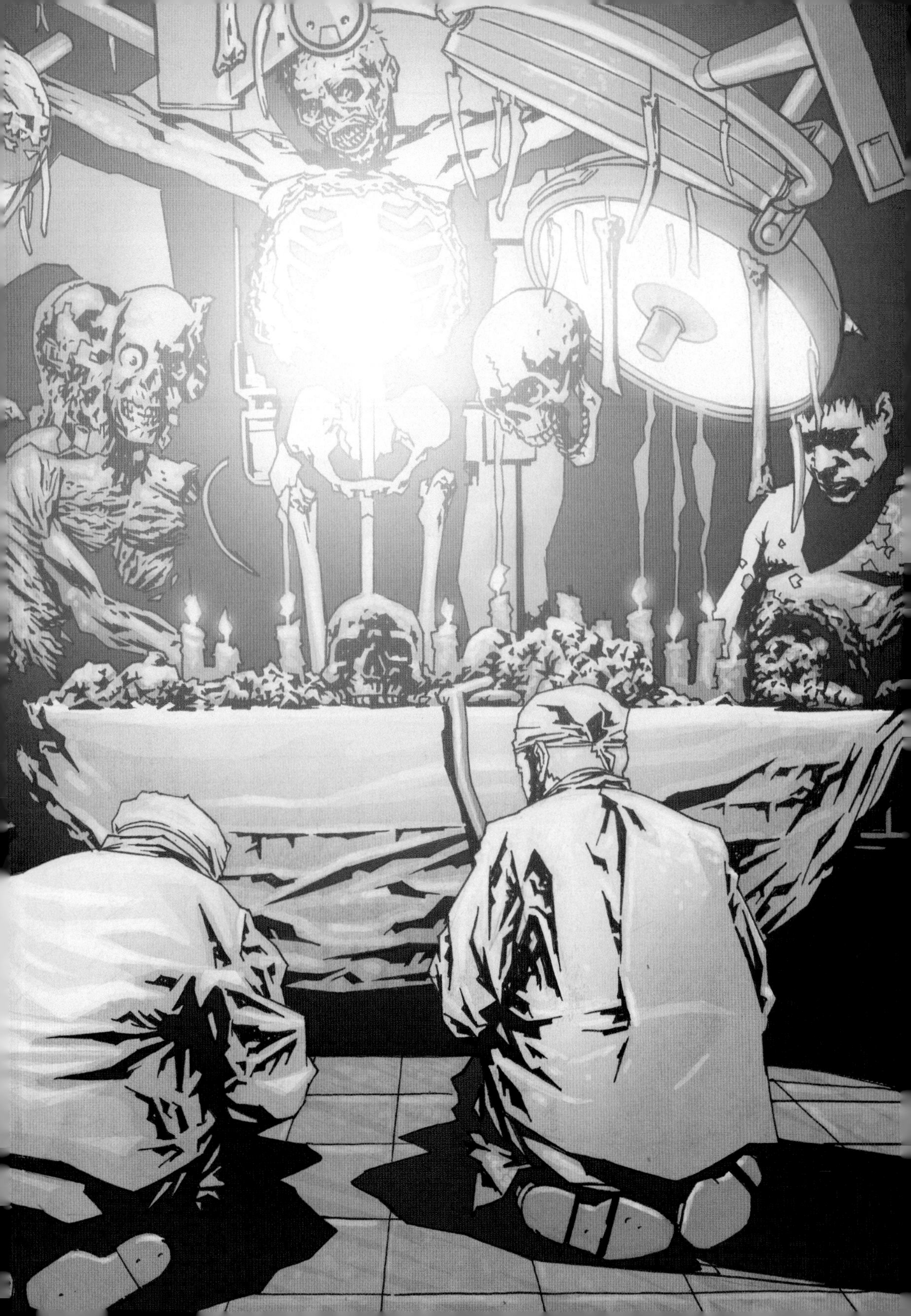

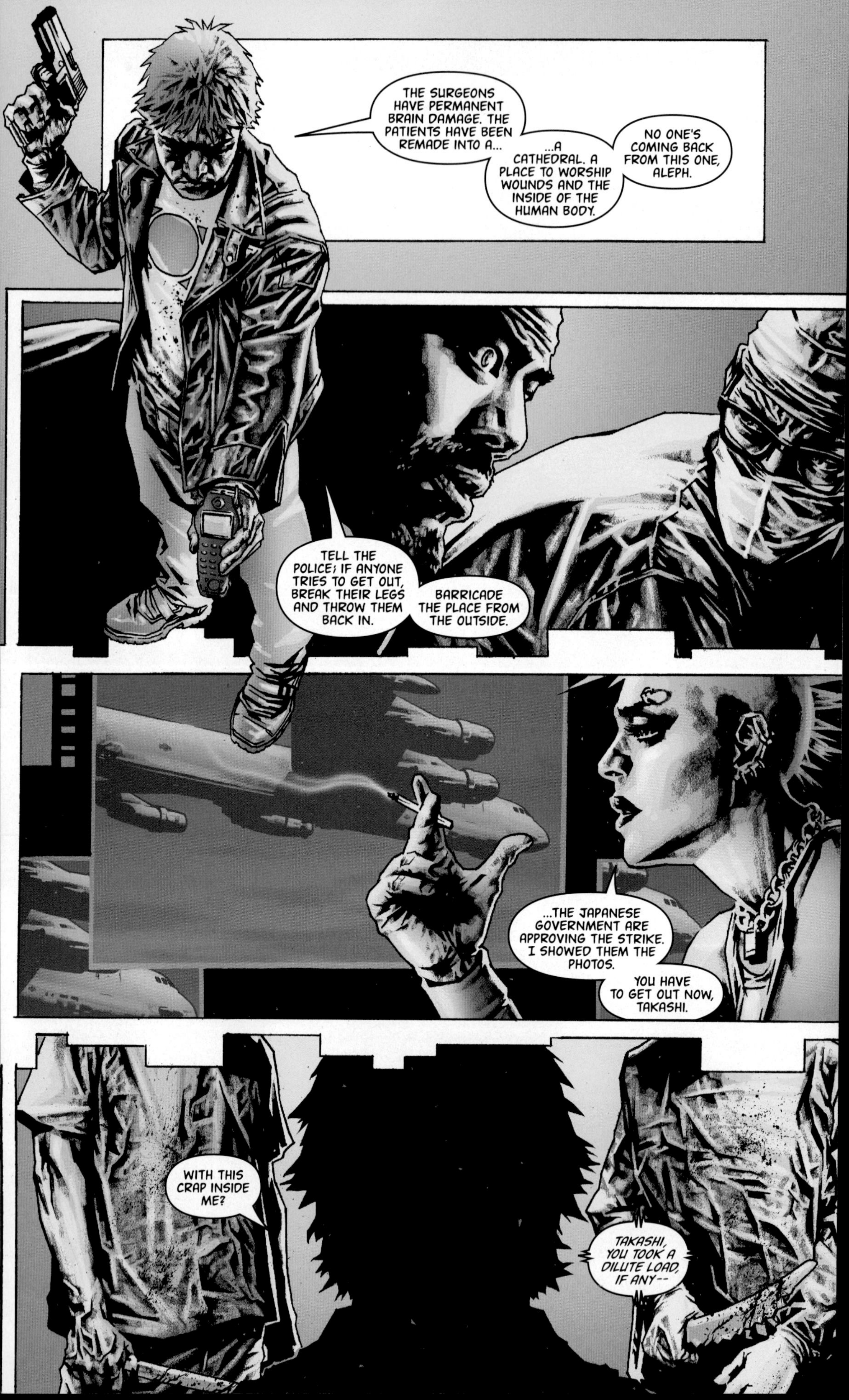
THE SURGEONS HAVE PERMANENT BRAIN DAMAGE. THE PATIENTS HAVE BEEN REMADE INTO A...
...A CATHEDRAL. A PLACE TO WORSHIP WOUNDS AND THE INSIDE OF THE HUMAN BODY.
NO ONE'S COMING BACK FROM THIS ONE, ALEPH.
TELL THE POLICE; IF ANYONE TRIES TO GET OUT, BREAK THEIR LEGS AND THROW THEM BACK IN.
BARRICADE THE PLACE FROM THE OUTSIDE.
...THE JAPANESE GOVERNMENT ARE APPROVING THE STRIKE. I SHOWED THEM THE PHOTOS.
YOU HAVE TO GET OUT NOW, TAKASHI.
WITH THIS CRAP INSIDE ME?
TAKASHI, YOU TOOK A DILUTE LOAD, IF ANY--

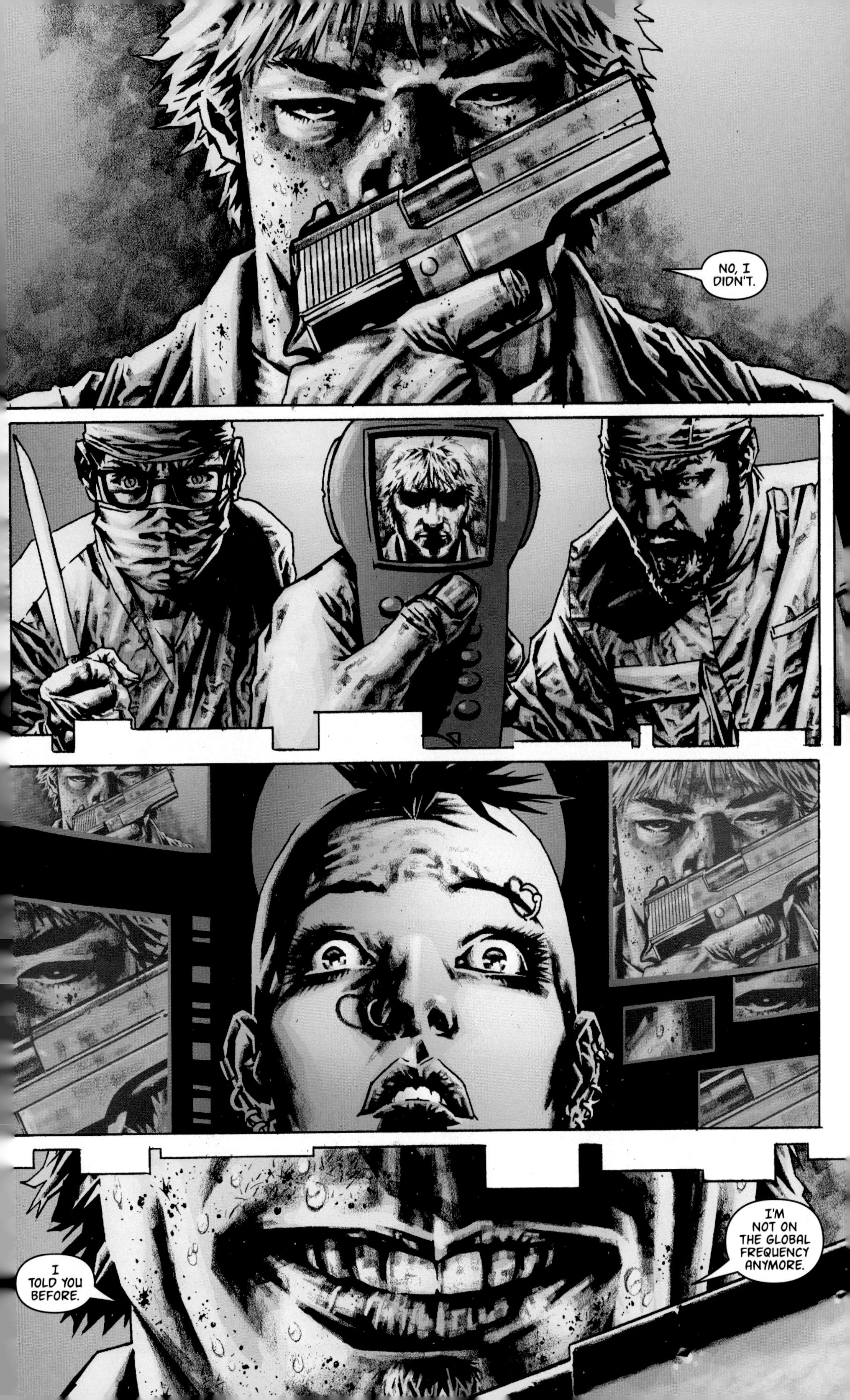
NO, I DIDN'T.
I TOLD YOU BEFORE.
I'M NOT ON THE GLOBAL FREQUENCY ANYMORE.

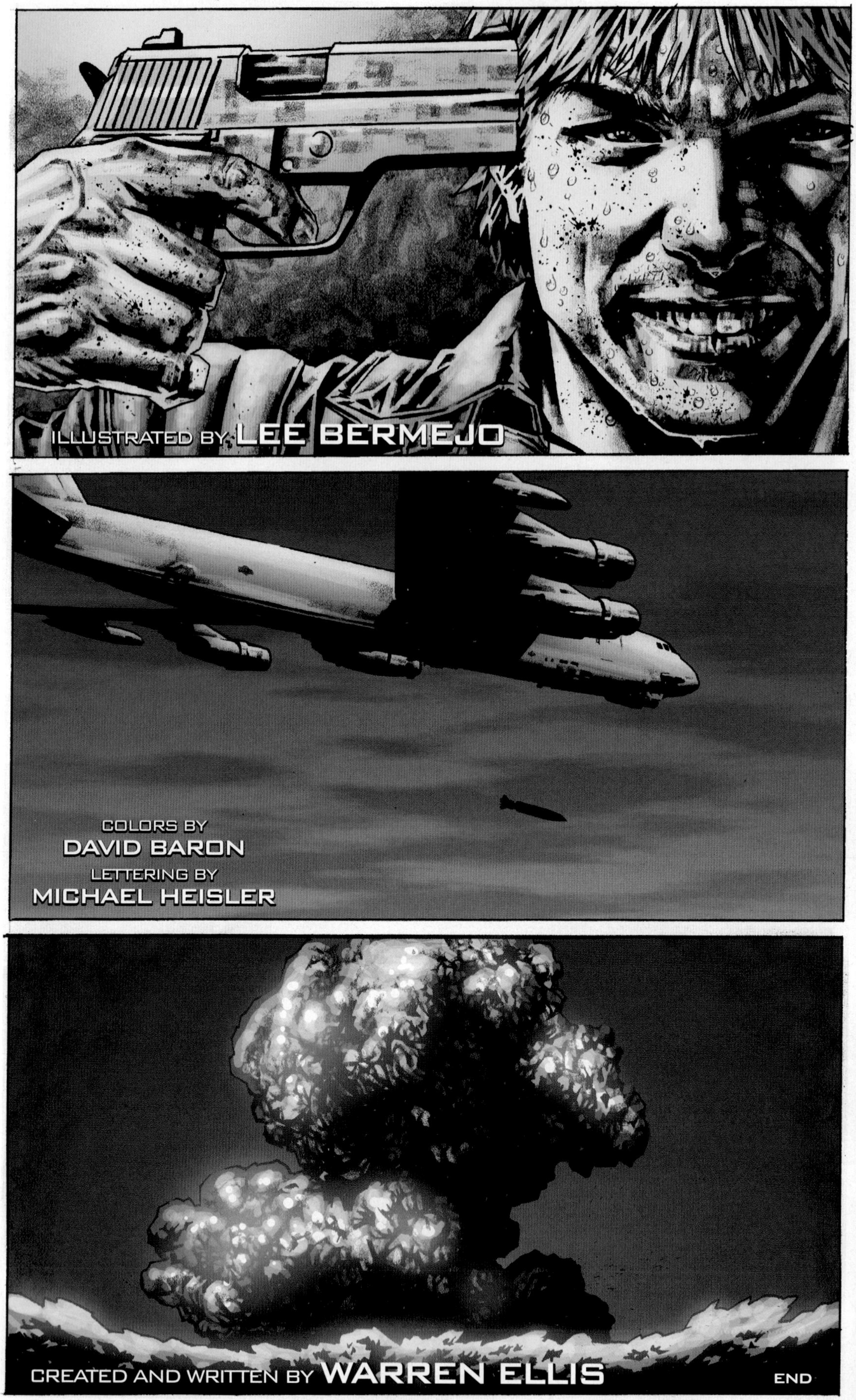
ILLUSTRATED BY LEE BERMEJO
COLORS BY
DAVID BARON
LETTERING BY
MICHAEL HEISLER
CREATED AND WRITTEN BY WARREN ELLIS
END

左パンチのフェイント
で右を向かせる。
ARE YOU ON THE
GLOBAL
FREQUENCY?
<後ろ回し蹴り>
フェイントの右回し蹴り。

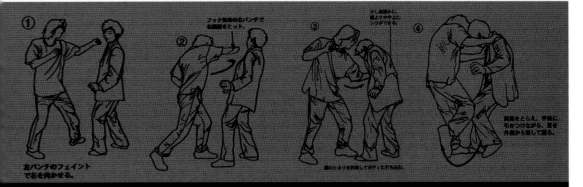

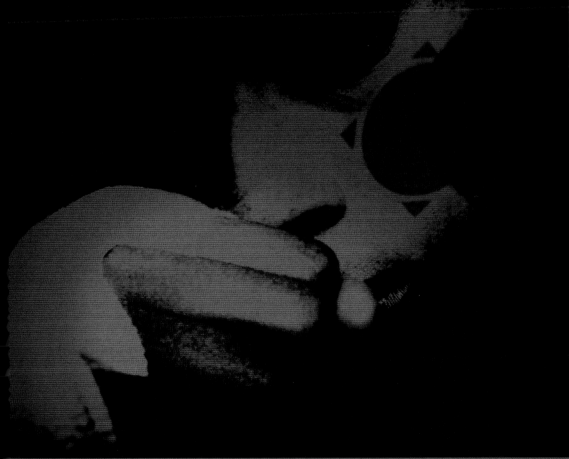

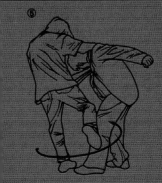

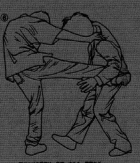

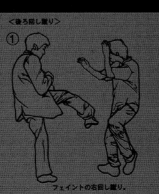

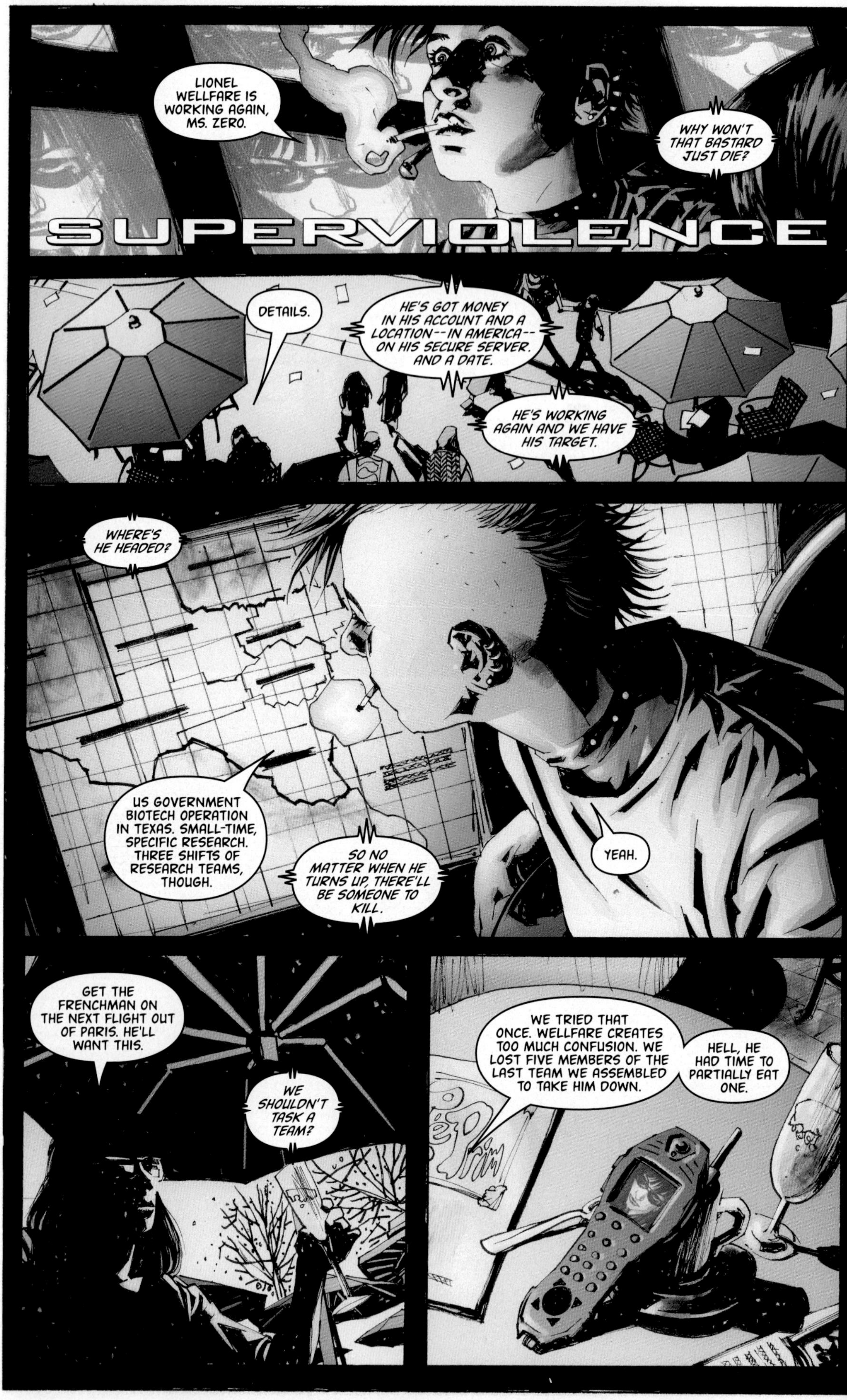
LIONEL WELLFARE IS WORKING AGAIN, MS. ZERO.
WHY WON'T THAT BASTARD JUST DIE?
SUPERVIOLENCE
DETAILS.
HE'S GOT MONEY IN HIS ACCOUNT AND A LOCATION--IN AMERICA--ON HIS SECURE SERVER. AND A DATE.
HE'S WORKING AGAIN AND WE HAVE HIS TARGET.
WHERE'S HE HEADED?
US GOVERNMENT BIOTECH OPERATION IN TEXAS. SMALL-TIME, SPECIFIC RESEARCH. THREE SHIFTS OF RESEARCH TEAMS, THOUGH.
SO NO MATTER WHEN HE TURNS UP, THERE'LL BE SOMEONE TO KILL.
YEAH.
GET THE FRENCHMAN ON THE NEXT FLIGHT OUT OF PARIS. HE'LL WANT THIS.
WE SHOULDN'T TASK A TEAM?
WE TRIED THAT ONCE. WELLFARE CREATES TOO MUCH CONFUSION. WE LOST FIVE MEMBERS OF THE LAST TEAM WE ASSEMBLED TO TAKE HIM DOWN.
HELL, HE HAD TIME TO PARTIALLY EAT ONE.

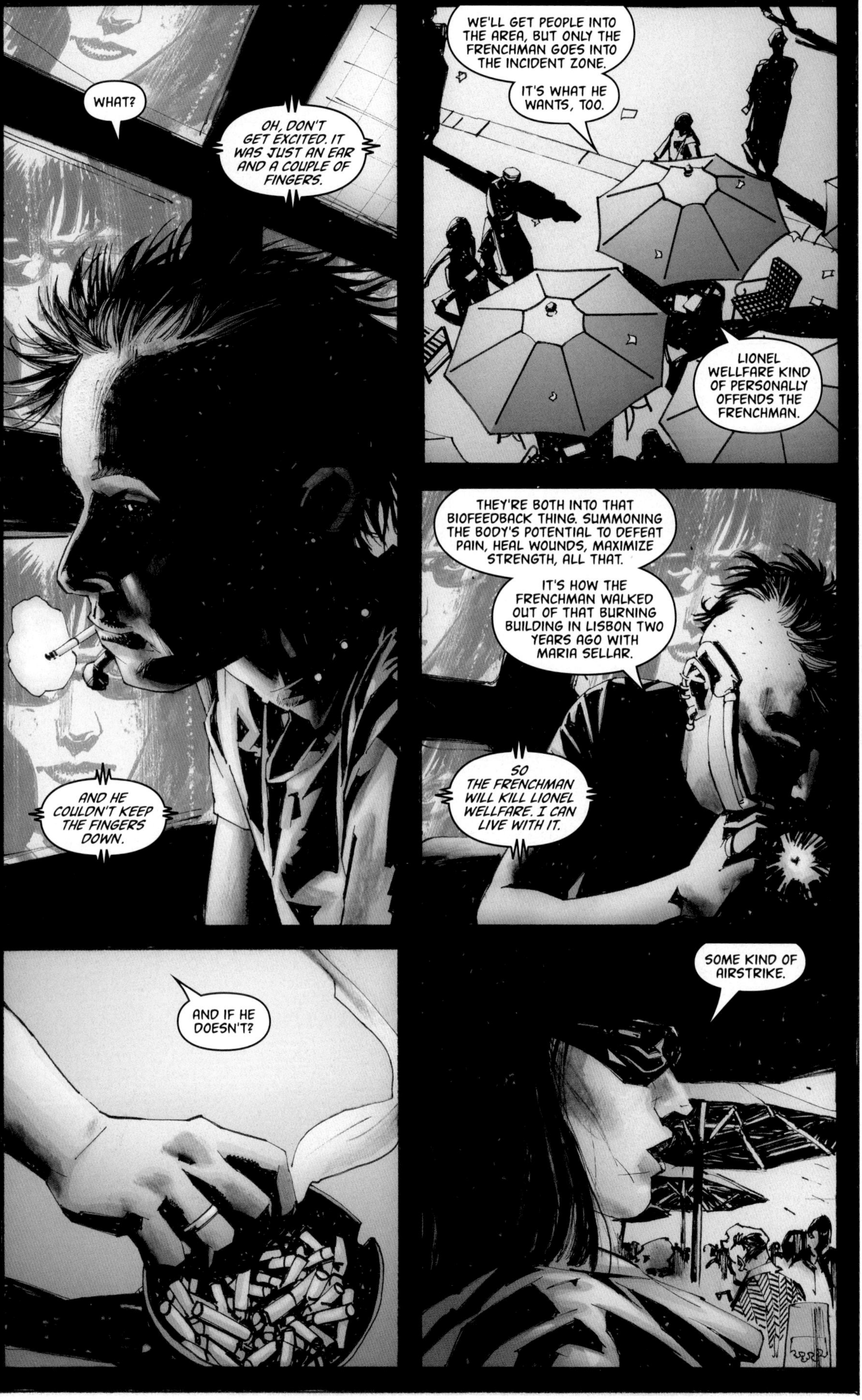
WHAT?
OH, DON'T GET EXCITED. IT WAS JUST AN EAR AND A COUPLE OF FINGERS.
AND HE COULDN'T KEEP THE FINGERS DOWN.
WE'LL GET PEOPLE INTO THE AREA, BUT ONLY THE FRENCHMAN GOES INTO THE INCIDENT ZONE.
IT'S WHAT HE WANTS, TOO.
LIONEL WELLFARE KIND OF PERSONALLY OFFENDS THE FRENCHMAN.
THEY'RE BOTH INTO THAT BIOFEEDBACK THING. SUMMONING THE BODY'S POTENTIAL TO DEFEAT PAIN, HEAL WOUNDS, MAXIMIZE STRENGTH, ALL THAT.
IT'S HOW THE FRENCHMAN WALKED OUT OF THAT BURNING BUILDING IN LISBON TWO YEARS AGO WITH MARIA SELLAR.
SO THE FRENCHMAN WILL KILL LIONEL WELLFARE. I CAN LIVE WITH IT.
AND IF HE DOESN'T?
SOME KIND OF AIRSTRIKE.

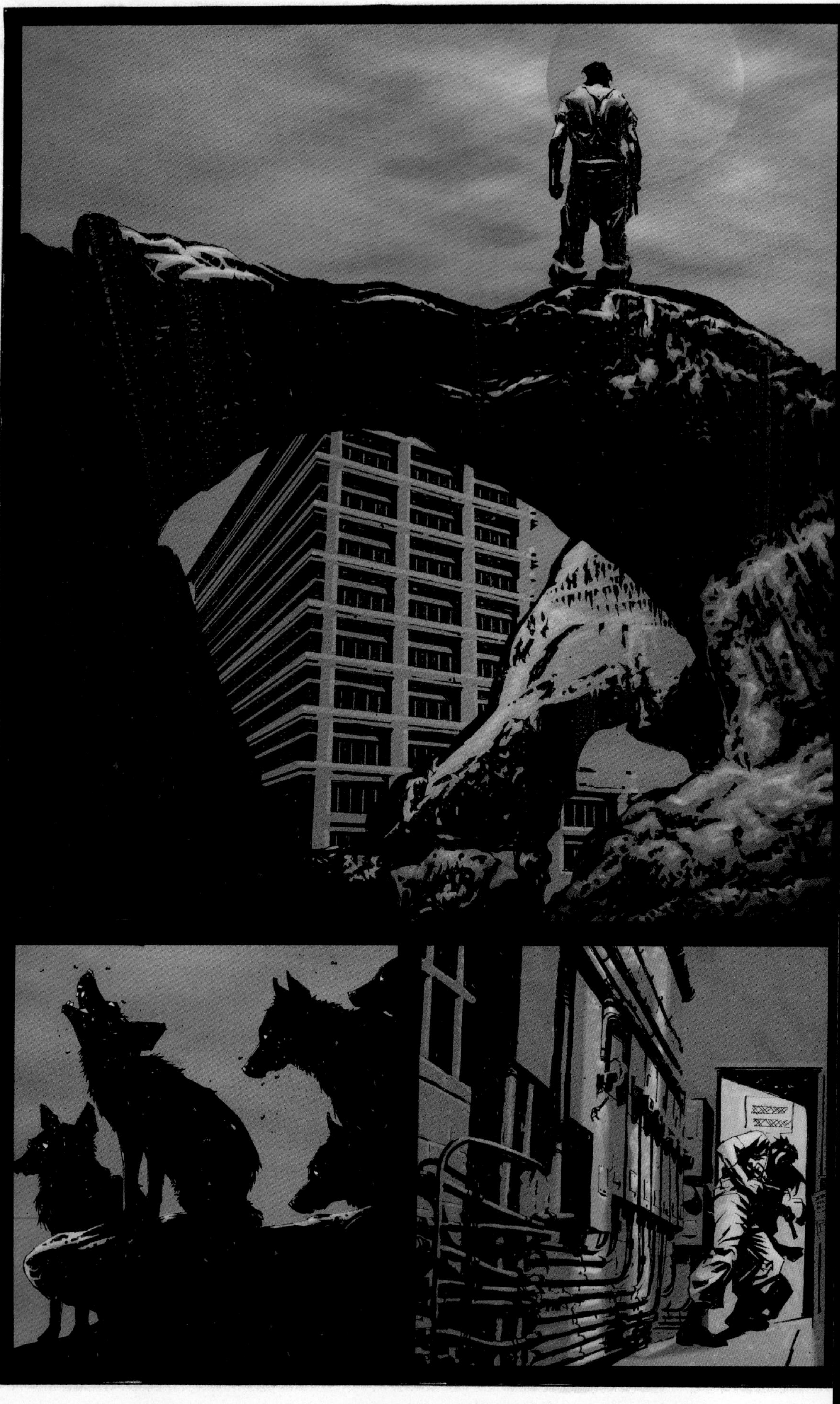

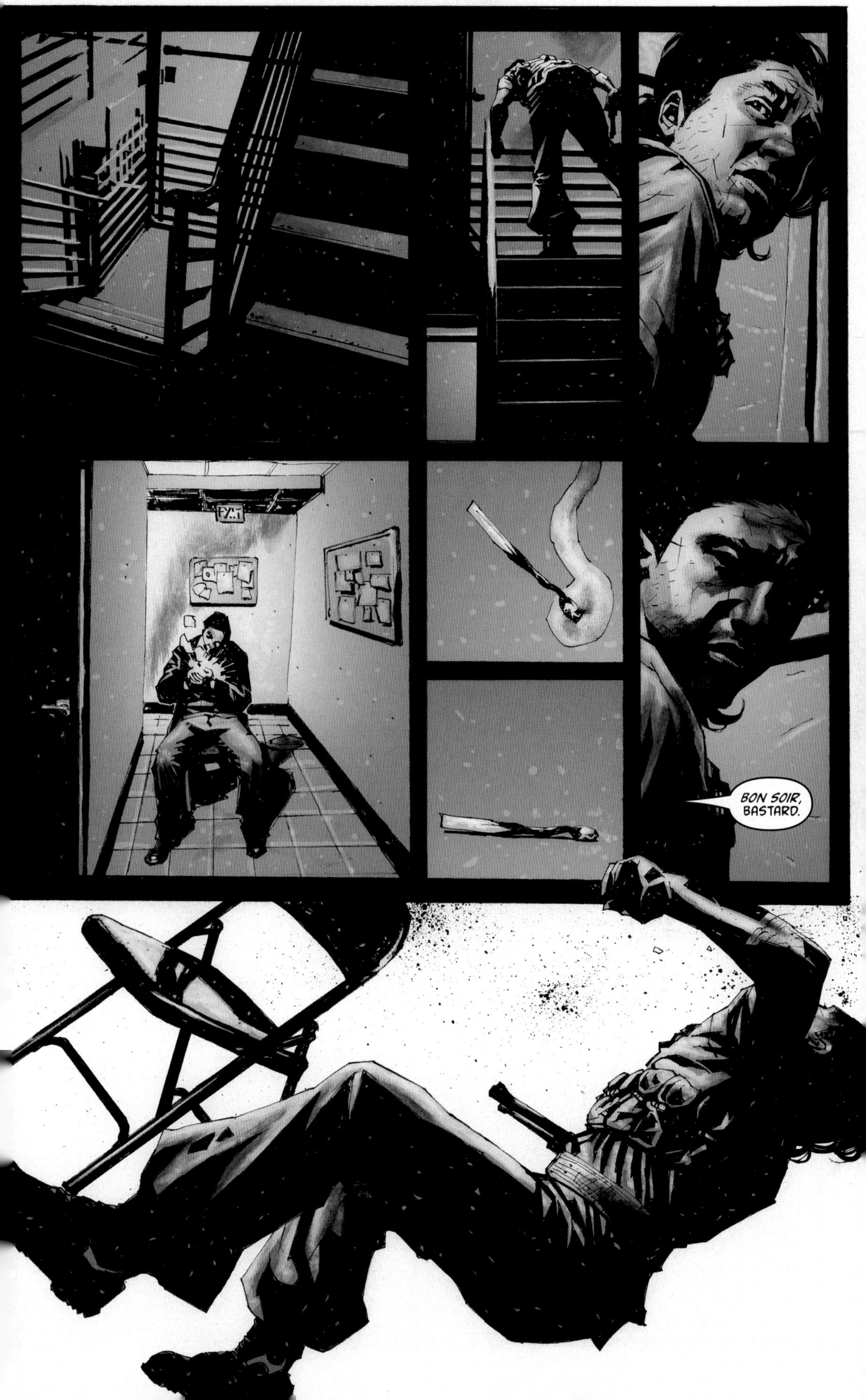
BON SOIR, BASTARD.

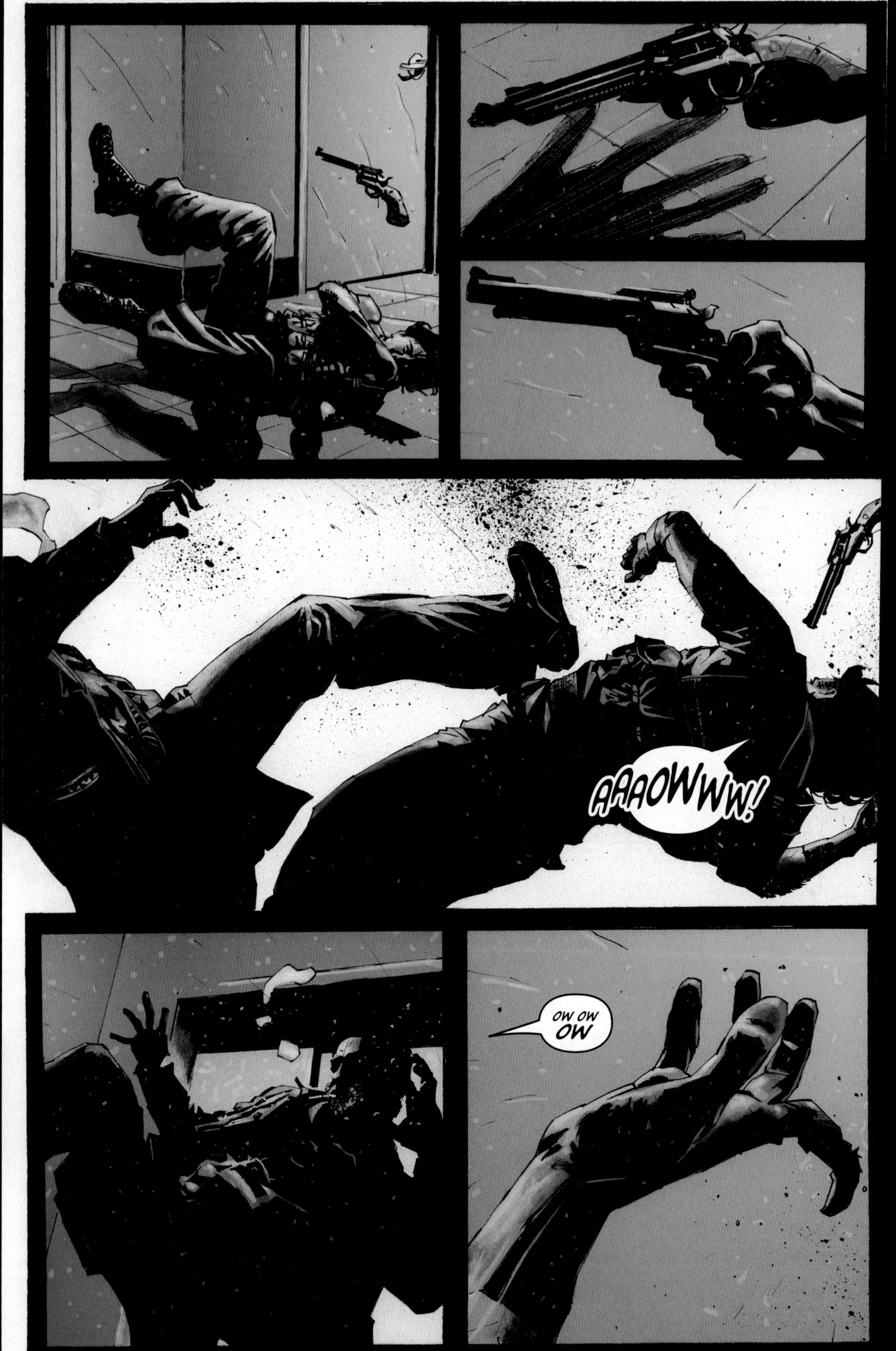
AAAOWWW!
OW OW OW

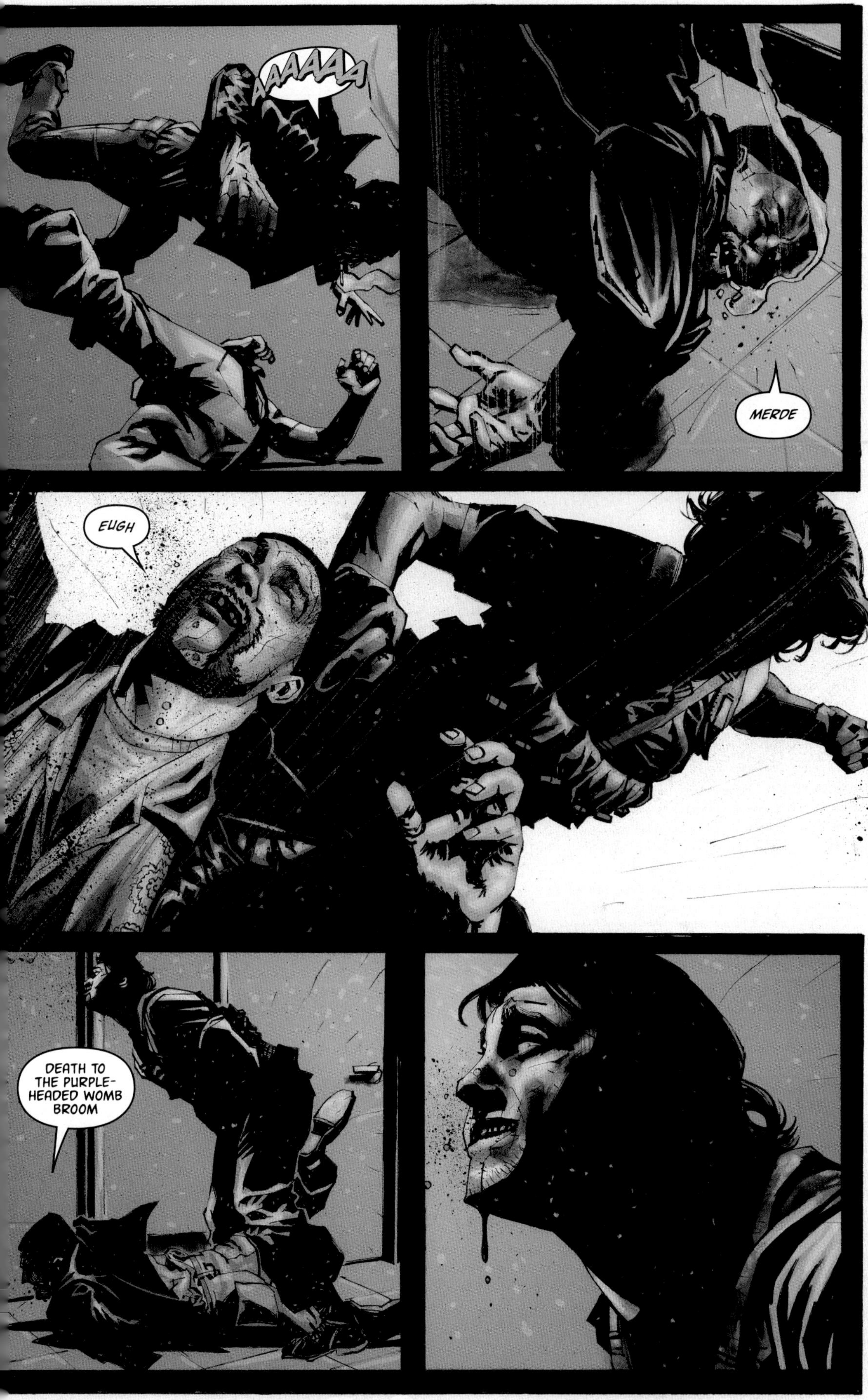

AAAAAA
MERDE
EUGH
DEATH TO THE PURPLE-HEADED WOMB BROOM

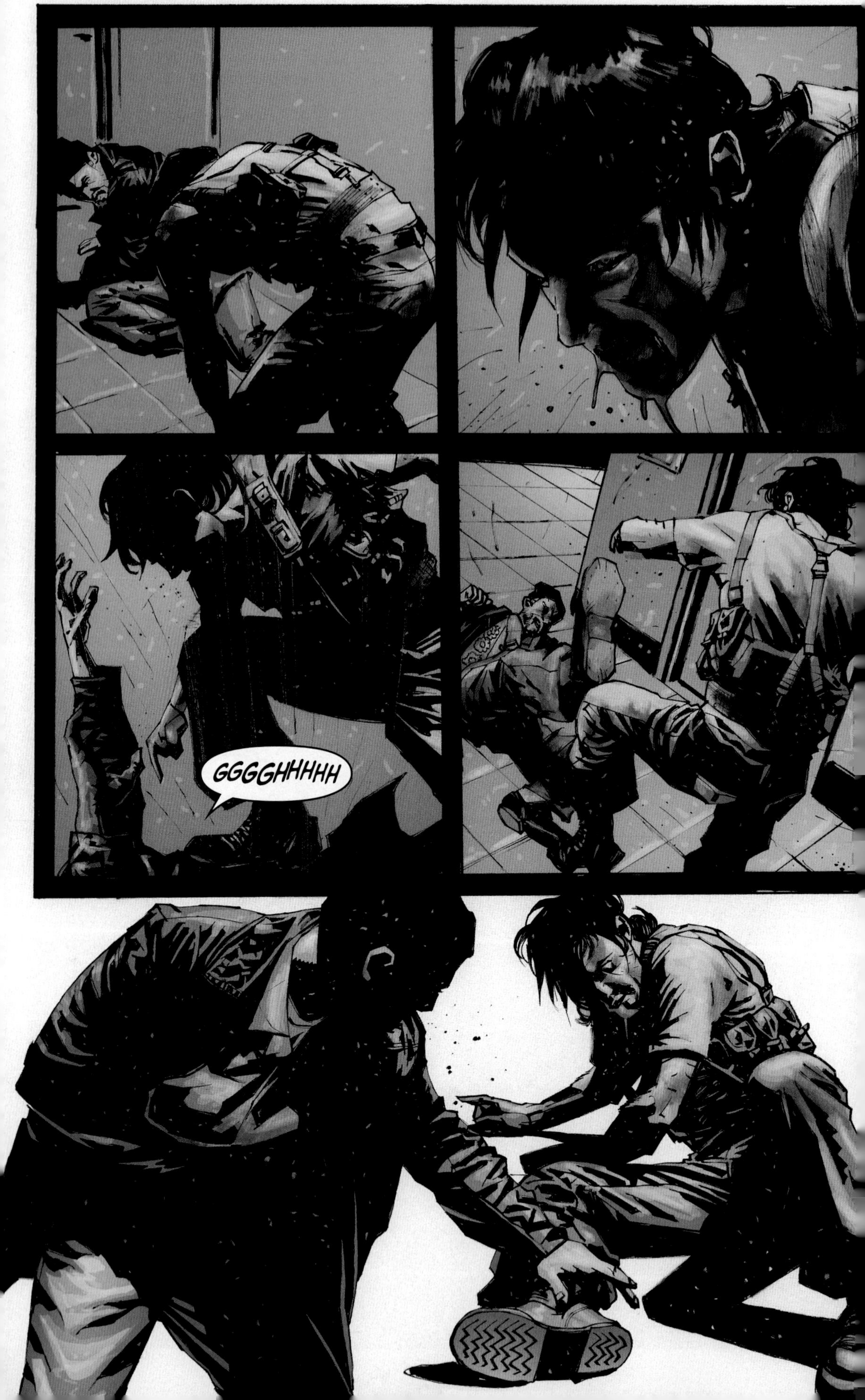
GGGGHHHHH

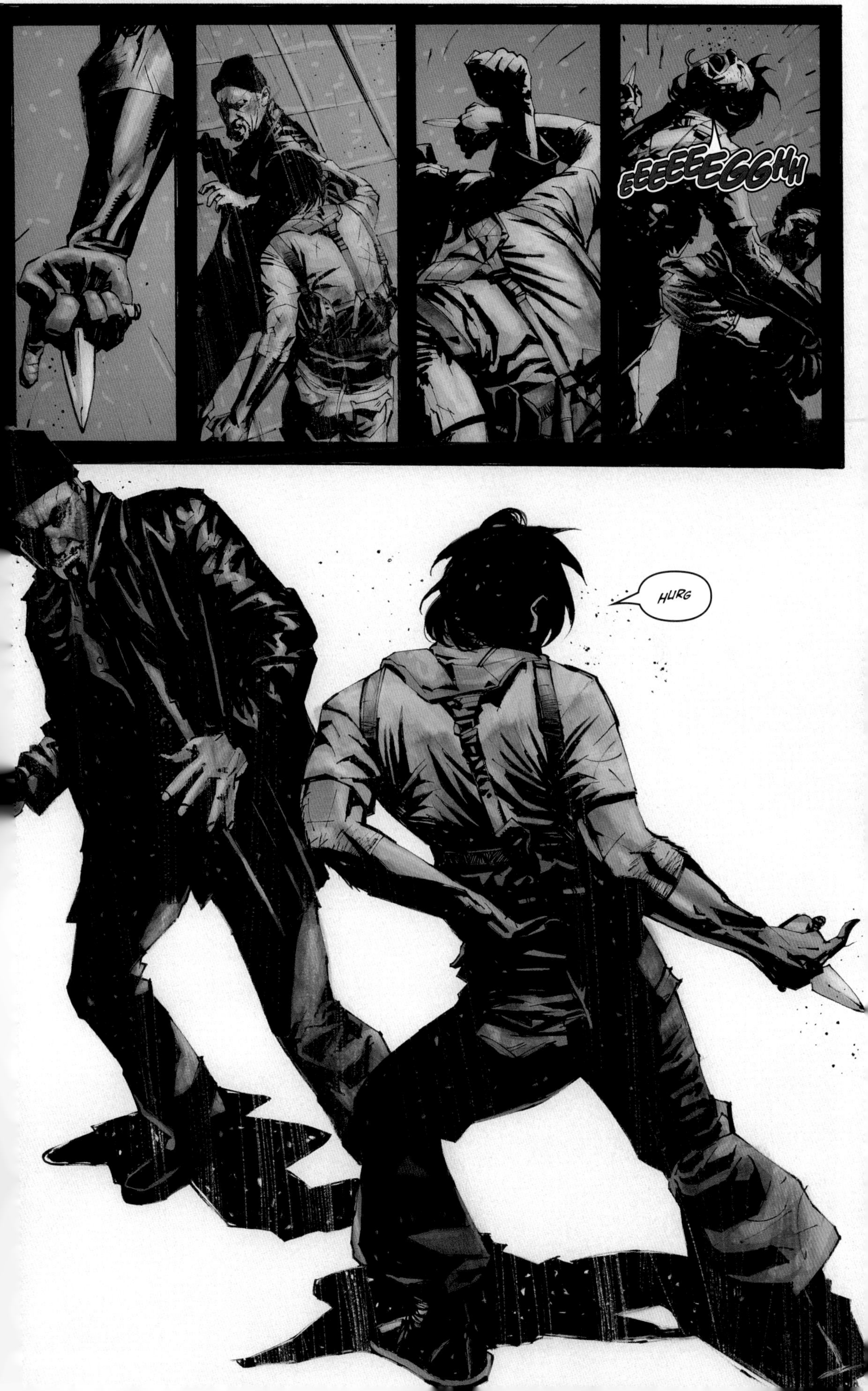
EEEEEEEGGHH
HURG

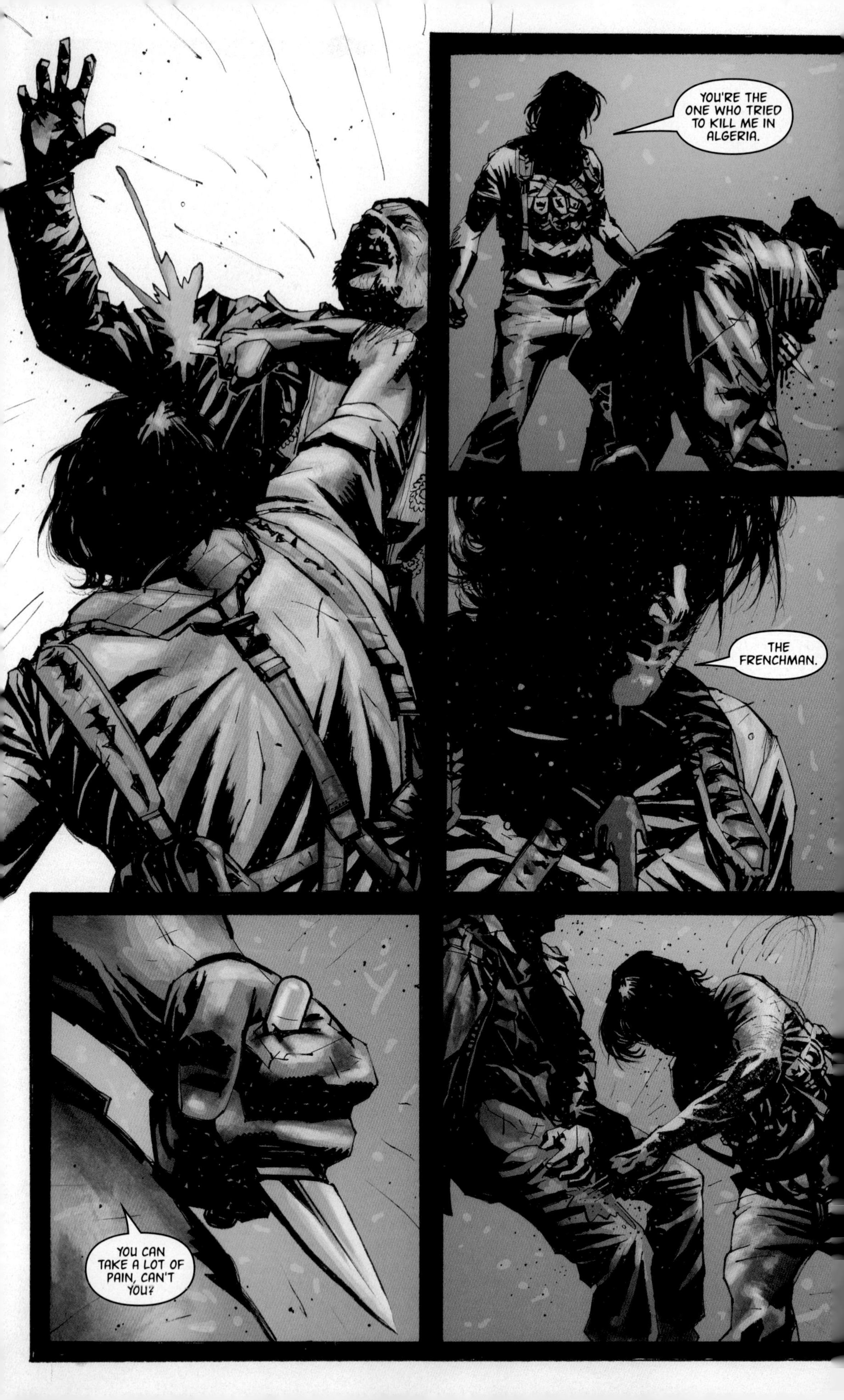
YOU'RE THE ONE WHO TRIED TO KILL ME IN ALGERIA.
THE FRENCHMAN.
YOU CAN TAKE A LOT OF PAIN, CAN'T YOU?

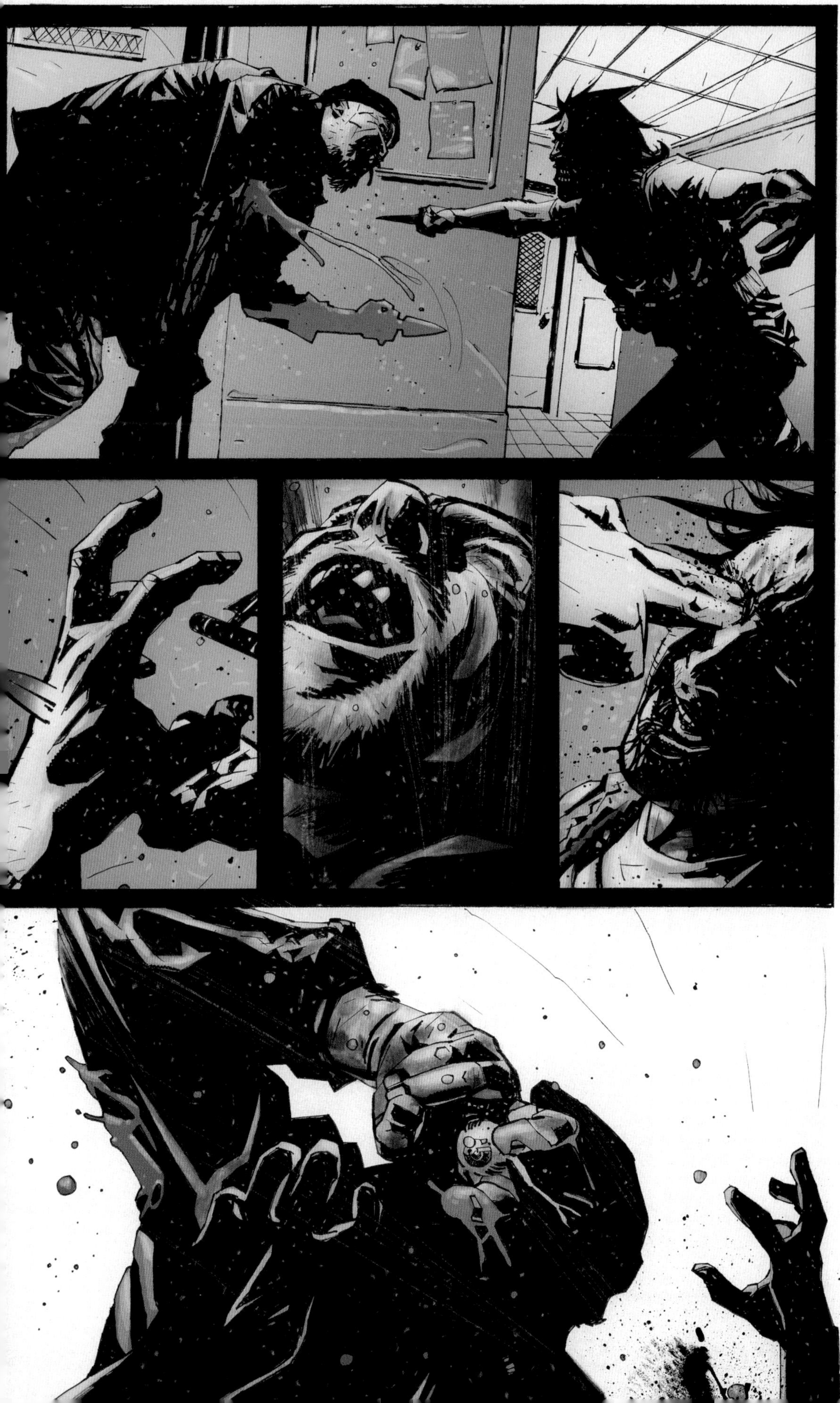

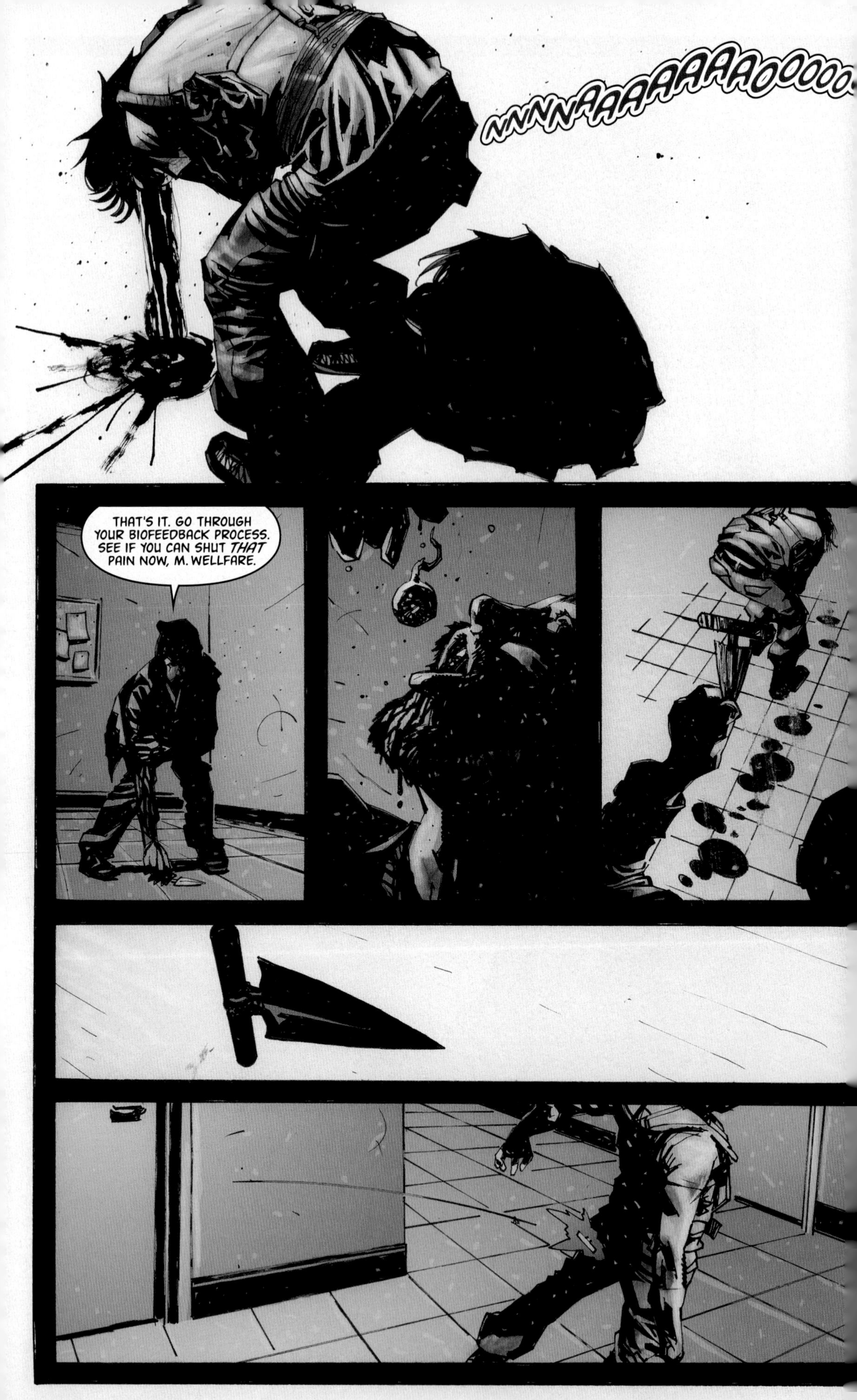
NNNNAAAAAAAAOOOOO
THAT'S IT. GO THROUGH YOUR BIOFEEDBACK PROCESS. SEE IF YOU CAN SHUT *THAT* PAIN NOW, M. WELLFARE.

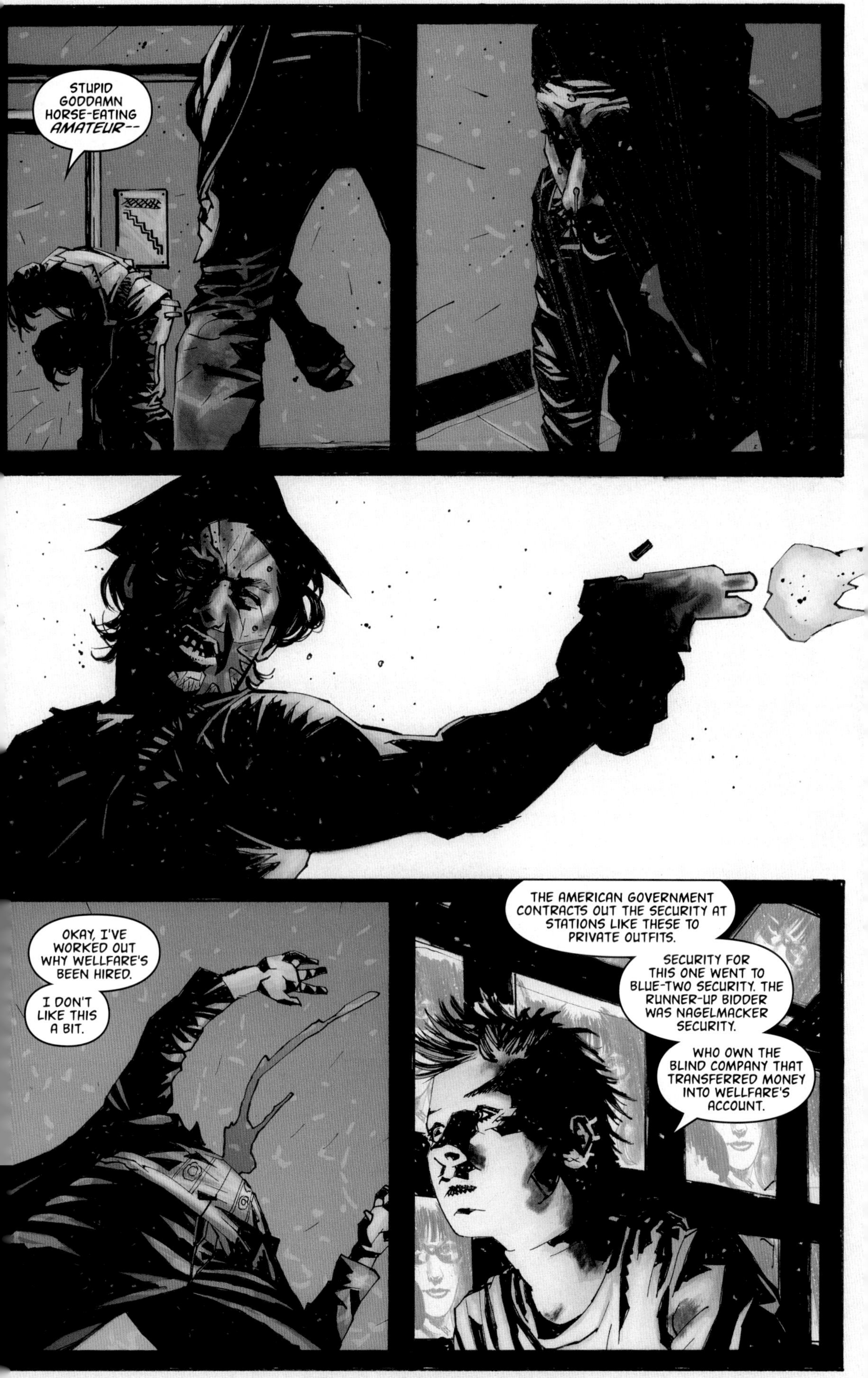
STUPID GODDAMN HORSE-EATING AMATEUR--
OKAY, I'VE WORKED OUT WHY WELLFARE'S BEEN HIRED.
I DON'T LIKE THIS A BIT.
THE AMERICAN GOVERNMENT CONTRACTS OUT THE SECURITY AT STATIONS LIKE THESE TO PRIVATE OUTFITS.
SECURITY FOR THIS ONE WENT TO BLUE-TWO SECURITY. THE RUNNER-UP BIDDER WAS NAGELMACKER SECURITY.
WHO OWN THE BLIND COMPANY THAT TRANSFERRED MONEY INTO WELLFARE'S ACCOUNT.

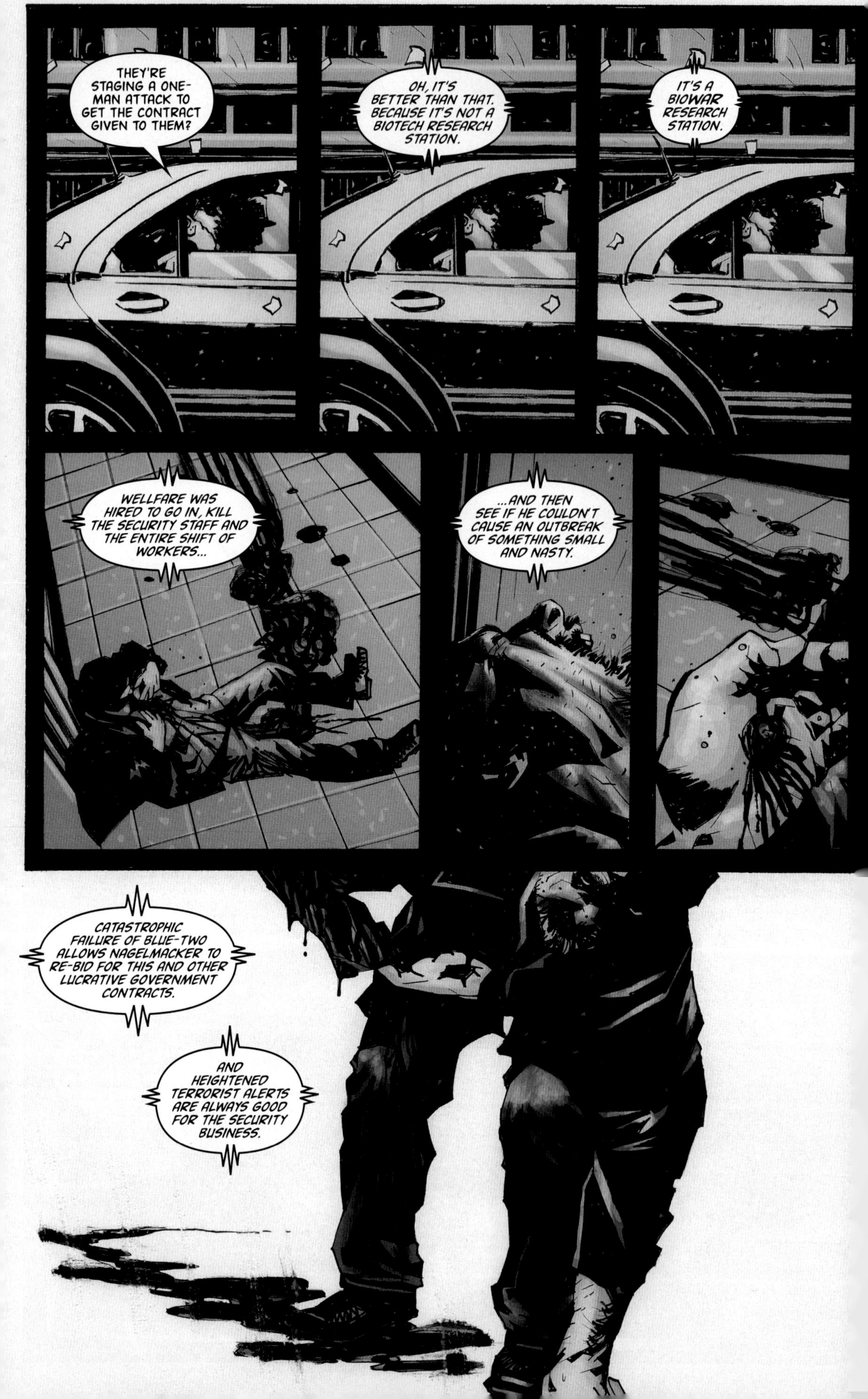
THEY'RE STAGING A ONE-MAN ATTACK TO GET THE CONTRACT GIVEN TO THEM?
OH, IT'S BETTER THAN THAT. BECAUSE IT'S NOT A BIOTECH RESEARCH STATION.
IT'S A BIOWAR RESEARCH STATION.
WELLFARE WAS HIRED TO GO IN, KILL THE SECURITY STAFF AND THE ENTIRE SHIFT OF WORKERS...
...AND THEN SEE IF HE COULDN'T CAUSE AN OUTBREAK OF SOMETHING SMALL AND NASTY.
CATASTROPHIC FAILURE OF BLUE-TWO ALLOWS NAGELMACKER TO RE-BID FOR THIS AND OTHER LUCRATIVE GOVERNMENT CONTRACTS.
AND HEIGHTENED TERRORIST ALERTS ARE ALWAYS GOOD FOR THE SECURITY BUSINESS.

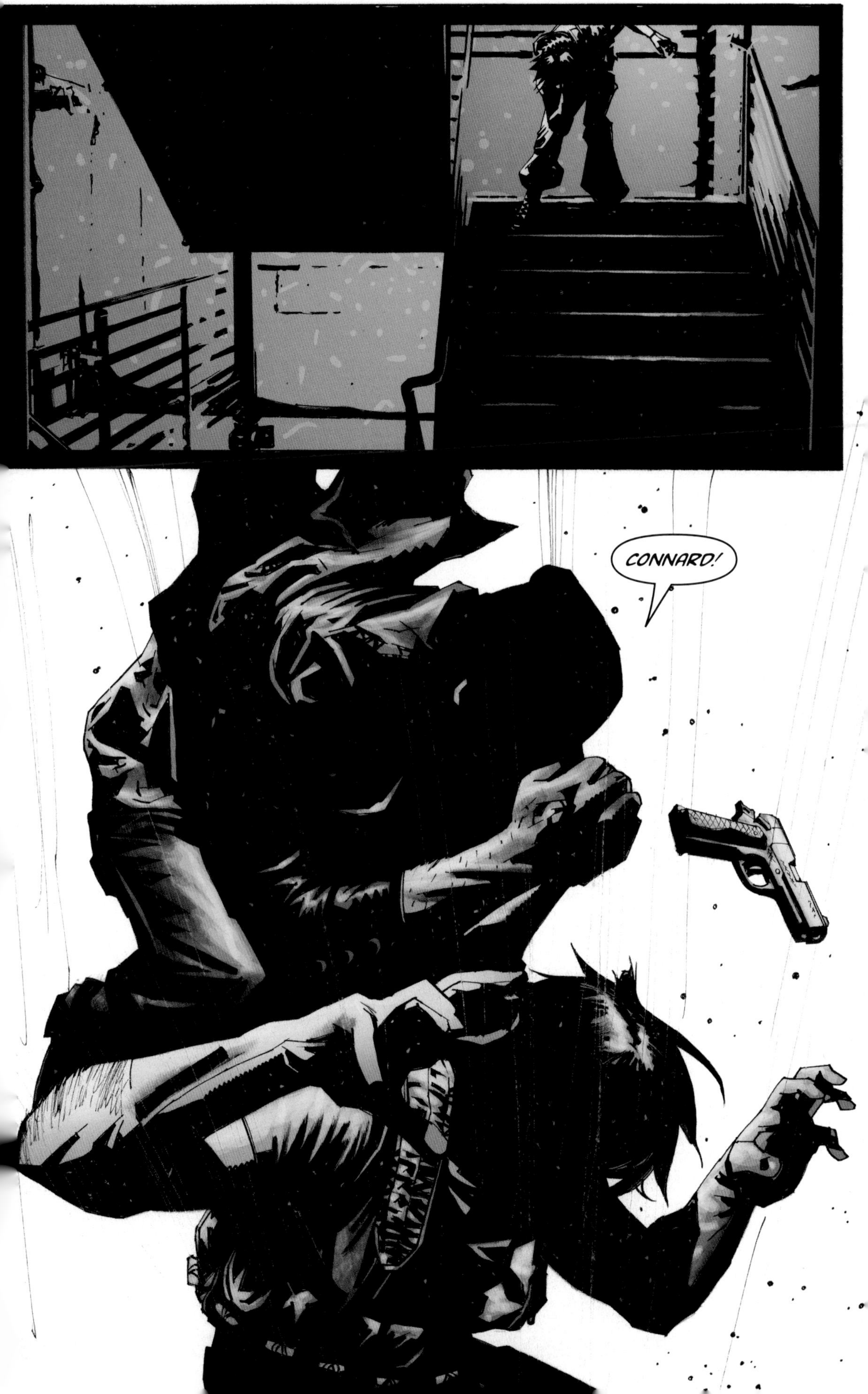
CONNARD!

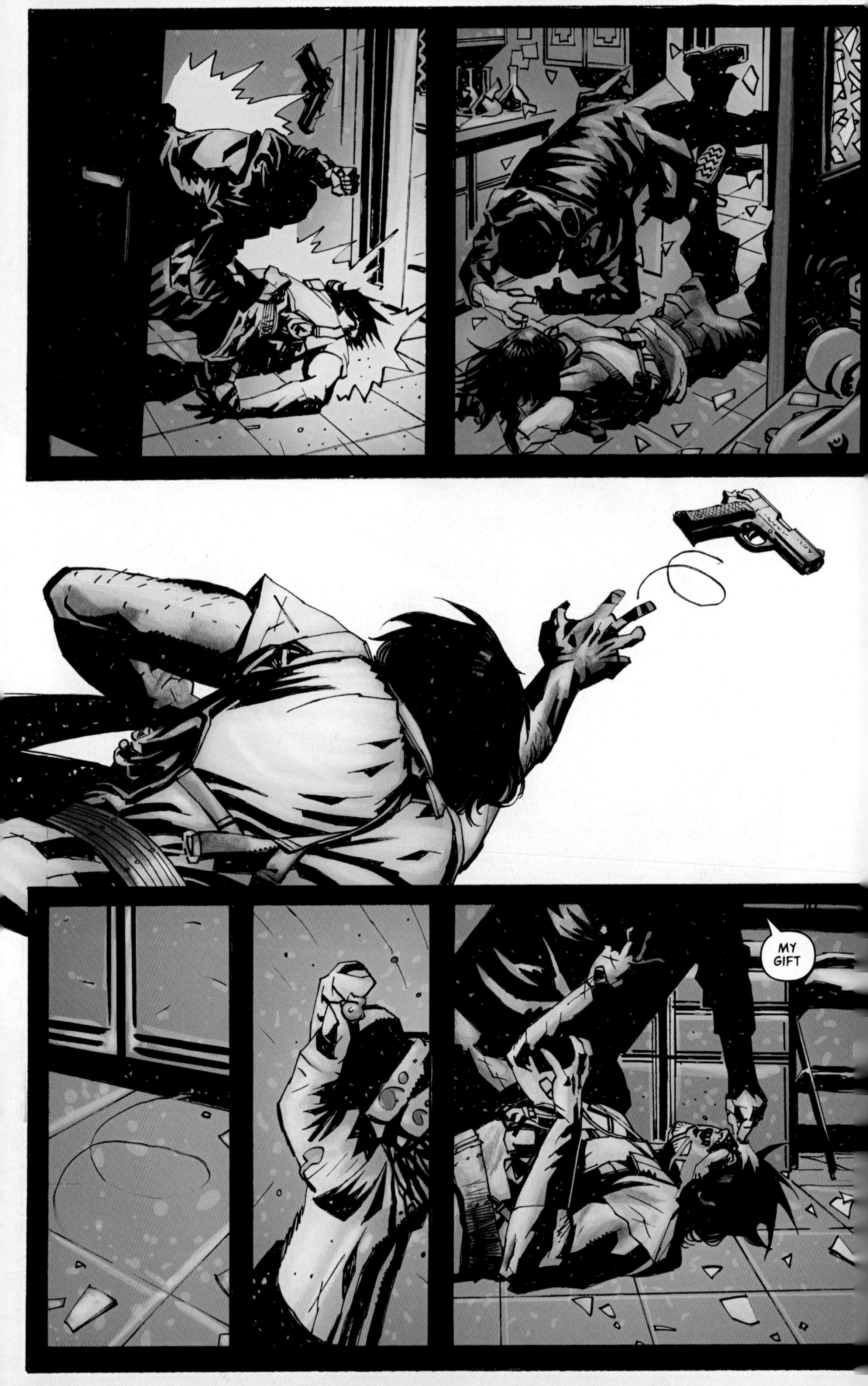
MY GIFT

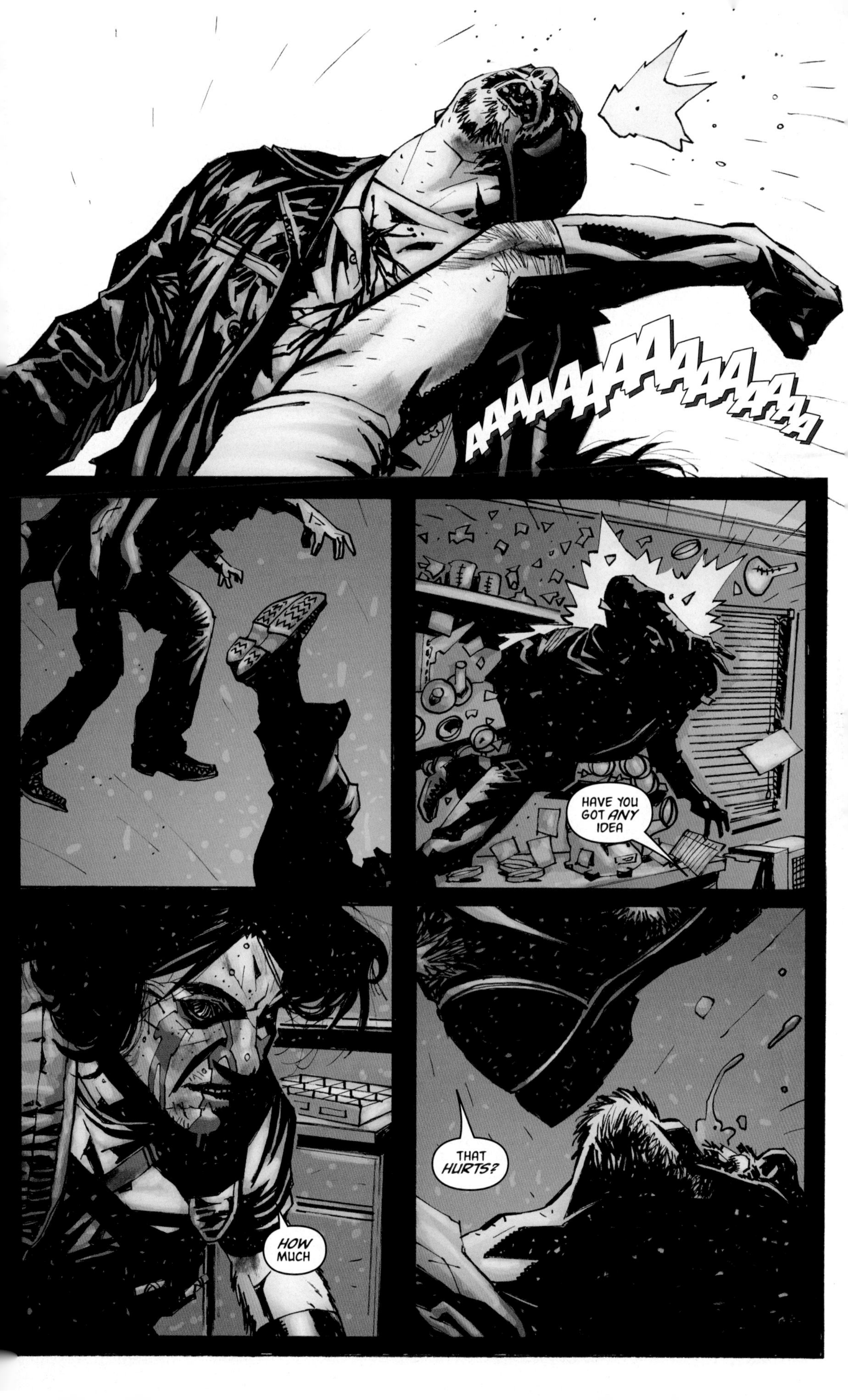
AAAAAAAAAAAAAAAAA
HAVE YOU GOT ANY IDEA
HOW MUCH
THAT HURTS?

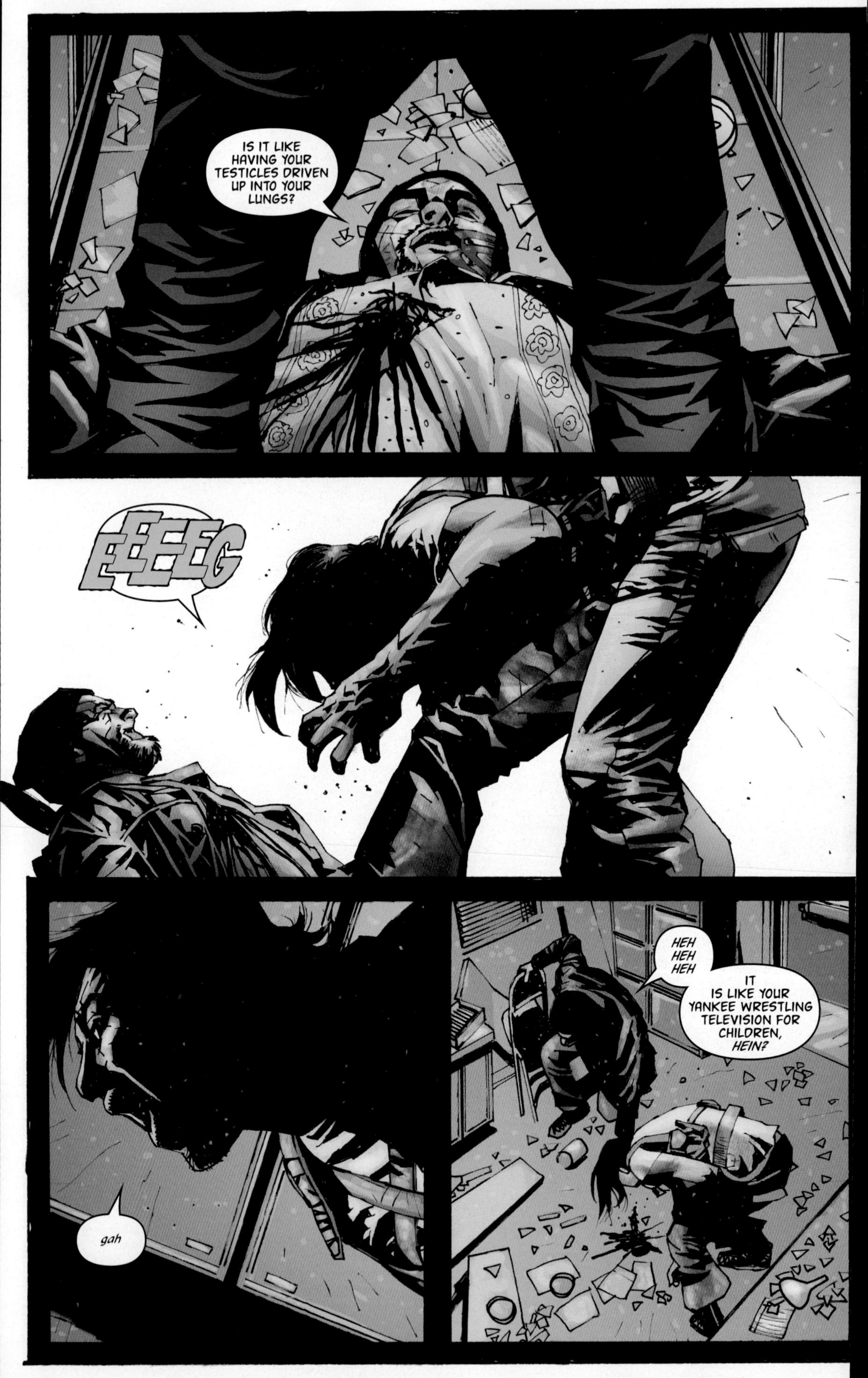
IS IT LIKE HAVING YOUR TESTICLES DRIVEN UP INTO YOUR LUNGS?
EEEEG
gah
HEH HEH HEH
IT IS LIKE YOUR YANKEE WRESTLING TELEVISION FOR CHILDREN, *HEIN?*

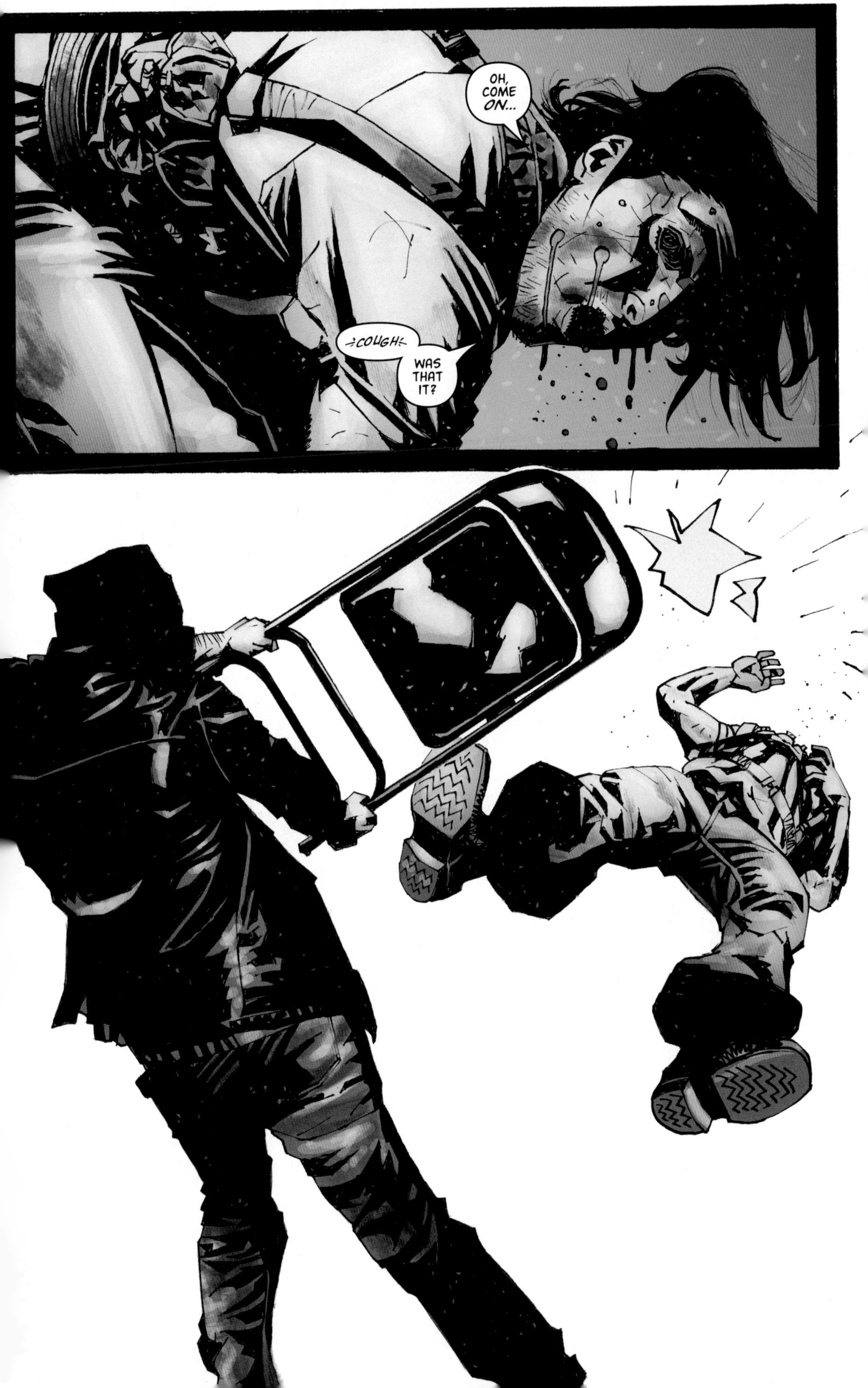
OH, COME ON...
COUGH
WAS THAT IT?

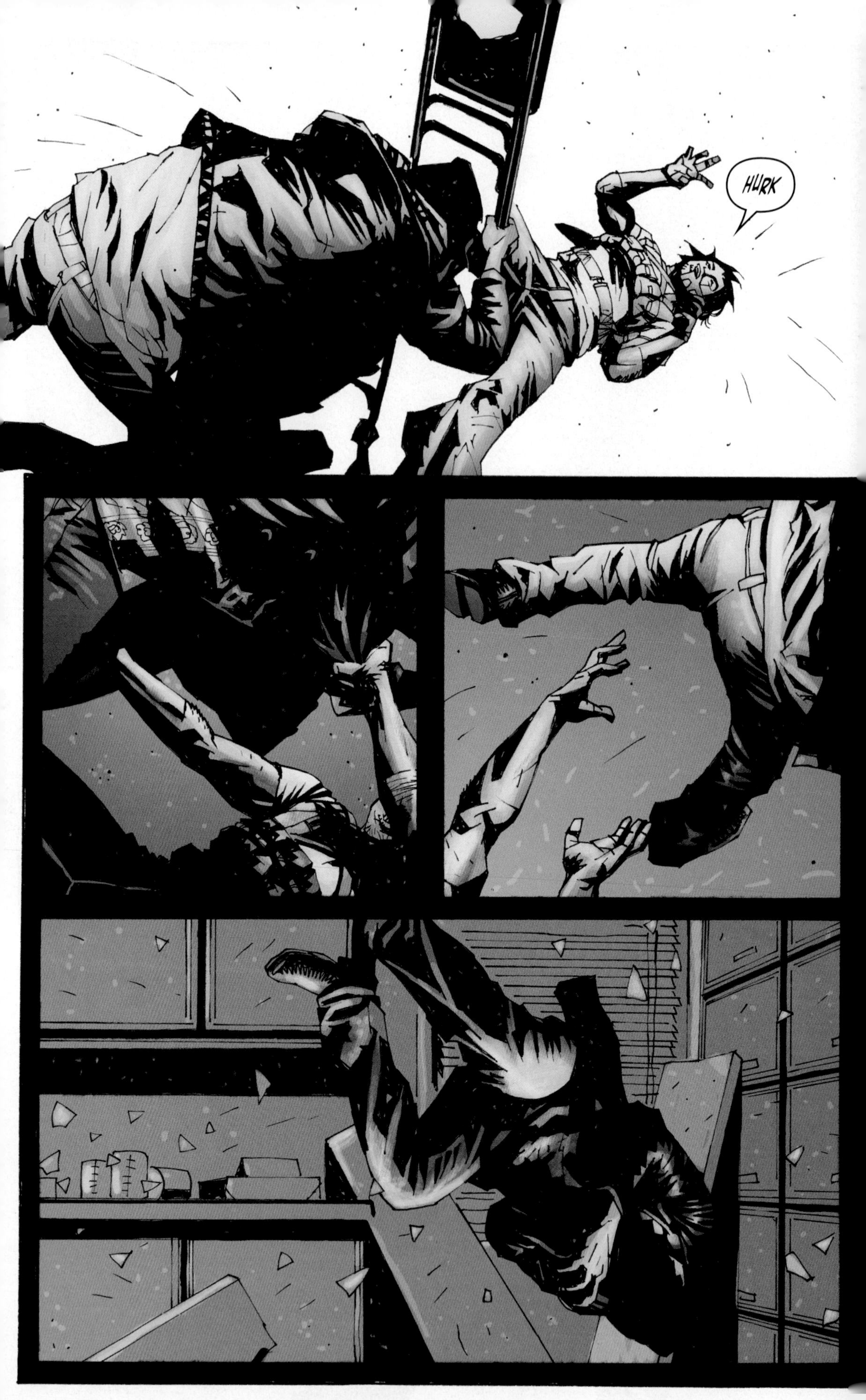
HURK

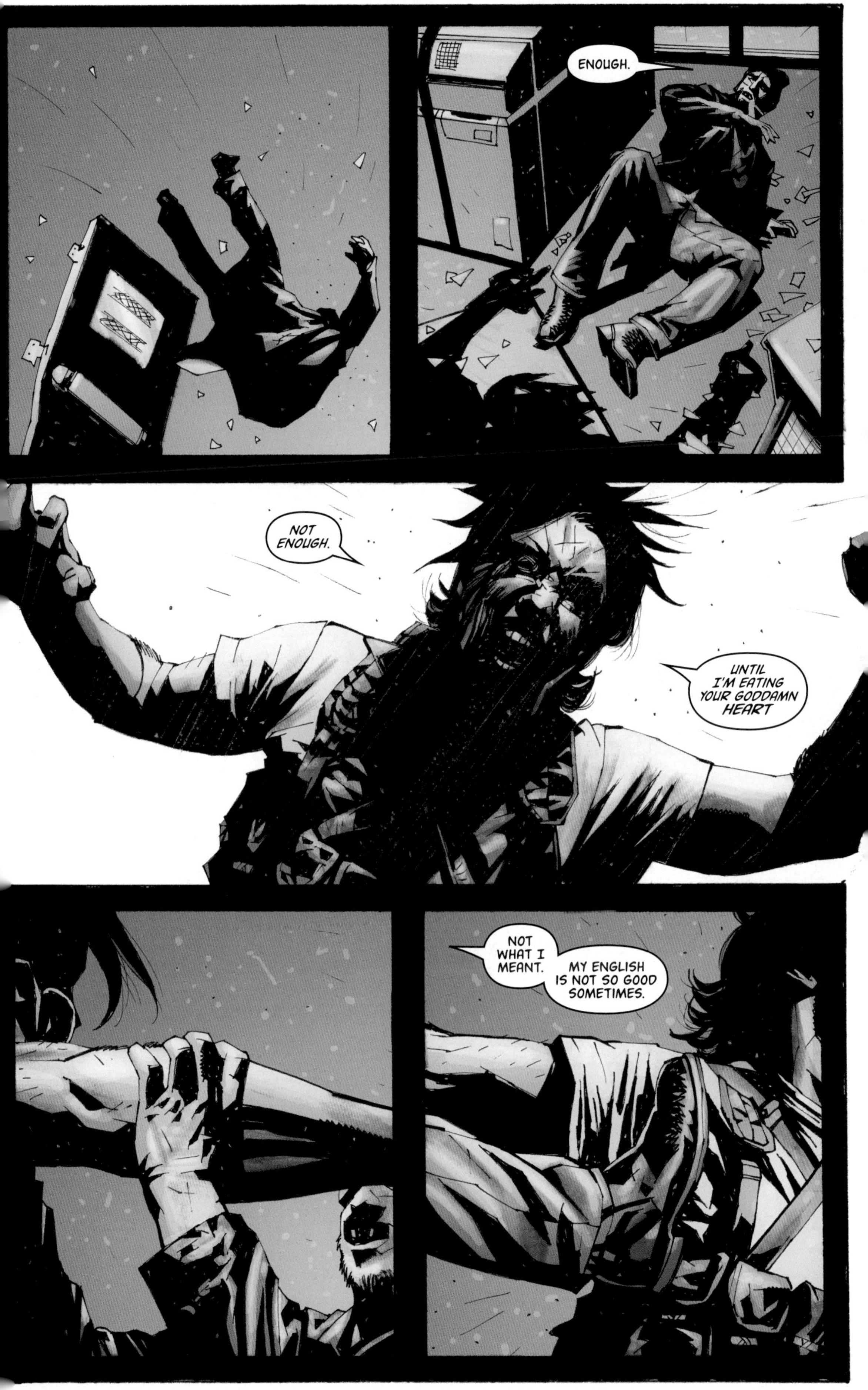
ENOUGH.
NOT ENOUGH.
UNTIL I'M EATING YOUR GODDAMN HEART
NOT WHAT I MEANT.
MY ENGLISH IS NOT SO GOOD SOMETIMES.

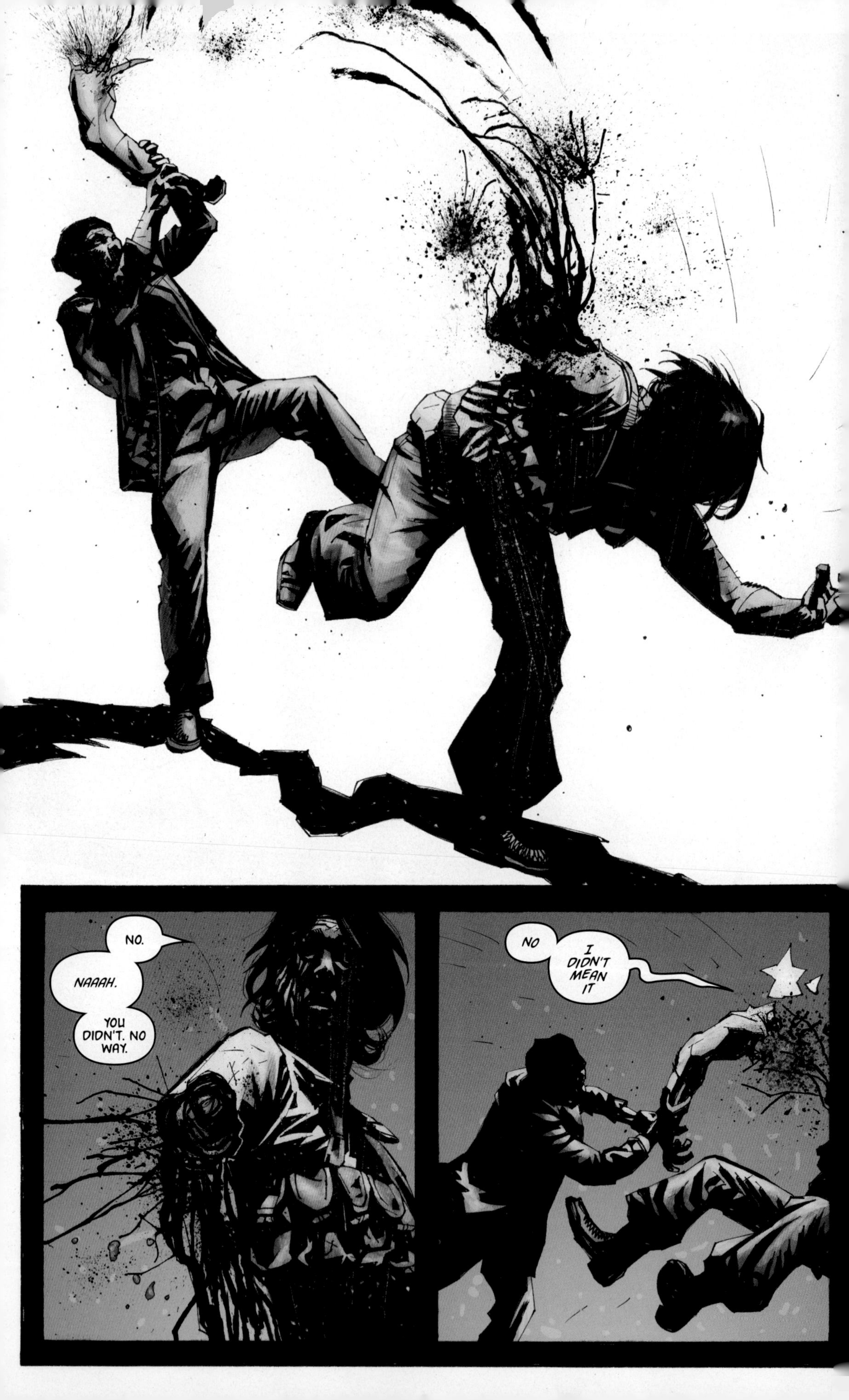
NO.
NAAAH.
YOU DIDN'T. NO WAY.
NO
I DIDN'T MEAN IT

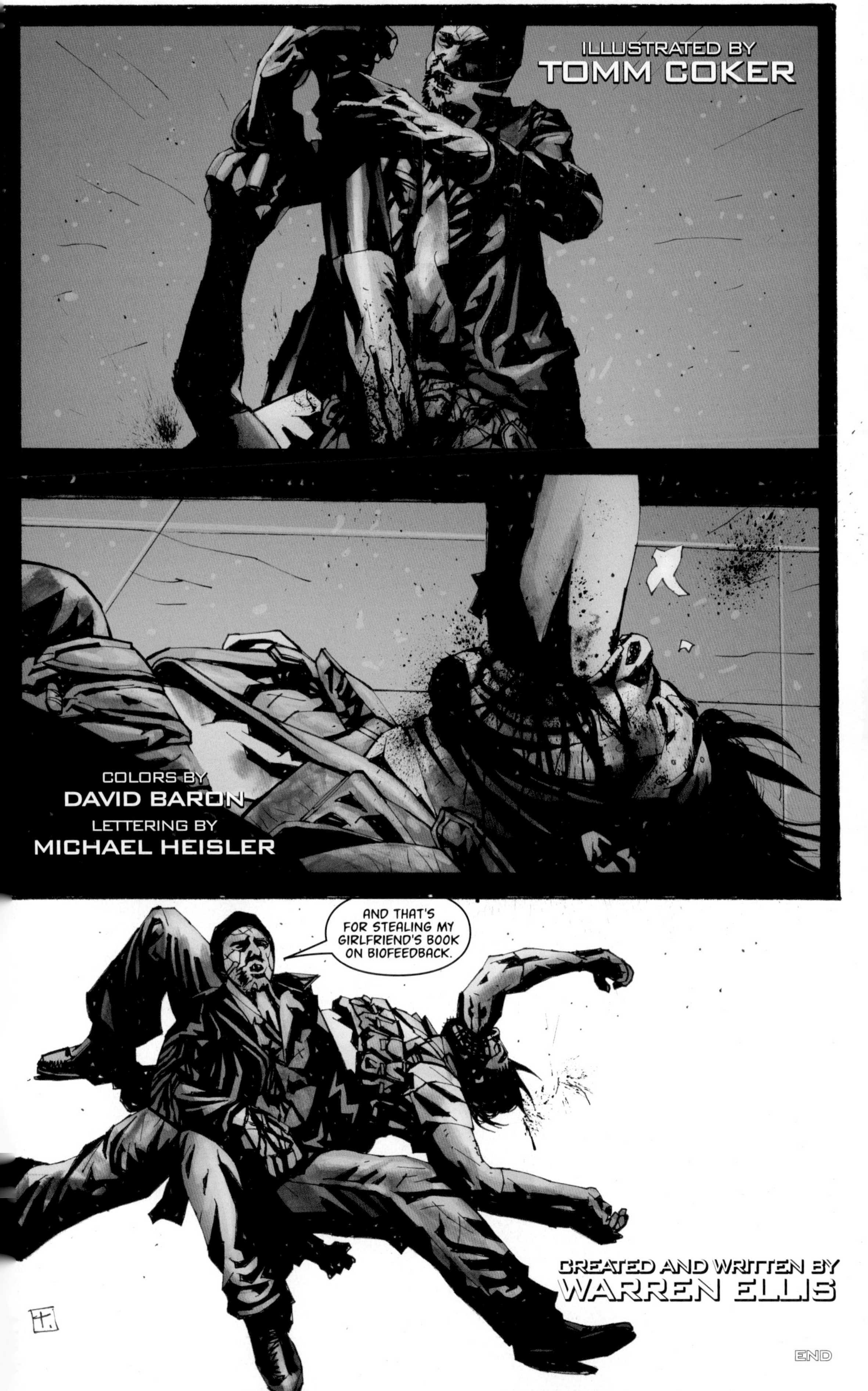
ILLUSTRATED BY
TOMM COKER
COLORS BY
DAVID BARON
LETTERING BY
MICHAEL HEISLER
AND THAT'S FOR STEALING MY GIRLFRIEND'S BOOK ON BIOFEEDBACK.
CREATED AND WRITTEN BY
WARREN ELLIS
END

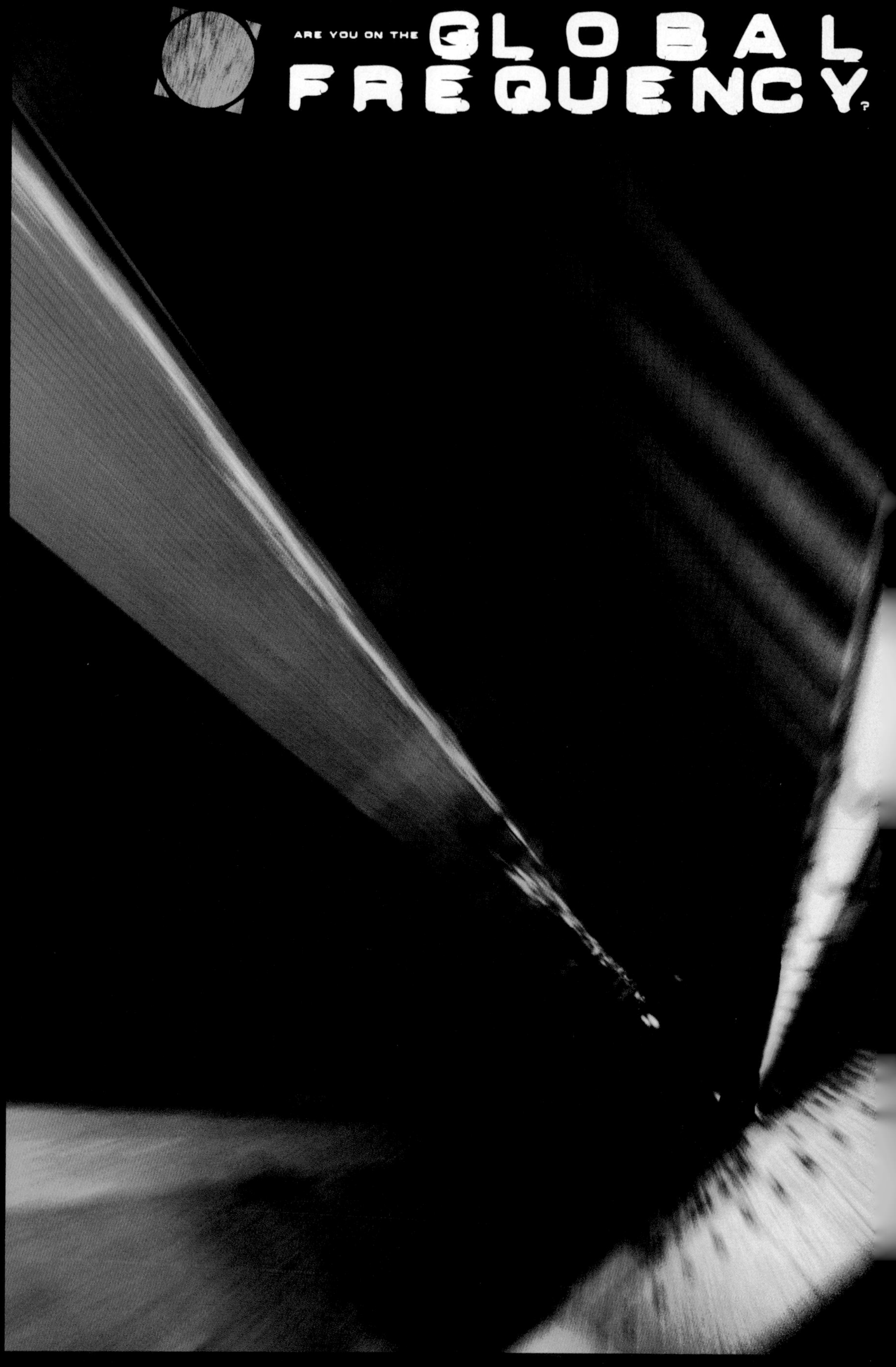
ARE YOU ON THE GLOBAL FREQUENCY?

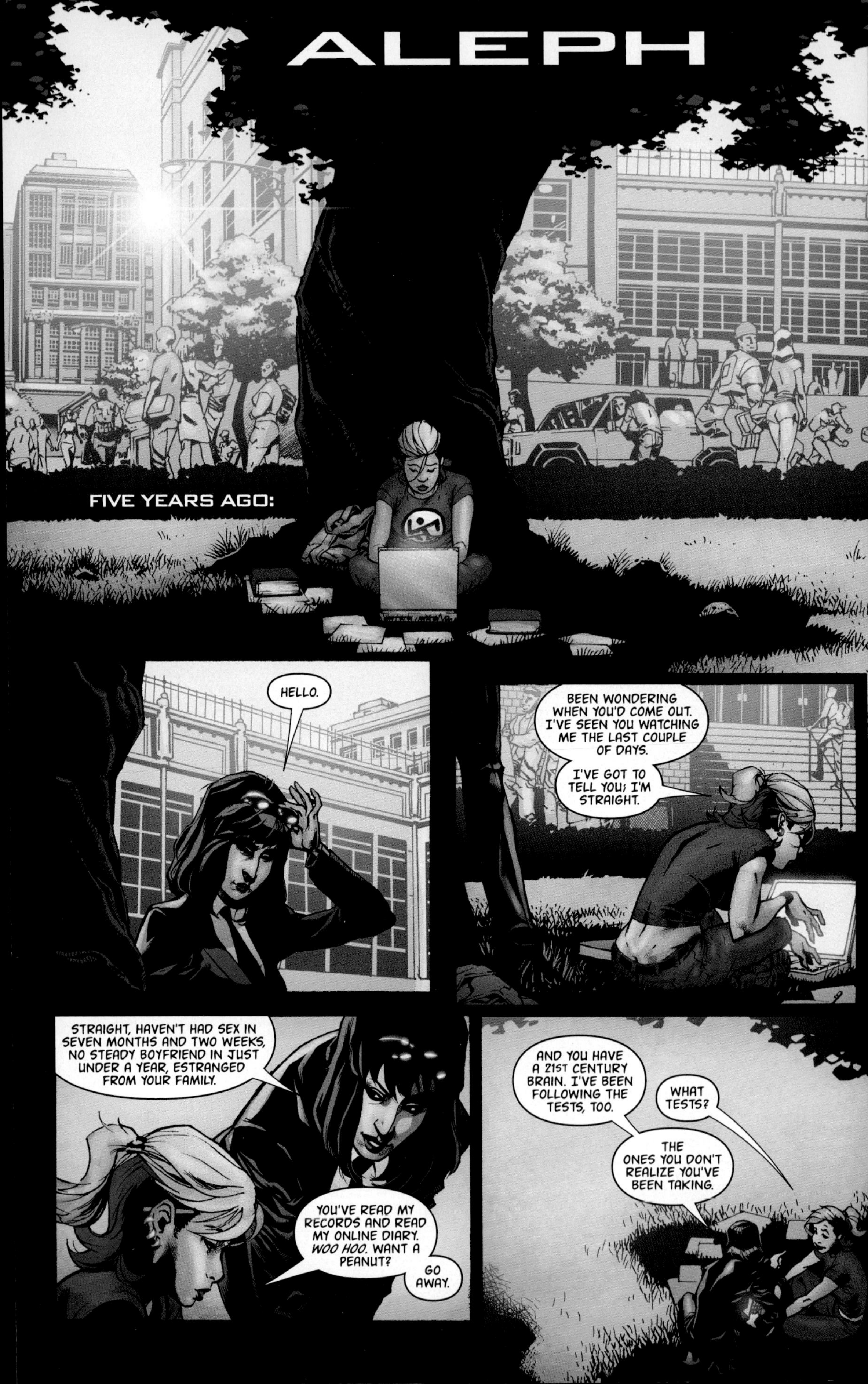
ALEPH
FIVE YEARS AGO:
HELLO.
BEEN WONDERING WHEN YOU'D COME OUT. I'VE SEEN YOU WATCHING ME THE LAST COUPLE OF DAYS.
I'VE GOT TO TELL YOU; I'M STRAIGHT.
STRAIGHT, HAVEN'T HAD SEX IN SEVEN MONTHS AND TWO WEEKS, NO STEADY BOYFRIEND IN JUST UNDER A YEAR, ESTRANGED FROM YOUR FAMILY.
YOU'VE READ MY RECORDS AND READ MY ONLINE DIARY. WOO HOO. WANT A PEANUT?
GO AWAY.
AND YOU HAVE A 21ST CENTURY BRAIN. I'VE BEEN FOLLOWING THE TESTS, TOO.
WHAT TESTS?
THE ONES YOU DON'T REALIZE YOU'VE BEEN TAKING.

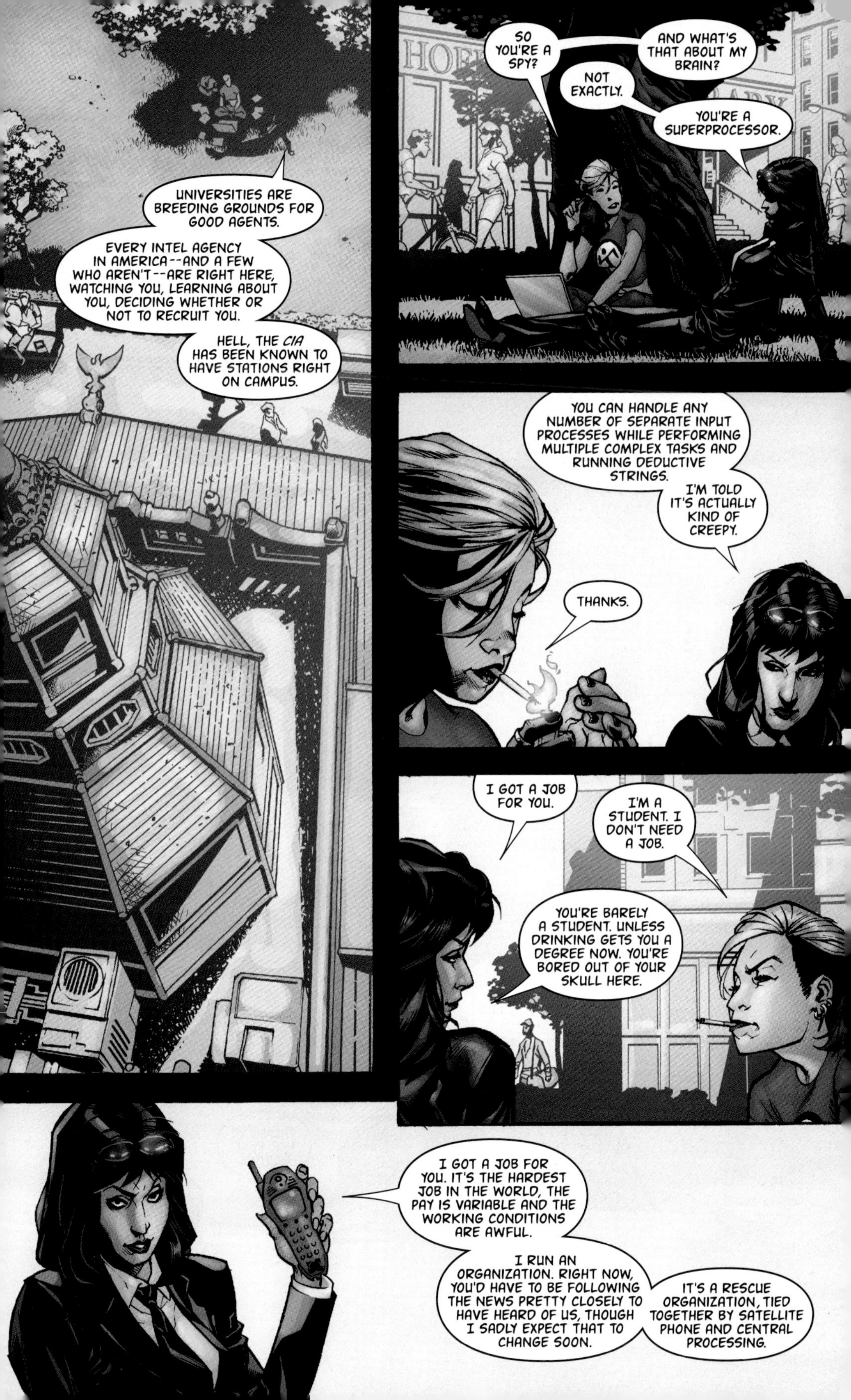
UNIVERSITIES ARE BREEDING GROUNDS FOR GOOD AGENTS.
EVERY INTEL AGENCY IN AMERICA--AND A FEW WHO AREN'T--ARE RIGHT HERE, WATCHING YOU, LEARNING ABOUT YOU, DECIDING WHETHER OR NOT TO RECRUIT YOU.
HELL, THE *CIA* HAS BEEN KNOWN TO HAVE STATIONS RIGHT ON CAMPUS.
SO YOU'RE A SPY?
AND WHAT'S THAT ABOUT MY BRAIN?
NOT EXACTLY.
YOU'RE A SUPERPROCESSOR.
YOU CAN HANDLE ANY NUMBER OF SEPARATE INPUT PROCESSES WHILE PERFORMING MULTIPLE COMPLEX TASKS AND RUNNING DEDUCTIVE STRINGS.
I'M TOLD IT'S ACTUALLY KIND OF CREEPY.
THANKS.
I GOT A JOB FOR YOU.
I'M A STUDENT. I DON'T NEED A JOB.
YOU'RE BARELY A STUDENT. UNLESS DRINKING GETS YOU A DEGREE NOW. YOU'RE BORED OUT OF YOUR SKULL HERE.
I GOT A JOB FOR YOU. IT'S THE HARDEST JOB IN THE WORLD, THE PAY IS VARIABLE AND THE WORKING CONDITIONS ARE AWFUL.
I RUN AN ORGANIZATION. RIGHT NOW, YOU'D HAVE TO BE FOLLOWING THE NEWS PRETTY CLOSELY TO HAVE HEARD OF US, THOUGH I SADLY EXPECT THAT TO CHANGE SOON.
IT'S A RESCUE ORGANIZATION, TIED TOGETHER BY SATELLITE PHONE AND CENTRAL PROCESSING.

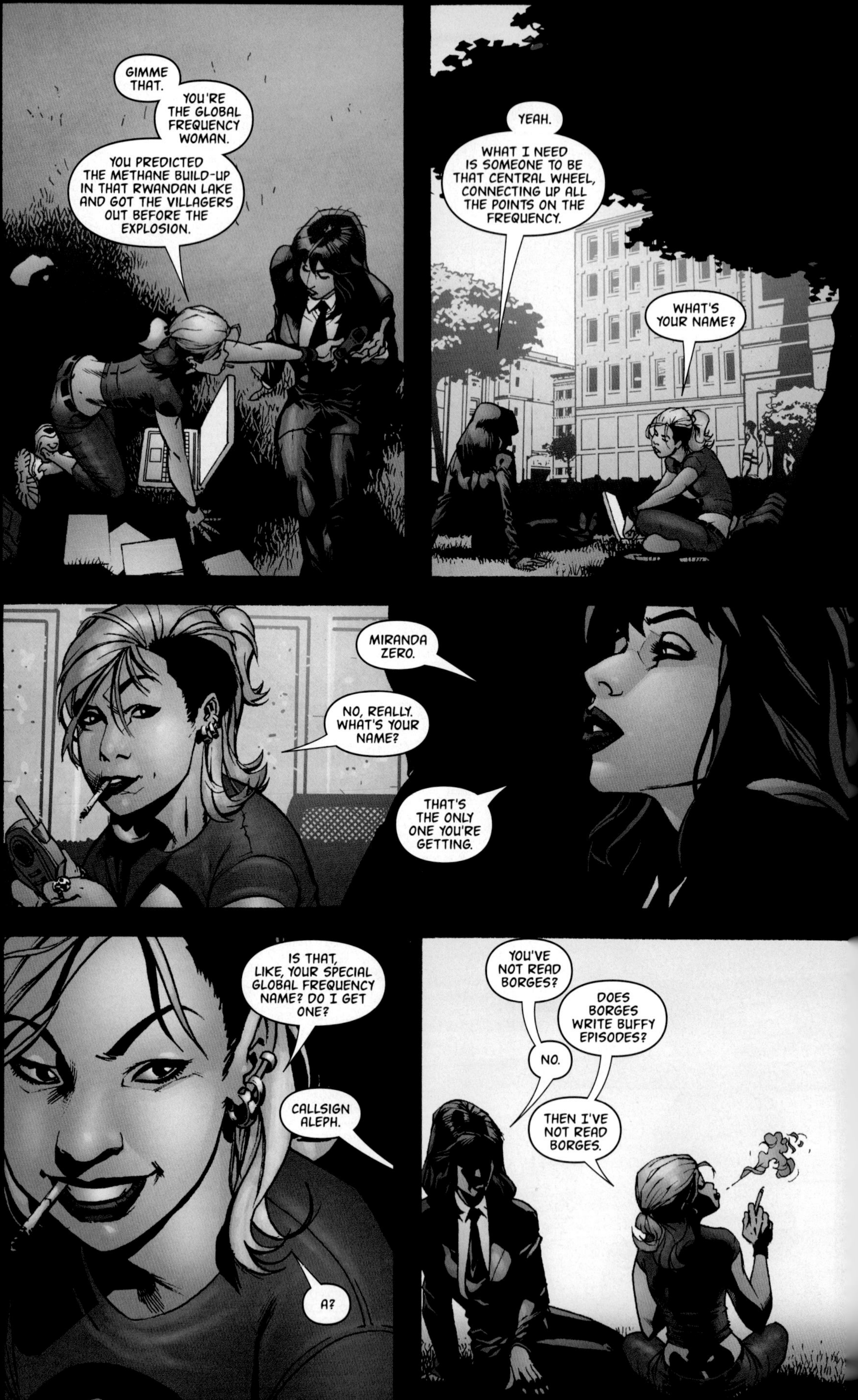
GIMME THAT.
YOU'RE THE GLOBAL FREQUENCY WOMAN.
YOU PREDICTED THE METHANE BUILD-UP IN THAT RWANDAN LAKE AND GOT THE VILLAGERS OUT BEFORE THE EXPLOSION.
YEAH.
WHAT I NEED IS SOMEONE TO BE THAT CENTRAL WHEEL, CONNECTING UP ALL THE POINTS ON THE FREQUENCY.
WHAT'S YOUR NAME?
MIRANDA ZERO.
NO, REALLY. WHAT'S YOUR NAME?
THAT'S THE ONLY ONE YOU'RE GETTING.
IS THAT, LIKE, YOUR SPECIAL GLOBAL FREQUENCY NAME? DO I GET ONE?
CALLSIGN ALEPH.
A?
YOU'VE NOT READ BORGES?
NO.
DOES BORGES WRITE BUFFY EPISODES?
THEN I'VE NOT READ BORGES.

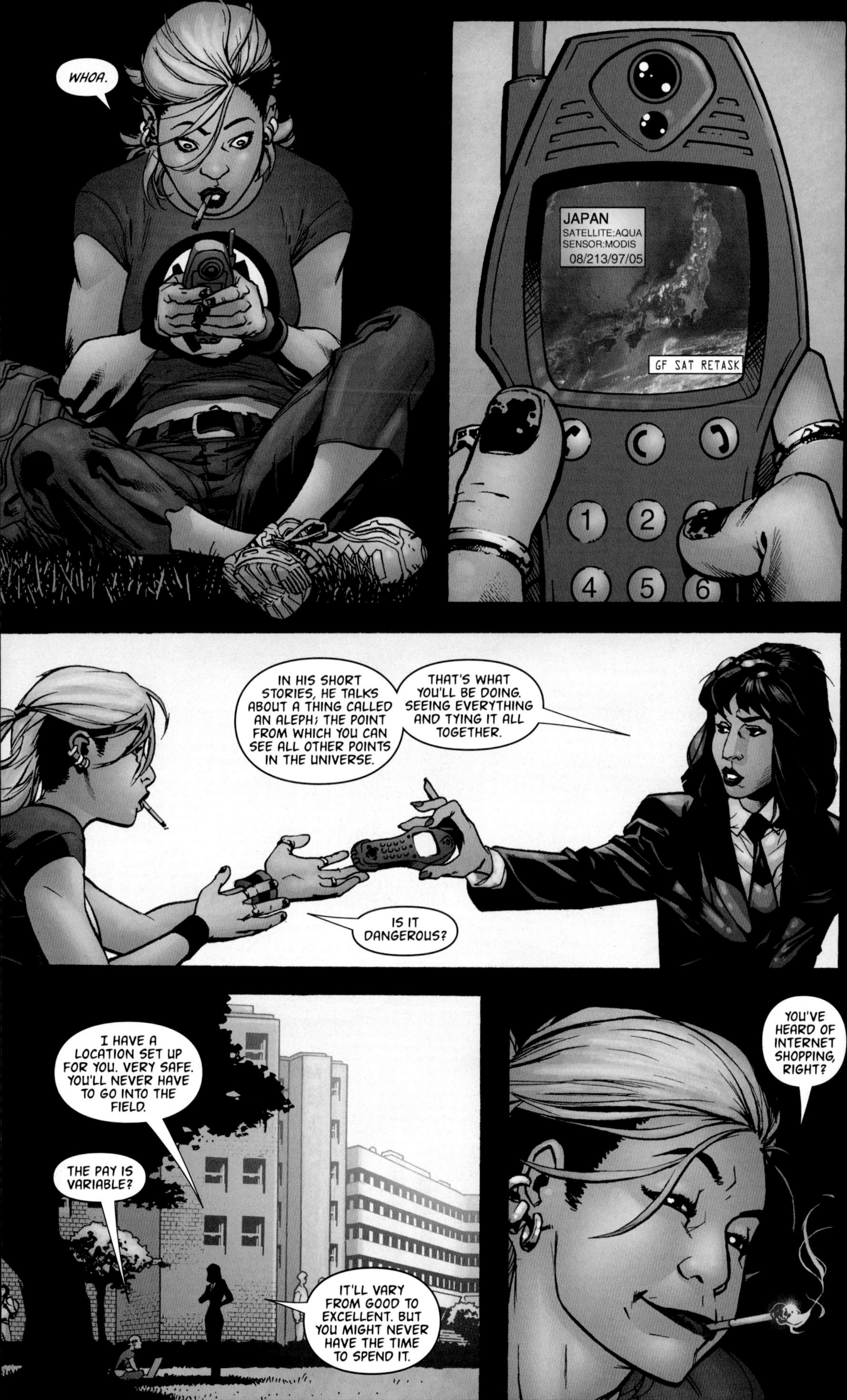
WHOA.
JAPAN
SATELLITE:AQUA
SENSOR:MODIS
08/213/97/05
GF SAT RETASK
IN HIS SHORT STORIES, HE TALKS ABOUT A THING CALLED AN ALEPH; THE POINT FROM WHICH YOU CAN SEE ALL OTHER POINTS IN THE UNIVERSE.
THAT'S WHAT YOU'LL BE DOING. SEEING EVERYTHING AND TYING IT ALL TOGETHER.
IS IT DANGEROUS?
I HAVE A LOCATION SET UP FOR YOU. VERY SAFE. YOU'LL NEVER HAVE TO GO INTO THE FIELD.
THE PAY IS VARIABLE?
IT'LL VARY FROM GOOD TO EXCELLENT. BUT YOU MIGHT NEVER HAVE THE TIME TO SPEND IT.
YOU'VE HEARD OF INTERNET SHOPPING, RIGHT?

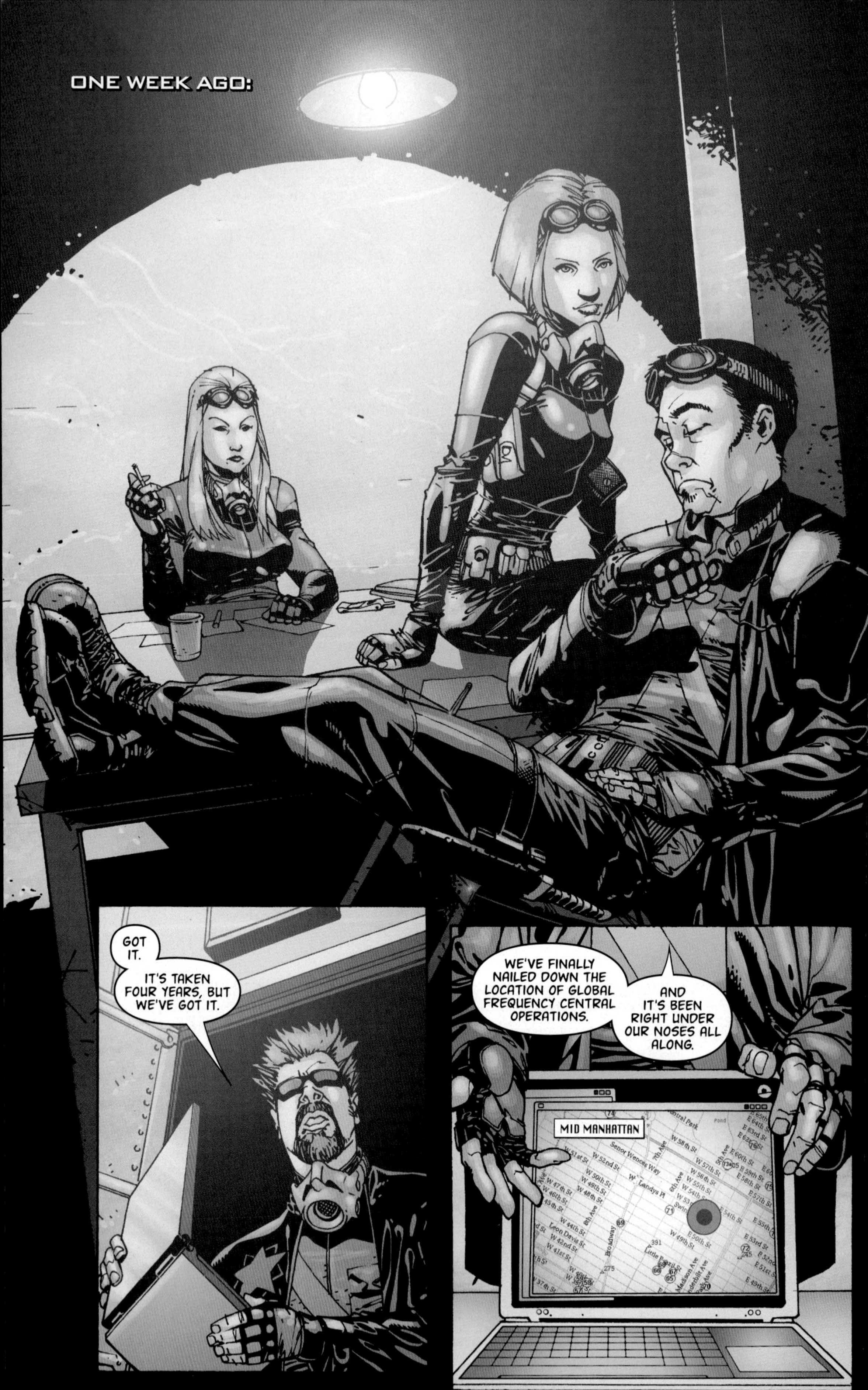
ONE WEEK AGO:
GOT IT.
IT'S TAKEN FOUR YEARS, BUT WE'VE GOT IT.
WE'VE FINALLY NAILED DOWN THE LOCATION OF GLOBAL FREQUENCY CENTRAL OPERATIONS.
AND IT'S BEEN RIGHT UNDER OUR NOSES ALL ALONG.
MID MANHATTAN

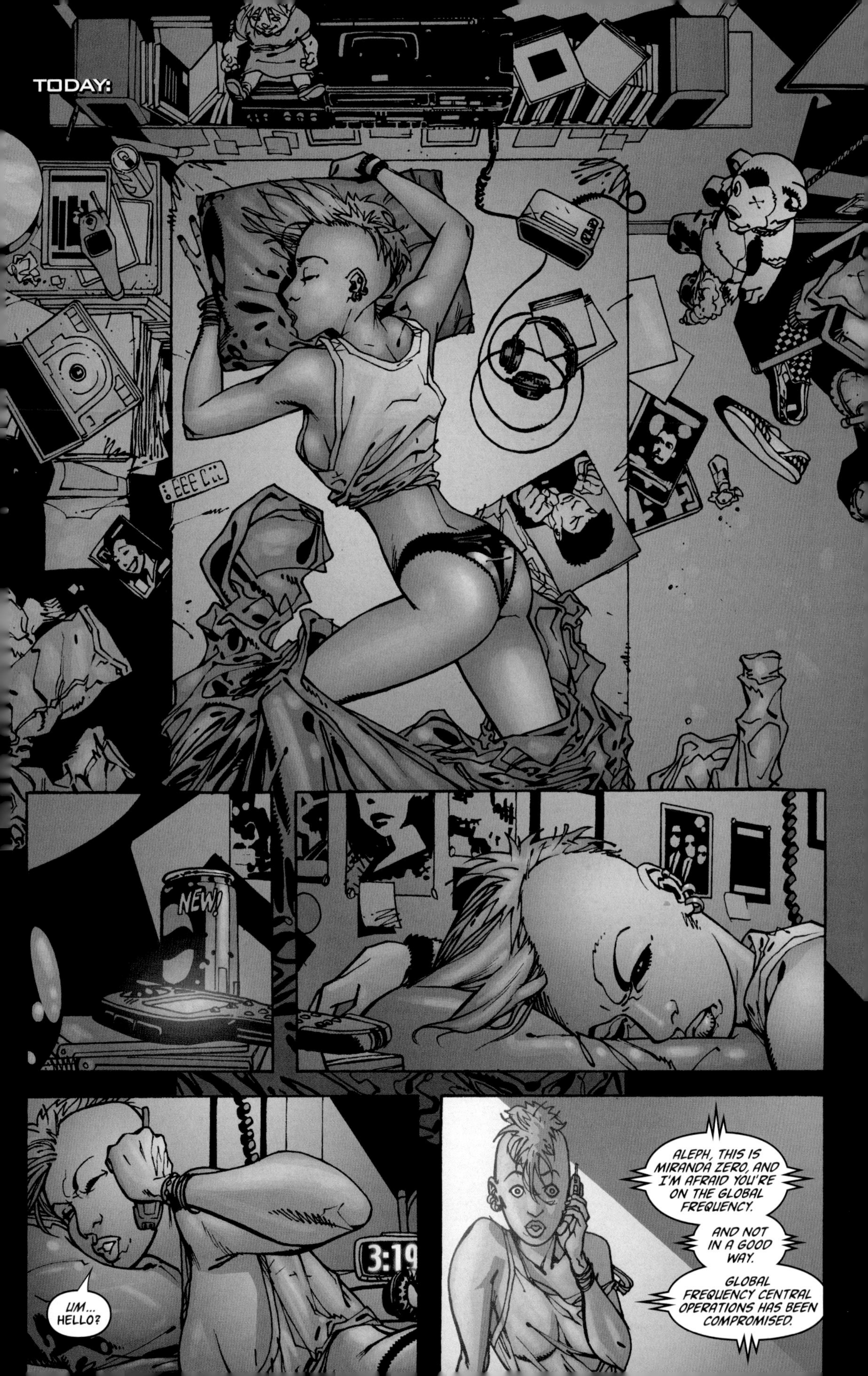
TODAY:
NEW!
3:19
UM... HELLO?
ALEPH, THIS IS MIRANDA ZERO, AND I'M AFRAID YOU'RE ON THE GLOBAL FREQUENCY.
AND NOT IN A GOOD WAY.
GLOBAL FREQUENCY CENTRAL OPERATIONS HAS BEEN COMPROMISED.

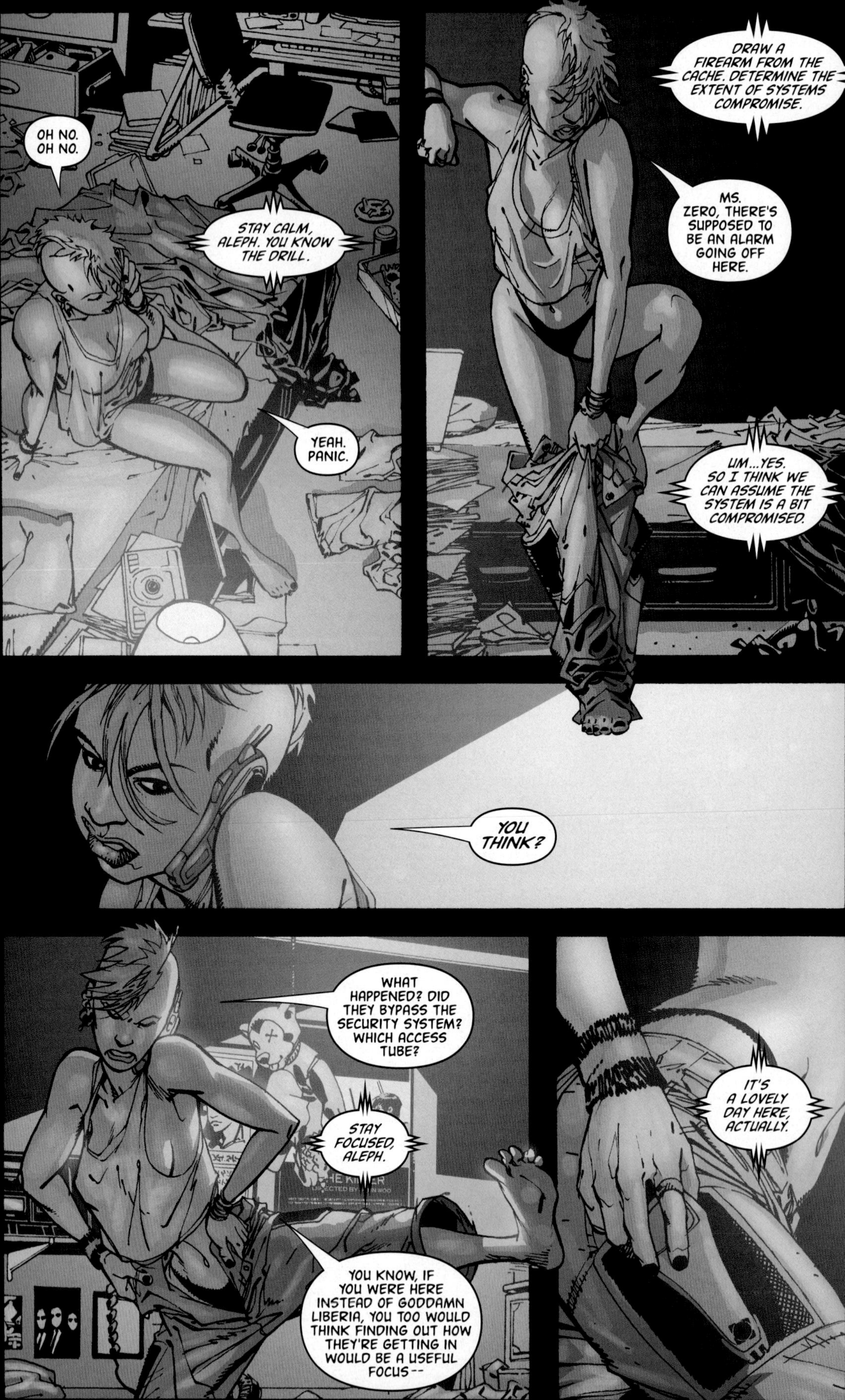
OH NO. OH NO.
STAY CALM, ALEPH. YOU KNOW THE DRILL.
YEAH. PANIC.
DRAW A FIREARM FROM THE CACHE. DETERMINE THE EXTENT OF SYSTEMS COMPROMISE.
MS. ZERO, THERE'S SUPPOSED TO BE AN ALARM GOING OFF HERE.
UM...YES. SO I THINK WE CAN ASSUME THE SYSTEM IS A BIT COMPROMISED.
YOU THINK?
WHAT HAPPENED? DID THEY BYPASS THE SECURITY SYSTEM? WHICH ACCESS TUBE?
STAY FOCUSED, ALEPH.
YOU KNOW, IF YOU WERE HERE INSTEAD OF GODDAMN LIBERIA, YOU TOO WOULD THINK FINDING OUT HOW THEY'RE GETTING IN WOULD BE A USEFUL FOCUS--
IT'S A LOVELY DAY HERE, ACTUALLY.

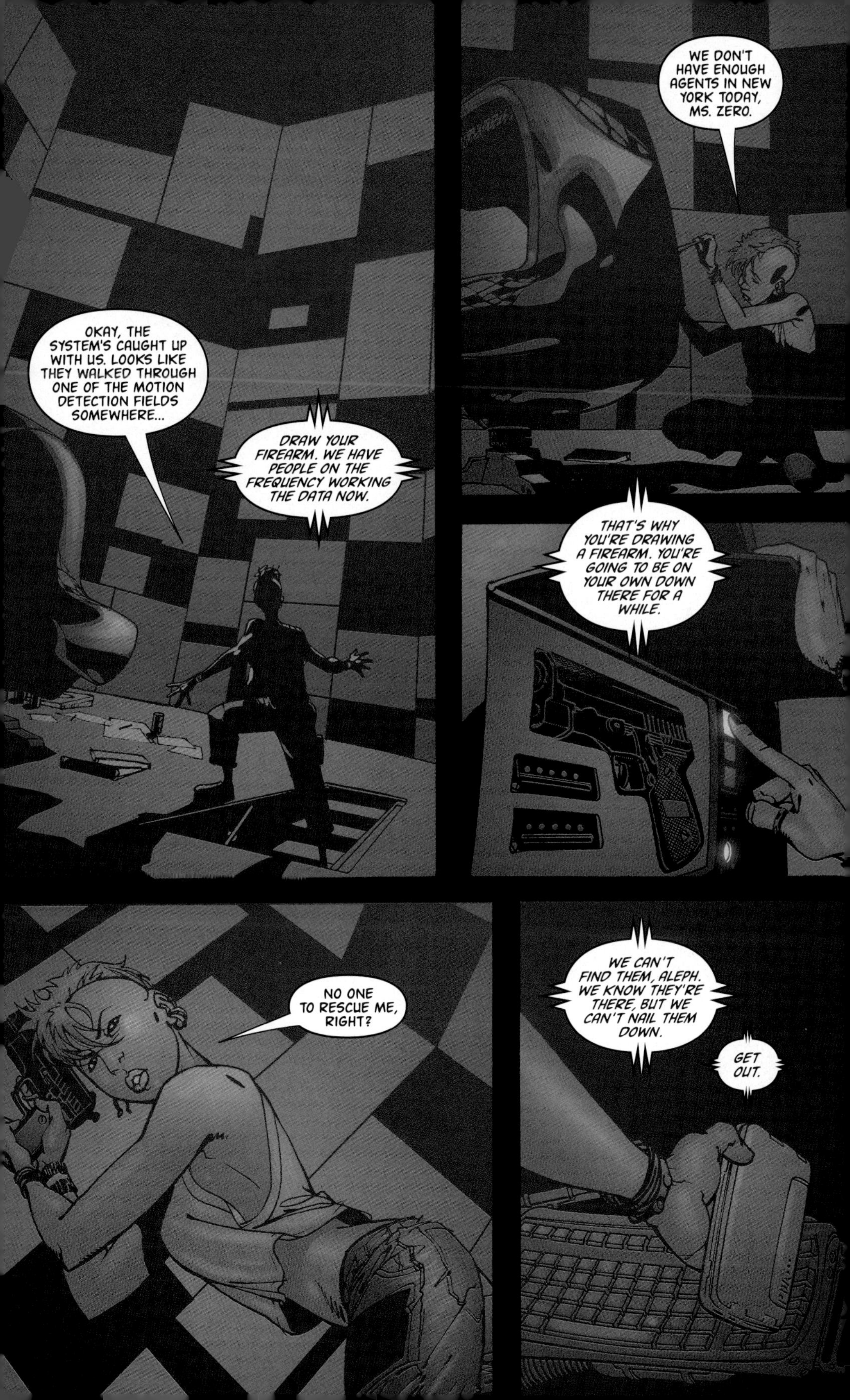
OKAY, THE SYSTEM'S CAUGHT UP WITH US. LOOKS LIKE THEY WALKED THROUGH ONE OF THE MOTION DETECTION FIELDS SOMEWHERE...
DRAW YOUR FIREARM. WE HAVE PEOPLE ON THE FREQUENCY WORKING THE DATA NOW.
WE DON'T HAVE ENOUGH AGENTS IN NEW YORK TODAY, MS. ZERO.
THAT'S WHY YOU'RE DRAWING A FIREARM. YOU'RE GOING TO BE ON YOUR OWN DOWN THERE FOR A WHILE.
NO ONE TO RESCUE ME, RIGHT?
WE CAN'T FIND THEM, ALEPH. WE KNOW THEY'RE THERE, BUT WE CAN'T NAIL THEM DOWN.
GET OUT.

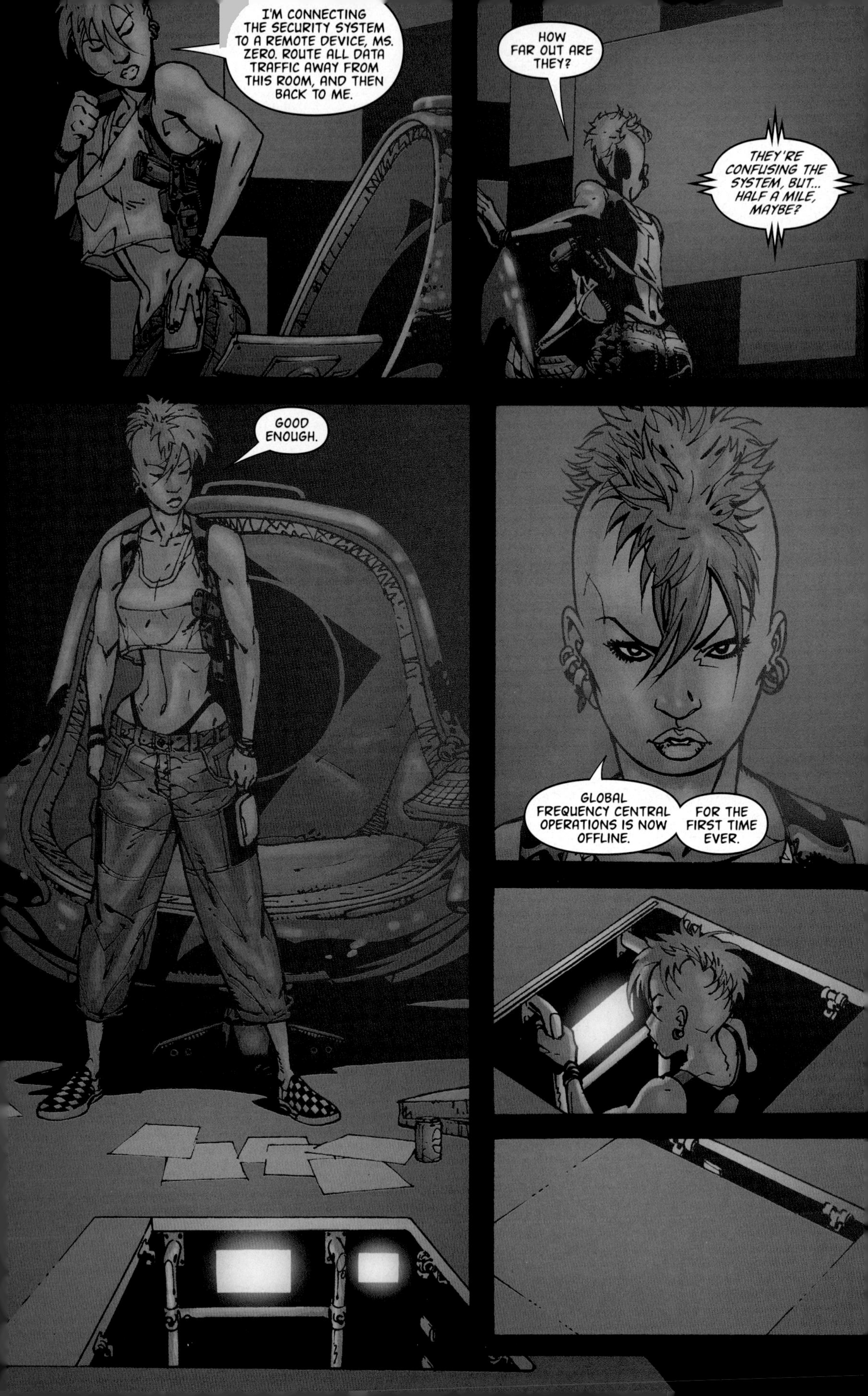
I'M CONNECTING THE SECURITY SYSTEM TO A REMOTE DEVICE, MS. ZERO. ROUTE ALL DATA TRAFFIC AWAY FROM THIS ROOM, AND THEN BACK TO ME.
HOW FAR OUT ARE THEY?
THEY'RE CONFUSING THE SYSTEM, BUT... HALF A MILE, MAYBE?
GOOD ENOUGH.
GLOBAL FREQUENCY CENTRAL OPERATIONS IS NOW OFFLINE.
FOR THE FIRST TIME EVER.

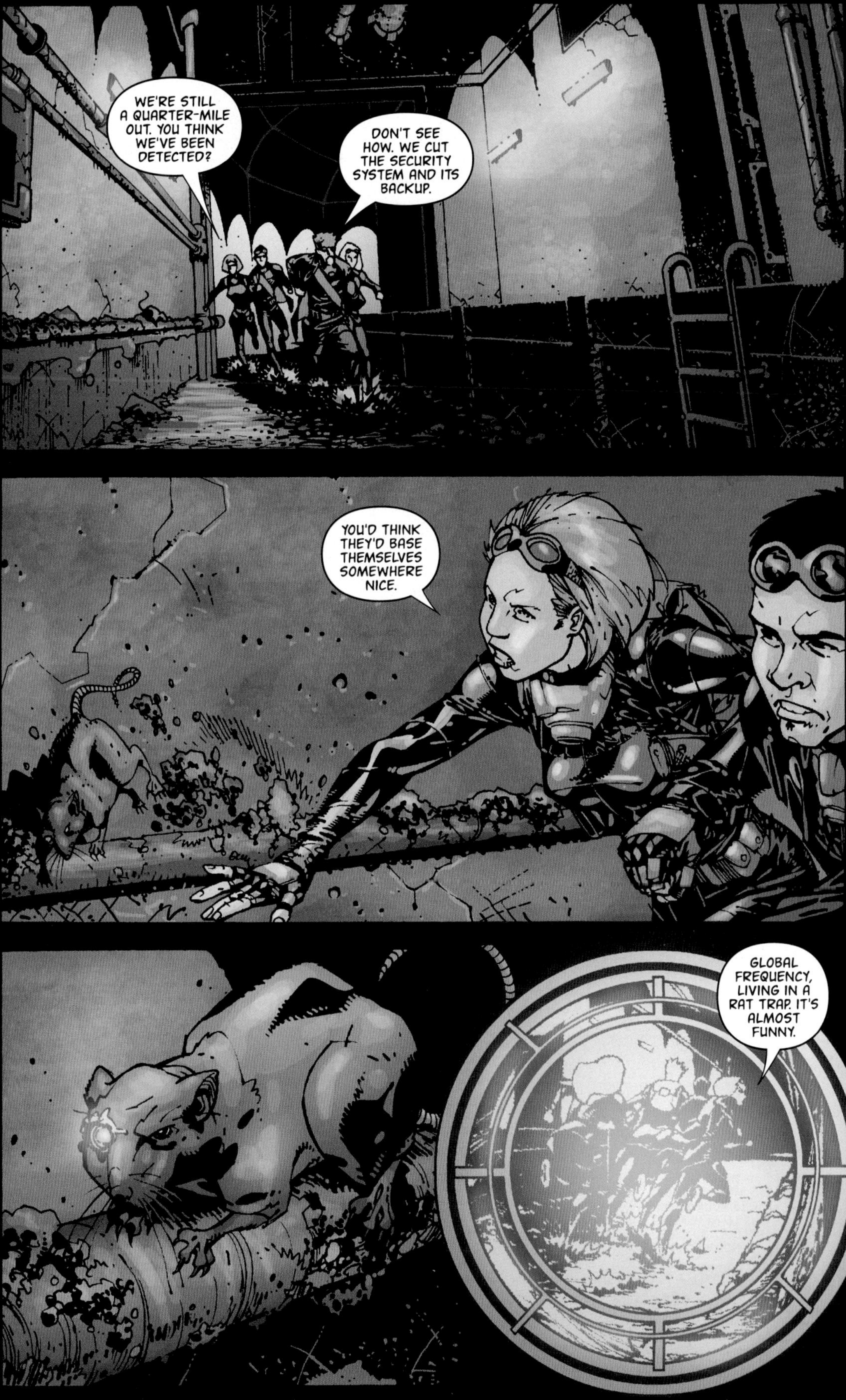
WE'RE STILL A QUARTER-MILE OUT. YOU THINK WE'VE BEEN DETECTED?
DON'T SEE HOW. WE CUT THE SECURITY SYSTEM AND ITS BACKUP.
YOU'D THINK THEY'D BASE THEMSELVES SOMEWHERE NICE.
GLOBAL FREQUENCY, LIVING IN A RAT TRAP. IT'S ALMOST FUNNY.

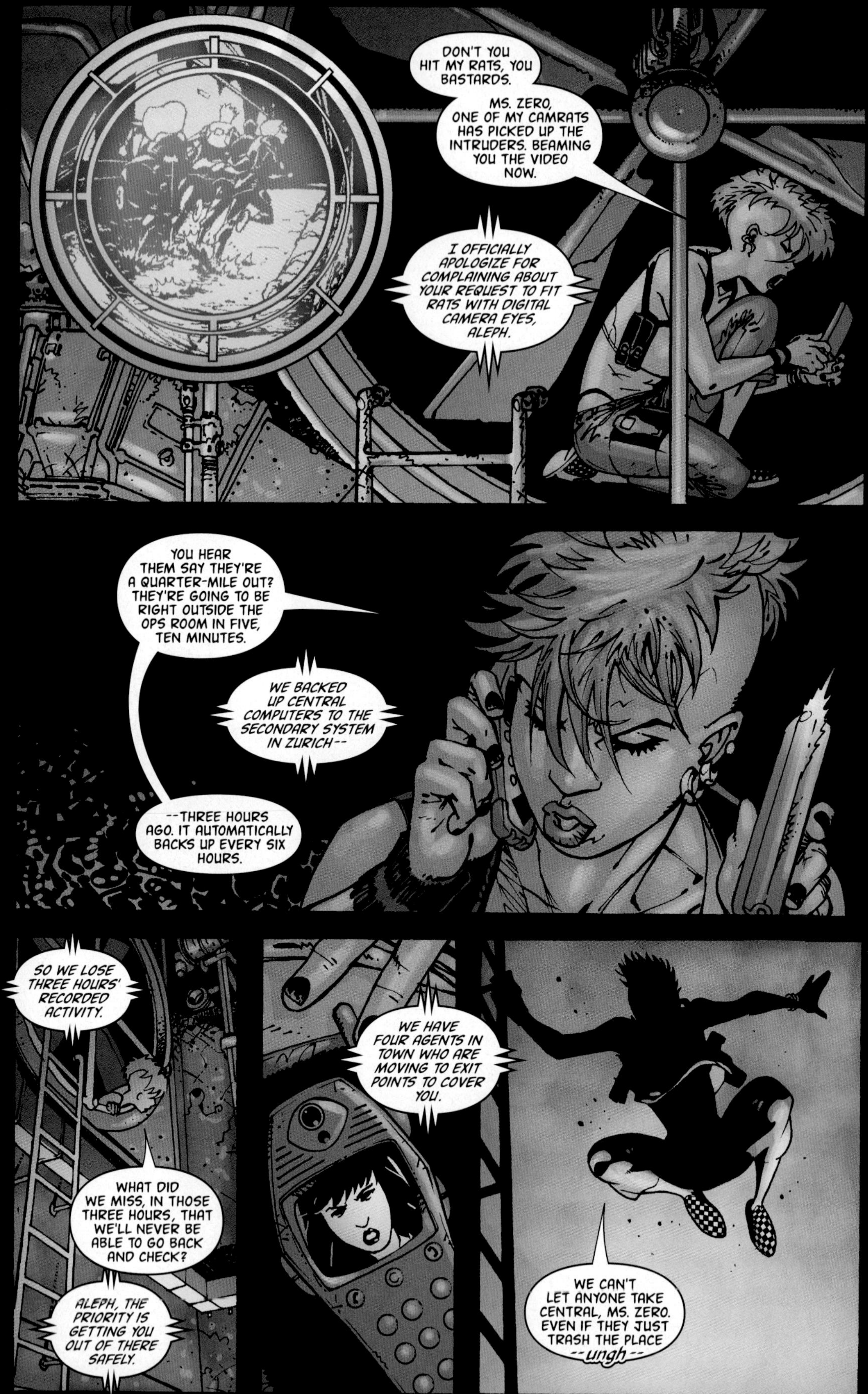
DON'T YOU HIT MY RATS, YOU BASTARDS.
MS. ZERO, ONE OF MY CAMRATS HAS PICKED UP THE INTRUDERS. BEAMING YOU THE VIDEO NOW.
I OFFICIALLY APOLOGIZE FOR COMPLAINING ABOUT YOUR REQUEST TO FIT RATS WITH DIGITAL CAMERA EYES, ALEPH.
YOU HEAR THEM SAY THEY'RE A QUARTER-MILE OUT? THEY'RE GOING TO BE RIGHT OUTSIDE THE OPS ROOM IN FIVE, TEN MINUTES.
WE BACKED UP CENTRAL COMPUTERS TO THE SECONDARY SYSTEM IN ZURICH--
--THREE HOURS AGO. IT AUTOMATICALLY BACKS UP EVERY SIX HOURS.
SO WE LOSE THREE HOURS' RECORDED ACTIVITY.
WHAT DID WE MISS, IN THOSE THREE HOURS, THAT WE'LL NEVER BE ABLE TO GO BACK AND CHECK?
ALEPH, THE PRIORITY IS GETTING YOU OUT OF THERE SAFELY.
WE HAVE FOUR AGENTS IN TOWN WHO ARE MOVING TO EXIT POINTS TO COVER YOU.
WE CAN'T LET ANYONE TAKE CENTRAL, MS. ZERO. EVEN IF THEY JUST TRASH THE PLACE
--ungh--

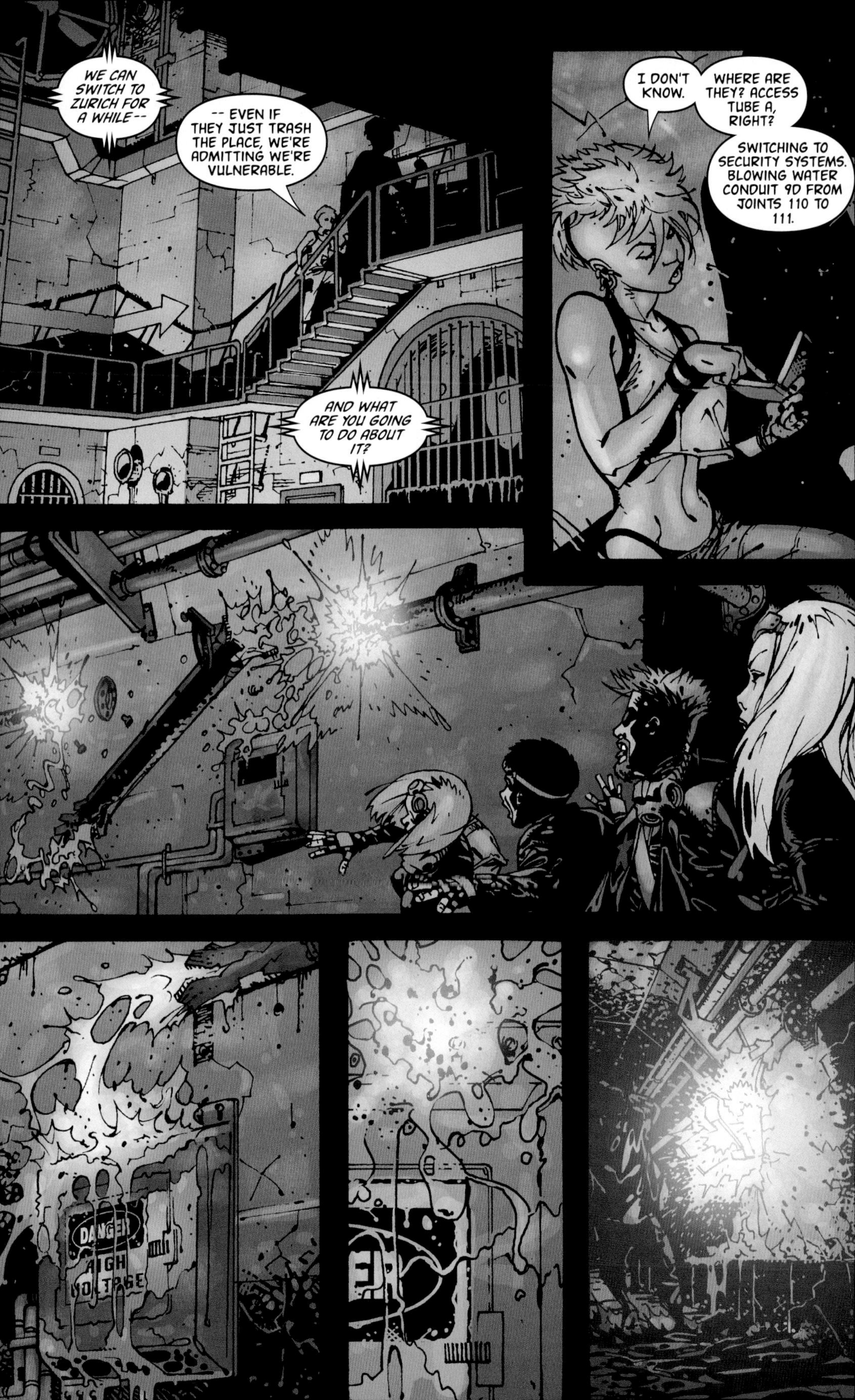
WE CAN SWITCH TO ZURICH FOR A WHILE--
-- EVEN IF THEY JUST TRASH THE PLACE, WE'RE ADMITTING WE'RE VULNERABLE.
AND WHAT ARE YOU GOING TO DO ABOUT IT?
I DON'T KNOW.
WHERE ARE THEY? ACCESS TUBE A, RIGHT?
SWITCHING TO SECURITY SYSTEMS. BLOWING WATER CONDUIT 9D FROM JOINTS 110 TO 111.
DANGER HIGH VOLTAGE

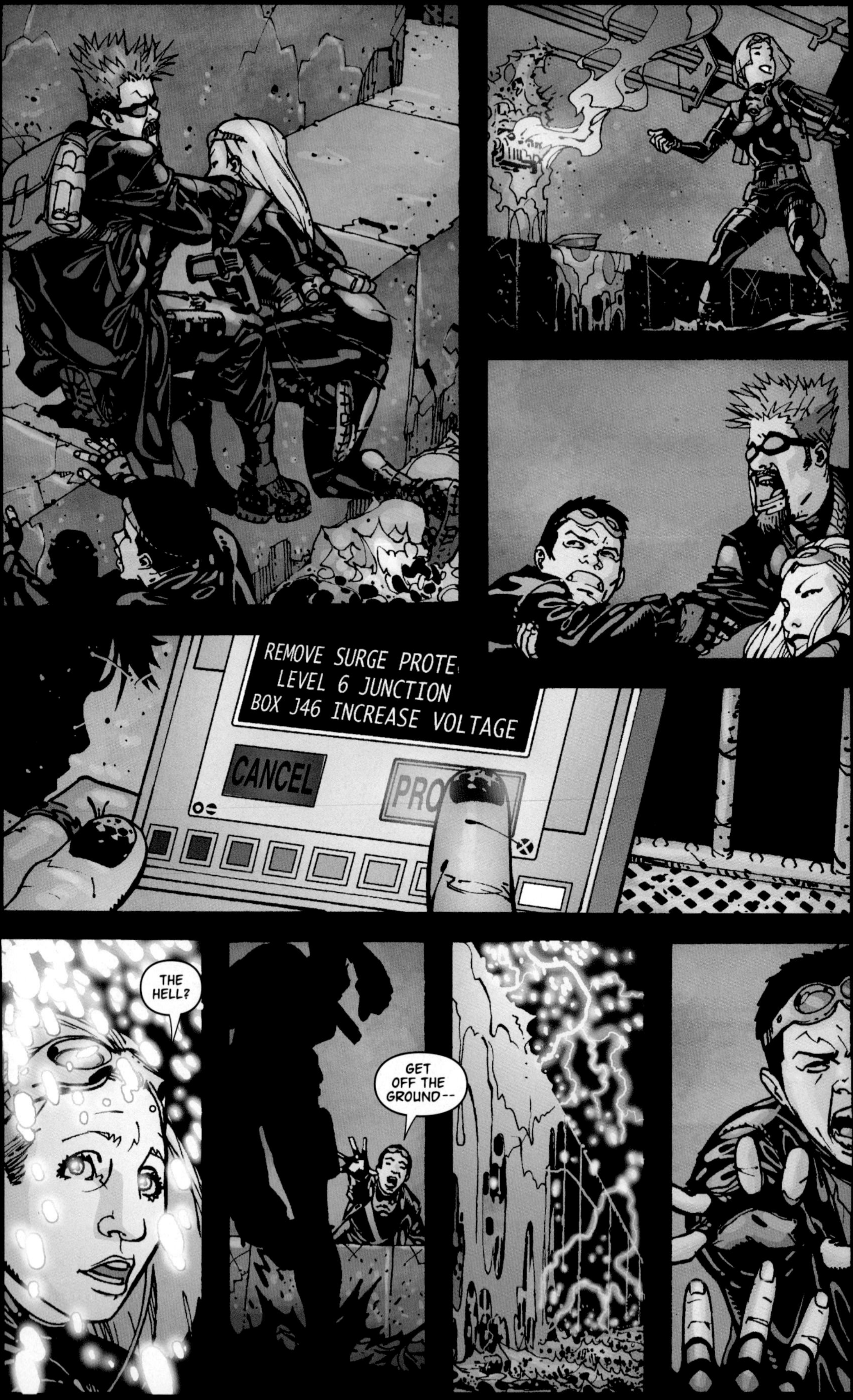
REMOVE SURGE PROTE
LEVEL 6 JUNCTION
BOX J46 INCREASE VOLTAGE
CANCEL
THE HELL?
GET OFF THE GROUND--

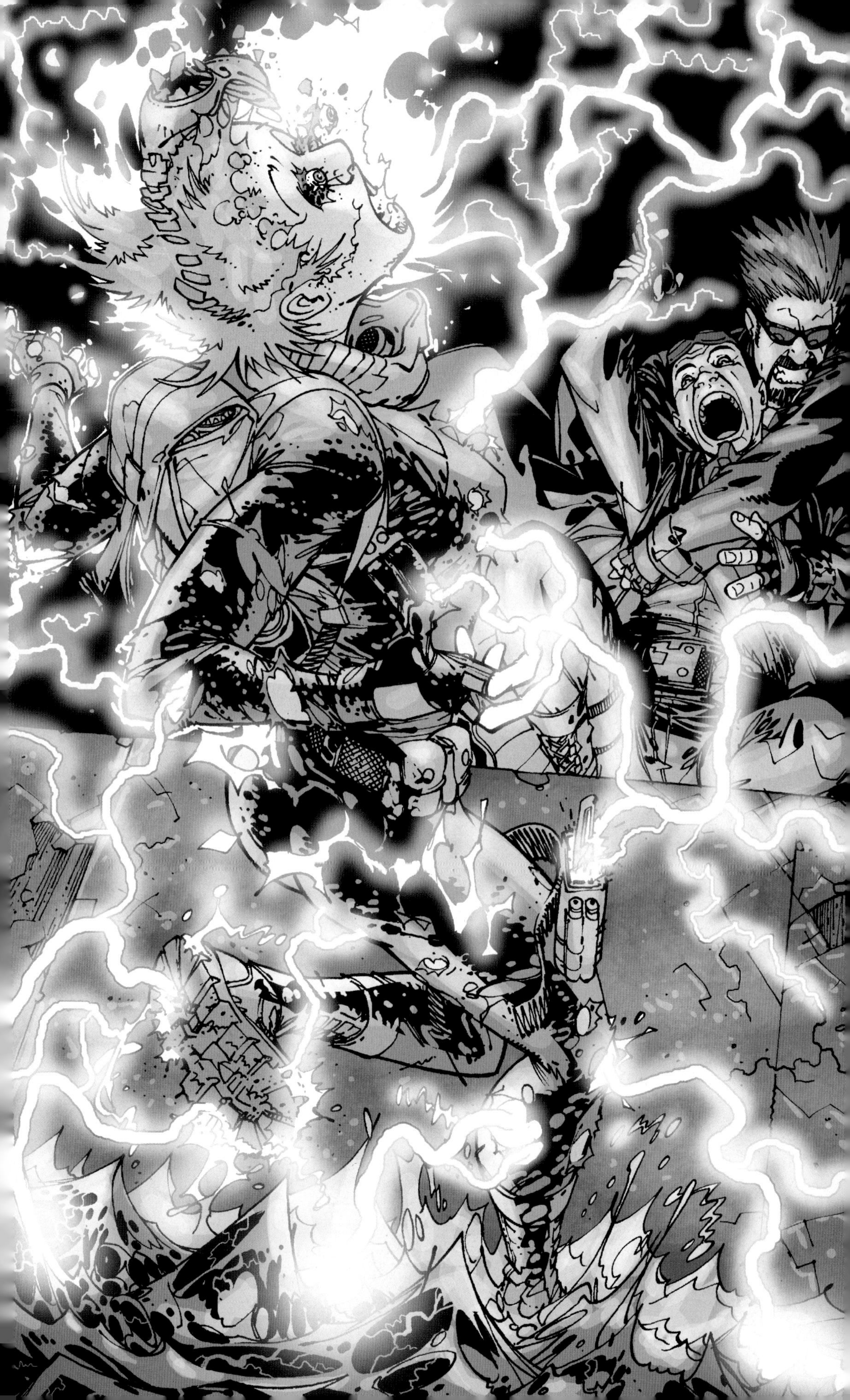

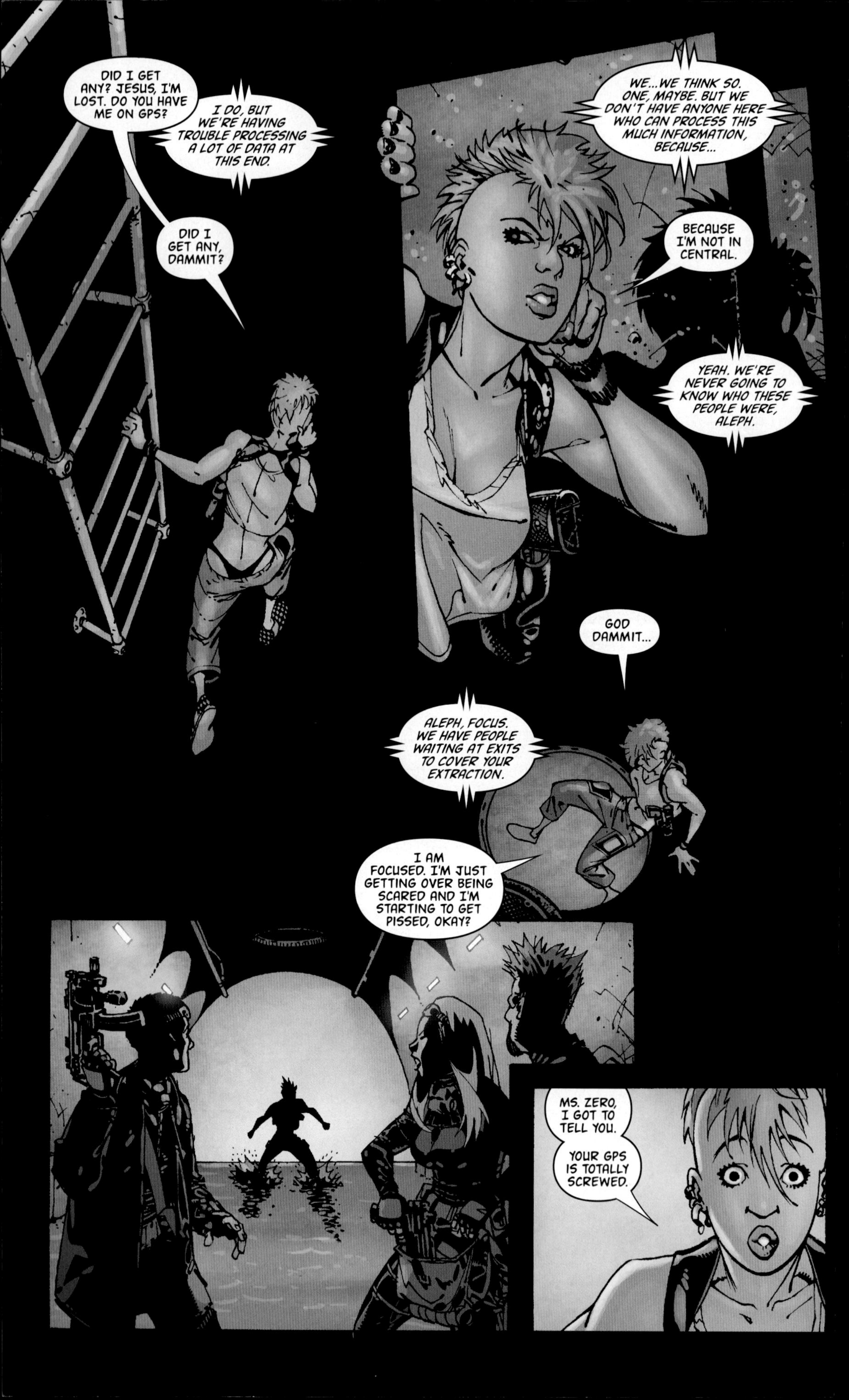
DID I GET ANY? JESUS, I'M LOST. DO YOU HAVE ME ON GPS?
I DO, BUT WE'RE HAVING TROUBLE PROCESSING A LOT OF DATA AT THIS END.
DID I GET ANY, DAMMIT?
WE...WE THINK SO. ONE, MAYBE. BUT WE DON'T HAVE ANYONE HERE WHO CAN PROCESS THIS MUCH INFORMATION, BECAUSE...
BECAUSE I'M NOT IN CENTRAL.
YEAH. WE'RE NEVER GOING TO KNOW WHO THESE PEOPLE WERE, ALEPH.
GOD DAMMIT...
ALEPH, FOCUS. WE HAVE PEOPLE WAITING AT EXITS TO COVER YOUR EXTRACTION.
I AM FOCUSED. I'M JUST GETTING OVER BEING SCARED AND I'M STARTING TO GET PISSED, OKAY?
MS. ZERO, I GOT TO TELL YOU.
YOUR GPS IS TOTALLY SCREWED.

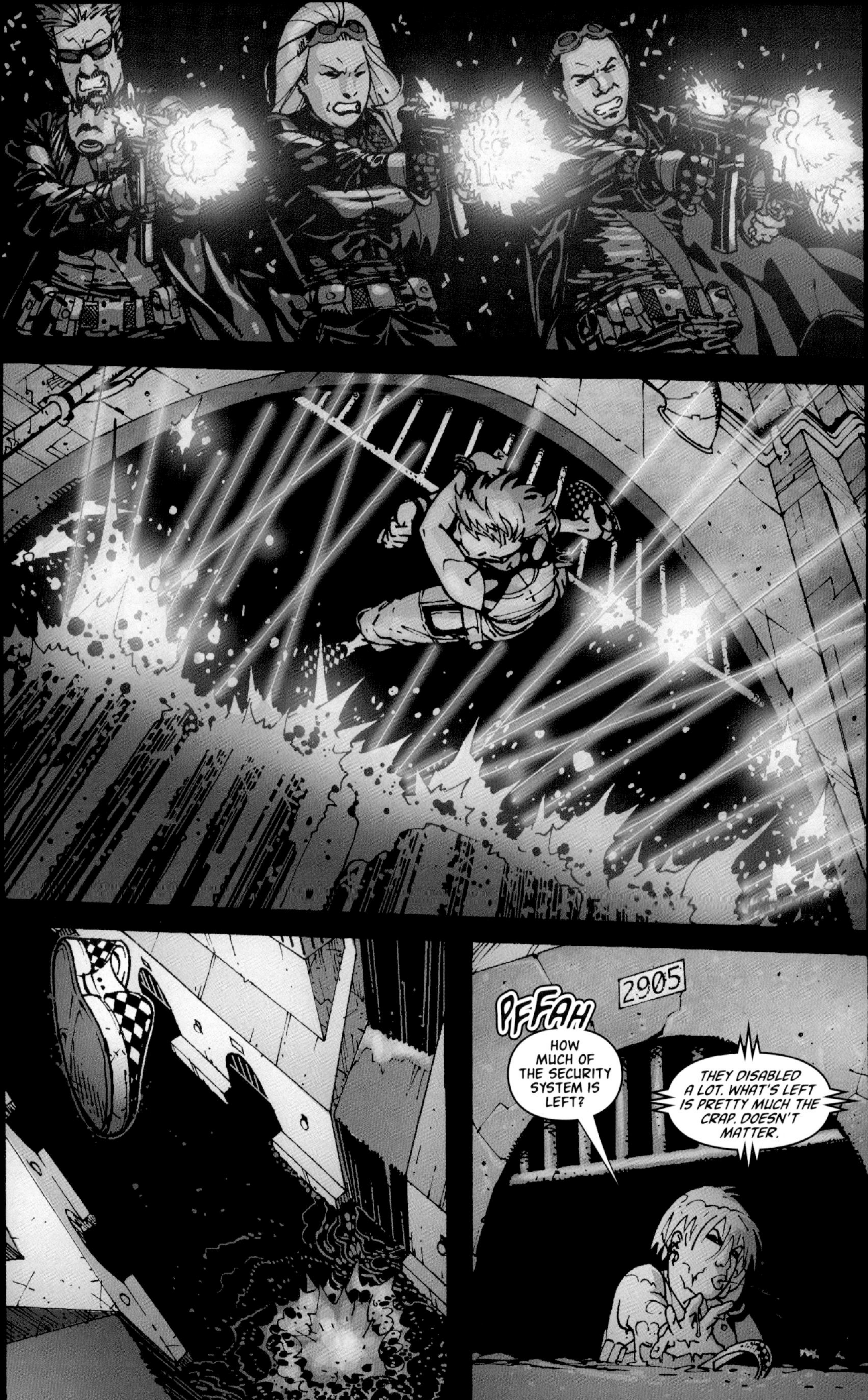
2905
PFFAH
HOW MUCH OF THE SECURITY SYSTEM IS LEFT?
THEY DISABLED A LOT. WHAT'S LEFT IS PRETTY MUCH THE CRAP. DOESN'T MATTER.

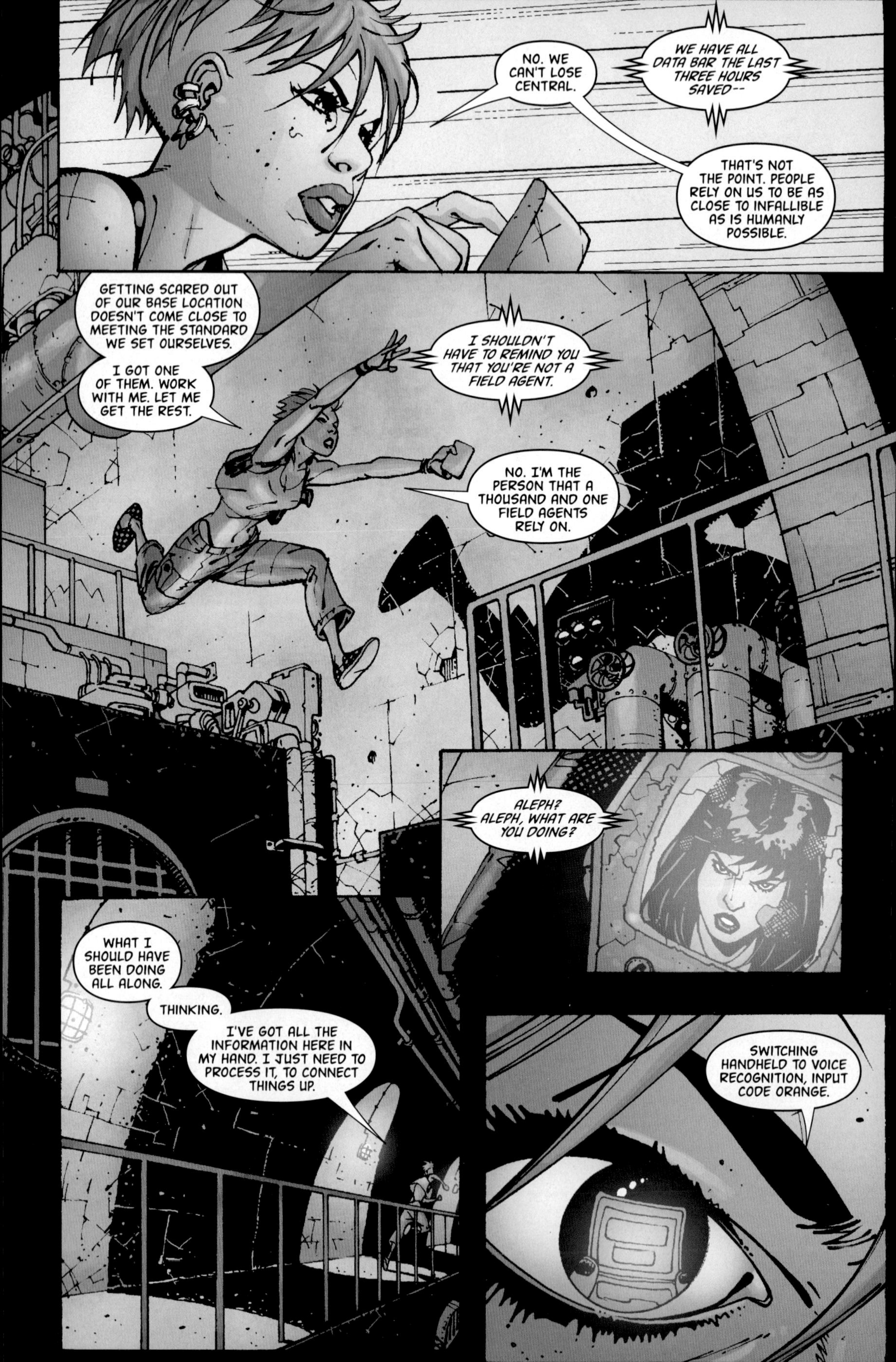
NO. WE CAN'T LOSE CENTRAL.
WE HAVE ALL DATA BAR THE LAST THREE HOURS SAVED--
THAT'S NOT THE POINT. PEOPLE RELY ON US TO BE AS CLOSE TO INFALLIBLE AS IS HUMANLY POSSIBLE.
GETTING SCARED OUT OF OUR BASE LOCATION DOESN'T COME CLOSE TO MEETING THE STANDARD WE SET OURSELVES.
I GOT ONE OF THEM. WORK WITH ME. LET ME GET THE REST.
I SHOULDN'T HAVE TO REMIND YOU THAT YOU'RE NOT A FIELD AGENT.
NO. I'M THE PERSON THAT A THOUSAND AND ONE FIELD AGENTS RELY ON.
ALEPH? ALEPH, WHAT ARE YOU DOING?
WHAT I SHOULD HAVE BEEN DOING ALL ALONG.
THINKING.
I'VE GOT ALL THE INFORMATION HERE IN MY HAND. I JUST NEED TO PROCESS IT, TO CONNECT THINGS UP.
SWITCHING HANDHELD TO VOICE RECOGNITION, INPUT CODE ORANGE.

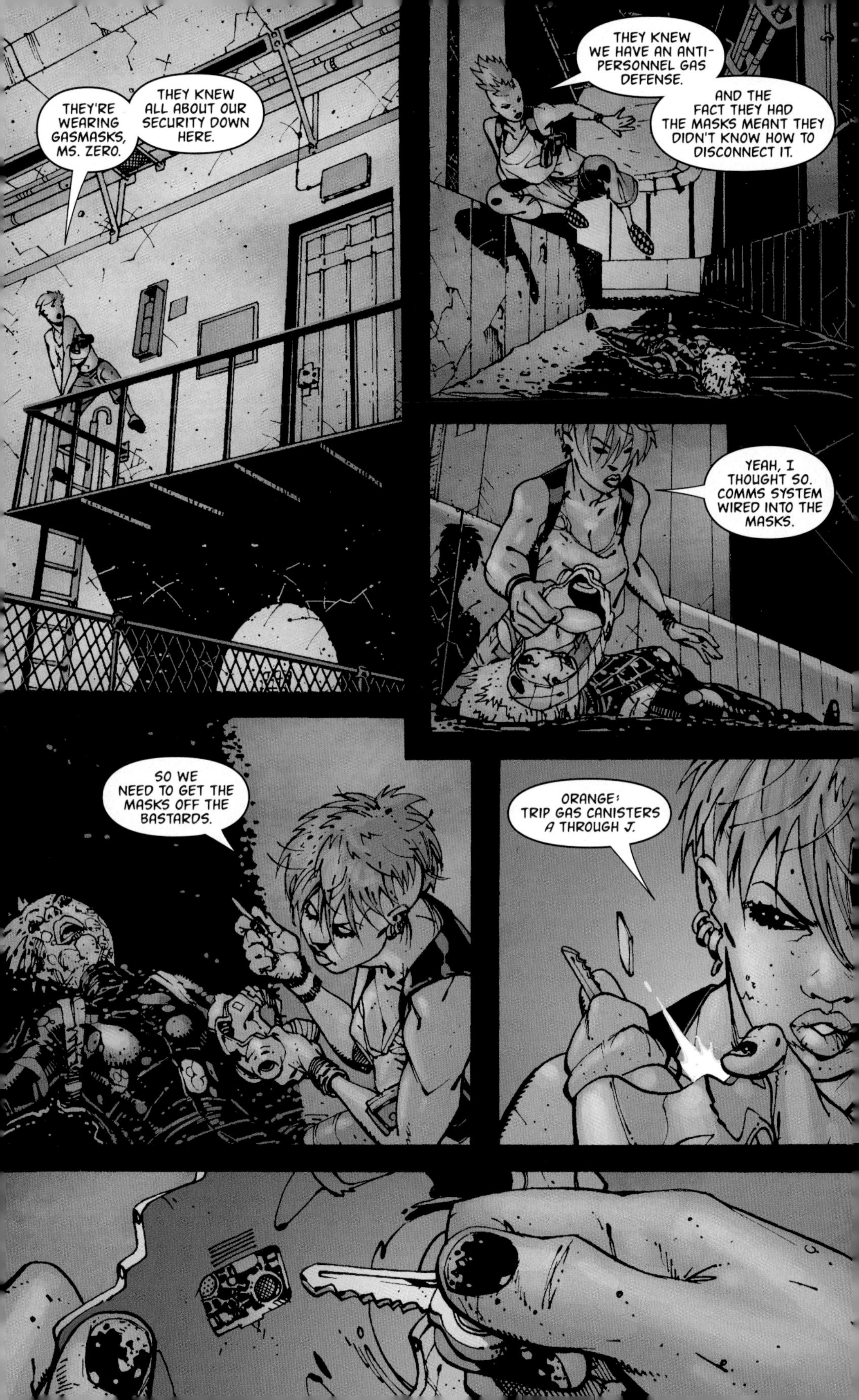
THEY'RE WEARING GASMASKS, MS. ZERO.
THEY KNEW ALL ABOUT OUR SECURITY DOWN HERE.
THEY KNEW WE HAVE AN ANTI-PERSONNEL GAS DEFENSE.
AND THE FACT THEY HAD THE MASKS MEANT THEY DIDN'T KNOW HOW TO DISCONNECT IT.
YEAH, I THOUGHT SO. COMMS SYSTEM WIRED INTO THE MASKS.
SO WE NEED TO GET THE MASKS OFF THE BASTARDS.
ORANGE: TRIP GAS CANISTERS A THROUGH J.

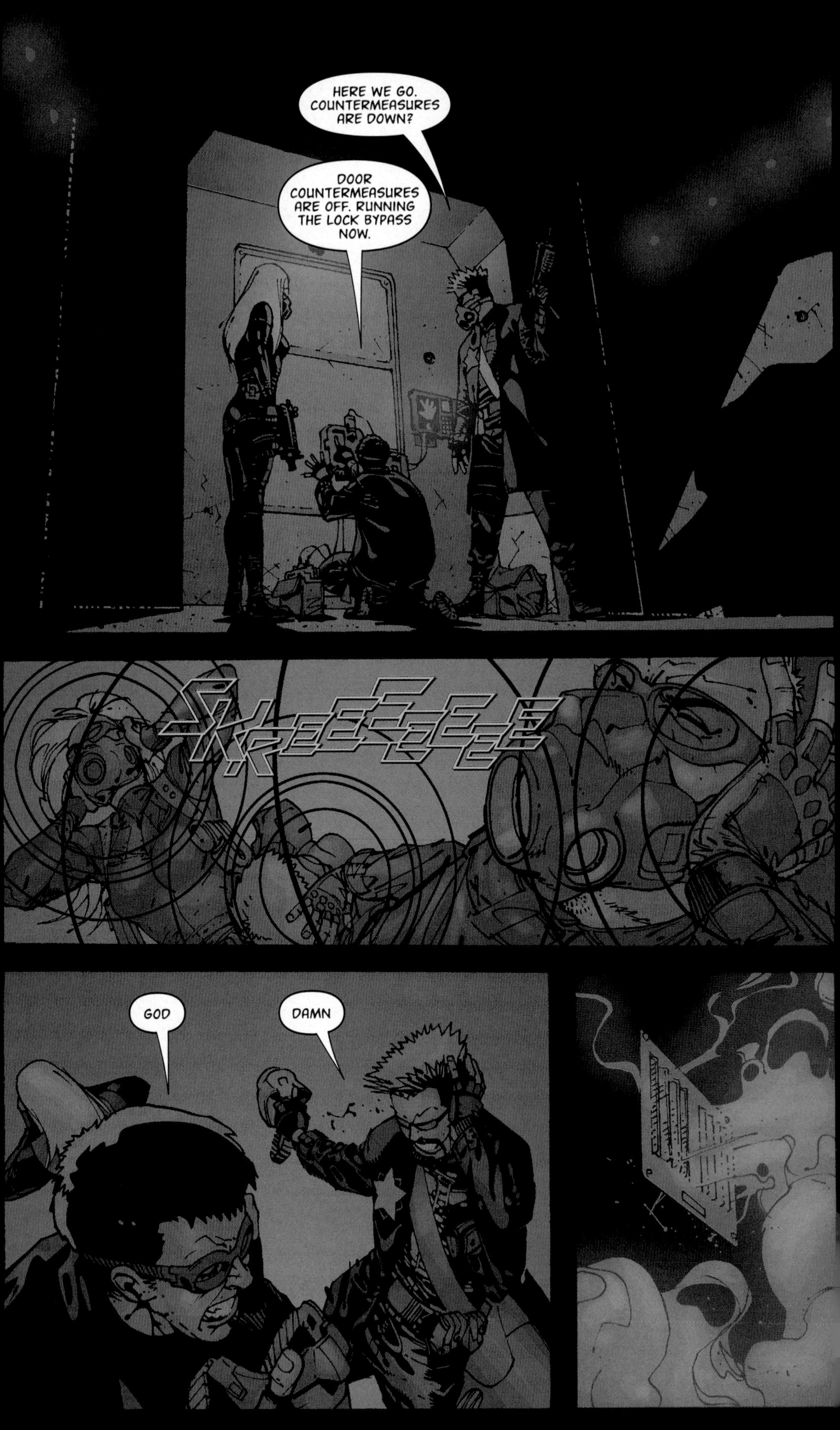
HERE WE GO. COUNTERMEASURES ARE DOWN?
DOOR COUNTERMEASURES ARE OFF. RUNNING THE LOCK BYPASS NOW.
SKREEEEEEEE
GOD
DAMN

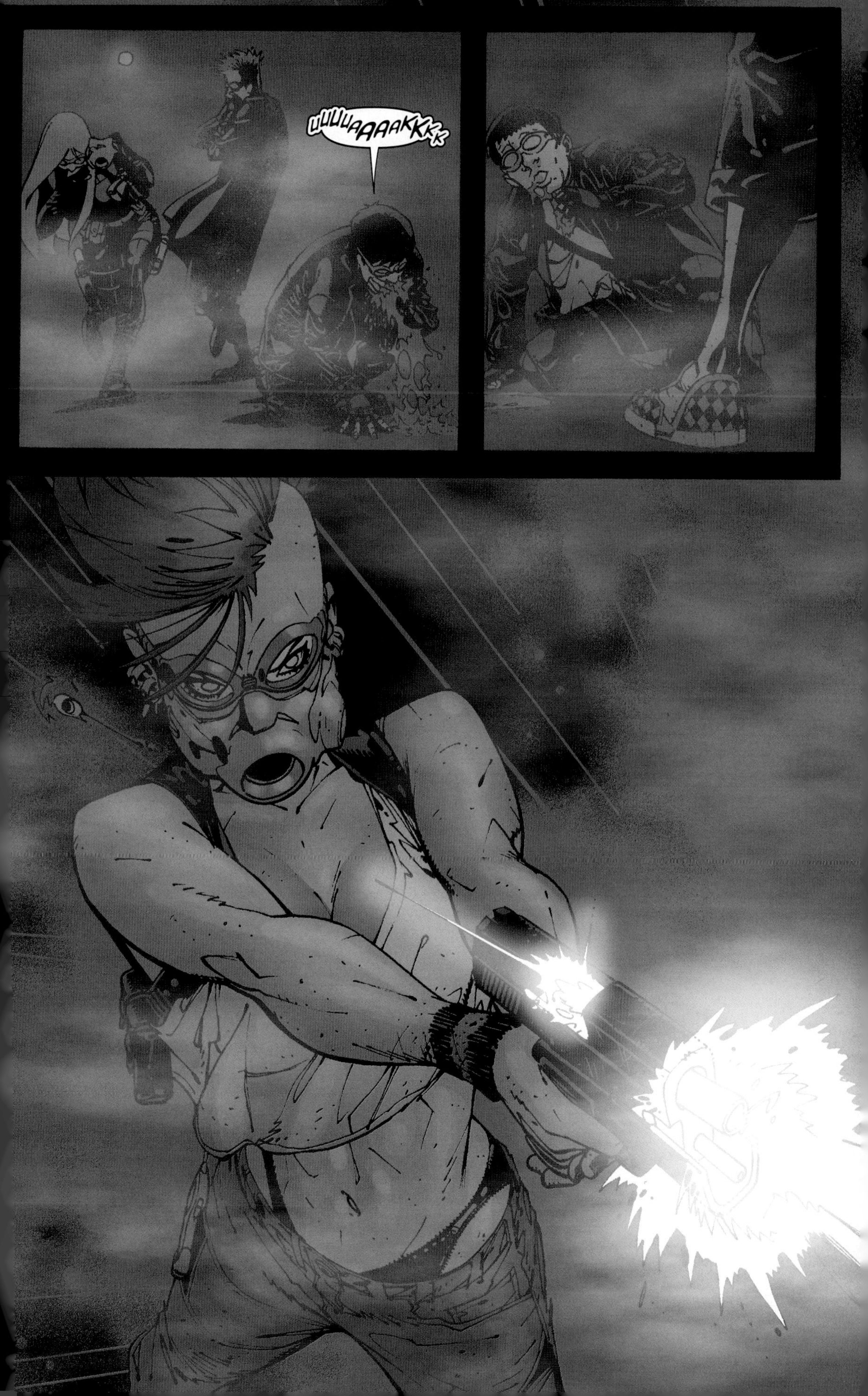
UUUUAAAAKKKK

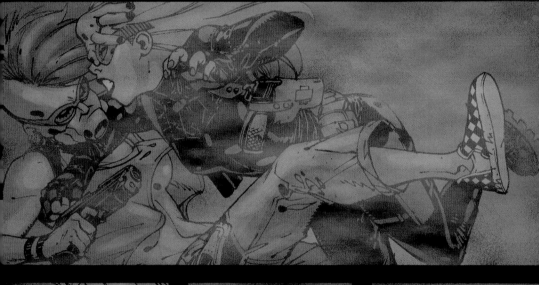

HEH

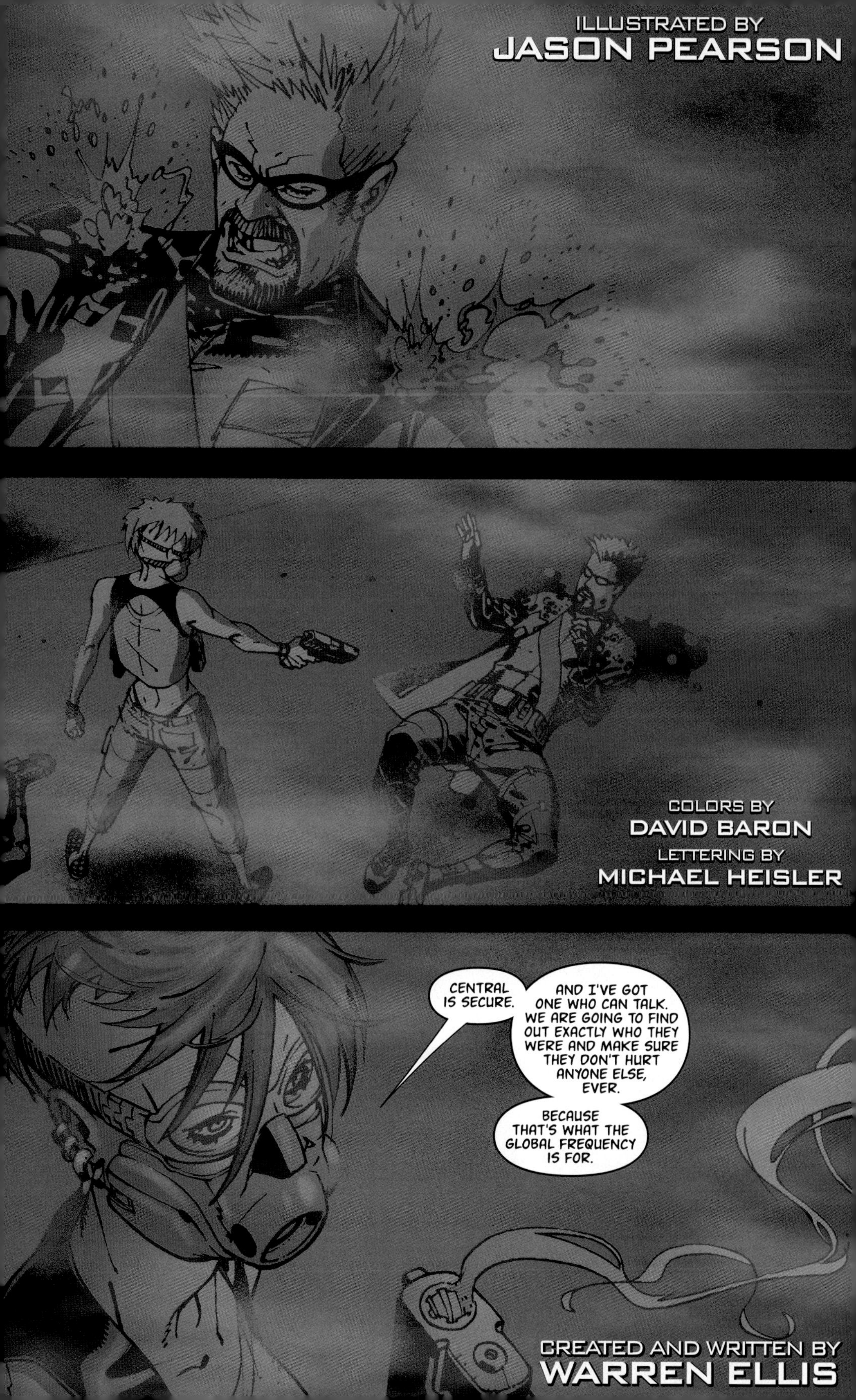
ILLUSTRATED BY
JASON PEARSON
COLORS BY
DAVID BARON
LETTERING BY
MICHAEL HEISLER
CENTRAL IS SECURE.
AND I'VE GOT ONE WHO CAN TALK. WE ARE GOING TO FIND OUT EXACTLY WHO THEY WERE AND MAKE SURE THEY DON'T HURT ANYONE ELSE, EVER.
BECAUSE THAT'S WHAT THE GLOBAL FREQUENCY IS FOR.
CREATED AND WRITTEN BY
WARREN ELLIS

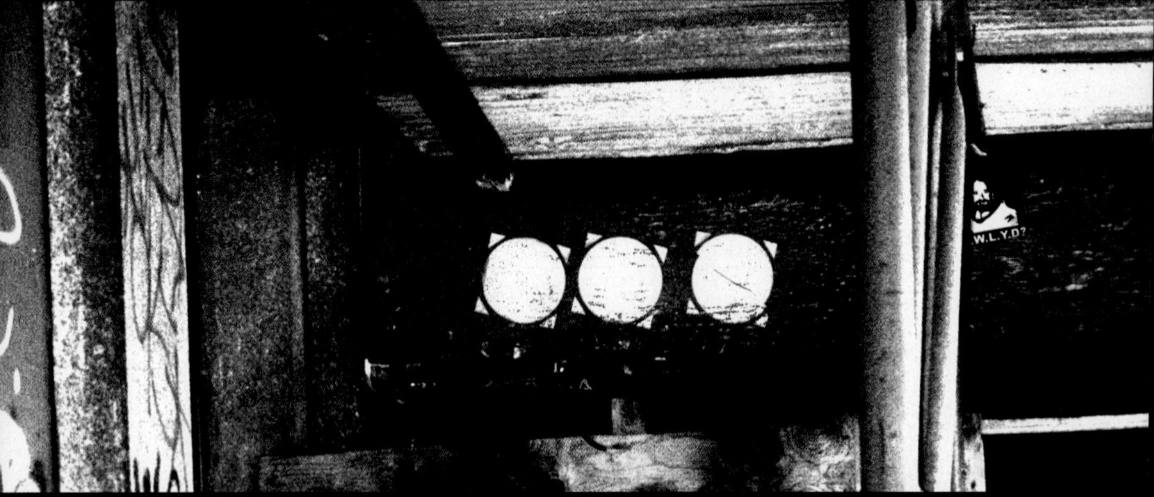
W.L.Y.D?

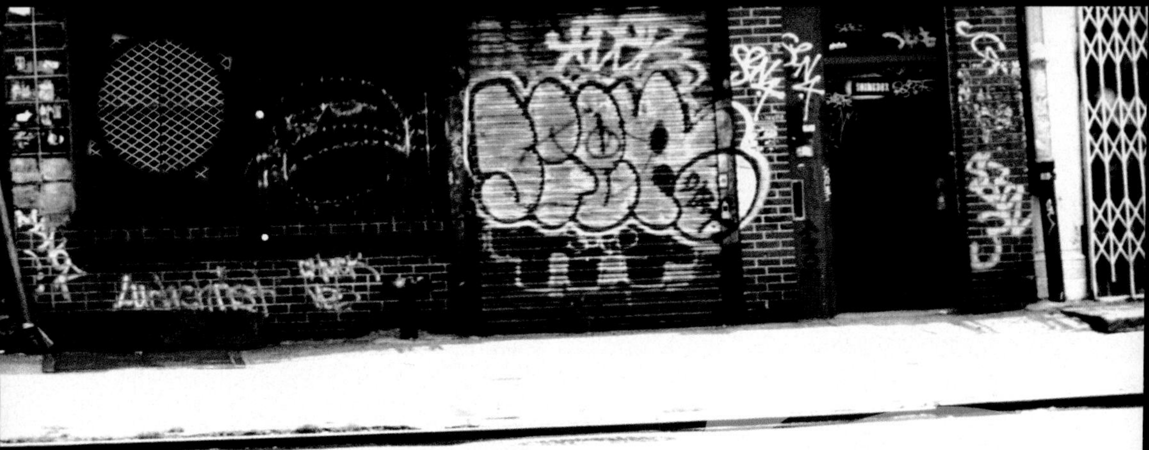

ARE YOU ON THE **GLOBAL FREQUENCY?**

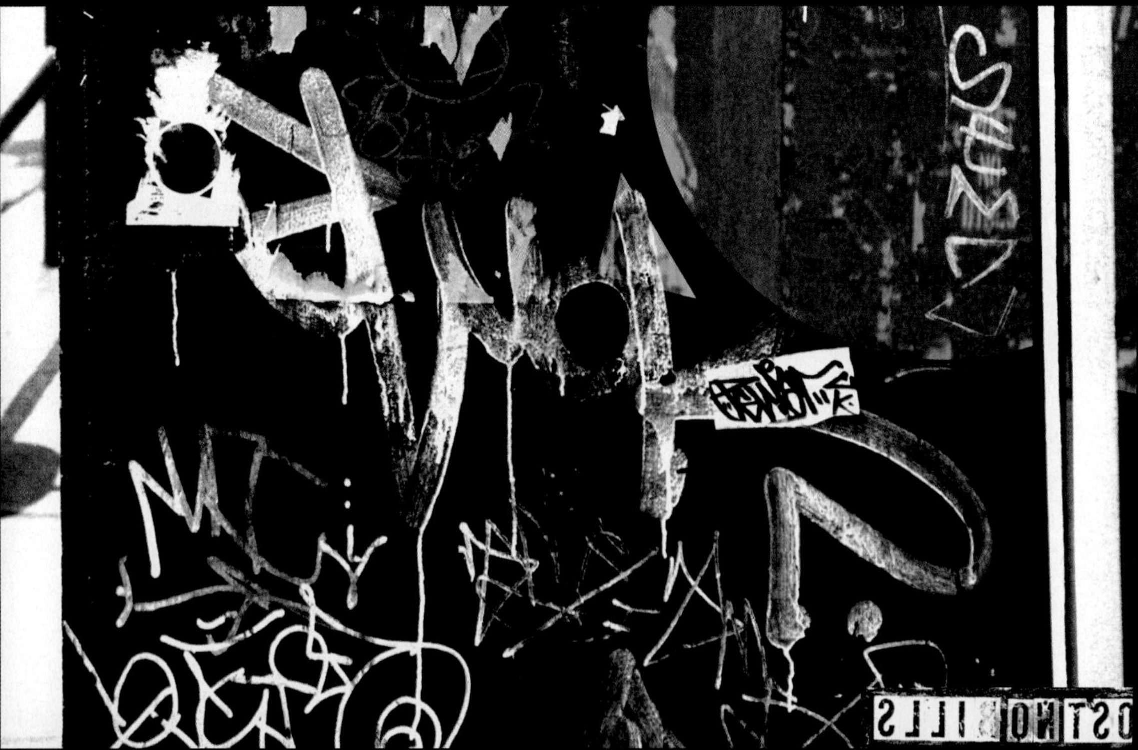

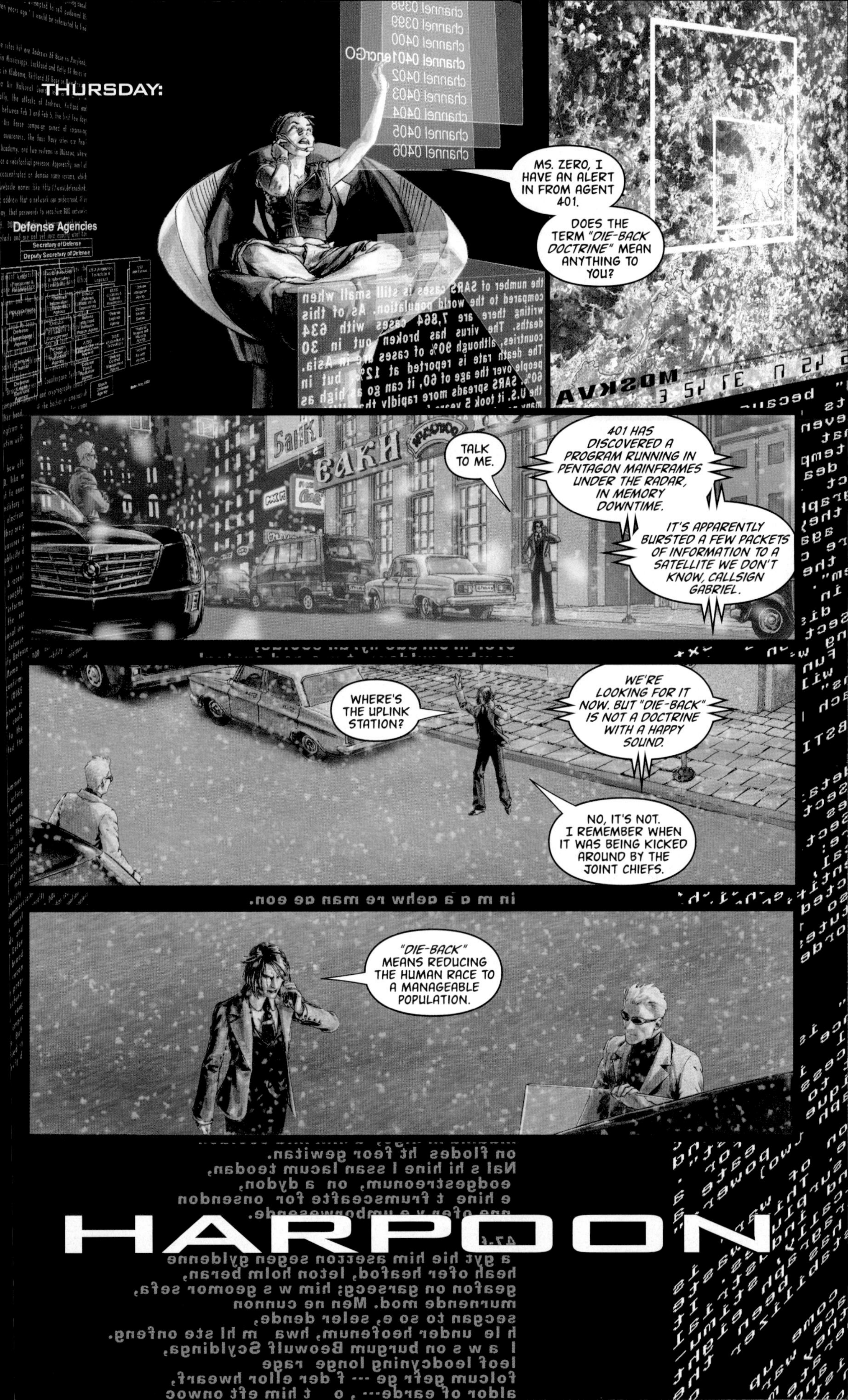
THURSDAY:
MS. ZERO, I HAVE AN ALERT IN FROM AGENT 401.
DOES THE TERM "DIE-BACK DOCTRINE" MEAN ANYTHING TO YOU?
TALK TO ME.
401 HAS DISCOVERED A PROGRAM RUNNING IN PENTAGON MAINFRAMES UNDER THE RADAR, IN MEMORY DOWNTIME.
IT'S APPARENTLY BURSTED A FEW PACKETS OF INFORMATION TO A SATELLITE WE DON'T KNOW, CALLSIGN GABRIEL.
WHERE'S THE UPLINK STATION?
WE'RE LOOKING FOR IT NOW. BUT "DIE-BACK" IS NOT A DOCTRINE WITH A HAPPY SOUND.
NO, IT'S NOT. I REMEMBER WHEN IT WAS BEING KICKED AROUND BY THE JOINT CHIEFS.
"DIE-BACK" MEANS REDUCING THE HUMAN RACE TO A MANAGEABLE POPULATION.
HARPOON

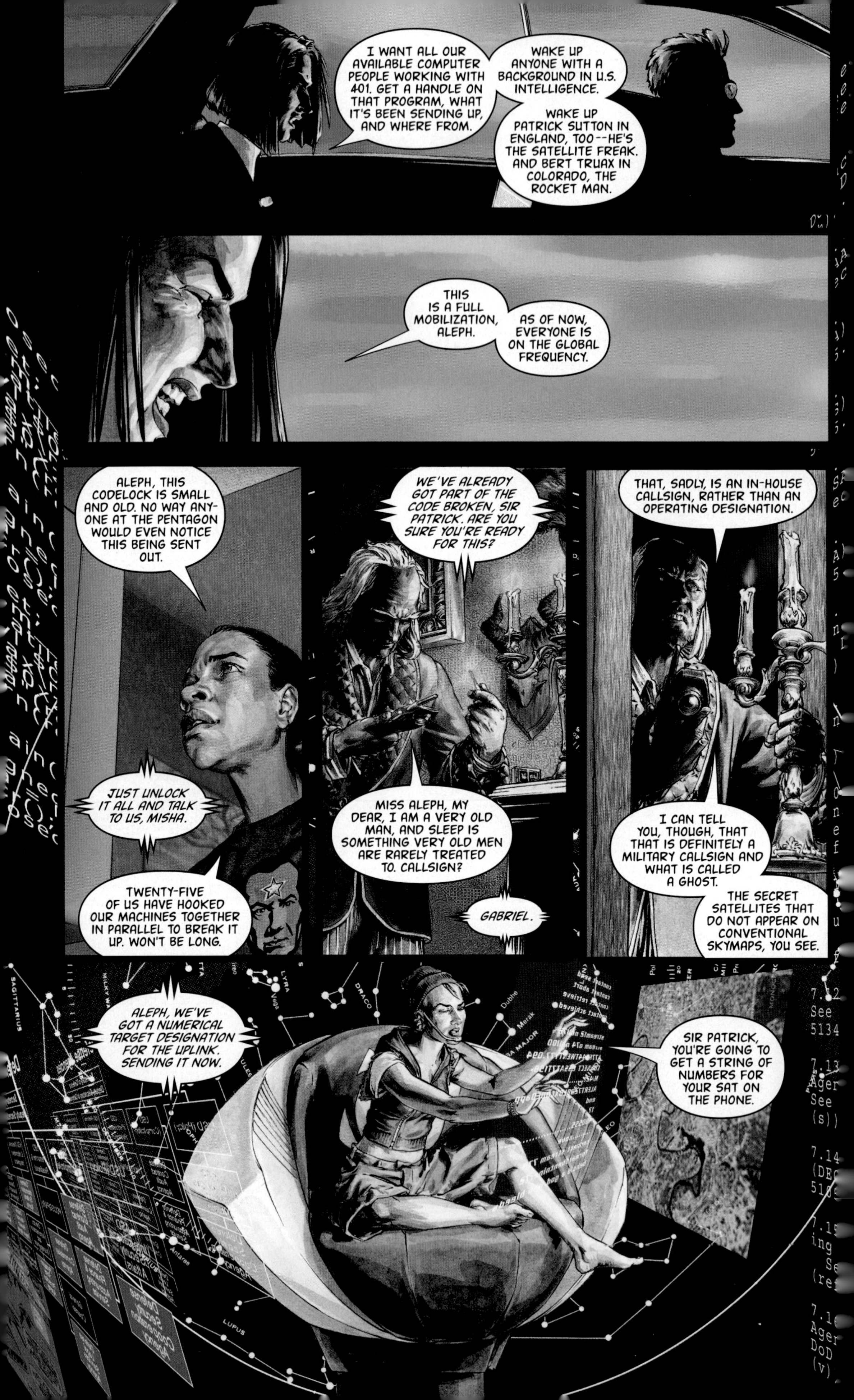
I WANT ALL OUR AVAILABLE COMPUTER PEOPLE WORKING WITH 401. GET A HANDLE ON THAT PROGRAM, WHAT IT'S BEEN SENDING UP, AND WHERE FROM.
WAKE UP ANYONE WITH A BACKGROUND IN U.S. INTELLIGENCE.
WAKE UP PATRICK SUTTON IN ENGLAND, TOO--HE'S THE SATELLITE FREAK. AND BERT TRUAX IN COLORADO, THE ROCKET MAN.
THIS IS A FULL MOBILIZATION, ALEPH.
AS OF NOW, EVERYONE IS ON THE GLOBAL FREQUENCY.
ALEPH, THIS CODELOCK IS SMALL AND OLD. NO WAY ANYONE AT THE PENTAGON WOULD EVEN NOTICE THIS BEING SENT OUT.
JUST UNLOCK IT ALL AND TALK TO US, MISHA.
TWENTY-FIVE OF US HAVE HOOKED OUR MACHINES TOGETHER IN PARALLEL TO BREAK IT UP. WON'T BE LONG.
WE'VE ALREADY GOT PART OF THE CODE BROKEN, SIR PATRICK. ARE YOU SURE YOU'RE READY FOR THIS?
MISS ALEPH, MY DEAR, I AM A VERY OLD MAN, AND SLEEP IS SOMETHING VERY OLD MEN ARE RARELY TREATED TO. CALLSIGN?
GABRIEL.
THAT, SADLY, IS AN IN-HOUSE CALLSIGN, RATHER THAN AN OPERATING DESIGNATION.
I CAN TELL YOU, THOUGH, THAT THAT IS DEFINITELY A MILITARY CALLSIGN AND WHAT IS CALLED A GHOST.
THE SECRET SATELLITES THAT DO NOT APPEAR ON CONVENTIONAL SKYMAPS, YOU SEE.
ALEPH, WE'VE GOT A NUMERICAL TARGET DESIGNATION FOR THE UPLINK. SENDING IT NOW.
SIR PATRICK, YOU'RE GOING TO GET A STRING OF NUMBERS FOR YOUR SAT ON THE PHONE.

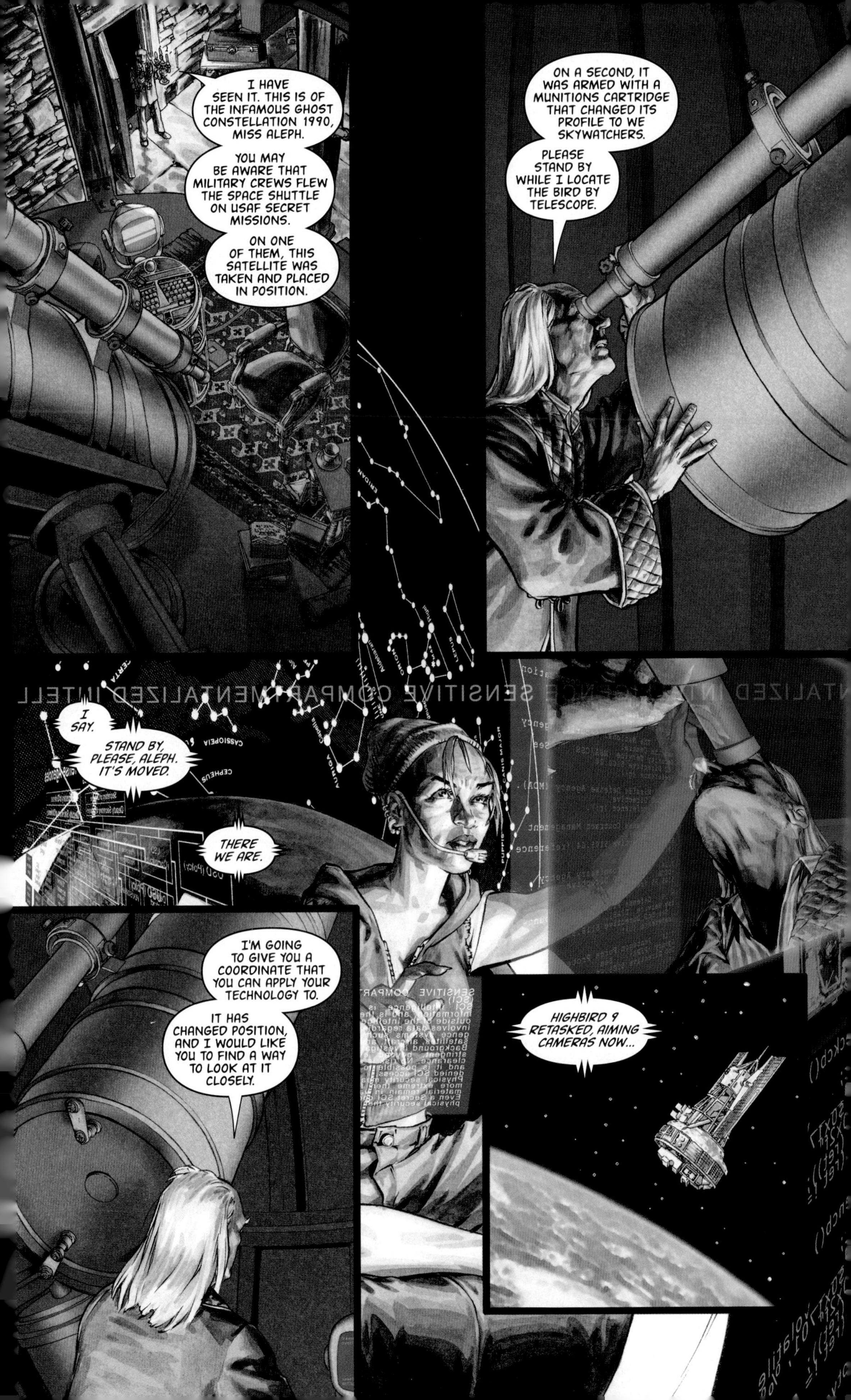
I HAVE SEEN IT. THIS IS OF THE INFAMOUS GHOST CONSTELLATION 1990, MISS ALEPH.
YOU MAY BE AWARE THAT MILITARY CREWS FLEW THE SPACE SHUTTLE ON USAF SECRET MISSIONS.
ON ONE OF THEM, THIS SATELLITE WAS TAKEN AND PLACED IN POSITION.
ON A SECOND, IT WAS ARMED WITH A MUNITIONS CARTRIDGE THAT CHANGED ITS PROFILE TO WE SKYWATCHERS.
PLEASE STAND BY WHILE I LOCATE THE BIRD BY TELESCOPE.
I SAY.
STAND BY, PLEASE, ALEPH. IT'S MOVED.
THERE WE ARE.
I'M GOING TO GIVE YOU A COORDINATE THAT YOU CAN APPLY YOUR TECHNOLOGY TO.
IT HAS CHANGED POSITION, AND I WOULD LIKE YOU TO FIND A WAY TO LOOK AT IT CLOSELY.
HIGHBIRD 9 RETASKED, AIMING CAMERAS NOW...

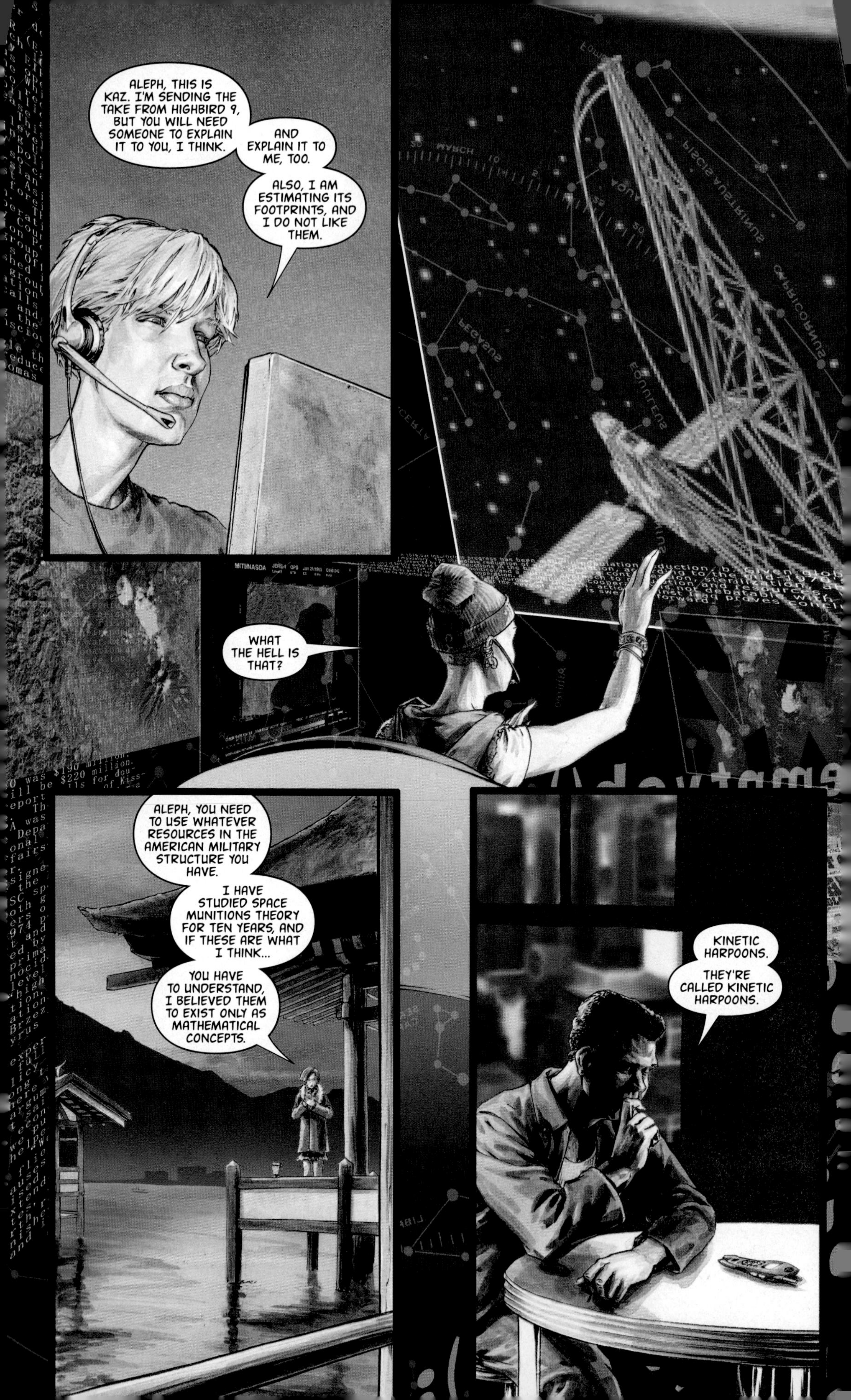
ALEPH, THIS IS KAZ. I'M SENDING THE TAKE FROM HIGHBIRD 9, BUT YOU WILL NEED SOMEONE TO EXPLAIN IT TO YOU, I THINK.
AND EXPLAIN IT TO ME, TOO.
ALSO, I AM ESTIMATING ITS FOOTPRINTS, AND I DO NOT LIKE THEM.
PISCIS AUSTRINUS
CAPRICORNUS
PEGASUS
EQUULEUS
MARCH
WHAT THE HELL IS THAT?
ALEPH, YOU NEED TO USE WHATEVER RESOURCES IN THE AMERICAN MILITARY STRUCTURE YOU HAVE.
I HAVE STUDIED SPACE MUNITIONS THEORY FOR TEN YEARS, AND IF THESE ARE WHAT I THINK...
YOU HAVE TO UNDERSTAND, I BELIEVED THEM TO EXIST ONLY AS MATHEMATICAL CONCEPTS.
KINETIC HARPOONS.
THEY'RE CALLED KINETIC HARPOONS.

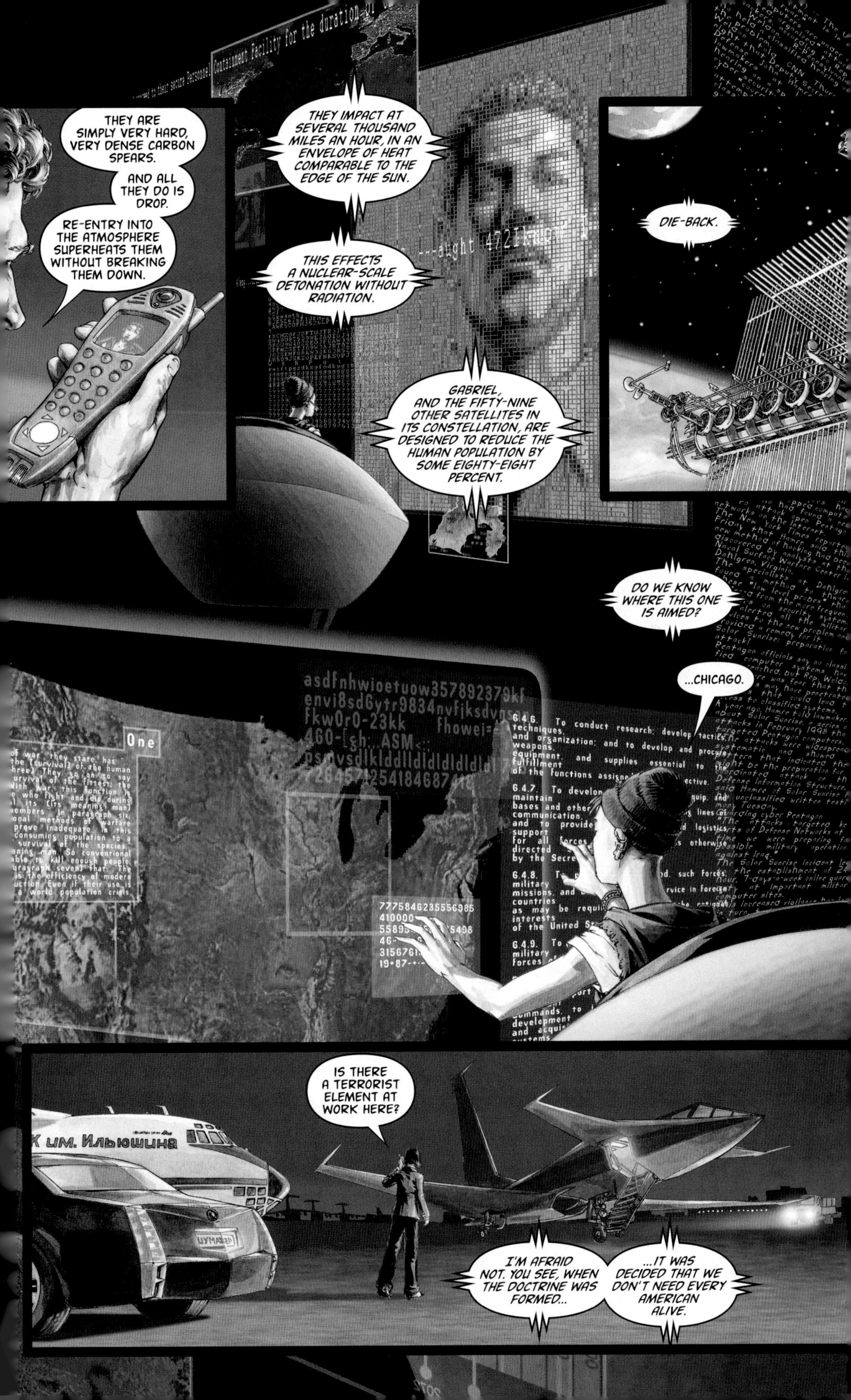
THEY ARE SIMPLY VERY HARD, VERY DENSE CARBON SPEARS.
AND ALL THEY DO IS DROP.
RE-ENTRY INTO THE ATMOSPHERE SUPERHEATS THEM WITHOUT BREAKING THEM DOWN.
THEY IMPACT AT SEVERAL THOUSAND MILES AN HOUR, IN AN ENVELOPE OF HEAT COMPARABLE TO THE EDGE OF THE SUN.
THIS EFFECTS A NUCLEAR-SCALE DETONATION WITHOUT RADIATION.
GABRIEL, AND THE FIFTY-NINE OTHER SATELLITES IN ITS CONSTELLATION, ARE DESIGNED TO REDUCE THE HUMAN POPULATION BY SOME EIGHTY-EIGHT PERCENT.
DIE-BACK.
DO WE KNOW WHERE THIS ONE IS AIMED?
...CHICAGO.
IS THERE A TERRORIST ELEMENT AT WORK HERE?
I'M AFRAID NOT. YOU SEE, WHEN THE DOCTRINE WAS FORMED...
...IT WAS DECIDED THAT WE DON'T NEED EVERY AMERICAN ALIVE.

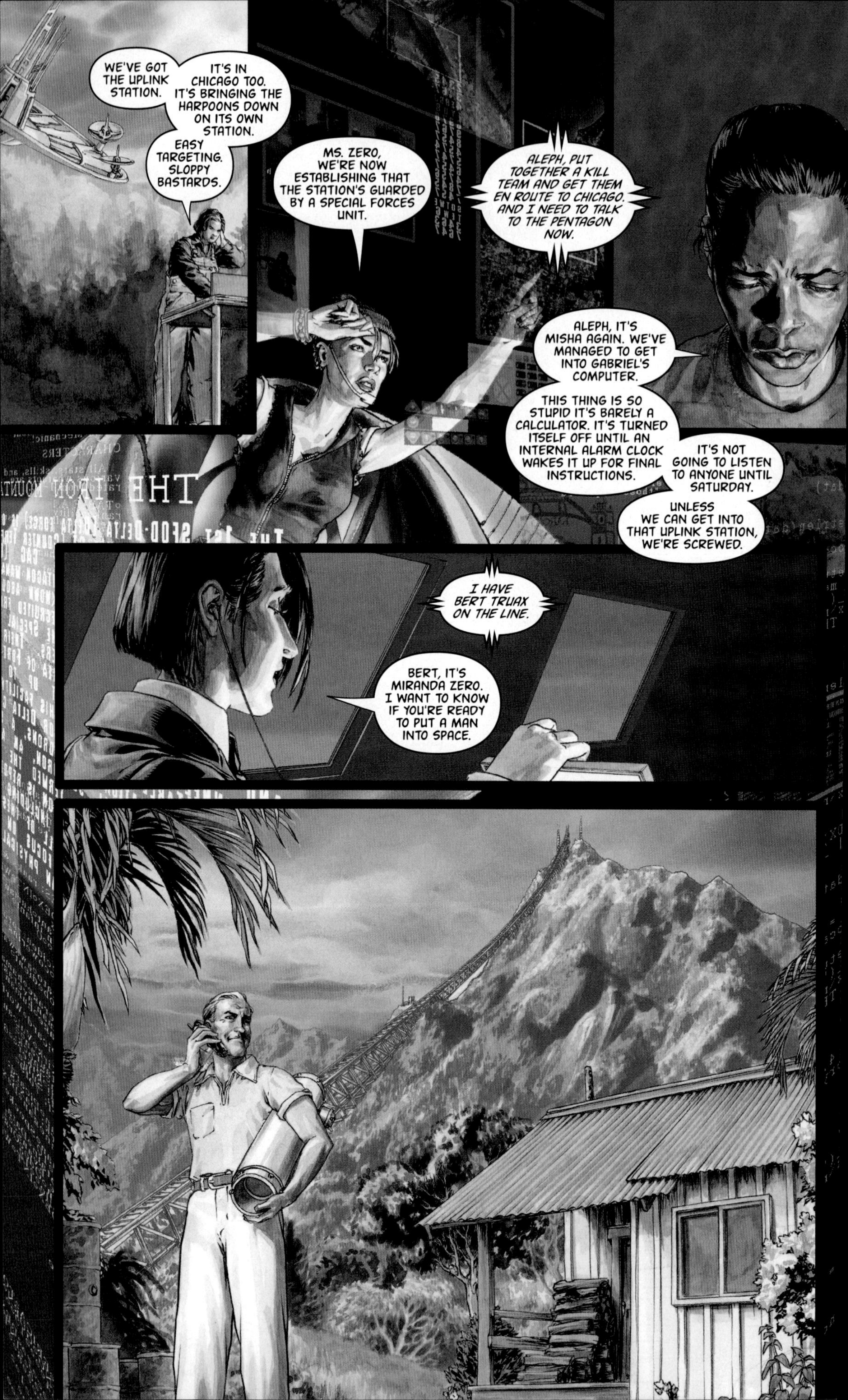
WE'VE GOT THE UPLINK STATION.
IT'S IN CHICAGO TOO. IT'S BRINGING THE HARPOONS DOWN ON ITS OWN STATION.
EASY TARGETING. SLOPPY BASTARDS.
MS. ZERO, WE'RE NOW ESTABLISHING THAT THE STATION'S GUARDED BY A SPECIAL FORCES UNIT.
ALEPH, PUT TOGETHER A KILL TEAM AND GET THEM EN ROUTE TO CHICAGO. AND I NEED TO TALK TO THE PENTAGON NOW.
ALEPH, IT'S MISHA AGAIN. WE'VE MANAGED TO GET INTO GABRIEL'S COMPUTER.
THIS THING IS SO STUPID IT'S BARELY A CALCULATOR. IT'S TURNED ITSELF OFF UNTIL AN INTERNAL ALARM CLOCK WAKES IT UP FOR FINAL INSTRUCTIONS.
IT'S NOT GOING TO LISTEN TO ANYONE UNTIL SATURDAY.
UNLESS WE CAN GET INTO THAT UPLINK STATION, WE'RE SCREWED.
I HAVE BERT TRUAX ON THE LINE.
BERT, IT'S MIRANDA ZERO. I WANT TO KNOW IF YOU'RE READY TO PUT A MAN INTO SPACE.

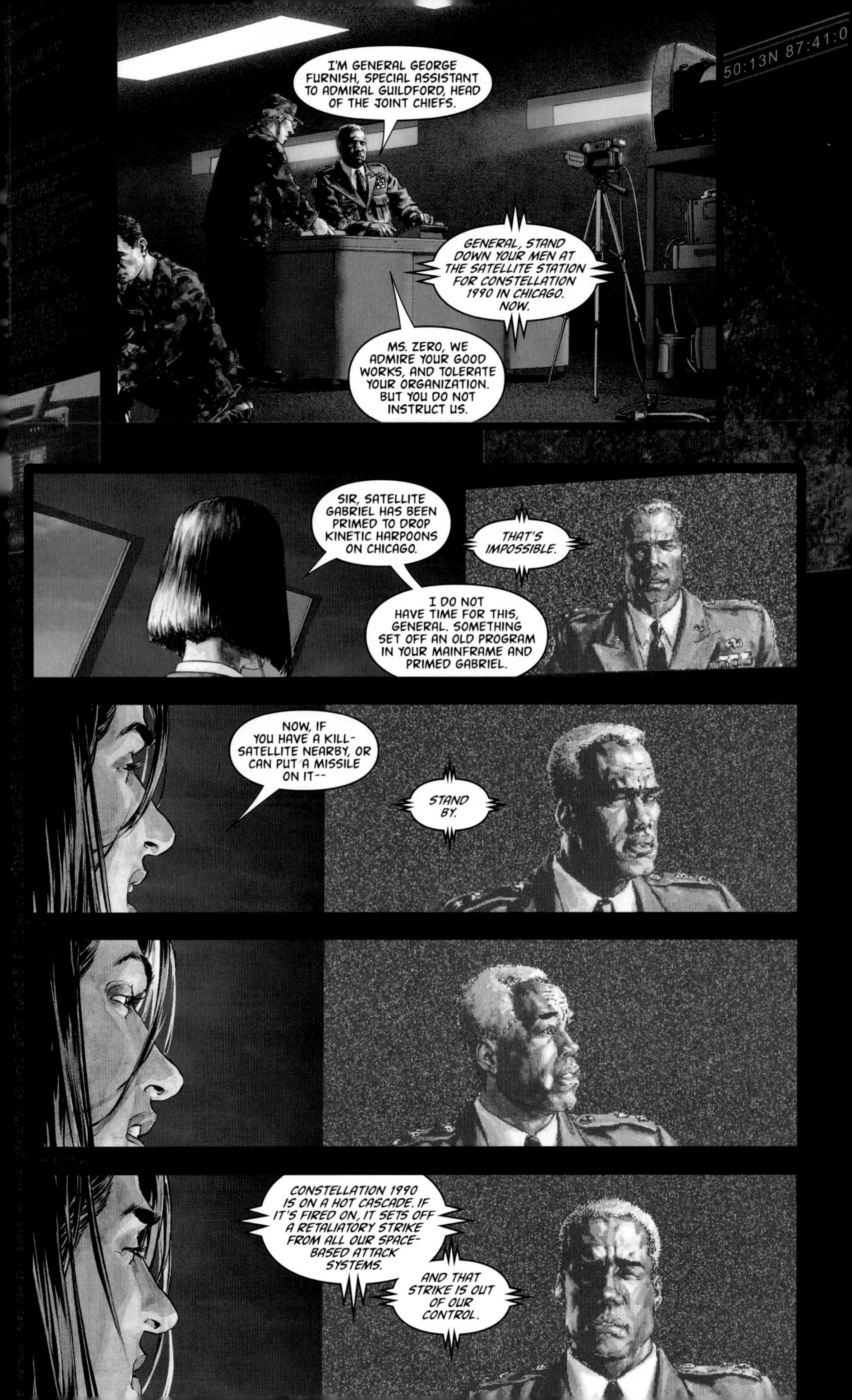
50:13N 87:41:0
I'M GENERAL GEORGE FURNISH, SPECIAL ASSISTANT TO ADMIRAL GUILDFORD, HEAD OF THE JOINT CHIEFS.
GENERAL, STAND DOWN YOUR MEN AT THE SATELLITE STATION FOR CONSTELLATION 1990 IN CHICAGO. NOW.
MS. ZERO, WE ADMIRE YOUR GOOD WORKS, AND TOLERATE YOUR ORGANIZATION. BUT YOU DO NOT INSTRUCT US.
SIR, SATELLITE GABRIEL HAS BEEN PRIMED TO DROP KINETIC HARPOONS ON CHICAGO.
THAT'S IMPOSSIBLE.
I DO NOT HAVE TIME FOR THIS, GENERAL. SOMETHING SET OFF AN OLD PROGRAM IN YOUR MAINFRAME AND PRIMED GABRIEL.
NOW, IF YOU HAVE A KILL-SATELLITE NEARBY, OR CAN PUT A MISSILE ON IT--
STAND BY.
CONSTELLATION 1990 IS ON A HOT CASCADE. IF IT'S FIRED ON, IT SETS OFF A RETALIATORY STRIKE FROM ALL OUR SPACE-BASED ATTACK SYSTEMS.
AND THAT STRIKE IS OUT OF OUR CONTROL.

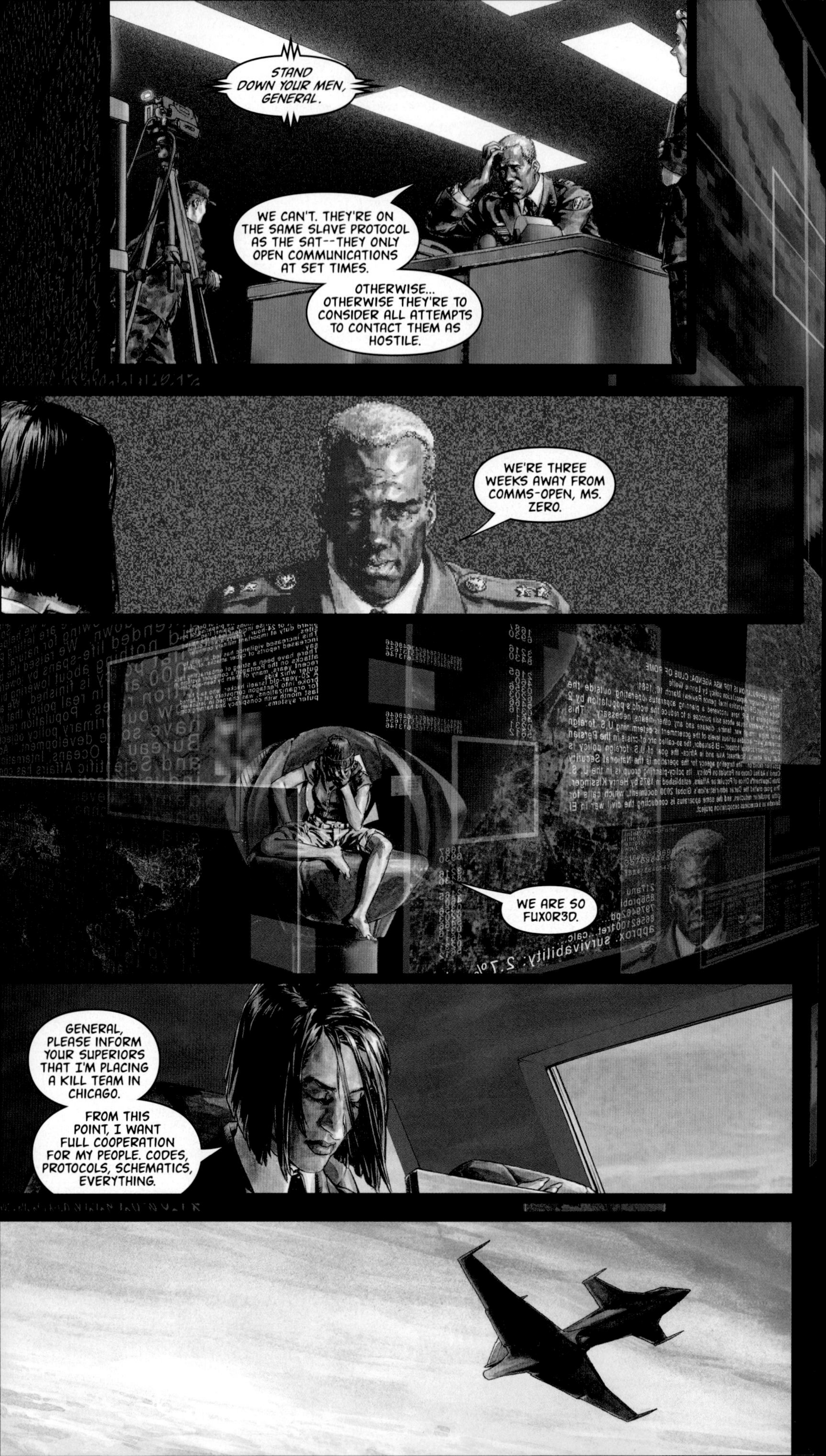
STAND DOWN YOUR MEN, GENERAL.
WE CAN'T. THEY'RE ON THE SAME SLAVE PROTOCOL AS THE SAT--THEY ONLY OPEN COMMUNICATIONS AT SET TIMES.
OTHERWISE... OTHERWISE THEY'RE TO CONSIDER ALL ATTEMPTS TO CONTACT THEM AS HOSTILE.
WE'RE THREE WEEKS AWAY FROM COMMS-OPEN, MS. ZERO.
WE ARE SO FUXOR3D.
GENERAL, PLEASE INFORM YOUR SUPERIORS THAT I'M PLACING A KILL TEAM IN CHICAGO.
FROM THIS POINT, I WANT FULL COOPERATION FOR MY PEOPLE. CODES, PROTOCOLS, SCHEMATICS, EVERYTHING.

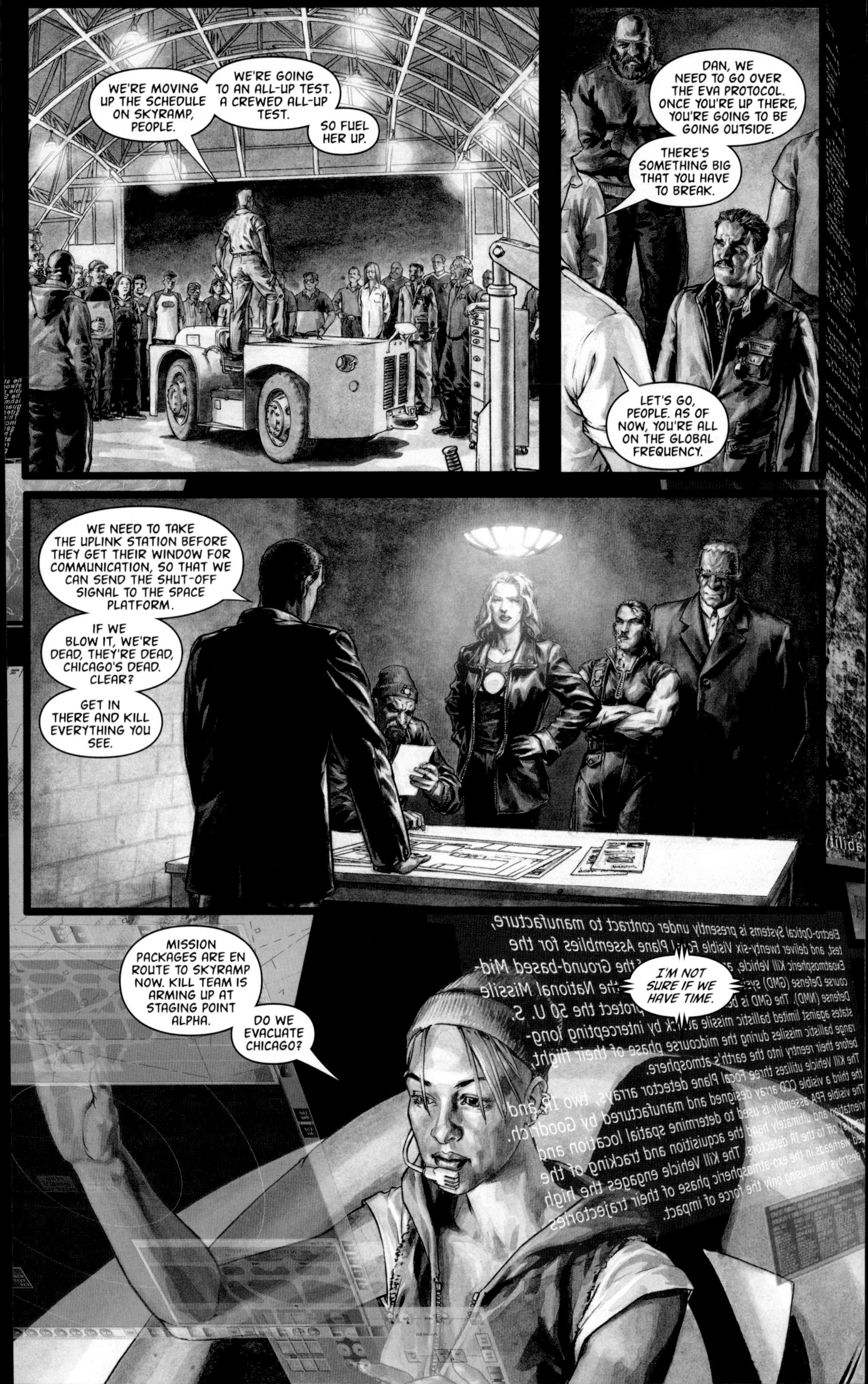
WE'RE MOVING UP THE SCHEDULE ON SKYRAMP, PEOPLE.
WE'RE GOING TO AN ALL-UP TEST. A CREWED ALL-UP TEST.
SO FUEL HER UP.
DAN, WE NEED TO GO OVER THE EVA PROTOCOL. ONCE YOU'RE UP THERE, YOU'RE GOING TO BE GOING OUTSIDE.
THERE'S SOMETHING BIG THAT YOU HAVE TO BREAK.
LET'S GO, PEOPLE. AS OF NOW, YOU'RE ALL ON THE GLOBAL FREQUENCY.
WE NEED TO TAKE THE UPLINK STATION BEFORE THEY GET THEIR WINDOW FOR COMMUNICATION, SO THAT WE CAN SEND THE SHUT-OFF SIGNAL TO THE SPACE PLATFORM.
IF WE BLOW IT, WE'RE DEAD, THEY'RE DEAD, CHICAGO'S DEAD. CLEAR?
GET IN THERE AND KILL EVERYTHING YOU SEE.
MISSION PACKAGES ARE EN ROUTE TO SKYRAMP NOW. KILL TEAM IS ARMING UP AT STAGING POINT ALPHA.
DO WE EVACUATE CHICAGO?
I'M NOT SURE IF WE HAVE TIME.

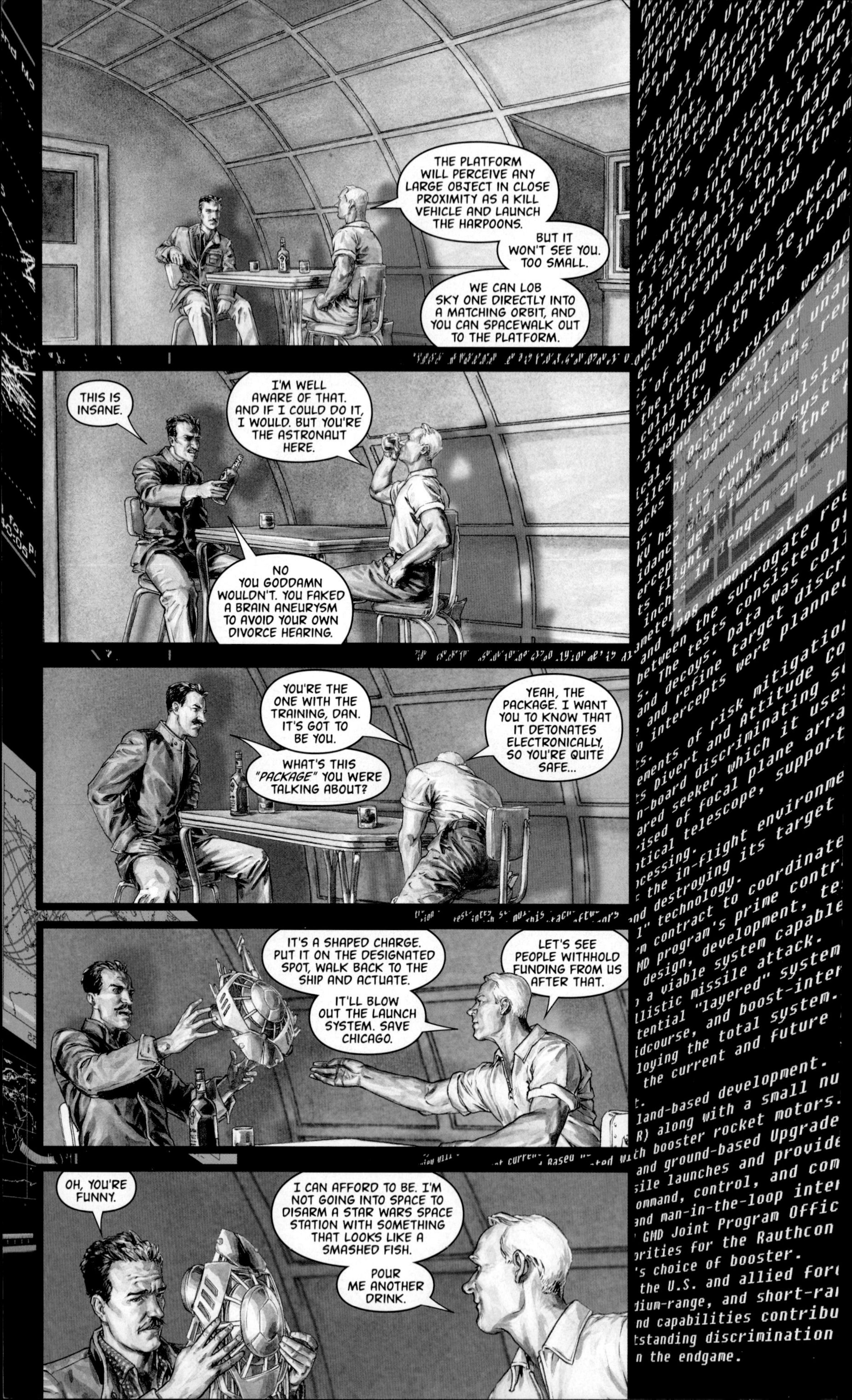
THE PLATFORM WILL PERCEIVE ANY LARGE OBJECT IN CLOSE PROXIMITY AS A KILL VEHICLE AND LAUNCH THE HARPOONS.
BUT IT WON'T SEE YOU. TOO SMALL.
WE CAN LOB SKY ONE DIRECTLY INTO A MATCHING ORBIT, AND YOU CAN SPACEWALK OUT TO THE PLATFORM.
THIS IS INSANE.
I'M WELL AWARE OF THAT. AND IF I COULD DO IT, I WOULD. BUT YOU'RE THE ASTRONAUT HERE.
NO YOU GODDAMN WOULDN'T. YOU FAKED A BRAIN ANEURYSM TO AVOID YOUR OWN DIVORCE HEARING.
YOU'RE THE ONE WITH THE TRAINING, DAN. IT'S GOT TO BE YOU.
WHAT'S THIS "PACKAGE" YOU WERE TALKING ABOUT?
YEAH, THE PACKAGE. I WANT YOU TO KNOW THAT IT DETONATES ELECTRONICALLY, SO YOU'RE QUITE SAFE...
IT'S A SHAPED CHARGE. PUT IT ON THE DESIGNATED SPOT, WALK BACK TO THE SHIP AND ACTUATE.
IT'LL BLOW OUT THE LAUNCH SYSTEM. SAVE CHICAGO.
LET'S SEE PEOPLE WITHHOLD FUNDING FROM US AFTER THAT.
OH, YOU'RE FUNNY.
I CAN AFFORD TO BE. I'M NOT GOING INTO SPACE TO DISARM A STAR WARS SPACE STATION WITH SOMETHING THAT LOOKS LIKE A SMASHED FISH.
POUR ME ANOTHER DRINK.

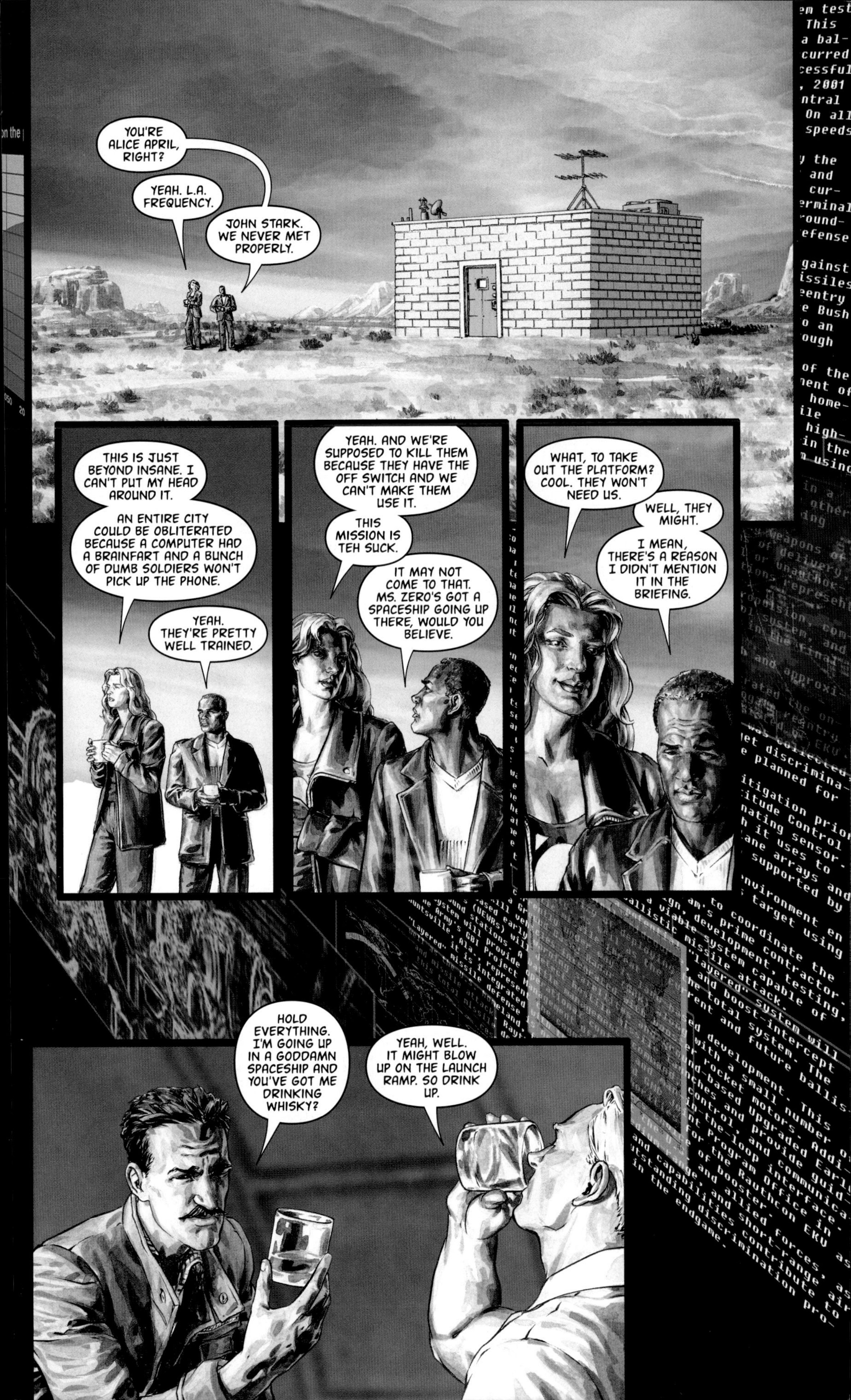

YOU'RE ALICE APRIL, RIGHT?
YEAH. L.A. FREQUENCY.
JOHN STARK. WE NEVER MET PROPERLY.
THIS IS JUST BEYOND INSANE. I CAN'T PUT MY HEAD AROUND IT.
AN ENTIRE CITY COULD BE OBLITERATED BECAUSE A COMPUTER HAD A BRAINFART AND A BUNCH OF DUMB SOLDIERS WON'T PICK UP THE PHONE.
YEAH. THEY'RE PRETTY WELL TRAINED.
YEAH. AND WE'RE SUPPOSED TO KILL THEM BECAUSE THEY HAVE THE OFF SWITCH AND WE CAN'T MAKE THEM USE IT.
THIS MISSION IS TEH SUCK.
IT MAY NOT COME TO THAT. MS. ZERO'S GOT A SPACESHIP GOING UP THERE, WOULD YOU BELIEVE.
WHAT, TO TAKE OUT THE PLATFORM? COOL. THEY WON'T NEED US.
WELL, THEY MIGHT.
I MEAN, THERE'S A REASON I DIDN'T MENTION IT IN THE BRIEFING.
HOLD EVERYTHING. I'M GOING UP IN A GODDAMN SPACESHIP AND YOU'VE GOT ME DRINKING WHISKY?
YEAH, WELL. IT MIGHT BLOW UP ON THE LAUNCH RAMP. SO DRINK UP.

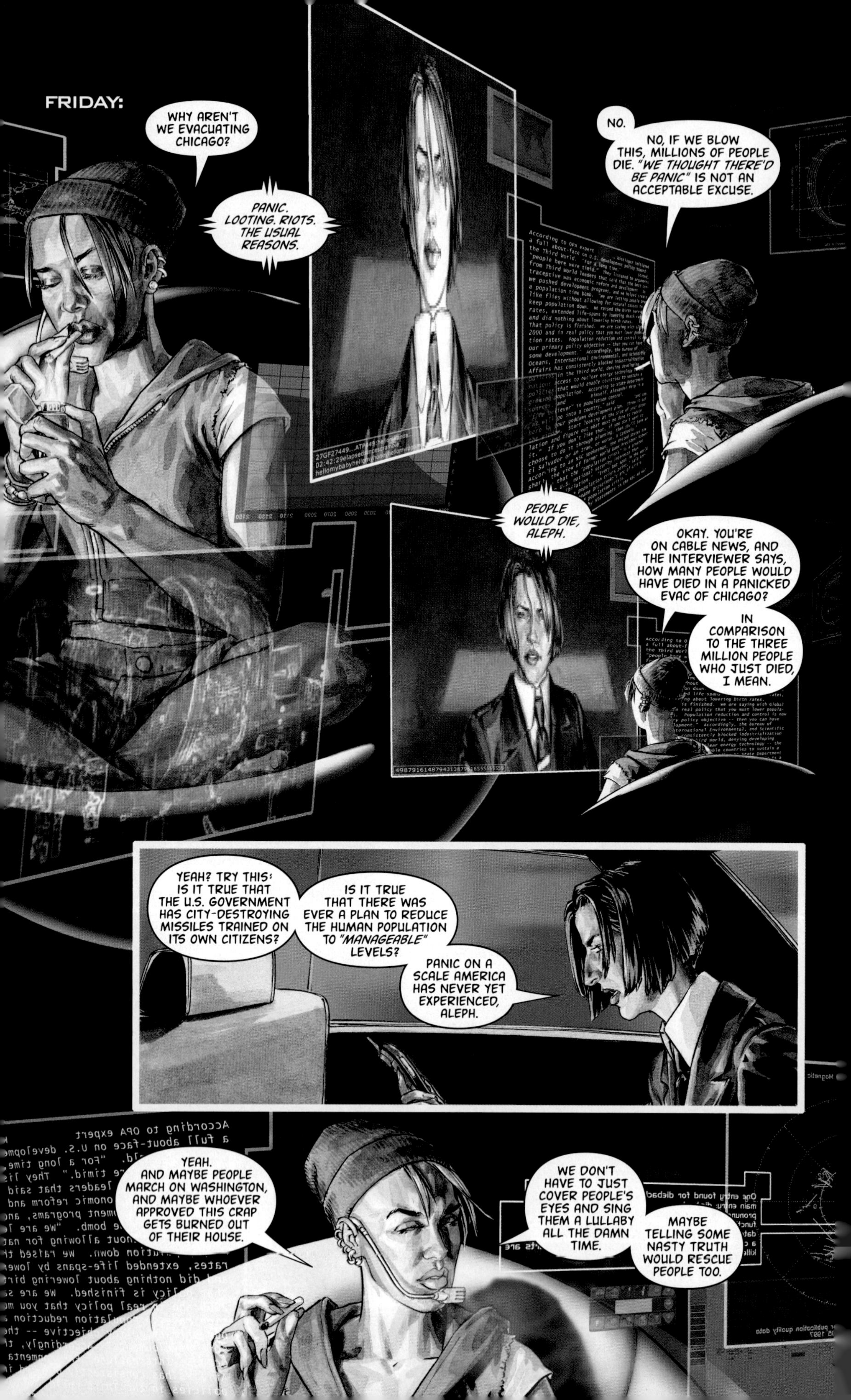
FRIDAY:
WHY AREN'T WE EVACUATING CHICAGO?
PANIC. LOOTING. RIOTS. THE USUAL REASONS.
NO.
NO, IF WE BLOW THIS, MILLIONS OF PEOPLE DIE. "WE THOUGHT THERE'D BE PANIC" IS NOT AN ACCEPTABLE EXCUSE.
PEOPLE WOULD DIE, ALEPH.
OKAY. YOU'RE ON CABLE NEWS, AND THE INTERVIEWER SAYS, HOW MANY PEOPLE WOULD HAVE DIED IN A PANICKED EVAC OF CHICAGO?
IN COMPARISON TO THE THREE MILLION PEOPLE WHO JUST DIED, I MEAN.
YEAH? TRY THIS: IS IT TRUE THAT THE U.S. GOVERNMENT HAS CITY-DESTROYING MISSILES TRAINED ON ITS OWN CITIZENS?
IS IT TRUE THAT THERE WAS EVER A PLAN TO REDUCE THE HUMAN POPULATION TO "MANAGEABLE" LEVELS?
PANIC ON A SCALE AMERICA HAS NEVER YET EXPERIENCED, ALEPH.
YEAH. AND MAYBE PEOPLE MARCH ON WASHINGTON, AND MAYBE WHOEVER APPROVED THIS CRAP GETS BURNED OUT OF THEIR HOUSE.
WE DON'T HAVE TO JUST COVER PEOPLE'S EYES AND SING THEM A LULLABY ALL THE DAMN TIME.
MAYBE TELLING SOME NASTY TRUTH WOULD RESCUE PEOPLE TOO.

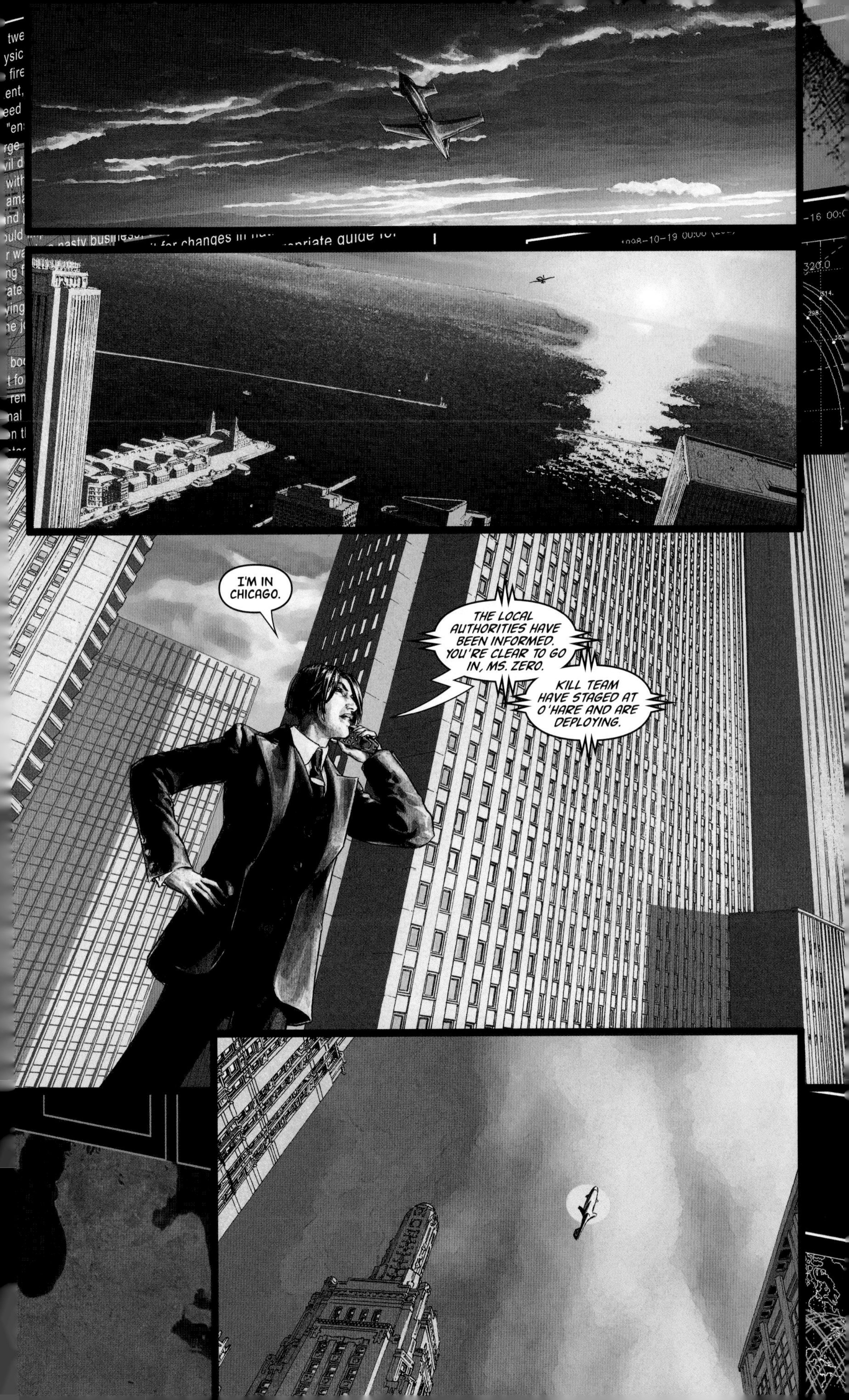
I'M IN CHICAGO.
THE LOCAL AUTHORITIES HAVE BEEN INFORMED. YOU'RE CLEAR TO GO IN, MS. ZERO.
KILL TEAM HAVE STAGED AT O'HARE AND ARE DEPLOYING.

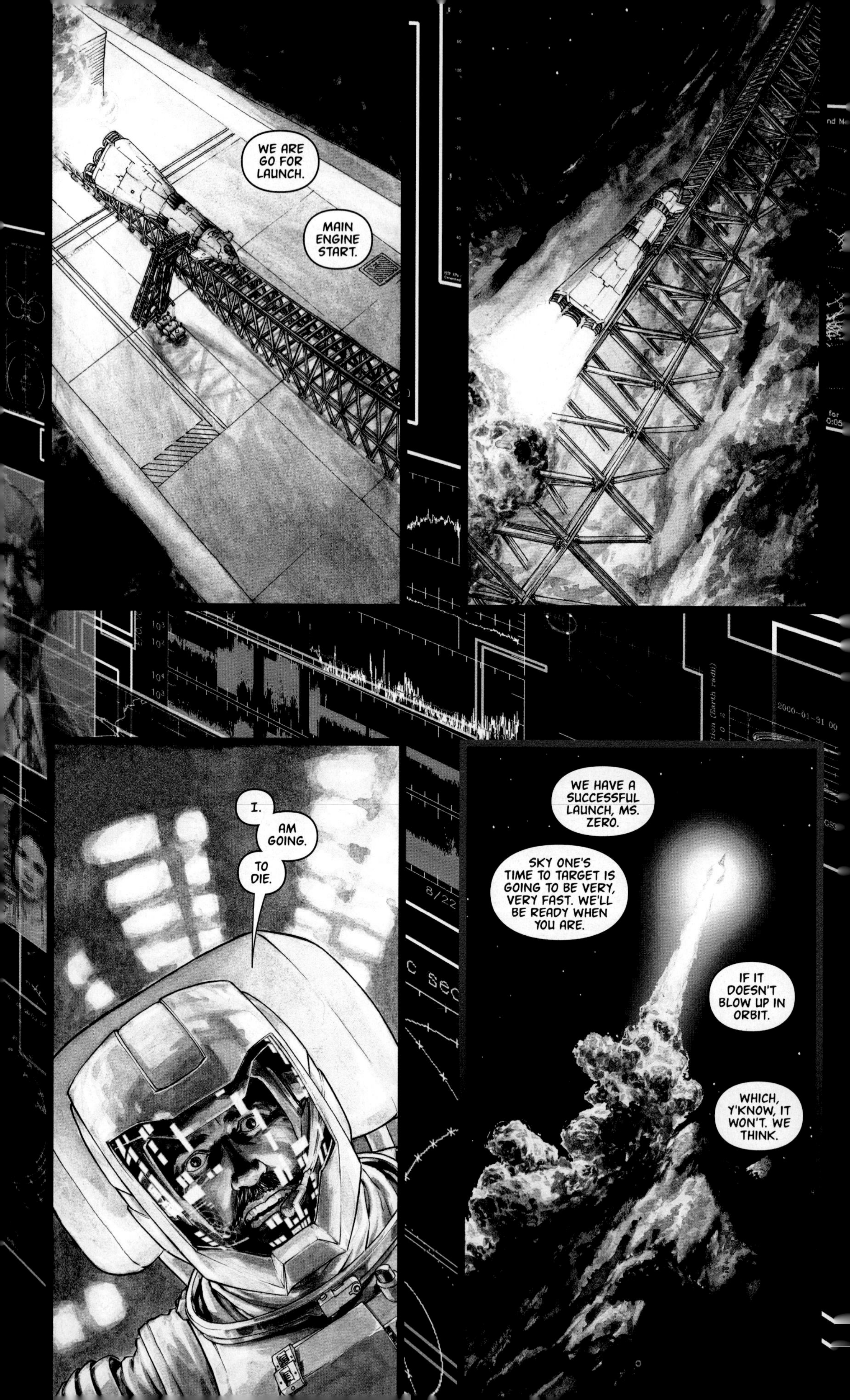
WE ARE GO FOR LAUNCH.
MAIN ENGINE START.
I.
AM GOING.
TO DIE.
WE HAVE A SUCCESSFUL LAUNCH, MS. ZERO.
SKY ONE'S TIME TO TARGET IS GOING TO BE VERY, VERY FAST. WE'LL BE READY WHEN YOU ARE.
IF IT DOESN'T BLOW UP IN ORBIT.
WHICH, Y'KNOW, IT WON'T. WE THINK.

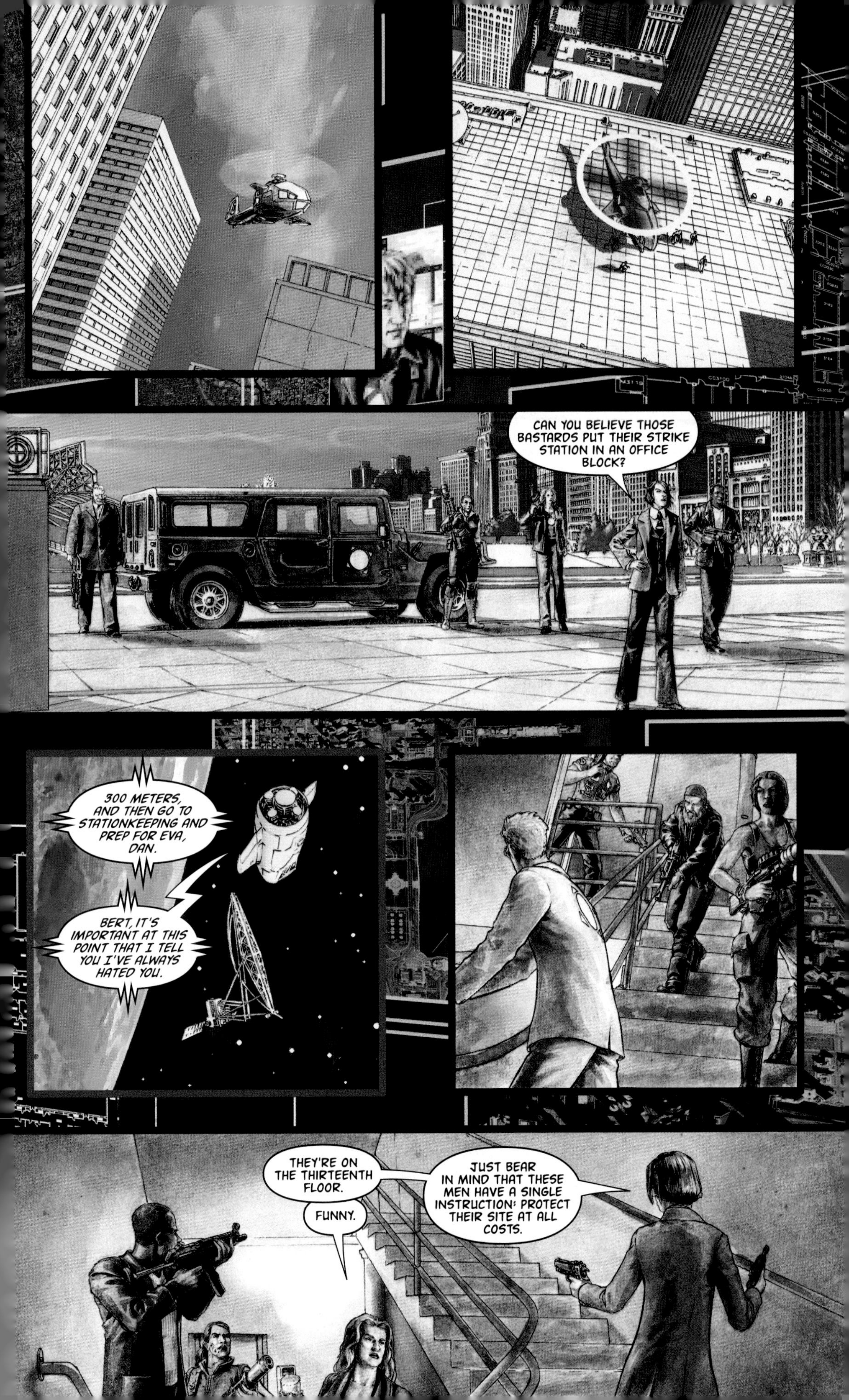
CAN YOU BELIEVE THOSE BASTARDS PUT THEIR STRIKE STATION IN AN OFFICE BLOCK?
300 METERS, AND THEN GO TO STATIONKEEPING AND PREP FOR EVA, DAN.
BERT, IT'S IMPORTANT AT THIS POINT THAT I TELL YOU I'VE ALWAYS HATED YOU.
THEY'RE ON THE THIRTEENTH FLOOR.
FUNNY.
JUST BEAR IN MIND THAT THESE MEN HAVE A SINGLE INSTRUCTION: PROTECT THEIR SITE AT ALL COSTS.

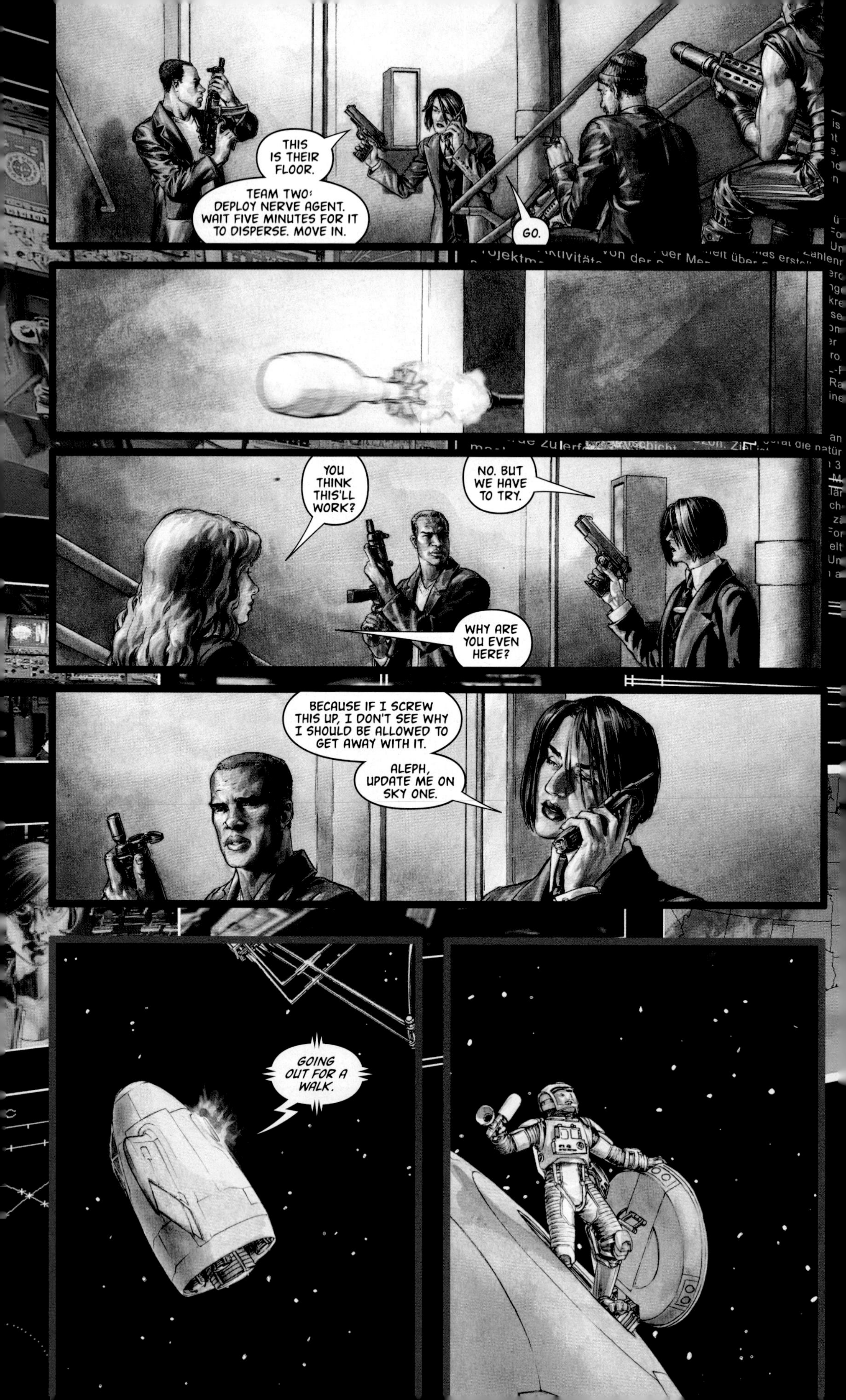
THIS IS THEIR FLOOR.
TEAM TWO: DEPLOY NERVE AGENT. WAIT FIVE MINUTES FOR IT TO DISPERSE. MOVE IN.
GO.
YOU THINK THIS'LL WORK?
NO. BUT WE HAVE TO TRY.
WHY ARE YOU EVEN HERE?
BECAUSE IF I SCREW THIS UP, I DON'T SEE WHY I SHOULD BE ALLOWED TO GET AWAY WITH IT.
ALEPH, UPDATE ME ON SKY ONE.
GOING OUT FOR A WALK.

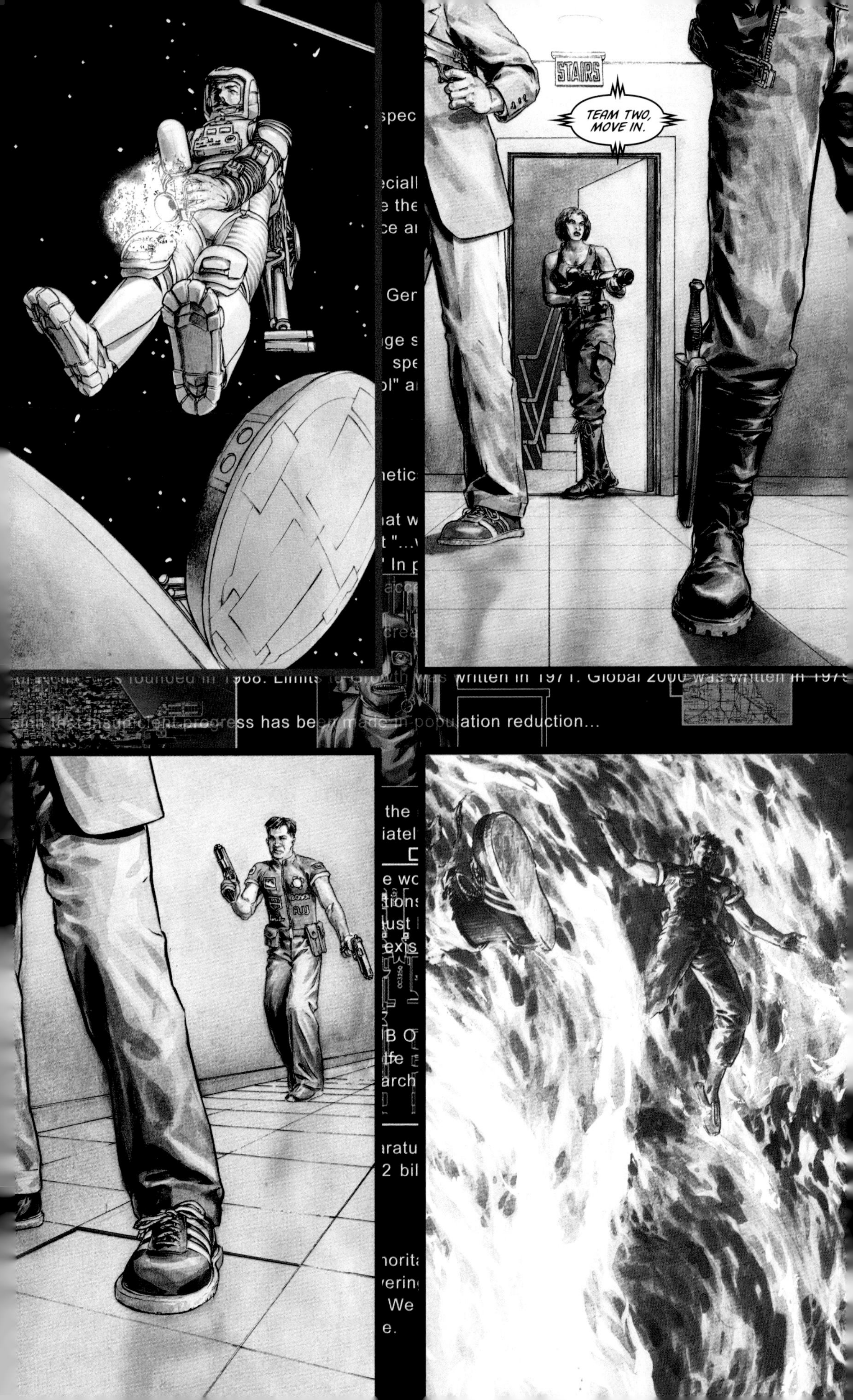
STAIRS
TEAM TWO, MOVE IN.

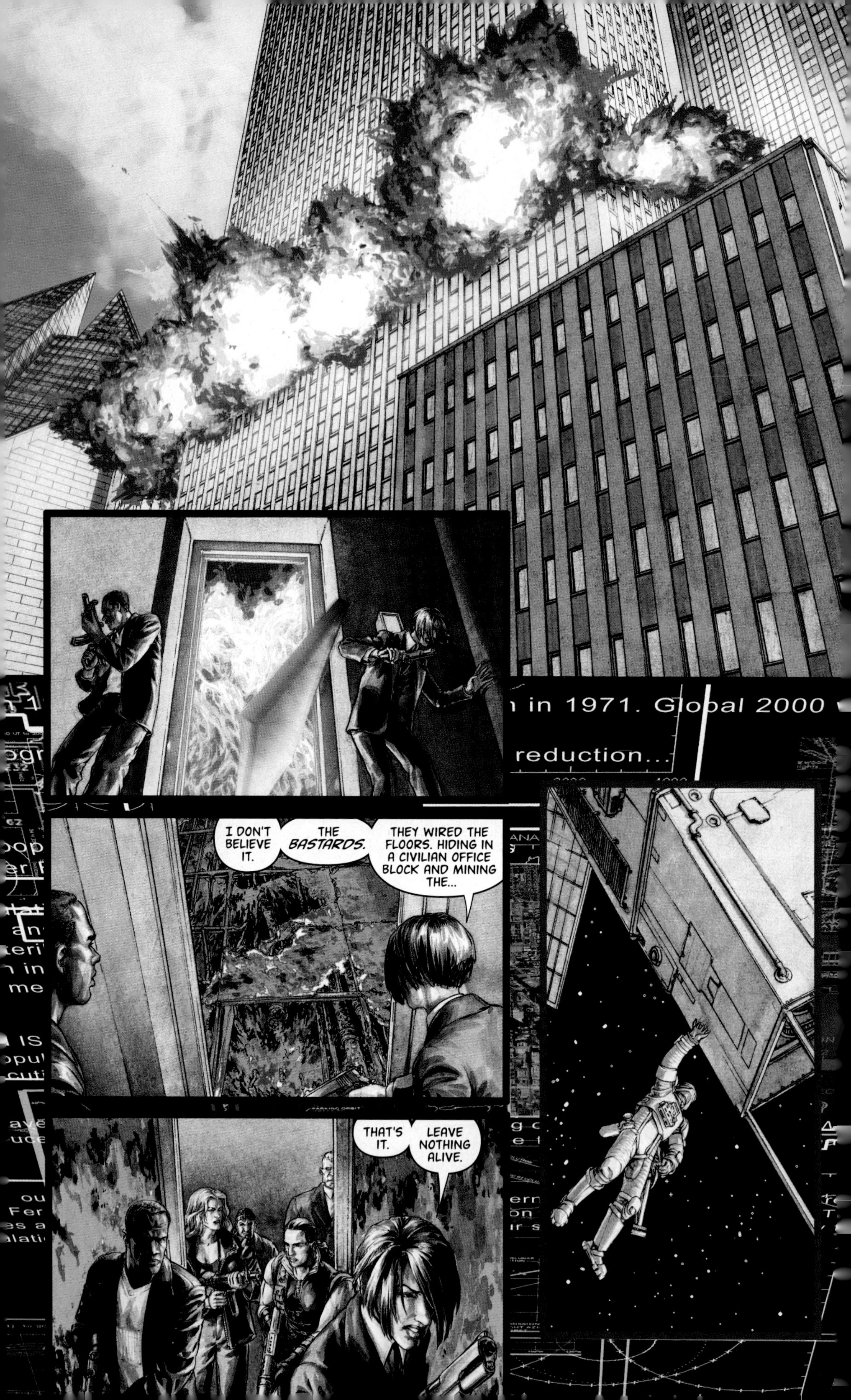
in 1971. Global 2000
reduction...
I DON'T BELIEVE IT.
THE BASTARDS.
THEY WIRED THE FLOORS. HIDING IN A CIVILIAN OFFICE BLOCK AND MINING THE...
THAT'S IT.
LEAVE NOTHING ALIVE.

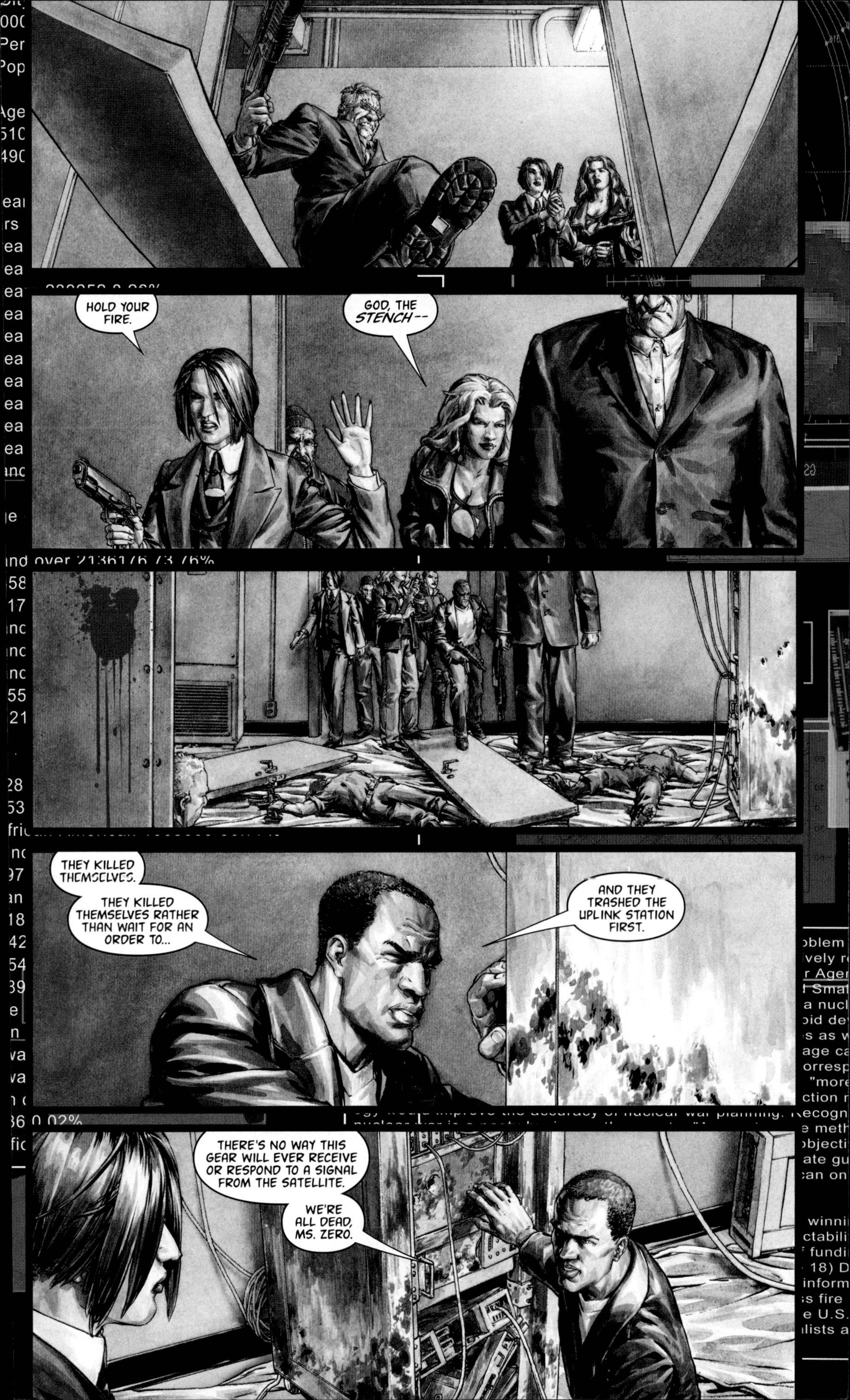
HOLD YOUR FIRE.
GOD, THE STENCH--
THEY KILLED THEMSELVES.
THEY KILLED THEMSELVES RATHER THAN WAIT FOR AN ORDER TO...
AND THEY TRASHED THE UPLINK STATION FIRST.
THERE'S NO WAY THIS GEAR WILL EVER RECEIVE OR RESPOND TO A SIGNAL FROM THE SATELLITE.
WE'RE ALL DEAD, MS. ZERO.

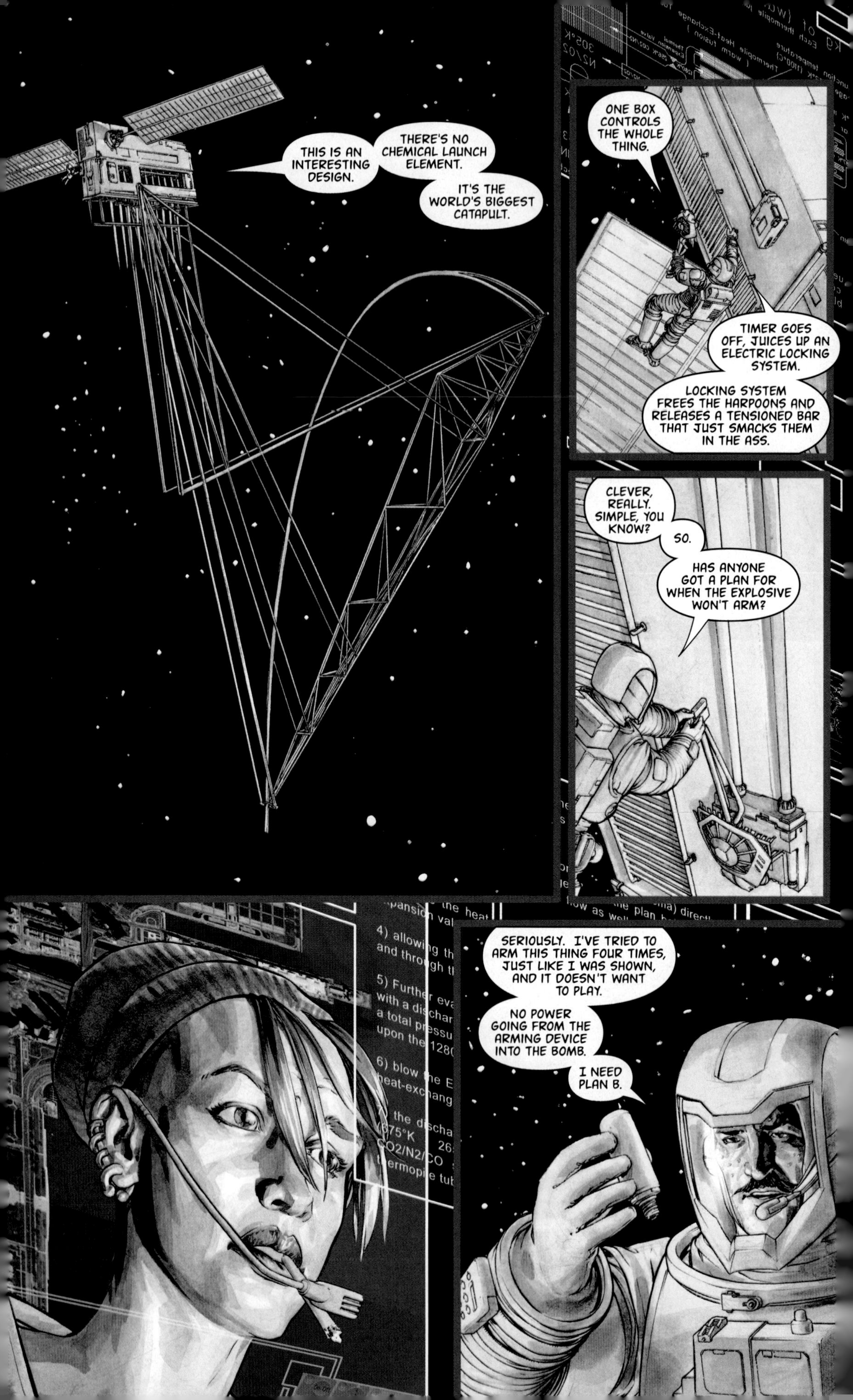
THIS IS AN INTERESTING DESIGN.
THERE'S NO CHEMICAL LAUNCH ELEMENT.
IT'S THE WORLD'S BIGGEST CATAPULT.
ONE BOX CONTROLS THE WHOLE THING.
TIMER GOES OFF, JUICES UP AN ELECTRIC LOCKING SYSTEM.
LOCKING SYSTEM FREES THE HARPOONS AND RELEASES A TENSIONED BAR THAT JUST SMACKS THEM IN THE ASS.
CLEVER, REALLY. SIMPLE, YOU KNOW?
SO.
HAS ANYONE GOT A PLAN FOR WHEN THE EXPLOSIVE WON'T ARM?
SERIOUSLY. I'VE TRIED TO ARM THIS THING FOUR TIMES, JUST LIKE I WAS SHOWN, AND IT DOESN'T WANT TO PLAY.
NO POWER GOING FROM THE ARMING DEVICE INTO THE BOMB.
I NEED PLAN B.

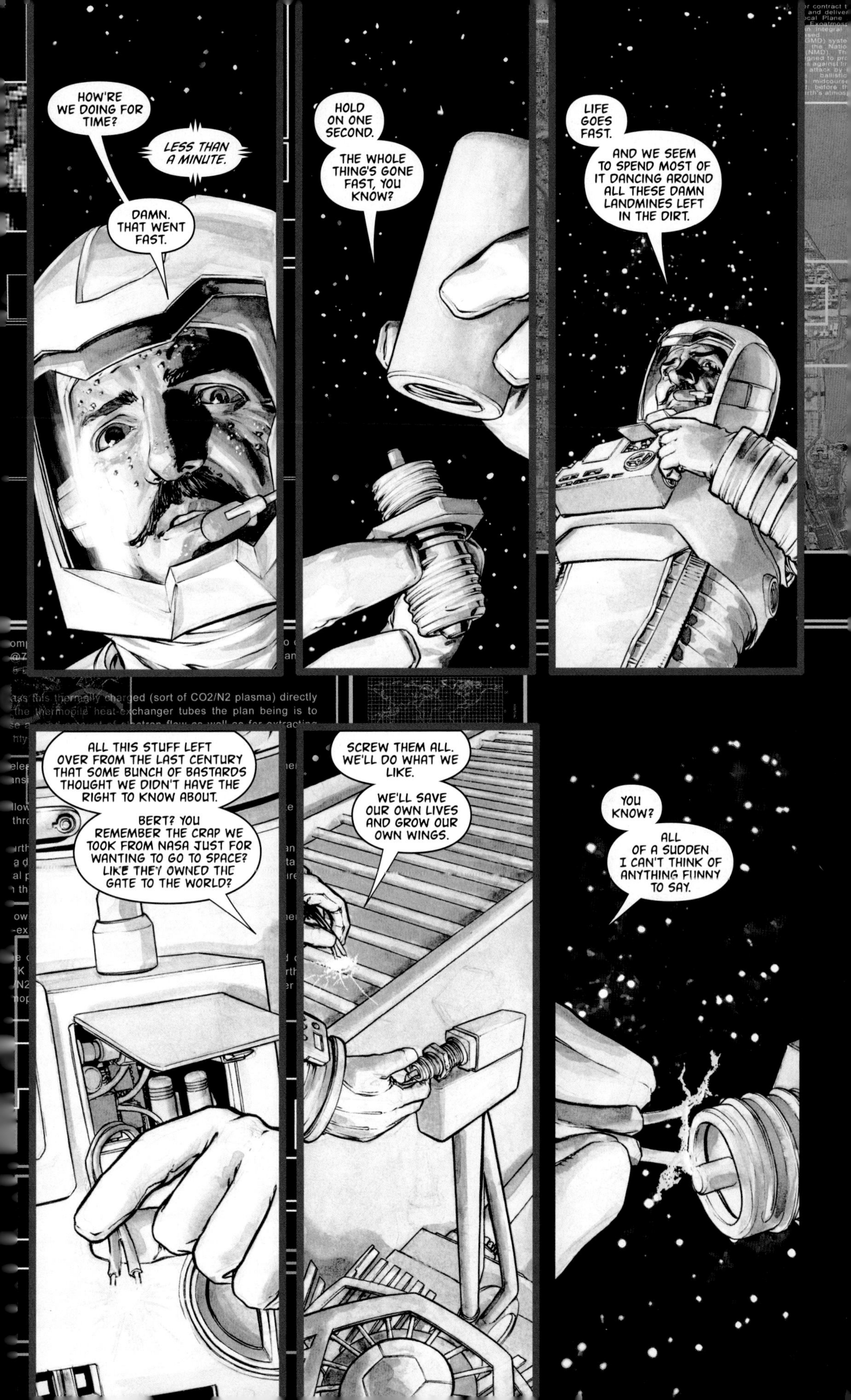

HOW'RE WE DOING FOR TIME?
LESS THAN A MINUTE.
DAMN. THAT WENT FAST.
HOLD ON ONE SECOND.
THE WHOLE THING'S GONE FAST, YOU KNOW?
LIFE GOES FAST.
AND WE SEEM TO SPEND MOST OF IT DANCING AROUND ALL THESE DAMN LANDMINES LEFT IN THE DIRT.
ALL THIS STUFF LEFT OVER FROM THE LAST CENTURY THAT SOME BUNCH OF BASTARDS THOUGHT WE DIDN'T HAVE THE RIGHT TO KNOW ABOUT.
BERT? YOU REMEMBER THE CRAP WE TOOK FROM NASA JUST FOR WANTING TO GO TO SPACE? LIKE THEY OWNED THE GATE TO THE WORLD?
SCREW THEM ALL. WE'LL DO WHAT WE LIKE.
WE'LL SAVE OUR OWN LIVES AND GROW OUR OWN WINGS.
YOU KNOW?
ALL OF A SUDDEN I CAN'T THINK OF ANYTHING FUNNY TO SAY.

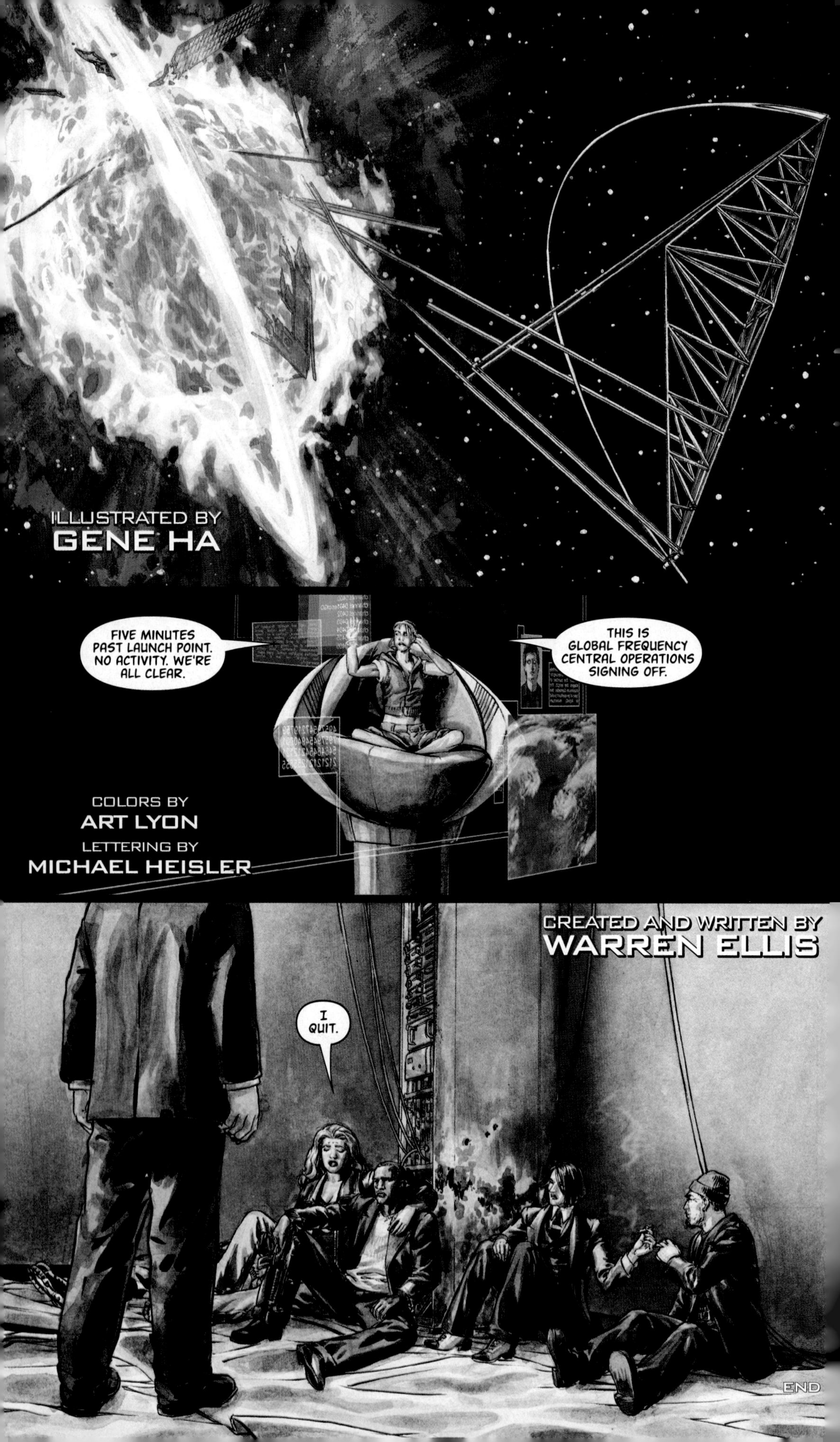
ILLUSTRATED BY
GENE HA
FIVE MINUTES PAST LAUNCH POINT. NO ACTIVITY. WE'RE ALL CLEAR.
THIS IS GLOBAL FREQUENCY CENTRAL OPERATIONS SIGNING OFF.
COLORS BY
ART LYON
LETTERING BY
MICHAEL HEISLER
CREATED AND WRITTEN BY
WARREN ELLIS
I QUIT.
END

GLOBAL FREQUENCY: PLANET ABLAZE
cover art by BRIAN WOOD

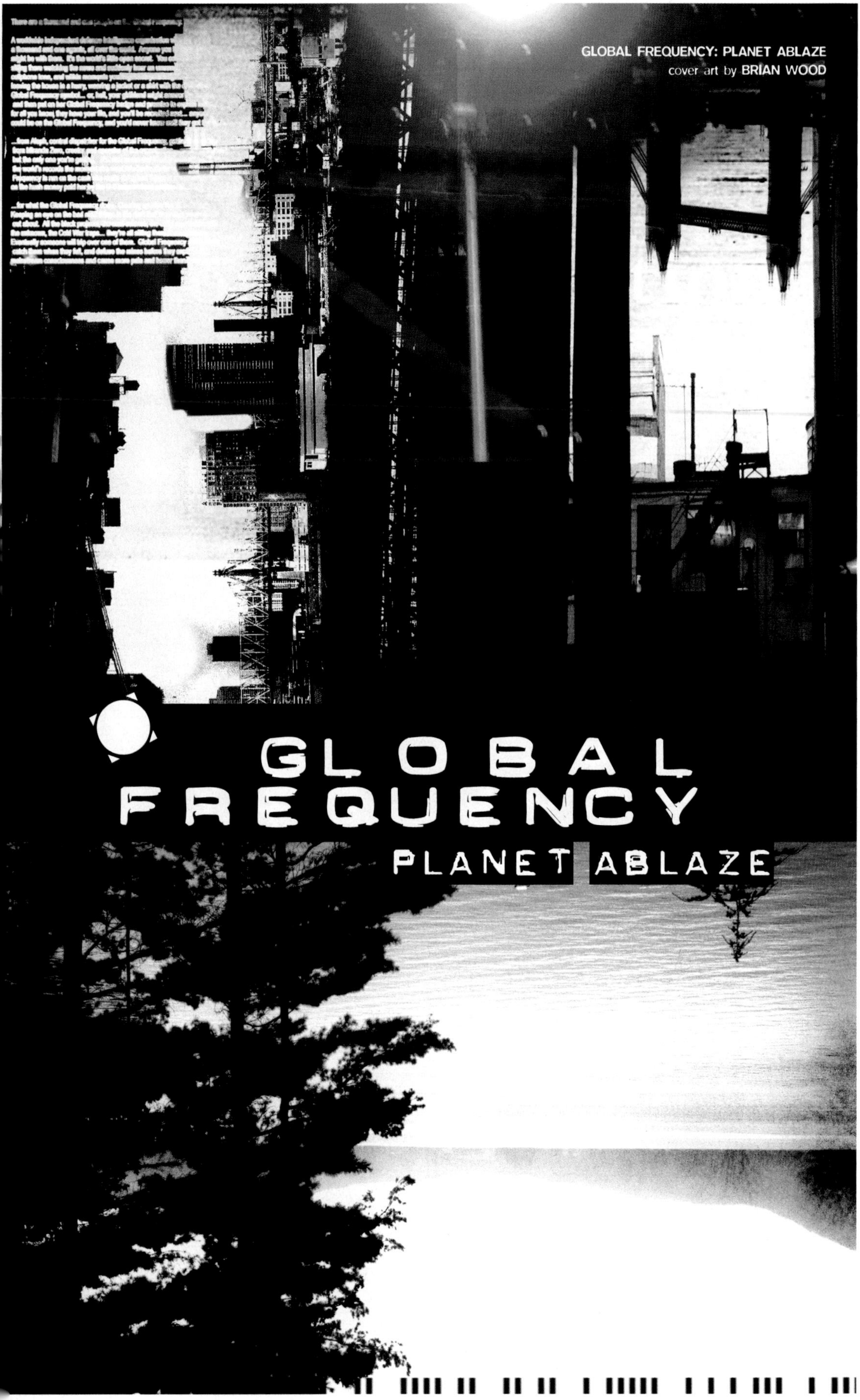
GLOBAL
FREQUENCY
PLANET ABLAZE

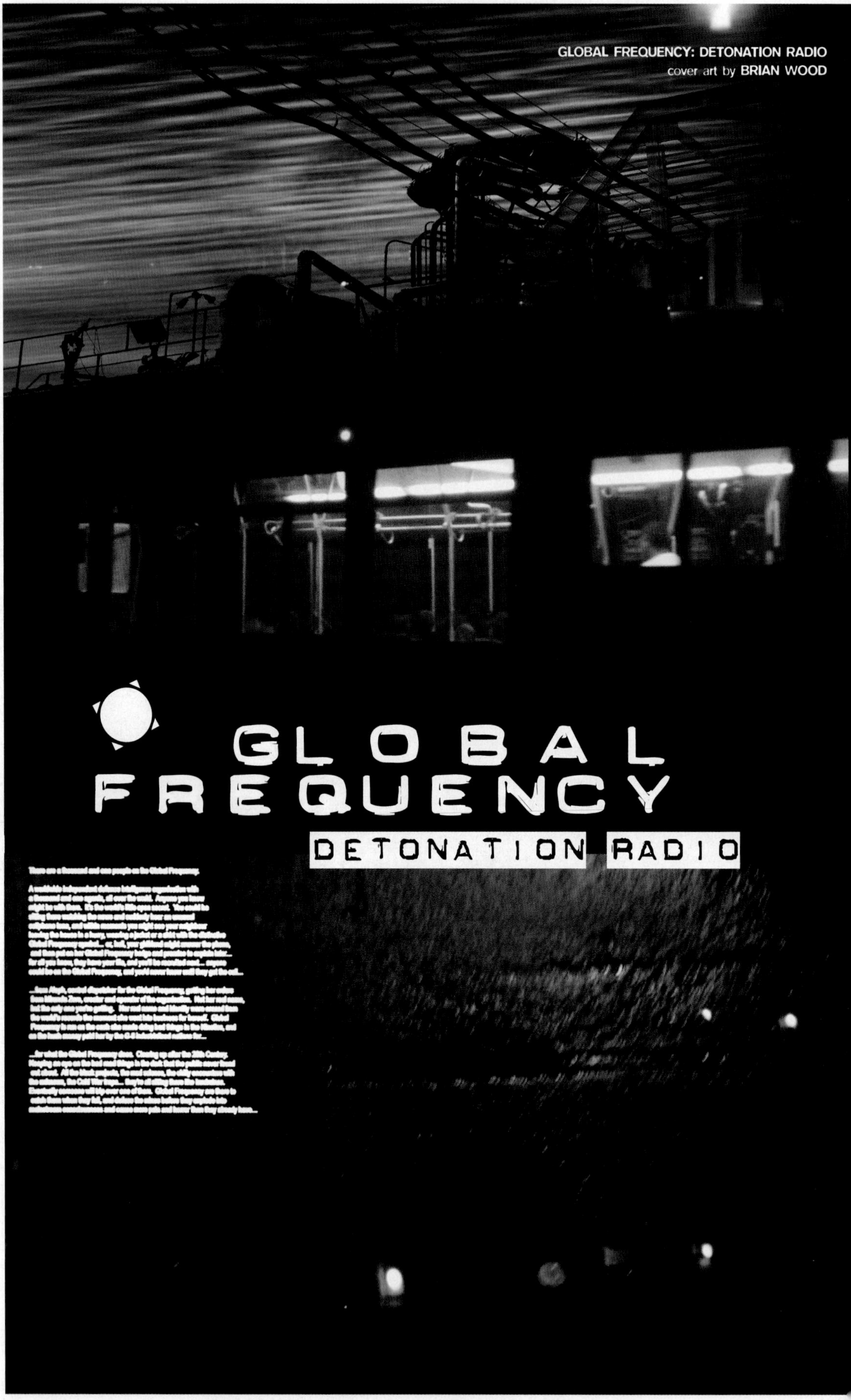
GLOBAL
FREQUENCY
DETONATION RADIO

GLOBAL FREQUENCY: DETONATION RADIO
cover art by **BRIAN WOOD**

VERTIGO

"Transmet is brilliant future-shock commentary."
—SPIN MAGAZINE

"It's angry political sci-fi and it's funny as hell."
—PLAYBOY

TRANSMETROPOLITAN VOL. 2: LUST FOR LIFE

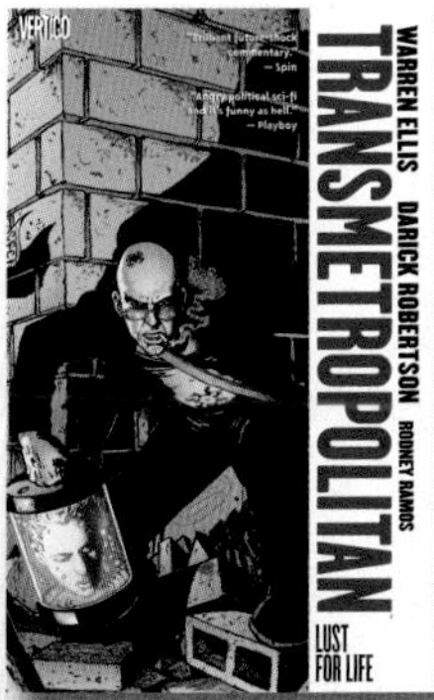
VERTIGO
WARREN ELLIS DARICK ROBERTSON RODNEY RAMOS
TRANSMETROPOLITAN
LUST FOR LIFE

TRANSMETROPOLITAN VOL. 3: YEAR OF THE BASTARD

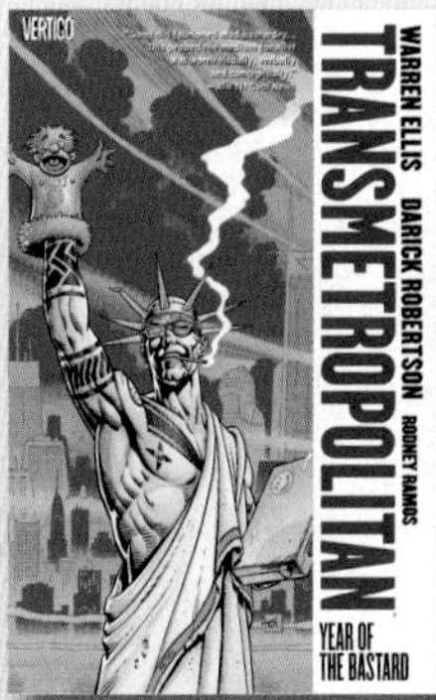
VERTIGO
WARREN ELLIS DARICK ROBERTSON RODNEY RAMOS
TRANSMETROPOLITAN
YEAR OF THE BASTARD

Read the Entire Series!

TRANSMETROPOLITAN VOL. 1: BACK ON THE STREET

TRANSMETROPOLITAN VOL. 2: LUST FOR LIFE

TRANSMETROPOLITAN VOL. 3: YEAR OF THE BASTARD

TRANSMETROPOLITAN VOL. 4: THE NEW SCUM

TRANSMETROPOLITAN VOL. 5: LONELY CITY

TRANSMETROPOLITAN VOL. 6: BACK ON THE STREET

TRANSMETROPOLITAN VOL. 7: SPIDER'S THRASH

TRANSMETROPOLITAN VOL. 8: DIRGE

TRANSMETROPOLITAN VOL. 9: THE CURE

TRANSMETROPOLITAN VOL. 10: ONE MORE TIME

FROM THE WRITER OF *PLANETARY*

WARREN ELLIS

TRANSMETROPOLITAN

with DARICK ROBERTSON

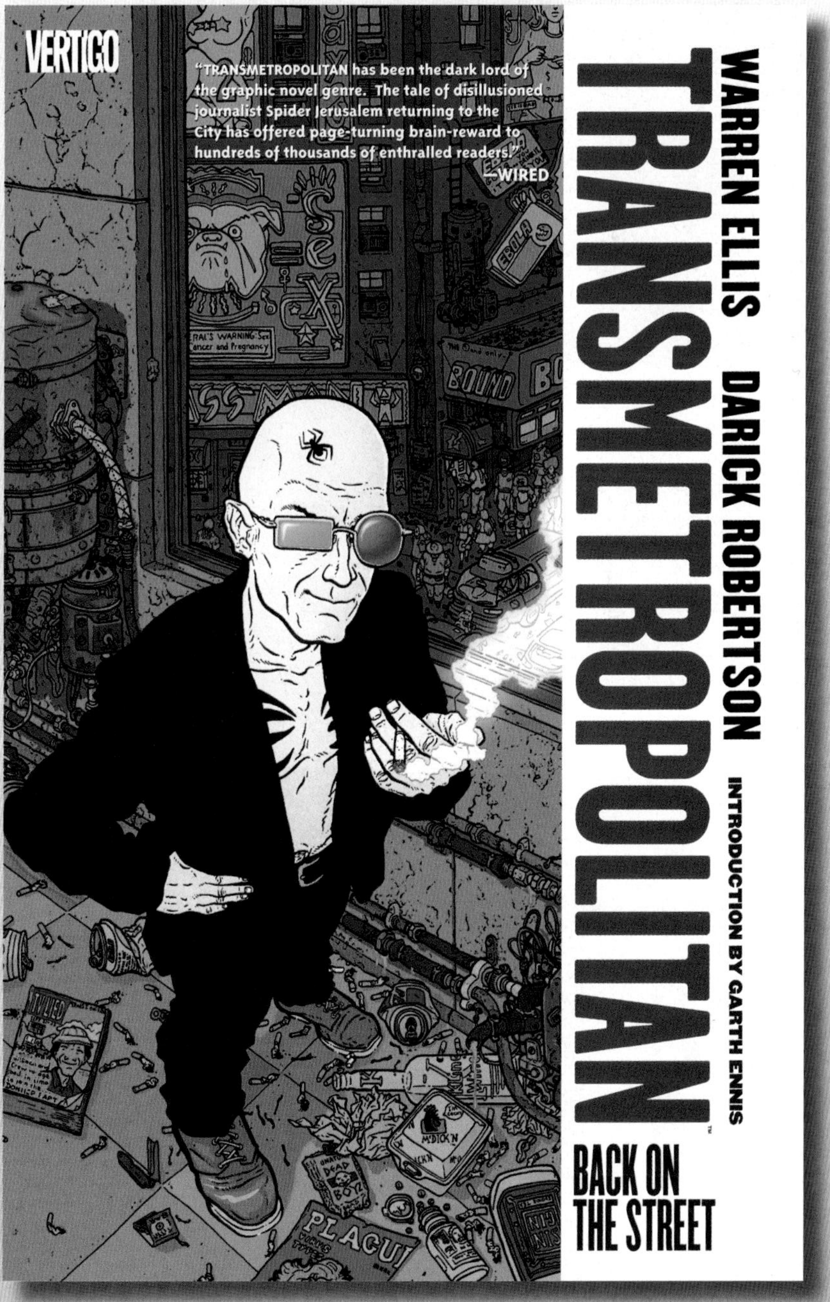
VERTIGO
"TRANSMETROPOLITAN has been the dark lord of the graphic novel genre. The tale of disillusioned journalist Spider Jerusalem returning to the City has offered page-turning brain-reward to hundreds of thousands of enthralled readers." —WIRED
WARREN ELLIS
DARICK ROBERTSON
TRANSMETROPOLITAN
INTRODUCTION BY GARTH ENNIS
BACK ON THE STREET

"Provocative, eminently addictive and top of its class."
—ENTERTAINMENT WEEKLY

"Darkly witty, breathtakingly illustrated takes on familiar characters."
—THE ONION / AV CLUB

FROM THE WRITER OF
TRANSMETROPOLITAN & THE AUTHORITY
WARREN ELLIS
with JOHN CASSADAY

**PLANETARY BOOK 2:
THE FOURTH MAN**

**PLANETARY BOOK 3:
LEAVING THE 20TH
CENTURY**

**PLANETARY BOOK 4:
SPACETIME
ARCHEOLOGY**